JUDICIAL REVIEW AND THE CONSTITUTION

Judicial Review and the Constitution

Edited by
CHRISTOPHER FORSYTH
Assistant Director of the Centre for Public Law,
University of Cambridge

·HART·
PUBLISHING

OXFORD – PORTLAND OREGON
2000

Hart Publishing
Oxford and Portland, Oregon

Published in North America (US and Canada) by
Hart Publishing c/o
International Specialized Book Services
5804 NE Hassalo Street
Portland, Oregon
97213-3644
USA

Distributed in the Netherlands, Belgium and Luxembourg by
Intersentia, Churchillaan 108
B2900 Schoten
Antwerpen
Belgium

Hart Publishing Ltd is a specialist legal publisher based in Oxford, England.
To order further copies of this book or to request a list of other
publications please write to:

Hart Publishing Ltd, Salter's Boatyard,
Folly Bridge, Abingdon Road, Oxford OX1 4LB
Telephone: +44 (0)1865 245533 or Fax: +44 (0)1865 794882
e-mail: mail@hartpub.co.uk
www.hartpub.co.uk

British Library Cataloguing in Publication Data
Data Available
ISBN 1 84113–105–9 (cloth)

Typeset in Sabon 10pt
by Hope Services (Abingdon) Ltd.
Printed in Great Britain on acid-free paper
by Bookcraft (Bath) Ltd.
Midsomer Norton, Somerset

Preface

Over the past three decades judicial review has become much more prominent in the administrative law of the United Kingdom. The judges have been active in their development of judicial review and today very few governmental decisions are beyond scrutiny in the courts. In these circumstances the focus has naturally shifted to the foundations of judicial review: have the judges been interfering in matters outside their bailiwick or have they being acting in accordance with classic constitutional principle and simply vindicating the rule of law? Over the past few years a lively debate has been carried on in the law journals in which the orthodox justification for judicial review, the ultra vires doctrine, has been both attacked and defended. (This doctrine holds the judges' task is simply to ensure that administrative authorities remain within the powers granted to them by the law, and thus all judicial intervention, however bold, must be linked, in one way or another, to the legal powers of the relevant public authorities.) This question of the proper basis of judicial intervention is one of the most important of all constitutional questions since it touches intimately, where it does not define, the relationship between the judiciary, the executive and the legislature.

The Centre for Public Law judged that it could make a contribution to this debate by calling a small expert conference in Cambridge on the Foundations of Judicial Review. This was held on the 22 May 1999. Most of those who had written about the topic in the law journals attended as did many other leading scholars – including leading practitioners and judges – and the occasion was lively and challenging. (The list of participants appears at p. 000.) A narrow view of the foundations of judicial review was not taken. Thus papers were given on both the jurisprudential aspects of the debate as well as the impact of devolution and the Human Rights Act 1998 on judicial review.

This volume contains all the papers given at the conference as well as written comments made after the conference by some participants. But it contains much more than that: most of the articles that contributed to the debate prior to the conference are reprinted here. Thus the interested reader can find in one place a thorough introduction to the debate over the foundations of judicial review as well as all the latest contributions. One recent paper not given at the conference is also included here. Dr Mark Elliott's paper "Fundamental Rights as Interpretative Constructs: the Constitutional Logic of the Human Rights Act 1998" complemented the other contributions and was so apposite to the theme of the conference that it is here included.

The conference was made possible through the support of the British Academy, St John's College, Cambridge and the Faculty of Law of the

University of Cambridge. The Centre for Public Law is very grateful to all these sponsors without whom its work would be impossible. Since several of the papers have been published elsewhere the Centre is also grateful for the authors and publishers of the works reprinted. Formally acknowledgement to copyright holders is made elsewhere.

30 January   2000 C.F.F .

Contents

PART I THE DEBATE BEGINS

PART III CONSTITUTIONAL REFORM
AND THE FOUNDATIONS OF JUDICIAL REVIEW

JUDICIAL REVIEW OF STATUTORY AND NON-STATUTORY DISCRETION

PART IV CONCLUSION

COMMENTS FROM SOME PARTICIPANTS

CHAPTER SEVEN — THE RULES

Acknowledgements

As explained in the preface this volume contains several important contributions to the debate originally printed elsewhere. Furthermore, four of the papers given at the conference were first published elsewhere. The Centre for Public Law is grateful to the authors of all these papers for consenting to publication in this volume. In addition the Centre is grateful to the original publishers, the Cambridge Law Journal, Sweet and Maxwell Ltd (publishers Public Law and the Hamlyn Lecture Series) and the Butterworths Division of Reed Elsevier (UK) Ltd (publishers of *Judicial Review*, 2nd ed eds. Supperstone and Goudie) for consenting to republication of the relevant contributions here.

The details are:

Reproduced through the permission of the Cambridge Law Journal:

Christopher Forsyth, "Of Fig Leaves and Fairy Tales: The Ultra Vires Doctrine, the Sovereignty of Parliament and Judicial Review" (1996) 55 CLJ 122

Paul Craig, "Ultra Vires and the Foundations of Judicial Review" (1998) 57 CLJ 63

Mark Elliott, "The Ultra Vires Doctrine in a Constitutional Setting: Still the Central Principle of Judicial Review" (1998) 57 CLJ 129

Reproduced through the permission of Sweet and Maxwell Ltd:

Dawn Oliver, "Is the Ultra Vires Rule the Basis of Judicial Review?" [1987] Public Law 543–565

Paul Craig and Mark Walters, "The Courts, Devolution and Judicial Review" [1999] Public Law 274–303

Jeffrey Jowell "Of Vires and Vacuums: The Constitutional Context of Judicial Review" [1999] Public Law 448–460

Paul Craig, "Competing Models of Judicial Review" [1999] Public Law 428–447

Sir Stephen Sedley, "Public Power and Private Power" from *Freedom, Law and Justice*, 1999 Hamlyn Lectures by the Rt. Hon. Lord Justice Sedley, 19–38.

Reproduced through the permission of the Butterworths Division of Reed Elsevier (UK) Ltd:

Lord Justice Laws, "Illegality: The Problem of Jurisdiction" in Supperstone and Goudie, *Judicial Review*, (2nd ed, 1997) and extract from 4.13–4.21.

Contributors

(including participants who made written comments)

T.R.S. Allan is Reader in Legal and Constitutional Theory and a Fellow of Pembroke College, Cambridge

Professor Stephen Bailey is Pro-Vice-Chancellor of the University of Nottingham

The Hon. Sir Robert Carnwath is a Justice of the High Court and Chairman of the Law Commission

Nicholas Bamforth is a Fellow of The Queen's College, Oxford

Professor Paul Craig, FBA is Professor of English Law, St John's College, Oxford

Professor David Dyzenhaus is Professor of Law and Philosophy, University of Toronto

Dr Mark Elliott is Fellow and Richard Fellingham Lecturer in Law, St. Catharine's College, Cambridge

Professor David Feldman is Dean of the Faculty of Law and Barber Professor of Jurisprudence at the University of Birmingham

Dr Christopher Forsyth is Assistant Director of the Centre for Public Law, Director of Studies and Fellow in Law of Robinson College, Cambridge.

Professor Brigid Hadfield is Professor of Public Law, The Queen's University of Belfast

Professor Jeffrey Jowell, QC is Dean of the Law Faculty, Professor of Public Law and Vice-Provost, University College London

The Rt Hon. Sir John Laws is a Lord Justice of Appeal

Professor Martin Loughlin is Dean of the Faculty and Professor of Law in the University of Manchester

Professor Dawn Oliver is Professor of Constitutional Law in the University of London (University College London)

The Rt Hon. Sir Stephen Sedley is a Lord Justice of Appeal

Professor Michael Taggart is Professor of Law in the University of Auckland

Mark Walters is a Lecturer in Law, New College, Oxford.

Professor Sir William Wade, QC, FBA was previously Rouse Ball Professor of Law in the University of Cambridge and Master of Gonville and Caius College

List of Participants

Lord Browne-Wilkinson
Lord Hope of Craighead
Lord Justice Laws
Lord Justice Sedley
Lord Steyn
Lord Woolf
The Hon Mr Justice Carnwath
The Hon Mr Justice Collins
The Hon Mr Justice Elias
The Hon Mr Justice Richards
Sir Derek Oulton, QC
Professor Sir William Wade,
    QC, FBA
Professor Stephen Bailey
Professor Jack Beatson, QC
Professor Anthony Bradley
Professor Paul Craig, FBA
Professor David Dyzenhaus
Professor David Feldman
Professor Brigid Hadfield
Professor Jeffrey Jowell, QC

Professor Martin Loughlin
Professor Gillian Morris
Professor David Mullan
Professor Dawn Oliver
Professor A.T.H. Smith
Professor Michael Taggart
Dr John Allison
Dr Yvonne Cripps
Dr Christopher Forsyth
Dr Stephanie Palmer
James Goudie, QC
Nigel Pleming, QC
Trevor Allan
Nick Bamforth
Mark Elliott
Ivan Hare
Richard Hart
Clive Lewis
Ronald Maines
Philip Sales

Table of Cases

Table of Legislation

Table of European Conventions

European Convention for the Protection of Human Rights and Fundamental Freedoms   251, 252, 291, 336, 339

Table of International Conventions

The Debate Begins

1

Is the Ultra Vires Rule the Basis of Judicial Review?*

DAWN OLIVER

The central principle of administrative law has long been that the court's juris-diction to review the acts and decisions of public authorities rests on the ultra vires rule. However, the trend in recent cases seems to be for the courts to pay little attention to questions of jurisdiction or the ultra vires rule (unless an ouster clause is involved): it was not relied on, for example, in the judgments of Lords Diplock, Scarman or Roskill in the *G.C.H.Q.* case.[1] It will be suggested in this article that judicial review has moved on from the ultra vires rule to a concern for the protection of individuals, and for the control of *power*, rather than *pow-ers*, or *vires*.

In considering whether ultra vires is the basis of judicial review, the phrase "judicial review" is used in the sense of the substantive rules applied by the courts when exercising a supervisory jurisdiction. This will usually nowadays involve an application for judicial review; but it should be remembered that the courts also exercise a supervisory jurisdiction, applying very similar principles to those applied in public law cases, when dealing with private decisions in areas such as company law, trusts, and (for present purposes, more relevant) private licensing decisions, expulsions, the "right to work" and so on.

These substantive rules that are applied when exercising a supervisory juris-diction could be grouped together as, to use Galligan's words,[2] "principles of good administration." They include the requirement of "fairness" in its various guises, and they prohibit the fettering or delegation of discretion, abuse of power, arbitrariness, capriciousness, unreasonableness, bad faith, breach of accepted moral standards, and so on. They require, in other words, legality, rationality, procedural propriety and possibly proportionality.

---

* This is a reprint of an article first published in [1987] Public Law 543.
[1] See *Council of Civil Service Unions* v. *Minister for the Civil Service* [1985] AC 374. However, Lord Fraser based his decision on the fact that the power was delegated to the Prime Minister by Order in Council (p. 399).
    A recent LEXIS search of English decisions indicated that since 1975 there have been 1,058 cases in which judicial review has been mentioned but not ultra vires or jurisdiction; by contrast, there have been 196 cases where ultra vires has been mentioned, and only 39 where both ultra vires and judicial review have been mentioned.
[2] D.J. Galligan, "Judicial Review and the Textbook Writers" (1982) 2 OJLS 257.

What is the relationship between these principles of good administration, and the ultra vires rule? This must depend upon what is meant by the ultra vires rule. The rule, stated briefly, is as follows: a public (or even a private[3]) body that has been granted powers, whether by statute, Order in Council, or some other instrument, must not exceed the powers so granted.[4] It will be taken to have exceeded its powers if either of two conditions are satisfied. First, that it has done or decided to do an act that it does not have the legal capacity to do. In other words if it has exceeded its jurisdiction in the narrow,[5] or strict,[6] sense.[7] I shall not be seeking in this article to challenge the ultra vires rule in this first strict, narrow sense. It is the next limb of the rule that is my main concern.

The second limb of the ultra vires rule has its roots in the *Wednesbury Corporation*[8] case and *Ridge* v. *Baldwin*,[9] among other leading cases. It means that an authority will be regarded as acting ultra vires if in the course of doing or deciding to do something that is intra vires in the strict or narrow sense, it acts improperly or "unreasonably" in various ways: these ways include disregard of the rules of natural justice, unfairness, taking into account irrelevant considerations, ignoring relevant considerations, bad faith, fettering discretion, attempting to raise taxation, interfering with the free exercise of individual liberties, and so on.

This second limb of the ultra vires rule rests on the interpretation of the instrument granting the power: Parliament, or the "donor" of the *vires* of the authority, is presumed not to have intended that the authority should act in breach of these principles of good administration. This presumption is, in theory at least, rebuttable, in the sense that if, but only if, the instrument granting the power clearly intends that these principles are not to apply,[10] the courts will

---

[3] For the ultra vires rule in relation to corporations see *Halsbury's Laws of England* (4th ed., 1974), vol. 9, title Corporations.

[4] See *e.g.* Craig, *Administrative Law* (1983) at p. 299: "The inherent power of the courts to review the findings of a tribunal has . . . been concerned with ensuring that the decision-maker remains within the jurisdiction *granted to him*" (my emphasis); see also Cane, *Introduction to Administrative Law* (1986) pp. 69–91; Foulkes, *Administrative Law* (6th ed., 1986), p. 168; Wade, *Constitutional Fundamentals* (1980) p. 62; Garner, *Administrative Law* (6th ed., 1985), p. 105; de Smith, *Judicial Review of Administrative Action* (4th ed., 1980), Chap. 3 and pp. 27, 28; Wade, *Administrative Law* (5th ed., 1982), p. 38.

[5] For this expression, see Lord Reid in *Anisminic Ltd.* v. *Foreign Compensation Commission* [1969] 2 AC 147, at p. 171; see also Lord Pearce at p. 195.

[6] This concept also applies to charitable trusts. For this use of the term, see Mervyn Davies J. in *Rosemary Simmons Memorial Housing Association Ltd.* v. *United Dominions Trust* [1987] 1 All ER 281, at pp. 285–286.

[7] A clear example of ultra vires action in this sense is provided by *White and Collins* v. *Minister of Health* [1939] 2 KB 838: power to acquire land provided that it does not form "part of any park, garden or pleasure ground . . ." does not permit acquisition of parkland. See G.L. Peiris, "Jurisdictional Review and Judicial Policy: The Evolving Mosaic" (1987) 103 LQR 66 for an analysis of this aspect of the ultra vires rule.

[8] *Associated Provincial Picture Houses* v. *Wednesbury Corporation* [1948] 1 KB 223.

[9] [1964] AC 40.

[10] See *e.g.* *Congreve* v. *Home Office* [1976] QB 629 (no taxing power without clear words); *R.* v. *Hillingdon London Borough Council, ex parte Royco Homes Ltd.* [1974] QB 720 (no limitation of property rights without express words).

give precedence to the terms of the Act or other instrument. However, the cases on ouster clauses indicate that the courts are very reluctant to allow statute to override these principles.[11]

I am aware of the bottomless pit of ambiguity and uncertainty into which one is, like Alice, liable to fall in defining anything in administrative law, especially the ultra vires rule. However, the rule as set out here has until recently provided an adequate explanation of the development of principles of judicial review (if that is not an exaggeration of the effect of the case law in this area). For the corollary of the rule that a body acts ultra vires if it breaches these rules of good administration is that a court may exercise its supervisory jurisdiction if, but only if, the body has acted ultra vires.

> Provided that they (the local authority) act, as they have acted, within the four corners of their jurisdiction this court cannot, in my opinion, interfere.[12]

It is in this sense that the ultra vires rule is said to be the basis of judicial review.

The vast majority of acts by public bodies are carried out under statutory authorisation, which lends itself to the ultra vires approach. However, significant areas of public administration are not carried out under statutory or other "granted" or delegated powers; and yet, as recent cases indicate, they may be subject to judicial supervision. It will be convenient to consider separately the ultra vires rule in relation to sources of power, institutions and functions, although there is an unavoidable overlap between those categories.

SOURCES OF POWER

A considerable part of the activity of central government is carried on under *de facto* or common law powers. It is not possible to analyse the exercise of such powers of government as being subject to express or implied terms imposed by the donor of the power. They do not lend themselves to the language of ultra vires.

Perhaps the most obvious area in which judicial review is available, but where the ultra vires doctrine is hard to apply, is the royal prerogative. This area of power is recognised by the common law, and is not "granted" by any donor whose intentions as to its proper use can be implied. This fact was implicitly recognised by the courts until the decision in the G.C.H.Q.[13] case. Until that

---

[11] The policy of the judges, as Sir William Wade has put it, is "to build up a code of rules of administrative fair play which they take for granted as intended by Parliament to apply to all statutory powers, and perhaps even to prerogative powers, and to insist on preserving their jurisdiction even in the face of legislation purporting to exclude it": Wade, *Constitutional Fundamentals* (1980) at p. 62. The passage, in referring to prerogative powers, illustrates the difficulty of applying the idea of Parliament's intention as justifying judicial review in the case of non-statutory powers such as those deriving from the royal prerogative.

[12] *Per* Lord Greene MR in *Associated Provincial Picture Houses* v. *Wednesbury Corporation* [1948] 1 KB 223, at p. 231; see also p. 228.

[13] *Council of Civil Service Unions* v. *Minister for the Civil Service* [1985] AC 374.

landmark decision, the courts would decide whether a power or capacity claimed as part of the prerogative had survived the gradual erosion by that power by Parliament,[14] but would not intervene to consider whether a power had been properly exercised in accordance with the principles of good administration which form the second limb of the ultra vires rule.

In the *G.C.H.Q.* case the power that had been exercised by the Prime Minister was in fact an indirect exercise of the prerogative: an instruction issued under the Civil Service Order in Council. In such as case the "interpretation" approach might be applied: the courts could presume that, in issuing the Order in Council, Her Majesty intended that the powers granted therein to the Minister for the Civil Service should be exercised in accordance with the principles of good administration developed in cases on judicial review. Lord Fraser chose to base his judgment on this approach:

> I am unable to see why the words should not bear the same meaning whatever the source of authority for the legislation in which they are contained. . . . Whatever their source, powers which are defined, either by reference to their object or by reference to the procedure for their exercise, or in some other way, and whether the definition is expressed or implied, are in my opinion normally subject to judicial control to ensure that they are not exceeded.[15]

However, in the *G.C.H.Q.* case the majority in the House of Lords decided that "the controlling factor in determining whether the exercise of prerogative power is subject to judicial review is not its source but its subject matter."[16] And, said Lord Diplock, "the source of the decision-making power may still be the common law itself"[17] and yet judicial review will be available.

It would seem to follow that if a power is in principle "justiciable", regardless of its source, then the supervisory jurisdiction will be available, and indeed it would have been available in the *G.C.H.Q.* case were it not for the national security issue. This is borne out, for example, by the *Take-over Panel*[18] case in which the Court of Appeal rejected the suggestion that judicial review was available only in respect of statutory or prerogative powers. The clear implication must be that judicial review is not based solely on principles of statutory (or other) interpretation, but on the application of some general principles of good administration to the exercise of power.

In enumerating the grounds of procedural impropriety, irrationality, illegality and, potentially, proportionality, Lord Diplock clearly had in mind that the exercise of power, whether it derives from the common law, whether it is simply *de facto* power, or whether it is statutory, would be subjected to the same

---

[14] See *Att.-Gen.* v. *De Keyser's Royal Hotel Ltd.* [1920] AC 508.

[15] [1985] AC at p. 399. See also Lord Brightman at p. 424.

[16] [1985] AC at p. 407 (*per* Lord Scarman). See also Lord Diplock at pp. 409, 410; Lord Roskill at p. 417.

[17] At p. 409.

[18] *R.* v. *Panel on Take-overs and Mergers, ex parte Datafin plc* [1987] 2 WLR 699, CA.

grounds[19] for judicial review, although of course statutory interpretation must enter into the question where statutory powers are in issue. Thus the decision in the *G.C.H.Q.* case, it seems, opens up new areas of public or state activity to judicial review outside any doctrine of ultra vires.

Lords Roskill and Diplock in the *G.C.H.Q.* case stated that the availability of judicial review depends upon the subject-matter of the power, and took the view that there will be few prerogative powers that are "justiciable".[20] Clearly matters of foreign relations and the like may not be justiciable; however, there are more prerogative powers than one might imagine, some of which could be exercised in a highly controversial and yet justiciable way. For example, the prerogative power to issue and distribute information to the public[21] is, in the light of experience with the campaigns against abolition of the G.L.C., the metropolitan counties and the I.L.E.A.,[22] power of a sort that is both open to abuse and in principle amenable to judicial review on grounds of illegality or irrationality. Similarly, the Home Secretary's prerogative power to supply equipment and weapons for keeping the peace (*e.g.* C.S. gas) might also at some time form the subject-matter of an application for judicial review.[23] The prerogative power to authorise the interception of communications, to the extent that it remains unregulated by statute,[24] is also subject to the supervisory jurisdiction.[25] In other words, prerogative powers are politically important and some of them are justiciable; but they are not subject to the second limb of the ultra vires doctrine, which is concerned with implied limitations in an instrument granting power.

Another area of activity opened up to review in recent years has been the issuing of circulars by government.[26] Where this is not authorised by statute, such action appears to be lawful in principle at common law, but subject to a supervisory jurisdiction if, for example, an incorrect statement of the law appears in a circular or if it advises action that is alleged to be unlawful. Hence the House of Lords in *Royal College of Nursing* v. *Department of Health and Social Security*[27] accepted that there was jurisdiction to make a declaration as to the legality of advice about law relating to abortion, although the advice was found

---

[19] And see Lord Scarman [1985] AC at p. 407. For the application of the rules of natural justice (procedural regularity) to a partly prerogative power, see *Mahon* v. *Air New Zealand Ltd.* [1984] AC 808, PC.

[20] [1985] AC at p. 418 (Lord Roskill) and p. 411 (Lord Diplock).

[21] See *Jenkins* v. *Att.-Gen., The Times*, August 14, 1971; [1971] CLY 1628.

[22] See *Local Authority Publicity*, Interim Report of the Committee of Inquiry into the Conduct of Local Authority Business (The Widdicombe Inquiry), 1985; *R.* v. *I.L.E.A., ex parte Westminster City Council* [1986] 1 WLR 28; *R.* v. *Greater London Council, ex parte Westminster City Council, The Times*, January 22, 1985. See now the Local Government Act 1985, ss. 2–4.

[23] See *R.* v. *Secretary of State for the Home Department, ex parte Northumbria Police Authority* [1987] 2 WLR 998, criticised by H.J. Beynon ([1987] Public Law 146).

[24] See Interception of Communications Act 1985.

[25] *R.* v. *Secretary of State for the Home Department, ex parte Ruddock* [1987] 2 All ER 518, Taylor J.

[26] There may be a prerogative power to issue circulars, at least to the extent that they consist of information rather than advice: *Jenkins* v. *Att.-Gen., supra* n. 21.

[27] [1981] AC 800.

not to be unlawful. And in *Gillick v. West Norfolk Area Health Authority*[28] a similar jurisdiction was accepted.

Both of these cases were applications for declarations and not for judicial review (though in *Gillick* some of their Lordships felt than an application for judicial review would have been more appropriate); this highlights the existence of supervisory jurisdictions applying similar rules to those applied in applications for judicial review, in other, private law, proceedings.[29]

Non-statutory self-imposed guidelines and rules, such as the immigration rules, also attract the supervisory jurisdiction, as evidenced by the *Asif Khan*[30] and *Kharrazi* cases.[31] Similarly, extra-statutory tax concessions may be subject to the supervisory jurisdiction through an application for judicial review.[32]

INSTITUTIONS

Many important "public" functions are carried on by organisations and institutions other than central or local government. Some of these quasi-governmental organisations derive both their existence and their authority from statute. Examples are the Independent Broadcasting Authority, the Monopolies and Mergers Commission, and London Regional Transport. These institutions may only do those things which they are authorised to do by their empowering legislation, and in their "public" activities they must act in accordance with principles of good administration, in order to comply with the intentions of their "parent" body.[33] Not all that they do will, of course, be subject to public law.

---

[28] [1986] AC 112. But see the criticism of this case by C. Harlow in "Gillick: A Comedy of Errors?" (1989) 49 MLR 768. In neither *Gillick* nor *Royal College of Nursing* was the weak locus standi of the plaintiffs a bar to their actions.

[29] See on this Lord Bridge in [1986] AC at p. 192.

[30] *R. v. Secretary of State for the Home Department, ex parte Asif Mahmood Khan* [1984] 1 WLR 1337, CA.

[31] *R. v. Chief Immigration Officer, ex parte Kharrazi* [1980] 1 WLR 1396; see also *R. v. Secretary of State for the Home Department, ex parte Ruddock* [1987] 2 All ER 518, in which Taylor J. held that a telephone subscriber had a legitimate expectation that the published criteria on the interception of telephone communications would be complied with by the Home Secretary. Compare *Connor v. Strathclyde Regional Council*, 1986 SLT 530, Outer House: although published guidelines gave rise to a legitimate expectation that they would be followed, this did not attract judicial review in the absence of any, or any sufficient, public element.

[32] *R. v. Inspector of Taxes, Reding, ex parte Fulford-Dobson* [1987] 3 WLR 277, McNeill J.

[33] But does the fact that a body is incorporated by statute necessarily involve that it is subject to public law and judicial review? In *R. v. Committee of Lloyds, ex parte Posgate, The Times*, January 12, 1983 [1983] CLY 2001, the action of the Committee of Lloyds in securing the dismissal of the applicant by his employers was held to be *ultra vires* and in breach of the duties of natural justice, and certiorari was granted. Lloyds was incorporated by a private Act in 1871 "for the effecting of Marine Insurance". The main concern of those provisions that were in issue was the protection of members or "names". It seems to have been assumed that certiorari was the correct remedy, thus implying (i) that Lloyds is in some respects a public body and (ii) that their influence over contracts to which the Committee was not a party had the necessary "public element" to admit of judicial review. Comparison may be made with *R. v. Independent Broadcasting Authority, ex parte the Rank Organisation plc*, Court of Appeal, March 26, 1986, discussed below at pp. 21–2.

Although the language of ultra vires may be readily applied to bodies of this kind, it is less easy to apply to organisations that are not governed by statute. Some public functions are carried out by individuals possessing the usual capacities of persons at common law,[34] together with special powers granted by statute or some other authority: chief constables, the Commissioner of Police for the Metropolis, registrars of births, deaths and marriages, the registrar of companies, for example. In principle, such an official is subject to judicial review in the conduct of his public duties to the extent that he has, or claims, powers over and above those possessed by private individuals. An illustration of this point may be drawn from *Thomas* v. *University of Bradford*[35] in which the House of Lords indicated that a university Visitor would be subject to the supervisory jurisdiction of the High Court.[36]

The ultra vires rule is not so readily applied where an official is using the powers which he possesses as an individual. As the *Malone*[37] case demonstrated, the courts may take the view that the addition of public functions does not necessarily detract from the private law liberties of the official so as to impose a civil tort liability. The exercise of such power may nevertheless be the subject of the supervisory jurisdiction, where for example legitimate expectations are involved.[38] The comments made below about economic power would apply equally here.

Royal charters provide another illustration of the inappropriateness of the ultra vires rule as the basis of judicial review. Examples of public or quasi-public chartered organisations include the British Broadcasting Corporation, and the universities. The Corporation of the City of London, the local authority for that area, is a corporation by prescription at common law[39] and has the same legal powers and capacities as an individual. When exercising statutory powers, the corporation is subject to judicial review; but who can doubt that the corporation is, or should be, also subject to judicial review when exercising its common law powers, such as the power to make contracts and own property, which in the case of statutory corporations are granted by the enabling legislation and are thus subject to judicial review? If, for example, the City of London acted as Leicester City Council did in *Wheeler* v. *Leicester City Council*[40] it would be remarkable if no remedy were available simply because the Corporation is chartered, and was exercising its powers as owner over a sports ground.

Inevitably, as with more obviously public bodies, much of the activity of organisations of this kind is entirely in the private domain, and subject only to the rules of contract, tort etc. "Like public figures, at least in theory, public

[34] *Malone* v. *Metropolitan Police Commissioner* [1979] Ch. 344.
[35] [1987] 2 WLR 677, HL.
[36] *Ibid*. at p. 695.
[37] *Malone* v. *Metropolitan Police Commissioner* [1979] Ch. 344.
[38] See *R.* v. *Secretary of State for the Home Department, ex parte Ruddock* [1987] 2 All ER 518, Taylor J.
[39] Blackstone's *Commentaries*, I, p. 473.
[40] [1985] AC 1054; and see below under *Functions*.

bodies are entitled to a private life.".[41] Chartered bodies may, however, have functions in the public domain which, at first sight at least, would appear to be subject to judicial review.[42] Yet there is House of Lords authority that the ultra vires rules does not apply to chartered corporations in their relationships with third parties, only in internal relationships:

> A chartered corporation is not, as a matter of vires, bound by its Charter. At common law it has all the powers of an individual and can legally and lawfully extend its activities beyond the objects of its Charter and indeed carry out activities prohibited by the Charter.[43]

It would seem to follow that, if and when chartered corporations are subjected to judicial review, this cannot be on the basis of the ultra vires rule in its normal sense, but on the basis of the application of a general supervisory jurisdiction which subjects activities having an impact on the public to the principles of good administration.[44]

More recently, the inappropriateness of the ultra vires rule as the basis of judicial review has been demonstrated in the *Take-over Panel* case,[45] where a body without granted or limited powers was held subject to the supervisory jurisdiction as long as there existed a "public"[46] element in its activities. What is not clear in the light of this case is the extent to which the supervisory jurisdiction

---

[41]   Woolf, "Public Law – Private Law: Why the Divide? A Personal View" [1986] PL 220, at p. 223.

[42]   See, *e.g. R. v. Pharmaceutical Society of Great Britain, ex parte Association of Pharmaceutical Importers, The Times*, April 11, 1987, DC.

[43]   See, *per* Lord Upjohn in *Pharmaceutical Society of Great Britain v. Dickson* [1970] AC 403, at p. 434. Lord Upjohn continues: "the appellant society, being the creation of a Royal Charter, is not bound by the doctrine of ultra vires in the same way as a corporation created by or pursuant to a statute . . . But its members, and only its members, can complain, for if the corporation goes outside its expressed objects or, worse still, performs acts prohibited by the terms of the Charter, the Crown may be *scire facias* proceed to forfeit the Charter; any member can, therefore, apply to the court to prohibit the corporation from risking such forfeiture by continuing such activities." See also *Wenlock (Baroness) v. River Dee Co.* (1885) 10 App.Cas. 354; *British South Africa Co. v. De Beers Consolidated Mines* [1910] 1 Ch. 354; *Jenkins v. Pharmaceutical Society of Great Britain* [1921] 1 Ch. 392. Compare *Finnigan v. New Zealand Rugby Football Union Inc.* [1985] 2 NZLR 159, where the Union, although a private body, was held liable to suit by non-members having a sufficient interest, in order to ensure that it did not act against its objects; standing was granted under the test in the *National Federation of Self-Employed and Small Businesses* case [1982] AC 617, because the Union was in a position of major national importance: "the case has some analogy with public law issues" (at p. 179).

[44]   In *R. v. Aston University, ex parte Roffey* [1969] 2 QB 538 the court, on an application for certiorari, found that the university (a chartered institution) owed a duty of natural justice to its students, but refused a remedy because of the applicant's delay: no point was taken on whether the university was subject to the ultra vires rule in public or private law, or internally or externally, nor on whether certiorari was an appropriate remedy: it seems to have been assumed that it would be. But see H.W.R. Wade (1969) 85 LQR 468. In *R. v. Broadcasting Complaints Commission, ex parte Owen* [1985] QB 1153 the court specifically left open the question whether the BBC would be subject to judicial review, though it is not clear whether this was because chartered institutions are not subject to the ultra vires rule, or because the BBC is not a public institution. The latter seems the more likely, though not a very convincing, ground.

[45]   *R. v. Panel on Take-overs and Mergers, ex parte Datafin plc* [1987] 2 WLR 699.

[46]   [1987] 2 WLR at pp. 712, 715, 722, 726, 727.

exercisable through the procedure of application for judicial review now reaches the actions of such institutions.

Does the public law supervisory jurisdiction extend, for example, to self-regulatory bodies in the field of sport (the Jockey Club; the British Board of Boxing Control; the British Greyhound Racing Club, and so on)? Here, unlike the Take-over Panel, the bodies were not established as a result of a decision of government and their powers are not buttressed by statute. In form they are contractual; and yet they perform functions important to the public. If they did not exist, the government might have to invent them.[47]

FUNCTIONS

An area of state activity that may have been opened up to the supervisory jurisdiction since the *G.C.H.Q.* case is the use of contractual and economic power, particularly the use of state economic power for political purposes.

Property[48] and contract have become increasingly important sources of power for state organisations since the Second World War. The property power is widely used by central government and local authorities for policy purposes.[49] Techniques (often referred to as "contract compliance") including imposing in contracts clauses that are designed to secure policy ends, such as equal opportunities in employment for disadvantages persons, a ban on bloodsports on publicly-owned tenanted farmland, or a boycott of South African products; adopting political criteria in tendering;[50] and punishing those dependent upon public property and contracts for non-compliance with public policy, for example by revoking licences, or refusing to renew licences or contracts.[51]

Could the supervisory jurisdiction be exercised where common law (rather than statutory) property and contracting powers are being exercised, whether by a private or a public body, so that questions of *vires* do not arise?

The question is of more than academic importance. The Crown possesses, as a corporation sole, property-owning and contracting powers at common law. This is true also of other corporations sole, and of other non-statutory legal

---

[47] If, as seems probable in the light of *Law v. National Greyhound Racing Club* [1983] 1 WLR 1302, self-regulatory bodies in sport are not subject to the application for judicial review, either because their sole source of power is contractual, or because they operate in the private domain, there nevertheless exists a private law supervisory jurisdiction exercisable on the principles set out in *Nagle v. Feilden* ([1966] 2 QB 633), *McInnes v. Onslow-Fane* ([1978] 1 WLR 1520), etc. This will be considered further in the next section.

[48] See J.K. Galbraith, *The Anatomy of Power*, 1983 at p. 32.

[49] See C. Turpin, *Government Contracts*, 1972; and T.C. Daintith, "Regulation by Contract: the New Prerogative" [1979] CLP 41; and G. Ganz, [1978] PL 333.

[50] The Local Government Bill (1987–88), Part II, will prohibit political discrimination in the award of contracts by local authorities.

[51] See for example *Wheeler v. Leicester City Council* [1985] AC 1054; see also the I.L.E.A. action in cancelling future orders from Rowntree Mackintosh for I.L.E.A. canteens because of the refusal to supply information about the ethnic composition of the workforce: *The Times*, April 4, 6 and October 15, 17, 1985.

persons, such as chartered corporations. Common law powers were used during the period of the blacklist policy 1975–78; they are potent weapons in the hands of government for the pursuit of policies and could involve interference with the free exercise of civil liberties of the kind experienced in *Wheeler* v. *Leicester City Council*[52]; they also permit detailed regulation of the conduct of private institutions and individuals. Certain statutory corporations (the Independent Broadcasting Authority, for example) use contract as a regulator and means of achieving policy ends.[53]

The question whether and when property and contracting powers are subject to judicial review is important in illustrating the fact that judicial supervision is not about *powers* or *vires*, but about the nature and location, the sources and instruments of *power*. Anomalously, the answer to the question whether property and contracting powers are subject to judicial review may depend on the "happenstance" of whether the property or contracting power in issue derives from statute or the common law.

It is often asserted that the exercise of non-statutory power of this kind is not susceptible to judicial supervision. Sir Harry Woolf, for example, discussing the "blacklist" policy operated by the government from 1976–78 commented:

> This by no means unique use of government contracts was never tested in the courts. There was, however, some concern expressed about its propriety, but it is doubtful whether at the present time the courts could provide any protection.[54]

This view is borne out by the decision in *R.* v. *Independent Broadcasting Authority, ex parte the Rank Organisation plc.*[55]

It is suggested that it is not certain whether this is still the case. The matter may be approached in two ways. First, there is a degree of judicial supervision of private contracting powers, and public contractors are in principle subject to at least the same degree of judicial supervision as private contractors. There is, in other words, a private law supervisory jurisdiction over certain aspects of contractual, quasi-contractual and property relations; and public bodies may be equally subject to that supervision. Secondly, in the light of the *G.C.H.Q.* case, the principles of good administration apply to an exercise of power that is in principle justiciable, regardless of whether the source of the power is statute or the common law. This consideration may extend judicial review in public law to matters of property and contract.

These arguments may be considered separately.

---

[52] [1985] AC 1054. In this case, the council's actions were based on statutory rather than common law powers.

[53] *R.* v. *Independent Broadcasting Authority, ex parte the Rank Organisation plc*, Court of Appeal, March 26, 1986.

[54] "Public Law – Private Law: Why the Divide? A Personal View" [1986] PL 220, at p. 225; see also Daintith [1979] CLP 41, at p. 45: "In domestic (*cf.* EEC) law, therefore, the scope for challenge to the use of precontractual powers by Ministers is not great."

[55] Court of Appeal, March 26, 1986.

Argument one: public bodies should be subject to at least the same degree of judicial supervision as private bodies

It is instructive to compare the supervisory jurisdiction in relation to private and public contracting. The starting point is that this sort of power, in private hands, is not generally subject to any supervisory jurisdiction; it would seem to follow that if public contractors are to be treated differently from private bodies and subjected to a supervisory jurisdiction, we have to devise a special doctrine of state power to produce that result – and our system is weak in distinguishing between state and private power,[56] although the concept of "public law" is producing some authority on state power.

However, that starting point (no supervisory jurisdiction over private contracting power) is not as clearly defined as might be supposed. Indeed, a supervisory jurisdiction with origins in nineteenth century cases began to develop in the mid 1960s in relation to private pre-contractual, even non-contractual relations, and contractual relations.

It is convenient to consider pre-contractual and non-contractual relations separately from contracts, although there is scope for cross-application of the principles. Freedom of contract in principle means that a contractor is entitled to enter into contractual relations with whom he will, and equally to refuse to enter into contractual relations with whomever he does not approve, whether for good, bad or indifferent reasons – subject to the sex and race discrimination legislation. It was against this background that Daintith wrote:

> ... in the precontractual phase, in selecting contractual partners and deciding the terms it will offer them the Government enjoys almost unfettered freedom and total immunity from judicial review by reason of the absence of general rules of domestic law to control this process.[57]

However, the position may have altered in some respects in the light of more recent developments.

Problems of privity and standing

On orthodox principles the application of the supervisory jurisdiction, in private law as in public law, should raise problems of privity and standing when applied to pre-contractual or non-contractual relationships. If there is no contract but only an invitation to treat or an application to contract, a person wishing to tender or contract would be regarded as a busybody if he sought to question the pre-contractual process. If there is a contract in existence, a stranger to it will not have standing to raise issues about *vires* conferred by the contract. Anyone seeking to invoke principles of good administration (natural

---

[56] See *Malone* v. *Metropolitan Police Commissioner* [1979] Ch. 344; see also G. Zellick, "Government beyond Law" [1985] PL 283.

[57] [1979] CLP at p. 59.

justice and so on) against another in private law can do so only by relying on the terms of a contract to which he is a party: this is borne out by cases such as *Law v. National Greyhound Racing Club Ltd.*[58] This is one respect in which public law and private law are supposedly very different, for in public law a "sufficient interest" is wider than contractual privity.[59]

However, this general principle has been somewhat eroded in recent years in the private sphere. There is an embryonic common law principle that a person may exceptionally raise issues about the *vires* or conduct of a private body with whom he has no contractual relationship. This trend involves extending aspects of the common law of good administration to non-contractual relationships.

The Court of Appeal in *Nagle v. Feilden*[60] held that (at least where a "right to work" is at stake) although there was no contractual relationship between the applicant for a trainer's licence and the stewards of the Jockey Club, the latter must not act "arbitrarily or capriciously" in rejecting the plaintiff's application. The reasons were (1) that the club exercised a "virtual monopoly in an important field of human activity" and (2) that the common law of England recognises that a man has a right to work at his trade or profession without being unjustly excluded from it. Given the similarity of function between the Jockey Club in this case and the Greyhound Racing Club in the *Law* case, and the finding in *Law* that the Greyhound Racing Club was not a public body, and that "there was no public element in the jurisdiction (of the club stewards) itself",[61] it must follow that there remains, even after *O'Reilly v. Mackman*[62] some precontractual and non-contractual supervisory jurisdiction over private bodies.

A similar principle – that a body must not act arbitrarily or capriciously in denying an opportunity to earn a living – was enunciated in *Weinberger v. Inglis*;[63] and in *McInnes v. Onslow-Fane*[64] a duty to act honestly, fairly, and without bias in dealing with applications was accepted. It will be noted that "arbitrariness and capriciousness" are close to "*Wednesbury* unreasonableness" or "irrationality".

Perhaps the strongest development in this direction comes from New Zealand, in the case of *Finnigan v. New Zealand Rugby Football Union.*[65] This was an application for an injunction and declaration against the Rugby Union

---

[58] [1983] 1 WLR 1302, CA. See also *R. v. Criminal Injuries Compensation Board, ex parte Lain* [1967] 2 QB 864, 882; *R. v. Post Office, ex parte Byrne* [1975] ICR 221; *R. v. BBC, ex parte Lavelle* [1983] 1 WLR 23.

[59] *R. v. Inland Revenue Commissioners, ex parte National Federation of Self-Employed and Small Businesses Ltd.* [1982] AC 617.

[60] [1966] 2 QB 633.

[61] [1983] 1 WLR 1302, at p. 1307.

[62] [1983] 2 AC 237.

[63] [1919] AC 606; in *Faramus v. Film Artistes Association* [1964] AC 925, Lords Hodson and Pearce indicated that unreasonable exclusionary rules adopted by a professional or trade association would be invalid at common law as being in restraint of trade; see also Lord Denning (dissenting) in that case at [1963] 2 QB 527.

[64] [1978] 1 WLR 1520.

[65] [1985] NZLR 159; compare however *Cowley v. Heatley and Others, The Times,* July 24, 1986, discussed below.

to prevent a proposed tour of South Africa. The Union is an incorporated association whose objects are to promote, foster and develop the game. The applicants did not have contracts directly with the Union but they were, as local club members, linked to it by a chain of contracts. They raised the issue that in permitting the tour the Union had acted against its objects, because the tour could not be regarded as promoting the game. It was held that the applicants had standing to bring the proceedings because this was not simply a matter of internal management or administration; it went to fundamentals. While technically a private and voluntary sporting association, the Union was in a position of major national importance.[66]

In the light of the English Court of Appeal decision in *Law*,[67] this factor alone would not make the Union a "public" body. Slade L.J. accepted "the importance to the general public of the activities which the National Greyhound Racing Club performs, not least its disciplinary functions", but he held nevertheless that the Club was not subject to Order 53. And in the *Take-over Panel* case, the assumption was that a voluntary body may be subject to Order 53 only if its foundation was the result of a decision of government and/or it is buttressed by statute. It would seem to follow that an organisation such as the New Zealand Rugby Union and other bodies regulating sport would not be regarded as "public" bodies to be subjected to Order 53. And yet a supervisory jurisdiction is exercisable in respect of them.

The New Zealand Court of appeal referred to the *National Federation of Self-Employed*[68] case in support of the general approach to standing, holding that the decision of the Union "affects the New Zealand community as a whole"; "in truth the case has some analogy with public law issues" though this approach was not to be pressed too far. The issue "falls into a special area where, in the New Zealand context, a sharp boundary between public and private law cannot realistically be drawn".

At a later hearing,[69] it was decided that there was an arguable case that the Union had deliberately shut their eyes to public concern over the tour (*i.e.* disregarded a relevant consideration) and had closed their minds to any genuine consideration of its effect on the welfare of rugby (*i.e.* fettered their discretion, or refused to exercise discretion). A most potent factor in the exercise of the court's discretion to grant an interim injunction was the public's and the nation's interest in the tour being cancelled.

It will be seen that in this case the boundaries between public and private law and their respective supervisory functions are breaking down, and that principles of good administration which bear a strong resemblance to the

---

[66] There are echoes here of Sir Harry Woolf's lecture on "Public law – private law: Why the Divide?" at [1986] PL 220.

[67] *Law* v. *National Greyhound Racing Club* [1983] 1 WLR 1302.

[68] [1982] AC 617.

[69] [1985] 2 NZLR 181.

substantive rules of judicial review were applied to a private body at the behest of applicants who had no contractual relationship with the Union.

In the *Finnigan* case the ultra vires rules entered into the picture because the Union may have been acting in breach of its general purposes. But it is remarkable that persons who were not in contractual relationship with the Union were entitled to rely on that rule. One can imagine situations where a court might interfere with private activity (*e.g.* of a chartered corporation) that has an impact on the public even if no question of *vires* arose. The doctrine of privity, which protects private organisations from judicial supervision, is breaking down in this area.

The limits of private non-contractual supervision

The supervisory jurisdiction in private pre-contract and non-contractual relations is at present limited. It would be misleading to imply that there exists, or should exist, a full-blown supervisory jurisdiction in this area. In *McInnes* v. *Onslow-Fane* Sir Robert Megarry, V.-C. was careful to emphasise that

> ... the courts must be slow to allow any implied obligation to be fair to be used as a means of bringing before the courts for review honest decisions of bodies exercising jurisdiction over sporting and other activities which those bodies are far better fitted to judge than the courts ... The concepts of natural justice and the duty to be fair must not be allowed to discredit themselves by making unreasonable requirements and imposing undue burdens.[70]

In *Cowley* v. *Heatley*,[71] the present Vice-Chancellor took the same line. The plaintiff applied for a declaration that she was eligible to compete for England in the Commonwealth Games. There was no contractual link between the plaintiff and the Commonwealth Games Federation. Sir Nicholas Browne-Wilkinson found that it was not necessary to decide whether the plaintiff had *locus standi*,[72] since the court would not in any event have exercised its jurisdiction to grant a declaration. It was the court's function to control illegality and to make sure that a functioning body did not act outside its terms. But no good cause would be served by attempting to regulate a domestic body such as the Commonwealth Games Federation.

Unless bias, unfairness, arbitrariness or capriciousness are established, there will be no interference by the courts in private bodies having no contractual relationship with the plaintiff.[73] Even if those grounds are established a court may in its direction refuse a remedy. But if those grounds are established, and if vital

---

[70] [1978] 1 WLR at p. 1535; this approach was echoed by the Court of Appeal in the *Take-over Panel* case [1987] 2 WLR 699.

[71] *The Times*, July 24, 1986, Sir Nicholas Browne-Wilkinson V.-C.

[72] Compare the finding of the New Zealand Court of Appeal that a party in no contractual relationship with the defendant did have standing, according to the test in the *National Federation of the Self-Employed* case: *Finnigan* v. *N.Z.R.F.U.* [1985] NZLR 159.

[73] R. v. *Trent Regional Health Authority, The Times*, June 19, 1986.

interests[74] or the public interest are affected, then a supervisory jurisdiction in private law may be exercisable. This, it is suggested, is an important and somewhat neglected development in private law.

Contracts and the supervisory jurisdiction

Once a private contract has been concluded, it would on the face of it be inconsistent with freedom of contract for any contracting party to deny the binding character of any of the terms, unless they fall within one of the classes of term that are void, for example as being in unreasonable restraint of trade, or for illegality. In a consensual relationship a party should not be entitled to go back on his consent, and hence the supervisory jurisdiction should not be available. The same applies in principle to contracts by public authorities. This was presumably what Diplock L.J. had in mind in *Ex parte Lain*[75] when he commented that the supervisory jurisdiction of the High Court "has not in the past been dependent upon the source of the tribunal's authority to decide issues submitted to its determination, *except where such authority is derived solely from agreement of parties to the determination*" (emphasis added). Despite this principle, however, the courts have on occasions implied terms or imposed obligations in private contracts which reflect some of the principles of good administration that are applied in applications for judicial review: the duty of natural justice or fairness is an obvious example, and was implied—or imposed—in *Herring* v. *Templeman*,[76] *Glynn* v. *Keele University*,[77] *Edwards* v. *SOGAT*,[78] *Breen* v. *AEU*[79] and, interestingly, in *R.* v. *Committee of Lloyds, ex parte Posgate*[80] (a forerunner of the *Take-over Panel* case). As in the pre-contractual phase these principles are devised to protect the "right to work", and possibly property rights.[81]

Quite apart from the use of express or implied terms in a contract, it seems that a private supervisory jurisdiction exists in certain circumstances in relation

---

[74] These include "rights to work". They do not, it seems, include mere reputation where no gainful activity is involved: *Currie* v. *Barber, The Times*, March 27, 1987; *cf. Fisher* v. *Keane* (1878) 11 Ch.D. 387. See also *Cowley* v. *Heatley, The Times*, July 24, 1986.

[75] *R.* v. *Criminal Injuries Compensation Board, ex parte Lain* [1967] 2 QB 864, at p. 884. See also *per* Lord Parker CJ: "Private or domestic tribunals have always been outside the scope of certiorari since their authority is derived solely from contract, that is, from the agreement of the parties concerned" (at p. 882).

[76] [1973] 3 All ER 569.

[77] [1971] 1 WLR 487.

[78] [1971] Ch. 354.

[79] [1971] 2 QB 175.

[80] Queen's Bench Divisional Court, January 11, 1983, *The Times*, January 12, 1983; see also *R.* v. *Committee of Lloyds, ex parte Moran*, Court of Appeal, March 5, 1985.

[81] See *R.* v. *Independent Broadcasting Authority, ex parte the Rank Organisation plc*, CA, March 26, 1986, where it was conceded by counsel for the authority that there was a duty in private law to exercise powers "bona fide and honestly", presumably because the IBA were interfering with the property rights of shareholders by denying them their voting rights. If the decision had come within the public law area, there would have been a more onerous duty of fairness.

to contractual or other established relationships. In *Wood* v. *Woad*,[82] a case on the expulsion of the plaintiff from a mutual insurance society, Kelly C.B. founded his decision in favour of the plaintiff not on implied contractual terms, but on the basis that the *audi alteram partem* rule "is applicable to every tribunal or body of persons invested with authority to adjudicate upon matters involving civil consequences to individuals".[83] And in *Fisher* v. *Keane*,[84] on expulsion of the plaintiff from his club, Jessel M.R. formulated the general principle that the committee,

> ought not, as I understand it, according to the ordinary rules by which justice should be administered by committee of clubs, or by any other body of persons who decide upon the conduct of others, to blast a man's reputation for ever – perhaps to ruin his prospects for life, without giving him an opportunity of either defending or palliating his conduct.[85]

In *Lapointe*,[86] which was concerned with the decision of the board of a pension fund trust to deprive the plaintiff of his pension, Lord Macnaghten based his decision that the rules of natural justice applied on both "the rules of the society" and "the elementary principles of justice".

In addition to imposing a duty of fairness, a duty not to impose haphazard or arbitrary rules or unreasonable restraints of trade on a contracting party was held to exist in *Pharmaceutical Society of Great Britain* v. *Dickson*.[87] These phrases are very reminiscent of "*Wednesbury* unreasonableness" and "irrationality". The courts will not always impose duties of this kind in contractual relationships. The position depends on the nature of the interest affected: the right to work may receive greater protection than other interests. In *Lewis* v. *Heffer*[88] there was no duty of natural justice where a decision was taken by the national executive committee of the Labour party to suspend a constituency party.[89]

There is thus, it seems, even in contract, a private law supervisory jurisdiction, though this may be achieved in part by implying terms in the contract.[90] As Daintith has put it,

> . . . one is struck by the similarity of the results obtained by applying, on the one hand, administrative law tests to the exercise of discretionary statutory powers, and on the other common law tests to discretionary contractual powers.[91]

---

[82] (1874) LR 9 Ex. 190.

[83] This statement was approved by Lord Macnaghten in *Lapointe* v. *L'Association de Bienfaisance et de Retraite de la Police de Montreal* [1906] AC 535, at pp. 538–540, PC; and by Lord Reid in *Ridge* v. *Baldwin* [1964] AC 40, 70.

[84] (1878) 11 Ch.D. 353. Compare *Hamlet* v. *G.M.B.A.T.U.* [1986] IRLR 293, 295.

[85] (1878) 11 Ch.D., at pp. 362–363. Jessel MR also suggested that there was a duty of proportionality (at p. 362).

[86] [1906] AC 535, PC.

[87] [1970] AC 403; see also *The "Vainqueur Jose"* [1979] 1 Lloyds Rep. 557, 574 (duty of subjective good faith); *Bonsor* v. *Musicians' Union* [1954] Ch. 479.

[88] [1978] 1 WLR 1061.

[89] See also *John* v. *Rees* [1970] Ch. 345.

[90] See Daintith [1979] CLP 41 at p. 58.

[91] *Ibid.*

Just as there is some supervision over private economic and contracting power, so some uses of such power in the hands of public bodies might be subjected to the same principles of good administration, involving requirements of fairness or natural justice,[92] *Wednesbury* reasonableness,[93] and so on.

Argument two: since the source of a power is irrelevant, property and contracting powers may be subject to judicial review

There is considerable similarity between statutory grant-giving and licensing, and statutory or common law pre-contractual decisions, and it is established that, for example, there may be judicial review of a statutory grant-giving policy,[94] and that duties of fairness apply in statutory licensing[95] and statutory grant-giving cases.[96] Complaints about the refusal of certain local authorities to purchase *The Times* newspaper for public libraries have been entertained in applications for judicial review.[97] On the surface these powers are statutory, but in reality they are exercises of purchasing and contracting power. Further, the grounds for review of property-owning and contractual decisions expounded by the House of Lords in *Wheeler* v. *Leicester City Corporation*[98] namely, illegitimate pressure, and punishment in the absence of wrong, are particularly appropriate to judicial review of property-owning and contractual or pre-contractual decisions.

Lord Diplock stressed in the *G.C.H.Q.* case that "I see no reason why simply because a decision-making power is derived from a common law and not a statutory source it should *for that reason only* be immune from judicial review."[99] On its face, this statement would seem to apply to decisions relating to property and contract. A difficulty here is that Lord Diplock also maintained that "for a decision to be susceptible to judicial review the decision-maker must be empowered by public law . . . to make decisions."[100] It is unlikely, however, that a minister or a local authority, in their tendering and procurement, decisions, would be regarded as "empowered by private law", since their duties (not at this point deriving from any contract) are related to promotion of the general public interest and not to their private freedoms or interests.

---

[92] See *R.* v. *Wear Valley D.C. ex parte Binks* [1985] 2 All ER 699, Taylor J.

[93] See *Roberts* v. *Hopwood* [1925] AC 578; *Pickwell* v. *Camden L.B.C.* [1983] QB 962.

[94] *British Oxygen Co. Ltd.* v. *Board of Trade* [1971] AC 610; *R.* v. *Secretary of State for the Environment, ex parte Brent L.B.C.* [1982] QB 593.

[95] *R.* v. *Barnsley M.B.C., ex parte Hook* [1976] 1 WLR 1052; *R.* v. *Liverpool Corporation, ex parte Liverpool Taxi Fleet Operators Association* [1972] 2 QB 299.

[96] n. 94, *supra*.

[97] *R.* v. *Ealing London Borough Council, ex parte Times Newspapers, The Times*, November 6, 1986.

[98] [1985] AC 1054.

[99] At p. 410; Lord Diplock's own emphasis.

[100] At p. 409.

Pre-contractual and non-contractual relationships

There is no generalised supervisory jurisdiction in relation to a public authority's pre-contractual conduct, as is demonstrated by *R. v. Trent Regional Health
Authority, ex parte Jones*[101] where a refusal of employment was not reviewed;
but the assumption[102] that judicial review of public pre-contract is never possible seems to me to be no longer justified, especially in the light of the *Take-over
Panel* case[103] and the development of private law supervision.

One aspect of tendering and procurement, and of other contracting activities
such as employment policies, that might lend itself to judicial review is the use
by public bodies of guidelines that regulate their procedures or set out their policies. Local authorities are required by section 135 of the Local Government Act
1972 to adopt standing orders respecting their contracting; other public authorities, though not required to adopt standing orders, may publish advice, minutes, and circulars setting out their tendering practice. In addition to published
guidelines, authorities may have informal policies on tendering, purchasing,
employment and so on.

Published policies of this kind may give rise to complaints of illegitimate pressure, which the House of Lords found unlawful in the *Wheeler* case;[104] and they
may raise legitimate expectations.[105] It is arguable therefore that the content,
and the implementation or non-implementation, of these policies, are subject to
judicial review.

The argument was put in *Connor v. Strathclyde Regional Council.*[106] An
unsuccessful applicant for a post as assistant head teacher at a local authority
school complained that the head teacher, who was present as an assessor during
his interview, was the uncle of the successful applicant; the relationship had not
been disclosed. The applicant claimed that he had a legitimate expectation that
he would be interviewed by a board as provided for in the authority's circular
setting out their procedures, in accordance with the rules of natural justice, and
that the rule against bias had been breached. It was held that the applicant did
have the legitimate expectation he claimed, but it was also held that the actings
of the board did not involve a sufficient element of public law to be subject to
judicial review.

---

[101] *The Times*, June 19, 1986.

[102] See *e.g.* Daintith [1979] CLP 41, at 45, 59.

[103] It is however clear that there is no general supervisory jurisdiction in pre-contract: *R. v. Trent
Regional Health Authority, ex parte Jones, The Times*, June 19, 1986.

[104] [1985] AC 1054.

[105] See *R. v. Chief Immigration Officer, ex parte Kharrazi* [1980] 1 WLR 1396; *Att.-Gen. of Hong
Kong v. Ng Yuen Shiu* [1983] AC 629, PC. See also Foulkes, *Administrative Law* (6th ed., 1986),
chap. 13; *R. v. Secretary of State for the Home Office, ex parte Asif Mahmood Khan* [1984] 1 WLR
1337; *R. v. Secretary of State for the Home Department, ex parte Ruddock,* [1987] 2 All ER 518; *R.
v. Commissioners of Inland Revenue, ex parte Fulford-Dobson and Another, The Times*, March 19,
1987.

[106] 1986 SLT 530, Outer House. And see [1987] Public Law 313.

This decision raises a number of difficulties. First, it envisages the existence of legitimate expectations which are not protected by law, a seeming contradiction in terms. Second, it is difficult to reconcile with *Malloch* v. *Aberdeen Corporation*,[107] where a public law element was found to exist in the statutory underpinning of teacher employment. And third, it invites the question why the contracting processes of public authorities should enjoy the same freedom from judicial supervision that is extended to private contracting. This last point is considered below.

Contractual and property transactions

The courts have generally been careful to exempt powers derived solely from contract from judicial review, unless there is a "statutory underpinning".[108] In the passage from the G.C.H.Q. case quoted earlier, Lord Diplock contrasted the position where a decision-maker is empowered by public law, and is therefore subject to judicial review, with the position where he is empowered "merely, as in arbitration, by agreement between private parties".[109] In *R.* v. *BBC, ex parte Lavelle*[110] Woolf L.J. held that judicial review was "confined to reviewing activities of a public nature as opposed to those of a purely private or domestic character". It is not entirely clear how these exemptions from judicial review operate.

The question whether the supervisory jurisdiction is available in respect of powers deriving from a contract arose in *R.* v. *Independent Broadcasting Authority, ex parte the Rank Organisation plc.*[111] The IBA had powers under the articles of association of a company, Granada Group, in which it was not a shareholder, to refuse to allow any shareholder with more than five per cent of the voting rights to exercise those rights. The IBA refused Rank, a shareholder in Granada Group, permission to exercise these rights. It was held that as the powers arose under the articles of association and not under the Broadcasting Act 1981, judicial review was not available. Lloyd L.J. expressed concern that there was a "gap in the armoury of the law".

---

[107] 1971 SC (HL) 85.

[108] *R.* v. *East Berkshire Health Authority, ex parte Walsh* [1985] QB 152, CA; *R.* v. *National Coal Board, ex parte National Union of Mineworkers* [1986] ICR 791; *R.* v. *BBC, ex parte Lavelle* [1983] 1 WLR 23; compare *R.* v. *Secretary of State for the Home Department, ex parte Benwell* [1985] QB 554. In *R.* v. *Civil Service Appeal Board, ex parte Bruce, The Times*, June 22, 1987, DC. May LJ held that even in a case of a civil servant employed under contract with the Crown, the circumstances of his dismissal and any appeal to the board might be subject to judicial review, although generally an industrial tribunal would be a more appropriate forum.

[109] At p. 409 (note the expression "private parties"); in *O'Reilly* v. *Mackman* [1983] 2 AC 237 Lord Diplock, referring to *ex parte Shaw* [1952] 1 KB 711, commented: "what was there rediscovered was that the High Court had power to quash by order of certiorari a decision of any body of persons having legal authority (not derived from contract only) to determine questions affecting the rights of subjects . . ."

[110] [1983] ICR 99, at p. 109.

[111] Court of Appeal, March 26, 1986, unreported.

The decision raises a number of problems, for the IBA's power arose under the articles of association, which had been altered by Granada Group plc in order to comply with a contract between Granada Television, a subsidiary of Granada Group, and the IBA. The articles constituted a contract between Granada Group and its shareholders, but not between shareholders and the IBA. In other words, the IBA derived its powers from a contract to which it was not a party; and it was enabled by that contract to enforce its powers (which interfered with the incidents of share ownership) against a third party, Rank, with whom it was not in contractual relationship. And it was not subject to judicial review.

This decision represents a far-reaching extension of the doctrine that powers deriving from contract are not subject to judicial review. It is one thing to provide that where a public body and a private organisation or individual are in a purely contractual relationship with one another with no statutory underpinning, their position is governed by their contract alone, as in *Walsh*.[112] It is quite another thing to deny parties who are bound to public institutions via contracts to which they are not parties access to the supervisory jurisdiction in public law, simply because the power derives from contract. Contracts of this kind are closer to by-laws than to true contracts.[113]

A contract that grants to a public authority powers of the type that were in issue in the *Rank* case, or other express powers or discretions, such as a right to inspect the employment records of a contractor or sub-contractor, or the right to terminate a contract for breach of the public authority's policies or guidelines, can hardly be said to be of a "purely private or domestic character", since the objective will be the promotion of public policies. Nevertheless it seems that there can be no recourse to judicial review, except possibly in private law.[114] This position derives from an inappropriate[115] analogy with arbitration clauses,[116] and it is not, it is suggested, immutable, especially given the "gap in the armoury of the law" that it leaves.[117]

Not all contracts entered into by public authorities are of this kind. Commonly contracting parties are able to influence one another's conduct and

---

[112] R. v. *East Berkshire Health Authority, ex parte Walsh* [1985] QB 152.

[113] See Lord Denning MR in *Bonsor v. Musicians Union* [1954] Ch. 479 at p. 485.

[114] *Supra*, pp. 17–19.

[115] See, *per* May LJ in the *IBA* case (*supra*, n. 12), after referring to Lord Diplock's statements about the exclusion from judicial review of certain contractual decisions: "But in none of those passages did Lord Diplock have in mind the case where the ultimate source of power is legislation, but the immediate source of power is a contract between the subject and the decision-maker, or, as in the present case, a contract between the shareholders of a public company conferring by its Articles of Association a power of decision on a third party. The contract between shareholders looks at first sight more like an agreement to appoint an arbitrator, the example given by Lord Diplock in the C.C.S.U. case. But a moment's thought reveals the difference. An arbitrator has (or should have) no interest whatever in the subject matter of his decision; whereas the IBA has a very direct interest in the granting or withholding of approval under Article 75A".

[116] See, *per* Lord Diplock in the G.C.H.Q. case [1985] AC 374, at p. 409; and *National Joint Council for the Craft of Dental Technicians (Disputes Committee), ex parte Neate* [1953] 1 QB 704.

[117] n. 12, *supra*.

rights, expectations or interests by virtue of the simple fact of the dependence of one upon another. Here the power does not derive from the terms of the contract, and judicial review may be available. Similarly, where a public authority has property at its disposal, access to which is sought by others, the authority is in a position of power which may attract judicial review. The point is illustrated by *R. v. Wear Valley District Council, ex parte Binks*.[118] In this case, the district council had revoked the contractual licence they had granted to a take-away hot food seller to park her van on council land. The chief executive alleged that the council could deal with its land as it saw fit at its absolute discretion, in the same way as any other land owner. Taylor J. rejected this claim and held that the rules of natural justice applied: "it seems to me that there is a public law element in the decisions of the council with regard to whom they license and whom they do not license to trade in the market place."[119]

If the land in the *Binks* case had been privately owned, there might not have been a duty of natural justice on the part of the owner before giving Mrs. Binks notice.[120] The rationale for this position is that a private owner is in principle free to decide who shall and who shall not enter and use his land, and on what terms; this is an aspect of the owner's personal liberty which constitutes a strong, though not insuperable, moral argument against imposing obstacles on the owner's exercise of his rights. Where however, as in the *Binks* case, land is publicly owned, an argument in terms of the "personal liberty" of the public authority is, or should be, less convincing – though a parallel and no more convincing argument succeeded in the *Malone* case.[121]

Even without a "public law element" in *Binks*, there may have been a private law duty of natural justice in that case on the strength of *Nagle v. Feilden*.[122] The "public element" was referred to mainly to support the exercise of jurisdiction under R.S.C. Order 53. Had the authority been exercising a statutory power in respect of the market, there would clearly have been a duty of natural justice, in accordance with *ex parte Hook*.[123] The point illustrates the anomalies that flow from treating regulatory powers differently where the supervisory jurisdiction of the court is concerned, simply because of the source of the power.

The courts have recently begun to develop principles for the control of the exercise of power derived from the ownership of property, in the absence of contract or statutory powers or duties. In *R. v. Brent London Borough Council, ex parte Assegai*[124] a local authority banned a member of the public from local authority property because he had made abusive and offensive remarks about two councillors. It was held that the local authority had an unfettered right to ban visitors from property which members of the public had no right to visit

---

[118] [1985] 2 All ER 699, Taylor J.
[119] At p. 703. See also *R. v. Brent L.B.C., ex parte Assegai, The Independent*, June 12, 1987, DC.
[120] But *cf. Wood v. Woad* (1874) LR 9 Ex. 190; and the *Lapointe* case [1906] AC 535, PC.
[121] *Malone v. Metropolitan Police Commissioner* [1979] Ch. 344.
[122] [1966] 2 QB 633; and *Wood v. Woad* (1874) LR 9 Ex. 190.
[123] *R. v. Barnsley M.B.C., ex parte Hook* [1976] 1 WLR 1052.
[124] *The Independent*, June 12, 1987, DC.

without an invitation, but that in the case of premises which were usually open to the general public the principles of fairness applied. The authority could not then discriminate against an individual on the basis of his conduct without following the requirements of natural justice. The banning was also faulted as being "wholly out of proportion to what the appellant had done."[125]

There are also cases where non-contracting parties have been able to invoke the supervisory jurisdiction over the exercise of contracting power by public authorities: *Roberts* v. *Hopwood*[126] and *Pickwell* v. *Camden L.B.C.*[127] are examples, although in both cases proceedings were initiated by the district auditor.

Judicial supervision of public and private economic power compared

It would be rash to suggest that a fully supervisory jurisdiction is developing, or ought to develop, in respect of private contracting and property power, or power of that kind in state hands. Yet, as the cases referred to above illustrate, economic and contracting power, whether in public or private hands, may be used to restrict the freedom of action of individuals and organisations without their true consent; and it may be used against the public interest in various ways. There is a strong case that such power, whether in public or private hands, should be subjected to supervision and application of the principles of good administration. Such an approach would also have the merit of subjecting common law and statutory power to similar controls.

Supervisory jurisdiction has to take account of some important differences between public and private power. Where purely private power is concerned, three factors argue against extensive judicial supervision. Respect for the individual liberty of the parties, certainty in the law, and the needs of the market,[128] would indicate that the courts ought not, in the name of good administration, to impose too many restraints on personal liberty, or introduce a general duty to subordinate private interests to the public interest unless a statute so requires.

However, where public economic and contracting power is concerned, the "liberty" of the public body or official should not be regarded as a reason to exempt that body from the principles of good administration.[129] Public power is supposed to be used in the public interest, whereas in the case of private power the rights of individuals having that power have to be weighed in the balance against the public interest. Further, it is often the case that the public authority

---

[125] *Per* Woolf LJ. See also *West Glamorgan C.C.* v. *Rafferty* [1987] 1 All ER 1005, CA, in which the authority's claim that it was entitled to evict trespassers at will in the same way as a private landowner was rejected because the authority was in breach of its duty to provide accommodation for the gipsies who were trespassing.

[126] [1925] AC 578.

[127] [1983] QB 962.

[128] The Court of Appeal was very conscious of the importance of this consideration in the *Takeover Panel* case [1987] 2 WLR 699.

[129] See, *e.g.* *Wheeler* v. *Leicester City Council* [1985] AC 1054.

is in a monopoly or near-monopoly position. These considerations would point towards increasing judicial supervision of public bodies in order to protect the free exercise of personal liberties by those affected by public power, an approach that was implicit in the dissenting judgment of Browne-Wilkinson L.J. in *Wheeler* v. *Leicester City Council.* As against this, there is a public interest in enabling public authorities to get on with the job of governing, and this argues for judicial restraint in dealing with complaints about the actions of public bodies. This argument, it is suggested, should be applied evenhandedly to the statutory and non-statutory activities of public bodies, and it is not in itself a persuasive argument against judicial review of contracting and property power.

There may be exercises of private and public power where no issues of individual liberty arise, but where the public interest is affected by a decision, as in the *Finnigan* case.[130] Here there may well be scope for the courts to develop, if Parliament does not do so, principles of good administration to which private bodies as much as public bodies should adhere.

CONCLUSIONS

As Lloyd L.J. put it in the *Take-over Panel* case:

> The express powers conferred on inferior tribunals were of critical importance in the early days when the sole or main ground for intervention by the courts was that the inferior tribunal had exceeded its powers. But those days are long since past.[131]

My purpose in this article has been to suggest that the ultra vires rules, though still very relevant in cases of judicial review, is not the basis of that jurisdiction. As has been written, "Notwithstanding the supremacy of Parliament, the courts impose standards of lawful conduct upon public authorities as a matter of common law, and it is arguable that the power to impose such standards is a constitutional fundamental."[132]

In place of the ultra vires rule a doctrine is emerging that, in the public sphere, the courts in exercising a supervisory jurisdiction are concerned both with the *vires* of public authorities in the strict or narrow sense referred to above, and with abuse of power. If abuse of power is established, the courts may properly intervene. If no abuse is established, the courts should leave to the political process the function of dealing with complaints about the exercise of power.[133] The judicial requirements about the exercise of public power, and even to an extent private power, are that the exercise of power should accord with certain broad principles of good administration, involving participatory procedures,

---

[130] n. 65, *supra.*
[131] *R.* v. *Panel on Take-overs* [1987] 2 WLR 699, 724.
[132] Wade and Bradley, *Constitutional and Administrative Law* (10th ed., 1985), at p. 594.
[133] See, *e.g.* Lord Scarman in *Nottinghamshire C.C.* v. *Secretary of State for the Environment* [1986] AC 240, at pp. 247, 249, 250.

rationality[134] and some substantive principles of compliance with "constitutional fundamentals".[135] For the most part, these principles are administered through the procedure of the application for judicial review. However similar principles, which developed before the introduction of Order 53 in 1977 and the decision in *O'Reilly* v. *Mackman*,[136] and the attempt to separate public and private law, may be applied to private bodies. Out of this is emerging a general theory about the exercise of power: the doctrine may apply to power whatever its source, if it affects vital private interests, or is in the "public domain", whether in public or private hands. To an extent, as Sir Harry Woolf commented, the two need to coalesce – and are beginning to do so:

> ... if public law has developed so rapidly that it now gives greater protection than does private law, should consideration be given to whether the type of review which takes place into administrative action should as at present be limited to public bodies? The interests of the public are as capable of being adversely affected by the decisions of large corporations and large associations, be they of employers or employees, and should they not be subject to challenge on *Wednesbury* grounds if their decision relates to activities which can damage the public interest? . . . Powerful bodies, whether they are public bodies or not, because of their economic muscle may be in a position to take decisions which at the present time are not subject to scrutiny and which could be unfair or adversely affect the public interest.[137]

It is remarkable that while the courts are striving to separate public and private law, the two are in some respects converging. An awareness of the nature of power, and of the "interpenetration of state and society", is leading the courts towards a willingness to supervise public and private power.

The weakness of the ultra vires rule as the basis for judicial review, and of the doctrines of separation of powers and parliamentary sovereignty on which the ultra vires rule rests, is symptomatic of the absence of workable concepts and of a framework of theory about the nature of power, whether public or private, upon which to build the supervisory jurisdictions of the courts.

Political theorists and philosophers can assist lawyers in their understanding of the nature and incidence of power; Galbraith's analysis in *The Anatomy of Power*[138] is useful for these purposes. Galbraith adopts Weber's definition of power as "the possibility of imposing one's will upon the behaviour of other persons".[139] Working from this definition, Galbraith identifies the instruments of power (public and private) as being condign power, compensatory power, and conditioned power. In legal terms, condign power is the use of coercive legisla-

---

[134] See D.J. Galligan, "Judicial Review and the Textbook Writers" (1982) 2 OJLS 257.

[135] See H.W.R. Wade, *Constitutional Fundamentals* (1980); and J.L. Jowell and A. Lester "Beyond *Wednesbury*: Substantive Principles of Administrative Law" at p. 368 *supra*.

[136] [1983] 2 AC 237.

[137] [1986] PL 220, at pp. 224–245.

[138] J.K. Galbraith (1983).

[139] *Max Weber on Law in Economy and Society* (1954), p. 323.

tion[140] backed up by powers of punishment imposed through the courts, and perhaps punishment imposed by public authorities through the withdrawal of co-operation, as in *Wheeler* v. *Leicester City Council*. Private bodies have similar powers of punishment through withdrawal of co-operation, as is illustrated from time to time in the field of labour relations, for example. By compensatory power, Galbraith means the power to win submission by the offer of affirmative reward, usually through the deployment of money or property, but also through the grant of licences and other privileges. Galbraith's "conditioned power" is the influence that a ruler or other individual or organisation derives from public belief in his or her authority – "legitimacy". Here it is important to recognise the potential for public and private bodies (for example, the press and those with access to advertising) to "condition" public attitudes to the authority of power-holders by the use of propaganda.

Galbraith distinguishes between the instruments of power and sources of power. The latter he identifies as property, organisation and personality. Property is very familiar to lawyers as an instrument of power.[141] Command of property may be used both to reward and to punish those over whom the property owner seeks to wield power. Hence there are strong links between property and condign and compensatory power. Organisation, or bureaucracy, whether public or private, is necessary to most exercises of power of any substance. Personality remains influential in the private sphere as a source of power, but in the public sphere the "charismatic" leader will normally require organisation and/or property in order to exert power effectively.

Galbraith's analysis of the anatomy of power casts light on the issues underlying the question whether and when the courts should concern themselves with the exercise and abuse of power. The courts in recent cases have intuitively begun to recognise some of these facts about power. Property is beginning to be perceived as a most potent source and instrument of power; and one that can be used both to reward and to punish. Organisation is essential to the exercise of power: hence the judicial recognition of and willingness to supervise organisations like the Take-over Panel, and self-regulatory bodies in sport and other areas. The importance of "conditioned power" and the potential for manipulation of public opinion were recognised by public authorities in the campaigns against the abolition of the metropolitan counties and the G.L.C., and the courts sought to accommodate it.

It is in this direction, it is suggested, that lawyers and the courts should be looking for an understanding of the nature of the problem which principles of good administration could help to solve. Once the nature and problem of power are recognised, the courts will be in a better position to develop a supervisory jurisdiction designed to prevent the abuse of power.

---

[140] See also T.C. Daintith on "imperium" in "The Executive Power Today: Bargaining and Economic Control", in Jowell and Oliver (eds.) *The Changing Constitution* (1985), at p. 174.
[141] See Daintith, n. 41 *supra*, on "dominium".

2

Of Fig Leaves and Fairy Tales: The Ultra Vires Doctrine, the Sovereignty of Parliament and Judicial Review*

CHRISTOPHER FORSYTH

I. INTRODUCTION

The doctrine of ultra vires has been aptly described by Sir William Wade as "the central principle of administrative law"[1] but in recent years it has been subjected to criticism. First the academics weighed in[2] and, increasingly, eminent judges speaking or writing extra-judicially have described the doctrine as a "fairy tale"[3] or a "fig leaf"[4] and declared its redundancy and lack of utility. The major grounds of criticism have been, first, that the doctrine is artificial in that the legislature could never have formed an intention, express or implied, on the many, subtle and various principles which form the modern law of judicial review. The content of the rules of natural justice, the concept of irrationality and the like are judicial, not legislative, constructs. And this should be recognised in the abolition of the doctrine of ultra vires. Secondly, it is argued that the concept of ultra vires can simply play no part in determining whether, as is clearly the case, non-statutory bodies which exercise no legal powers at all are subject to judicial review.

The purpose of this article is to defend the orthodox doctrine of ultra vires from these criticisms and to show that it remains vital to the developed law of

---

* This is a reprint of an article first published in 55 [1996] CLJ 122. I am grateful to Sir William Wade, Dr Yvonne Cripps, Trevor Allan and Ivan Hare for their comments on a draft of this article; I remain responsible for all errors.

[1] Wade and Forsyth, *Administrative Law* (7th ed., 1994), p. 41. The present writer is the co-author with Sir William Wade of the 7th ed. of this book, but he has no desire to assume any credit for passages which, although they appear in the 7th ed., are substantially unchanged from earlier editions.

[2] Dawn Oliver, "Is the ultra vires rule the basis of judicial review?", [1987] *Public Law* 543 and Chapter One, pp. 3–26 above; Craig, *Administrative Law* (3rd edn., 1994), pp. 12, pp. 3–26 above.

[3] Lord Woolf of Barnes "Droit Public – English Style" [1995] *Public Law* 57 at 66 adopting the phrase coined by Lord Reid ("The Judge as Lawmaker" [1972] *The Journal of Public Teachers of Law* 22) to describe those who denied the judiciary any law making role.

[4] This metaphor was first used in print by Sir John Laws in "Illegality: the problem of jurisdiction" in Supperstone and Goudie (eds), *Judicial Review* (1992) 67. It has since been used many times.

judicial review. The burden of the argument will be that the prime role of the doctrine is to provide the necessary constitutional underpinning for the greater part (albeit not the whole) of judicial review. Thus to knock away that under-pinning in the absence of alternative support is to undermine the basis of judi-cial review. Moreover, constitutional considerations aside, this change will render judicial review much less effective. Furthermore, it will be shown that to abandon the doctrine implies the abandonment of legislative supremacy. Such a profound change in the constitutional order, should not, it will be argued, be undertaken by the judiciary of their own motion.

The defence may start with the point that, notwithstanding the eminence of the critics, the views of the House of Lords, as expressed recently in *R.* v. *Lord President of the Privy Council, ex parte Page*,[5] remain unhesitatingly orthodox. Lord Browne-Wilkinson, speaking for the majority, said:

> The fundamental principle [of judicial review] is that the courts will intervene to ensure that the powers of public decision-making bodies are exercised lawfully. In all cases[6] . . . this intervention . . . is based on the proposition that such powers have been conferred on the decision-maker on the underlying assumption that the powers are to be exercised only within the jurisdiction conferred, in accordance with fair procedures and, in a *Wednesbury* sense, reasonably. If the decision-maker exercises his powers outside the jurisdiction conferred, in a manner which is procedurally irregular or is *Wednesbury* unreasonable, he is acting ultra vires his powers and therefore unlaw-fully.[7]

It is this statement of the orthodox position that this article will defend.

However, before turning to the heart of that defence, there is a preliminary issue to discuss. As adumbrated, one of the commonest criticisms of the ultra vires doctrine is that it can provide no explanation for the fact that non-statutory bodies exercising non-legal powers may be subject to judicial review. There is, it is submitted, a satisfactory but relatively novel answer to this objec-tion that can be dealt with immediately before turning to the other criticisms.

---

[5] [1993] AC 682. Sir John Laws argues in "The power of the public law court: who defines it?" (an unpublished paper delivered at Queen Mary College in 1995) (at p. 22) that because Lord Browne-Wilkinson refers elsewhere (at 702F) to a body acting ultra vires "if it reaches its conclusion on a basis erroneous under the *general law*" his view of ultra vires is not orthodox. But when Lord Browne-Wilkinson's dicta on ultra vires are read as a whole it seems undeniable that he has the orthodox view in mind.

[6] Lord Browne-Wilkinson recognises one qualification to this statement: the power to quash for error of law on the face of the record which does not depend upon ultra vires. A further area of juridical review which does not depend upon ultra vires concerns non-statutory bodies which do not exercise legal powers (discussed below in Section II).

[7] See the speech of Lord Browne-Wilkinson at 701C–G, 702F–G citing Wade's views with approval.

II. JUDICIAL REVIEW AND THE EXERCISE OF NON-LEGAL POWERS BY NON-STATUTORY BODIES

Elementarily the developed law of judicial review extends to non-statutory bodies that do not exercise legal powers.[8] The Panel on Takeovers and Mergers is but the most prominent of several examples of this phenomenon.[9] Self-evidently, it is not meaningful, when a body lacks legal power, to talk about it acting in excess of its legal powers. Thus some juridical basis, other than the doctrine of ultra vires, is needed to justify judicial intervention in such cases.

Although the constitutional basis of this extension of judicial review has seldom been discussed, there is, it is submitted, ready at hand a common law root for such judicial intervention. Very usefully Paul Craig has pointed out that it has been "almost forgotten" that the common law imposed a duty to act reasonably on those who exercised monopoly power even where that power simply existed *de facto*.[10] This principle has, behind it the venerable authority of Lord Chief Justice Hale who stated in *De Portibus Maris*,[11] that:

> A man for his own private advantage, may in a port or town set up a wharf or crane and may take what rates he and his customers may agree for cranage, houselage, pesage, for he doth no more than is lawful for any man to do, *viz*, make the most of his own . . . [But] If the King or subject have a public wharf, unto which all persons who come to that port must come and unlade or lade their goods . . . because there is no other wharf in that port as it may fall out where a port is newly erected; in that case there cannot be taken arbitrary and excessive duties for cranage, wharfage, pesage etc. . . .; but the duties must be reasonable and moderate, though settled by the King's license or charter. For now the wharf, and crane and other conveniences are affected with a public interest, and they cease to be *jus privati* only . . .

This principle was then adopted in *Alnutt and Another* v. *Inglis*,[12] where the London Dock Company which owned the only warehouses in London in which wine importers could bond their wine (*i.e.* lodge and secure it without paying duty immediately) was held bound by law to charge only a reasonable hire for receiving wines into bond. Such a monopoly attached a public interest to their property.

---

[8] See Wade and Forsyth, *op. cit.* pp. 659–667 for a review of this development. The limits and constitutional implications of this extension of judicial review have yet to be worked out.

[9] See *R.* v. *Panel on Take-overs and Mergers ex parte Datafin* [1987] QB 815 discussed in Wade and Forsyth, *op. cit.* pp. 662–663. The Court of Appeal recognised that the Panel wields "immense *de facto* power" governing company take-overs and mergers "without visible means of legal support" and, hence, held that it should act "in defence of the citizenry" and grant judicial review in appropriate cases to prevent abuse of those powers. The quotations come from the judgment of Sir John Donaldson MR.

[10] Craig, *Administrative Law* (3rd ed.), pp. 222–225 and, in more detail, "Constitutions, Property and Regulation". [1991] *Public Law* 538.

[11] 1 Harg L. Tr., 78 (1787).

[12] (1810) 12 East 527, and see the several other nineteenth century cases following this principle (primarily *Corporation of Stamford* v. *Pawlett* (1830) 1 C. & J. 57).

All the cases cited by Craig as well as all the American cases in which the principle has been adopted are concerned with imposing upon the owners of monopolies the duty to make only reasonable charges for the use of their property or the provision of related services. However, why should the common law not impose on those who exercise monopoly power, whether that power derives from the ownership of property or otherwise, a more general duty to act reasonably, for instance, to heed the rules of natural justice, not to act irrationally and not to abuse their powers? That indeed, it is submitted, is implicit in the modern case of *Nagle* v. *Fielden*[13] where, in the days before legislation against sexual discrimination, a woman who had been refused a trainer's licence by the Jockey Club merely because of her sex, sought relief against the club. On public policy grounds Lord Denning M.R. refused the Jockey Club's application to strike out her action. The Jockey Club exercised "a virtual monopoly in an important field of human activity" and were not free to deny the right to work. Salmon L.J. also spoke of the common law preventing the club denying a livelihood to the trainer "capriciously and unreasonably". It is but a small step from such statements to the proposition that those who exercise monopoly power should act fairly, heed the rules of natural justice and not act irrationally etc.

Thus it is submitted that in this common law power of the courts to control the abuse of monopolies lies their power to subject bodies such as the Take-over Panel, which clearly exercise monopoly powers, to judicial review.[14] Sir Edward Coke speaks in *Calvin's Case*[15] of "the Common Law of England [being] a science sociable and copious: sociable, in that it agreeth with the principles and rules of other excellent sciences, divine and human, copious for that . . . there should be such a multitude and *farrago* of authorities . . . for the deciding of the point of so rare an accident". Here then is the common law revealed once more to be both sociable and copious. Sociable in that it agrees with the excellent science of common sense that the great monopoly powers of such non-statutory bodes should be regulated; and copious in that it is from within the common law itself that the solution is waiting to be found.

We must return to the doctrine of ultra vires but there are two final points to be made about the judicial review of non-statutory bodies. First of all, the recognition that the common law regulation of monopolies is the underlying basis of this extension of judicial review may extend the boundaries of the judicial review of non-statutory bodies. In particular, the courts have been reluctant to subject "non-governmental" bodies (typically religious and sporting bodies) to

---

[13] [1966] 2 QB 633 approved in several later decisions (*Endersby Town Football Club Ltd.* v. *Football Association Ltd.* [1971] Ch. 591 and *McInnes* v. *Onslow-Fane* [1978] 1 WLR 1520).

[14] The problem of procedural exclusivity may arise but it is not intended to discuss it in detail here (see Wade and Forsyth, *op. cit.*, pp. 680ff). The form of action in *Nagle* v. *Fielden* was a writ action but *ex parte Datafin* was an application for judicial review in terms of R.S.C. Order 53. It is submitted that once the common law principle of the control of monopolies is recognised, then it should make no difference whether that principle is vindicated by action or by judicial review proceedings provided that the form of proceedings chosen is otherwise appropriate.

[15] (1608) 7 Co. Rep. 1a, 28a.

judicial review, even where they exercise great powers. But the common law clearly draws no distinction between monopoly powers that exist by virtue of some governmental intervention and those that exist as a matter of fact. The factual circumstances which create the monopoly may transmute what might otherwise be an unregulated *ius privati* into an regulated *ius publici*. Lord Woolf seems aware of just these considerations when he remarks that "As a matter of principle the present approach of the [judicial] authorities to religious and sporting activities and 'private' ombudsmen appears questionable. The controlling bodies of a sport and religious authorities can exercise monopolistic powers, and the ombudsman is administering a system which provides an alternative method of resolving disputes to that provided by the courts. How then as a last resort can the courts be justifiably excluded?"[16] Here then, in the common law, lies the juristic basis for an extension of judicial review on the lines envisaged by Lord Woolf.

Secondly, it should be made clear that the ultra vires doctrine has never been the sole justification for judicial review. The valuable jurisdiction to quash for error of law on the face of the record, although little used today because, save in special circumstances, all errors of law have become jurisdictional, never depended upon ultra vires.[17] Indeed, it was the blight cast by "parliamentary interference, prompted by judicial pedantry"[18] that led to the eclipse of error of law on the face of the record and the development of the doctrine of ultra vires in the form that we have it today.

The importance of this for the argument of this article is that the recognition that the common law provides the basis for judicial review in some circumstances is not an admission of the failure of ultra vires. Ultra vires retains its central position as far as decisions made under statutory powers are concerned. Moreover, it should be remarked for the avoidance of doubt that recognition of a common law basis for part of judicial review does not challenge legislative supremacy; it is always open to the legislature to intervene to regulate the position. Let us now return to the other criticisms of the doctrine.

III. "WEAK" AND "STRONG" CRITICISMS OF THE ULTRA VIRES DOCTRINE

It is useful to begin by drawing a distinction between what may be termed the "weak" criticisms of the ultra vires doctrine and the "strong" criticisms.[19] Some of the criticisms stresses the artificiality of the doctrine against the background of the developed and extensive modern law of judicial review. As Sir John Laws writes:

---

[16] Lord Woolf of Barnes, "Droit Public-English Style" [1995] *Public Law* 57 at 64.
[17] Wade and Forsyth, *op. cit.*, pp. 306–307.
[18] Wade and Forsyth, *op. cit.*, p. 307.
[19] As we shall see some critics launch both "weak" and "strong" criticisms at the doctrine, but we are concerned with the criticisms not the critics.

> [It] cannot be suggested that all these principles [*viz.*, the modern principles of admin-
> istrative law in particular, natural justice, improper purposes, the protection of legit-
> imate expectations and *Wednesbury* unreasonableness], which represent much of the
> bedrock of modern administrative law, were suddenly interwoven into the legisla-
> ture's intentions in the 1960s and 70s and onward, in which period they have been
> articulated and enforced by the courts. They are, categorically, judicial creations.
> They owe neither their existence nor their acceptance to the will of the legislature.
> They have nothing to do with the intention of Parliament, save as a fig leaf to cover
> their true origins. We do not need the fig-leaf any more.[20]

In the result these "weak" critics either call for or assert that it is the common
law, rather than the implied will of the legislature, that requires that decisions
should be fairly and reasonably made. Consequently, when the judicial review
court quashes a decision of a public body, it is vindicating the common law, not
heeding the will of the legislature.

"Weak" criticisms do not directly challenge the legislative supremacy of
Parliament and do not expressly assert a judicial power to overrule statutes. But
there are, on the other hand, "strong" criticisms which use the deficiencies, real
or perceived, of the ultra vires doctrine as the base for a direct challenge to the
legislative supremacy of Parliament. They assert that the courts enjoy a power
which, although it should be sparingly used in exceptional cases, enables them
to strike down Parliamentary statutes. Parliament, in other words, has lost its
sovereignty; and the judges may in appropriate circumstances pronounce upon
the validity of Acts of Parliament. Lord Woolf, for instance, has said that "if
Parliament did the unthinkable [and undermined substantially the role of the
High Court on judicial review], then I would say that the courts would also be
required to act in a manner which would be without precedent . . . I myself
would consider that there were advantages in making it clear that there are even
limits on the supremacy of Parliament which it is the courts' inalienable responsibility to identify and uphold . . . [These limits] are no more than are necessary
to enable the rule of law to be preserved".[21] Sir John Laws has gone rather further in his published writings, arguing with characteristic vigour that:

> The democratic credentials of an elected government cannot justify its enjoyment of a
> right to abolish fundamental freedoms . . . [T]he need for higher-order law is dictated
> by the logic of the very notion of government under law . . . [T]he doctrine of
> Parliamentary sovereignty cannot be vouched by Parliamentary legislation; a higher
> order law confers it and must of necessity limit it . . . It is characteristic of the intel-
> lectual insouciance which marks our unwritten constitution that though higher order
> law is an imperative required for the establishment of institutions to govern a free
> people, not only is it nowhere to be found, but its emphatic denial, in the shape of the
> absolute sovereignty of Parliament is actually represented by our traditional writers
> such as Dicey as a constitutional cornerstone . . .[22]

---

[20] "Law and Democracy" [1995] *Public Law* 72 at 79.
[21] [1995] *Public Law* 57 at 69.
[22] [1995] *Public Law* 72 at 81–93.

This too is a powerful argument which will need to be effectively countered in order to defend the orthodox view. We will return to it in due course.

An attack on the sovereignty of Parliament may appear to be unrelated to criticism of the ultra vires doctrine. The "strong" critics direct their fire on to the foundations of the constitution, while the "weak" critics seek to undermine only the constitutional justification for judicial review. Yet the abolition of parliamentary sovereignty implies that the final word on the lawfulness of administrative action is not to be found in the implied intent of the legislature. Moreover, in the writings of the critics, "weak" criticism of the doctrine of ultra vires often seems to open the path to "strong" criticism of legislative supremacy. Thus the distinction between "strong" and "weak" criticisms is useful.

The defence of orthodoxy against the "weak" criticisms, however, is different from its defence against the "strong" criticisms. The "weak" criticisms must be engaged with arguments enmeshed in the technicalities of administrative law. It will be shown that if the alternatives of the "weak" critics were adopted there would be grave, but largely unrealised, consequences for judicial review. If ultra vires were abolished, ouster clauses would be much more effective at excluding judicial review than they are today. And, although not generally expressed in the "weak" criticisms, it will be shown that the abandonment of ultra vires inevitably involves the judicial review court in indirectly challenging legislative supremacy.

Nonetheless, supporters of the orthodox view and the "weak" critics are readily reconciled – and that reconciliation will also be attempted below – in a common appreciation of the creativity of the judicial role in developing the principles of judicial review and the value of the task of the judges in subjecting the exercise of executive power (as well as delegated legislative power) to those principles.

The "strong" criticisms, on the other hand, must be countered not with the technicalities of administrative law but with the sword of constitutional principle. And in the end there is no easy reconciliation that can be reached with the "strong" critics. Before doing this let us respond to the "weak" criticisms.

IV. THE RESPONSE TO "WEAK" CRITICISM

The course that supporters of the "weak" criticisms urge upon the judges has, probably unbeknown to the "weak" critics, been tried elsewhere. The ultra vires doctrine, previously considered the basis of judicial review in South African law,[23] was abandoned by that country's highest court in *Staatspresident en*

---

[23] See Lawrence Baxter, *Administrative Law* (Juta & Co., 1984), pp. 307–312 dealing with and rejecting alternative views (primarily those of Taitz, Wiechers and Rose-Innes). These writers were concerned that a narrow concept of ultra vires, based on a literalist construction of statutory words, would unduly restrict judicial review. But as Baxter remarks "[t]he courts cannot hope to get away with modifying the content of the legislation of a sovereign Parliament . . . without a proper theoretical justification – which requires Parliament's imprimatur through the fiction of intention" (p. 312 n. 56).

andere v. *United Democratic Front en 'n ander*[24] with consequences which every thoughtful critic has considered disastrous.[25] Those who urge this same course upon English administrative law should study this case carefully.[26]

The case concerned a challenge to several emergency regulations made by the State President in terms of the Public Safety Act 1953. During the several states of emergency declared under the 1953 Act during the 1980s the State President made far-reaching emergency regulations controlling many aspects of everyday life including in particular, for present purposes, regulations severely restricting freedom of the press. Regulations designed to prevent the dissemination of information about the unrest sweeping the country prohibited the presence of journalists at the scene of "unrest", the publications in newspapers of information about "unrest" and the taking of photographs of "unrest". The United Democratic Front sought to challenge the regulations on the ground, *inter alia*, that the concept of "unrest"[27] was so vague as to render the regulations null and void. The detail of why "unrest" was considered vague need not concern us.[28]

All the emergency regulations made by the State President were protected by an ouster clause, to be found in section 5B of the 1953 Act, that provided that "no court shall be competent to enquire into or to give judgment on the validity of any . . . proclamation" made "under section 3" of the 1953 Act; and the regulations attacked purported to be made under that section. However, on classic *Anisminic* principles it was clear that if the regulations were ultra vires, judicial review would not be precluded by the ouster clause.[29] *Ultra vires* regulations,

---

[24] 1988 (4) S.A. 830(A). There was one earlier case which has also abandoned ultra vires (also with disastrous results): *Lipschitz* v. *Wattrus*. NO 1980(1) S.A. 662(T).

[25] The Constitution of the Republic of South Africa 1993, section 24, however, now provides that "Every person shall have the right to . . . lawful administrative action where any of his or her rights or interests is affected or threatened". Since the constitution is the supreme law (section 4), this prevents an ouster clause being effective through the application of *United Democratic Front* reasoning.

[26] This is not an easy task since all the judgments are written in Afrikaans. Criticisms in English, however, is readily available. See, *inter alia*, N. Haysom and C. Plasket, "The War Against Law: Judicial Activism and the Appellate Division" (1988) 4 *South African Journal on Human Rights* 303; E. Mureinik "Pursuing Principle: the Appellate Division and Review under the State of Emergency" (1989) 5 S.A.J.H.R. 60 and Grogan (1989) 106 S.A.L.J. 14.

[27] There were similar arguments about the concept of "security action" but it would burden unnecessarily this article to go into them here.

[28] In brief the argument was the following: Regulation 1(1) defined "unrest" as "any activity or conduct" which "a reasonable bystander" would consider a prohibited gathering (*i.e.* prohibited under other regulations), a physical attack on a member of the security forces or conduct which constituted a riot or public violence. The difficulty which the court at first instance had with this definition was whether it meant that a bystander in possession of more knowledge than the reasonable bystander could publish information about an incident with impunity? For instance, if a bystander knew that the particular gathering had been prohibited but that was not widely known (and so not known to the reasonable bystander), could that information about that gathering be freely published? This is a somewhat simplified definition of the concept of "unrest". For the detail see 1987(3) SA 296(N) at 318H–319F.

[29] *Anisminic Ltd.* v. *Foreign Compensation Commission* [1969] 2 AC 147. For the detail, see Wade and Forsyth, *op. cit.* pp. 734–739. Similar principles apply to ouster clauses in South African law: *Minister of Law and Order* v. *Hurley* 1986(3) SA 568 (A).

the argument ran, were not made "under section 3" of the 1953 Act and so were not protected from review by the ouster clause.

The first instance court had found that the definition of "unrest" was so vague as to be ultra vires and void; and in consequence the ouster clause did not preclude the court from quashing the offending regulations. But Rabie A.C.J. giving the majority judgment[30] in the Appellate Division took a rather different view. Far from wrestling with the technical arguments about vagueness, the acting chief justice accepted the appellants' submission that, even if the regulations were vague, they were still made "under section 3" and thus protected from review by the ouster clause, *i.e.* vague regulations were *intra vires*. The judge said that ". . . in order to be protected from being declared invalid by section 5B, a regulation does not have to comply with all the requirements for validity".[31] The doctrine of ultra vires was rejected in terms. The ultra vires approach, the acting chief justice, said "was unjustified. In my opinion it is artificial and false, and I think that vagueness must be seen as a self-standing ground on which subordinate legislation . . . may be attacked, and not as an example of ultra vires."[32] It was the Roman-Dutch common law, not the doctrine of ultra vires, which required that subordinate legislation should not be vague. Thus although vague regulations could in theory be struck down by the court in the exercise of its common law powers, such regulations were made "under the Act" and thus protected by the ouster clause from being struck down. The regulations were *intra vires* and thus the ouster clause was effective to shield the regulations from judicial challenge. Since the heart of modern judicial review consists of grounds – irrationality, procedural impropriety, abuse of power, etc. – which may be presented as coming from outside the enabling legislation (and are so presented by the "weak" critics), the effect of this finding is to eviscerate judicial review (at any rate where there is a relatively straightforward ouster clause).[33]

Perhaps even more clearly than Rabie A.C.J.'s judgment, Hefer J.A.'s judgment is cast in the language of "weak" criticism. He refers to classic statements of the extended or stretched ultra vires doctrine (including Sir William Wade's),[34] but relates it to the "conceptualism" and "the formalism of the available remedies" in Britain; and concludes that South African law "has no need of this kind of conceptualism or of an all embracing ground rule for the exercise by the courts of their review jurisdiction".[35]

---

[30] There was a separate concurring judgment by Hefer J.A. (discussed below). Van Heerden J.A. dissented, upholding the traditional approach to ultra vires.

[31] At 853F–G.

[32] At 855F–H. An alternative translation for "artificial and false" is "forced and impure".

[33] Following *Staatspresident* v. *U.D.F.* it has been confirmed that an ouster clause prevents judicial review on the ground of vagueness (*Catholic Bishops Publishing Co.* v. *State President* 1990(1) SA 849 (A)); and in *Natal Indian Congress* v. *State President* 1989(3) SA 588 (N) an ouster clause successfully prevented review on the ground of *Kruse* v. *Johnson* [1898] 2 QB 91 unreasonableness.

[34] *Administrative Law* (5th ed.), p. 40; a very similar passage occurs in the 7th ed. at p. 41. The judge also relies on Craig's account and criticism of the doctrine in *Administrative Law* (2nd ed.).

[35] At 867G, 868.

The views of Rabie A.C.J. and Hefer J.A. are of a piece with those "weak" critics who complain about the artificiality of the doctrine of ultra vires. Just like the views of Sir John Laws quoted above they open the way to the recognition that a distinction may be drawn between different kinds of defect in a decision; and those on which the heart – Sir John Laws calls it "the bedrock" – of judicial review rests will be excluded by straightforward ouster clauses. This is, of course, not what the "weak" critics of the ultra vires doctrine have in mind; but it is the inevitable consequence of abandoning ultra vires.[36]

It will, of course, be said that this is all very well but it could not happen here. The attack on ultra vires is not prompted by a desire to eviscerate judicial review. But the consequences that result from change are often not those intended. Once ultra vires has been abandoned the logic of the *U.D.F.* case could clearly be adopted in English law. *Anisminic Ltd.* v. *Foreign Compensation Commission*[37] itself could have been differently decided. The Foreign Compensation Act 1950, section 4(4) provided that "no determination by the Commission on any claim made to them under the Act shall be called in question in any court of law". If a determination was challenged on the ground of a failure of natural justice,[38] and the duty to heed the rules of natural justice came from the common law, a determination in breach of natural justice would still be "a determination by the Commission on [a] claim made . . . under the Act" and thus protected by the clause. If ultra vires is abandoned it follows as the night the day that Treasury counsel will ere long be heard to submit that even if the decision in dispute was flawed through a failure of natural justice, the decision remains *intra vires* and is thus unchallengeable because of an ouster clause. It is, of course, to be hoped that judges would resist this argument. But with the abandonment of ultra vires the judiciary will have discarded the strongest and most straightforward ground on which to do so.

A further example of the evisceration of judicial review on the abandonment of ultra vires is found in the exclusive statutory remedy (available in a wide range of planning, compulsory purchase and similar matters)[39] that allows "any person aggrieved" to apply to the High Court within six weeks of the confirmation of a contested order for an appropriate remedy. It is made available in lieu of the application for judicial review under R.S.C. Order 53; and strong ouster

---

[36] Sir John Laws, it is believed, is the only one of the "weak" critics to discuss the position of ouster clauses (in Supperstone and Goudie, *Judicial Review*, pp. 61ff). But he only does so in the context of voidness, arguing that ouster clauses may be effective even in the absence of voidness, the true question being in each case whether Parliament intended the body protected by an ouster clause to have the power to make final determinations of questions of law. This is, of course, entirely consistent with the doctrine of ultra vires.

[37] [1969] AC 147.

[38] Under the current ouster clause (Foreign Compensation Act 1969, section 3) it is specifically provided that challenging a determination on the "ground that it is contrary to natural justice" shall not be precluded by the clause (section 3(10)).

[39] See, to give but one example, Town and Country Planning Act 1990, ss. 284–288 for the current legislation in planning matters. For compulsory purchase see the Acquisition of Land Act 1981, s. 25.

clauses generally provide that apart from the statutory application a contested order "shall not . . . be questioned in any legal proceedings whatsoever".[40] Even without the abandonment of ultra vires such ouster clauses have generally been interpreted as creating an exclusive procedure; and once the six weeks has elapsed the "person aggrieved" has no remedy.[41] However, such legislation into invariably provides that the challenge to the validity of the order can only be made "on the ground that it is not within the powers of [the relevant] Act or that any requirement of the Act has not been complied with . . .".[42] Without the ultra vires doctrine, it is clear these words must mean that orders would not be able to be challenged on any of the "bedrock" grounds, since those grounds now derive from the common law not the Act. In *Smith* v. *East Elloe Rural District Council*[34] Lord Morton of Henryton in his much criticised minority judgment took a similar view, holding that if all the express statutory requirements had been complied with the applicant was bound to fail – whatever his grounds of complaint. As Sir William Wade points out this meant "that many kinds of unlawful action would not be challengeable even within the six weeks. This extraordinary conclusion would allow uncontrollable abuse of statutory power and cannot conceivably have been intended by Parliament".[44] Yet this is exactly the consequence that results from the abandonment of ultra vires.

From these overlooked practical consequences of the abandonment of ultra vires, let us turn to consider some of the analytical consequences. Suppose that a Minister in the apparent exercise of a statutory power to make regulations, makes certain regulations which are clearly so vague that their meaning cannot be determined with sufficient certainty. Classic theory tells us that Parliament never intends to grant the power to make vague regulations – this seems an entirely reasonable and realistic intention to impute to Parliament – and thus the vague regulations are ultra vires and void;[45] there would no difficulty in the court striking down the regulations.[46] But classic theory has been abandoned: the grounds of review derive, not from the implied intent of the legislature, but from the common law. It follows that although the regulations are *intra vires* the minister's powers, they are none the less invalid because they are vague.

The analytical difficulty is this: what an all powerful Parliament does not prohibit, it must authorise either expressly or impliedly. Likewise if Parliament

[40] Acquisition of Land Act 1981, s. 25.

[41] See, Wade and Forsyth, *op. cit.*, pp. 745–748 discussing particularly *Smith* v. *East Elloe Rural District COuncil* [1956] AC 736 and *R.* v. *Secretary of State for the Environment ex parte Ostler* [1977] QB 122.

[42] This is the formula used in the Housing Act 1930, s. 11.

[43] [1956] AC 736.

[44] Wade and Forsyth, *op. cit.*, pp. 751–752.

[45] See *McEldowney* v. *Forde* [1971] AC 632 per Lord Diplock at 665B, "A regulation whose meaning is so vague that it cannot be ascertained with reasonable certainty cannot fall within the words of delegation". Admittedly Lord Diplock was here dissenting but Lord Hodson for the majority is to similar effect (643F).

[46] There is no ouster clause so no question of it being effective to prevent the operation of judicial review.

grants a power to a minister, that minister either acts within those powers or outside those powers. There is no grey area between authorisation and prohibition or between empowerment and the denial of power. Thus, if the making of the vague regulations is within the powers granted by a sovereign Parliament, on what basis may the courts challenge Parliament's will and hold that the regulations are invalid? If Parliament has authorised vague regulations, those regulations cannot be challenged without challenging Parliament's authority to authorise such regulations.

The same conclusion is reached using Hohfeldian analysis.[47] The crucial relationship is that between jural opposites. If Parliament has given a Minister the **power** to make clear regulations, then the Minister is **disabled** from doing the opposite – making vague regulations. He lacks the **power** to do so. Of course, it may be said (implausibly, I submit) that Parliament in fact granted to the Minister a **privilege** to make either clear or vague regulations in exercising his regulation-making **power**. If which case, common sense requires that the Minister should also be under a **duty** to make clear regulations. If that **duty** derives from the statute then we are back where we started: the Minister's **power** is limited to making clear regulations. If that **duty** derives from the common law (as the "weak" critics would assert), then that **duty** is inconsistent with the will of Parliament in granting the **privilege** to make either clear or vague regulations to the Minister.

The upshot of this is that whether one follows a traditional analytical route or the Hohfeldian analysis, one is led inevitably to the conclusion that to abandon ultra vires is to challenge the supremacy of Parliament. "Weak" critics, whether they intend it or not, are transmuted into "strong" critics.

Some "weak" critics will have no difficulty with this; they accept that they are latent "strong" critics. But, for those who do not wish to challenge legislative supremacy and for those who do not favour the evisceration of judicial review let us turn to the reconciliation of the "weak" criticisms with orthodoxy.

V.   RECONCILING THE "WEAK" CRITICISMS WITH ORTHODOXY

It clearly is the case that the modern law of judicial review is a judicial creation. It is the judges that have made it; and they rightly enjoy the admiration of administrative lawyers for their achievement. And it is unarguable that judicial attitudes and insights have been predominant in determining all aspects of the developed law. It cannot be plausibly asserted that the implied intent of the legislature provides any significant guidance to the reach of the rules of natural justice or the fine distinctions to be drawn between decisions that are unreasonable but not irrational and the like. The "weak" critics make a powerful case.

---

[47]   W. Hohfeld, *Fundamental Legal Conceptions* (1923). The words in **bold** in what follows refer to Hohfeldian concepts.

But the judicial achievement in creating the modern law did not take place in a constitutional vacuum. It took place against the background of a sovereign legislature that could have intervened at any moment (and sometimes did).[48] This was recognised by the judiciary in many of their most creative decisions. More importantly, however, since the legislature took no steps to overturn the extension and development of judicial review by the judges, it may reasonably be taken to have accepted the creativity of the judicial role. The consequence is that the legislature may reasonably be taken to have given tacit approval to the development by the judiciary of the principles of judicial review, subject, crucially, to the recognition of legislative supremacy.

In this more subtle account of the relationship between statutory powers and judicial review, the "implied intention" of the legislature does not provide the key to enable the judge to measure the precise degree of natural justice required or to distinguish an improper purpose from a proper one. Instead, the legislature is taken to have granted an *imprimatur* to the judges to develop the law in the particular area. This again is not that novel. After all Lord Browne-Wilkinson in his statement of the orthodox position in R. v. *Lord President of the Privy Council, ex parte Page*,[49] spoke of "the underlying assumption" by the legislature that powers would only be reasonably exercised in accordance with fair procedures in a context in which he thought that Parliament had left it to the judiciary to assess that fairness and reasonableness. It is a commonplace for the legislature to give such evaluative tasks to the judiciary. This is inevitable – neither the legislature nor the executive can evaluate everything. It is also common sense; and, most importantly, implies no infraction of the principle of legislative supremacy. In these circumstances an assumption that the judges have been given the task of so developing the law, within any limits which may be set by the legislature, seems entirely reasonable. And it implies no breach of the doctrine of ultra vires; in so developing the law the judges are doing what Parliament intended, or may reasonably be taken to have intended, them to do.

It must be recognised that this reconciliation of "weak" criticism and orthodoxy still leaves the judiciary with little concrete guidance as to the reach of judicial review and the scope and content of the various grounds of review. That is both a burden and a challenge of their office. But they would receive no better guidance if ultra vires had been abolished. Moreover, great advantages have been secured by its retention. The judges no longer challenge legislative

---

[48] The legislature, to its credit, however, rarely intervened and when it did generally acted in a constructive way. See, for instance, the Tribunals and Inquiries Act 1992 (discussed in Wade and Forsyth, *op. cit.*, pp. 920ff) and the Supreme Court Act 1981, s. 31. *Cf.* War Damage Act 1965, s. 1 and see G. Zellick [1985] *Public Law* 283 especially 290. See also, R. Cranston, "Reviewing Judicial Review" in G. Richardson and H. Genn, *Administrative Law and Government Action* (OUP, 1994) at pp. 69–75.

[49] [1993] AC 682 at 701C–G. And see also R. v. *The Home Secretary, ex parte Doody* [1994] 1 AC 531 where Lord Mustill said "where an Act of Parliament confers an administrative power there is a presumption that it will be exercised in a manner that is fair in all the circumstances . . . The standards of fairness are not immutable . . ." (at 540).

supremacy, the effectiveness of ouster clauses remains attenuated, and there is a sound constitutional basis for judicial review.

VI. THE UTILITY OF FIG-LEAVES AND FAIRY TALES

Good metaphors may sometimes mislead; and articles such as this one should engage in argument rather than the construction of more elaborate figures of speech that add little to understanding. But it is, perhaps, worth pointing out that Sir John Laws has misunderstood the fig-leaf metaphor when he says that the intention of Parliament serves only "as a fig-leaf to cover [the] true origins [of the grounds of review]. We do not need the fig-leaf any more."[50] The point about the fig-leaf metaphor (and why it is so apt) is that fig-leaves do not deceive anyone as to what lies beneath them. The fig-leaf, like the swimming costume on a crowded beach, is to preserve the decencies. It enables individuals to interact in an appropriate manner without threatening the social order. The doctrine of ultra vires plays a similar role in public law. No one is so innocent as to suppose that judicial creativity does not form the grounds of judicial review; but by adhering to the doctrine of ultra vires the judiciary shows that it adheres to its proper constitutional position and that it recognises that Parliament is free to dispense with the judicially developed principles of judicial review.

Those who consider that the fig-leaf should be stripped away to reveal the awful truth to all the world do not, with respect, appreciate the subtlety of the constitutional order in which myth but not deceit plays so important a role and where form and function are often different. The unwritten constitution consists very largely of things that appear to be one thing but are in fact another. A Prime Minister who lacks significant legal powers but who is in fact all powerful. A Crown that appears very powerful but which is, save in special circumstances, without significant power. To some this is a valuable characteristic of the constitution; it spurs others to seek a new constitutional settlement. But it is undeniable that it is inherent in the existing constitutional order.

The fig-leaf of ultra vires is of a piece with that. Setting aside the practical and analytical consequences of abandonment discussed above, its crucial role is to provide the constitutional justification of judicial review. Under our present constitution judicial review does not challenge but fulfils the intention of parliament.[51] By their ready acceptance of ultra vires the judges show that they are the guardians, not the subverters, of this existing constitutional order. This fact is not a "fig-leaf" nor is it a "fairy tale"; it marks the maintenance of the proper balance of powers between the elected and non-elected parts of the constitution.

[50] [1995] *Public Law* 72 at 79.

[51] An apt phrase first used by Roger Cotterell in "Judicial Review and Legal Theory" in *Administrative Law and Government Action* (1994) edited by Genevra Richardson and Hazel Genn at p. 16.

Adherence to ultra vires is a gentle but necessary discipline. And it is worrying that some judges chafe against it.

VII. THE RESPONSE TO "STRONG" CRITICISM

A. Flying Office Latham and Sir John Laws

Sir John Laws's adoption of the "strong" criticisms (particularly in the long passage cited above) is clearly significantly influenced by the views of Richard Latham, Fellow of All Souls, whose life was cut short by enemy action in the air off the Norwegian coast in 1944.[52] In his book, *The Law and the Commonwealth*,[53] Latham made a very important contribution to the debate over the Sovereignty of Parliament.[54] In much cited words on the nature of legislative sovereignty he said:[55]

> Where the purported sovereign is any one but a single actual person, the designation of him must include the statement of rules for the ascertainment of his will, and these

---

[52] Laws, "Law and Democracy" [1995] *Public Law* 72 at 86. The other influence on Sir John is Sir William Wade's article "The Legal Basis of Sovereignty" [1955] CLJ 172 which Sir John uses to establish that Parliamentary Sovereignty is vouchsafed not by legislation but by the courts. As Wade says, the rule that Acts of Parliament have the force of law "in unique in being unchangeable by Parliament – it is changed by revolution, not by legislation; it lies in the keeping of the courts, and no Act of Parliament can take it from them . . . [I]t is always for the courts to say what is a valid Act of Parliament; and . . . the decision of this question is not determined by any rule of law which can be laid down or altered by any authority outside the courts. It is simply a political fact." But there is no suggestion here that the courts are justified (as Sir John would have us believe) in imposing substantive limits on Parliamentary enactments in accordance with the judicial estimation of the severity with which Parliament intrudes upon fundamental rights. The "ultimate legal principle" that is unchangeable by Parliament is a formal not a substantive principle, *viz.*, that properly enacted statutes, whatever their content, will be obeyed by the courts.

[53] OUP, 1949. An intriguing book. It is in fact a reprint in facsimile form of an essay first published in W.K. Hancock, *Survey of British Commonwealth Affairs, Volume 1 Problems of Nationality 1918–1936* (OUP, 1937). For this reason, the first page of the essay is p. 510.

[54] It is not intended to provide here a full account of the debate over the Sovereignty of Parliament. But the following point may be made: in certain circumstances EU legislation prevails over later Parliamentary legislation (see Wade and Forsyth, *op. cit.*, pp. 30–31; *R. v. Secretary of State for Transport ex parte Factortame Ltd. (No. 2)* [1990] 1 AC 603); but this is the result (and only the result) of the enactment of the European Communities Act 1972, s. 2(4). This, it is submitted, does not show the curtailment of sovereignty but its strength. For so long as Parliament retains the power (as a matter of legal principle rather than political reality) to repeal the 1972 Act, Parliament remains sovereign.

[55] At p. 523. Elsewhere he makes the same point more colourfully: ". . . the extraction of a precise expression of will from a multiplicity of human beings is . . . an artificial process and one which cannot be accomplished without arbitrary rules. It is, therefore, an incomplete statement to say that in a state such and such an assembly of human beings is sovereign. It can only be sovereign when acting in a certain way prescribed by law. At least some rudimentary manner and form is demanded of it: the simultaneous incoherent cry of a rabble, small or large, cannot be law, for it is unintelligible. The minimum would be rule prescribing some sort of majority – simple, plurality, absolute majority, unanimity or some arbitrary portion. . . ." (1939 King's Counsel 152 cited at length in R.F.V. Heuston, *Essays in Constitutional Law* (1961, Stevens & Co), p. 8).

rules, since their observance is a condition of the validity of his legislation, are rules of law logically prior to him.

It is this passage that leads Sir John to conclude that "the need for higher-order law is dictated by the logic of the very notion of government under law ... [T]he doctrine of Parliamentary sovereignty cannot be vouched by Parliamentary legislation; a higher order law confers it and must of necessity limit it".

However, it is submitted, that Sir John's conclusion is inconsistent with Flying Officer Latham's views. The rules that Latham considers to be logically prior to the effective expression of the legislative will are rules of manner and form that determine *how* that legislative will is to be expressed. They have no substantive content, *i.e.* they do not limit the power of the legislature *operating in accordance with those rules*. In the late Professor Beinart's telling phrase, Latham's rules "defined the sovereign, not sovereignty".[56]

Latham's approach has been adopted at least twice by Commonwealth courts.[57] In the clearest case, *Harris and others* v. *Minister of the Interior and another*,[58] the question was whether the sovereignty of the South African Parliament could be reconciled with the effectiveness of provisions of the South Africa Act 1909 which required a two thirds majority of both houses sitting unicamerally for certain matters (such as the matter in dispute, *viz*, the removal of coloured persons from the common voters' roll). Centlivres C.J. accepted the nub of Latham's reasoning in holding that the South Africa Act 1909 defined what Parliament was and showed how it was to be distinguished from the "incoherent cry of a rabble". "One is doing no violence to language," he said in the crucial part of his judgment, "when one regards the world 'Parliament' as meaning Parliament sitting either bicamerally or unicamerally in accordance with the requirements of the South Africa Act, 1909."[59] Thus Parliament, as so defined, had not expressed its will on the question of the coloured vote; and the Separate Representation of Voters Act 1951, which purported to be such an expression of Parliament's will, was void.

The great theoretical strength of this judgment (as well as Latham's reasoning on which it is based) is that it reconciles the sovereignty of the South African Parliament with the effectiveness of the "entrenched" clauses. This judgment expressed the court's disapproval of the government's course in purely formal and juristic terms. It was not a crass descent into party politics, but it did vindicate (for a time) constitutional rights.[60]

---

[56] B. Beinart, "Parliament and the Courts" [1954] *Butterworths SA Law Review* 134 at 136/7. Beinart was referring to a particular example of such "Latham rules" – those contained in the South Africa Act 1909.

[57] In *Harris and others* v. *The Minister of the Interior and another* 1951(2) SA 428 (A) by the Appellate Division of the Supreme Court of South Africa and by the Privy Council (on appeal from Ceylon) in *Bribery Commissioner* v. *Ranasinghe* [1956] AC 172.

[58] Above.

[59] At 468.

[60] For the detail of how these constitutional rights were eventually lost see, C.F. Forsyth, *In Danger for Their Talents: A Study of the Appellate Division of the Supreme Court of South Africa 1950–1980* (Juta & Co, 1985), pp. 61–74.

B. The consequences of striking down an Act of Parliament

Yet consider the course that Sir John would urge upon the judiciary: that judges would oppose and strike down Acts of Parliament on substantive grounds because in the judicial estimation these Acts threatened the democratic order and fundamental rights. Were Parliament to enact such measures, we may be sure that the issues involved would be the subject of intense, passionate and doubtless vituperative debate in Parliament and elsewhere. The measures, thoroughly bad though they might be, would enjoy the support of a majority of the elected representatives of the people and there would be large swathes of opinion in the country that supported the measures.

Any judge who struck down the legislation in these circumstances, not on some formal ground founded in non-compliance with a Latham rule, but on substantive grounds touching the merits of the measure would cast the judiciary into a political maelstrom from which it could not emerge unscathed. Even if judges were not removed from office, the judiciary would be perceived as politically motivated; its jurisdiction would be ousted in many cases; and, perhaps most gravely, appointments to the bench would be politicised.

But is this not all speculation? Such legislation is not about to be enacted; and if it were it would not be the judges who would restore democracy. As Lord Irvine of Lairg remarks:

> many would regard as inconceivable, on the part of any Parliament we can presently contemplate, any assault on the basic tenets of democracy which might call for the invocation of the judicial power claimed . . . [There is] the need for eternal vigilance. But, if there ever were such an assault, it would surely be on the political battlefield that the issue would be resolved. I have to wonder whether it is not extra-judicial romanticism to believe that a judicial decision could hold back what would, in substance, be a revolution.[61]

VIII. CONCLUSIONS

The argument of this article should not be misunderstood. The orthodox approach to ultra vires has not been defended as the only possible, or the ideal, basis for judicial review. The argument has been that, for reasons of principle and pragmatism, it is not for the judges, acting on their own motion, to abolish ultra vires. It may well be that at some point in the future there is a new constitutional settlement, a Bill of Rights will be enacted, and judicial review will be placed on a different, and perhaps better, constitutional footing. But until that happens another juristic basis for judicial review is required; the ultra vires doctrine is, and should remain, that basis. Similarly, prior to a fresh constitutional

---

[61] "Judges and Decision-makers: the Theory and Practice of Wednesbury Review" [1996] *Public Law* 59 at 77.

settlement the sovereignty of Parliament, for good or ill, remains a fundamental element of the constitutional order; and it is not for the judges acting on their own motion to try to change that.

The most fundamental reason for this is that in a democratic polity change in the constitutional order must – or at any rate should – come about through the democratic process. And the judiciary, as important as its independence is to the rule of law, is a non-elected part of the constitutional order. How can some judges suppose they are entitled to change the fundamentals of the constitution without reference to the elected elements of that constitution? It may very well be a good thing if the judges were to have the task of protecting democracy and fundamental rights against the legislature, but they should be given that task by the people; it is unseemly that they should seize it themselves.

Sir William Wade has remarked that one possible result "from our lack of a written constitution [is] that the closer judges come to the constitutional bedrock, the more prone to disorientation they seem to be".[62] The attack by some judges on the doctrine of ultra vires and the sovereignty of Parliament is but the latest example of judges missing their footing on that bedrock. It is to be hoped that it is the last.

---

[62] Wade and Forsyth, *op. cit.*, p. vi.

3

Ultra Vires and the Foundations of Judicial Review*

PAUL CRAIG

There is a growing literature concerning the role of the ultra vires doctrine and its place within administrative law. For some the doctrine is the central principle of administrative law, without which judicial intervention would rest on uncertain foundations.[1] For others, it constitutes at best a harmless fiction, which is incapable of explaining all instances of judicial intervention, and at worst a device which allows the judiciary to conceal the real justifications for developments in judicial review.[2] Christopher Forsyth falls into the former camp. He has written a vigorous defence of the ultra vires principle, contending that "it remains vital to the developed law of judicial review".[3] The purpose of this article is to contribute to the debate on this issue by putting the opposing view. The article will be divided into four sections.

The first section will draw together the criticisms of the ultra vires principle. More specifically it will be argued that it is indeterminate, unrealistic, beset by internal tension, and that it cannot explain all instances where the judiciary has applied public law principles. The second and third sections will consider the arguments of those who believe that the ultra vires principle is indeed central to administrative law. Christopher Forsyth has helpfully articulated this position and has contended that certain undesirable consequences would ensue if we were to rest judicial intervention on any other ground. It will be argued that these fears are misplaced and that those who are opposed to the ultra vires principle would not be forced to accept such undesirable consequences. The final section will develop the analysis in two related ways. It will be argued from an historical perspective that judicial intervention was not posited on the idea of

---

* This is a reprint of an article first published in [1998] CLJ 63. I am grateful for the comments of Jack Beatson, Mark Freedland, Elizabeth Fisher, Sir John Laws, Dawn Oliver and Sir Stephen Sedley. I remain responsible for all errors.

[1] Wade & Forsyth, *Administrative Law* (7th ed., 1994), p. 41; Forsyth, "Of Fig Leaves and Fairy Tales: The Ultra Vires Doctrine, The Sovereignty of Parliament and Judicial Review" [1996] C.L.J. 122 and Chapter Two, p. 29 above.

[2] Oliver, "Is the Ultra Vires Rule the Basis of Judicial Review?" [1987] P.L. 543 and Chapter One p. 3 above; Craig, *Administrative Law* (3rd ed., 1994), pp. 12–17; Sir John Laws, "Illegality: The Problem of Jurisdiction", in Supperstone and Goudie (eds.), *Judicial Review* (1992) and Chapter Four (extract) p. 73 below; Lord Woolf, "Droit Public – English Style" [1995] P.L. 57 at 66.

[3] Forsyth, *op. cit.* n. 1, p. 122 and 29 above.

effectuating the intent of the legislature, and that therefore to regard this as the classic theory underpinning judicial review is misconceived. It will be further argued from a conceptual perspective that it is possible to provide an alternative justification for judicial review which is sound, which fits with the seminal case law on the foundations of judicial review and which captures the proper relationship between the courts and the administration.

It should be made clear at the outset that this article does not seek to address criticisms of the ultra vires principle which amount to direct challenges to the sovereignty of Parliament, what Christopher Forsyth terms "strong" criticisms of the principle.[4] This is not because I disagree with such criticisms of the ultra vires principle. It is rather simply because of lack of space: discussion of sovereignty, and of possible changes to what is commonly perceived as the traditional doctrine of Parliamentary sovereignty, is a complex topic in its own right.[5]

It should also be made clear that references to judicial review refer to the substantive and procedural norms which comprise this topic, and not to the way in which a remedy is obtained.

I. THE CRITICISMS OF THE ULTRA VIRES DOCTRINE

The precise meaning of the ultra vires principle is, as will be seen below, more complex and contentious than is commonly acknowledged. This section of the article will, however, accept the meaning of the principle which is adopted by those who are minded to defend it as the only viable basis for judicial review in this country. The core idea can be expressed as follows.

The ultra vires principle is based on the assumption that judicial review is legitimated on the ground that the courts are applying the intent of the legislature. Parliament has found it necessary to accord power to ministers, administrative agencies, local authorities and the like. Such power will always be subject to certain conditions contained in the enabling legislation. The courts' function is to police the boundaries stipulated by Parliament. The ultra vires principle was used to achieve this end in two related ways. In a narrow sense it captured the idea that the relevant agency must have the legal capacity to act in relation to the topic in question: an institution given power by Parliament to adjudicate on employment matters should not take jurisdiction over non-employment matters. In a broader sense the ultra vires principle has been used as the vehicle through which to impose a number of constraints on the way in which the power given to the agency has been exercised: it must comply with rules of fair

---

[4] Forsyth, *op. cit.* n. 1, pp. 127–129 and pp. 33–5 above.

[5] My own views on this topic can be found in "Sovereignty of the United Kingdom Parliament after *Factortame*" (1991) 11 Y.B.E.L. 221 and "Public Law, Sovereignty and Citizenship", in *Rights of Citizenship* (Blackburn ed., 1993), Chap. 16. Further development of these ideas can be found in "Public Law, Political Theory and Legal Theory" (forthcoming).

procedure, it must exercise its discretion to attain proper and not improper purposes, it must not act unreasonably etc.

The ultra vires principle thus conceived provided both the basis for judicial intervention and also established its limits. Judicial intervention was increasingly posited on the idea that the objective was to ensure that the agency did remain within the area assigned to it by Parliament. The limits to judicial review were also profoundly affected by the ultra vires principle. If the agency was within its assigned area then it was prima facie performing the tasks entrusted to it by the legislature and hence not contravening the will of Parliament. Controls over the way in which the agency exercised its discretionary power had, therefore, to be framed with this in mind. The courts should not substitute their judgment for that of the agency. The controls over the way in which discretionary power was exercised were, moreover, justified by reference to legislative intent: it would be argued, for example, that Parliament did not intend the agency to make decisions based on irrelevant considerations or improper purposes.

The ultra vires principle is thus regarded as both a necessary and sufficient basis for judicial intervention. It is necessary in the sense that any ground of judicial review has to be fitted into the ultra vires doctrine in order for it to be acceptable. It is sufficient in the sense that if such a ground of review can be so fitted into the ultra vires principle it obviates the need for further independent inquiry.

When reading the criticisms of the ultra vires principle set out below it is important to bear two related points in mind in order to avoid confusion. One is that those who are critical of the ultra vires principle as the foundation of judicial review are not committed in any sense to regarding legislative intent as being irrelevant in determining the extent and incidence of such review. It is self-evident that the enabling legislation must be considered when determining the ambit of a body's powers. This is not, however, the same thing as saying that the heads of review, their meaning or the intensity with which they are applied can be justified by reference to legislative intent. The other point to bear in mind is that critics of the ultra vires principle are of course concerned to keep bodies within their assigned spheres. The central issue is how far the relevant legal rules and their application can be satisfactorily explained by reference to legislative intent.

(a) The indeterminacy of the ultra vires principle

One potent critique of the ultra vires principle is its very indeterminacy. This can be exemplified by its application to judicial review of jurisdictional issues such as those presented in cases such as *Bolton*,[6] *Brittain*,[7] *Anisminic*[8] or *Page*.[9]

---

[6] R. v. *Bolton* (1841) 1 Q.B. 66.
[7] *Brittain* v. *Kinnaird* (1819) 1 B. & B. 432.
[8] *Anisminic Ltd.* v. *Foreign Compensation Commission* [1969] 2 A.C. 147.
[9] R. v. *Lord President of the Privy Council, ex p. Page* [1993] 2 A.C. 682.

A statute states, for example, that if an employee is injured at work then an agency may or shall grant compensation. It is clear from the face of the legislation that there are three conditions which must be satisfied before the agency can proceed further: the existence of an employee, an injury and the fact that the injury has occurred while at work.

It is indisputable as a matter of legal history that the courts in this country have adopted a number of different approaches to defining jurisdictional error. These have been considered in detail elsewhere,[10] but suffice it to say for the present that three such approaches can be detected within the courts' jurisprudence: limited review, the collateral fact doctrine and the more modern test of extensive review under which all relevant errors of law are open to challenge.

It is equally indisputable that the ultra vires doctrine provides no guidance as such as to which of these standards of review ought to be applied. It does not tell us whether the correct standard of judicial review should be for the court to substitute judgment on the meaning of each of these conditions, or whether it should substitute judgment on certain of the conditions but not others, or whether it should adopt some other test. Any of these tests can be formally reconciled with the ultra vires principle. It can always be maintained that, for example, Parliament only intended that certain preliminary issues should be subject to judicial review, or by way of contrast that Parliament intended that the ordinary courts should substitute judgment on all relevant questions of law for that of the agency being reviewed. Courts which have been eager to promote a particular doctrine of jurisdictional error have sought to validate their chosen view by invoking Parliamentary intent in this manner.[11]

The flexibility in the ultra vires principle can preserve the veneer that the courts are simply obeying the legislative mandate, but it is this very flexibility which ultimately robs the reasoning of any conviction. It is precisely because legislative intent can be used to legitimate almost all types of judicial control that it loses its potency to legitimate any particular one.[12] As Sir John Laws has remarked,[13] the ultra vires principle in this area is simply a fig leaf which enables the courts to intervene to the degree to which they think is appropriate without too nakedly confronting the authority of the executive. How far the courts ought to be intervening in this area and the factors which are of relevance in this respect will be considered in more detail below. The ultra vires principle is capable of accommodating a variety of conclusions on this issue. It is not however able to provide any independent *ex ante* guidance.

[10]   Craig, *Administrative Law* (3rd ed., 1994), Chap. 10.

[11]   See, e.g., *R. v. Commissioners for Special Purposes of Income Tax* (1888) 21 Q.B.D. 313; *Colonial Bank of Australasia v. Willan* (1874) L.R. 5 P.C. 417; *Page, op. cit* n. 9.

[12]   It is, moreover, even more difficult to conceive of intervention in this area being based on legislative intent determining the limits of validity if the courts employ a functional as opposed to an analytical sense of the term "error of law". See generally, J. Beatson, "The Scope of Judicial Review for Error of Law" (1984) 4 O.J.L.S. 22.

[13]   "Illegality: The Problem of Jurisdiction", in *Judicial Review* (Supperstone and Goudie eds., 1992), Chap. 4 and Chapter Four (extract) p. 73 below.

(b) The lack of reality of the ultra vires principle

Another telling criticism of the ultra vires doctrine is that it does not accord with reality. This can be exemplified by considering the controls which the courts have imposed on the exercise of discretion. The orthodox approach has been to legitimate these controls by reference to Parliamentary intent: the legislature only intended such power to be exercised on the basis of relevant considerations, reasonably and for proper purposes. There are two problems with this rationalisation of judicial behaviour.

Firstly, the legislation which is in issue in a particular case will often not provide any detailed guide to the courts as to the application of these controls on discretion. There will often be scant guidance to be gained from the enabling legislation as to what should be considered to be relevant as opposed to irrelevant considerations. Nor is it realistic to think of the legislative process being conducted in these terms.[14] This is particularly so in relation to legislation which is framed in broad, open textured terms. The court will of necessity have to make its own considered judgment on such matters.

Secondly, the orthodox justification for the controls which exist on discretion makes little if any sense when we consider the development of these controls across time. The constraints which exist on the exercise of discretionary power are not static. Existing constraints evolve and new types of control are added to the judicial armoury. Changes in judicial attitudes towards fundamental rights, the acceptance of legitimate expectations, and the possible inclusion of proportionality as a head of review in its own right are but three examples of this process. These developments cannot plausibly be explained by reference to legislative intent. Let us imagine that, for example, the UK courts were to decide in 1998 that proportionality was an independent head of review. Can it plausibly be maintained that this is to be justified by reference to changes in legislative intent which occurred at this time? Would the legislature in some manner have indicated that it intended a new generalised head of review in 1998 which had not existed hitherto? The question only has to be posed for the answer to be self-evident.[15] Sir John Laws captures this point when speaking of developments in judicial review,[16]

> They are, categorically, judicial creations. They owe neither their existence nor their acceptance to the will of the legislature. They have nothing to do with the intention of Parliament, save as a fig leaf to cover their true origins. We do not need the fig leaf any more.

[14] See Sir Stephen Sedley, "The Common Law and the Constitution" in Lord Nolan and Sir Stephen Sedley, *The Making and Remaking of the British Constitution* (1998) at 16.

[15] The same point can of course be made about other developments which have occurred in judicial review. For example, the expansion of the head of jurisdictional error cannot plausibly be explained by changes in legislative intent which occurred at the time of the decision in *Page* [1993] 2 A.C. 682.

[16] "Law and Democracy" [1995] P.L. 72 at 79.

(c) Tensions within the ultra vires principle

A further problem with the ultra vires doctrine is that it is beset by internal tensions. These are most apparent in the context of statutory provisions which seek to exclude the courts from judicial review through the presence of preclusive or finality clauses. If the rationale for judicial review is that the courts are thereby implementing legislative intent this leads to difficulty where the legislature has stated in clear terms that it does not wish the courts to intervene with the decisions made by the agency. As is well known such clauses have not in fact served to exclude judicial review. The courts have used a number of interpretative techniques to limit the effect of such clauses, most notably in *Anisminic*[17] where their Lordships held that the relevant provision did not serve to protect decisions which were nullities.

Various attempts can and have been made to square such decisions with the orthodox ultra vires principle. It might be argued that Parliament really did not intend such clauses to cover decisions which could otherwise be rendered null. It might alternatively be contended that Parliament acquiesced in the actual decision reached by the courts in the instant case. It might be further argued that in the future Parliament would know that any such clause would be interpreted in this manner and that it signalled its consent in this respect by its willingness to include such clauses in legislation while being fully cogniscent of their limited legal effect.

While such arguments can be made they are susceptible to two complementary objections, one substantive, the other formal.

In substantive terms, arguments of this nature should not be allowed to conceal the reality of what the legislature was attempting to achieve, nor should it be allowed to mask the judicial response. Such clauses were clearly designed to exclude the courts. This might be for a "legitimate" reason, in the sense that the legislature was merely trying to signal that it preferred the view of a specialist agency to that of the reviewing court. It might be for a more "dubious" reason, as where the legislature was merely seeking to immunise the decisions of a minister from any challenge. We should be equally honest about the nature of the courts' response. Although it is capable of being reconciled with orthodoxy in the above manner, the reality is that the courts were reaching their decision by drawing upon a constitutional principle independent of Parliamentary intent. The essence of this principle was that access to judicial review, and the protections which it provides, should be safeguarded by the courts, and that any legislative attempt to block such access should be given the most restrictive reading possible, irrespective of whether this truly accorded with legislative intent or not.

The other objection to the arguments made above is more formal in nature. Even if one believes that the decisions in this area can be reconciled with ultra

---

[17] [1969] 2 A.C. 147.

vires orthodoxy this reconciliation is only bought at a price. The price in this instance is the straining of the ultra vires doctrine itself. The malleability of the doctrine allows it to be formally stretched in the above manner. Yet the more contrived the search for the legitimation of legislative intent, the more strained and implausible does the whole ultra vires doctrine become. This tension has indeed been exacerbated by more recent developments in judicial review. The House of Lords in *Anisminic* could at least contend that there was some space left for the ouster clause to operate on, given that they held that the concept of error of law within jurisdiction still existed. The death knell of the idea of non-jurisdictional error of law which was sounded in *Page*[18] has removed this line of argument.

(d) The ultra vires principle and the scope of public law

For all its difficulties it is at least plausible to think of the ultra vires principle as being the basis of judicial review in relation to those bodies which derive their power from statute. The courts have, however, expanded the principles of judicial review to cover institutions which are not public bodies in the traditional sense of the term, in circumstances where these bodies do not derive their power from statute or the prerogative. This trend has been more marked as of late because of reforms in the law of remedies.[19] It would none the less be mistaken to think of this as a recent development. The courts have applied public law, or analogous principles to such bodies for a very considerable period of time, irrespective of whether this was in the context of an action for judicial review as such. Trade associations, trade unions and corporations with *de facto* monopoly power have, for example, been subject to some of the same principles as are applied to public bodies *stricto sensu*.[20]

It is difficult to apply the ultra vires principle to such bodies without substantially altering its meaning.[21] These bodies do not derive their power from statute and therefore judicial control cannot be rationalised through the idea that the courts are delineating the boundaries of Parliament's intent. The very language of ultra vires can only be preserved by transforming it so as to render the principles of judicial review of generalised application to those institutions which wield a certain degree of power; these principles are then read into the articles of association or other governing document under which the body operates. While this step can be taken it serves to transform the ultra vires doctrine. It can no longer be regarded as the vehicle through which the courts effectuate the will

---

[18] *Op. cit.* n. 9.

[19] Craig, *op. cit.* n. 10, Chap. 15.

[20] On some occasions the courts will justify this by reference to the supposed intent of the relevant parties; on others, they will impose the relevant obligation without reference to the parties' intent, see generally, D. Oliver, "Common Values in Public and Private Law and the Public Private Divide" [1997] Public Law 63.

[21] Oliver, *op. cit.* n. 2.

of Parliament. It becomes rather a juristic device through which these private or quasi-public bodies are subject to the controls which the courts believe should operate on those who possess a certain type of power.

II. THE DEFENCE OF THE ULTRA VIRES PRINCIPLE: THE DANGERS OF
ITS ABANDONMENT

It is unsurprising, given the nature of these criticisms, that there should have been a defence of the ultra vires principle and Christopher Forsyth has made a valuable contribution to the debate by articulating this point of view. His defence in effect entails two complementary lines of analysis: one set of arguments is designed to show the dangers of abandoning the ultra vires principle; the other is designed to address and meet some of the criticisms of that principle. The first set of arguments will be considered within this section; the second in the section which follows.[22]

(a) The particular danger: ouster clauses

One of the primary arguments advanced by Forsyth[23] is that if we abandon the ultra vires principle the courts will be unable to circumvent ouster clauses in the manner which they have done in cases such as *Anisminic*.

The argument is based on the decision of the South African court in the *UDF* case.[24] The case concerned judicial review of emergency regulations made by the State President which were designed to prevent the dissemination of information about "unrest". The UDF sought to challenge these regulations on the ground that the definition of unrest was so vague as to render the regulations void. The regulations were protected by an ouster clause, which would not have served to immunise them from attack had the court employed the type of reasoning used in cases such as *Anisminic*.

Rabie A.C.J. who gave the majority judgment in the Appellate Division of the South African court reasoned, however, that even if the regulations were vague they were still made pursuant to the legislation and hence still protected by the ouster clause. Rabie A.C.J. also rejected the ultra vires doctrine as the basis of judicial review, holding that it was Roman–Dutch common law and not the ultra vires doctrine which required that subordinate legislation should not be vague. While such regulations could in theory be struck down by the court in the exercise of these common law powers, the regulations were still made "under the Act" and thus were protected by the ouster clause.

---

[22] It should be pointed out for the sake of clarity that this method of dividing Christopher Forsyth's argument is mine and not his.

[23] Forsyth, *op. cit* n. 1, pp. 129–133 and pp. 000–000 in this volume.

[24] *Staatspresident en andere* v. *United Democratic Front en "n ander* 1988(4) S.A. 830A.

Forsyth contends that if we abandoned the ultra vires doctrine then such results could happen here too, and that the reasoning adopted by Rabie A.C.J. could be applied even if the ground of challenge was irrationality, procedural impropriety, or abuse of power. An ouster clause could operate to immunise such errors from attack. Judicial review would in Forsyth's words be "eviscerated" and this would be "the inevitable consequence of abandoning ultra vires", even though it was not the intended consequence.[25]

Christopher Forsyth is clearly correct to alert us to the reasoning used in the *UDF* case, and to point out the consequences of abandoning the ultra vires principle which occurred in that case. The reasoning of Rabie A.C.J. is indisputable. It happened. It could therefore happen in another legal system which chose to reject the ultra vires principle.

Forsyth is however mistaken in contending that this is the inevitable consequence of abandoning the ultra vires principle, or even the likely consequence. The argument posits a link between the abandonment of the ultra vires doctrine and the treatment of ouster clauses which does not in reality exist. Let us imagine that a court is minded to abandon the ultra vires doctrine as the basis of judicial review and to maintain instead that the controls on the exercise of public power are based not on the will of Parliament, but rather on common law created doctrines and principles. It is important to recognise at this juncture that these common law created doctrines and principles will include not only the established heads of review, but also other principles of public law which are relevant, for example, to the treatment of fundamental rights and indeed ouster clauses. How does such a judge deal with a case in which there is an ouster clause? Is he or she forced to reason in the manner exemplified by Rabie A.C.J. and hold that the clause protects errors which would otherwise be susceptible to challenge under one of the established heads of review? No. Such a judge would reason as follows.

The judge would begin by making explicit and honest what is implicit in the current approach of the courts to ouster clauses. The limited effect to be given to such clauses would not be based on the strained idea that Parliament did not intend such clauses to protect nullities. It would rather be based on what is any event the reality underlying the current law in this area. This is the existence of a common law constitutional principle to the effect that the inherent power of the courts should not readily be taken to be wholly excluded from review, a principle recognised and forcefully expressed by Professor Wade.[26] A clause which purported to do this would therefore be restrictively construed so as to apply only to decisions which were not vitiated by errors of the kind which

---

[25] Forsyth, *op. cit.* n. 1, p. 131 and p. 38 above.

[26] See, H.W.R. Wade, *Constitutional Fundamentals* (1980), p. 66, stating that Parliament's attempts to exempt public bodies from the jurisdiction of the courts is tantamount to giving them dictatorial power and is a constitutional abuse of power by Parliament; that judicial control over discretionary power is a constitutional fundamental, akin to an entrenched constitutional provision, p. 68; and that it ought not to be left to Whitehall to say how much judicial control will or will not be tolerated, p. 70.

could be challengeable under standard heads of review. A court could therefore in a case such as *UDF* or *Anisminic* proceed to consider the alleged error and strike down the regulations or government action if the error were proven to exist.

A final point on this topic is warranted here. Not only is the approach adopted in the *UDF* case not the logical or necessary consequence of abandoning the ultra vires principle. We should also recognise that the result reached in *Anisminic* was not a foregone conclusion, in some way logically derived from the very use of the ultra vires principle. In other words the mere fact that a legal system does employ the ultra vires principle does not mean that it will necessarily use it to interpret ouster clauses in the manner adopted by the House of Lords. We have already seen the strain which this very approach placed upon the ultra vires doctrine itself.

(b) The general danger: the analytical impasse?

The second perceived danger of abandoning the ultra vires principle is captured in the following quotation from Christopher Forsyth's article.[27]

> Suppose that a Minister in the apparent exercise of a statutory power to make regulations, makes certain regulations which are clearly so vague that their meaning cannot be determined with sufficient certainty. Classic theory tells us that Parliament never intends to grant the power to make vague regulations – this seems an entirely reasonable and realistic intention to impute to Parliament – and thus the vague regulations are ultra vires and void: there would be no difficulty in the court striking down the regulations. But classic theory has been abandoned: the grounds of review derive, not from the implied intent of the legislature, but from the common law. It follows that although the regulations are intra vires the minister's powers, they are none the less invalid because they are vague.
>
> The analytical difficulty is this: what an all powerful Parliament does not prohibit, it must authorise either expressly or impliedly ... Thus, if the making of the vague regulations is within the powers granted by a sovereign Parliament, on what basis may the courts challenge Parliament's will and hold that the regulations are invalid?

The argument in this quotation is powerfully presented. It should be noted at the outset that no such analytical impasse has ever in fact been perceived by the courts which developed review and did so independently of ideas of legislative intent. The argument must none the less be answered by those who seek to challenge the ultra vires principle as the basis of judicial review. It is however capable of being met.

The fact that some might choose to reject the ultra vires doctrine based on legislative intent as the justification for judicial review does not for any reason mean that the limits to an agency's powers thereby alter. The argument as put

---

[27] Forsyth, *op. cit.* n. 1, p. 133 and p. 42 above.

thus elides the existence of limits to an agency's power with the conceptual basis for those limits. The limit on power is that regulations should not be too vague, but it might equally be that they should not be manifestly unreasonable,[28] or that they should be interpreted so as not to infringe fundamental rights[29] etc. The live issue is whether one believes that such limits are really to be derived from legislative intent or more honestly from judicial creation through the process of the common law. Under the latter approach one would simply say that there is a common law principle that regulations cannot be too vague, that statutes which empower the making of regulations will be read subject to this principle and therefore that the minister did *not* have power to make such vague regulations.

It is no answer in this respect to state that what an all powerful Parliament does not prohibit it must authorise either expressly or impliedly. This is not in reality a problem. The orthodox reading of the ultra vires principle is itself based on the assumption that Parliament will be presumed not to have intended the making of regulations which are vague, unreasonable etc. The presumption is therefore that vague or unreasonable regulations are prohibited. There is no substantive difference in this respect with the alternative conceptual basis for judicial review, which sees the heads of review based on the common law. On this view there would be a common law presumption that the common law proscription against the making of vague or unreasonable regulations could be operative, and hence such regulations would be prohibited, unless there was some very clear indication from Parliament to the contrary.

Now of course if Parliament *were* to state explicitly in the enabling legislation that the minister should be thus empowered then judicial review would be correspondingly curtailed. But this would be equally true irrespective of whether one perceived review to be based upon legislative intent or the common law. If it were the former, and assuming that the courts really were seeking to apply such intent, then the minister would be empowered to make vague regulations. If the principles of review were seen to be based on the common law then these could be overridden by legislation which was sufficiently clearly phrased and which was inconsistent with the common law norm, unless of course one chose to mount a direct or "strong" challenge to the sovereignty of Parliament.

(c) The symbolic argument: the utility of fig-leaves

Christopher Forsyth reinforces his analysis with an argument of a more symbolic nature. He takes Sir John Laws to task for misunderstanding the fig-leaf metaphor. The point about the fig-leaf metaphor is, says Forsyth, precisely that fig-leaves "do not deceive anyone as to what lies beneath them".[30] The fig-leaf,

---

[28] *Kruse* v. *Johnson* [1898] 2 Q.B. 91; *McEldowney* v. *Forde* [1971] A.C. 632.
[29] *R.* v. *Secretary of State for the Home Department, ex p. Leech* [1993] 4 All E.R. 539.
[30] Forsyth, *op. cit.* n. 1, p. 136 and 42 above.

"like the swimming costume on a crowded beach, is to preserve the decencies".[31] On this view the ultra vires doctrine plays a similar role in public law: while no one is so innocent as to deny the existence of judicial creativity in this area, the ultra vires doctrine serves to preserve the proper balance of power and the correct formal relationship between the judiciary and Parliament.

This is an interesting argument which undoubtedly contains an element of truth. There are however two counter arguments which are of relevance here.

The first is that the argument assumes a particular vision of the relationship between courts and Parliament, with the ultra vires doctrine based on legislative intent as the constitutional justification for judicial review. It is by no means self-evidently correct as the discussion in the last section of this article will reveal.

Secondly, we should in any event be mindful of the "costs" of the strategy which Forsyth advocates: fig-leaves are not harmless and do in fact naturally lead to concealment as to the proper basis for developments in judicial review. This can be exemplified by the changes in the law of jurisdictional error. The courts have, as we have seen, shifted ground on this issue over the years, moving from a doctrine of limited review, to the collateral fact doctrine and on to the present position which renders all relevant errors of law open to challenge. It is, at present, all too easy for the courts when minded to develop the law in a particular direction simply to "justify" this by some general invocation of legislative intent. Thus courts have said that they should, for example, review all errors of law because Parliament intends all such questions of law to be decided by the ordinary courts. Similar formal reliance on legislative intent served to justify the earlier legal positions on this topic.

This invocation of mystical legislative intent serves to conceal the much richer set of issues which are really at stake in this area concerning the appropriate balance of power between courts and agencies. It leaves entirely unanswered a whole series of significant questions. Why did the courts in the eighteenth, nineteenth and twentieth century persist with the other more limited doctrines of jurisdictional error? Was it simply because they felt in some way analytically constrained to do so? Was it because they were in some way under a mistaken impression about the possible limits of judicial intervention in this area? A close reading of the case law in this area would indicate a negative answer to all of these questions.[32] Alternative doctrines of jurisdictional error were based rather on differing views about the proper balance of power between courts and agencies when interpreting the conditions of jurisdiction. Although this can be divined from some of the court's jurisprudence, many of the cases were simply content to rest their chosen conclusion behind the impenetrable formalism of legislative intent. The contrast between the level of judicial debate on this topic in Canada or the USA as opposed to the UK is marked indeed. The case law in these countries is replete with explicit judicial discussion of the real issues which

---

[31] *Loc. cit.*

[32] The relevant case law can be found in Craig, *op. cit.* n. 10, Chap. 10, fns. 33 and 34.

do and should affect the legal doctrine which is applied in this area.[33] The outcome of such judicial discourse might be the same as the legal status quo as expressed in the *Page* decision. It might not. The answer either way is irrelevant to the point being made here. An important cost of using the ultra vires doctrine based on legislative intent is to conceal the true policy considerations which affect the law in this area.

III. THE DEFENCE OF THE ULTRA VIRES PRINCIPLE: MEETING THE OBJECTIONS

Christopher Forsyth does not merely point out what he perceives to be the dangers of abandoning the ultra vires doctrine. He also seeks to meet some of the objections which have been put in the first section of this article. Two arguments are advanced in this respect, one particular, the other general. They will be considered in turn.

(a) The particular defence: the exercise of power by non-statutory bodies

Forsyth concedes that the ultra vires doctrine cannot explain all instances in which the courts exercise the power of judicial review. He accepts that "it is not meaningful, when a body lacks legal power, to talk about it acting in excess of its legal powers", and that therefore "some juridical basis, other than the doctrine of ultra vires, is needed to justify judicial intervention in such cases".[34] Forsyth is willing to accept that this juridical basis can be found in the common law. He draws upon work, including that of the present author,[35] which has shown that the common law imposed a duty to price reasonably on those who exercised monopoly power, even where that power existed *de facto* rather than *de jure*. Forsyth then seeks to generalise from this case law in order to sustain the proposition that the common law should impose a more general duty to act reasonably on such bodies, which would include an obligation not to act irrationally or to abuse their powers.[36]

It would be surprising, given the views which I have expressed earlier, if I were to object to this line of argument. I do not, although there is considerable room for discussion as to which types of bodies should be subject to public law principles in this manner, and also as to which principles of public law should be

---

[33] Madame Justice L'Heueux-Dube, "The 'Ebb' and 'Flow' of Administrative Law on the 'General Question of Law'", in *The Province of Administrative Law* (Taggart ed., 1997), 308–330; Craig, "Jurisdiction, Judicial Control and Agency Autonomy", in *A Special Relationship: American Influences on Public Law in the UK* (Loveland ed., 1995), Chap. 7.

[34] Forsyth, *op. cit.* n. 1, p. 124 and pp. 31–3 above.

[35] Craig, "Constitutions, Property and Regulation" [1991] P.L. 538.

[36] Forsyth, *op. cit.* n. 1, p. 125 and p. 32 above.

applied to them. This is not the place for detailed discussion of such matters and my own views can be found elsewhere.[37]

The following point is however of direct relevance to the present debate. Forsyth remains firmly of the belief that the ultra vires principle based on legislative intent should retain its central position so far as decisions made under statutory powers are concerned.[38] If we were to accept this view then we should be very clear of the consequences. We would be saying that the heads of review which could apply to bodies which do and which do not derive their power from statute would be generally the same, but that the conceptual basis for such review powers would be strictly distinguished. In relation to the former type of body, the traditional ultra vires doctrine would continue to provide that justification. In relation to the latter type of body, we would be willing to ground such controls on the common law's capacity to control public power.

This dichotomy does little service to a rational system of public law. This is in part for empirical reasons, in that the very dividing line between bodies which do and do not derive their power from statute can be difficult to draw. It is in part for conceptual reasons, in that it begs the central question: if the common law is to be regarded as the legitimate basis for controls on bodies which do not depend on statute for their powers, why then cannot it be so regarded for bodies which do derive their powers from statute? This question will be addressed in the final section of this article.

(b) The general defence: tacit consent and legislative delegation to the judiciary

Christopher Forsyth also seeks to reconcile the broader criticisms of the ultra vires principle with orthodoxy. He accepts that judicial review is a judicial creation. He recognises that the implied intent of the legislature cannot plausibly provide any significant guidance as to "the reach of the rules of natural justice or the fine distinctions to be drawn between decisions that are unreasonable but not irrational and the like".[39] He argues however that these judicial developments did not take place in a constitutional vacuum, but rather against the background of a sovereign legislature that "could have intervened at any moment", and sometimes did.[40] The fact that it generally did not do so is taken by Forsyth to be tacit approval by the legislature of the principles of judicial review, subject to the recognition of legislative supremacy. While the implied intent of the legislature cannot therefore provide the key to the precise application of the rules of natural justice, reasonableness etc which will apply in a particular case, "the

---

[37] Craig, "Public Law and Control over Private Power" in *The Province of Administrative Law* (Taggart ed., 1997), pp. 196–216.

[38] Forsyth, *op. cit.* n. 1, p. 126 and p. 33 above.

[39] *Ibid.* p. 134 and p. 40 above.

[40] *Ibid.* p. 135 and p. 41 above.

legislature is taken to have granted an *imprimatur* to the judges to develop the law in the particular area".[41]

Proponents of the traditional ultra vires doctrine pay a heavy price for this mode of reconciliation. It is accepted that legislative intent provides no sure guide as to the precise application of the heads of review in a particular case. It is acknowledged that the general meaning to be ascribed to an established head of review, such as jurisdictional error, is similarly to be decided by the judiciary. It would seem also to follow that legislative intent can furnish no adequate explanation for the introduction of a new head of review at a particular time. In truth, this mode of reconciliation robs the traditional orthodoxy of virtually all content. On this view the only relevance of legislative intent comes in the form of tacit approval by the legislature for the principles of judicial review developed by the courts and tacit consent for the continuance of this judicial role. On this interpretation the ultra vires doctrine becomes a mere shadow of its former self, capable only of performing a residual role by implicitly legitimating what the courts have chosen to do, while being incapable of providing any more specific guidance.

Even this residual role can be questioned. While Parliament could in theory choose to intervene and overturn a development of which it disapproved, thereby giving positive life to the residual notion of legislative intent, this could be more difficult than might initially be imagined. If the courts were, for example, to recognise proportionality as an independent head of review, and the legislature disapproved of this step, could the legislature enact a general statute which prohibited its use? In theory yes, subject of course to more general discussion of the sovereignty of Parliament. But even accepting traditional notions of sovereignty can one realistically imagine such a statute being drafted and enacted?

IV. THE FOUNDATIONS OF JUDICIAL REVIEW

The discussion thus far has been concerned with the current debate concerning the relevance of the ultra vires doctrine as the foundation for judicial review. This section of the article will seek to broaden the discussion both historically and conceptually. It will be argued that in historical terms judicial review was not originally founded on the idea of effectuating legislative intent, and that this only became a central focus in the nineteenth century. The analysis will then shift to the conceptual level, and it will be argued that there are valid reasons for basing the principles of judicial review on a common law foundation.

---

[41] *Loc. cit.*

(a) The historical perspective

The very meaning of the ultra vires doctrine is more complex than often thought and the foundations for judicial review have varied across time. This will become apparent from the historical discussion. It may be helpful at the outset to exemplify this in a modern context before considering the historical materials.

The decision of the House of Lords in *Page*[42] is cited by those who seek to defend the ultra vires doctrine as support for their position.[43] Lord Browne-Wilkinson who gave the leading judgment based the court's power squarely on the ultra vires principle. His Lordship stated that *Anisminic*[44] had rendered obsolete the distinction between errors of law on the face of the record and other errors of law and that it had done this by extending the ultra vires doctrine. Thenceforth it was to be taken that "Parliament had only conferred the decision-making power on the basis that it was to be exercised on the correct legal basis"[45] with the consequence that a misdirection in law when making the decision rendered the decision ultra vires. This passage clearly does provide support for the ultra vires doctrine as articulated earlier: judicial review is explicitly posited on the assumption that Parliament intended that all errors of law should be open to challenge. A rather different reading of the ultra vires doctrine is however to be found but a page later in Lord Browne-Wilkinson's judgment. His Lordship was once again considering the rationale for judicial control over all errors of law, in order to determine whether the same degree of control should be applied to a University Visitor. Here a rather different meaning was ascribed to the ultra vires doctrine.[46]

> . . . the constitutional basis of the courts' power to quash is that the decision of the inferior tribunal is unlawful on the grounds that it is ultra vires. In the ordinary case, the law applicable to a decision made by such a body is the general law of the land. Therefore, a tribunal or inferior court acts ultra vires if it reaches its conclusion on a basis erroneous under the general law.

On its face this dictum provides a different foundation for judicial review: ultra vires is equated with the general law of the land, which clearly includes the common law. On this view the ultra vires doctrine is no longer based exclusively on legislative intent. It simply becomes the vehicle through which the common law courts develop their controls over the administration. Whether Lord Browne-Wilkinson actually intended this result is unclear.

What is clear is that uncertainty as to the precise foundation of the courts' review powers is not new and that the effectuation of legislative intent was not an important feature in this respect until the nineteenth century.

---

[42] [1993] A.C. 682.
[43] Forsyth, *op. cit.* n. 1, p. 123 and p. 30 above.
[44] [1969] 2 A.C. 147.
[45] [1993] A.C. 682, 701.
[46] *Ibid.* p. 702F.

The history of judicial review is inextricably bound up with the development of remedies as opposed to the creation of new heads of review. The elaboration of grounds for review took place within, and was framed by, the evolution of adjectival law. We must therefore look to the prerogative writs in order to understand the foundations of judicial review. Space precludes a detailed analysis of this topic which could easily occupy a book let alone an article. The established case law and literature[47] can none the less be drawn on to provide a general picture.

Mandamus was the earliest of the prerogative writs to be transformed into a more general purpose tool for the remedying of administrative error. *Bagg's* case[48] was the seminal judgment in this respect. Henderson captures the importance and novelty of the decision.[49] A "writ of restitution" existed prior to *Bagg's* case. Its primary focus was, however, to protect the privilege of a claimant who had been deprived of an office so as to ensure that he or she could consult with a King's Bench counsel. If such a person was therefore arrested while attempting to exercise this right a writ would be sought to command the prison to release the person thus detained. By 1613–15 the writ had been transformed and *Bagg's* case was of central importance in this respect. The colourful case concerned the disenfranchisement of James Bagg who had been a burgess of Plymouth. He had made a succession of abusive comments about the mayor and other burgesses. Coke in the King's Bench found for Bagg: the offensive words were an insufficient cause for disenfranchisement from a freehold office. This conclusion on the facts was buttressed by a more important finding as to the general jurisdiction of King's Bench. It was held that this court had the authority "not only to correct errors in judicial proceedings, but other errors and misdemeanors extra-judicial, tending to the breach of the peace, or oppression of the subjects, or to the raising of faction, controversy, debate or to any manner of misgovernment; so that no wrong or injury, either public or private, can be done but that it shall be (here) reformed or punished by due course of law".[50]

The decision was of far reaching importance both in terms of the development of the remedy itself, and also because of the types of error which were now said to be reviewable. Henderson captures the former point well.[51]

> ... by 1613–15 a new writ had appeared with a definite though potentially very flexible form. Moreover, by this writ King's Bench did something quite different from its traditional activities. It was not addressed to the sheriff or any other law enforcement official ... Nor was it directed to other judicial authority like the writs of prohibition, error ... and some of the medieval forms of certiorari. By this new writ a public

---

[47] Henderson, *Foundations of English Administrative Law* (1963); Rubinstein, *Jurisdiction and Illegality* (1965); de Smith, "The Prerogative Writs" [1951] C.L.J. 40 and "Wrongs and Remedies in Administrative Law" (1952) M.L.R. 189; Jaffe and Henderson, "Judicial Review and the Rule of Law: Historical Origins" (1956) 72 L.Q.R. 345.

[48] (1615) 11 Co. Rep. 93b.

[49] Henderson, *op. cit* n. 42, pp. 46–58.

[50] (1615) 11 Co. Rep. 93b, 98a.

[51] Henderson, *op. cit.* n. 47, pp. 61–62. Italics in the original.

official outside the normal law enforcement system was required to do something . . .
All this was a very far-reaching departure from tradition. Yet as may be seen, the writ
as it was now worded said nothing to explain why King's Bench could do this, beyond
the bare generality that an injustice had been done and that it ought to be set right.

The significance of the latter point, the scope of errors which King's Bench
could address, was not lost on those who read the judgment. Thus in the
Observations on the Lord Coke's Reports Lord Ellesmere,[52] having noted that
the case was simply concerned with the legality of removal from an office, had
this to say about the broader dicta concerning the scope of the King's Bench
power.[53]

> Herein (giving excess of authority to K.B.) he hath as much as insinuated that this
> Court is all-sufficient in itself to manage the State; for if the King's Bench may reform
> any manner of misgovernment (as the words are) it seemeth that there is little or no
> use either of the King's Royal care and authority exercised in his person, and by his
> proclamations, ordinances, and immediate directions, nor of the council table, which
> under the King is the chief watch tower for all points of government . . . and besides
> the words do import as if the King's Bench had a superintendency over the government
> itself, and to judge wherein any of them do misgovern.

Theoretical justification for the expansive power arrogated by King's Bench was
not immediately forthcoming. We can none the less draw some conclusions
both negative and positive from the existing materials.

In *negative* terms, there was no attempt to legitimate this exercise of judicial
power by reference to ultra vires in the sense of legislative intent, howsoever it
might be defined. This is clear in part because of the very absence of any such
indication in the judgment of *Bagg's* case which might suggest this as the foundation for review. This conclusion is reinforced by the fact that Parliament was
not at this time the fount of all authority. Power was divided between the King
and Parliament, and it was to take a civil war and consequent settlement before
it would even begin to become meaningful to speak of a Parliament which had
truly sovereign capacity in the modern sense of the term. Yet one suspects that
even if Parliament had attained this status at the time of *Bagg's* case it would not
have suited Coke's temperament and intellectual leanings to rest judicial review
on the foundation of legislative intent. It is of course true that Coke was a real
supporter of Parliament in its struggles with the King, as manifested in the seminal decisions concerning the prerogative.[54] Yet his enduring belief was in the
power of the common law itself. Given that this was so it is doubtful in the
extreme if Coke would have been content to rest judicial intervention on the vindication of Parliamentary intent.

---

[52] The observations are attributed to Lord Ellesmere, although Henderson, *op. cit* n. 47, p. 70,
questions whether he was indeed the author.

[53] The quotation can be found in (1615) 11 Co. rep. 93b, 98a fn B.

[54] *Prohibitions del Roy* (1607) 12 Co. Rep. 63; *Case of Proclamations* (1611) 12 Co. Rep. 74. For
a discussion see, Craig, "Prerogative, Precedent and Power", in *The Golden Metward and the
Crooked Cord, Essays in Honour of Sir William Wade* (1998) 65–90.

One hundred and fifty years later the "parties' have changed but the story remained the same. Parliament's position had improved considerably during this time, although the monarch still exercised real power. The leading judicial decisions declined none the less to rest review powers on ideas of legislative intent. What was true of Coke in this respect was true also of Mansfield. It was Lord Mansfield in *R. v. Barker*[55] who produced the seminal eighteenth century rationalisation of mandamus.

> The original nature of the writ, and the end for which it was framed, direct upon what occasions it should be used. It was introduced, to prevent disorder from a failure of justice, and defect of police. Therefore it ought to be used upon all occasions where the law has established no specific remedy, and where in justice and good government there ought to be one.

Nor should we forget in this respect that even in the nineteenth century, when it was more common for judges to invoke legislative intent as the justification for review, there were still notable instances where the courts would honestly admit that the common law was supplying the omission of the legislature.[56]

In *positive* terms a number of possible justifications for the newly created judicial power were advanced. Coke himself sought to rest it in part upon Magna Carta and the protections for freehold offices derived therefrom, although as Henderson has pointed out it was by no means self-evident that a municipal alderman did possess such a freehold in his office.[57] More generally, Coke advanced a theory of delegation, whereby the King was taken to have committed all his judicial power to the courts, including in this respect the power to do justice.[58] There are however both empirical and conceptual difficulties with this explanation.[59] In truth, we would do well to pay attention to the actual language used by both Coke and Mansfield, and to acknowledge that both jurists based their conclusions on the capacity of the common law to control governmental power. Indeed, as Jaffe and Henderson aptly remark,[60] Coke's doctrine of irrevocable delegation was in truth but a corollary of "his boldest and most spacious notion", the autonomy of the common law. This conceptual justification for judicial review will be considered more fully below.

The evolution of certiorari into a generalised remedy capable of catching a variety of governmental errors was to post-date the developments in mandamus which have been charted above. While there was therefore a temporal difference in the elaboration of the remedies, the conceptual foundation for the expansion in the remit of certiorari paralleled that which we have identified in the context of mandamus.

---

[55] (1762) 3 Burr. 1265, 1267.

[56] *Cooper v. Wandsworth Board of Works* (1863) 14 C.B. (N.S.) 180.

[57] Henderson, *op. cit.* n. 47, pp. 77–78.

[58] Coke, *The Fourth Part of the Institutes of the Laws of England* (1648), p. 71, cited by Henderson, *op. cit.* n. 47, pp. 70–71. See also, Jaffe and Henderson, *op. cit* n. 47, p. 361.

[59] Henderson, *op. cit.* n. 47, pp. 71–72.

[60] *Op. cit.* n. 47, p. 362.

Certiorari certainly existed during the medieval period, and was used for many purposes, most notably as a means for calling up the record on a particular matter. Certiorari to quash emerged rather later. The judgment in *Commins* v. *Massam*[61] was of central importance. It arose out of a decision by the Commissioners for Sewers to charge the cost of repairs to a sea wall to the lessee of the land. The court was divided as to whether certiorari would lie or not. Mallett J. was of the view that it would not, but Heath J. and Bramston C.J. held to the contrary. Heath J. was firmly of the opinion that certiorari would lie since there was no court which could not be corrected by King's Bench.[62] It seems that this newly created remedy of certiorari to quash was originally only available against courts of record.[63] It was Holt C.J. who built on these foundations to fashion a remedy of more wide ranging application. In the *Cardiff Bridge* case[64] he held that certiorari would lie whenever a new jurisdiction was created, whether by private or public Act of Parliament. This same theme was developed in *Groenvelt* v. *Burwell*[65] where Holt C.J. held that where any court was created by statute, certiorari would lie, for it was a consequence of all jurisdictions to have their proceedings examined by King's Bench. Moreover, although the statute did not "give authority to this Court to grant a certiorari", this was not conclusive since "it is by the common law that this Court will examine if other Courts exceed their jurisdictions".[66]

The concept of jurisdiction was then to be the touchstone through which King's Bench controlled the inferior bodies which it had bought within its purview. This is not the place for any general exegesis on the meaning ascribed by the courts to jurisdiction. This can be found elsewhere.[67] What is of importance for the purposes of the present discussion is to be clear how far the particular meaning accorded to jurisdiction was determined by reference to legislative intent, and how far it was the result of a choice made by the reviewing court of its own volition in the exercise of its inherent common law power.

There is no doubt that in one sense the determination of jurisdiction must necessarily make reference to the enabling legislation. It is only by doing so that one can begin to determine the ambit of authority given to any particular body. In this sense the legislation provides a necessary focus for judicial review. This bears out the point made earlier, that those who are opposed to the traditional ultra vires doctrine as the basis for judicial review, none the less accept that the enabling legislation will always be of relevance.[68] There is however a world of difference between acknowledging that the legislation is of relevance in this respect, and accepting that the intent of the legislature can provide any real guid-

---

[61] (1643) March N.C. 196.
[62] *Ibid.* p. 197.
[63] Henderson, *op. cit.* n. 47, p. 112.
[64] (1700) 1 Ld. Raym. 580.
[65] (1700) 1 Ld. Raym. 454.
[66] *Ibid.* p. 469.
[67] Craig, *op. cit.* n. 2, Chap. 10; Rubinstein, *op. cit.* n. 47; Henderson, *op. cit.* n. 47.
[68] See above, p. 49.

ance as to, for example, the scope of jurisdictional error or the types of control which should exist over the exercise of discretion.

It is clear that the varying answers which were given to these latter questions in the seventeenth and eighteenth centuries were not generally based upon legislative intent. Nor was any general theory of jurisdiction provided by Coke, Blackstone or Hale.[69] It was left to individual courts to reach decisions which they felt expressed the appropriate standard to be imposed pursuant to the common law power of judicial review. Not surprisingly views differed on this, in much the same manner as they do in the modern day. Some such as Heath J. in *Commins*[70] expressly acknowledged that the court could intervene to examine jurisdiction and not justice, but then so applied jurisdiction so as to embrace in effect any error of law. Others, such as those who gave judgment in *Woodsterton*,[71] construed the concept of jurisdiction more narrowly. It is in the nineteenth century that we begin to see the courts more commonly seeking to justify their chosen interpretations of jurisdiction by reference to legislative intent, in order thereby to imbue them with greater legitimacy.[72] Yet as we have already seen, it was the very malleability of legislative intent which rendered it capable of legitimating virtually any of the chosen meanings of jurisdiction adopted by the courts, thereby robbing it of the capacity to legitimate any particular one.

(b) The conceptual perspective

We have already seen that proponents of the traditional ultra vires doctrine defend it on the ground, *inter alia*, that it legitimates judicial review, by making it referable to Parliamentary intent. They question whether any other conceptual justification for the courts' powers of judicial review could be found, and maintain this position even while acknowledging some of the shortcomings of the ultra vires doctrine. This is an important argument which must be directly addressed.

The most dramatic way of doing so is, of course, to attack the foundations of the argument directly, by challenging established ideas of Parliamentary supremacy. This is a possible line of argument and as indicated earlier I believe that there are indeed strong reasons for rethinking traditional ideas of Parliamentary supremacy. The justifications for altering our constitutional foundations must however be addressed in their own right, and the detailed historical, legal and conceptual parts of the analysis cannot be examined here.[73]

It will however be argued that a sound conceptual foundation for judicial review can be found even if Parliamentary supremacy remains unaltered. The essence of the argument can be put quite simply.

[69] Henderson, *op. cit.* n. 47, pp. 126–127.
[70] (1643) March N.C. 196.
[71] (1733) 2 Barnard K.B. 207.
[72] See above, n. 11.
[73] See above n. 5.

It is common for lawyers to think in the pigeon-holes represented by their specialty. We all try to compensate for this and broaden our horizons, but exigencies of time and the growing sophistication of differing legal disciplines render this increasingly difficult. Testing the fundamental assumptions which underlie one area against accepted judicial behaviour in other areas can however be rewarding. This is particularly true when we consider public and private law. Important work has been done on the differences and similarities between the two fields, but a significant difference has not been noted.

In public law, the view is, as we have seen, that controls on public power must be legitimated by reference to legislative intent. In private law, there is no such assumption. It is accepted that constraints on the exercise of private power can and have been developed by the common law in and of itself, and there are numerous examples of this in contract, tort, restitution and property law.[74]

When we consider the matter in this light the historical material considered above appears less surprising. The absence of any formal divide between public and private law helps us to understand why it would not have appeared at all odd to a Coke, Heath, Holt or a Mansfield to base judicial review on the capacity of the common law to control public power. It is the very same absence of a formal divide which can help us to understand the willingness of the courts to extend common law created doctrine to bodies which possessed a de facto monopoly.

There are consequential interesting differences in the sense of legitimation which operates in the two areas. In public law, the traditional ultra vires model sees legitimation in terms of the *derivation* of judicial authority, flowing from legislative intent. The prime focus is not on the *content* of the heads of review. We are of course concerned about content, but this is not the primary focus when we are thinking about the legitimacy of judicial review itself. This is in part a consequence of the fact that, as we have seen, the ultra vires doctrine is capable of vindicating virtually any chosen heads of review. In private law, by way of contrast, we tend to think of legitimation in terms of the *content* of the common law norm which the courts have imposed, and more specifically about its *normative justification*. We ask whether certain constraints imposed on the exercise of private power in, for example, contract and tort, are sensible, warranted and justified in the light of the aims of the particular doctrinal area in question. It should be made very clear at this juncture that no claim is being

---

[74] In the law of tort see, e.g., the economic torts which place limitations on the legitimate scope of competitive activity in the market place or the way in which the courts have limited the *volenti* doctrine so as to render it inapplicable where real free choice is not available. In the law of contract see, e.g., the common law rules which condition the acceptability of exemption clauses, or the rules concerning illegality which relate to the restraint of trade doctrine. In the law of restitution see, e.g., doctrines such as duress. On some occasions, limits are rationalised by reference to the supposed intent of the parties, on others by the courts will openly impose the limits. It is of course the case that Parliament could overrule common law norms created by the courts related to private law. This does not alter the point being made in the text: neither the courts, nor writers seek to deny that some of these controls are common law creations in the manner described above.

made either way as to whether the *content* of the constraints imposed on public and private power should be the same or different. It is the *approach* to this topic which is in issue here.

An important consequence of conceiving of judicial review in this manner is that it better expresses the relationship between courts and legislature in a constitutional democracy. The fact that the legislature could ultimately limit review, given traditional notions of sovereignty, does not mean that the institution of review has to be legitimated by reference to legislative intent in the absence of any such limits being imposed. The constitution assigns a role to the courts as well as the legislature. This latter point has been powerfully captured by Professor Wade.[75]

> If we respect what little is left of our own constitution, it ought not to be left to Whitehall to say how much judicial control they will or will not tolerate. It is just as much for the judges to say how much abuse of power they will or will not tolerate. This is the part that the constitution assigns to them and they should be allowed to play it, free from threats and accusations and without talk of government by judges.

The challenge can then be presented squarely. Why is it that some now feel that judicial review can only be properly grounded on legislative intent, given that this was not felt to be so for public law by earlier jurists, and given also that controls on private power are not perceived to operate in this manner? Three different answers might be suggested.

The first possible response is that we must preserve the ultra vires doctrine since we would otherwise encounter problems with ouster clauses and be faced with analytical difficulties. This argument has been addressed above.[76]

The second is that to rest judicial review on the common law would still constitute a challenge to sovereignty, since these controls on the exercise of public power would always be operative. This will not withstand examination. There is nothing in principle inconsistent in positing the existence of judicial review on the capacity of the common law to control public power, while accepting at the same time that Parliament might, with sufficiently clear words etc, limit such common law constraints. In historical terms it has been convincingly argued that this is in fact what Coke had in mind in *Dr. Bonham's Case*,[77] rather than the more radical idea of overturning legislation.[78] Even when construed in this manner Coke's doctrine did lay the foundation for a "highly autonomous and powerful judiciary", which would insist that "legislation would be interpreted in the light of 'reason' and the 'common law', that official action would be subject to legal control, and that the authority of courts would be accepted by Parliament and Crown".[79]

---

[75] *Constitutional Fundamentals, op. cit.* n. 26, p. 70.
[76] See above, pp. 54–7.
[77] (1610) 8 Co. Rep. 107.
[78] Gough, *Fundamental Law in English Constitutional History* (1955), pp. 43–45.
[79] Jaffe and Henderson, *op. cit.* n. 47, p. 362.

The third possible argument is that we must preserve the idea of ultra vires based on legislative intent, since otherwise there would be no limits as to the types of common law constraints which the courts could impose. Even leaving aside the residual capacity of Parliament to intervene, this argument is still open to two counter objections. On the one hand, the ultra vires doctrine itself has never, as we have seen, provided any meaningful guidance concerning the heads of review, their limits or their precise content. On the other hand, if we accept that such review powers rest on the common law we can then employ the same approach which we bring to bear in the context of private law. The focus would be where it ought to be, on the existence of a reasoned justification, which was acceptable in normative terms, for the particular head of review which was in question. Thus, for example, rather than "justifying" a particular reading of jurisdictional error by reference to legislative intent, there should instead be a reasoned argument as to why this view of jurisdictional error was felt to be correct.

V. CONCLUSION

Debate about the foundations of a body of law is important in any legal system. This is especially so in relation to public law, given the importance of the subject matter. Few would doubt that a democratic polity requires some measure of judicial review. For some the primary focus may be on the need to constrain public power. For others it may be directed towards ensuring that affected interests are represented in the administrative process. Other views are clearly possible.

When we think about the foundations for this body of law we should be mindful of the analytic consequences of adopting a particular view, and mindful also of our historical heritage. Both have been addressed in this article. Christopher Forsyth is clearly correct to point out the analytic consequences which have, for example, attended the demise of the ultra vires doctrine in South Africa. We do however differ markedly as to whether these are necessary or even likely results of departing from established orthodoxy. Our historical heritage is equally important. An appreciation of the historical foundations for judicial review can prevent a potent form of "temporal parochialism". It can help us to understand that the orthodoxy of today is less permanent and more ephemeral than might have been imagined. The ultra vires doctrine conceived in terms of legislative intent, which is now regarded as the unshakeable foundation for review, would never have appeared so to Coke, Heath, Holt or Mansfield, nor to many of the other judges who participated in the development of review during this period. There is little doubt but that these judges would have felt more at home with the vision of dual constitutionalism or bi-polar sovereignty articulated by Sir Stephen Sedley,[80] and also with the autonomous capacity of the

---

[80] "Human Rights: A Twenty-First Century Agenda" [1995] P.L. 386.

common law to develop review advanced in the work of Sir John Laws.[81] Important traces of similar ideas are also to be found in the work of those associated with the traditional ultra vires doctrine, such as Professor Wade.[82]

There is no doubt that the institution of judicial review must be justified, as too must the heads of review and the particular meaning accorded to them. The ultra vires doctrine conceived in terms of legislative intent cannot provide this. We should recognise what was self-evident to our intellectual ancestors that review is the creation of the common law. We should recognise also that the ambit of review can only be legitimated in the same way as other common law powers, by asking whether there is a reasoned justification which is acceptable in normative terms for the controls which are being imposed. The institution of judicial review both demands and deserves legitimation in this manner.

[81] See above, ns. 2 and 16.
[82] *Constitutional Fundamentals, op. cit.* n. 26, pp. 66, 68, 70–71.

4

An Extract from:
Illegality: The Problem of Jurisdiction*

SIR JOHN LAWS

In what I regard as a very important and distinguished article[1] Dr Christopher Forsyth of Robinson College Cambridge, co-author of Wade's 7th edition, roundly attacks the view that the ultra vires doctrine no longer affords a true justification or analysis of the court's judicial review jurisdiction. His defence of orthodoxy (as he regards it) consists in no little measure of a series of assaults on arguments put forward by myself. I recognise the tedium that can readily be induced by the prospect of riposte and counter-riposte in a debate where the protagonists take starkly contrasting positions. My reason for addressing Dr Forsyth's paper in some detail is that its quality is such that since its publication no discussion of ultra vires can claim to grapple with the subject without doing so.

Forsyth's approach is subtle and imaginative. First he seeks to come to terms with the difficulty facing the ultra vires theory that the court reviews decisions made by bodies whose authority is not derived from statute at all,[2] citing *Ex p Datafin*. Forsyth's answer is that "the constitutional basis of this extension of judicial review" (the use of the term "extension" is a nice begging of the question) is to be found in what Dr Paul Craig called the "almost forgotten" jurisprudence by which "the common law imposed a duty to act reasonably on those who exercised monopoly power even where that power simply existed *de facto*."[3] Forsyth cites the authority of Hale LCJ in *De Portibus Maris*[4] as stating the old jurisprudence:

> A man, for his own private advantage, may in a port or town set up a wharf or crane and may take what rates he and his customers may agree for cranage, houselage,

---

* "Illegality: The Problem of Jurisdiction" was first published in M. Supperstone and J. Goudie (eds.), *Judicial Review* (London, 1997) 2nd edn.

[1] 'Of Fig Leaves and Fairy Tales: The *Ultra Vires* Doctrine, the Sovereignty of Parliament and Judicial Review", Vol. 55 [1996] CLJ 122 and Chapter Two above.

[2] Review of non-statutory bodies is a significant dimension in Professor Dawn Oliver's article, "Is the Ultra Vires rule the basis of Judicial Review?" [1987] *Public Law* 543 and Chapter One p. 3 above to which I should pay tribute.

[3] Forsyth, p. 124 and Chapter One p.29 above. Craig's texts are his "Administrative Law" (3rd edn.), pp. 222–225 and "Constitutions, Property and Regulation" [1991] *Public Law* 538.

[4] 1 Harg LTr, 78 (1787).

pesage, for he doth no more than is lawful for any man to do, *viz.* make the most of his own . . . [But] if the King or subject have a public wharf, unto which all persons who come to that port must come and unlade or lade their goods . . . because there is no other wharf in that port as it may fall out where a port is newly erected; in that case there cannot be taken arbitrary or excessive duties for cranage, wharfage, pesage etc . . .; but the duties must be reasonable and moderate, though settled by the King's license or charter. For now the wharf, and crane and other conveniences are affected with a public interest, and they cease to be *jus privati* only . . .

Forsyth continues:[5]

All the cases cited by Craig as well as all the American cases in which the principle has been adopted are concerned with imposing upon the owners of monopolies the duty to make only reasonable charges for the use of their property or the provision of related services. However, why should the common law not impose on those who exercise monopoly power, whether that power derives from the ownership of property or otherwise, a more general duty to act reasonably, for instance, to heed the rules of natural justice, not to act irrationally and not to abuse their powers? That indeed, it is submitted, is implicit in the modern case of *Nagle* v. *Fielden*[6] where, in the days before legislation against sexual discrimination, a woman who had been refused a trainer's licence by the Jockey Club merely because of her sex, sought relief against the club. On public policy grounds Lord Denning MR refused the Jockey Club's application to strike out her action. The Jockey Club exercised "a virtual monopoly in an important field of human activity" and were not free to deny the right to work.

I find no difficulty with this; it supports my thesis, because it illustrates the court's abiding concern with abuse of power, which in my view is much closer to the fundamentals of judicial review than is the idea of ultra vires.[7] But Forsyth is not interested merely in reconciling the ultra vires doctrine with the fact of review of non-statutory bodies. He proceeds to confront the critics of ultra vires directly. He addresses what he calls "weak" and "strong" criticisms. The "weak" criticism consists in the proposition, for which he cites[8] a passage in my article "Law and Democracy",[9] that the developed doctrines of modern administrative law – *Wednesbury, Padfield* and the requirements of fairness and proper procedure; "are, categorically, judicial creations. They owe neither their existence nor their acceptance to the will of the legislature. They have nothing to do with the intention of Parliament, save as a fig-leaf to cover their true origins. We do not need the fig-leaf any more."[10] Forsyth proceeds to categorise the "strong" criticisms as amounting to the proposition that "the judges may in

---

5   Page 125 and p. 32 above.

6   [1966] 2 QB 633.

7   Mr Justice Sedley refers to the link, consisting in the court's hostility to abuses of power, between the old monopoly cases and modern judicial review principles in "Public Law and Contractual Employment" 23 (1994) *Industrial Law Journal* 201. I have discussed this, and also the restraint of trade cases, in "Public Law and Employment Law: Abuse of Power" [1997] *Public Law* 455.

8   At p. 127 and p. 34 above.

9   [1995] *Public Law* 72 at 79.

10   Op cit at 79.

appropriate circumstances pronounce upon the validity of Acts of Parliament".[11] He cites Lord Woolf's extra-judicial statement:[12]

> . . . if Parliament did the unthinkable [and undermined substantially the role of the High Court on judicial review], then I would say that the courts would also be required to act in a manner which would be without precedent . . . I myself would consider that there were advantages in making it clear that there are even limits on the supremacy of Parliament which it is the courts' inalienable responsibility to identify and uphold . . . [These limits] are no more than are necessary to enable the rule of law to be preserved.

Forsyth's assault on the "weak" criticism is mounted both on pragmatic and theoretical grounds. As for the first, Forsyth's view is that the abandonment of ultra vires will or may actually "eviscerate" the judicial review jurisdiction. In developing this argument he draws on the jurisprudence of South Africa (in which he is a distinguished expert). In *Staatspresident* v. *United Democratic Front*[13] the issue was the validity of certain emergency regulations, severely restricting press freedom, made by the State President purportedly acting under powers granted by main legislation. It was said that the regulations were so vague as to be null and void. But on the face of it they were protected by an ouster clause in the enabling Act: "no court shall be competent to enquire into or to give judgment on the validity of any . . . proclamation" made under the relevant section. If the regulations fell to be regarded as ultra vires, then on *Anisminic* principles they were not made under the section and the court's power to strike them down could not be excluded by the ouster provision. However the Supreme Court, by a majority, upheld the regulations: while the Roman-Dutch common law might presume against vague regulations, nevertheless the regulations were made under the Act (were intra vires) and so protected by the ouster clause. Dicta from Rabie ACJ and Hefer JA cited by Forsyth show that this conclusion was arrived at by a rejection of the conventional ultra vires approach, so that *Anisminic* principles had no application. Thus in short Forsyth argues[14] that abandonment of ultra vires unwrites the *Anisminic* doctrine and deprives the courts of their best weapon to ensure that unfair or irrational decisions are not protected by ouster clauses.

Forsyth advances another instance of what he sees as the "evisceration" of judicial review if ultra vires is left behind: the provisions in planning and other legislation allowing a statutory appeal by "any person aggrieved" against action "not within the powers of the Act", which typically must be brought within 6 weeks; and ouster clauses in such statutes have been held to prohibit other forms of challenge. Forsyth's position is that without ultra vires such an appeal could only succeed on strict illegality grounds – not *Wednesbury* or unfairness.

---

[11] Page 127 and p. 34 above.
[12] [1995] *Public Law* 57 and 69.
[13] 1998(4) SA 830(A).
[14] Pages 131–132 and pp. 35–8 above.

In order to address these points it is necessary to confront Forsyth's theoretical argument. This is how it is put:[15]

> The analytical difficulty is this: what an all powerful Parliament does not prohibit, it must authorise either expressly or impliedly. Likewise if Parliament grants a power to a minister, that minister either acts within those powers or outside those powers. There is no grey area between authorisation and prohibition or between empowerment and the denial of power. Thus, if the making of the vague regulations is within the powers granted by a sovereign Parliament, on what basis may the courts challenge Parliament's will and hold that the regulations are invalid? If Parliament has authorised vague regulations, those regulations cannot be challenged without challenging Parliament's authority to authorise such regulations. The same conclusion is reached using Hohfeldian analysis . . . one is led inevitably to the conclusion that to abandon ultra vires is to challenge the supremacy of Parliament. "Weak" critics, whether they intend it or not, are transmuted into "strong" critics.

Forsyth, however, proposes to reconcile the "weak" criticisms with what he regards as the orthodox doctrine of ultra vires. He accepts that[16] "It cannot plausibly be asserted that the implied intent of the legislature provides any significant guidance to the reach of the rules of natural justice or the fine distinctions to be drawn between decisions that are unreasonable but not irrational and the like. The 'weak' critics make a powerful case." His reconciliation consists in the proposition that Parliament could have intervened at any time to limit or negate the developing common law principles of administrative law such as *Wednesbury*.[17] Subject to the correctness of the rule of Parliamentary supremacy, this of course is right; but it does not show that these principles are creatures of the legislature's intention. However, this is the way it is put by Forsyth: ". . . the legislature is taken to have granted an *imprimatur* to the judges to develop the law in the particular area . . . It is a commonplace for the legislature to give such evaluative tasks to the judiciary. This is inevitable – neither the legislature nor the executive can evaluate everything . . . an assumption that the judges have been given the task of so developing the law, within any limits that may be set by the legislature, seems entirely reasonable. And it implies no breach of the doctrine of ultra vires; in so developing the law the judges are doing what Parliament intended, or may reasonably be taken to have intended, them to do."[18]

It is an elegant, but doomed, attempt to dress a fiction in the garb of reality. It confuses two propositions: (1) it is in actual fact the intention of the legislature that the judges should confine the powers of Parliament's delegates by such doctrines as *Wednesbury* and so forth, and *for that reason only* they are authorised to do so, and (2) while the development of such doctrines is a function of the courts' free-standing constitutional role, it is open to Parliament at any time

---

[15] Pages 133–134 and pp. 39–40 above.
[16] Page 134 and p. 40 above.
[17] Pages 134–136 and pp. 39–40 above.
[18] Page 135 and p.41 above.

to intervene and curtail it. The first proposition is plainly false, and in reality is not supported by Forsyth. The second is plainly true, at least so long as the legislative supremacy of Parliament remains accepted. Forsyth is driven to treat (2) as if it were (1) because of his twin concerns about the evisceration of judicial review and Parliamentary sovereignty.

These concerns are misplaced. As regards the first of them the correct starting-point is to recognise the obvious, namely that in addressing statutory powers the courts are first concerned with the construction of the Act. The rules of construction are judge-made. A developing rule of construction is this: a statute will only be interpreted to allow breaches of fundamental or constitutional rights if its permission to do so is given expressly.[19] This is entirely unsurprising. No one would suggest that a power of imprisonment might be conferred by Parliament upon the executive by a mere implication; nor in my view might statute nowadays permit by implication a public body to act in breach of the *Wednesbury* principles or such requirements of fairness as in the context otherwise applied to it. But in that case, the general words of an ouster provision will not suffice to exclude the court's jurisdiction to review such breaches; nor will the general words of such provisions in the planning Acts as are referred to by Forsyth suffice to exclude them from scrutiny upon a statutory appeal. (In that latter context, however, in my view the language of the relevant sections in the planning Acts and associated legislation – ". . . not within the powers of the Act or . . . any requirement of the Act has not been complied with" – is out of date. It has been reproduced in successive statutes from the late 1940s (the *nadir* of administrative law) onwards. The right of appeal should simply be expressed as arising in respect of any error of law,as has been done in the Tribunals and Inquiries Acts.)

I discuss ouster clauses, and the material provisions of the planning Acts, in greater detail below.

Nor does the approach I take fall foul of Forsyth's other concern, the doctrine of Parliamentary sovereignty. While as it happens I am one of Forsyth's "strong" critics, cited by him as such,[20] it is no part of my purpose in this chapter to mount any assault on the doctrine, which remains the plainest constitutional fundamental at the present time; a departure from it will only happen, in the tranquil development of the common law, with a gradual re-ordering of our constitutional priorities to bring alive the nascent idea that a democratic legislature cannot be above the law. I am, rather, here concerned to refute Forsyth's argument that "weak" criticism is, like it or not, "strong" criticism in disguise. I think his reasoning as to the "analytical consequences" of the abandonment of ultra vires is faulty. I do not accept that "what an all powerful Parliament does

---

[19] An example of this, in a decision of a Divisional Court constituted by Rose LJ and myself, is *R. v. Lord Chancellor, ex p Witham* [1997] 2 All ER 779, concerning the constitutional right of access to the courts.

[20] Page 128 and p. 34 above. The reference is to "Law and Democracy" [1995] *Public Law* 72, pp. 81–93.

not prohibit, it must authorise either expressly or impliedly" (save as a tautology: what Parliament does not forbid it does not forbid, which of course like any tautology is true but empty). The absence of a legislative prohibition does not entail the existence of a legislative permission. So also the proposition "if Parliament grants a power to a minister, that minister either acts within those powers or outside those powers" tells one nothing; it provides no basis for the view that the extent of Parliament's remit is the *only* condition of the lawful exercise of power by the minister. Forsyth's argument is vitiated by an implicit mistake: the mistake of assuming that because Parliament can authorise or prohibit anything, all authorities and prohibitions must come from Parliament. It is a *non sequitur*. It neglects what the logicians call the "undistributed middle" – an obscure, but useful, academic expression, meaning that although X and Y may be opposites, like praise and blame, they do not cover the whole field; there might be Z, which involves neither. Thus Forsyth mistakes the nature of legislative supremacy, which is trumps, not all four suits; specific, not wall-to-wall. How could it be otherwise? A legislature makes and unmakes laws when it thinks it needs to; the fact that in England the common law allows it to make or unmake any law it like confers upon it no metaphysic of universality.

On the face of it the position I take does not look very different from Forsyth's "reconciliation" of the "weak" criticisms with what he regards as orthodoxy. We agree that Parliament may at any stage legislate so as to change, curtail, or qualify the common law doctrines of rationality and the rest. However the differences between us *en route* to that conclusion are, I think, more important than the conclusion itself. I assert that the developed doctrines of modern public law, including an increasing recognition of fundamental constitutional rights, are not in fact and logically cannot be a function of Parliament's law. Forsyth asserts that they should be regarded as such, although in effect he concedes the fictional nature of such a position. Thus, as it seems tome, ultra vires builds constitutional theory on a pretence; that might not matter (for Forsyth it is a virtue),[21] but for its substantive effects in comparison with the effects of the true position.

Once you concede the fiction, all the public law decisions of the courts must be credibly represented as executing Parliament's will. That puts an impossible, or at least very difficult, strain upon the development of principles of construction which will give effect to constitutional rights, and therefore to the benign modernising of the British constitution; especially, perhaps, is this so since the decision of the House of Lords in *Pepper* v. *Hart*,[22] whose implications for the ultra vires theory have I think not been noticed. Suppose a statute confers

---

[21] See p. 136 and p. 42 above. "Those who consider that the fig-leaf should be stripped away . . . do not . . . appreciate the subtlety of the constitutional order in which myth but not deceit plays so important a role and where form and function are often different. The unwritten constitution consists very largely of things that appear to be one thing but are in fact another." This last statement is quite true. But it cannot justify a false doctrine about the nature of legal power.

[22] [1993] AC 593.

discretionary power which is then deployed so as to extinguish or at least curtail a constitutional right. An example might be the power in Schedule 2 to the Immigration Act 1971 to detain an illegal entrant. This power does not of itself (on any sensible view) infringe constitutional rights. But if it were exercised so as to confine the immigrant for an unreasonable period, it would; and the courts have held[23] that it cannot be so exercised. Now, if reference to *Hansard* positively demonstrated that the intention in promoting the Bill, presumed then to be inherent in the Act, was that such detainees should be confined indefinitely until the Home Office found it possible or convenient to remove them, given *Pepper* v. *Hart* the court would have to be loyal to that intention if on any challenge it proceeded on the conventional ultra vires basis.

No doubt better examples can be found. But the point of principle is clear. The judges' duty is to uphold constitutional rights: to secure order, certainly, but to temper the rule of the state by freedom and justice. In our unwritten legal system the substance of such rights is to be found in the public law principles which the courts have developed, and continue to develop. Parliament may (in the present stage of our constitutional evolution) override them, but can only do so by express, focussed, provision. Since ultra vires consigns everything to the intention of the legislature, it may obscure and undermine the judges' duty; and *Pepper* v. *Hart* should not be seen to contribute to any such process.

More deeply, ultra vires must logically reduce the constitutional norms of public law to the same condition of moral neutrality as in principle applies to legislation, because by virtue of it the decisions of the courts are only a function of Parliament's absolute power. It means that the goodness of the common law is as short or as long as the legislature's wisdom. But the common law does not lie on any such Procrustean bed.

R. V HULL UNIVERSITY VISITOR EX P PAGE[24]

As we have seen, Wade regards this as an important case. So does Forsyth.[25] The question, relevant for my purposes, which the House of Lords had to decide was whether judicial review would lie against a university visitor in respect of a decision by him as to the correct interpretation of the internal law of the university. It was accepted that he was amenable to review on other grounds, such as unfairness. But by a majority of three to two the House decided that his interpretation of the university's internal law was not subject to supervision by certiorari. The leading speech in support of the majority view was given by Lord Browne-Wilkinson. Lord Mustill and Lord Slynn disagreed. It is important to identify the essential basis of Lord Browne-Wilkinson's reasoning. It was that "the applicable law is not the common law of England but a peculiar or

---

23 *Ex p Harjiat Singh* [1984] 1 WLR 704.
24 [1993] AC 682.
25 See p. 135 and p. 41 above.

domestic law of which the visitor is the sole judge. This special status of a visitor springs from the common law recognising the right of the founder to lay down such a special law subject to adjudication by a special judge, the visitor". (700E–F)

So far, however, this tells us nothing to throw light on the general question, whether the ultra vires rule is a sensible touchstone of the court's power to control the exercise of statutory discretions, or is to be condemned on the basis I have advanced. But the defenders of the ultra vires rule would draw attention to later passages in Lord Browne-Wilkinson's speech. Responding to counsel's argument that if the visitor was amenable to review on some grounds (such as procedural impropriety) he must be amenable on all grounds which the law recognises (a proposition which the minority accepted), Lord Browne-Wilkinson said this:

> The fundamental principle [sc. of judicial review] is that the courts will intervene to ensure that the powers of public decision-making bodies are exercised lawfully. In all cases, save possibly one, this intervention by way of prohibition or certiorari is based on the proposition that such powers have been conferred on the decision-maker on the underlying assumption that the powers are to be exercised only within the jurisdiction conferred, in accordance with fair procedures and, in a *Wednesbury* sense, reasonable. If the decision-maker exercises his powers outside the jurisdiction conferred, in a manner which is procedurally irregular or is *Wednesbury* unreasonable, he is acting ultra vires his powers and therefore unlawfully . . . (701C–E)

Then a little later:

> In my judgment the decision in *Anisminic* . . . rendered obsolete the distinction between errors of law on the face of the record and other errors of law by extending the doctrine of ultra vires. Thenceforward it was to be taken that Parliament had only conferred the decision-making power on the basis that it was to be exercised on the correct legal basis: a misdirection in law in making the decision therefore rendered the decision ultra vires. (701F–G)

I must cite one further passage, at 702F–G:

> . . . the constitutional basis of the court's power to quash is that the decision of the inferior tribunal is unlawful on the grounds that it is ultra vires. In the ordinary case, the law applicable to a decision made by such a body is the general law of the land. Therefore, a tribunal or inferior court acts ultra vires if it reaches its conclusion on a basis erroneous under the general law. But the position of decisions made by a visitor is different . . .

Now, I recognise at once that Lord Browne-Wilkinson uses the language of ultra vires. And he uses it in the course of his formulation of the constitutional basis for the judicial review power. Not only that, he describes it as the premise on which Parliament is, since *Anisminic*, to be taken to have acted in conferring decision-making powers on public bodies. But none of this establishes the proposition that the judicial review principles are nothing but a function of the legislative will. Indeed, Such a notion is implicitly, but necessarily, contradicted by the last passage which I have cited: a public body "acts ultra vires if it reaches its conclusion on a basis erroneous under the *general law*" (my emphasis). Lord Browne-Wilkinson does not mean what Sir William means by the ultra vires rule. He is not saying that the judge, if he is to intervene, must find "an implied term or condition in the Act, violation of which then entails the condemnation of ultra vires". He is not categorising the doctrines of our developed public law as no more than functions of the rules concerning the construction of statutes.

However, not only *Page*, but very many other authorities, use the language of ultra vires. Wade and Forsyth are certainly entitled to claim that by and large it is the argot in which the judicial review jurisdiction has hitherto been spoken by the judges. But is is characteristic of the common law that old principles are constantly refashioned. The doctrine of ultra vires has been a builder's scaffold; when the house is built, you take the scaffold away. It is not to say, of course, that judicial review is a complete edifice. But it has reached the point where it can stand by itself.

5

The Ultra Vires Doctrine in a Constitutional Setting: Still the Central Principle of Administrative Law*

MARK ELLIOTT

I. INTRODUCTION

Few branches of English law have grown so rapidly in scope and significance over recent decades as the law of judicial review. After the neglect of administrative law in the early part of the twentieth century, the judges have now rediscovered their constitutional duties. The supervisory jurisdiction has been reinvigorated and extended, so that by the early 1980s "the courts were waiting with refined instruments of torture for ministers and departments . . . who took their public law obligations cavalierly".[1] It is perhaps this expansion of judicial review at "breakneck speed"[2] which has led to so much uncertainty concerning its juridical basis. As Sir John Laws has remarked, "there may be a price to pay for so speedy a development; it carries the risk that principles are built on a foundation with too much sand and not enough rock".[3]

Although the constitutional foundations of judicial review have, to some extent, been overlooked in the past, such criticism can no longer be sustained. This matter is now the subject of intense and often divisive debate amongst public lawyers, both academic and judicial. The protagonists can be broadly separated into two camps.

In orthodox theory, the principles of good administration which the courts apply in order to secure fairness and rationality in public decision-making are said to amount to nothing more than judicial enforcement of legislative intention. For reasons which will be discussed in detail later, this theory holds that considerations of parliamentary sovereignty dictate that judicial review should lie on the sole ground that administrative action is ultra vires, or beyond the

* This is a reprint of an article first published in Vol. 58 [1999] CLJ 129. I am grateful to Dr. Christopher Forsyth for his valuable comments on an earlier draft of this paper.

[1] Sir Stephen Sedley, "The Sound of Silence: Constitutional Law Without a Constitution" (1994) 110 L.Q.R. 270, 283.
[2] P. Cane, *An Introduction to Administrative Law* (Oxford 1996), 3rd ed., describes the growth of judicial review in such terms at p. v.
[3] "The Ghost in the Machine: Principle in Public Law" [1989] P.L. 27.

powers granted by Parliament. Thus the familiar obligations which are incumbent on the executive – to observe the rules of natural justice; to take all relevant (but no irrelevant) considerations into account; to make only reasonable decisions – are all said to spring from unwritten legislative intention. Sir William Wade has long been the leading proponent of this view. He has expressed it, which characteristic clarity, in the following terms:

> The simple proposition that a public authority may not act outside its powers (ultra vires) might fitly be called the central principle of administrative law . . . Having no written constitution on which he can fall back, the judge must in every case be able to demonstrate that he is carrying out the will of Parliament as expressed in the statute conferring the power. He is on safe ground only where he can show that the offending act is outside the power. The only way in which he can do this, in the absence of an express provision, is by finding an implied term or condition in the Act, violation of which then entails the condemnation of ultra vires.[4]

Opponents of this traditional approach argue, for reasons which will be addressed below, that the values which the courts vindicate through judicial review are not, and do not need to be, related to legislative intention. Rather, it is said, administrative law embodies a series of principles that are the fruit of judicial creativity and which are founded in the common law. These ideas were expressed in an influential paper by Dawn Oliver in 1987[5] and have been articulated more recently by Sir John Laws who, through a series of lectures and articles, has become a leading exponent of this theory:

> [The principles of judicial review] are, categorically, judicial creations. They owe neither their existence nor their acceptance to the will of the legislature. They have nothing to do with the intention of Parliament, save as a fig leaf to cover their true origins. We do not need the fig leaf any more.[6]

In 1996, Christopher Forsyth[7] published an important article on this subject, which has since prompted thoughtful responses from Professor Paul Craig[8] and Sir John Laws.[9] Although Forsyth has generally been interpreted as defending the traditional ultra vires doctrine, such a view is not wholly accurate. In fact, Forsyth seeks to lay the foundations of a new approach to the justification of judicial review which embraces the best features of the two contrasting models described above.

It is the purpose of this paper to build on that approach by demonstrating that any attempt to choose between legislative intention and judicial endeavour as

---

[4] H.W.R. Wade and C.F. Forsyth, *Administrative Law* (Oxford 1994), 7th ed., pp. 41 and 44.

[5] "Is the Ultra Vires Rule the Basis of Judicial Review?" [1987] P.L. 543 and Chapter One p. 3 above.

[6] Sir John Laws, "Law and Democracy" [1995] P.L. 72, 79.

[7] "Of Fig Leaves and Fairy Tales: The Ultra Vires Doctrine, the Sovereignty of Parliament and Judicial Review" [1996] C.L.J. 122 and Chapter Two p. 29 above.

[8] "Ultra Vires and the Foundations of Judicial Review" [1998] C.L.J. 63 and Chapter Three p. 47 above.

[9] "Illegality: The Problem of Jurisdiction" in M. Supperstone and J. Goudie (eds.), *Judicial Review* (London 1997), 2nd edn. and Chapter Four (extract), p. 73 above.

the real basis of the supervisory jurisdiction is ultimately futile. In reality, both the will of Parliament and the creativity of the judges have important roles to play. However, the true foundations of judicial review can be fully appreciated only when this branch of public law is located within its broader constitutional setting.

II. THE IMPORTANCE OF JUSTIFYING JUDICIAL REVIEW

In recent decades, the role of judicial review has steadily expanded. As the comparative lawyer Mauro Cappelletti observes, the rise of the administrative state has led to the courts in many jurisdictions "becoming themselves the 'third giant' to control the mastodon legislator and the leviathan administrator".[10] The growth of judicial review of executive action in English law is certainly consistent with this trend.

It is, perhaps, this increasing prominence of judicial review which has inspired commentators to search for constitutional foundations of the supervisory jurisdiction which have deeper roots than those which the ultra vires doctrine acknowledges. Whereas the methodology of ultra vires confines the judicial function to the implementation of Parliament's will, the more modern approach recognises the creative role which the judges undoubtedly play in the development of legal limits on public power. In this way, it has been possible to relate judicial review to broader constitutional principles such as the rule of law and the separation of powers which, many writers have cogently argued, furnish a more convincing – and more constitutionally satisfying – basis for judicial review.

This question of *how* judicial review is to be justified must be returned to later. First, it is necessary to evaluate the premise on which that question is founded, by asking *whether* it is necessary to justify judicial review at all. That premise has been challenged by Sir John Laws. In an essay which was first published in 1991, he set out the following view of the constitutional position of the courts:

> [F]or every body other than the courts, legal power depends upon an imprimatur from an external source; but this is not true of the High Court and its appellate hierarchy. In point of theory, there exists no higher order of law for them. It follows that any analysis of their jurisdiction, if it is not to be confined to the simplest statement that the court reviews what it chooses to review, must consist in a description of the nature and extent of judicial review in practice . . . [T]he ultimate freedom of movement which on my analysis the judges enjoy needs to be understood in order to appreciate that the court, if it decides in effect to push out the boundaries of judicial review in the particular case, is not guilty of any constitutional solecism.[11]

[10] M. Cappelletti, *The Judicial Process in Comparative Perspective* (Oxford 1989), p. 19.
[11] "Illegality: The Problem of Jurisdiction" in M. Supperstone and J. Goudie (eds.), *Judicial Review* (London 1991), 1st ed., at pp. 69–70.

Similarly, Laws has written that:

> "Jurisdiction", like "reasonableness", is a protean word. Its easiest application is the case where a body has express but limited powers conferred on it by another body: so if it acts outside those powers, it exceeds its jurisdiction. But the superior courts in England are not constituted on any such basis. They have, in the last analysis, the power they say they have.[12]

The essence of this argument is that the constitution prescribes no limits to judicial power, and that the only true limits on the powers of the other branches of government are those which the courts choose to recognise. This is indeed a "trailer for a constitutional theory of judicial supremacism"[13] which demands the closest inspection.

Laws's approach is inconsistent with any legal duty of judicial fidelity to the legislative will of Parliament. Consequently it sweeps away the constitutional theory of sovereignty on which the ultra vires doctrine is based. However, Laws's thesis goes further still. His conceptualisation of judicial power would, if accepted, render otiose *any* attempt to justify judicial review. If the judges have "the power they say they have",[14] then Laws is correct to argue that any analysis of the courts' public law jurisdiction[15] must either "be confined to the simplest statement that the court reviews what it chooses to review" or "consist in a description of the nature and extent of judicial review in practice"[16] since, in the absence of fixed constitutional constraints on the courts, there exists no yardstick by which to assess the constitutional legitimacy of their jurisprudence. Thus Laws's thesis questions the relevance of both the orthodox justification for judicial review and the more modern theories, based on the rule of law and the separation of powers, which have been put forward.[17]

However, this view of the British constitution must be challenged. Laws argues that the courts are in the unique and privileged position of possessing legally unlimited power. The basis of this proposition is unclear. Although it is true that, at root, all power is factual in nature, it must be recognised that developed societies employ power-allocation methodologies which are based in law and which regulate the distribution of power to the various branches of government. These processes can be observed most transparently in countries which have adopted written constitutions. For instance, the first three articles of the United States Constitution set out, in clear terms, the manner in which power is allotted to the three branches of government. The only alternative to such con-

---

[12] *Op. cit.* n. 9, at p. 4.1 and *op. cit.* n. 11, at p. 51.
[13] Sir Stephen Sedley [1993] P.L. 543, 544.
[14] Laws, *op. cit.* n. 9, at p. 4.1.
[15] And, for that matter, any other jurisdiction.
[16] Laws, *op. cit.* n. 11, at p. 69.
[17] Within the framework which Laws sets out, constitutional principles such as the rule of law and the separation of powers could still be used to guide the courts in their control of public power: see Laws's treatment of the rule of law, *op. cit.* n. 9, at pp. 4.30–4.35. Crucially, however, such concepts would be fulfilling an *explanatory* rather than a *justificatory* function, since justification would be unnecessary according to Laws's constitutional model.

stitutional power-allocation is the approach which obtains in primitive and undemocratic societies, where governmental power is exercised by those who are best able to arrogate it to themselves. If Britain is not to be likened to such societies, then it must be recognised that it is the constitution – its unwritten character notwithstanding – which assigns and, where necessary, limits the powers of the different branches of government.

This conclusion has important implications for the conception of the judicial function which Laws propounds. The power of the courts is not unlimited. They do not have "the power they say they have". In truth, the courts – like every other branch of government[18] – have the power which the constitutional order says they have.[19] The implications of this for the courts have been outlined by Lord Woolf, who remarked that, "Our parliamentary democracy is based on the rule of law . . . [T]he courts derive their authority from the rule of law . . . and can not act in manner which involves its repudiation."[20] More specifically, this view has important consequences for judicial review. As Lord Scarman observed, "Judicial review is a great weapon in the hands of the judges: but the judges must observe the constitutional limits set by our parliamentary system upon their exercise of this beneficent power."[21]

Thus, in approaching the power which the courts exercise over the executive by way of judicial review, it is crucial to be aware of the sensitive power-allocation issues which arise in this area. The judges must be alert to the importance of ensuring that they do not transgress the bounds of their allotted constitutional province, as the following dictum of Lord Mustill emphasises:

> As the judges constantly remark, it is not they who are appointed to administer the country. Absent a written constitution much sensitivity is required of the parliamentarian, administrator and judge if the delicate balance of the unwritten rules [of judicial review] evolved . . . in recent years is not to be disturbed, and all of the recent advances undone . . . [T]he boundaries [between the proper functions of the different branches of government] remain; they are of crucial significance in our private and public lives; and the courts should I believe make sure that they are not overstepped.[22]

---

[18] This argument is not inconsistent with the doctrine of legislative supremacy. There is no reason why the constitution should not embody a consensus which ascribes to Parliament legislative competence over all matters.

[19] In the words of H.R. Hahlo and E. Kahn, *The South African Legal System and its Background* (Cape Town 1968), p. 39, "The law should be [the judges'] only master." This comment formed part of an argument that judges should be independent and fearless in the face of government; however, it is also relevant to the present contention that the courts must recognise legal and, in particular, constitutional constraints. The constitution imposes on the judges imperatives of both activism and self-restraint.

[20] "*Droit Public* – English Style" [1995] P.L. 57, 68.

[21] *Nottinghamshire County Council* v. *Secretary of State for the Environment* [1986] A.C. 240, 250–251.

[22] *R.* v. *Secretary of State for the Home Department, ex p. Fire Brigades Union* [1995] 2 A.C. 513, 567–568. As the Lord Chancellor, Lord Irvine of Lairg, pointed out in a lecture given to the Historical Society of the United States Supreme Court (May 1998, Washington D.C.), it is an awareness of these sensitive power-allocation issues which has deterred the British courts from establishing a substantive, rights-based review jurisdiction. The Human Rights Act will provide the courts

It is, therefore, broadly accepted that any claim of judicial power must be scrutinised and evaluated against the delimitation of governmental functions prescribed by the constitutional order. Nowhere is this more important than in relation to judicial review since, in exercising their supervisory jurisdiction, the judges risk usurping both legislative functions (because it has traditionally been Parliament which promotes responsible government) and executive functions (since if review is too intensive, the courts, in substance, become the primary decision-makers). It should be emphasised that it is no part of the present argument that the courts have in fact transgressed the boundaries of their proper constitutional province. Rather, it is the *existence* of those boundaries, and the imperative of justifying judicial review by reference thereto, which is propounded.

Having established the importance of justifying judicial review, it is necessary to consider how this may best be achieved.

III.   THE RELATIONSHIP BETWEEN LEGISLATIVE INTENTION AND JUDICIAL REVIEW

The modern tendency within public law scholarship is to challenge the received wisdom that the grounds of judicial review are related to the intention of Parliament.[23] Recently, this argument has been articulated with particular force by Paul Craig, who contends that the principles of good administration which the courts enforce are simply part of the common law.[24] There are many attractions in such an approach. The implausibility of the direct connection between legislative intention (or, in reality, legislative silence) and the grounds of review, which the ultra vires doctrine postulates, is avoided. Moreover, the common law potentially provides a foundation for all types of judicial review, whether or not the source of the power scrutinised is statutory.

However, Christopher Forsyth has argued that in spite of these attractions of a supervisory jurisdiction resting on common law foundations, constitutional logic dictates that judicial review of statutory power must ultimately be related to the sovereign will of Parliament. The following passage captures the essence of Forsyth's thesis:

> [W]hat an all-powerful Parliament does not prohibit, it must authorise either expressly or impliedly. Likewise if Parliament grants a power to a minister, that minister either acts within those powers or outside those powers. There is no grey area between authorisation and prohibition or between empowerment and the denial of power. Thus, if the making of . . . vague regulations is within the powers granted by a sovereign Parliament, on what basis may the courts challenge Parliament's will and hold that the regulations are invalid? If Parliament has authorised vague regulations,

with the constitutional warrant which is necessary to confer democratic legitimacy on such a development.

[23] See, for example, Oliver, *op. cit.* n. 5, especially pp. 543–545 and pp. 3–5 above.
[24] *Op. cit.* n. 8. See also Woolf, *op. cit.* n. 20 and Laws, *op. cit.* nn. 6, 9 and 11.

those regulations cannot be challenged without challenging Parliament's authority to authorise such regulations . . . The upshot of this is that . . . to abandon ultra vires is to challenge the supremacy of Parliament. "Weak" critics [who purport to criticise only the ultra vires doctrine, and not the sovereignty of Parliament], whether they intend it or not, are transmuted into "strong" critics [who challenge parliamentary sovereignty].[25]

Thus, for Forsyth, when Parliament grants executive power, it is either a condition of that grant that the decision-maker must act fairly, reasonably and consistently with all the other requirements of good administration, or it is not. According to this view, logic dictates that any requirements of fairness and rationality which obtain must be internal to the grant itself. If Parliament chooses not to attach such a requirement to a grant of administrative power, such that, in effect, executive power is created free from any obligation to act fairly and rationally, it would be improper for a court to seek to impose such obligations, since to do so would be to set up the common law against the sovereign will of Parliament: the common law prohibition on unfair or unreasonable decisions would cut across the broader statutory power to make such decisions.[26]

Both Laws[27] and Craig[28] disagree fundamentally with this reasoning. It is necessary to set out Laws's critique in some detail:

I think . . . [Forsyth's] reasoning as to the "analytical consequences" of the abandonment of ultra vires is faulty. I do not accept that "what an all powerful Parliament does not prohibit, it must authorise either expressly or impliedly" . . . The absence of a legislative prohibition does not entail the existence of a legislative permission . . . Forsyth's argument is vitiated by an implicit mistake: the mistake of assuming that because Parliament can authorise or prohibit anything, all authorities and prohibitions must come from Parliament. It is a *non sequitur*. It neglects what the logicians call the "undistributed middle" – an obscure, but useful, academic expression,

---

[25] Forsyth, *op. cit.* n. 7, at pp. 133–134 and pp. 39–40 above.

[26] I have argued elsewhere that this analysis holds true even if the traditional conception of full parliamentary supremacy is rejected. See M.C. Elliott, "The Demise of Parliamentary Sovereignty? The Implications for Justifying Judicial Review" (1999) 115 L.Q.R. 119 and below, for a summary of this argument.

[27] *Op. cit.* n. 9, at pp. 4.13–4.19 and pp. 77–8 above.

[28] *Op. cit.* n. 8, at pp. 73–75 and pp. 56–8 above. However, notwithstanding his expressed dissatisfaction with Forsyth's approach, Craig – somewhat paradoxically – appears to embrace the logic of Forsyth's point. Craig argues that if the common law is adopted as the legal basis of review, "there would be a common law presumption that the common law proscription against the making of vague or unreasonable regulations could be operative, and hence such regulations would be prohibited, unless there was some very clear indication from Parliament to the contrary". The difference between this approach and that of Forsyth is semantic only. The effect of Craig's common law presumption that Parliament does not prohibit common law rules of good administration acknowledges that legislative intention *is* relevant: Craig must be understood as conceding that, ultimately, judicial review is constitutionally justified only to the extent that Parliament so permits. Thus, it is difficult to see how Craig's "common law presumption" differs in substance from Forsyth's notion of the "imprimatur" which, he argues, Parliament grants to the courts to allow them to develop the law of judicial review (on which see Forsyth, *op. cit.* n. 7, at pp. 134–136 and pp. 40–2 above).

meaning that although X and Y may be opposites, like praise and blame, they do not cover the whole field; there might be Z, which involves neither. Thus Forsyth mistakes the nature of legislative supremacy, which is trumps, not all four suits; specific, not wall-to-wall. How could it be otherwise? A legislature makes and unmakes laws when it thinks it needs to; the fact that in England the common law allows it to make or unmake any law it likes confers upon it no metaphysic of universality.[29]

Laws's central argument is that the common law *can* constitute a satisfactory legal basis for the supervisory jurisdiction, and that there is no need to relate judicial review to the intention of Parliament. He arrives at this conclusion by holding that the analytical reasoning of Forsyth – which was summarised above, and which provides that judicial review must be related to parliamentary intention – is faulty. This disagreement lies at the very heart of the debate concerning the theoretical underpinnings of judicial review, and it is the issues which it raises that must now be addressed.

A. The nature and consequences of legislative supremacy

It has already been seen that, for Forsyth, the proposition that "what an all powerful Parliament does not prohibit, it must authorise either expressly or impliedly" dictates the logical necessity of relating judicial review to legislative intention. It is this proposition which Laws seeks to challenge. He ascribes to Forsyth the view that "because Parliament can authorise or prohibit anything, all authorities and prohibitions must come from Parliament".[30] Thus, according to Laws, Forsyth presents a "wall-to-wall" view of parliamentary sovereignty. He concludes that Forsyth misunderstands the nature of legislative supremacy and that his argument is consequently undermined.

The conception of sovereignty which Laws ascribes to Forsyth would, indeed, be open to serious doubt. For instance, if all prohibitions really had to come from Parliament, then it would not even be constitutionally possible for the courts to impose such classic common law requirements as the duty to take care to avoid harming one's neighbour.[31] Similarly, the development of the criminal law by the courts[32] would not be permissible. Such a view of sovereignty would clearly be inaccurate.

[29] *Op. cit.* n. 9, at pp. 4.17–4.18 and p. 78 above.

[30] *Ibid.*

[31] This pre-eminent common law duty was first articulated in its general form (as distinct from the earlier context-specific duties in negligence) by Lord Atkin in *Donoghue* v. *Stevenson* [1932] A.C. 562. His Lordship did not, of course, seek to justify this general private law prohibition on careless conduct by reference to legislative intention, and it would be unthinkable for anyone to question the legitimacy of the modern law of negligence on this ground. Naturally, if Parliament enacted legislation dealing with the general duty of care owed to one's neighbours, it would necessarily follow that, as regards the common law rule on this subject, Parliament would either have repealed it (expressly or impliedly) or ordained (expressly or impliedly) that the common law rule should continue. In the absence of such legislation, however, the courts are clearly free to develop the law in this area in accordance with traditional common law method.

[32] For a notable example, see *R.* v. *R. (Rape: Marital Exemption)* [1992] 1 A.C. 599.

However, in truth, the consequences of sovereignty which Forsyth identifies are much more modest. By stating that "what an all-powerful Parliament does not prohibit, it must authorise either expressly or impliedly",[33] Forsyth is simply asserting that once Parliament has created a power, the limits which the courts impose on that power must logically either coincide with or cut across the scope of the power which Parliament actually conferred. This is apparent from Forsyth's statement that "if Parliament grants a power to a minister, that minister either acts within those powers or outside those powers. There is no grey area between authorisation and prohibition or between empowerment and the denial of power."[34]

An analogy may be drawn with the effect of European Union legislation on the competence of national legislatures. Once the Community institutions have adopted a regulation in relation to a particular matter, it is no longer open to member states to legislate on the same topic. The position has been expressed thus: "Under the 'classic' preemption doctrine, once the Community legislates in a field, it occupies that field, thereby precluding Member State action. The Community has assumed exclusive competence in the field."[35] Consequently, the European Court of Justice has held that "there can be no question . . . that the States may . . . take measures the purpose of which is to amend [a regulation's] scope or to add to its provisions. In so far as the Member States have conferred on the Community legislative powers . . . they no longer have the power to issue independent provisions in [that] field."[36]

Thus, once the Community has enacted legislation in the form of a regulation (which is, of course, a supreme form of law in all member states), it is not open to national legislatures to interfere in that field. No-one would suggest that this means that the Community legislature enjoys "wall-to-wall" competence in the sense that "all authorities and prohibitions" must come from that legislature. On the contrary, in the majority of cases it is open to member states to enact their own legislation until such time as the Community legislature "occupies the field".

This is precisely the approach which Forsyth envisages as regards the sovereignty of the United Kingdom Parliament. Thus, in the absence of a statutory framework, it is for the courts – by imposing common law requirements of rationality and fairness – to regulate the use of de facto public power. It has been argued that the courts do this through their long-established jurisdiction to control monopoly power.[37] However, once de facto public power is replaced with

---

[33] Forsyth, *op. cit.* n. 7, at p. 133 and p. 39 above.

[34] *Ibid.*

[35] S. Weatherill, "Beyond Preemption? Shared Competence and Constitutional Change in the European Community" in D. O'Keefe and P.M. Twomey (eds.), *Legal Issues of the Maastricht Treaty* (Chichester 1994), p. 16.

[36] Case 74/69, *Hauptzollamt Bremen* v. *Krohn* [1970] E.C.R. 451, 459. See also Case 40/69, *Hauptzollamt Hamburg-Oberelbe* v. *Firma Paul G. Bollman* [1970] E.C.R. 69, 79.

[37] There is broad agreement on this point. See Forsyth, *op. cit.* n. 7, at pp. 124–127 and pp. 31–3 above; Craig, *Administrative Law* (London 1994), 3rd ed., pp. 222–225; Laws, "Public Law and Employment Law: Abuse of Power" [1997] P.L. 455.

statutory power, regulated by a statutory framework, any limits which the courts subsequently impose on the use of such power through the judicial review process must, in orthodox theory, relate to the scope of the power which Parliament granted. Once Parliament has "occupied the field", it is improper for the courts to use the common law (which is inferior to parliamentary law) to impose limits on the power concerned different from those limits which inhere in the grant of power itself – just as national legislatures are not permitted to invoke domestic law (which is inferior to Community law) to modify the scope of regulations adopted by the Community legislature.

Neither of these propositions ascribes a "wall-to-wall" sovereignty to the legislature concerned, in the sense that "all authorities and prohibitions must come from" that legislature; in reality, the position is more subtle. Properly understood, Forsyth's approach to statutory discretionary power simply involves the notion that once Parliament has occupied the field by creating an administrative competence, no legitimate opportunity exists for the common law to determine the scope of that power since, logically, the scope of a power created by Parliament can only be determined by reference to the terms of the parliamentary grant itself.[38]

B. The argument of logic

As well as arguing that Forsyth's central point – that "what an all power Parliament does not prohibit, it must permit expressly or impliedly" – is based on a misconception of sovereignty, Laws contends, more broadly, that it is simply illogical. He submits that Forsyth's approach "neglects what the logicians call the 'undistributed middle' – an obscure, but useful, academic expression, meaning that although X and Y may be opposites, like praise and blame, they do not cover the whole field; there might be Z, which involves neither".[39]

It is noteworthy that this argument is fundamentally inconsistent with some of Laws's earlier work. In a lecture delivered in 1994, he remarked that no government can "be *neutral* about free speech. If it is not to be denied, it must be permitted; there is no room for what the logicians would call an undistributed middle."[40] By way of illustration Laws cited the biblical passage, "He that is not with me is against me."[41] It is difficult to see how these comments can be reconciled with Laws's more recent attempt to undermine Forsyth's analysis, which

---

[38] Of course, background common law values are relevant to the *interpretation* of legislation and, therefore, to the identification of any limits which apply to statutory power. However, for the reasons discussed, the common law cannot *independently* delimit the scope of statutory power. The nature of the interpretive process and the relevance of the common law in this regard are discussed further below.

[39] *Op. cit.* n. 9, at p. 4.18 and p. 78 above.

[40] *Op. cit.* n. 6, at p. 84 (original emphasis).

[41] St. Matthew's Gospel, Ch. 12, v. 30, quoted by Laws, *ibid.*, at n. 32.

is based on precisely the same logic as that which underpinned Laws's comments on free speech.

In spite of this inconsistency, Laws's most recent argument is that there *does* exist an "undistributed middle". Thus he contends that, when Parliament grants discretionary power, the grant itself is not exhaustive of the conditions which apply to the exercise of the power. While some limits may be related to legislative intention (such as those appearing expressly in the enabling provision), as regards other limitations (for instance, the rules of natural justice) it is assumed that Parliament possesses no intention whatsoever.[42] It is, so the argument runs, this "undistributed middle" which creates the opportunity for the common law to intervene and supply the duty of fairness. This, it is said, occurs without any constitutional impropriety because the common law is not being set up against legislative intention; rather, it is filling a gap where no intention exists.

Prima facie this is a persuasive argument against the intention-based model. It appears to clear the way for a common law approach which avoids the problems usually associated with the methodology of ultra vires.[43] Ultimately, however, the common law model does not withstand analysis, as the following discussion seeks to demonstrate.

C. Alternative conceptions of the relevance of legislative intention to judicial review

The disagreement between proponents of the intention-based and common law models stems from the question of what role, if any, should be ascribed to parliamentary intention vis-a-vis the grounds of judicial review. It is submitted that the entire range of possible views on this subject can be expressed in a series of five competing propositions. It will be argued that all but one of these propositions must be rejected.

The first possibility is that, when Parliament confers discretionary power, it actually intends that there should be no implied limits on that power. On this approach, judicial enforcement of common law requirements of good administration would be constitutionally improper because it would infringe the doctrine of parliamentary sovereignty. The only limits which could legitimately be enforced would be those mentioned explicitly in the enabling provision. Any additional common law limits would cut across the power which Parliament had intended should be fettered only by those limits set out in terms in the empowering provision.

---

[42] This attempt to divide the grounds of review into two categories – one based on legislative intention, the other resting on different foundations – is reminiscent of the analytical approach adopted by the South African Appellate Division in *Staatspresident* v. *United Democratic Front* 1988 (4) S.A. 830. See E. Mureinik [1988] Annual Survey of South African Law 34, 63–64 for criticism.

[43] These problems, some of which have been mentioned already, are considered in greater detail in section IV below, where it is argued that the shortcomings of the traditional ultra vires doctrine are overcome once it is placed in its proper constitutional setting.

However, it could not reasonably be assumed, in the absence of express contrary enactment, that Parliament would wish to create administrative power free from any duties to exercise it fairly, rationally, in conformity with the purpose of the legislative scheme and according to the other general principles which usually limit executive discretion. For this reason, this first view of the role of legislative intention must be rejected because it involves attributing to Parliament an absurd intention.

Secondly, it may be that, when Parliament creates discretionary power, it specifically intends every detail and nuance of the principles of good administration which the courts apply. According to this view there exists a direct relationship between legislative intention and the grounds of review. However, this approach is at least as absurd as the first. It is simply unrealistic to suggest that Parliament possesses specific intention as regards the detailed requirements of good administration, as critics of the ultra vires doctrine such as Craig point out:

> [T]he ultra vires doctrine . . . does not accord with reality . . . The orthodox approach has been to legitimate [the principles of good administration] by reference to Parliamentary intent . . . [However,] the legislation which is in issue in a particular case will often not provide any detailed guide to the courts as to the application of these controls on discretion . . . This is particularly so in relation to legislation which is framed in broad, open textured terms. The court will of necessity have to make its own considered judgment on such matters.[44]

Indeed, even those, such as Forsyth, who argue in favour of *some* role for legislative intention reject the existence of any *direct* relationship between the grounds of review and the will of Parliament:

> It cannot be plausibly asserted that the implied intent of the legislature provides any significant guidance to the reach of the rules of natural justice or the fine distinctions to be drawn between decisions that are unreasonable but not irrational and the like.[45]

Thus this second view of the role of legislative intention must also be discarded.

The third possibility is that Parliament may have no choice but to grant discretionary power subject to the condition that it must be exercised in accordance with the rules of good administration. On this view legislative intention would be beside the point. Equally there would be no need for common law principles of good administration. The grounds of review would derive straightforwardly from the limited nature of the grant of power which Parliament would be capable of making.

This approach presupposes an attenuated conception of parliamentary sovereignty. It is traditionally held that Parliament can enact any legislation it chooses. Therefore, in orthodox theory, Parliament can always elect whether to grant discretionary power subject to or free from the obligation to abide by the

---

[44] *Op. cit.* n. 8, at p. 67 and p. 51 above.
[45] *Op. cit.* n. 7, at p. 134 and p. 40 above.

principles of good administration. However, although this received view of the sovereignty of Parliament has been questioned,[46] I have argued elsewhere that the recognition of limits on parliamentary competence does not necessarily impact on the basis of judicial review.[47] This third approach could only operate if such significant inroads were made into legislative supremacy as to render Parliament incapable of modifying or, where appropriate, suspending the operation of the principles of good administration (presumably on the basis that the procedural rights of individuals are so important that they should be placed beyond the possibility of legislative interference). However, none of the leading commentators posits the erosion of parliamentary sovereignty on such a grand scale. Indeed, given that the substantive rights which will be protected under the Human Rights Act 1998 are not to be accorded this fundamental status, there is certainly no case for such treatment of the procedural values currently vindicated by judicial review. Thus, as Laws recognises, it is still the case that "Parliament may at any stage legislate so as to change, curtail, or qualify the . . . doctrines of rationality and the rest" which are enforced through judicial review.[48]

So long as this position continues to subsist, it will not be possible to justify review by reference to the limits of Parliament's legislative capacity. Provided that Parliament retains the choice whether to create discretionary power subject to or free from the requirements of good administration, the role of legislative intention must be grappled with. The attempts of the first two propositions to deal with this complex issue have been rejected. It is now necessary to consider two further, and more subtle, approaches to this question.

The fourth model holds that when Parliament confers power on an administrative agency, it must follow in logic that it either grants or withholds the authority to act unfairly and unreasonably. It is this principle which lies at the core of Forsyth's reasoning. However, it is, prima facie, difficult to appreciate the nature of the relationship between this legislative intention and the complex rules of good administration which the courts enforce. In order to resolve this difficulty, it is necessary to have recourse to the constitutional setting within which legislation is enacted by Parliament and interpreted by the courts.

The rule of law, which is a fundamental of the British constitution, clearly favours the exercise of public power in a manner that is fair and rational. It is entirely reasonable to assume that, in the absence of clear contrary enactment, Parliament intends to legislate in conformity with the rule of law. As Lord Steyn remarked in a recent decision of the House of Lords, "Parliament does not legislate in a vacuum. Parliament legislates for a European liberal democracy

---

[46] See, *inter alios*, Sir Robin Cook, "Fundamentals" [1988] N.Z.L.R. 158; Woolf, *op. cit.* n. 20; Laws, *op. cit.* nn. 6, 9 and 11; Sir Stephen Sedley, "Human Rights: A Twenty-First Century Agenda" [1995] P.L. 386; T.R.S. Allan, "The Limits of Parliamentary Sovereignty" [1985] P.L. 614 and "Parliamentary Sovereignty: Law, Politics, and Revolution" (1997) 113 L.Q.R. 443.

[47] See Elliott, *op. cit.* n. 26.

[48] *Op. cit.* n. 9, at p. 4.18 and p. 78 above.

founded on the principles and traditions of the common law. And the courts may approach legislation on this initial assumption."[49]

Thus, Parliament, intending to legislate in conformity with the rule of law, is taken only to grant such administrative power as is consistent with the requirements of that constitutional principle.[50] It is therefore taken to withhold from decision-makers the power to act unfairly and unreasonably, while recognising that the detailed requirements of fairness and rationality can most appropriately be determined incrementally by the courts through the forensic process. Hence, Parliament grants to the judges a margin of freedom – or, as Forsyth puts it, an "imprimatur"[51] – to set the precise limits of administrative power. It is the simple – and wholly plausible – assumption that Parliament intends to legislate consistently with the rule of law which bridges the apparent gulf between legislative silence and the developed body of administrative law which today regulates the use of executive discretion.

Consequently there *is* a relationship between parliamentary intention and the grounds of review. However, whereas the traditional ultra vires doctrine conceptualises the relationship as direct in nature, the present approach maintains that the relationship exists in indirect form. While the details of the principles of review are not attributed to parliamentary intention, the judicially-created rules of good administration should nevertheless be viewed as having been made pursuant to a constitutional warrant granted by Parliament.

This proposition involves no conceptual novelty, since Parliament often delegates interpretive functions to the courts. Sometimes this occurs explicitly. For instance, the Occupiers' Liability Act 1957 requires an "occupier" of premises to take reasonable care for the safety of his visitors.[52] The sphere of operation of the legislation turns, inter alia, on the meaning of the term "occupier". The Act states that, for the purposes of the legislation, the term is to be accorded the same meaning as that which it bears at common law.[53] Thus, recognising that the notion of occupation is complex, Parliament has explicitly delegated to the courts the task of determining the precise meaning of the concept.

It is more common for Parliament implicitly to assign this type of function to the judiciary. For example, a great deal of protective legislation extends only to

[49] R. v. *Secretary of State for the Home Department, ex p. Pierson* [1998] A.C. 539, 587. Similarly, at pp. 573–574, Lord Browne-Wilkinson observed that, "Parliament does not legislate in a vacuum: statutes are drafted on the basis that the ordinary rules and principles of the common law will apply to the express statutory provisions . . . Where wide powers of decision-making are conferred by statute, it is presumed that Parliament implicitly requires the decision to be made in accordance with the rules of natural justice." See also Lord Steyn, "Incorporation and Devolution – A Few Reflections on the Changing Scene" [1998] European Human Rights Law Review 153, 154–155.

[50] See R. v. *Secretary of State for the Home Department, ex parte Doody* [1994] 1 A.C. 531, 560, *per* Lord Mustill: "where an Act of Parliament confers an administrative power there is a presumption that it will be exercised in a manner which is fair in all the circumstances".

[51] *Op. cit.* n. 7, at p. 135 and p. 41 above.

[52] See s. 2(1).

[53] See s. 1(2). Similarly, "visitor" is defined as a composite term embracing the common law notions of "invitee" and "licensee". The same approach is adopted by the Occupiers' Liability Act 1984, which regulates the liability of the occupier to persons other than his visitors.

individuals who are parties to a particular class of legal relationship. Hence tenants acquire many more statutory rights than mere licensees,[54] and employees benefit from a much more generous regime of employment protection than independent contractors.[55] Yet the protective legislation which confers such benefits on tenants and employees, while withholding them from licensees and independent contractors, does not define those types of relationship. As with "occupation", so with "tenancy" and "employment": Parliament, recognising the complexity of such concepts, realises that it is desirable to leave to the courts the task of determining their exact content.

No-one would question the existence of a relationship between the intention of Parliament and the courts' jurisprudence on the meaning of terms such as "occupier", "tenant" and "employee". The courts are, quite clearly, determining the reach of the protective legislation pursuant to an explicit or implicit legislative warrant. There is no conceptual distinction between the courts' activities in these private law fields and their public law jurisprudence on the ambit of discretionary power created by Parliament. Since it is not reasonable to assume that Parliament intends to confer unlimited discretionary power, and impossible to maintain that legislative intention predetermines the exact limits on such power, the only reasonable assumption is that Parliament has delegated to the courts the task of determining the precise scope of executive discretion. The relationship between legislative intention and the grounds of review is directly analogous to the relationship between parliamentary intention and the meaning attributed to terms such as "employee". No-one would maintain that Parliament intends the nuances of the complex definition of that term which the courts have, in the best traditions of the common law, developed incrementally over many years; but nor would they deny the existence of a relationship between legislative intention and the courts' jurisprudence on the point. By the same token it cannot realistically be maintained that Parliament intends the precise details of the limits which the courts impose on discretionary power. However, as the private law analogies demonstrate, this does not mean that there exists no relationship between the legislature's intention and the courts' jurisprudence. In each case the relationship exists, but in an indirect form.

Hence, the ultra vires doctrine, once placed in its proper constitutional setting by acknowledging the important contribution of judicial creativity within an interpretive framework based on the rule of law, provides a convincing account of the theoretical basis of the supervisory jurisdiction. It reconciles judicial review with the doctrine of legislative supremacy, while eschewing the implausible, direct relationship between parliamentary intention and the grounds of review which the traditional approach posits.

[54] For example, tenants (but not licensees) enjoy protection under the Rent Act 1977 and benefit from the statutory schemes regulating assured tenancies (under the Housing Act 1988) and business tenancies (under the Landlord and Tenant Act 1954).

[55] Thus, under the Employment Rights Act 1996, only employees are capable of qualifying for such benefits as the rights not to be unfairly dismissed, to receive a redundancy payment and to be permitted to return to work after taking maternity leave.

The fifth, and final, conceptualisation of the relevance of legislative intention to judicial review is articulated by Sir John Laws.[56] He argues that there is actually no relationship at all between parliamentary intention and the grounds of review. Rather, it is for the common law to supply the principles of good administration, Parliament having desisted from occupying the logician's "undistributed middle". The logical basis of this model – which directly challenges the approach favoured by Forsyth – has already been questioned. However, Laws's methodology must also be doubted on another ground.

It is necessarily implicit in this fifth model that Parliament is wholly neutral about the extent of the administrative power which it grants and the manner in which such power is exercised: Parliament is to be taken to have no opinion on the matter, neither prescribing nor proscribing limits to the executive power which it creates. For this reason, it is said, the common law can, and does, supply this legislative omission without constitutional impropriety: there is no risk of the common law being set up against legislative intention, because there exists no intention capable of contradiction.

The choice between the fourth and fifth models is therefore stark. The former attributes to Parliament a reasonable, plausible and straightforward intention – that the rule of law should be upheld – while leaving it to the good sense and experience of the courts to determine precisely how this outcome can best be secured. In sharp contrast, the fifth model necessarily imputes to Parliament an intention which is both absurd and implausible, requiring the assumption to be made that Parliament is entirely unconcerned about the use and misuse of the governmental power which it creates. For this reason – together with the failure of common law theorists to rebut the argument that the limits of statutory power must, logically, be determined by reference to the extent of the parliamentary grant – the fifth approach must be rejected. The fourth model stands alone in accommodating the theory of legislative supremacy and the practice of judicial review in a manner which is both logical and plausible.

Indeed, the modest role for legislative intention which is being argued for is, in some respects, supported by opinions which Sir John Laws has himself expressed, both judicially and extra-curially.

In the *Witham* decision, the Divisional Court struck down regulations made by the Lord Chancellor in order to raise court fees and to remove the exemption which persons receiving income support had previously enjoyed.[57] The reasoning of Laws J., with which Rose L.J. concurred, is clearly consistent with the present argument which holds that a relationship exists between the standards of legality applied by the courts on review, and the legislative intention of Parliament:

> [T]he primary submission is that there exist *implied limitations* upon the Lord Chancellor's power to prescribe the fees to be taken in the Supreme Court. Section 130

---

[56] Craig makes a similar argument.
[57] *R. v. Lord Chancellor, ex p. Witham* [1998] Q.B. 575.

[of the Supreme Court Act 1981, which was the putative legal basis on which the Lord Chancellor relied] does not permit him to exercise the power in such a way as to deprive the citizen of what has been called his constitutional right of access to the courts.[58]

Moreover, in his conclusion, Laws J. rejected counsel's submission "that there is no vires argument here".[59] Such references to "implied limitations" and "vires" appear to acknowledge some form of relationship between legislative intention and the grounds of review. Indeed, this is entirely consistent with a number of House of Lords decisions, such as *Page*[60] and *Pierson*,[61] which have affirmed the importance of the ultra vires doctrine. Most recently, the centrality – and practical consequences – of the ultra vires principle have been underscored by the House of Lords in *Boddington* v. *British Transport Police*.[62] Lord Steyn could see "no reason to depart from the orthodox view that ultra vires is the 'central principle of administrative law'[63] . . . This is the essential constitutional underpinning of the statute based part of our administrative law."[64] Lord Irvine L.C.[65] and Lord Browne-Wilkinson[66] were equally supportive of the ultra vires doctrine.[67]

---

[58] *Ibid.*, at pp. 579–580, *per* Laws J. (emphasis added).

[59] *Ibid.*, at p. 586.

[60] R. v. *Lord President of the Privy Council, ex parte Page* [1993] A.C. 682. See Lord Browne-Wilkinson at pp. 701–702: "[Judicial review] is based on the proposition that [administrative] powers have been conferred on the decision-maker on the underlying assumption that the powers are to be exercised only within the jurisdiction conferred, in accordance with fair procedures and, in a *Wednesbury* sense, reasonably . . . [Therefore,] the constitutional basis of the courts' power to quash [administrative decisions] is that the decision of the inferior tribunal is unlawful on the grounds that it is ultra vires."

[61] R. v. *Secretary of State for the Home Department, ex parte Pierson* [1998] A.C. 539. The speech of Lord Steyn provides a particularly striking illustration of the methodology of ultra vires operating in precisely the manner contended for in the present article. The question whether it was within the Home Secretary's powers under the Criminal Justice Act 1991, s. 35(2), to increase the tariff of a prisoner serving a mandatory life sentence had to be resolved by construing the enabling provision within the context of the rule of law: "Unless there is the clearest provision to the contrary, Parliament must be presumed not to legislate contrary to the rule of law. And the rule of law enforces minimum standards of fairness, both substantive and procedural" (see p. 591). The rule of law required that a tariff period, once set and communicated to the prisoner, should not be increased, and nothing in the Act displaced this presumption. Lord Browne-Wilkinson's reasoning is also consistent with the thesis of this paper, although in his dissenting speech he concluded that the decision was not unlawful (because his Lordship took a different view of precisely what the rule of law required of the Home Secretary).

[62] [1998] 2 W.L.R. 639. For comment on this decision, see M.C. Elliott, "*Boddington*: Rediscovering the Constitutional Logic of Administrative Law" [1998] Judicial Review 144.

[63] This term is, of course, Sir William Wade's: see Wade and Forsyth, *op. cit.* n. 4, at p. 41.

[64] *Boddington*, at p. 662.

[65] See *ibid.*, at p. 650: "The *Anisminic* decision established . . . that there was a single category of errors of law, all of which rendered a decision ultra vires. No distinction is to be drawn between a patent (or substantive) error of law or a latent (or procedural) error of law."

[66] See *ibid.*, at p. 655: "I adhere to my view that the juristic basis of judicial review is the doctrine of ultra vires."

[67] Lords Slynn and Hoffmann gave only very short, concurring speeches, and therefore did not discuss the ultra vires doctrine.

It is also instructive to refer to the following passage from Laws's contribution to the recently-published *Festchrift* in honour of Sir William Wade:

> In an age when respect for human rights has received the imprimatur of civilized society, which regards it not as a political option but as a moral necessity, the reasonable public decision-maker is bound to entertain a bias against any infraction of such rights . . . A public authority cannot be *neutral* about the demands of individual freedom without building a wall between itself and current public morality. So, in the name of reasonableness, the law insists that the decision-maker is not neutral.[68]

The essence of this argument is that it is unreasonable to be neutral about individual freedoms. If it is unreasonable to be neutral about the substantive freedoms with which the excerpt is concerned, then this must be equally true of the procedural rights which are presently vindicated by way of judicial review. Furthermore, if – as Laws contends – neutrality on this matter is unreasonable on the part of administrative authorities, then it is equally (or perhaps even more) unreasonable on the part of the legislature. Laws argues that "in the name of reasonableness", the law (by which he means the judiciary) precludes such neutrality. However, it is submitted that in relation to the scope of discretionary power created by Parliament, the courts do not need to *insist* that the limits of such power are biased in favour of, rather than neutral about, the protection of individuals' procedural rights. If Parliament is not to be taken as neutral – and, therefore, on Laws's own argument, unreasonable – then it must be assumed that Parliament itself is biased in favour of the limitation of public power in accordance with the precepts of the rule of law, while leaving it to the courts to determine the detailed requirements necessary to give effect to this bias. The courts do not possess a monopoly on reasonableness. Parliament can be reasonable too, and should be taken to be so – by presuming an intention to legislate in conformity with the rule of law – unless strong evidence exists to the contrary. It is this straightforward proposition which lies at the heart of the ultra vires principle within its proper constitutional setting.

IV. A CONSTITUTIONAL SETTING FOR THE ULTRA VIRES DOCTRINE:
OVERCOMING THE SHORTCOMINGS OF THE TRADITIONAL MODEL

The charge most frequently levelled against the ultra vires doctrine is its inability to explain the connection between legislative intention and the rules of good administration which the courts enforce through judicial review. It has already been argued that, once the ultra vires principle is located within its proper constitutional setting, this criticism can no longer be sustained.

However, this is certainly not the only criticism which has been made of the traditional model. It is the purpose of the remainder of this paper to address the

---

[68] Sir John Laws, "*Wednesbury*" in C.F. Forsyth and I.C. Hare (eds.), *The Golden Metwand and the Crooked Cord* (Oxford 1997), p. 195 (original emphasis).

other principal shortcomings of the orthodox ultra vires doctrine – helpfully set out by Craig in his recent article on the subject[69] – and to demonstrate that those problems do not beset the ultra vires principle once it is understood within its constitutional setting.

A. The development of administrative law across time

The direct connection between legislative intention and the grounds of review which the traditional ultra vires doctrine seeks to establish is placed under particular strain when the development of administrative law across time is considered, as Craig observes:

> The constraints which exist on the exercise of discretionary power are not static. Existing constraints evolve and new types of control are added to the judicial armoury. Changes in judicial attitudes towards fundamental rights, the acceptance of legitimate expectations, and the possible inclusion of proportionality as a head of review in its own right are but three examples of this process. These developments cannot plausibly be explained by reference to legislative intent.[70]

This is a strong criticism of the orthodox view of ultra vires. However, once the ultra vires doctrine is properly understood, the development of administrative law over time is readily comprehensible. Within the modified ultra vires model which has been set out, the task of the courts is not to ascertain and effectuate a crystallised legislative intention regarding the limitation of discretionary power. Rather, the creativity of the judicial function can be openly acknowledged. It is for the courts to decide how discretionary power should be limited in order to ensure that its exercise complies with the requirements of the rule of law. Consequently, instead of relating the development of administrative law to putative changes in legislative intention, the modified ultra vires model holds that such developments relate to the evolution, across time, of the content of the constitutional principle of the rule of law. As the fluid and dynamic British constitution develops, so the courts rightly draw on changing constitutional norms in order to fashion new principles of judicial review and reformulate old ones.

This approach to statutory interpretation, according to which legislative provisions are construed in light of prevailing conditions, is widely accepted, as Professor Jack Beatson explained in a lecture dealing with the modern role of the common law within a legal system which is increasingly dominated by legislation:

> The vitality of the common law is preserved by the presumption that Parliament intends the court to apply to an ongoing statute . . . a construction that continually

---

[69] *Op. cit.* n. 8, especially pp. 64–70 and pp. 48–54 above.

[70] *Ibid.*, at p. 68 and pp. 51–2 above. A similar point is made by Laws, *op. cit.* n. 6, at pp. 78–79.

updates its meaning to allow for changes since it was initially framed. This means that in its application on any date the language of the Act, though necessarily embedded in its own time, is nevertheless to be construed in accordance with the need to treat it as current law . . . [For example,] at the time the Land Registration Act 1925 was passed giving a person "in actual occupation" of property an overriding interest, the balance of authority suggested that a wife residing with her husband where the husband alone was the legal owner of the property was not "in actual occupation". But by the beginning of the 1980s the social and legal status of husband and wife had changed and it was held that the wife was "in actual occupation" and entitled to the statutory protection. The solution was derived from a consideration of the statute in the light of current social conditions.[71]

Just as the courts' interpretation of legislation changes according to social conditions, so their view of what limits on discretionary power are required by the rule of law alters as the constitution develops over time.[72]

The evolution of judicial review to date can be related to the constitutional changes which have been prompted by the massive expansion of the administrative state, necessitating the development of safeguards for individuals as they interact with government in order to ensure that citizens are treated in accordance with rule of law. In this manner, it is possible to understand the development of administrative law within an analytical model which ascribes a relevance to legislative intention, but without resorting to the strained proposition that changes in judicial control correspond directly to the will of Parliament.

B. Preclusive clauses

The traditional methodology of ultra vires also encounters problems in relation to the courts' treatment of legislative provisions which – at least on their face – seek to curtail or exclude judicial review of a particular decision-making process. As Craig points out, "If the rationale for judicial review is that the courts are thereby implementing legislative intent this leads to difficulty where the legislature has stated in clear terms that it does not wish the courts to intervene with the decisions made by the agency."[73]

These difficulties can be observed in their most acute form in the celebrated decision of the House of Lords in *Anisminic Ltd.* v. *Foreign Compensation Commission.*[74] In spite of a legislative enjoiner that determinations of the administrative agency in question could "not be called in question in any court

---

[71] "Has the Common Law a Future?" [1997] C.L.J. 291, 302–303.

[72] See R. v. *Secretary of State for the Home Department, ex p. Doody* [1994] 1 A.C. 531, 560, *per* Lord Mustill: "The standards of fairness are not immutable. They may change with the passage of time, both in general and in their application to decisions of a particular type."

[73] *Op. cit.* n. 8, at p. 68 and p. 52 above.

[74] [1969] 2 A.C. 147.

of law",[75] the court nevertheless intervened, holding that Parliament could not have intended to insulate unlawful decisions from judicial review.[76]

As Craig points out, if judicial review is about nothing more than ascertaining and enforcing the literal meaning of the words which Parliament uses, then cases like *Anisminic* cannot be accommodated within such a model. However, it has been argued that the exercise of the judicial review jurisdiction occurs within a constitutional setting that leads the courts to impute to Parliament an intention to legislate consistently with the rule of law. As a long line of authorities attests, the rule of law strongly favours citizens' access to the courts.[77] Consequently, ouster provisions present the courts with a tension which must be resolved, since the literal meaning of the provision appears to be inconsistent with the deeply embedded canon of construction that Parliament intends to legislate in conformity with the rule of law. Two countervailing forces are therefore at work. The court must attempt to find the right constitutional balance between the prima facie meaning of the provision and the strong preference for access to justice which the rule of law embodies.

This interpretive methodology is certainly not peculiar to the construction of ouster provisions. British courts have long been required to look beyond the plain meaning of national legislation in order to construe it, compatibly with European Community law, whenever possible.[78] A comparable interpretive obligation will be imposed on the judiciary by the Human Rights Act 1998, which will enjoin the courts to read and give effect to primary and secondary legislation in a way which is compatible with fundamental rights, so far as it is possible to do so.[79] In each instance, the interpretive function of the judiciary transcends the mechanical implementation of the words which Parliament employs. The doctrine of indirect effect and the Human Rights Act contribute to the rich tapestry which forms the backdrop against which British courts

---

[75] Foreign Compensation Act 1950, s. 4(4).

[76] The success of this argument depended, of course, on precisely what was meant by an "unlawful decision". It was the House of Lords' expansive reformulation of the notion of jurisdiction which permitted judicial review to lie in spite of the ouster clause. By holding that any contravention of the principles of good administration constituted an excess of jurisdiction on the part of the decision-maker, it was possible to characterise all unreasonable and unfair decisions as unlawful and, therefore, unprotected by the preclusive provision which operated only on determinations within jurisdiction.

[77] In addition to *Anisminic*, a number of other decisions confirm the importance which is attached to the right of access to the courts. See, inter alia, *Raymond* v. *Honey* [1982] 1 All E.R. 756; *R* v. *Secretary of State for the Home Department, ex parte Leech* [1994] Q.B. 198; *R* v. *Lord Chancellor, ex parte Witham* [1998] Q.B. 575.

[78] The European Court of Justice articulated this interpretive obligation, known as the doctrine of indirect effect, in order to secure some effect in national law for Community provisions which lack direct effect. See Case 14/83, *Von Colson* v. *Land Nordrhein-Westfalen* [1984] E.C.R. 1891 and Case C–106/89, *Marleasing SA* v. *La Comercial Internacional de Alimentacion SA* [1990] E.C.R. I–4135. For an imaginative example of this interpretive approach in the English courts see *Webb* v. *Emo Air Cargo (UK) Ltd. (No. 2)* [1995] 1 W.L.R. 1454.

[79] Section 3(1).

discharge their interpretive duties. The rule of law also constitutes a fundamental part of that backdrop.[80]

To the extent that the traditional ultra vires doctrine denies to the courts any interpretive role beyond effectuating the literal meaning of enactments, it is indeed incapable of accommodating the creative approach which has been adopted in such cases as *Anisminic*. This has led some writers to argue that, in their decisions concerning preclusive clauses, the courts must be enforcing some deeper constitutional logic which is prior even to the sovereignty of Parliament.[81]

However, such attempts to rationalise the courts' jurisprudence on ouster provisions is fundamentally inconsistent with the British constitutional framework. In contrast, by placing the ultra vires doctrine within its proper constitutional setting, it is possible to articulate an explanation of the courts' approach to ouster clauses which accommodates both the theory of parliamentary sovereignty and the constitutional duty of the judges to uphold the rule of law.

Such an approach will not always make it possible for the courts to construe ouster provisions so as to preserve some role for judicial review. For example, the courts give effect to the literal meaning of clauses which preclude review only after a certain period of time has expired: in this area, there is less tension between the plain meaning of the provision and the dictates of the rule of law, because judicial review is not precluded altogether by the clause.[82]

The field of collateral challenge also illustrates judicial acceptance that Parliament can reduce the scope for vindication of public law values in the courts. Thus, in *R. v. Wicks*,[83] the House of Lords recognised that, although the rule of law generally requires defendants in criminal proceedings to be able to raise as a defence the invalidity of the secondary legislation under which they are charged, such collateral challenge will not be permitted when this would be inconsistent with the statutory scheme which Parliament has established. As Lord Nicholls observed, "the general principles [which favour the availability of collateral challenge] . . . must always take effect subject to any contrary indication in the relevant legislation".[84] However, the court is more likely to conclude that Parliament truly intended to prevent collateral challenge when the defen-

---

[80] See Lord Steyn, "Incorporation and Devolution – A Few Reflections on the Changing Scene", *op. cit.* n. 49, at p. 154: "So much of public law concerns interpretation of statutes . . . Too often courts have asked: Is there an ambiguity in the statute? . . . It is sometimes a misguided journey to search for an ambiguity. The principle of legality may apply: it is in the words of Rupert Cross a constitutional principle not easily displaced by a statutory text." See also T.R.S. Allan, "Legislative Supremacy and the Rule of Law: Democracy and Constitutionalism" [1985] C.L.J. 111 on the importance of the rule of law in the interpretive context.

[81] See Wade and Forsyth, *op. cit.* n. 4, at p. 737 and T.R.S. Allan, "Parliamentary Sovereignty: Law, Politics, and Revolution", *op. cit.* n. 46, at p. 448.

[82] See *Smith v. East Elloe Rural District Council* [1956] A.C. 736 and *R. v. Secretary of State for the Environment, ex parte Ostler* [1977] Q.B. 122 and, generally, Wade and Forsyth, *op. cit.* n. 4, at pp. 742–756.

[83] [1998] A.C. 92.

[84] *Ibid.*, at p. 109.

dant had sufficient opportunity to question the validity of the delegated legislation by administrative means since, in this situation, the threat to the rule of law is not so serious.[85]

Nevertheless, in our constitutional system, any *irreconcilable* conflict between the intention of Parliament and the rule of law must ultimately be resolved in favour of the former,[86] and judicial decisions which fail to respect this axiom must be rejected as lacking constitutional legitimacy. Some ouster provisions enacted since the *Anisminic* decision seek to circumvent the reasoning employed in that case by, for example, providing that even "purported determinations"[87] or decisions "as to jurisdiction"[88] are not reviewable. It may well be that such clauses would, if put to the test, be held to evince a legislative intention which is sufficiently clear to preclude judicial review. It would then be the duty of the courts to enforce those provisions.

However, it is the function of the judiciary to ensure that, so far as possible, legislation is interpreted in a manner which is consistent with the rule of law. The values which underlie our constitution dictate that Parliament cannot be assumed – in the absence of very clear countervailing evidence – to intend anything else. Understood thus, the judicial attitude to ouster clauses and the view of the ultra vires doctrine which is propounded are of a piece with one another: in each case, the courts' jurisprudence springs from the interpretation of legislation within a framework based firmly on the rule of law.[89]

C. Judicial review of non-statutory power

It is often said that a further shortcoming of the traditional ultra vires principle is its inability to justify the entirety of judicial review.[90] The courts now

---

[85] See *Boddington* v. *British Transport Police* [1998] 2 W.L.R. 639, 653, *per* Lord Irvine L.C., who argued that the outcome in *R.* v. *Wicks, op. cit.* n. 83, turned on the point that it concerned an administrative act "specifically directed" at the defendant who, in turn, had enjoyed "clear and ample opportunity" to challenge administratively the legality of the act in question before being charged with an offence.

[86] Indeed, it is this principle which lies at the heart of the Human Rights Act. The respect for fundamental rights which is facilitated by the interpretive machinery set out in s. 3 must give way to the sovereign will of Parliament when legislation cannot be reconciled with the European Convention. This is clear from ss. 3(2)(b) and 4(6)(a), which provide that neither the duty of consistent construction nor the issue of a declaration of incompatibility shall affect the "validity, continuing operation or enforcement" of primary legislation.

[87] See Foreign Compensation Act 1969, s. 3(3) and (9).

[88] See Interception of Communications Act 1985, s. 7(8), and Security Service Act 1989, s. 5(4).

[89] Moreover, the logic of ultra vires generally enhances the courts' ability to vindicate the rule of law by narrowly interpreting ouster clauses. When the South African Appellate Division abandoned the ultra vires doctrine in favour of a common law basis for certain grounds of review in *Staatspresident* v. *United Democratic Front* 1988 (4) S.A. 830, it found itself unable to apply *Anisminic* reasoning to an ouster provision. For discussion, see Forsyth, *op. cit.* n. 7, at pp. 129–133 and pp. 000–000 in this volume.

[90] See, *inter alios*, Oliver, *op. cit.* n. 5; Craig, *op. cit.* n. 37, at pp. 15–16 and *op. cit.* n. 8, at p. 70 and pp. 53–4 above.

confidently supervise not only the use of statutory power, but also the exercise of prerogative and de facto power.[91] This raises important problems for proponents of the traditional ultra vires doctrine. As Paul Craig clearly explains, judicial review of non-statutory power "cannot be rationalised through the idea [embodied in the traditional ultra vires principle] that the courts are delineating the boundaries of Parliament's intent".[92] Thus, Sir William Wade has remarked – in response to the review of non-statutory power in the *Gillick* case[93] – that, "The dynamisn of judicial review is such that it has burst through its logical boundaries".[94]

If the boundaries of judicial review are taken to be wholly delimited by the ultra vires rule, then review of prerogative and other non-statutory power is indeed unjustifiable. However, our constitution would be highly defective if it were incapable of legitimising judicial review of non-statutory forms of governmental power. Indeed, in light of its capacity to adapt to changing circumstances – which derives from its unwritten and flexible character – the British constitution should be well-placed to rise to new challenges such as the need to regulate the exercise of different forms of public power.

Consequently, proponents of the traditional ultra vires doctrine may argue that while the orthodox view of ultra vires explains judicial review of statutory power, a different justification must be articulated in relation to review of other types of power. Unfortunately, this view is also problematic, since it raises a difficult paradox. It means that the justifications for judicial review of statutory and non-statutory power are entirely distinct, the former being found in judicial vindication of legislative intention, with the latter – of logical necessity – resting on wholly separate foundations. However, it must be recalled that – considerations of justiciability aside – the courts apply very similar grounds of review to all forms of governmental power which have been held amenable to judicial supervision.[95] If it is maintained that wholly distinct constitutional foundations

---

[91] See principally *R v. Criminal Injuries Compensation Board, ex parte Lain* [1967] 2 Q.B. 864; *Council of Civil Service Unions v. Minister for the Civil Service* [1985] A.C. 374; *R v. Panel on Takeovers and Mergers, ex parte Datafin plc* [1987] Q.B. 815.

[92] *Op. cit.* n. 8, at p. 70 and p. 53 above. See also Craig, *op. cit.* n. 37, at pp. 15–16.

[93] *Gillick v. West Norfolk and Wisbech Area Health Authority* [1986] A.C. 112. This case concerned judicial review of ministerial guidance to doctors relating to the provision of contraceptive advice to minors. In fact, Lords Fraser and Scarman (at pp. 166 and 177, respectively) thought that the advice *was* issued pursuant to a statutory discretion created by the National Health Services Act 1977, s. 5(1)(b), so that the traditional ultra vires doctrine could apply. However, Lord Brandon did not take this point, and Lords Bridge and Templeman (at pp. 192 and 206, respectively) agreed that the advice was not issued under any statutory authority, but that review could nevertheless lie.

[94] H.W.R. Wade, "Judicial Review of Ministerial Guidance" (1986) 102 L.Q.R. 173, 175.

[95] For example, in *Council of Civil Service Unions v. Minister for the Civil Service* [1985] A.C. 374, 411, Lord Diplock stated that the grounds of review based on "illegality" and "procedural impropriety" apply both to statutory and prerogative power; he also said that there is "no a priori reason to rule out 'irrationality' as a ground for judicial review of ministerial decisions taken in exercise of prerogative powers", although he explained that the fields which are still governed by prerogative power are such that judicial review will lie less frequently because "[s]uch decisions will generally involve the application of government policy" and are therefore likely to be non-justiciable.

underpin the review of statutory and non-statutory power, it is difficult to explain why the two regimes are nevertheless, in substance, the same as one another.[96]

These shortcomings do not beset the modified ultra vires principle. This model does not seek to justify judicial review of statutory power purely in terms of legislative delegation, and nor does it require the justifications for judicial review of different types of power to be separated into watertight compartments. It recognises that the whole of judicial review rests on one foundation, *viz.* the rule of law. In relation to review of statutory power, the operation of the sovereignty principle raises special considerations which require the rule of law to be vindicated *presumptively* in order to ensure that judicial review can be reconciled with constitutional principle. Outside the realm of statutory power, the rule of law can be effectuated *directly*, since the constraints which the sovereignty principle imposes on review of statutory power do not operate in relation to non-statutory power.

Consequently, the ultra vires doctrine, within its proper constitutional setting, is consistent with a judicial review regime which transcends the supervision of statutory power and which applies identical principles of good administration, based on the rule of law, to all types of governmental power. The fact that the interpretive methodology of ultra vires is applicable only to the review of statutory power should not be perceived as a criticism of the modified ultra vires model but, rather, as an important strength. It is this feature of the model which allows requirements of legality to be applied to powers created by Parliament in a way which is compatible with the doctrine of legislative supremacy, yet within a coherent framework which embraces judicial review of all forms of governmental power.

V. CONCLUSION

The uncertainties surrounding the juridical basis of administrative law become increasingly conspicuous and unsatisfactory as the importance of judicial review grows. The need to address this question is made more urgent by the impending changes which will occur within administrative law when the

---

[96] Of course, the precise content of the grounds of review, and the intensity with which they are applied, varies according to the context. As regards review of statutory power, the legislative framework may well indicate, for example, what fairness requires and which considerations are relevant and irrelevant. In relation to non-statutory power similar guidance may exist, but in more diffuse form. For instance, in *R. v. Panel on Take-overs and Mergers, ex parte Datafin plc* [1987] Q.B. 815, 841, Lord Donaldson M.R. said that the court could intervene if (inter alia) the Panel misconstrued its Code, thereby leading it to commit what would be an "error of law" but for the non-legal character of the Code. However, the Panel had to be given a generous margin of appreciation in discharging this interpretive function because it could choose to change the rules at any time, and because of their open-textured nature. Nevertheless, in spite of this context-sensitivity in judicial application of the grounds of review, it remains the case that, at root, the courts apply the same broad requirements of fairness and rationality irrespective of the source of the power concerned.

Human Rights Act 1998 is enacted and brought into force. The courts' public law jurisdiction will assume an even higher profile once the judiciary is charged with the important task of protecting not only individuals' procedural rights, but also their substantive rights.

Some – although by no means all – commentators who have, thus far, participated in the stimulating debate concerning the constitutional basis of judicial review have tended to polarise the potential solutions to this difficult problem, by presenting the traditional justification based on parliamentary intention and the theory which credits the judges with developing a common law of judicial review as two stark alternatives which must be chosen between.

It is submitted that such an approach is ultimately misguided. It is important to recognise that, for the reasons discussed above, the vast majority of judicial review – *viz.* that which regulates the use of statutory power – must be reconciled with parliamentary intention. Only in this manner is it possible to avoid the heterodoxy of challenging legislative supremacy, which would inhere in any attempt to divorce judicial review from the will of Parliament.

The impetus which underlies the desire of many critics to articulate an autonomous justification for judicial review, based on independent principles of the common law, is complex. Undoubtedly, however, it stems in a substantial part from a wish to abandon the fictitious direct relationship between legislative intention and judicial review which forms the focus of the orthodox ultra vires doctrine, and to acknowledge and give credit to the fundamental role which the judiciary has played in fashioning the important safeguards which citizens now enjoy as they interact with governmental agencies. These ideas have been expressed with particular clarity by Sir John Laws:

> The judges' duty is to uphold constitutional rights: to secure order, certainly, but to temper the rule of the state by freedom and justice. In our unwritten legal system the substance of such rights is to be found in the public law principles which the courts have developed, and continue to develop. Parliament may (in the present stage of our constitutional evolution) override them, but can only do so by express, focussed provision. Since ultra vires consigns everything to the intention of the legislature, it may obscure and undermine the judges' duty . . . More deeply, ultra vires must logically reduce the constitutional norms of public law to the same condition of moral neutrality as in principle applies to legislation, because by virtue of it the decisions of the courts are only a function of Parliament's absolute power. It means that the goodness of the common law is as short or as long as the legislature's wisdom. But the common law does not lie on any such Procrustean bed.[97]

It is the contention of this paper that it is possible to deal with these issues *without* taking the constitutionally unacceptable step of challenging the sovereignty of Parliament by denying any role to legislative intention in explaining the basis of judicial review. The manner in which the courts have developed the law of judicial review to date, and the further development which will no doubt take

---

[97] *Op. cit.* n. 9, at pp. 4.18–4.19 and p. 79 above.

place in the future,[98] undeniably amounts to the articulation of a substantive body of public law which has its basis in judicial creativity. Located within its constitutional setting, the ultra vires doctrine does not consign this judicial achievement to the intention of the legislature; nor does it reduce the emerging and developing norms of public law to a position of moral neutrality. In truth, the courts' public law jurisprudence is based on the vindication of the rule of law, which forms part of the bedrock of the British constitution. Neither constitutional propriety nor the ultra vires doctrine, properly understood, requires the courts to conceal the true nature of their enterprise in this regard.

Nevertheless, so long as the common law accords a legislative supremacy to Parliament, it must be possible to reconcile the courts' public law jurisprudence with this constitutional principle. It is the interpretive methodology of ultra vires – and *only* this methodology – which is capable of securing this reconciliation. It does so not through any sleight of hand or trick of logic, but simply by recognising the good sense in the dual propositions that Parliament ought to be taken to intend that the rule of law should be upheld, and that the limitation of discretionary power which is consequently required is a task most appropriately left to the judgment of the courts. Understood thus, the achievement of the ultra vires principle is the provision of a conceptual basis for judicial review which truly comes to terms with the existing constitutional order, in contradistinction to competing explanations of review which must ultimately founder because they are not firmly anchored to the realities of – and the limitations imposed by – the prevailing constitutional framework.

It has been written that "the [British] constitution possesses its own harmony, in which the protection of individual liberties can coexist with recognition of the ultimate supremacy of the democratic will of Parliament".[99] Indeed, this is so, and can be appreciated nowhere more clearly than in the operation of the ultra vires doctrine within its proper constitutional setting.

---

[98] Particularly in light of the likely impact of the Human Rights Act.
[99] T.R.S. Allan, *op. cit.* n. 80, at p. 112.

The Jurisprudential Debate

6

Ultra Vires and Institutional Interdependence

NICHOLAS BAMFORTH

The debate about whether the ultra vires principle forms the basis of judicial review highlights in particularly vivid form the interconnection between constitutional propriety and administrative law. For its supporters, the ultra vires principle can be justified by normative considerations of constitutional necessity – by reference, for example, to the need for unelected judges to defer (or at least, to give the appearance of deferring) to the will of an elected Parliament[1] – while opponents talk of the unhealthiness of concealing the true dynamics of our constitution beneath "fig-leaves" or "pretences".[2] What both sides of the debate would appear to share is the conviction that one's view concerning the basis (and, in consequence, the proper parameters) of judicial review will be heavily influenced, if not determined, by one's normative view concerning the appropriate constitutional relationship between the courts and Parliament.[3] It will be suggested in this chapter that normative arguments are, however, insufficient for resolving the debate. For the normative stance adopted by supporters of the ultra vires principle fails to take account of – and, indeed, can be defeated by – an *analytical* argument concerning the way in which the constitutional model they defend would work in practice. Their account of the English legal system presupposes – as, indeed, do orthodox accounts of legal systems in general – the existence of an institutional interdependence between the legislature and the judiciary, in that the powers of each institution seem ultimately to depend upon the other. One consequence of this interdependence is that the ultra vires

---

[1] See Christopher Forsyth, "Of Fig Leaves and Fairy Tales: The Ultra Vires Doctrine, the Sovereignty of Parliament and Judicial Review" (1996) 55 *CLJ* 122 (hereafter "Of Fig Leaves and Fairy Tales") p. 27 above. See, more broadly, Lord Irvine of Lairg, "Judges and Decision-Makers: The Theory and Practice of *Wednesbury* Review" [1996] *PL* 59, 75–8.

[2] See, for example, Sir John Laws, "Illegality – the Problem of Jurisdiction" in Michael Supperstone and James Goudie (eds), *Judicial Review* (London, Butterworths, 2nd edn., 1997) 4.18, p. 73 (extract) above; T.R.S. Allan, "Fairness, Equality, Rationality: Constitutional Theory and Judicial Review" in Christopher Forsyth and Ivan Hare (eds), *The Golden Metwand and the Crooked Cord: Essays on Public Law in Honour of Sir William Wade* (Oxford, Clarendon Press, 1998) – an essay which also contains a more overtly normative attack on ultra vires.

[3] A point emphasised in Mark Elliott's defence of ultra vires: "The Ultra Vires Doctrine in a Constitutional Setting: Still the Central Principle of Administrative Law" (1999) 58 *CLJ* 129 (hereafter "The Ultra Vires Doctrine in a Constitutional Setting") p. 83 above.

principle can provide no more reliable a defence for parliamentary sovereignty – understood in terms of Sir William Wade's theory[4] – than can rival common law bases for judicial review relating to the rule of law, fundamental rights, or control of public power.[5] In consequence, the ultra vires principle loses what is – according to its supporters – one of its major advantages, at least for so long as it rests on Sir William Wade's account of sovereignty. It will be argued that the proper limits of judicial review *cannot* reliably be set using a theory like ultra vires, which relates merely to the appropriate *exercise* of judicial power. It is only through a more detailed and thorough political theory – relating to the political and moral values which the judges should enforce *via* judicial review – that this can be done.

The first section of the chapter will discuss the possible criteria which might be used in order to assess the comparative merits of ultra vires and its rivals. It is important to articulate these criteria clearly in order to have a solid basis for comparison between the rival theories. It will be argued in the second section that the ultra vires principle can set no more definite a limit to the proper exercise of judicial power through judicial review than can its common law rivals – the reason being that supporters of ultra vires overlook the interdependence between the courts and Parliament, which is inherent in Sir William Wade's account of parliamentary sovereignty. The third section of the chapter will seek to reinforce this claim by suggesting that an analogous interdependence can be seen in Professor H.L.A. Hart's analaysis of the nature of legal systems in general – an analysis with which Wade's account of English law is often associated. The fourth section of the chapter will suggest that an analogous but not identical interdependence can be found in the case law relating to parliamentary privilege. The final section will outline some of the issues which are likely to arise in determining the true basis of judicial review.

CRITERIA FOR ASSESSING THE MERITS OF A LEGAL THEORY

In determining whether ultra vires is a preferable constitutional basis for judicial review to any of its common law rivals, it is plainly important to have in mind a set of criteria which might be used for the purpose of evaluating the competing theories. Unless we keep some such criteria in mind, we will be reduced to making comparisons on the basic of *ad hoc* intuitions. Furthermore, by specifying exactly which criteria we regard as relevant, we can tailor the focus of our inquiry to suit our particular purposes.

As a general matter, quite a large number of criteria can be employed in order to compare the merits of rival theories of a particular area of law. Perhaps the most preliminary criteria ask how well a particular theory fits the case law it is supposed to explain. Such criteria are preliminary in the sense that they are not

---

[4] Articulated in "The Basis of Legal Sovereignty" [1955] *CLJ* 172 and "Sovereignty – Revolution or Evolution?" (1996) 112 *LQR* 568.

concerned with the substance of the theory under evaluation, whether in terms of that theory's merits or its consistency. They are far from being neutral or value-free criteria, however, since they require us first to define what it is about a group of cases which allows them to be treated as a set and to adopt a view about what a theory must do in order to "fit" that set – something which in turn requires us to make certain substantive judgments as to what constitutes an ordered understanding of the common law. The second set of criteria go to consistency, in the sense that they ask whether a theory works on its own terms. Such criteria might require us to consider whether a theory of law is consistent with any underpinning political or constitutional theory on which it is based, and whether all elements within the theory are internally consistent. These criteria are concerned, at heart, with an argument's analytical validity. A third set of criteria go to the substantive merits of a theory. Any assessment of a theory's merits will, of course, depend to an extent on the definition of "merit" which is favoured by the person conducting the assessment. Two specific criteria – plausibility and acceptability – are particularly important. The plausibility criterion asks whether the reasoning contained within or the conclusions reached by a theory appear sensible, given the circumstances in which that theory must operate. A mathematical theory might be described as implausible, for example, if it rested on the assumption (that is, if it lacked coherent reasoning which established, in the face of mathematical orthodoxy) that two plus two equalled five. The acceptability criterion is more clearly subjective, in that it relates to the substantive appeal of a theory. This criterion asks whether a theory's implications or ramifications are acceptable, normatively-speaking, in terms of our background theories of the nature of law and of the constitution. This criterion explicitly appeals to the theorist's own position, and it must therefore be accepted that different people may well give different, subjective answers to the question whether a particular theory is substantively attractive.

On some occasions, a particular theory may seem more attractive than its rivals in terms of some of these criteria, but less attractive in terms of others. Where this is the case, we are forced to make an all-things-considered judgment about whether the theory is worth supporting. On other occasions, the discovery of a flaw in a theory using any one of these criteria might be enough to knock that theory out of consideration. The arguments addressed in this chapter will be of a largely analytical nature – that is, they concern the consistency of ultra vires as a theory, in the sense of asking whether it in fact succeeds in its goal of protecting parliamentary sovereignty, or at least of giving the appearance of doing so. Given that defenders of ultra vires often characterise the protection of sovereignty – or at least, preservation of the appearance of deference to Parliament – as the normative goal or goals of their theory, proof that ultra vires fails in such a task must force us to conclude that there is an inconsistency between the theory's aims and its outcome. Such a conclusion *must* fatally undermine the theory's claims to be seen as substantively attractive, given that its appeal – for its supporters – rests on the normative goal or goals claimed for it. In consequence, the arguments which are considered in this chapter are not particularly affected by the number of cases which can be cited as supporting or undermining the ultra vires principle[6] – although the degree to which any theory of judicial review can ultimately be considered plausible will depend to an extent on how well it fits the case law as a whole.

ULTRA VIRES AS THE CONSTITUTIONAL FOUNDATION OF JUDICIAL REVIEW

According to Sir William Wade, "The simple proposition that a public authority may not act outside its powers (ultra vires) might fitly be called the central principle of administrative law".[7] Every administrative act can be categorised as either intra or ultra vires, the courts being empowered to condemn only ultra vires acts.[8] Any ultra vires act is void in law – in other words, without legal effect – because "in order to be valid it needs statutory authorisation, and if it is not within the powers given by the Act, it has no legal leg to stand on".[9] For Sir William Wade and his supporters, ultra vires is thus the constitutional basis (or at least, the principal constitutional basis)[10] for judicial review.

In this section of the chapter, the soundness of this view will be questioned. It will be suggested that save in relation to the efficacy of ouster clauses (which may or may not, according to perspective, become more effective if ultra vires was to be discarded as the basis of judicial review),[11] supporters and opponents of ultra vires broadly agree that ultra vires cannot, in and of itself, provide

[5] The principal accounts of this sort are: Sir John Laws, "Illegality: the Problem of Jurisdiction", above at n.2, and "Law and Democracy" [1995] *PL* 72; Lord Woolf MR, "Droit Public – English Style" [1995] *PL* 57; Paul Craig, "Ultra Vires and the Foundations of Judicial Review" (1998) 57 *CLJ* 63 and p. 47 above; Dawn Oliver, "Is the Ultra Vires Rule the Basis of Judicial Review?" [1987] *PL* 543 and p. 3 above; David Dyzenhaus, "Reuniting the Brain: The Democratic Basis of Judicial Review" (1998) 9 *PLR* 98; T.R.S. Allan, "Fairness, Equality, Rationality: Constitutional Theory and Judicial Review", above at n.2.

[6] The most prominent examples being *CCSU* v. *Minister for the Civil Service* [1985] AC 374 and *R.* v. *Panel on Take-overs and Mergers, ex p. Datafin* [1987] QB 815 (often used against ultra vires); and *R.* v. *Hull University Visitor, ex p. Page* [1993] AC 682 and *Boddington* v. *British Transport Police* [1998] 2 WLR 639 (generally seen as supporting ultra vires).

[7] H.W.R. Wade and C.F. Forsyth, *Administrative Law* (Oxford, Clarendon Press, 7th edn., 1994) 41 (hereafter "Wade and Forsyth"). Despite his co-authorship of the book, Dr Forsyth expresses himself as having "no desire to assume any credit" for any of the passages cited here, since they were originally drafted by Sir William and are "substantially unchanged from earlier editions" – "Of Fig Leaves and Fairy Tales" above at n.1, 122, n.1 and p. 27 above.

[8] Wade and Forsyth above at n.7, 44.

[9] Ibid., 43.

[10] Forsyth concedes that judicial review of non-statutory bodies cannot be explained using ultra vires, but instead turns on a common law jurisdiction to regulate the exercise of monopoly power: "Of Fig Leaves and Fairy Tales" above at n.1, 124–7 and pp. 31–3 above. *Cf.* Paul Craig, "Ultra Vires and the Foundations of Judicial Review" above at n.5, 70, 77–8 and pp. 53, 59–60 above. One unanswered difficulty facing Forsyth's concession is that it fails to explain (any more than does the ultra vires principle itself) the basis on which judicial review of the exercise of common law prerogative power might be justified.

[11] Compare Christopher Forsyth, ibid., 129–134 and pp. 35–40 above; Paul Craig, ibid., 71–3 and p. 54 above.

detailed guidance to the judiciary as to how the grounds of judicial review should be developed. Both sides accept that in reality, it is the judges who have developed – and who will continue to develop – the detailed grounds and principles of judicial review. The *real* disagreement between supporters and opponents of ultra vires instead concerns the appropriate constitutional rôle of the courts in judicial review, particularly in relation to parliamentary sovereignty. For Dr Christopher Forsyth has argued that the removal of ultra vires would inevitably lead the courts into conflict with parliamentary sovereignty – a view reinforced by Mark Elliott[12] and apparently shared by Sir William Wade,[13] but rejected by Professor Paul Craig.[14] Whether Forsyth's argument is right is thus of great importance in assessing the adequacy of ultra vires as the basis of judicial review. It will be suggested here that Forsyth's and Elliott's sovereignty-based defences of ultra vires cannot be sustained, at least for so long as they rely upon Sir William Wade's account of parliamentary sovereignty. For both defences overlook the notion of institutional interdependence contained within Wade's account. Once institutional interdependence is taken into account – and as, it will be suggested, Sir William Wade's own analysis of sovereignty in fact demonstrates – parliamentary sovereignty turns out to be no more secure in an ultra vires-based régime of judicial review than it would be in an openly common law-based régime, thereby removing the principal normative argument in favour of ultra vires and laying the principle open to the charge that its operation is inconsistent with its goals.

The apparent consensus surrounding the rôle of the judiciary in developing the grounds of judicial review in day-to-day cases can be seen by comparing the arguments of Wade, Forsyth and Craig. Wade suggests that the courts have conceptualised just about every available ground of judicial review as falling within the ultra vires framework:

> The tendency, accordingly, is towards a unified theoretical basis for all the numerous grounds on which the courts may assert their control [through judicial review], namely that every reviewable error is a species of ultra vires.[15]

As well as explaining the classic cases of jurisdictional error, ultra vires therefore explains, for example, judicial review for breach of natural justice, for *Wednesbury* unreasonableness, and in cases where the decision-maker has paid regard to irrelevant considerations.[16] Wade suggests that these should be seen as breaches of implied statutory conditions, which render an offending decision

---

[12] Mark Elliott, "The Demise of Parliamentary Sovereignty? The Implications for Justifying Judicial Review" (1999) 115 *LQR* 119, 120 (hereafter "The Demise of Parliamentary Sovereignty?"): the "principal virtue of ultra vires" is "its capacity to accommodate the coexistence of judicial review and legislative supremacy".

[13] Sir William Wade, "Habeas Corpus and Judicial Review" (1997) 113 *LQR* 55, 66, n.51 – Forsyth's article described as a "spirited and effective reply" to critics of ultra vires.

[14] "Ultra Vires and the Foundations of Judicial Review" above at n.5, 86–9 and pp. 67–70.

[15] Wade and Forsyth above at n.7, 47.

[16] Ibid., 44. Wade admits at this point that judges sometimes say that decisions flawed by procedural errors are "within jurisdiction", but suggests that this is a misdescription.

ultra vires in just the same way as if it had violated an express condition.[17] Since the courts can only set aside ultra vires decisions and actions, these additional grounds of judicial review have to be placed within the ultra vires heading to enable the courts to intervene.[18] Government might therefore be seen as working against a background of judge-made rules of statutory interpretation, which are used to ensure that public power is exercised properly.[19]

For Professor Craig, the "central issue" is how far the rules of judicial review and their application *can* in fact "be satisfactorily explained by reference to legislative intent".[20] Craig suggests that ultra vires is indeterminate in that it cannot explain what standards or intensity of review the courts should adopt. In jurisdictional error cases, for example, the courts have applied at least three contrasting approaches – characterised by Craig as limited review, the collateral fact doctrine and extensive review[21] – yet the ultra vires principle:

> provides no guidance as to which of these standards of review ought to be applied. It does not tell us whether the correct standard of judicial review should be for the court to substitute judgment on the meaning of each of these conditions, or whether it should substitute judgment on certain of the conditions but not others, or whether it should adopt some other test. Any of these tests can be formally reconciled with the ultra vires principle.[22]

While ultra vires preserves the "veneer" that courts are obeying the will of Parliament, its flexibility "ultimately robs the reasoning of any conviction".[23] Craig makes an analogous point in relation to judicial regulation of the exercise of statutory discretion by a decision-maker. Discretion-conferring legislation rarely provides the courts with real guidance as to how to regulate, leaving judges to make their own assessment. Requiring the courts to legitimate the controls they impose by reference to Parliamentary intent therefore "does not accord with reality"[24] – especially since the courts have, over time, altered the controls without any indication from Parliament of a change in legislative intent.[25] Furthermore, entirely contrasting interpretations of Parliamentary intent are possible – for example, in cases where a court has to decide whether Parliament's intention was for an ouster clause wholly to exclude judicial review – and ultra vires can provide no guidance as to which interpretation is preferable.[26]

---

[17] Ibid., 42.

[18] Ibid., 44.

[19] Ibid., 42.

[20] "Ultra Vires and the Foundations of Judicial Review" above at n.5, 66 pp. 49–50 above.

[21] For further discussion of these concepts, see P.P.Craig, *Administrative Law* (London, Sweet & Maxwell, 4th edn., 1999), chapter 15.

[22] "Ultra Vires and the Foundations of Judicial Review" above at n.5, 66 pp.49–50 above.

[23] Ibid., 67.

[24] Ibid., 67.

[25] Ibid., 67–8.

[26] Ibid., 68–70. For an obvious example, see the reasoning of the House of Lords in *Anisminic* v. *Foreign Compensation Commission* [1969] 2 AC 147.

Professor Craig's criticisms are certainly forceful;[27] and for present purposes, it is important to observe that they appear – at least in terms of their general thrust – to be acknowledged by supporters of ultra vires. For example, Sir William Wade has accepted that it involves "a high degree of artificiality"[28] to categorise every ground of judicial review as an example of ultra vires, and has conceded that the courts "can make the doctrine mean almost anything they wish by finding implied limitations in Acts of Parliament".[29] Wade maintains, however, that this artificiality is explicable and necessary for a constitutional reason:

> Having no written constitution on which he can fall back, the judge must in every case be able to demonstrate that he is carrying out the will of Parliament as expressed in the statute conferring the power. He is on safe ground only where he can show that the offending act is outside the power. The only way in which he can do this, in the absence of an express provision, is by finding an implied term or condition [requiring the decision-maker to act reasonably, with procedural fairness, with regard only to relevant considerations, etc.] in the Act, violation of which then entails the condemnation of ultra vires.[30]

For Wade, the courts will be safe from charges of constitutional impropriety so long as they base judicial review on the ultra vires principle, since this enables them to claim that they are "carrying out the mandates of Parliament".[31]

Forsyth frames the argument in still stronger terms. He accepts that the modern law of judicial review is a judicial creation, and that it "cannot be plausibly asserted that the implied intent of the legislature provides any significant guidance to the reach of the rules of natural justice or the fine distinctions to be drawn between decisions that are unreasonable but not irrational and the like".[32] Instead of providing judges with a key to enable them to measure *exactly how* a particular ground of review should be developed or applied, the real meaning of the "implied intention" of the legislature is that "the legislature is taken to have granted an *imprimatur* to the judges to develop the law in the particular area".[33] Furthermore, by adhering to the ultra vires principle, the judiciary shows that it is remaining within its proper constitutional rôle – according to which it is free to develop the grounds of judicial review, while recognising that Parliament is sovereign and is free to dispense with those grounds should it so choose.[34] The ultra vires principle might therefore be said to legitimate the

[27] See also the analogous critique developed by Sir John Laws in "Illegality – the Problem of Jurisdiction" above at n.2, 4.3 to 4.30 and pp. 73–81 (extract) above.

[28] Wade and Forsyth above at n.7, 43.

[29] Ibid., 43.

[30] Ibid., 44.

[31] Ibid., 46.

[32] "Of Fig Leaves and Fairy Tales" above at n.1, 134 and p. 40 above. Elliott appears also to accept that ultra vires involves artificiality: see "The Demise of Parliamentary Sovereignty?" above at n.12, 119–120; "The Ultra Vires Doctrine in a Constitutional Setting" above at n.3, 148–156 and pp.100–7 above.

[33] "Of Fig Leaves and Fairy Tales" above at n.1, 135 and p. 41 above.

[34] Ibid., 136–7 and pp. 41–43 above.

exercise of judicial power within an established constitutional order in which Parliament is sovereign, maintaining a proper balance of power between elected and non-elected institutions.[35] Forsyth suggests that:

> the legislature may reasonably be taken to have given tacit approval to the development by the judiciary of the principles of judicial review, subject, crucially, to the recognition of legislative supremacy.[36]

In consequence, it seems fair to conclude that – rhetorical differences aside – supporters and opponents of ultra vires would broadly agree that it can, as a principle, involve a high degree of artificiality in day-to-day judicial review cases. However, supporters of ultra vires maintain that this artificiality is necessary for a constitutional reason – namely that it preserves the appearance of judicial adherence to the established constitutional order – whereas most opponents are clear that it is not. At first sight, this divergence might appear to boil down to an issue of presentation – namely, whether it is necessary to preserve the *appearance* of deference to Parliament's will via the ultra vires principle – in response to which one might argue that constitutional theory should be concerned with the *substance* of the allocation of power, not the appearance. However, Forsyth's argument contains a deeper substantive distinction between ultra vires and the rival common law theories of judicial review: namely that abandonment of ultra vires would *inevitably* lead to challenges to parliamentary sovereignty itself. Forsyth uses the example of vague regulations made by a minister in purported exercise of a statutory power. The ultra vires principle enables the courts to rule that Parliament could not have intended to allow the minister to make vague regulations, enabling the regulations to be struck down without challenging parliamentary sovereignty. But if ultra vires is removed, no judicial attack can be made on the regulations by reference to Parliament's implied intent – leaving the courts with no choice but to attack the regulations directly, using the common law as their basis for doing so. Forsyth suggests that this would amount to a direct attack on parliamentary sovereignty, since what a sovereign parliament has not prohibited, it must be taken to have authorised – including, presumably, vague regulations.[37] One might express the point more broadly, by saying that ultra vires is necessary since it sets one definite limit to the judicial review jurisdiction – namely that outside cases which involve an element of EU law, it allows the courts to *interpret* and *apply*, but not to *challenge*, statutes. According to this argument, ultra vires can therefore serve to restrain the judicial review court in constitutionally sensitive cases in which a challenge to parliamentary sovereignty might otherwise be possible.

---

[35] "Of Fig Leaves and Fairy Tales", 137 and pp. 42–3 above.

[36] Ibid., 135 and p. 41 above.

[37] Ibid., 133–4 pp. 39–40 above. Note, however, that Forsyth's assertion that a sovereign Parliament must expressly or impliedly authorise that which it does not prohibit may well fall into the confusion between subordination and derivation of criteria of validity identified by Professor H.L.A. Hart: *The Concept of Law* (Oxford, Clarendon Press, 2nd edn., 1994) 101. See also Sir John Laws' critique in "Illegality – the Problem of Jurisdiction" above at n.2, 4.17 to 4.18 and pp. 73–81 above.

If this argument is correct, then the crucial test of the utility of ultra vires would seem to be whether, in the *exceptional* cases in which the appropriate *limits* of judicial review are in issue, it is in fact better able than any common law theory to recognise and accommodate parliamentary sovereignty.[38] An obvious – but often overlooked – point is that any answer to this question must turn as much on the workings of parliamentary sovereignty as on ultra vires itself: for if the ultra vires principle is adequately to defend parliamentary sovereignty, the two principles must fit coherently together. Given its shared authorship – as a theory – with ultra vires, the most obvious starting point for any answer would appear to lie in Sir William Wade's account of parliamentary sovereignty.[39] The crux of Wade's argument is that at root, parliamentary sovereignty turns not on the attitudes of Parliament but on those of the courts: "the seat of sovereign power is not to be discovered by looking at Acts of Parliament but by looking at the courts and discovering to whom they give their allegiance".[40] No *statute* can establish the rule of law that courts obey Acts of Parliament because no statute can alter or abolish such a rule.[41] Instead, the rule of judicial obedience to statutes is the ultimate *political* fact on which the constitutional system hangs, although it is also a rule of common law.[42] In consequence, the relationship between the courts and Parliament is ultimately a political reality: legislation owes its authority to the rule of judicial obedience, rather than vice versa. As Wade succinctly puts it,

> To say that Parliament can change the rule [of judicial obedience], merely because it can change any other rule, is to put the cart before the horse.[43]

The rule of judicial obedience cannot be changed by *Parliament* through legislation, but only by a constitutional revolution in which the *courts* abandon their loyalty to the legislature as at presently constituted: the rule "lies in the keeping of the courts, and no Act of Parliament can take it from them".[44] In practical day-to-day terms, establishing whether or not we have parliamentary sovereignty thus requires us to focus on the case law. Wade was confident in

[38] This concern is of heightened importance in the light of Dr.Forsyth's assertion that it is impossible to challenge ultra vires without challenging parliamentary sovereignty – for if ultra vires cannot itself defend Parliament's power, a key advantage (from the standpoint of those concerned to defend Parliament's power) must disappear.

[39] Unless, that is, Forsyth's defence of ultra vires rests on a different theory of sovereignty from that advanced by Wade – a point which is unclear from "Of Fig Leaves and Fairy Tales", in which Forsyth merely makes reference to (without approving) Richard Latham's account of sovereignty – above at n.1, 137–9 and pp. 43–4 above. Forsyth's suggestion (at 137, n.52 and p. 43 above) that Wade's account of sovereignty maintains that "properly enacted statutes, whatever their content, *will* be obeyed by the courts" (emphasis added) is, with respect, difficult to reconcile with Wade's more recent argument that the decision in *Factortame (No.2)* entails a revolutionary switch in judicial allegiance.

[40] "The Basis of Legal Sovereignty" above at n.4, 196.

[41] Ibid., 187.

[42] Ibid., 188.

[43] Ibid., 188.

[44] Ibid., 189. For evaluation and critique of Wade's position, see A.W. Bradley, "The Sovereignty of Parliament – in Perpetuity?" in J. Jowell and D. Oliver (eds), *The Changing Constitution* (Oxford, Clarendon Press, 3rd edn., 1994), pp. 89, 104, 105–7.

1955 that *Ellen Street Estates* v. *Minister*[45] was the crucial case in English law, and stood as authority for the proposition that the Westminster Parliament was not bound by constraints as to the content or form of future legislation.[46] *Attorney-General of New South Wales* v. *Trethowan*[47] – in which a "manner-and-form" constraint had been upheld – could be distinguished because it concerned a non-sovereign legislature.[48]

Wade's description of the situations which might be described as "revolutionary" is, perhaps inevitably, a little hazy. He suggested that since any "revolution" is assessed in terms of judicial behaviour, it is a "purely political forecast" rather than something directly achievable by legislation.[49] A "revolution" is a "legal discontinuity, a fundamental change which defies the existing rules of law – as when James II was succeeded by William and Mary in 1688"[50] – or, more broadly, something which happens when the judges, faced with a novel situation, "elect to depart from the familiar rules for the sake of political necessity".[51] In practice, this would mean that if the Westminster Parliament sought to bring about a radical change of affairs in relation to its own ability effectively to legislate – for example, by passing an Act granting full political and legal independence to a colony – there would be a "revolution" if the *courts* of the former colony threw off their allegiance to the Westminster Parliament.[52] After a successful revolution, it would then be for the courts to find new ultimate legal principles for themselves.[53]

Wade's court-based account of sovereignty and "revolutions" is of profound importance for the ultra vires principle. For ultra vires maintains that the development of judicial review is in the keeping of the courts, *subject to* the limits imposed by parliamentary sovereignty. Yet, according to Wade's account of sovereignty, the courts are able – in the event of a constitutional "revolution" – to depart even from *those* limits by overthrowing sovereignty. The obvious logical implication must be that in the circumstances of a "revolution", there would in fact be *no* limits on the courts save for those laid down by the dictates of practical politics.[54] In a "revolutionary" situation, parliamentary sovereignty *cannot* therefore act as a definite check on judicial review – with the consequence that ultra vires is no more able to provide a solid basis for limiting the ambit of judi-

---

[45] [1934] 1 KB 590; see also *Vauxhall Estates* v. *Liverpool Corporation* [1932] 1 KB 733.

[46] "The Basis of Legal Sovereignty" above at n.4, 175–6.

[47] [1932] AC 526.

[48] "The Basis of Legal Sovereignty" above at n.4, 173, 182–4.

[49] Ibid., 190.

[50] Wade and Forsyth, *Administrative Law* above at n.7, 30.

[51] "Sovereignty – Revolution or Evolution?" above at n.4, 574.

[52] "The Basis of Legal Sovereignty" above at n.4, 196. Wade treats the South African case *Harris* v. *Donges* [1952] 1 *Times LR* 1245 as an example of a successful judicial "revolution" – ibid. at 173, 190–2. For a more complex but related account of *Harris*, see Professor Hart's *The Concept of Law* above at n.37, 122–3.

[53] "The Basis of Legal Sovereignty" above at n.4, 192.

[54] Wade has even suggested that for the academic in a "revolutionary" situation "the prudential course may be to . . . turn a blind eye to constitutional theory altogether", "Sovereignty – Revolution or Evolution" above at n.4, 575.

cial review in such a situation than might any rival common law basis for the jurisdiction. There is, in short, a lacuna in Wade's argument: on the one hand, the ultra vires principle maintains that the courts should ultimately defer to parliamentary sovereignty; yet on the other, sovereignty lies in the keeping of the courts and can be overthrown by them – unhindered by ultra vires – should a "revolutionary" situation manifest itself before the courts in judicial review.[55] For so long as Forsyth's account of ultra vires rests upon Wade's theory of sovereignty, his constitutional justification for the ultra vires principle – that it is necessary in order to defend sovereignty – thus loses its force in exactly the "revolutionary" situations where it should be at its strongest. Due to the nature of Wade's theory of sovereignty, ultra vires can provide no more effective a limit to the ambit of judicial review in "revolutionary" situations than can any rival common law basis such as the rule of law or respect for fundamental rights. Furthermore, if ultra vires is unable to guarantee the protection of parliamentary sovereignty in substance, it seems implausible to assume that it will successfully preserve the *appearance* of judicial deference to Parliament – an issue to which we shall return below.

Much the same point can be made concerning Mark Elliott's defence of ultra vires. Elliott's defence contains two strands, the first of which relates the ultra vires principle to parliamentary sovereignty and the second to the rule of law. In relation to sovereignty, Elliott asserts that provided:

> it is accepted that, for the time being at least, the traditional conception of Parliamentary sovereignty continues to hold true in theoretical terms, then it becomes clear that . . . the ultra vires principle remains essential to the justification of judicial review of action taken under statutory powers.[56]

In fact, the true issue is not whether the "traditional conception" of sovereignty holds good, but whether the "revolutionary" aspect of Wade's theory fatally undermines any sovereignty-related constitutional justification for judicial review based upon it. The essential problem facing Elliott is that, like Forsyth, he seems to have overlooked the lacuna in Sir William Wade's account of parliamentary sovereignty. The remainder of his sovereignty-related argument – concerning the *necessity* of ultra vires – can be of little practical utility when it rests on such an insecure foundation.[57] Related difficulties undermine the second, rule of law-based strand of Elliott's defence. Elliott suggests that "the true foundations of judicial review can be fully appreciated only when this branch of public law is located within its broader constitutional setting".[58] This can be achieved if we construe Parliament's intention, in the absence of clear contrary enactments, as being to legislate in conformity with the rule of law – which has the consequence that Parliament can be taken to have intended to withhold

---

[55] For an analogous argument, see Sir John Laws, "Illegality – the Problem of Jurisdiction" above at n.2, 4.6, 4.13.
[56] "The Demise of Parliamentary Sovereignty?" above at n.12, 128.
[57] A point which can be levelled at most of the argument found at ibid., 130–7.
[58] "The Ultra Vires Doctrine in a Constitutional Setting" above at n.3, 131 and p. 85 above.

from decision-makers the power to act unfairly, unreasonably, and so on, providing a new constitutional linkage between Parliamentary intention and the grounds of judicial review.[59] One weakness of this argument, however, is that Elliott provides no real basis for explaining why his definition of the rule of law is to be preferred, given its content, to any other – something which is plainly problematical given the wide variety of possible definitions of the rule of law, ranging from the purely procedural to the fully substantive.[60] Elliott does make plain that he regards it as necessary to opt for a definition of the rule of law which gives way to parliamentary sovereignty, at least where Parliament's expression of its sovereign will is clear[61] (as opposed to, say, the type of definition which maintains that legislation may be set aside where it contradicts whatever conception of the rule of law is in play[62]) – and seeks to justify this by asserting that the courts only have the power which the constitutional order allocates to them according to its delimitation of governmental functions.[63] This argument, however, falls victim to the same objection raised against the sovereignty-based strand of Elliott's reasoning: namely that since we are concerned with situations in which the existing constitutional order has either been called into question (potentially "revolutionary" situations, in Wade's terminology) or is open to a series of radically divergent interpretations, merely appealing to the *existing* power-allocation principles of that order is unlikely to take us very far.

The lacuna in Wade's account is not just of interest as a matter of abstract theory, as two practical examples will demonstrate. The first relates to Britain's membership of the European Union. Wade has recently argued that there *has* in fact been a "revolution" in English constitutional law via the House of Lords' decision in *Factortame (No.2)*.[64] Wade claims that for the House of Lords to "disapply" the Merchant Shipping Act 1988 for incompatibility with provisions of EC law deriving their authority in domestic law from the European Communities Act 1972 "was a revolutionary change".[65] As a result of the House of Lords' decision,

> The Parliament of 1972 had succeeded in binding the Parliament of 1988 and restricting its sovereignty, something that was supposed to be constitutionally impossible.[66]

The rule that Parliament cannot bind its successors is thus now subject, Wade suggests, to one exception in the case of the European Communities Act 1972 (although this exception would presumably disappear were the 1972 Act to be

[59] "The Ultra Vires Doctrine in a Constitutional Setting" n. 3, 143–5 and pp. 96–8 above.
[60] In relation to which, see Paul Craig, "Formal and Substantive Conceptions of the Rule of Law: An Analytical Framework" [1997] *PL* 467.
[61] "The Ultra Vires Doctrine in a Constitutional Setting" above at n.3, 145, 153, 157 and pp. 98, 105, 108–9 above.
[62] See, for example, Lord Woolf's "Droit Public – English Style" above at n.5, 67–9.
[63] "The Ultra Vires Doctrine in a Constitutional Setting" above at n.3, 131–4 and pp. 85–8 above.
[64] "Sovereignty – Revolution or Evolution?" above at n.4.
[65] Wade and Forsyth above at n.7, 31.
[66] "Sovereignty – Revolution or Evolution", above at n.4, 568.

expressly repealed).[67] In consequence, for so long as Britain remains a member of the EU, "we are in a regime in which Parliament has bound its successors successfully, and which is nothing if not revolutionary".[68] Wade also suggests that Lord Bridge took it for granted, in his judgment in *Factortame (No.2)*, that Parliament was able to bind its successors via the 1972 Act – and that "[I]f that is not revolutionary, constitutional lawyers are Dutchmen".[69]

Wade's account of *Factortame (No.2)* is certainly open to criticism: in particular, it might be felt that the term "revolution" is too blunt and crude a description of a situation in which Parliament can still recover its sovereignty by repealing the 1972 Act, and in which the courts continue by-and-large to accord deference to Parliament in cases where no EC law issue is involved (criticisms which might be applied to Wade's notion of a constitutional "revolution" more broadly).[70] Wade's account is important for present purposes, however, because it demonstrates very clearly the fragility of ultra vires when parliamentary sovereignty is ultimately in the hands of the courts. For by suggesting that a "revolution" has occurred – implying a decisive break with the past – Wade is logically forced to accept that there may now be all to play for in our constitutional order. For example, Wade himself acknowledges the implications of categorising the decision in *Factortame (No.2)* as "revolutionary" by suggesting that it is now "guesswork" to predict whether other limitations on sovereignty might be possible: on the one hand, courts might now suggest that it is possible for Parliament voluntarily to limit its sovereignty at any time; on the other hand, they might decide that accession to the EC was a unique legal event; or, as a middle course, they might find that certain legal provisions – for example, those relating to fundamental rights – are capable of entrenchment, while others are not.[71] Some of Wade's comments go even further. For instance, he casually asserts that:

> Now that Parliament has proved capable of binding its successors [in the EC law context], novel possibilities are emerging. It may be that where legislation is buttressed by treaty obligations the courts will give it overriding effect.[72]

He also suggests that as a result of Lord Bridge's categorisation in *Factortame (No.2)* of Parliament as having voluntarily accepted any limitations on its sovereignty in the EC law context,[73] parliamentary sovereignty is "now a freely adjustable commodity whenever Parliament chooses to accept some

---

[67] Wade and Forsyth above at n.7, 31.
[68] "Sovereignty – Revolution or Evolution" above at n.4, 571.
[69] Ibid., 573.
[70] The present author would certainly agree with these criticisms. For rival accounts of the effect of *Factortame (No.2)*, see P.P. Craig, "Sovereignty of the United Kingdom Parliament after *Factortame*" (1991) *YBEL* 221; T.R.S. Allan, "Parliamentary Sovereignty: Law, Politics, and Revolution" (1997) 113 *LQR* 443.
[71] "Sovereignty – Revolution or Evolution?" above at n.4, 575.
[72] Wade and Forsyth above at n.7, 31–2.
[73] [1991] 1 AC 603, 658.

limitation".[74] In a constitutional world as unpredictable as that in which Wade claims we now live, it is surely improbable to expect that ultra vires – a principle which *demands* deference to a Parliament whose sovereignty has, we are told, been "overthrown" in a "revolution" – could automatically be expected to survive intact. If the constitutional justification for characterising judicial review as being based on the ultra vires principle is the need to defend parliamentary sovereignty (or at least to give the appearance of doing so), it is difficult to see why ultra vires should remain if – at least, according to Wade – sovereignty does not.

The second example can be found in the controversial extra-judicial assertions of Lord Woolf MR[75] and Sir John Laws[76] concerning possible common law limitations to parliamentary sovereignty. It should immediately be acknowledged that Sir John has since conceded – speaking judicially in *R. v. Lord Chancellor's Department, ex p. Witham* – that judicial review *is* constrained by parliamentary sovereignty.[77] Nonetheless, the earlier observations of both judges provide a useful illustration of the analytical fragility of ultra vires in situations which Wade would categorise as potentially "revolutionary". In his observations, Sir John Laws directly employs Sir William Wade's argument that sovereignty lies in the keeping of the courts, using it to suggest that:

> The thrust of this reasoning is that the doctrine of Parliamentary sovereignty cannot be vouchsafed by Parliamentary legislation; a higher-order law confers it, and must of necessity limit it.[78]

In making this comment, Sir John is referring *specifically* to a situation in which the courts would be required to determine how to respond to a statute of a constitutionally controversial nature – for he makes clear that he is talking of "the existence of a power in the courts to strike down a statute as inconsistent with a fundamental right or, were it to happen, with democracy itself".[79] Sir John Laws is, in other words, using Wade's *own* account of sovereignty to show that in a potentially "revolutionary" situation – *i.e.* where a court is required to respond to a constitutionally novel scenario – it is analytically possible for the court to opt to set aside a statute.

In similar vein, Lord Woolf MR has suggested (relying on the decision in *Anisminic* v. *Foreign Compensation Commission*)[80] that:

> if Parliament did the unthinkable [and sought by legislation to exclude the judicial review jurisdiction of the High Court], then I would say that the courts would also be

---

[74] "Sovereignty – Revolution or Evolution?" above at n.4, 573.

[75] "Droit Public – English Style" above at n.5, 67–9.

[76] "Law and Democracy" above at n.5, 84–8.

[77] [1998] QB 575. It may be the case that a similar concession is contained in Sir John's extra–judicial observations in his article "Public Law and Employment Law: Abuse of Power" [1997] PL 455.

[78] "Law and Democracy" above at n.5, 87.

[79] Ibid., 87.

[80] Above at n.26.

required to act in a manner which would be without precedent. Some judges might choose to do so by saying that it was an unrebuttable presumption that Parliament could never intend such a result. I myself would consider there were advantages in making it clear that ultimately there are even limits on the supremacy of Parliament which it is the courts' inalienable responsibility to identify and uphold.[81]

Like Sir John Laws, Lord Woolf is talking about how judges might respond to a statute which did something controversial and constitutionally novel – in other words, he too is talking about a potentially "revolutionary" situation. While neither judge is, at least extra-judicially, a supporter of the ultra vires principle as the basis of judicial review – Sir John Laws has explicitly rejected it,[82] while Lord Woolf has described it as at best useful for the sake of constitutional respectability[83] – their comments starkly beg the question whether ultra vires is worth defending as a means of protecting parliamentary sovereignty when Wade's *own* theory suggests that sovereignty can be swept aside in "revolutionary" situations.

These extra-judicial assertions also demonstrate the fragility of ultra vires as a mechanism for preserving the *appearance* of judicial deference to Parliament. Supporters of ultra vires, it will be recalled, regard the appearance of deference as important even if this involves artificiality in practice: Forsyth thus argues that ultra vires, like a swimming costume worn on a crowded beach, serves to "preserve the decencies".[84] Everyone knows what the swimming costume conceals, in just the same way that "[n]o one is so innocent as to suppose that judicial creativity does not form the grounds of judicial review; but by adhering to the doctrine of ultra vires the judiciary shows that it adheres to its proper constitutional position".[85] However, as was suggested earlier, if ultra vires cannot in practice offer an adequate defence of parliamentary sovereignty in potentially "revolutionary" situations, it seems implausible to claim that it can serve as an effective guarantor of the *appearance* of judicial deference. As we have seen, Sir John Laws was able to rely on Wade's own account of sovereignty in order to argue that courts might be able to set aside statutes of a constitutionally controversial nature – an argument which gave rise to public controversy given that it was made during a period of political debate concerning the powers of the judiciary in relation both to judicial review and sentencing.[86] Shortly after Lord Woolf's and Sir John Laws' extra-judicial observations, Lord Irvine – then Shadow Lord Chancellor – initiated a debate in the House of Lords concerning the rôle of the judiciary. Lord Irvine – a defender of ultra vires and sovereignty – began by suggesting that:

---

[81] "Droit Public – English Style" above at n.5, 69.
[82] In "Illegality – the Problem of Jurisdiction" above at n.2, esp. 4.3 to 4.5.
[83] "Droit Public – English Style" above at n.5, 66.
[84] "Of Fig Leaves and Fairy Tales" above at n.1, 136 and p. 42 above.
[85] Ibid.
[86] For a useful discussion of this controversy, see Andrew Le Sueur, "The Judicial Review Debate: From Partnership to Friction" (1996) 31 *Government & Opposition* 8.

> the country must believe that there is unprecedented antagonism between the judges
> and the Government . . . over judicial review of ministerial decisions . . . The public
> must be perplexed by what they perceive as a major clash over the distinct roles of
> Parliament, Ministers and the judges . . . I regard as . . . unwise a number of recent
> extra-judicial statements by distinguished judges that in exceptional cases the courts
> may be entitled to hold invalid statutes duly passed by Parliament. This causes ordi-
> nary people not only to believe that judges may have got over and above themselves
> but that perhaps they are exercising a political function in judicial review cases instead
> of simply upholding the rule of law.[87]

Whatever Lord Irvine's intentions, the very fact that he felt it necessary to make
these comments highlights the inability of ultra vires to preserve us from public
controversy concerning the proper allocation of power between the judiciary
and Parliament.

The argument so far should now be summarised. I have suggested that there
appears to be a consensus among supporters and opponents of the ultra vires
principle to the effect that ultra vires can provide at best loose guidelines as to
how courts should apply and develop the grounds and detailed rules of judicial
review in day-to-day cases. This being so, the utility of ultra vires needs to be
tested by evaluating how strong a defence of parliamentary sovereignty it can
provide in the constitutionally controversial cases in which sovereignty comes
under threat. To understand the operation of ultra vires in such cases – which
would be categorised by Sir William Wade as potential opportunities for a constitutional "revolution" – it is necessary to read the principle in conjunction
with Wade's account of sovereignty. When we do so, however, we can see that
ultra vires cannot provide any stronger a defence of sovereignty than its common law rivals, for the reason that according to Sir William Wade, sovereignty
lies ultimately in the hands of the courts and – interpreted in this way – can provide no normative ammunition against a "revolution". Logically, there can be
no stronger a constraint on judicial review overthrowing parliamentary sovereignty (defined using Wade's theory) where the jurisdiction is based on ultra
vires than where it is based on any rival common law theory. In consequence –
and as the extra-judicial utterances of Sir John Laws and Lord Woolf MR
demonstrate – it is difficult to see how ultra vires can be expected reliably to
uphold the appearance of judicial deference to parliamentary sovereignty.

The fact that ultra vires and parliamentary sovereignty cannot, in and of
themselves, set definite limits to the ambit of judicial power in constitutionally
controversial cases suggests that Sir William Wade's account of the English constitutional order must ultimately run up against the interdependence of the powers of Parliament and the courts. For while the courts – according to Wade's
analysis of parliamentary sovereignty – have the final say in determining the
ambit of Parliament's legislative power, Parliament can attempt to restrict judicial activism by legislation, while the success of that legislation will ultimately

[87] HL Deb, 5 June 1996, cols.1254–5. Lord Irvine's position is set out more broadly in "Judges
and Decision-Makers: the Theory and Practice of *Wednesbury* Review" above at n.1.

depend on the manner in which it is interpreted and applied by the courts. The powers of the two institutions are therefore interdependent both analytically and practically. On a day-to-day basis, the comparative power of each institution vis-à-vis the other will be an issue of some political importance. Michael Beloff QC has suggested, for example, that the late twentieth century expansion of judicial review has been influenced by:

> the diminution in the power and effectiveness of political control over the Executive; the subservience of backbenchers disciplined by whips and ambition alike; the limitations on the powers of the opposition, hampered by lack of access to information – except at the discretion of disobedient civil servants; inadequate powers and resources for the Select Committees compared, say, with their American counterparts; the decline, it may be, of the number of MPs with the stamina to inquire and the wit to criticise. It is for political scientists to debate the relative significance of these factors. But that there has been a vacuum cannot be doubted; and the judges have filled it.[88]

Sir Stephen Sedley – writing extra-judicially – makes a related point: that the growth of judicial review is the result of a *judicial* refashioning, with "*popular* support sufficient to mute political opposition to it, of our organic constitution".[89] This may mean that we now have "a bi-polar sovereignty of the Crown in Parliament and the Crown in its courts, to each of which the Crown's ministers are answerable – politically to Parliament, legally to the courts".[90] Lord Woolf MR – also writing extra-judicially – suggests that in day-to-day terms, the balance of power between the executive or Parliament and the judiciary will vary. Tensions between the executive or Parliament and the judiciary will appear – for example, when the courts seek to develop judicial review in the absence of other effective checks on executive power – but this is a necessary part of maintaining the constitutional balance of power.[91] While the day-to-day balance of power may reflect political factors, however, it is important to be aware that any view about whether an *appropriate* balance of power exists at any given moment will depend on the range of philosophical, political and moral values (for example, conceptions of rights and duties) which we believe the judiciary should enforce via judicial review. This issue will be considered in further detail at the end of the chapter.

---

[88] Michael Beloff, "Judicial Review – 2001: A Prophetic Odyssey" (1995) 58 *MLR* 143, 145.

[89] Sir Stephen Sedley, "Human Rights: a Twenty-First Century Agenda" [1995] *PL* 386, 389 (emphasis added).

[90] Ibid., 389. See also Sir Stephen's *Freedom, Law and Justice* (London, Sweet & Maxwell, 1999), pp.7–8.

[91] Lord Woolf MR, "Judicial Review – the Tensions between the Executive and the Judiciary" (1998) 114 *LQR* 579. The most recent period of "tension" is surveyed in Andrew Le Sueur, "The Judicial Review Debate: From Partnership to Friction" above at n.86.

INSTITUTIONAL INTERDEPENDENCE AND HART'S RULE OF RECOGNITION

It was argued in the previous section that the ultra vires principle can provide no more solid a defence of parliamentary sovereignty than can its common law rivals, at least for so long as it is tied to Professor Sir William Wade's theory of sovereignty. The present section of the chapter will provide theoretical reinforcement for this argument by analysing Professor H.L.A. Hart's positivist account of the nature of a legal system.[92] It is not my intention to suggest that Hart's account is necessarily correct, nor that it can necessarily be defended against the detailed critique developed by Professor Ronald Dworkin,[93] nor that it necessarily provides the best account of the nature of the English legal system.[94] Instead, Hart's account is relevant because it contains analyses both of the nature of legal systems in general, and of the nature of the English legal system in particular, which are strongly analogous to Sir William Wade's account of English constitutional law. Indeed, Hart's and Wade's accounts are often associated with one another:[95] for Hart believed – like Wade – that it was possible to identify the foundational rules of a legal system, and that questions concerning the nature and scope of such rules must ultimately be resolved by the courts.[96] Given these similarities, the presence of an institutional interdependence between Parliament and the courts in Hart's analysis of legal systems *in general* may suggest that the presence of a similar interdependence in Wade's *particular* analysis of English law is inevitable – with the consequence that any sovereignty-based defence of the ultra vires principle is likely to fail.

One of Hart's main concerns was to explain what it was that turned an otherwise random array of rules into a unified legal system. The way in which he did this was to characterise a legal system as a union of primary and secondary rules. Primary rules are those which impose obligations or duties, and most individual rules of law fall within this category. Hart argued, however, that a body of rules could only be categorised as a legal *system* if it also contained rules, first, for determining whether something *counted* as an authoritative rule of law, and if so what its scope was; secondly, for explaining how existing rules of law could be *adapted* in response to changing circumstances – whether, for example, by eliminating old rules or adopting new ones; and thirdly, for empowering a

---

[92] Developed in *The Concept of Law* above at n.37.

[93] Developed principally in Dworkin's books *Taking Rights Seriously* (London, Duckworth, 1977), chs. 2–4 and *Law's Empire* (London, Fontana Press, 1986), pp. 31–44, chs. 2, 4. For Hart's response, see the Postscript to the second edition of *The Concept of Law* above at n.37, 244–268.

[94] For a Dworkinian account of the English legal system, see T.R.S. Allan's *Law, Liberty, and Justice: The Legal Foundations of British Constitutionalism* (Oxford, Clarendon Press, 1993), especially – in relation to parliamentary sovereignty and the courts – chs. 3, 4 and 11. Note, however, that Allan's arguments in these chapters may go beyond Dworkin's own position as set out in *Law's Empire* above at n.93, 401–2.

[95] See, for example, T.R.S. Allan, "Parliamentary Sovereignty: Law, Politics, and Revolution" above at n.70, 443–4; Martin Loughlin, *Public Law and Political Theory* (Oxford, Clarendon Press, 1992), 184–190, 246.

[96] H.L.A. Hart, *The Concept of Law* (hereafter "*The Concept of Law*") above at n.37, 147–54.

specified agency or person to determine whether an individual rule had been violated in any given circumstances. Unless supplemented by rules of this type, a set of primary rules would be too uncertain, too static and too inefficient to administer to make up a functioning legal system.[97] Rules which fulfilled these three functions could be categorised as secondary rules, in that:

> they are concerned with the primary rules themselves. They specify the ways in which the primary rules may be conclusively ascertained, introduced, eliminated, varied, and the fact of their violation conclusively determined.[98]

Hart suggested that any legal system needed three types of secondary rule. First, rules of recognition, which "will specify some feature or features possession of which by a suggested rule is taken as a conclusive affirmative indication" that it is a valid (primary) rule of the legal system concerned.[99] To say that a primary rule is valid is therefore to recognise that it has passed "all the tests provided by the rule of recognition".[100] In a modern legal system, rules of recognition identify primary rules by some general characteristic they share, which "may be the fact of their having been enacted by a specific body, or their long customary practice, or their relation to judicial decisions".[101] Hart acknowledged that where more than one of these characteristics is treated as an authoritative identifying criterion for valid primary rules, the characteristics will need to be listed in order of superiority in order to explain, for example, that a statute takes priority over a rule of common law.[102] A crucial feature of any rule of recognition is that while it may be the supreme criterion for assessing the validity of primary rules, there is "no rule providing criteria for the assessment of its own legal validity".[103] For, since the rule of recognition provides the criteria for assessing the validity of other rules, it can itself "be neither valid nor invalid but is simply accepted for use in this way", in much the same way that "we assume, but can never demonstrate, that the standard meter bar in Paris which is the ultimate test of the correctness of all measurement in meters, is itself correct".[104] Thus, while the rule of recognition supplies the criteria by which other rules are identified as valid law, it can itself be said to "exist" only if it is followed *in practice* by the courts (and, Hart at least initially suggested, by other officials and private persons) in identifying the law by reference to those criteria.[105]

The concept of the "rule of recognition" is the most well-known of Hart's secondary rules. For a legal system to work, however, a second and third set of secondary rules must be in operation. The second set are rules of change, which

---

[97] Ibid., 92–4.
[98] Ibid., 94.
[99] Ibid., 94; see, more generally, 100–1.
[100] Ibid., 103.
[101] Ibid., 95.
[102] Ibid., 95; see further 101, 105–7.
[103] Ibid., 107.
[104] Ibid., 109.
[105] Ibid., 110, 112, 116–7. In his Postscript to the second edition, Hart focuses solely on the acceptance of the rule of recognition by the *courts*; see 250, 258, 266–7.

empower "an individual or body of persons to introduce new primary rules for the conduct of the life of the group, or of some class within it, and to eliminate old rules".[106] These rules therefore explain the concepts of legislative enactment and repeal. The third set are rules of adjudication, which empower individuals "to make authoritative determinations of the question whether, on a particular occasion, a primary rule has been broken".[107] Such rules identify which individuals are to adjudicate and what procedures are to be followed in adjudicating. For example, rules of adjudication confer judicial powers and accord an authoritative status to judicial declarations about breaches of primary rules; they thus define "the concepts of judge or court, jurisdiction and judgment".[108]

Hart's account of the nature of legal systems in general clearly presupposes a degree of institutional interdependence, exhibited in the inter-relationship between the three secondary rules, and the rules of recognition and adjudication in particular. Hart observed that if any legal system has rules of adjudication then it is necessarily committed to having at least an elementary rule of recognition. For if the courts are empowered authoritatively to determine the fact that a primary rule has been broken, such determinations "cannot avoid being taken as authoritative determinations of what the [primary] rules are".[109] So a rule conferring jurisdiction to adjudicate is also a rule of recognition, identifying the primary rules through the judgments of the courts, the judgments themselves becoming "sources" of law.[110] More fundamentally, Professor Neil MacCormick has asked whether there is in fact a circular relationship between the rule of recognition and the rule of adjudication.[111] For, while the rule of recognition presupposes the existence of judges – that is, a person or group of persons empowered authoritatively to determine legal disputes (for how else, for example, could we be sure that a particular rule was definitely a valid law of the system?) – the power to adjudicate is conferred by the rule of adjudication. And, while the rule of adjudication can only be valid if it complies with the criteria set out in the rule of recognition, the rule of recognition presupposes the existence of judges empowered by the rule of adjudication. MacCormick's answer is that "rules of recognition, change and adjudication are indeed necessarily interlocking and interacting, so that change in or redefinition of one must be mirrored by change in or redefinition of another".[112] He suggests, however,

---

[106] Ibid., 95

[107] Ibid., 96.

[108] Ibid., 97.

[109] Ibid., 97.

[110] Ibid., 97.

[111] Neil MacCormick, *H.L.A. Hart* (London, Edward Arnold, 1981), 108–9. MacCormick's question in fact asks whether there is an interconnection between all three secondary rules. However, it is not strictly necessary to discuss the rule of change in the context of this chapter, and MacCormick's own discussion of that rule appears to be somewhat inelegant. For example, if Hart's analytical distinction between the subordination and derivation of criteria of validity – discussed in *The Concept of Law* above at n.37, 101 – is to be followed, then any "circularity" involving the rules of recognition and change can relate only to judicial responses to legislation rather than to legislation and existing common law rules, as MacCormick's discussion appears to imply.

[112] Neil MacCormick, *H.L.A. Hart*, above at n.111, 119.

that conceptual circularity can be avoided if we remember that the rules are interlocking for historical rather than logical reasons. A society's rules of adjudication, change and recognition evolve in response to changing power-relationships between its institutions – in some political circumstances, the legislature will attempt to redefine the power of the courts and vice versa (through legislation and interpretation respectively), and we may venture that the result of either might ultimately be a change in the rule of recognition. In consequence, we might fairly say that in a developed legal system, proper discharge of the legislative function necessarily presupposes a judiciary capable of identifying which rules are valid primary laws – requiring the courts to have a view as to the proper limits of the legislative function (even if the courts in fact define the proper limit as "none") – while the rôle of the judiciary in discharging this task presupposes the existence of a body capable of creating valid primary laws. In short, Hart's account of the nature of legal systems in general assumes a degree of institutional interdependence in which the rules of recognition, adjudication and change are inter-related.

This point can be reinforced by considering Hart's assessment of the nature of the English legal system. Hart categorised the formula "Whatever the Queen in Parliament enacts is law" as an adequate description of the English rule of recognition for "the overwhelming majority of cases".[113] Echoing Wade, Hart was clear that doubts concerning the meaning and scope of this rule were to be settled by the courts – for at any given moment, some aspects of the rule might be clear but others would not be.[114] As an example, Hart suggested that if Parliament enacted a law prescribing a minimum wage for engineers and stipulated in the relevant legislation that no alteration could have effect as law unless confirmed by the engineers' union, it would be attempting to use a "manner-and-form" provision in order to entrench a particular wage level in practice.[115] Arguments about whether this was possible had no predetermined answer, given that the issue fell into "the area of open texture of the system's most fundamental rule".[116] An authoritative answer could be provided only when a court ruled on the question. In doing so, the court would have "made determinate . . . the ultimate rule by which valid law is identified"[117] given that it would have to pronounce on the existence and scope of Parliament's powers effectively to entrench legislation. Echoing MacCormick, Hart acknowledged that this appeared to involve a circularity, in that courts would be exercising "creative powers which settle the ultimate criteria by which the validity of the very laws, which confer upon them jurisdiction as judges, must itself be tested".[118]

Hart's first response to this apparent circularity was to suggest that while every rule is doubtful at some points, it is a necessary condition of the existence

[113] *The Concept of Law* above at n.37, 148.
[114] Ibid., 150.
[115] Ibid., 150–1.
[116] Ibid., 151.
[117] Ibid., 152.
[118] Ibid., 152.

of a legal system that not every rule is open to doubt on all points. The judiciary's authority to resolve uncertainties concerning the rule of recognition thus depends on the fact that the application of that rule to "a vast area of law" – including the rules that confer the courts' own authority – raises no doubts, although its precise scope and ambit might do so in particular cases.[119] This suggestion is clearly insufficient to resolve the circularity, however. For its explanatory power is purely contingent, depending entirely on the nature and seriousness of the particular cases which arise. It also assumes that there are no cases – or sets of inter-related cases concerning different manifestations of the same issue – that are of sufficient seriousness that they threaten the rule of recognition's application more generally. Hart may have been thinking of these points when he conceded that his first suggestion was "too short a way" to resolve the circularity.[120] His second suggestion was effectively to counsel that we simply ignore it. It was possible, Hart observed, that

> when courts settle previously unenvisaged questions concerning the most fundamental constitutional rules, they *get* their authority to decide them accepted after the questions have arisen and the decision has been given. Here all that succeeds is success.[121]

Some constitutional questions may divide society too fundamentally to be settled effectively by judicial decision. However:

> where less vital social issues are concerned, a very surprising piece of judicial lawmaking concerning the very sources of law may be calmly "swallowed". Where this is so, it will often in *retrospect* be said, and may genuinely appear, that there always was an "inherent" power in the courts to do what they have done.[122]

Normatively or analytically, one may disagree with this as an account of judicial decision-making in cases of constitutional controversy. The crucial point, however, is that Hart's second suggestion acknowledges the existence of institutional interdependence in practice. In Hart's example of a case involving "less vital social issues", the legislature is dependent upon the courts for clarification of its powers – something which threatens to create a problem since it is unclear where the courts get *their* power to clarify from. Hart's pragmatic response is effectively to say that if the clarification offered by the courts allows the institutions to rub along together, then the circularity can simply be glossed over or ignored. People will assume that the courts always had the power to offer the clarification, which will just be accepted. Of course, this solution may or may not work in practice. For present purposes, its importance lies in the fact that it requires us to acknowledge that the powers of the courts and Parliament are in practice inter-dependent – for in situations of potential constitutional controversy, each ultimately depends upon the other to keep the system intact.

---

[119] *The Concept of Law* above at n.37, 152.
[120] Ibid., 153.
[121] Ibid., 153.
[122] Ibid., 153.

Hart's general account – with its clear institutional interdependence – is thus reflected in his analysis of the English legal system. In fact, as Hart's analysis of the English legal system demonstrates, it is unlikely that his general model could work in practice without such an interdependence. Given the similarities between Wade's and Hart's accounts – their shared focus on the rule of recognition as a "political fact", together with the fundamental rôle of the courts (and, in Hart's case, officials more generally) in the identification and operation of a legal system[123] – the presence of an interdependence in both accounts is unsurprising. Indeed, given that institutional interdependence is in-built within Hart's positivist account of the nature of legal systems *in general*, it would be remarkable if it was not also in-built within Wade's positivist theory of parliamentary sovereignty. The very inevitability of institutional interdependence in Wade's account must, in consequence, undermine still further the scope for claiming that the ultra vires theory is *necessarily* more capable than its rivals of defending parliamentary sovereignty.

AN ANALOGY: PARLIAMENTARY PRIVILEGE

It has been argued that as an analytical matter, parliamentary sovereignty is no better protected by the ultra vires principle than by any rival common law basis for judicial review, given that the powers of the courts and Parliament can ultimately be categorised as interdependent. While this interdependence – significant in practical terms for its implications for the rôle of the courts in recognising valid legislation (in other words, in recognising the expressions of a sovereign Parliament's will) – might be said to lie at the root of the English legal system,[124] a more subtle form of interdependence can be seen in the rules relating to parliamentary privilege. Analysis of these rules sheds further light on the nature of the relationship between Parliament and the courts in relation to judicial review.

Any analysis of parliamentary privilege must begin with Article 9 of the Bill of Rights 1689, which makes clear:

> That the freedome of speech and debates or proceedings in Parlyament ought not to be impeached or questioned in any court or place out of Parlyament.

The great analytical difficulty with Article 9 – as the saga of *Stockdale* v. *Hansard*[125] and the *Case of the Sheriff of Middlesex*[126] powerfully demonstrates – is that both Parliament and the courts claim to have the last say in delimiting

---

[123] See further T.R.S. Allan, "Parliamentary Sovereignty: Law, Politics, and Revolution" above at n.70.

[124] The intricacies of the Scottish position concerning sovereignty – as to which, see *MacCormick* v. *Lord Advocate* [1953] SC 396 – will not be considered here.

[125] (1839) 9 Ad & E 1.

[126] (1840) 11 Ad & E 273.

the scope of the phrase "proceedings in Parliament".[127] As Keir and Lawson have succinctly suggested:

> there may be at any given moment two doctrines of privilege, the one held by the courts, the other by either House, the one to be found in the Law Reports, the other in *Hansard*, and no way of resolving the real point at issue should conflict arise.[128]

The mere *fact* that this point remains unresolved is not especially significant, given that it simply highlights the existence of a disagreement between Parliament and the courts as to which body should have ultimate responsibility for determining the boundaries of Parliamentary privilege. What *is* significant is Lord Browne-Wilkinson's suggestion on behalf of the Judicial Committee of the Privy Council in *Prebble* v. *Television New Zealand* that Article 9 is in fact "but one manifestation" of a "wider principle" – namely that the "courts and Parliament are both astute to recognise their respective constitutional roles".[129] In the context of *Prebble*, this dictated that the courts should avoid trespassing into Parliament's territory – with the consequence that words spoken in the course of a Parliamentary debate could not be used as part of a defence in a libel action. However, the *mutuality* of concern suggested by Lord Browne-Wilkinson implies a deeper constitutional interdependence between the courts and Parliament, in that each must be sensitive to the need to avoid undermining the privileges of the other in order for those privileges to be maintained. This point is captured in *R. v. Parliamentary Commissioner for Standards, ex p. Fayed*, where Lord Woolf MR approved Sedley J's suggestion at first instance that Lord Browne-Wilkinson's "wider principle" rested on "a mutuality of respect between two constitutional sovereignties".[130] More broadly, Keir and Lawson have implied that difficulties concerning the ambit of parliamentary privilege can be avoided so long as there is a "sufficient measure of tacit agreement" between the courts and the legislature.[131]

There is, of course, an important difference between parliamentary sovereignty and parliamentary privilege: for, whereas sovereignty goes to the very foundation of the constitution, privilege is but one element of it. It would thus be quite feasible to imagine a constitutional system containing a principle of parliamentary privilege but no principle of parliamentary sovereignty (although the reverse would – depending on the ambit of the privilege rules in play – be difficult if not impossible to achieve if the Parliament concerned was not to be

---

[127] For a useful and up-to-date survey, see the essays collected in Dawn Oliver and Gavin Drewry (eds), *The Law and Parliament* (London, Butterworths, 1998).

[128] D.L. Keir and F.H. Lawson, *Cases in Constitutional Law* (Oxford, Clarendon Press, 6th edn. By F.H. Lawson and D.J. Bentley, 1979), 255.

[129] [1995] 1 AC 321, 332.

[130] [1998] 1 WLR 669, 670; Sedley J's judgment – which echoes his extra-judicial observations concerning "bi-polar sovereignty" (above at n.89) is reported at [1997] COD 376; see also *Hamilton v. Fayed* [1999] 3 All ER 317. For comment, see Nicholas Bamforth, "Judicial Review, Parliamentary Privilege, and the Parliamentary Commissioner for Standards" (1998) 57 *CLJ* 6.

[131] D.L. Keir and F.H. Lawson above at n.128, 255.

bound by "manner-and-form" constraints when legislating).[132] Nonetheless, an analogy can be drawn between the two concepts in that neither is capable, in and of itself, of specifying the exact legal boundary between the territories of Parliament and the courts. Rather, each depends for its operation on the existence of a continuing *dialogue* between the two institutions (the dialogue consisting in legislation, judicial interpretation of that legislation and judicial decision-making more broadly, Parliament's response to judicial decisions and extra-judicial pronouncements, etc.). In both cases, this dialogue becomes tense when the "tacit agreement" envisaged by Keir and Lawson breaks down – in the case of sovereignty where, for example, the judges are drawn into a debate with Parliament as to the limits (if any) of the latter's legislative powers, and in the case of privilege where the two bodies adopt divergent views as to the scope of that principle. The important lesson which privilege offers here is that such disputes cannot, in general, be resolved by conceptual analysis of the notion of privilege *itself* – indeed how could they, given the uncertainty as to which institution has ultimate control over the interpretation of privilege? Instead, such disputes are usually resolved by invoking notions of constitutional principle which stand behind and are broader than the concept of privilege – for example, the need for the courts and Parliament to preserve a mutuality of respect – or due to a pragmatic concern to find a workable solution to the problem immediately facing the courts.[133] At root, the legal status of parliamentary privilege might therefore be said to turn on the principled and pragmatic considerations which *inform* the dialogue between Parliament and the courts.

Given that Wade's view of parliamentary sovereignty entails an even more basic interdependence between the two institutions – in that that the powers of the legislature depend ultimately upon the stance of the courts – it is submitted that a similar point can be made concerning the resolution of any sovereignty-related dispute. Mere invocation of terms such as "sovereignty", "ultra vires", "the rule of law" and "fundamental rights" can tell us little or nothing about the respective powers of Parliament and the courts in cases where the correct interpretation of those powers is in dispute. Instead, the matter can only be resolved by reference to broader considerations of political and moral principle.

---

[132] It is to be regretted that the House of Lords did not emphasise the analytical distinction between sovereignty and privilege more clearly in *British Railways Board* v. *Pickin* [1974] AC 765. Lord Morris's judgment was framed in the language of privilege (at 790), while Lords Reid, Wilberforce and Cross avoided general discussion of the terms "sovereignty" and "privilege", Lord Reid merely suggesting at 782 that the case did not involve any attempt "to question the general supremacy of Parliament". However, Lord Simon – mistakenly, it is submitted – went so far as to describe privilege as a "concomitant" of parliamentary sovereignty (at 798).

[133] As Geoffrey Lock has argued in relation to parliamentary privilege: "Cases involving Parliament have obliged judges to establish lines of demarcation between the courts and the legislature; they may have to choose between remaining faithful to their judicial principles and fermenting constitutional ferment, though all-out conflicts are fortunately rare" (in Dawn Oliver and Gavin Drewry (eds) above at n.127, 51).

CONCLUSION: MAKING EXPLICIT THE BASIS OF JUDICIAL REVIEW

Although the ultra vires principle is defended by its supporters on the normative basis that it is necessary in order to defend parliamentary sovereignty – or at least, to give the appearance of judicial deference to Parliament – it has been argued that it cannot succeed in doing so given the institutional interdependence inherent in Sir William Wade's account of parliamentary sovereignty. Ultra vires fails as a theory since it cannot work on its own terms – it is inconsistent, in the sense discussed earlier in the chapter, whatever normative arguments might be advanced in its favour. Supporters of ultra vires might in consequence attempt to abandon Wade's account of parliamentary sovereignty in order to find a new constitutional grounding for their principle.[134] To mount a watertight defence of ultra vires, however, they would need to find a constitutional foundation which contained *no* institutional interdependence whatever between the legislature and the courts – a task of enormous philosophical difficulty, if not impossibility. It is submitted that the simpler and more attractive option would be to acknowledge that an alternative constitutional foundation for judicial review is necessary.

This chapter is not the place to compare in detail the merits of the various alternatives.[135] It should be clear, however, that any successful alternative would need to take account of the difficulty of avoiding some sort of institutional interdependence, at least in the context of our present constitutional structure. In reality, it would probably be sensible simply to accept the existence of an institutional interdependence between Parliament and the courts as part of any alternative, and to acknowledge that judicial review tends to expand in the face of weak parliamentary scrutiny of government. This ongoing process of give-and-take between Parliament and the courts is of great political importance – for it concerns the distribution of power at a high level within the constitution – but it should be guided and shaped by considerations of political and moral principle, rather than naked concern for power.[136] In seeking to make such considerations explicit, the framers of any alternative basis for judicial review will doubtless be assisted by the growing body of scholarship highlighting the competing theories of justice and political morality which have shaped the development of public law thought – and the case law itself – from the late nineteenth century onwards.[137] For it seems fairly clear that one's support for or opposition

[134] Something which might be possible given the ambiguities in "Fig Leaves and Fairy Tales" concerning Christopher Forsyth's exact view of the nature of sovereignty – see above at n.39.

[135] See further the materials discussed above at n.5.

[136] A concern raised, among others, by Mark Elliott: "The Ultra Vires Doctrine in a Constitutional Setting above at n.3, 131–4 pp. 131–5 above.

[137] See Martin Loughlin, *Public Law and Political Theory* above at n.95, esp. chs. 4, 8 and 9; Carol Harlow and Richard Rawlings, *Law and Administration* (London, Butterworths, 2nd edn., 1997), chs. 1 to 5; Paul Craig, *Public Law and Democracy in the United Kingdom and the United States of America* (Oxford, Clarendon Press, 1990), esp. chs. 4, 6, 8, 10 and 11. For one account based explicitly on a background theory of justice, see T.R.S.Allan, *Law, Liberty, and Justice: the Legal Foundations of British Constitutionalism* above at n.94.

to a particular constitutional relationship between Parliament and the courts – whether one thinks, normatively, that a given relationship is or is not substantively attractive – will depend to a large extent on one's background theories of justice and political morality. A theory of justice concerns the proper distribution of entitlements – rights, liberties and the like – between individuals or groups in a society, while a theory of political morality concerns the ways in which state power should rightfully be exercised. In combination, these theories determine the range of rights which citizens should be able to assert against the state and against one another, and how far it is appropriate for the state to interfere with those rights. Some theories of justice and political morality favour weak protection of individual rights by the courts, coupled with judicial deference to the legislature or the executive, while others favour a more assertive judiciary which is determined to protect individual rights. Theories of the first sort – which will need to take account of the institutional interdependence issue – tend to stress the need for greater internal parliamentary or governmental scrutiny of legislative measures or executive action, preferably before legislation is passed or final administrative decisions are taken. Theories of the second sort tend to assume that internal scrutiny alone is inadequate – necessitating a stronger rôle for the courts – although they face the difficult task of demonstrating authoritatively which rights the courts are to protect and to what extent. Nonetheless, it is substantive considerations of justice and political morality which must ultimately form the basis and dictate the boundaries of judicial review. By bringing such considerations to the forefront – by asking, for example, what level of protection our theory of justice demands that a court should grant a particular right, whether on its own or considered alongside competing rights – we might encourage a more intellectually honest and perhaps normatively appealing approach to judicial review.

7

Form and Substance in the Rule of Law: A Democratic Justification for Judicial Review?

DAVID DYZENHAUS*

INTRODUCTION

This essay takes up a debate about the rule of law, liberalism, democracy and the justification for judicial review. The last issue is never far beneath the surface of discussions of administrative law. When it surfaces, the argument often is that judicial review is justified because it preserves democracy or liberalism, or some combination.

This debate is in some sense as old as the debate in philosophy of law between positivists and antipositivists. The central question of philosophy of law is the relationship between law and morality. And the claim that judicial review is justified because it protects values that are democratic and integral to the rule of law, or liberal and integral to the rule of law, or rule of law values that are somehow both democratic and liberal, is a claim about the connection between law and morality. As such, it sets itself against those legal positivist positions which unite around the separation thesis that there is no necessary connection between law and morality.[1]

Here I want to examine a striking revival of the rule of law debate which has taken place in the United Kingdom in the last ten or so years. That revival has looked both to the future and to the past. It has looked to the future because of the anticipation that British judges will at some point get direct statutory authority to test the legality of administrative action against human rights norms. It has looked to the past because of questions made urgent in the wake of the massive project of privatisation undertaken in Thatcher's Britain,

---

* This essay was prepared for the Conference on "The Foundations of Judicial Review" held in Cambridge in May 1999. I have revised it in the light of the debates occasioned by the papers at that conference. I thank John Allison, Paul Craig, Christopher Forsyth, Nils Jansen, Cheryl Misak and – especially – Trevor Allan and Mike Taggart for comments on a draft of this paper. I also thank Clare Hall and the Faculty of Law of Cambridge University for the hospitality which made writing this essay possible, and the Social Sciences and Humanities Research Council of Canada for providing research funding.

[1] Hobbes, the founder of legal positivism, did not subscribe to this thesis. Nor, in my view, did Bentham.

questions about when a power is sufficiently public for it to be amenable to judical review. Of course, both future and past come together on the issue of the "horizontal effect" of the Human Rights Act 1998, that is, on the extent to which judges will hold non-state actors accountable to its requirements.[2]

I will argue that the basis for judicial review is democratic rather than liberal, antipositivist rather than positivist, and procedural rather than substantive. I put these contrasts in a somewhat tentative form in order to capture a theme of the argument, which is that these contrasting terms are best seen as the poles of a continuum, so that where one places oneself should be more a matter of emphasis than of plumping for one or other side of a sharp distinction.

The two standard packages in the debate are, or so I will suggest, the democratic position which is positivist and procedural in orientation and the liberal position which is antipositivist and substantive. So my argument, with its combination of democracy, proceduralism and antipositivism seeks to strike out in a new direction, one which disputes the separation thesis through a connection between law and politics rather than one between law and morality.

Unlike some of the other participants in the rule of law debate, I make no claim to the banner of the "orthodox" position, the one which is closest to the history and traditions of English constitutionalism. That both of the main camps – common law and ultra vires – can plausibly make this claim may show that the debate cannot be decided, as it were, empirically. It may even show that any claim to represent orthodoxy should not take an either/or stance, but should somehow attempt to articulate the foundation of the rather large consensus between the two camps.[3] But while my task at times comes close to an attempt to articulate a foundation for the consensus, it is for the most part a different one. It is to chase down the theoretical commitments and underpinnings of the different camps, and so my arguments operate at a relentlessly abstract level.

PROCEDURE AND SUBSTANCE IN POLITICAL THEORY

My starting place is the process/substance distinction as it is drawn in political theory rather than in administrative law. My claim is that liberalism as a political philosophy is more oriented to substance, while democratic theory is more oriented to process. In a well-known passage, Isaiah Berlin said of the liberal conception of liberty, that it is:

> principally concerned with the area of control, not with its source. Just as a democracy may, in fact, deprive the individual citizen of a great many liberties which he

[2] See Murray Hunt, "The 'Horizontal Effect' of the Human Rights Act" [1998] *PL* 423 and Stephen Sedley, "Public Power and Private Power", in *Freedom, Law and Justice* (1999) and pp. 291–305 below.

[3] Mark Elliott has taken a significant step in this direction – see his "The Ultra Vires Doctrine in a Constitutional Setting: Still the Central Principle of Administrative Law" (1999) 58 *CLJ* 129 and pp. 83–109. However, as his title suggests, he is still rather too occupied with showing that one camp must win.

might have in some other form of society, so it is perfectly conceivable that a liberal-minded despot would allow his subjects a large measure of personal freedom . . . Freedom in this sense is not, at any rate logically, connected with democracy or self-government.[4]

Berlin here gestures towards an important distinction in political theory between the citizen who has the positive right to participate in political deliberation and decision-making on fundamental matters and the passive subject, content to receive his due as long as his negative rights against coercion by others are preserved.

This distinction is also one between process rights and substance rights, where process rights are the rights to participate in producing a result that will affect us and substance rights the rights to have particular results, whatever the process. It follows from Berlin's claim about liberalism that it is concerned with substance not process. What matters is what you get, not how you got it. Of course, process rights will matter but only in so far as they serve to secure substance rights. Process or democracy is entirely subordinated or instrumentalised to securing liberal substance.

As one surveys the terrain of political theory, so the map gets more complex. One has, first, to note a dispute within liberalism. For libertarian liberals the negative space of liberty is all important. It must be protected against intrusions, especially those that come armed with the coercive authority of the state. Thus the legitimate scope for democracy – for collective decision-making about the common good – is very limited.

For egalitarian liberals, in contrast, the space of protected substance is more limited, thus giving more scope for collective decision-making. The limits of state action are not set by a libertarian principle which argues that the more extensive the space of negative liberty for the individual the better. Rather the limits are set by a neutrality principle which says that the state may act in any way it likes, as long as it does not act on the basis of a view about what the good life is for individuals. What makes these liberals into egalitarians is that they think the state, subject to the constraints of the neutrality principle, should act in order to secure equality for all. The space of collective decision-making is then the space in which the people express their judgment through their legislative representatives about what policies will best promote equality.

This disagreement within liberalism about protected substance is a family squabble. In large part it is a disagreement about the scope of the neutrality principle since libertarians also subscribe to that principle. They argue that any intrusion by the state into the space of negative liberty which is not justified by what is strictly necessary to secure that space will involve an illicit and coercive judgment about the good life. What I called earlier the libertarian principle – the more extensive the space of negative liberty for the individual the better – is for

---

[4] "Two Concepts of Liberty", in Isaiah Berlin, *Four Essays on Liberty* (Oxford, Oxford University Press, 1969) 118, 129–30.

libertarians merely the most coherent conception of the basic liberal commitment to neutrality.

The second complicating factor I need to mention is that the debate between liberals and democrats can also plausibly be seen as one about the scope of the neutrality principle. The egalitarian camp within liberalism is also the liberal democratic camp because of the greater scope it allows for collective decision-making. And no democrat today argues for the priority of procedure over substance in a way that detaches the worth of procedures from substance. Moreover, the substantive value of giving priority to procedure over substance is said by democrats to reside in principles to do with the rights and freedoms of the individual. Though the rights and freedoms emphasised will have to do with securing participation in collective decision-making, ultimately the democrat will concede that some minimum space of negative liberty has to be guaranteed to the individual in order to secure effective participation.[5]

In sum, even radical democratic proceduralism seems to presuppose some protected liberal substance so that all involved in the great debates of political theory are part of one big, though sometimes rancorous family. The various positions in that debate no longer seem greatly at odds with each other. Rather, they look like points along a continuum marked by the extent of protected liberal substance. The less the extent of protected substance, the more faith is put in the outcomes of procedures, and vice versa. Hence it may well seem that the distinction between citizen and subject with which I started is overdrawn.

I want to leave this point for the moment in order to explore another, the extent to which this debate in political theory translates into debates about the rule of law and judicial review. It may seem that the translation is obvious. The closer one is to the libertarian end, the more one will be tempted to put forward a picture of the rule of law in which judges are the guardians of a constitutional morality protective of liberal substance. Conversely, the closer one is to the democratic end of the continuum, the more modest the role for judges. Hence, one answers questions about the rule of law and judicial review by first settling the great questions of political theory.

However, if one switches from political to legal theory, one notices that one prominent position in legal theory argues that this translation exercise has nothing to do with debate about the rule of law. Rather, it is about what political vision should be embedded in the positive law. I will now try to show that once we see the difficulties of that position, we will have a better grip on the politics of the rule of law and, as a result, be further along in providing a foundation for judicial review.

---

[5] And this observation is true also of those communitarians who ally themselves with democratic proceduralism because localised collective decision-making seems to hold out the best promise of securing the good of community.

Legal positivists say that it is a mistake to confuse the tasks of political and legal theory. In this section, I will examine two influential positions on the rule of law and judicial review which have recently been put forward by administrative lawyers in the United Kingdom, Paul Craig and Christopher Forsyth. As we will see, tensions internal to these positions as well as tensions between them show positivism, at least in these forms, to be an unsatisfactory guide in the area of administrative law. However, there are still valuable insights to be gleaned from the main positivist challenge to an antipositivist conception of the rule of law, a challenge which I will try to meet in the last section of this essay.

Paul Craig takes his bearings from the sophisticated account of the rule of law put forward by Joseph Raz.[6] He distinguishes between formal and substantive meanings of the rule of law, claiming that this "dichotomy is . . . of crucial importance in determining the nature of the specifically legal precepts which can be derived from the rule of law".[7] Formal conceptions of the rule of law do not pass judgment on the content of the law:

> Formal conceptions of the rule of law address the manner in which the law was pro-
> mulgated (was it by a properly authorised person, in a properly authorised manner,
> etc.); the clarity of the ensuing norm (was it sufficiently clear to guide an individual's

---

[6] Paul Craig, "Formal and Substantive Conceptions of the Rule of Law: An Analytical Framework" [1997] *PL* 466. For Raz, see "The Rule of Law and its Virtue" in Raz, *The Authority of Law: Essays on Law and Morality* (Oxford, Clarendon Press, 1997) 210; "The Politics of the Rule of Law" in Raz, *Ethics in the Public Domain: Essays in the Morality of Law and Politics* (Oxford, Clarendon Press, 1994) 354; and, most recently, "On the Authority and Interpretation of Constitutions: Some Preliminaries" in Larry Alexander, (ed.), *Constitutionalism: Philosophical Foundations* (Cambridge, Cambridge University Press, 1998) 152. In what follows, I generally take Craig's account as a definitive account of Raz's positivist position. My critique latches at times onto certain nuances in Craig's argument which may not be exactly Raz's, but I will mention only some possible differences below. My view is that the tensions on which I focus are all to be found in any version of that positivist position, though they may manifest themselves differently following differences in nuance.

In personal communications, Craig has objected strongly to my categorisation of his own position on the rule of law as positivistic. Indeed, he claims to be a Dworkinian substantivist – a protagonist of the common law camp – and points to his articulation of a substantive basis for judicial review in his textbook on administrative law: see Paul Craig, *Administrative Law* (London, Sweet & Maxwell, 1994, third edition), Chapter 1, esp. 17–40 and in *Public Law and Democracy in the United Kingdom and the United States of America* (Oxford, Clarendon Press, 1994). However, the either/or structure of his argument – either a formal conception of the rule of law or a substantive theory of justice – is one which only a positivist should make as it attempts to disqualify by definition any theory of the rule of law that goes beyond law's formal attributes. As I will show below, it follows from this way of setting up the debate that a theory of adjudication has to be substantive in Craig's sense. In other words, there is no inconsistency between Craig's own development of a substantive theory of judicial review and his positivist commitments and this may well be evidence of the fact that, as I suggested in a review of *Public Law and Democracy in the United Kingdom and the United States of America*, it is not clear that he has moved beyond Dicey's shadow; see David Dyzenhaus, "Dicey's Shadow" (1993) 43 *University of Toronto Law Journal* 127.

[7] Craig, "Formal and Substantive Conceptions of the Rule of Law: An Analytical Framework", 467.

conduct so as to enable a person to plan his or her life, etc.); and the temporal dimension of the enacted norm (was it prospective or retrospective, etc.). Formal conceptions of the rule of law do not however seek to pass judgment upon the actual content of the law itself. They are not concerned with whether the law was in that sense a good law or a bad law, provided that the formal precepts of the rule of law were themselves met.[8]

A substantive conception, in contrast, for example, Ronald Dworkin's, derives its theory of the rule of law from an account of justice. "On this view the rule of law is nothing more or less than a synonym for a rights-based theory of law and adjudication".[9]

Craig suggests that there are two main reasons for preferring a formal account. The first is that, while a substantive conception of the rule of law will attempt to incorporate the formal rule of law values which legal positivism identifies as the values of the rule of law, they do not have any independent status in that conception. Put differently, the formal values are subordinated to the substantive values.[10] And that tells us that substantive conceptions rest not on an account of the rule of law but on a full and controversial theory of justice which is better debated undistracted by claims about the rule of law. In this regard, Craig suggests that the issue is not just clarity since the phrase "the rule of law" has weight from its historical usage – a "weight and force of its own" – which necessarily puts in a bad light governmental action contrary to the rule of law. Hence, there is something politically dangerous in a claim that such a substantive position is also a theory of the rule of law, since it seeks a weight for itself to which it is not entitled.[11]

Second, what gives force to the rule of law is that it is "rightly regarded as a central principle of constitutional governance",[12] but we lose our understanding of what is involved in governance under the rule of law if we are not clear about its formal status. Here Craig refers to what he calls, following Raz, the "negative value of the rule of law". It is a necessary but not sufficient requirement of the rule of law that laws are enacted in accordance with the requisite procedures for producing valid law. If it were treated as sufficient it would have the effect that the fact that a law is properly enacted means that the rule of law is in place, which could lead to such obvious absurdities as saying that the rule of law exists when a dictator causes to be enacted an enabling law which gives him unfettered discretion to do what he likes.[13] The other important aspect of the rule of law is that the laws properly enacted "should be capable of guiding one's conduct in

[8] Craig, "Formal and Substantive Conceptions of the Rule of Law: An Analytical Framework", 467.

[9] Ibid., 477–9, at 479.

[10] Ibid., 478, and see Craig's third point against Trevor Allan at 482.

[11] Ibid., 478, 487.

[12] Ibid., 487.

[13] Ibid., 469 and see Raz, "The Rule of Law and its Virtue", 212–13. The specific example is mine and refers to Hitler's Enabling Act of 1933, *Das Gesetz zur Behebung der Not von Volk und Reich (Ermächtigungsgesetz)* 24 March 1933, RGBl. S.141.

order that one can plan one's life". Other specific attributes follow from this general precept including:

> that laws should be prospective, not retrospective; that they should be relatively stable; that particular laws should be guided by open, general and clear rules; that there should be an independent judiciary; that there should be access to the courts; and that the discretion which law enforcement agencies possess should not be allowed to undermine the purposes of the relevant rules.[14]

The negative value of the rule of law is thus that though

> the law can empower the state to do all manner of things the rule of law . . . minimises the danger created by the law itself. It does so by ensuring that whatever the content of the law, at least it should be open, clear, stable, general and applied by an impartial judiciary. It would however be mistaken not to recognise the more positive side of the rule of law when viewed in this manner. Even if the actual content of the law is morally reprehensible, conformity to the rule of law will often be necessary to ensure that individuals actually comply with the demands which the law imposes.[15]

Craig can also invoke a feature of debate about the rule of law in legal theory that there is general agreement in legal theory (to which Dworkin is party) that an account of law, and thus of the rule of law, is different from an account of the requirements of justice. If there is no difference between a substantive account of the rule of law and an account of justice, then substantive accounts of the rule of law fail by a criterion they themselves accept.[16] It is this feature of the debate that provides the main challenge to antipositivist accounts of the rule of law, whatever the merits of positivist accounts. I draw attention to this feature because although I shall now argue that positivist accounts are flawed, antipositivism cannot win by default. It must still meet the challenge just articulated.

According to Craig, a positivist account of the rule of law is formal in that its primary focus is on the procedures for producing valid law. Indeed, Craig himself suggests at one point that the form/substance distinction is the same as the procedure/substance distinction.[17] And it is not substantive because it permits any substance or content to become part of the law as long as a law with that substance is enacted in accordance with the requisite procedures.

---

[14] Craig, "Formal and Substantive Conceptions of the Rule of Law: An Analytical Framework", 469.

[15] Ibid.

[16] Ibid., 487. Dworkin has always accepted this criterion; see his distinction between "two forms of political rights": "background rights, which are rights that hold in an abstract way against decisions taken by the community or the society as a whole, and more specific institutional rights that hold against a decision made by a specific institution. Legal rights may then be identified as a distinct species of a political right, that is, an institutional right to the decision of a court in its adjudicative function"; Ronald Dworkin, *Taking Rights Seriously* (London, Duckworth, 1981, 2nd impression) xii. The positivist argument is that any conception of the rule of law that goes beyond positivism cannot make this distinction, hence, as I suggested above, Craig's place in the positivist tradition.

[17] Craig, "Formal and Substantive Conceptions of the Rule of Law: An Analytical Framework", 481.

But the positivist account is substantive in one sense, given to us by the second criterion that has to be met before the rule of law is in place – that the law must be capable of guiding individual planning. This criterion is about substance since it tells us that particular laws must have a determinate substance before they do their job as law. Craig's account here follows a positivist tradition that stretches back to Thomas Hobbes in requiring that the substance must be one which is determinable as a matter of fact – the tests for identifying the content of the law must, that is, be capable of being applied without resort to moral argument.[18] And, as in Hobbes, the specific attributes of the rule of law that follow from a formal conception of the rule of law, including the existence of an independent and impartial judiciary, are attributes that serve to make the law better able to meet its aspiration – to be law capable of effective guidance for legal subjects because it has a factually determinable content.

This understanding of the rule of law is highly problematic, especially in administrative law. The problems all arise out of the unstable relationship between the two aspects of a formal conception of the rule of law: the claim that the formality of the rule of law lies in the fact that it specifies procedures for enacting and finding valid law without connecting the procedures to substance; and the insistence that the point of such procedures is to specify a substance, but not one from a particular set derived from a theory of justice.

Recall that the second aspect is considered crucial in order to provide effective guidance for legal subjects, guidance which they would not have if, for example, a dictator causes to be enacted an enabling law which gives him unfettered discretion to do what he likes. However, this dictatorial situation is exactly the situation which A.V. Dicey, Lord Hewart and F.A. Hayek thought characterised administrative law, since legislatures in common law legal orders took to delegating unfettered authority to the administrative agencies and officials charged with implementing the programmes of the administrative state. Those subject to the authority of this state seemed to Dicey, Hewart and Hayek subject to the arbitrary authority of the officials who staffed it and not to the rule of law.

There is, as Craig notes in his discussion of Dicey, an ambiguity in the idea of arbitrariness, as it is not always clear whether Dicey meant by it lack of determinate content and thus arbitrariness in the formal sense of unforseeability of what will be decided, or substantive arbitrariness and thus arbitrariness from the perspective of a theory of justice.

Craig suggests that the formal sense of arbitrariness is what Dicey intended. Dicey's first pillar of the rule of law follows John Austin's legal positivism in holding that the legislature is sovereign in the sense of having legally unlimited law-making power so that judges are required to defer to all clear expressions of legislative will. So it seems crucial to Dicey's understanding of the rule of law that law has a determinate content and that one should be able – Dicey's second

[18] See Joseph Raz, "Legal Positivism and the Sources of Law", in Raz, *The Authority of Law: Essays on Law and Morality* 37, 3–40.

pillar of the rule of law – to have that law determined by an impartial body of judges.[19]

Craig is right that there is an ambiguity here and indeed it infects in varying degrees the work of Hewart and Hayek as well. All three belonged to the libertarian camp of liberalism but seemed unable at times to decide whether what was *legally* wrong with the administrative state was its assault on laissez-faire or the fact that so much discretion was given to officials to achieve its goals.[20]

There is, however, a significant difficulty in supposing that Dicey thought that the only concern from the point of view of the rule of law is formal arbitrariness, since Dicey also seemed to find a third pillar of the rule of law in the constitutional morality made up of rights protected by the common law. Craig deals with this difficulty by saying that Dicey's point was not that the rule of law has to have a substantive content equivalent to this constitutional morality. Rather, what Dicey meant is that if you wished to have such a constitutional morality, the common law was better suited to protecting it than methods adopted by other legal systems.[21]

Craig's explanation of the role of Dicey's third pillar of the rule of law makes Dicey into what current legal theory describes as an inclusive or incorporationist positivist. But, as I will now show, this explanation is far from helpful to Craig's account of formalism.

Briefly put, legal positivism today divides between exclusive and inclusive legal positivists. Exclusive legal positivists say that the law and the rule of law have to be understood in the formal way we have seen Craig outline. As a result, when interpretation of the law has to rely on moral considerations and arguments, it follows necessarily that the interpreter has stepped beyond the law.

Inclusive legal positivists, in contrast, say that if the law requires the interpreter to rely on moral considerations and arguments, then the conclusion of the best argument as to what morality requires is the law. They reckon that they retain their place in the positivist tradition by emphasising that it is an entirely contingent matter whether such considerations and arguments have a secure place in a particular legal order through incorporation over time in a fashion recognised by the formal tests for law.

Craig has so far refrained from stating his views on this dispute between legal positivists, in which Raz is the most powerful proponent of what seems now to be the minority exclusive position.[22] At times he seems attracted to Raz's position which sticks to the claim about law's formal nature by positing an ever increasing scope for legally uncontrolled judicial and official discretion, which

---

[19] Craig, "Formal and Substantive Conceptions of the Rule of Law: An Analytical Framework", 470–3.

[20] See F.A. Hayek, *The Constitution of Liberty* (London, Routledge, 1993) 247–9, and Lord Hewart, *The New Despotism* (London, Ernest Benn Limited, 1929) 44–6.

[21] Craig, "Formal and Substantive Conceptions of the Rule of Law: An Analytical Framework", 473–4.

[22] Ibid., 483, including note 44 at that page.

means that formal law plays little role in interpretation.[23] At other times, most notably in his critique of the claim that the ultra vires doctrine is the foundation of judicial review, Craig tells a story about the role of the common law as foundation which seems more in keeping with inclusive legal positivism.[24] But if one takes the view of the tradition that stretches from Hobbes to Bentham, rather than the perspective of H.L.A. Hart's postwar amendments to Austinian positivism, it does not matter which of these options one adopts since both undermine the spirit of the positivist tradition.

As we have seen, Raz's exclusive legal positivism retains its commitment to the formal view of the law and of the rule of law by asserting that the role of formal law is severely limited in legal interpretation. He suggests that a realistic understanding of interpretation recognises that it involves the exercise of discretion or law-making power. Administrative law seems then to be a situation in which discretion is piled on top of discretion – judicial discretion on top of official discretion. The result is, from the positivist perspective, the state of "administrative lawlessness" which led, according to Lord Hewart, to the new despotism. The difference between Raz, on the one hand, and Hewart, Hayek and Dicey, on the other, is only that Raz says that one should not make a fetish of the rule of law – justice might well require its sacrifice.[25] But that concession results in a picture of legal order as a hierarchy of officials with discretion in which law understood as positive law ceases to play any significant role.[26]

Inclusive legal positivism also loses its grip on law as positive law. With Raz it accepts that, in a legal order like that of the United Kingdom, a formal understanding of law and of the rule of law might do little, even no work. Unlike Raz, it holds that a substantive account of law and of the rule of law might well tell us what the law of a legal order is. As already suggested, its connection to formalism is only through its claim that not all legal orders necessarily incorporate such substantive accounts. Further, those that do incorporate a substantive account do so because, as a matter of contingent historical fact, the formal tests for law have come to include substantive moral criteria for the identification of law.

But there is hardly any difference in character between this kind of inclusive legal positivism and a Dworkinian substantive account when one is operating in a legal order which contingently incorporates moral criteria among its criteria for the validity of law. In particular, from the perspective of a judge working in

---

[23] Craig, "Formal and Substantive Conceptions of the Rule of Law: An Analytical Framework", 483–4.

[24] Paul Craig, "Ultra Vires and the Foundations of Judicial Review" (1998) 57 *CLJ* 63 and pp. 47–71. Craig's critique is directed at Christopher Forsyth's argument for ultra vires, which I discuss below.

[25] Raz, "The Rule of Law and its Virtue", 226–9, where Hayek is his target.

[26] As Hermann Heller pointed out of Hans Kelsen's legal positivism; Heller, *Staatslehre* (1934) in Christoph Müller (ed.), Heller, *Gesammelte Schriften* (Tübingen: J.C.B. Mohr (Paul Siebeck), 2nd edn., 1992) vol iii, 79, 304–5. For discussion, see David Dyzenhaus, *Legality and Legitimacy: Carl Schmitt, Hermann Heller and Hans Kelsen in Weimar* (Oxford, Clarendon Press, 1997) chapters 3 and 4. F.A. Hayek made the same point much later than Heller – see F.A. Hayek, *Law, Legislation and Liberty* (London, Routledge & Kegan Paul, 1982) ii, 47–56.

such a legal order, which is the perspective in play when Dicey outlines his second and third pillars of the rule of law, judges are duty bound to apply the substantive theory of justice articulated in the common law. From their perspective, the rule of law is substantive.

As Trevor Allan points out, it follows that Craig's attempt to enlist Dicey in the formalist camp fails to account for much of what Dicey says:

> To interpret Dicey's discussion as presenting a purely formal conception of the rule of law – or, even more prosaically, as a hymn to mere legality – is to misunderstand his theory by overlooking its context. The purpose of subjecting officials to the jurisdiction of the ordinary courts, applying primarily the rules of private law, was to make government subservient to principles of justice which protected fundamental interests in personal liberty. A formal equality between citizen and officials would thereby be transmuted into a substantive equality, imposed by the faithful application of a body of consistent legal principle. Moreover, there were limits to the ability of statute to undermine the rule of law, by conferring extensive discretionary power on officials: statutes would be interpreted by common law judges, familiar with the values underlying the private law . . .[27]

But while Craig might be wrong in his explanation of the role of Dicey's third pillar of the rule of law, his explanation does have the merit of seeking to rescue Dicey from falling into the trap of proposing a substantive theory of justice disguised as an account of the rule of law. To equate a general account of the rule of law with the principles of the common law of nineteenth century England seems at best parochial, at worst an attempt to smuggle a political vision of the superiority of private order into legal theory.[28] And the ambiguity in Dicey's understanding of arbitrariness together with the fact that his first pillar of the rule of law requires complete judicial deference to the clearly expressed will of the legislature, are evidence of his own sense of the problems encountered by his account of the rule of law, as a substantive theory.

It is more productive, in my view, to understand Dicey as caught in an irresolvable tension between a formalistic positivism, which he inherited via John Austin from Jeremy Bentham, and a common law tradition of judicial antipositivism. His formalistic positivism is expressed in the first pillar of the rule of law, which requires utter judicial deference to clearly expressed legislative intent. His judicial antipositivism is expressed in an understanding of the importance of the second pillar of the rule of law – access to the courts – as instrumental to access to the third pillar – access to the constitutional morality of the common law.

In other words, Dicey lays the foundation for two very different understandings of the rule of law and of the judicial role in upholding it. Two sorts of judges can find a basis in his account: those who think their job is to make the

---

[27] Trevor Allan, "The Rule of Law as the Rule of Reason: Consent and Constitutionalism", (1999) 115 *LQR* 221, at 243.

[28] See Judith N. Shklar, "Political Theory and the Rule of Law" in Allan C. Hutchinson and Patrick Monahan (eds), *The Rule of Law: Ideal or Ideology* (Toronto, Carswell, 1987) 1.

law live up to an aspiration to be formal law and those who seek to make the law live up to the aspirations of a certain vision of the common law. The ambiguity which Craig rightly detects in Dicey's account of arbitrariness also affects Dicey's account of the judicial role since that role is pulled in two different directions – towards the formalistic understanding of legislative intent and towards the substantive account of the morality of the common law. Judges who take seriously everything he seems to say about the judicial role will find themselves caught in what I have called in other work a "pragmatic contradiction".[29]

In such a situation, the choice which judges exercise in deciding between the formal vision of law and the substantive vision seems a highly political one. Craig recognises this, as he concludes his essay on the rule of law by saying that "it is of course open to public lawyers, and indeed, anyone else, to choose between the contending views of the rule of law presented above".[30] He also suggests that it would be "intellectually honest" if those who put forward substantive views would be clear about exactly what their substantive account of justice is.[31]

This suggestion strikes me as odd since the lawyers who put forward substantive accounts of the rule of law, on Craig's classification, have generally argued that all such accounts are political and thus have felt it incumbent to flesh out the politics of their own accounts. The call to come clean about politics is better addressed to those positivistic accounts of the judicial role and the rule of law which seek to make an apolitical entry into a fray in which a foundation for judicial review has to be sought in a political theory of the rule of law.

However, while odd, the suggestion is not untypical of legal positivism in this century. For positivists have sought to finesse the political debate about the rule of law by claiming that it should take place on a terrain established by a prior allegedly apolitical argument about the nature of law. And then it somehow turns out that their account of the rule of law is both politically superior to others and immune from political challenge because its foundation is not political.[32]

This curious stance does not come about because of any desire on the part of legal positivism to perform some theoretical or political sleight of hand. Rather its origins lie in the way in which legal positivism has lost its moorings in this

---

[29] David Dyzenhaus, *Hard Cases in Wicked Legal Systems: South African Law in the Perspective of Legal Philosophy* (Oxford, Clarendon Press, 1991) 236–8.
[30] Craig, "Formal and Substantive Accounts of the Rule of Law: An Analytical Framework", 487.
[31] Ibid.
[32] See my discussion of Kelsen in *Legality and Legitimacy: Carl Schmitt, Hans Kelsen and Hermann Heller in Weimar*, chapter 3.
Nils Jansen has suggested to me that different accounts may be more or less political, and that the formal account may be the least political and focus on values which all accounts agree to be values of the rule of law. Substantive accounts would then be accounts which departed from the consensus because they wish to add some other values. However, once formal accounts are rooted in political theory – as I argue below they have to be to make sense – they are no less political than any substantive account. In addition, though I do not argue for this claim here, the role that so called formal values – e.g. certainty or the principle against retrospective legal change – play in an account of the rule of law will depend significantly on the political theory underpinning the account.

century, and the best illustration of this is in Christopher Forsyth's attempt to show that the ultra vires doctrine – one based in the intent of the legislature – is the foundation of judicial review in the United Kingdom.[33]

Forsyth, following Sir William Wade,[34] has sought to put the first pillar of Dicey's account of the rule of law – judicial deference to legislative will – on a better theoretical foundation than Dicey's Austinian positivism, in which the central institution is a legally unconstrained, sovereign law-maker. Forsyth finds this foundation, via the work of R.T.E. Latham, in Hans Kelsen.[35]

As Latham noted, Kelsen posits a basic rule or *Grundnorm* as the foundational rule of any legal system. In Latham's summary:

> The *Grundnorm* is the ground of validity of the system which depends on it, and its supremacy constitutes the assurance that there will be no conflict within that system. It may therefore be said to embody and express the formal unity of the system. From the point of view of their form, of their validity, all other rules in the system are particularizations of the *Grundnorm*.[36]

What this tells us, according to Latham, is that the Austinian idea of legally unlimited sovereignty - the "tacit jurisprudence" of "English constitutional writings" – is wrong. Austin's understanding of sovereignty, which identifies the sovereign as a legally unlimited legislature, is at best a "legitimate special case under Kelsen's general theory of the *Grundnorm*". But even this is doubtful, since the designation of such a sovereign "must include the statement of rules for the ascertainment of his will, and these rules, since their observance is a condition of the validity of his legislation, are rules of law logically prior to him".[37]

Of course, the possibility remains that the idea of a legally unlimited sovereign is really meant to refer to the situation of a legal order where there are only formal and no substantive limits on sovereign authority. There the sovereign's commands will be recognised as law as long as he complies with certain minimal criteria pertaining to the steps that have to be followed in the law-making process. In such a legal order, it would follow that the only legitimate basis for judicial review of administrative action is something like the ultra vires doctrine, which says that the judges must enforce only those legal limits on administrative action which the legislature intended them to enforce. That is, since the

---

[33] See Christopher Forsyth, "Of Fig Leaves and Fairy Tales: The Ultra Vires Doctrine, the Sovereignty of Parliament and Judicial Review" (1996) 55 *CLJ* 122 and p. 29 above. What follows draws partly on my detailed response to Forsyth – David Dyzenhaus, "Reuniting the Brain: The Democratic Basis of Judicial Review" (1998) 9 *PLR* 98.

[34] See H.W.R. Wade and C.F. Forsyth, *Administrative Law* (Oxford, Clarendon Press, 1994, 7th edn.).

[35] R.T.E. Latham, *The Law and the Commonwealth* (Oxford, Oxford University Press, 1949) 522–5. (The book is a reprint of an essay first published in 1937). For reliance on Latham by Sir William Wade, see his classic "The Basis of Legal Sovereignty" (1955) *CLJ* 172, 187–8, and more explicitly, Forsyth, "Of Fig Leaves and Fairy Tales: The Ultra Vires Doctrine, the Sovereignty of Parliament and Judicial Review", 137–9 and pp. 43–4. Peter Oliver is engaged in research which will provide a full account of Latham's innovative work.

[36] Latham, *The Law and the Commonwealth*, 523.

[37] Ibid., footnotes omitted.

legislature delegated authority to public officials, the limits on their authority are exactly the limits intended in that delegation. For judges to conclude otherwise, for example, by finding limits in common law principles, would amount to an illegitimate arrogation of authority.

But Latham's point also leaves open the possibility that the limits on sovereign authority are substantive, a possibility explored by one of the substantivists in the United Kingdom debate, Sir John Laws, who finds those limits in the common law.[38]

Forsyth argues for the first possibility but his argument is flawed. He claims that Laws's substantivist approach is inherently "inconsistent with . . . Latham's views":

> The rules that Latham considers to be logically prior to the effective expression of the legislative will are rules of manner and form that determine *how* that legislative will is to be expressed. They have no substantive content, *i.e.* they do not limit the power of the legislature *operating in accordance with those rules*.[39]

But nothing in Kelsen, or in Latham's account of Kelsen, licences Forsyth's inference. Just as Hart's later articulation of the same idea in the rule of recognition takes no stand on the issue whether the rule of recognition of a particular legal order includes substantive criteria among the criteria for the validity of law, so Kelsen's *Grundnorm* is agnostic on this issue.[40]

Forsyth does offer some political reasons for preferring ultra vires as the foundation of legitimate judicial review rather than common law substantive accounts. These include the claims that if judges base their review authority in the common law this will be seen by a democratic electorate as a political power grab by unelected officials, that an assertion of such authority in a confrontation with the legislature will lead to a political row whose consequence will be the politicisation of judicial appointments, and, more generally, that the ultra vires doctrine encourages an appropriately modest or restrained judicial stance.[41] And all of these claims are clearly linked to Forsyth's sense that ultra vires is the least intrusive way of understanding the limits on legislative authority in a

---

[38] Sir John Laws, "Law and Democracy" [1995] *PL* 72, 86 and see Forsyth, "Of Fig Leaves and Fairy Tales: The Ultra Vires Doctrine, the Sovereignty of Parliament and Judicial Review", 137–8 and pp. 42–3 above.

[39] Forsyth, "Of Fig Leaves and Fairy Tales: The Ultra Vires Doctrine, the Sovereignty of Parliament and Judicial Review", 138 and p. 43 above, his emphasis.

[40] See Hart's own remarks on this topic in his (posthumous) Postcript to P. Bulloch and J. Raz (eds), Hart, *The Concept of Law* (Oxford, Clarendon Press, 2nd edn. 1994) and see Kelsen, "Wesen und Entwicklung der Staatsgerichtsbarkeit", in Hans Klecatsky et. al. (eds). *Die Wiener Rechtstheoretische Schule:Schriften von Hans Kelsen, Adolf Merkl, Alfed Verdross* (Vienna, Europa Verlag, 1968) 1813, 1851–4. Indeed, Forsyth and Laws seem to make the same mistake of equating the constitution, written or unwritten, with the ultimate legal rule of a legal order. See Joseph Raz, "On the Authority and Interpretation of Constitutions" in Larry Alexander, (ed.), *Constitutionalism: Philosphical Foundations* (Cambridge, Cambridge University Press, 1998) 152, 160–2.

[41] Forsyth, "Of Fig Leaves and Fairy Tales: The Ultra Vires Doctrine, the Sovereignty of Parliament and Judicial Review", 136–9 and pp. 41–5.

democracy where judges have not been given by statute an explicit basis for test-ing legislative intent against substantive principles.[42]

However, insofar as these claims rest on concerns about judges' adopting a political role, they have no weight if they are advanced within a debate in which all conceptions of the rule of law are political. This is why we also find the thought that the role Forsyth advocates is somehow apolitical because it derives from a correct – i.e. formal – understanding of the rule of law. But not only do his theoretical reference points in Kelsen and Latham fail to support that deriva-tion, he also wishes to assert that his account is the appropriate one for a demo-cratic polity (though he provides no argument for this assertion).

Most damaging of all to Forsyth's position is that he approves of the stance taken by English courts following *Anisminic*[43] of reading out of statutes the ouster clauses which sought to preclude judges from exercising their review authority. And his approval seems to be predicated in part on the fact that this stance permits the courts to go on imposing the common law principles of nat-ural justice on statutory bodies.[44]

Forsyth is compelled by his claims about the justification for judicial review to assert that the basis for this stance is ultra vires. But an ouster clause is a direct statutory command to courts to refrain from regarding themselves as the ulti-mate interpreters of the law. To invoke a statutory basis for review in order to evade the statutory command in the ouster clause not only begs the question of what authorises this judicial exercise of power, but seems on its face incoherent. And so much is granted by Wade in an account of *Anisminic* on which Forsyth relies. For Wade says that the *Anisminic* approach to interpretation involved the judges in an act of "disobedience" of Parliament.[45]

In Wade's view, the judges are justified in taking that stance because they are preserving a constitutional basis for review – a "constitutional fundamental" which even a "sovereign parliament cannot abolish".[46] The judges, "with their eye on the long term and the rule of law, have made it their business to preserve a deeper constitutional logic, based on their repugnance to allowing any subor-dinate authority to obtain uncontrollable power".[47]

This point manifests the ambiguity we saw earlier between lack of control or arbitrariness in the sense of lack of formal constraints and arbitrariness in the sense of lack of substantive restraints. But if, as both Forsyth and Wade seem to grant, among the legal constraints on which judges have their eye are the

---

[42] Ibid., 140 and pp. 45–6 above.

[43] *Anismimic Ltd.* v. *Foreign Compensation Commission* [1969] 2 AC 147.

[44] Forsyth, "Of Fig Leaves and Fairy Tales: The Ultra Vires Doctrine, the Sovereignty of Parliament and Judicial Review", 124–5 and pp. 31–3 above.

[45] See Forsyth, ibid., footnote 29, 130, referring to Wade and Forsyth, *Administrative Law*, 734–9. (In footnote 1 at 122 of "Of Fig Leaves and Fairy Tales: The Ultra Vires Doctrine, the Sovereignty of Parliament and Judicial Review", Forsyth says that, despite his co-authorship of the book, he has "no desire to assume any credit for passages . . . substantially unchanged from earlier editions". But the scope of this disclaimer cannot include footnote 29). See p. 36 n. 29 above.

[46] Wade and Forsyth, *Administrative Law*, 737.

[47] Ibid., 738.

constraints of common law principles, then the constitutional morality of the rule of law goes well beyond rules of manner and form. For the rule of law then includes substantive principles.

Forsyth seems to have two responses to this problem. First, he offers a version of Raz's and Craig's challenge to substantive accounts of the rule of law. He says that, if the claim that the common law is the basis of judges' review power is to be coherent, it must ultimately be the strong claim that judges can, without any statutory basis for doing so, resist even the clearest legislative derogations from the common law.[48] His challenge, that is, is not so much one that directly supports the formalist account as asserts that no alternative can work. Any substantive alternative must ultimately rest not in a theory of law but in a theory of justice to which all formal elements of law are subordinate. I will deal with his challenge at the same time as I deal with Raz's and Craig's claim that alternative accounts of the rule of law cannot stop short of being a full theory of justice.

Forsyth's second response is that the judicial stand in *Anisminic* is about preserving the idea that there are legal limits, but not any particular legal limits. The common law does no justificatory work here. Rather, once it is seen that the ouster clause can legitimately be read out of the statute, then there is a question of what fills the void of legal controls; and common law principles are merely among the candidates. But as both Craig and I have pointed out, this response only deepens the incoherence of the ultra vires doctrine, since its application gives no guidance to judges at all. It replaces the unfettered discretion which the legislature sought to give officials with the unfettered discretion of judges.[49]

Forsyth's formalism has much in common with the tradition of legal positivism. And it can be made more coherent in the light of that tradition, though one has to reach back to pre-Austinian positivism – to Bentham – for such coherence to be achieved. But this coherence comes at a price since Bentham's legal positivism is best understood as a subordinate though important component of a general theory of law and politics in which the political component – the theory of justice – is dominant. For Bentham is clear that legal institutions are to be structured in order to promote what I call a culture of reflection.[50]

---

[48] Forsyth, "Of Fig Leaves and Fairy Tales: The Ultra Vires Doctrine, the Sovereignty of Parliament and Judicial Review", 137–9 and pp. 43–5.

[49] Craig, "Ultra Vires and the Foundations of Judicial Review", 78–9 and pp. 60–1; Dyzenhaus, "Reuniting the Brain: The Democratic Basis of Judicial Review", 107. In his comments at the Cambridge Conference on "The Foundations of Judicial Review", Forsyth repeated his claim that his position on ultra vires is supported by the decision by the Appellate Division of South Africa in *Staatspresident en andere* v. *United Democratic Front en 'n ander* 1988 (4) SA 830 (A). He said that it was the rejection of ultra vires by the majority that led to their pernicious conclusion. It is important to know that Forsyth's appeal to this and other South African examples is problematic. The leading article on the decision, while highly critical of it, rejects the ultra vires doctrine – see Andrew Breitenbach, "The Justifications for Judicial Review" (1992) 8 *South African Journal on Human Rights* 512. In "Reuniting the Brain", I deal with this issue and also show how Forsyth's interpretation of the South African constitutional cases of the 1950s is controversial. Indeed, I argue that these cases might be better interpreted as undermining Forsyth's position.

[50] Here and below I rely on earlier work: David Dyzenhaus, "Law as Justification: Etienne Mureinik's Conception of Legal Culture" (1998) 14 *South African Journal on Human Rights* 11.

The idea of law as promoting a culture of reflection works in the service of a radical democratic theory, in which statute law accurately reflects through the medium of the legislature the preferences of the majority. The judicial duty is to apply the law as it is and the citizen's duty to obey the law as it is.[51] For Bentham law (properly so called) is statute law, the reflection of the results of public rational reason, while the common law is the subjective opinions of judges masquerading as public reason. Judges are therefore to be disempowered as far as possible by depriving their judgments of legal force, except as between the parties.

It is because the political component is dominant in the general theory that Bentham is able to declare the common law to be an institutional mistake. And it is the same component that leads him to express even greater aversion to what he regards as the arbitrariness of common law adjudication writ large. For Bentham detests the kind of constitutionalism which writes individual rights and liberties into law and gives judges the authority to invalidate statutes in light of their understandings of these values.

So it is in Bentham that we find unadulterated what I called earlier the standard package of positivism, proceduralism, and democracy. Democracy is fundamental because it provides the institutional mechanisms for ascertaining what the majority thinks will make them happy. Law provides the instrument for implementing the policies which reflect that majority sense. And the procedures for determining what that law is should be entirely subservient to the goal of accurate reflection. In Bentham, the relationship between the formality of his conception of law and the idea that law, to do its job, must have a substance is entirely stable. But it is stable because formal values are rooted in a democratic political theory which informs the structure of legal institutions and guides the behaviour of actors within those institutions.

Since the formal aspects of Bentham's understanding of the rule of law are entirely subordinate to his political theory, it may seem both that he falls on the substantive side of Craig's formal/substantive divide and that, therefore, he does not exemplify the standard democratic package. I will return to this point below and simply remark for the moment that Bentham's theory of justice is not substantive in the sense of seeking to fill in a set of substantive principles of justice, since its point is to permit such principles to emerge through the procedures of democracy. It is substantive then only in that it is political since it subordinates its account of legal form to its account of democratic politics.

However, ever since Austin insisted that the positivist distinction between law as it is and law as it ought to be is a conceptual rather than a political one, positivism has lost its moorings in political theory. In Kelsen's and Hart's hands, it

---

[51] Bentham does countenance the institutional possibility of a judge finding the law as it is to be unjust, not applying it to the parties before him, and informing a legislative committee of the problem detected. He can countenance this possibility for the same reason that Hobbes is prepared to give equity such a large role in judicial intepretation – the judge's decision is to have no legal force beyond a ruling about the particular case.

is advertised as the value free or scientific way of understanding the law. Since that commitment to value freedom requires that every substance that is formally incorporated into law be acknowledged as law properly so called, even substances which are in tension with the role of effective guidance are given legal status. It is no longer open to legal positivists to say that the common law or rights-based constitutionalism are institutional mistakes from the perspective of legal as well as political theory – not law (properly so called) because they are politically misguided.

However, positivists are still often tempted by the political past of their tradition to say exactly these sorts of things, as one can see in Forsyth's attempt to exclude Laws's substantivist view, his aversion to the common law as the basis for judicial review, and the democratic credentials he claims for his formalism.[52] I am not, however, suggesting that all positivism needs to do to supply a foundation for judicial review is to moor itself once again in a Benthamite theory of justice. From Bentham's perspective, the administrative state is surely at least as big a mistake as the common law since it licenses official discretion just as the common law licenses judicial discretion. The mistake here lies not in adopting redistributive political goals but in implementing them through the administrative state.

But if it is the case that the administrative state is required in order to implement those goals, then, as lawyers associated with the London School of Economics and Political Science discovered, there is only one way to be true to Bentham's legacy. They argued that to pile judicial discretion on top of official discretion not only compounds the problem but invites interference by judges who are at best ignorant of and at worst hostile to the programs of redistributive welfarism. The problem of discretion was then solved, not by judicially imposed controls, but by treating administrative officials as part of the legislative process.[53] But these lawyers also discovered that unrestrained public power

[52] Moreover, the distinction between legal and political theory made by contemporary positivists has, as already suggested, a certain kind of political force. Just as the claim that one's political theory is also the theory of the rule of law seeks political advantage by claiming a weight that attaches to the rule of law, so the claim that one's theory of the rule of law is scientific claims a weight that attaches to science. And that involves a kind of political move. For how is it not political to claim to be able to put the rule of law on a secure footing above the controversial claims of substantive political argument, thus ruling out of court the arguments of positivism's opponents?

[53] This stance might well be able to find a theoretical correlate in Hart's legal theory. Roger Cotterrell rightly points out that in Hart's legal theory judicial discretion is to be understood no differently from official discretion and that the common law then provides no "special authority for judicial review"; Roger Cotterrell, "Judicial Review and Legal Theory" in Genevra Richardson and Hazel Genn (eds), *Administrative Law and Government Action: The Courts and Alternative Mechanisms of Review* (Oxford, Clarendon Press, 1994) 13, 26. It must surely follow that any legislative delegation of authority to an official rather than a judge should be taken as definitive of the issue of who should decide. Cotterrell's point depends on imputing to Hart's legal theory a political agenda, however he himself conceives it. In my view, this imputation is the only way to make sense of contemporary positivism, whether of the Hartian or the Kelsenian variety. (See chapter 4 of my *Legality and Legitimacy: Carl Schmitt, Hans Kelsen and Hermann Heller in Weimar* for an attempt to locate Kelsen's Pure Theory of law willy-nilly in a democratic theory.) But one has to be clear that it is at odds with the self-understanding of contemporary positivists and that this self-

can be as problematic for the citizens in whose interests it is supposed to work as unrestrained private power. They thus have mostly joined in a project of trying to conceive of appropriate legal controls on administrative action, controls which require the institution of judicial review even though more modestly conceived.[54]

But positivist legal theory plays no part in this project, I think for the reason suggested by my analysis so far. Positivism cannot supply a foundation for judicial review since it is politically committed to minimising the role of judges in legal order. Positivism should treat as illegitimate conceptions of the judicial role which depend on a view of law different from the positivist one described by Lon L. Fuller as a "one-way projection of authority originating with government and imposing itself upon the citizen".[55] The constraints on law-making power are only those that assist in giving law its determinate content, with the whole process legitimised if, and only if, that content reflects the judgment of the people.

Once detached from those political commitments positivism is consistent with any role for judges you like, even one totally antithetical to the positivist tradition. It becomes a purely formal or empty doctrine about the nature of law, one which contains only the weakest of traces of what was once a vibrant project of political and legal reform.

We have seen Craig suggest that any account of judicial review that tries to be a little bit substantive cannot avoid going all the way, thus collapsing into a controversial theory of justice. Since even substantivists agree that a theory of the rule of law must be somewhat distinct from a theory of justice, they fail on their own terms. And we have seen Forsyth make an analogous criticism when he says that any coherent attempt to found judicial review in the constitutional morality of the common law must be prepared to give judges the authority to strike down legislation which violates that morality.

In the next section, I will agree with Craig that Dworkin's account of the rule of law cannot meet the positivist challenge and that any similar account must likewise fail. Here my focus will be Trevor Allan's recent essay on the rule of law, which defends, via Lon Fuller, a Dworkinian approach to the rule of law.[56]

understanding has real effects within their theories, for example, the agnosticism about formal or substantive accounts of the rule of law mentioned above.

[54] This story is well told by Carol Harlow and Richard Rawlings, *Law and Administration* (London, Butterworths, 1997, 2nd edition), who also present an imaginative project for reconceiving administrative law. As Michael Taggart notes in his laudatory review of that book, there are still some Benthamite holdouts, in the United Kingdom J.A.G. Griffith and in Canada Harry Arthurs – "Reinvented Government, Traffic Lights, and the Convergence of Public and Private Law" [1999] *PL* 124. Taggart also observes that there is some confusion in administrative law writing about how different positions fit into the positivist/anti-positivist categories. Harlow and Rawlings, for example, categorise "red light" theorists, those opposed to the administrative state, as positivists, while those who are on the Benthamite side of things – who show a "green light" to the State – are not so categorised; 125, note 3. My argument in this essay aims in part to show why such confusions arise.

[55] Lon L. Fuller, *The Morality of Law* (New Haven, Yale University Press, rev. edn., 1969) 204. For the same point, see Cotterrell, "Judicial Review and Legal Theory", 13.

[56] "The Rule of Law as the Rule of Reason: Consent and Constitutionalism".

However, I will argue that one can meet the challenge only if one treats Fuller as terminus rather than detour.

We have seen that Craig detects an ambiguity in Dicey's understanding of the evil of arbitrariness, whether he meant arbitrariness in the sense of unforsee-ability or arbitrariness from the perspective of a substantive account of justice. I suggested that this ambiguity is located in Dicey's understanding of judicial review, whether it is directed towards the formal pillar of the rule of law – def-erence to facts about legislative intent – or to the substantive pillar – the consti-tutional morality of the common law. This ambiguity is not, however, just a fact about Dicey. It is to be found in all discussions of the rule of law which assume that there is a distinction between a theory of justice and a theory of the rule of law.

In developing his substantive account of the rule of law, Trevor Allan finds the foundation for judicial review in the common law. But his ambition is to expand the idea of legality without going the length of providing a full theory of justice. He thus shares the aspiration of some positivist accounts which seek to avoid the controversial claims of political theory by finding in the rule of law a consensual basis for criticising governmental action "even when we may dis-agree about the merits of rival conceptions of justice".[57]

Allan notes that the ambiguity Craig detects in Dicey also plagues Fuller's account of the "inner morality" of law. Fuller argues that there are eight prin-ciples of legality which are inherent in the idea of law and which together make up its inner morality: generality, promulgation, non-retroactivity, clarity, non-contradiction, possibility of compliance, constancy through time, and, the one which he took to be the most complex, congruence between official action and declared rule.[58] A system which fails completely to meet one of these require-ments, or fails substantially to meet several, would not, in his view, be a legal system. It would not qualify as government under law – as government subject to the rule of law.

Fuller contrasts his understanding of law with the positivist "managerial model" which, as we have seen him claim, understands law as a "one-way pro-jection of authority originating with government and imposing itself upon the citizen." His own account of law understands it as directed towards the promo-tion of individual interaction:

> law is not, like management, a matter of directing other persons how to accomplish tasks set by a superior, but is basically a matter of providing the citizenry with a sound

[57] Allan, "The Rule of Law as the Rule of Reason: Consent and Constitutionalism", 221.

[58] These are set out in detail in Lon L. Fuller, *The Morality of Law* (New Haven, Yale University Press, rev. edn., 1969).

and stable framework for their interactions with one another, the role of government being that of standing as a guardian of the integrity of this system.[59]

But, as Allan argues, Fuller's principles can be viewed from two very different perspectives:

> The capacity of the law to provide its subjects with determinate guidance may be viewed from the perspective of the law-giver, who wishes to use the law as an instrument to achieve his purposes; or it may instead be viewed from the perspective of the law's subject, who wishes to avoid punishment for disobedience and, more generally, to use his knowledge of the law in planning and conducting his affairs safely and effectively. The ambiguity is important because the general notion of providing guidance will generate different principles according to the perspective adopted.[60]

Raz and other positivists trade on this ambiguity, converting the principles into formal principles of legality which serve to make the law into an effective means of exercising power, of implementing the objectives of the powerful. But this neglects, Allan contends, the "role of law as set of constraints and limitations on the pursuit of such objectives".[61] The rule of law provides an "overall constitutional scheme", one "quite as much concerned with ensuring that state officials – both executive and the judiciary – are able to obey the law, and required to do so, as with affording guidance to the private citizen".[62]

According to Allan, the way to resolve the ambiguity in Fuller's favour is to see how the idea of formal equality before the law is necessarily connected to substantive equality. The idea of formal equality is expressed in the requirement that laws be general in the sense that "all are subject to the law, and no one is exempted from compliance with the law, even if the law's content varies (perhaps quite unfairly) from person to person".[63] These are the formal understandings of equality and generality which positivists take to be attributes of the rule of law.

A different understanding of generality is that "similar rules govern the conduct of all citizens placed in similar circumstances".[64] Allan regards this understanding as the one which animates the idea that the rule of law provides a constitutional scheme for interaction between citizens and between citizen and government and it brings a requirement of substantive equality into the rule of law. Here is his full articulation of the connection:

> At the heart of the ideal of the rule of law, properly understood, is a principle requiring governmental action to be rationally justified in terms of some conception of the common good. The formal equality ensured by the regular and impartial application of rules to all those within their purview is supplemented by a more substantive

---

[59] Ibid., 210. For a sensitive exploration of the ideas in this passage, see Gerald J. Postema, "Implicit Law" (1994) 13 *Law and Philosophy* 361.

[60] Allan, "The Rule of Law as the Rule of Reason: Consent and Constitutionalism", 226.

[61] Ibid., 229.

[62] Ibid.

[63] Ibid., 230.

[64] Ibid.

equality, or notion of equal citizenship. The substantive principle does not prohibit the imposition of special burdens, or grant of special benefits, to particular groups or classes: it requires only that all legislative and administrative classifications should be reasonably related to legitimate, defensible public purposes. The principle of equality does not disallow discrimination between persons or groups of persons, but the relevant distinctions must be capable of a reasoned justification, whose merits will in turn be open to public debate and scrutiny. The rule of law does not, then, embody any particular theory of equal justice; but it does enforce a requirement that government should adhere faithfully and consistently to some coherent conception of justice, however controversial. It insists that all governmental acts and decisions affecting the fortunes of particular persons should be capable of justification, and be explicitly defended, on the basis of a publicly avowed, even if politically contentious, view of the common good.[65]

And Allan adds that Dworkin's understanding of the ideal of the rule of law as "integrity" best captures the way in which substantive equality is inherent in the rule of law. In Dworkin's words, citizens may insist that the state act on "a single coherent set of principles even when its citizens are divided about what the right principles of justice and fairness really are".[66]

In sum, to get rid of the ambiguity in Fuller, one has to see that equality before the law is not just equality before the formal law, but equality before the substantive vision of justice within the law.

However, I do not think that Allan has answered Craig's challenge that there is no middle way between formal/positivist and substantive accounts of the rule of law. Allan's argument is that the form of law is not mere form since it will lead to a substance. His understanding of substance is of course different from the one we saw Craig articulate on behalf of contemporary positivism, where the substance is the content of a particular law. On Allan's Dworkinian approach, the substance is the coherent conception of the common good – a vision of justice – which should inform interpretation of all the particular laws. That vision binds together – gives integrity to – the legal order.

But it is not clear that this formulation of integrity is incompatible with contemporary positivist understandings of the rule of law, especially in their inclusive versions.[67] Positivists think that they can without cost recognise that in any relatively stable society over time the law will come to express some or other

---

[65]   Ibid., 231–2, footnote omitted.

[66]   Ibid., 232; the quotation is from Ronald Dworkin, *Law's Empire* (London, Fontana, 1986) 165–6.

[67]   Allan says that this point is of little concern to him as he is interested in developing the middle way and not in whether it can be categorised as positivist. However, with Dworkin I think that there is no point in trying to develop a middle way account of the rule of law unless one also supposes that there is good reason to reject positivism. The point of a middle way account is surely to contest the (exclusive) legal positivist claim that one either has a formal theory of the rule of law or a substantive account of justice. If there is nothing wrong with positivism, one could (as Craig suggests) rest content with working out one's theory of justice. Moreover, as already indicated in the last section, there is no difference between exclusive and inclusive legal positivism on this issue. Inclusive legal positivism differs from exclusive legal positivism only in the status it is willing to grant the results of legal reasoning based on contingently incorporated morality.

vision of the common good. That vision will provide the substantive values which get implemented and enforced through the institutions which together make that society into one governed by the rule of law. Indeed, in his 1958 essay, "Positivism and the Separation of Law and Morals", Hart noted that Austin "spoke of the 'frequent coincidence' of positive law and morality and attributed the confusion of what law is with what law ought to be to this very fact".[68] In Fullerian terms, there is likely under stable conditions to be some significant overlap between the substance of external morality – the morality outside the law – and the substance of the law. But as Hart said then, and as contemporary positivists have hammered home in response to Dworkin, if that external morality is a pernicious moral ideology, that ideology will inform the substantive content of the law – the coherent conception of the common good.[69]

Put differently, the claim which has to be made to contest contemporary positivism is not that some substantive vision of justice might have been incorporated into the law, or even that every legal order will express one or other vision of justice. The claim has to be that only a very limited set of visions, moreover a set of basically sound visions, can be so incorporated. Just such a claim was made by F.A. Hayek, whose account of the rule of law is in many respects the exact converse of Bentham's culture of reflection. But as we will now see, once one makes that claim one is in the business of offering a substantive account of justice, rather than an account of the rule of law.

To Hayek the formality of the rule of law means something very different from the sense in which it has been used so far, since it is designed to exclude the law being used in the service of any substantive objectives. That emphasis on form often leads Hayek to emphasise process as the essence of the rule of law, but ultimately he always makes it clear that process is subordinated to substance. The rule of law is explicitly put in the service of what I call a culture of

---

[68] H.L.A. Hart, "Positivism and the Separation of Law and Morals" in Hart, *Essays in Jurisprudence and Philosophy* (Oxford, Clarendon Press, 1983) 49, at 54. In the very same passage Hart says that "Bentham too was certainly ready to admit" the existence of this "causal connection" between law and morality. *Pace* Hart, Bentham's understanding of the rule of law is incompatible with contemporary positivism since Bentham and Austin cannot be so easily paired on this point. On the account of Bentham in the last section, he thought it important to exclude moral principles from being incorporated into law in such a way that judges were thereby licenced to rely on them as criteria for the validity of law. As I said there, Bentham's theory of justice is not substantive in the sense of seeking to fill in a set of substantive principles of justice, since its point is to permit such principles to emerge through the procedures of democracy. But excluded are principles which, once embedded in the law, become substantive constraints on that process. What I called the culture of reflection requires that the procedures for making law and for identifying its content be purely formal. Raz's exclusive legal positivism is perhaps then best understood as an orphaned version of Bentham. He inherits from Bentham the idea that substantive moral values have no place in legal order. But he cannot deal with that idea in the way prompted by the political reasons which underpinned it for Bentham – that is, the democratic reasons which exclude moral values from playing any role. Rather, he differs from inclusive legal positivists only in so far as he gives a different account of the role such values play when they are incorporated. As I suggested in the last note, exclusive legal positivists will insist that a judgment based on such values is discretionary in nature while inclusive legal positivists say that it is fully determined by law.

[69] Ibid., 70.

neutrality, the liberal attempt to use law to preserve a realm of principles safe from democracy.

It is a culture of neutrality because the main criterion for illegitimate state action is that the state has acted non-neutrally in infringing the individual's right to decide for himself how to live. Neutralist liberals hold that the principles which together make up the culture of neutrality, whether at common or constitutional law, represent the essence of law. These principles are supposed to express the true voice of public reason, since they demarcate the limits of the state's legitimate scope for interfering with individual liberty. Statutes are an inferior form of law, the transient expressions of majority preference as to government policy, legitimate only so long as they do not run up against the judges' understanding of the limits of public reason.[70]

Hayek's version of the culture of neutrality is extreme because of his libertarian commitments. While he shares with Bentham the idea of structural subordination of legal to political theory, his subordination of legal theory is to a liberal account of justice not to a democratic account of politics. But the problem then is that his account seems to cease to be one of law; rather it is a substantive account of justice.

Dworkin's position is very similar. He is also a neutralist liberal[71] and he shares with Bentham and Hayek the view that legal theory is but part of a general theory of law which includes a dominant political component.[72] It is true that, as an egalitarian liberal, Dworkin understands the scope of neutrality in a far more restrictive way than does Hayek. But his understanding of the judicial role is no different from Hayek's – the judicial role in upholding the rule of law is to be the guardian of liberal principle.

This substantive account of the rule of law – one which founds judicial review on liberal principle – puts Dworkin in a dilemma. Either he admits that it does not hold in those legal orders where a different conception of the common good is dominant, in which case his position is no different from inclusive legal positivism, or he simply disqualifies those legal orders from legal status, in which case Craig is right that a Dworkinian account of the rule of law collapses into a substantive account of justice.

In either case Dworkin fails to establish a connection between law and morality which can contest positivism's separation thesis.[73] And in either case what

[70] The most complete recent articulation of the liberal idea of public reason is John Rawls, *Political Liberalism* (New York, Columbia University Press, 1993). Note that in Hayek's first and best known treatment of this topic – "Planning and the Rule of Law" in F.A. Hayek, *The Road To Serfdom* (Chicago, University of Chicago Press, 1994, 50th anniversary edition), he had not yet discovered the full potential of common law style judicial review and so relied much more on continentalist arguments about the form of statute law.

[71] Not all liberals make neutrality a central principle of their theory and my argument does not address their positions.

[72] See Dworkin's remarks about Bentham in his rather neglected but important "Introduction" to Ronald Dworkin, *Taking Rights Seriously*, ix.

[73] He is in fact in a trilemma, since much of of what he said in *Taking Rights Seriously* suggested that he supposes that a connection between law and sound morality is established merely because a

started off life as an antipositivist position becomes something like a "one-way projection of authority" in which a particular substantive vision of justice is enforced by judges.[74]

This issue transcends abstract legal theory – it is just the most abstract form of a concrete problem in the practice as well as the theory of judicial review of administrative action. The first component of the problem is institutional – the "supremacist" place of judges in "Law's Empire". Dworkin accepts a doctrine about the separation of powers in which the legislature makes law, judges interpret the law, and the executive implements the law.[75] No less than Dicey, he understands legislatures as having a monopoly on making law and judges a monopoly on its interpretation.[76] There is no place in Dworkin's understanding of legal order for administrative agencies which have an authority to make or interpret the law in the sense that such administrative decisions are ones to which courts have reason to defer. At most, he can concede to administrative agencies the authority to make decisions about the policy implications of their constitutive statutes, that is, utilitarian calculations about what decision will best advance the policy, or decisions about what the policy effects of different arrangements of natural justice might be. But they have no authority over legal principles – the exclusive province of the judiciary.[77]

The second component is substantive – the assumption that the essence of law is some particular substance, a coherent conception of the common good. Generally speaking, it does not matter so much what the precise content of that vision is, more or less libertarian, more or less egalitarian, as that there is such

judge has shown that the outcome of reasoning in a hard case is supported by the conception of the public good embedded in the positive law. In later work, Dworkin denied that this is his position – see Dworkin, "A Reply" in Marshall Cohen, *Ronald Dworkin and Contemporary Jurisprudence* (London, Duckworth, 1983), 247, 257–60 and my discussion in *Hard Cases in Wicked Legal Systems: South African Law in the Perspective of Legal Philosophy*, 253–7.

[74] Note that Fuller argued that the positivist view of law as a one-way projection of authority makes two important mistakes, one of which is to conceive of legal order as managerial. The other is to deny law has any effect on morality. And he claimed that Dworkin made the second mistake along with other legal theorists influenced by Hart; see Fuller, *The Morality of Law*, 204–5. In "Fuller's Novelty" (in Willem Witteveen and Wibren van den Burg, (eds), *Rediscovering Fuller* (Amsterdam, University of Amsterdam Press, forthcoming)), I argue that the trajectory of Dworkin's legal theory vindicates Fuller's claim that Dworkin is a positivist, once one sees that the hallmark of positivism is not so much the separation thesis as the "insulation thesis", one which seeks to insulate morality from the reach of law.
In "Judicial Review and Legal Theory", Roger Cotterrell makes a distinction between two models of law – *imperium* and community – which tracks Fuller's distinction between managerial and interactive models of law. But as he notes, Dworkin's model of law as the expression of liberal community "rarely shows citizens shaping law. More often, the rhetoric of community obscures the reality that when judges and politicians purport to determine law by appealing to the values of 'the community' they almost invariably invoke values they ascribe to such a community rather than any that its members are actually known to share"; 23 (note omitted).
What this shows, in my view, is that Dworkin's model ends up on the *imperium* side of the divide.
[75] See, for example, his "Introduction" to *Taking Rights Seriously*, vii–viii.
[76] For the ideas of legislative and interpretative monopoly in Dicey, see Craig, *Administrative Law*, chapter 1.
[77] See Ronald Dworkin, "Principle, Policy, Procedure" in Dworkin, *A Matter of Principle* (Cambridge, Mass., Harvard University Press, 1985) 72, at 99–101.

an assumption. For it is the assumption that there is such a substance, rather than particular judicial understandings of what exactly the substance is, which requires that judges have the institutional place just sketched. However, it may also be the case that there is a natural tendency among judges who share the assumption to drift towards the libertarian pole of liberalism if, as libertarians suggest, the most coherent conception of liberal neutrality is the claim that individual liberty should be maximised.

Together these two components create difficulties very familiar to administrative lawyers. On the one hand, Dworkin's understanding of the imperialism of principles over which judges preside invites the extension of principles derived from one area of law into another, and thus, for example, invites judges to attempt to govern the public law regimes of administrative law in the light of their understandings of private law.[78] On the other hand, the distinction between principle and policy on which Dworkin's whole account of adjudication rests suggests that when one is on the policy side of the divide, no crucial issues of legal principle arise.[79] But this is exactly the distinction between quasi-judicial and the administrative functions which has so plagued the common law of judicial review. The administration either gets squeezed into a procrustean common law bed or left to its own devices because it is somehow not for the most part involved in law, properly so called.[80]

So far I have compared two different ways of understanding law and the rule of law, each situated in a particular kind of political culture. Law in the culture of reflection is simply the formal or procedural means of implementing the judgments of utility, and judicial review has at most a very small role to play in such a culture. Law in the culture of neutrality is similarly instrumental – it provides a resource of principles on which judges should rely in order to work the law pure, to bring it more into line with what they understand as the substance which has been – or which should have been – incorporated into the law.

---

[78] The imperial project is subject to the principle of local priority, which allows "departments of law" to deviate somewhat from pure integrity – see Dworkin, *Law's Empire*, 250–4. But all such deviations are a matter of regret and, given judges' place in the imperial project, it is highly unlikely that a judge should pause to take seriously an administrative agency's sense that the principles of, say, the common law of contract should not govern the interpretation of a collective agreement.

[79] See Dworkin's discussion of the distinction between moral harm and bare harm, "Principle, Policy, Procedure", 84 ff. and see Genevra Richardson, "The Legal Regulation of Process" in Richardson and Genn, (eds), *Administrative Law and Government Action* 105, at 112–13: "This is a powerful argument for procedural rights in relation to substantive rights. The corollary is, however, that there are no procedural rights in relation to bare interests. The harm which may result from interference with bare interests is bare harm; there is no moral harm since nothing has been lost to which there is a right, and it is only moral harm that attracts procedural protection. It seems that for Dworkin, once outside the sphere of substantive rights, procedures are essentially matters of policy with any claim to specific procedures being so weak as to be negligible".

[80] The choice is the unsatisfactory one between "activist" and "inactive" "formalism" described by Martin Loughlin in an important essay on the quasi-judicial/administrative distinction – "Procedural Fairness: A Study of the Crisis in Administrative Law Theory" (1978) 28 *University of Toronto Law Journal* 214.

On the one hand, the culture of reflection is too hostile to judicial review to provide anything like a foundation for it. On the other, the culture of neutrality goes too far, finding a foundation for judicial review in an implausible and impracticable equation of law with the principles of one or other liberal conception of the good.[81]

We seem then to be back to the claim that different understandings of the rule of law are simply different substantive political positions translated into legal theory. The closer one is to the libertarian end of the political theory continuum, the more one will be tempted to put forward a picture of the rule of law in which judges are the guardians of a constitutional morality protective of liberal substance. Conversely, the closer one is to the democratic end of the continuum, the more modest the role one will give to judges. And the hope, shared by formalists and substantivists alike, of finding in the rule of law some refuge from the darkling plain of political controversy is vain.

I will now argue that the rule of law offers no refuge from political controversy, though I will conclude that there is a way of understanding it which offers a more productive foundation for judicial review. And the toehold here is the mistake in Forsyth's version of the challenge to accounts of the rule of law that go beyond formalism.

THE PLEASING PERSISTENCE OF PROCESS BASED THEORIES

Recall that Forsyth says that for a claim that the common law is the basis of judges' review power to be coherent, that claim must ultimately be the strong one that judges can, without any statutory basis for doing so, resist even the clearest legislative derogations from the common law.[82] A tacit premise on which he relies here is supplied by his substantivist opponents that, if there is a foundation for substantive review, it must lie in the common law since it does not reside in statute. But, as Forsyth points out, the common law is subordinate to statute. It follows that common law-based judicial review is always subject to statutory countermand and hence that statute is the true foundation of judicial review. It also follows, he thinks, that if one really wants substantive review – judicial review on the basis of moral principles – one should get those principles incorporated into law by statute.

[81] In discussion Trevor Allan has indicated that one bit of the Dworkinian picture which he does not accept is the idea of neutrality. It seems to me that one cannot ditch that idea without significant alteration to the whole of the Dworkinian construction. Allan's desire to emphasise the idea of constraints inherent in the rule of law on public officials – constraints which get their content from a particular substantive vision of justice – is a venerable one within the tradition of liberal rule of law thought, and neutrality is just the contemporary slogan adopted for articulating that idea. Liberalism without that idea ceases, in my view, to be liberalism. What one gets is a democratic theory in which individual rights and liberties are important but do not have quite the status liberalism accords them, and so cannot require the central role of judges as guardians of the constitution.

[82] Forsyth, "Of Fig Leaves and Fairy Tales: The Ultra Vires Doctrine, the Sovereignty of Parliament and Judicial Review", 137–9 and pp. 42–5 above.

Since most proponents of substantive accounts of the rule of law also argue for statutory incorporation there is in some respects very little between Forsyth and the substantivists on this point. The disagreement is in part political – is it desirable to have such a constitutional morality in place? And it is in part empirical – is such a constitutional morality already to some extent in place? But there is agreement that at issue is judicial review founded on substantive standards which must be located in some positive source of law.

Indeed, Craig's distinction between formal/positivistic accounts of the rule of law and their rivals assumes that any rival which genuinely challenges formalism must be substantive. Allan, as we have seen, agrees. It is no wonder, then, that positivism seems to win the day in the sense that the issue becomes one about what substantive theory of justice should be incorporated into the law. But, as I have argued, that is a pyrrhic victory for positivism. Legal theory becomes at best a side show in a political debate and one puts paid to the aspiration of those who debate the rule of law to show how law is not just politics by other means.

There is, however, a response to Forsyth's challenge which offers an important clue to a way out of this theoretical impasse, a way which in my view holds out the best hope of becoming the "middle way" between formalism and substantivism which positivists regard as non-existent. Recall here the manner in which Dicey, operating in formal mode, dealt with the thought experiment which might be deployed to show counterfactually that there are limits on what he argued to be legislative omnipotence. He said that the fact that a British parliament would not enact a morally obnoxious statute, one which, for example, required all blue eyed babies to be put to death, showed not that there are legal limits on legislative power but that there are moral limits – limits to be found in the conscience of the legislators and their subjects.[83]

That thought experiment, however, was too contrived to help Dicey's case since it depends on the claim that any limit must be a substantive moral limit. It would have been more interesting to know how Dicey, again in formal mode, would have coped with examples where an allegedly omnipotent legislature enacts a statute obnoxious to legal form rather than to moral substance. For it is only such examples which force a formalist to confront the point of form.

Just such an example was forced on administrative lawyers of all sorts by ouster or privative clauses because on their face such clauses seemed to make public officials omnipotent or, at least, judges impotent. But ouster clauses were not the most effective example just because they are so radical. One could understand their radical message more or less literally by taking the view that other than absurd arrogations of authority by a tribunal, for example, an immigration tribunal setting itself up as a competition tribunal, tribunals are indeed a law unto themselves. Or one could say that they are so radical that, from a constitutional perspective, they have to be treated as a nullity – the legislature

---

[83]   A.V. Dicey, *An Introduction to the Study of the Law of the Constitution* (London, MacMillan, 1985, 10th edn.) 81. Dicey took the example from Leslie Stephen.

could not have been serious when it inserted the clause. But either option left the issue of the point of legal form unanswered, leading to the problem already noted in Wade's explanation of the justification for *Anisminic*.[84]

Far more effective are examples where a statute explicitly and totally excludes one or other principle of the common law of judicial review when such a principle seems obviously required, for example, *audi alteram partem* where a person's liberty interest is at stake. Forsyth deals with such examples by simply biting the bullet, an especially effective strategy if it works since it copes with the pain by shifting its locus to the substantivists.

The attempt, however, fails if the opponent is the antipositivist proceduralist rather than the antipositivist substantivist, as we can see by returning to Dicey's example. In the case of the legislature which enacts the statute requiring the execution of blue eyed babies our reaction would be, as Dicey said, that the legislators had engaged in an act of moral madness – they had taken themselves beyond the moral pale. But surely there is a legal equivalent – a claim that legislators have gone legally mad, taking themselves beyond the legal pale. Once we see this it does not matter so much how we think that we or judges ought to deal with the problem as that we correctly characterise it. For to fail to see that the problem is one for the rule of law is to empty the idea of the rule of law of all meaning, something which nearly all positivists and formalists are reluctant to do.

Once the problem is correctly characterised, there are direct implications for legal practice, even if these do not come about through judicial declarations of invalidity. As Edwin Cameron, an eminent South African judge, put it in his written submission to the Truth and Reconciliation Commission's Hearing on the role of lawyers during apartheid, where judges were unable to use the law to curtail apartheid, they could still "criticise the profanation of *legal* values that apartheid laws represented".[85] And since that Hearing, three Zimbabwe judges have shown how effective such criticism can be when they called publicly on Robert Mugabe to declare his government's allegiance to the rule of law.[86]

In sum, one's account of the rule of law need not stand or fall by a criterion of whether it cashes out directly in judicial authority to make declarations of invalidity. And Forsyth's acceptance of that criterion might evidence the same pull towards judicial supremacism which bedevils substantive accounts of the rule of law.

---

[84] Canadian judges opted for a (perhaps typically Canadian) compromise solution – they tried to make sense of privative clauses as requiring review of a functionalist sort. In effect, though this read the privative clauses out of statutes, the logical end to this process was a focus – productive in my view – on the interplay between formal and substantive considerations in a functionalist approach. For my own account of the process, see David Dyzenhaus, "The Politics of Deference: Judicial Review and Democracy" in M. Taggart (ed.), *The Province of Administrative Law* (Oxford, Hart Publishing, 1997) 279.

[85] My emphasis; for the quotation and discussion, see David Dyzenhaus, *Judging the Judges, Judging Ourselves: Truth, Reconciliation and the Apartheid Legal Order* (Oxford, Hart Publishing, 1998), 150–1.

[86] For an account, see R.W. Johnson in (1999) 21 *London Review of Books*, 32–3.

Moreover, once one sees the problem as one for the rule of law, one is on a path away from the claim that the issue is mere or pure form. And that path does not have to end in substance, either the standards that protect Dworkin's or Hayek's neutralism, or the positivist claim that the rule of law requires a substance. Rather, the path can end in the idea of legality.

I use the term "legality" in order to stress process over the more substantive sounding "law". But process or form here is not mere or pure process or form. As in Bentham's general theory of law and politics, the focus on process or form is ultimately anchored in political commitments. And again as in Bentham, the political commitments do not make up a theory of justice in the liberal sense of substantive constraints on legislation but rather a theory of politics. The commitments are not, that is, to a particular set of moral principles, but to the political principles which give shape to institutions of democratic government. However, this procedural view departs from Bentham since it understands democracy not as a political culture of reflection but as a political culture of justification.[87]

As I understand it, the idea of law as a culture of justification shares with Bentham the thought that the primary mode of making law is legislation, so that the role that judges have in legal order is one derived from a theory of democratic legislation rather than from a substantivist theory of adjudication like Dworkin's.[88] And it shares with the culture of neutrality the notion that judicial guardianship of fundamental principles of law is important to maintaining the rule of law. But those principles do not have the kind of judicially fixed content which liberals desire – they are not principles with a content against which statutes or executive decisions must not offend if they are to be valid. Rather, they are principles which make internal to the law the ideals of both democracy and administrative law – participation and accountability.

Bentham subscribed to both these ideals, but he did not make them into principles of law, preferring to provide after-the-fact political controls on the content of law.[89] The culture of reflection is legitimate only if political and legal institutions are highly responsive to legislative reform in the light of citizens' experience of the effects of the law. Bentham's famous slogan that the good citizen is the one who obeys punctually and censures freely makes sense because he envisages political and legal channels for effective criticism of the law. If you didn't like the law, you could try to get it changed through institutional channels which ensured legislative responsiveness to criticism.

But while every democrat would welcome such an attractive institution, it is an impoverished theory of democracy which does not countenance controls

---

[87] This term was coined by Etienne Mureinik. For discussion, on which I rely below, see Dyzenhaus, "Law as Justification: Etienne Mureinik's Conception of Legal Culture".

[88] These embryonic ideas share much with the project sketched in Jeremy Waldron, *Law and Disagreement* (Oxford, Clarendon Press, 1999), especially section I, "A Jurisprudence of Legislation". Waldron, however, seems to want to remain firmly within the Benthamite culture of reflection.

[89] See Gerald Postema, "Review of Rosen" (1986) 3 *Philosophical Review* 483.

which operate in the very determination of what law is. This point is underscored when one takes into account that the form of law has changed in ways unanticipated by Bentham, and by Hobbes – the founder of the positivist tradition. That is, the form has changed in just those ways that required the development of the body of law we now call administrative law – the principles that govern the activity of the officials who do not merely implement the law, but to whom the law delegates both policy-making and interpretative roles.

The emphasis on process here does not come about because substance is unimportant. Indeed, it is so important that we should try to ensure that what it is is decided in the most productive fashion and that our decisions are amenable to revision in the light of experience. The debate about the rule of law is then the debate about the process by which such decisions are best made and revised since the institutions of legality are the institutions which we have developed for making such decisions.

If we return to the passage quoted above where Allan outlines his vision of the rule of law,[90] it may seem then that there is very little difference between my sketch of the culture of justification and what he has to say. But there is an important shift in emphasis in the understanding of the importance of the ideal of equal citizenship which we both claim to be an essential element of the rule of law. For Allan, that ideal leads one to the substance of the law before which the citizen is equal. In the culture of justification, by contrast, the focus is on the citizen as active participant in legal order and not on the substance incorporated into law.

Put differently, it is a mistake to try to get rid of the ambiguity between substance and form which I claimed exists in all accounts of the rule of law which assume that there is a distinction between a theory of justice and a theory of the rule of law. Rather, one should attempt to design legal institutions in order that they might bring to the surface and productively deal with that ambiguity. Indeed, Dworkin's great contribution to legal theory is, in my view, not so much his claim that liberal principles revealed through judicial interpretation are the basis of law. Rather, his contribution lies in the way in which he has illuminated the justificatory character of the rule of law – law is not only about setting clear goals but also about argument as to what those goals should be.[91] That contribution shows that an important part of the rule of law is the idea – internal to the law – of justification.

Dworkin also tries to argue for a set of ultimate principles immanent in the law which must guide judicial interpretation. But one can accept his account of the process without accepting those principles. One can, in my view, make this move without falling into the inclusive legal positivist camp. One risks that fall only if one accepts that the debate about judicial review and the rule of law is one about the necessary presence of a particular set of substantive standards in

[90] See n. 65 above.
[91] Compare Neil MacCormick, "Rhetoric and the Rule of Law" in David Dyzenhaus (ed.), *Recrafting the Rule of Law: The Limits of Legal Order* (Oxford, Hart Publishing, 1999) 163.

the (positive law). But if one argues for a connection between law and morality which is about (in Habermasian terms) the legitimacy of legality, one's focus is on the way in which a decision to govern through law makes government, at least to some extent, legitimate. And what makes it legitimate is that a commitment to process is ultimately a commitment to what we might think of as a substantive ideal – the ideal of free and equal citizenship.

This is the ideal of the active citizen who is not a mere subject of the law content to receive his due as long as what he gets lives up to one or other political theory. The active citizen can require more than a legal warrant in positive law for official coercion, for he is equipped with resources to participate in the making of the law and to hold officials to account by principles of fair participation.

If the ideal of the active citizen is in place in a legal order, it would be more than surprising if the positive law contained contents greatly obnoxious to the liberal tradition. But that is because of the constraints of a process of public rational justification. It was for this reason that when Fuller first articulated his faith in the moral resources of law he suggested that when people "are compelled to explain and justify their decisions, the effect will generally be to pull those decisions towards goodness, by whatever standards of ultimate goodness there are".[92] And elsewhere I have argued that even a wicked legal system, to the extent that it is a legal system, will contain some of the fundamental principles of legality that together make up the basis of an antipositivist, democratic and procedural account of the rule of law.[93]

An elaborate exploration of what these principles are is beyond the scope of this essay.[94] Suffice it to say here that one of the important consequences of uncoupling the justificatory part of Dworkin's theory from the substantive liberal "neutralist" part is that one can then try to conceptualise and design legal institutions in general – not just the judiciary – in order fully to realise the culture of justification. This allows one to take seriously what John Allison has usefully termed the "procedural reason for judicial restraint", that the limits of adjudication which Fuller identified because of the problem of polycentricity have to be taken even more seriously than Fuller thought.[95]

But I take that suggestion to be one which requires that debate about the rule of law, and hence about the foundations of judicial review, be guided not by substantive theories of justice, but by close attention to what is required in order to achieve the rule of law in democracy: a political and controversial but fundamentally still law-focused inquiry.

[92] Lon L. Fuller, "Positivism and Fidelity to Law: A Reply to Professor Hart" (1958) 71 *Harvard Law Review* 630, at 636. I explore this passage in Fuller in detail in "The Legitimacy of Legality" (1996) 82 *Archiv für Rechts- und Sozialphilosophie* 324; (1996) 46 *University of Toronto Law Journal* 129.

[93] See *Hard Cases in Wicked Legal Systems: South African Law in the Perspective of Legal Philosophy*, esp. chapter 10, and more recently, *Judging the Judges, Judging Ourselves: Truth, Reconciliation and the Apartheid Legal Order*, esp. chapter 4.

[94] My sense is that such an exploration will begin at the level of fine-grained analysis of administrative law, rather than at the level of theory .

[95] John Allison, "The Procedural Reason for Judicial Restraint" [1994] *PL* 452.

8

Judicial Review and the Meaning of Law

SIR JOHN LAWS

INTRODUCTORY

Our system of public law in the English jurisdiction has flowered over the last generation. In light of it, and especially in this time of constitutional change, we ought to reflect on the constellation of law, people and government. In particular we should examine the relation between what the law schools call jurisprudence – I prefer to call it legal philosophy – and law in practice. These two have long been regarded as separate spheres; but this (to use a fruitful self-contradiction) is an unconscious conspiracy of academics and practitioners. We stand to make better law if we choose to grasp the theory of the thing; particularly where our subject, public law, is one where conflicting norms and ideals swim and struggle against one another. There are three great conflicts: the clash of freedom and order, the clash of rights and duties, the clash of democratic power and the legal control of government. Sometimes the clash is visceral. They are, all three, the stuff of public law. At every turn the decisions of the courts are about which ideal shall prevail. And they rest on moral perceptions, more often than not unspoken, about the values of these ideals. How are we to forge legal principles, whose operation in practice will serve and not disrupt the tranquillity of the State, on so unruly an anvil?

THE COMMON LAW

I must first say a word about the nature of the common law. Its great virtue is that it builds principle case by case. It never starts with a premise given *aliunde*, from which in the particular field all else is said to follow. It has no premise *outside itself*. Seemingly basic principles, such as the court's duty to obey and give effect to primary legislation, are not given to the common law; they are a creature of it. It owes its power not to dictat, but to history. There is, therefore, nothing *dirigiste* about the common law. Sir Gerard Brennan said this:[1]

---

[1] At p. 18 in "*The Purpose and Scope of Judicial Review*", one of the papers presented at a conference at the University of Auckland in February 1986 and published in *Judicial Review of Administrative Action in the 1980s* (OUP and the Legal Research Foundation Inc. 1986).

The political legitimacy of judicial review depends, in the ultimate analysis, on the assignment to the Courts of that function by the general consent of the community. The efficacy of judicial review depends, in the ultimate analysis, on the confidence of the general community in the way in which the Courts perform the function assigned to them. Judicial review has no support other than public confidence.

This is acutely true of judicial review, but true also of the common law generally. Social consent and public confidence are pragmatic requirements without which the common law's authority would very soon be lost. They are the compulsory frame within which the common law's ambitions must be set, and they also explain or justify its evolutive nature. But the common law must lead as well as follow; it must be a voice, and not an echo. If it followed merely, it could not function as a coherent system for the decision of disputes, for public opinion is a many-headed hydra, and what issues from its innumerable mouths is so unformed, various, quixotic and self-contradictory as never to be the stuff of which principles are made (though great *movements* may be made from it). And it is the creation, the elaboration, of reasoned principle that is above all else the mark of the common law. It gives coherence and discipline to instinctive moral perceptions; it exposes the weaknesses of some opinions, and the strengths of others; it gives shape, clarity, and depth to the raw material of diverse and strident claims and assertions. It finds compromise, without sacrificing the idea of principle itself.[2]

Let me give what is at once the most obvious, and perhaps the most important, concrete instance of this alchemy at work. It consists in the imperative of what the Americans call due process. The evidence of a heinous terrorist crime, perhaps involving many deaths, may be formidably stacked against the defendant; the public – more accurately, the popular newspapers – may cry out for his conviction. The police may be tempted (as sometimes they have been, with disastrous consequences) to cut corners with the nature of the material they provide to the Crown Prosecution Service. But the defendant is entitled to every proper procedural protection; if he is convicted on inadmissible or tainted evidence, his conviction is rightly quashed in the Court of Appeal, whether in fact he is guilty or not. He will later parade his success in the Court of Appeal as vindication of his innocence, which it may well not be. Many members of the public will think he has been let out on a technicality, and (depending on the case, and on what one means by "technicality" – a much overworked expression) this may well be true; but the Court of Appeal will have upheld a vital though elementary principle, that a defendant is only to be convicted of any offence by due process of law. It applies alike, and without any distinction, to

---

[2] Some criticise the modern Church of England for failing to achieve a like result, and allege the pronouncements of its leaders to be all compromise and no principle. The question is not relevant to my present discussion, save to point this contrast: the Church by its own lights has to accommodate what it sees as the eternal with what it sees as the day-to-day; the common law is not burdened (or enlightened) with any vision of the eternal. If it were, given its power, it would be a very dangerous beast. If the secular law of any State has apocalyptic pretensions, it is at once an engine of tyranny.

the trivial shoplifter and to the mass murderer. The importance of due process can only be appreciated by reflection on the consequences of its absence; reflection which travels beyond the agonising, pressing merits of the immediate case in hand. So it is the law's duty to travel beyond the instant case, and develop principles by which all cases may be justly accommodated.

Many other instances to illustrate the need and ideal of principle spring readily to mind; some concerned with due process, some with substantive law. In every case its hallmarks consist in a series of balances. There is the balance between due process and getting a result on the merits. In the substantive law, there are many balances: in the law of libel, between free speech and the protection of reputation; in the law of negligence, between the instinct to compensate for suffering and the need not to make the rest of the world an insurer; in the law of contract, between the traditional conception of freedom of contract and the more modern conception of inequality of bargaining power; in the law of trusts, between the need to preserve the trust property, and the chance of opportunity to enhance it. Most particularly, given our present subject, there is the balance in the public law jurisprudence between the courts' respect for democratic power and their insistence that objective standards of legality, reason, and fairness be imposed on democratic decision-makers. In many instances in the private law sphere, statute has intervened to change the balance. But at every turn the judge-made law, though sometimes overruled by Parliament, has evolved principles by the reflective process of building case on case, which has enabled it to move the law forward in light of the conditions of the time.

In all of this the command of public confidence is met, so far as it is met, by two different factors. First, the law must not stray too far from what the common man – he used to travel on the Clapham omnibus – thinks. But secondly, and much more important for my purpose, public confidence requires a reasoned, reflective law which elaborates principles, even if its results are sometimes unpopular. Here is the reconciliation of echo and voice. It is an irony, perhaps a paradox, that a system of law which substituted populist reaction for the elaboration of principle (it would hardly be a *system*) would very soon lose any popular appeal which it might at first possess. Public confidence surely requires that the law provides an armoury of principles, honed by close argument and intelligent reasoning, which survives the arrows of individual cases; though individual cases will sometimes change its shape, and hone it further. The way the common law develops was described by Cardozo J in words which cast light on its seduction of public confidence:

> The work of a judge is in one sense enduring and in another sense ephemeral. What is good in it endures. What is erroneous is pretty sure to perish. The good remains the foundation on which new structures will be built. The bad will be rejected and cast off in the laboratory of the years. Little by little the old doctrine is undermined. Often the encroachments are so gradual that their significance is at first obscured. Finally we discover that the contour of the landscape has been changed, that the old maps must be cast aside, and the ground charted anew.

This central characteristic of the common law, the elaboration of principle, is likely to come under greatly increased scrutiny as the judges embark on the tasks given them by the Human Rights Act 1998 and the devolution legislation. Public law, and constitutional law, will be the focus of a heightened interest in judicial activity. The three great conflicts which I mentioned at the beginning will be at the heart of it, certainly in relation to human rights. In that context, the judges of the appellate courts will be much more overtly engaged in ethical dilemmas at the theoretical level than has traditionally been the case. They will do it, however, by the traditional common law means, building principles by cases.

PHILOSOPHY

In the future this task will involve a richer diet of abstract reasoning. We need, therefore, to articulate more closely what is *meant* by the elaboration of legal principles. The philosopher RG Collingwood (who should nowadays be read more than he is) said this:[3]

> There are some things which we can do without understanding what we are doing; not only things which we do with our bodies, like locomotion and digestion, but even with things which we do with our minds, like making a poem or recognizing a face. But when that which we do is in the nature of thinking, it begins to be desirable, if we are to do it well, that we should understand what we are trying to do. Scientific and historical thought could never go very far unless scientists and historians reflected on their own work, tried to understand what they were aiming at, and asked themselves how best to attain it. Most of all, this is true of philosophy. It is possible to raise and solve philosophical problems with no very clear idea of what philosophy is, what it is trying to do, and how it can best do it; but no great progress can be made until these questions have been asked and some answer to them given.

Very much the same, I think, applies to law, and will increasingly apply to it as the three great conflicts attract more piercing searchlights. Collingwood continued thus:[4] "Philosophy, moreover, has this peculiarity, that reflection upon it is part of itself". This is not generally true of law. Now, I do not suggest that all good lawyers must hereafter be philosophers also. But we do need to reflect on the nature of what we will be doing in the field of constitutional principles. There is an alchemy here; we shall be making new lamps from old. Understanding it is a philosophical inquiry.

I must say a little, therefore about the nature of such an inquiry. Philosophy is not like other disciplines, and not only for the reason that Collingwood gave. Its practitioners debate questions first raised by the Greeks 2,500 and more years ago. While it is true that any question, in any discipline, may remain unsolved through so many centuries, the intelligent inquirer may reasonably suppose that

---

[3] *Philosophical Method* (Oxford, 1933) p. 1.
[4] *Ibid.* p. 1.

once the question is identified a definitive answer will at length be found. And this is broadly true in the world of factual inquiry. We have learnt that the earth is not flat, that the blood circulates in the body, that antibiotics may combat infection; we have learnt the properties of gunpowder, electricity, steam, uranium, and the micro-chip. But we cannot agree on what it means to be *good*. It is because the philosopher is not seeking after a truth which is external to him, or at least that is not all he seeks. By the force of his ideas he forges himself what seems in his time to be true; and unlike the scientist, he is, usually at least, a victim or a creature of the *zeitgeist*. The influence of utilitarianism in western philosophy since the time of Bentham and Mill has been germinated in receptive soil, in an increasingly post-religious age. The "greatest happiness of the greatest number" owes its appeal to social forces which outstrip the reasoning of its intellectual founders. So it is with other philosophies, all or most moral and political philosophies. So it was with the devout philosophers of the Middle Ages: witness the valiant attempts of Aquinas to harness the logic of Aristotle to the Catholic faith. A morality in which rights predominate will have appeal at a particular time; at another, a philosophy of duties will possess the greater force. In one age government by dictatorship is for a time acceptable to the people, for the security it may bring and because there is no concept of the brotherhood, or equality, of all men. In another, as it is now in the developed western world, it is anathema. In one age homosexuality is not condemned; in another it is excoriated as an unnatural vice. In some of these areas, especially those of personal morality, religion is appealed to as a source of universal and eternal truth.

Through the ages philosophy's dream has often been to escape from the parochial, the temporary, the immediate, and to find and describe an unchanging universal truth. It is a great mistake, at least in the field of moral and political philosophy, to treat the dream as if it were reality. I may dream of standing outside a door, on whose other side are all the answers to the questions of the universe; but I cannot find the key. Philosophy tries to find the key. It is a doomed enterprise, because there is *no door*. There is a door, many doors, for science, for history, for anthropology, for other disciplines; not for philosophy. All the stuff of reality is around us; it is not locked away in a place where 2,500 years and more of hard thinking have failed to find the "Open Sesame". And if there were a door, and there were a key, some might say that only hell would lie on the other side. If we found perfection, it would by definition be unchanging and unchangeable. There would be no striving any more. There would be no inquiry into big disputes. There would be no *thought*: at least not about things that really mattered. They would all have been settled. There would be no debate or disputation in John Donne's figurative description of a blissful hereafter:

> no Cloud nor Sun, no darkness nor dazling, but one equall light, no noyse nor silence, but one equall musick, no fears nor hopes, but one equal possession, no foes nor friends, but an equall communion and Identity, no ends nor beginnings; but one equall eternity.

I think it is a frightening prospect. No hopes? No friends? One virtuous sameness? A sameness in which there is no vice – therefore, it may be said, no virtue.

Philosophers, therefore, should (*pace* Plato) be standard-bearers, not kings. If good philosophy cannot prescribe an ideal world, as certainly it cannot, we can at least harness its disciplines to make this world better, not least in the light it can cast on the discipline of the law. Unfortunately it has in this field largely let us down. Millions of words have been expended in academic disputation of the question, what law *is*. I am afraid I think very many of them have been wasted. What law *is* is a deceptive question. It suggests that there is a *single* answer. That is a false proposition; just as, on a somewhat grander scale, the proposition that the concept of *goodness* describes a single quality, ascertainable by factual enquiry, is false. You can have a good man, a good golf club, a good book, or, as Sir Tom Stoppard said,[5] a good bacon sandwich. Terms like goodness, and law, refer to a whole range or family of situations. Very roughly, the family of meanings attributable to goodness connotes the idea of commendation, moral or otherwise. The family of meanings attributable to law connotes the idea of rule, consensual or otherwise. What law *is* is only a sensible question if one means by it either of two things: (a) how the term is and has in fact been used over time in different societies, or any particular society one is considering; that is a linguistic and sociological enquiry; (b) what law *ought to be*, or in what it should consist, either ideally or in a given society at a given epoch. (a) is factual. (b) is normative. There has been too much confusion between the two.

POSITIVISM

One may perceive the extent to which legal philosophy has been less than helpful to the law's rigorous development by means of a brief consideration of the notion of *positivism*, and how it has been treated. Positivism has been traditionally contrasted with *natural law*. Put very crudely, the debate has been between those who believe that law, to qualify as such, must exemplify moral characteristics, or possess a moral content, and those (the positivists) who assert only that it must fulfil certain defining criteria which may be value-free. One of the leading post-war British thinkers on the subject has been Professor HLA Hart, the influence of whose book *The Concept of Law*[6] has been very considerable in the common law world. Hart claims to be what is called a positivist. In the Notes to the second edition of Hart's book (for which the editors are presumably responsible, and in their frankness they have done us a service) this is said:[7]

---

[5] In his wonderful play, *Jumpers*. The first production, with Diana Rigg and Michael Hordern, cannot be overestimated.

[6] Oxford University Press, 1961; the second edition was published posthumously by the OUP in 1994 (editors Penelope Bulloch and Joseph Raz), and includes a lengthy and fascinating postscript in which Hart addresses criticisms of his book made over the intervening years, principally by Professor Ronald Dworkin.

[7] Page 302.

The expression "positivism" is used in contemporary Anglo-American literature to designate one or more of the following contentions: (1) that laws are commands of human beings; (2) that there is no necessary connection between law and morals, or law as it is and law as it ought to be; (3) that the analysis or study of meanings of legal concepts is an important study to be distinguished from (though in no way hostile to) historical inquiries, sociological inquiries, and the critical appraisal of law in terms of morals, social aims, functions, &c; (4) that a legal system is a "closed logical system" in which correct decisions can be deduced from predetermined legal rules by logical means alone; (5) that moral judgments cannot be established, as statements of fact can, by rational argument, evidence or proof ("non cognitivism in ethics"). Bentham and Austin[8] held the views expressed in (1), (2), and (3) but not those in (4) and (5); Kelsen holds those expressed in (2), (3), and (5) but not those in (1) or (4) . . .

In continental literature the expression "positivism" is often used for the general repudiation of the claim that some principles or rules of human conduct are discoverable by reason alone . . .

The word "positivism" means nothing to the ordinary intelligent person. It has been invented by the academics. It means what they say it means; it has no other credentials. If it had been invented to expose an important concept previously hidden in the language, well and good. But on the account given above it may mean all sorts of things, variously connected or unconnected with each other. As a term of art, which is its only possible justification, it is so opaque and multi-faceted as to be almost useless. It is disgraceful that it has been so casually applied, tossed like a ping-pong ball from one idea to another. This unrespectable state of affairs is not improved by the fact that in other branches of philosophy the word is also used to denote a range of ideas whose connection is not always clear.[9]

To be fair to Hart, he makes it unambiguously plain what he means by positivism:

Here we shall take Legal Positivism to mean the simple contention that it is in no sense a necessary truth that laws reproduce or satisfy certain demands of morality, though in fact they have often done so.[10]

I think this is true but uninteresting. Plainly a vile regime may promulgate and enforce compulsory rules by which its citizens are constrained. It seems to me simply idle to suggest that such a regime is not law. It only means, it is not law of which we approve. Equally plainly, in civilised societies, including our own, laws may be made which are morally contentious, giving rise to bitter disputes about their merits; disputes which, largely, will fall to be resolved on the political plane. The absence of any perceptible moral value in a legal system cannot debar the regime in question from qualifying, on linguistic or sociological

---

[8] John Austin, *The Province of Jurisprudence Determined* (1832).

[9] I have in mind the "logical positivists" and the Vienna Circle: see Ayer, *Language Truth and Logic*, 1936, a brilliant but misconceived book.

[10] *The Concept of Law* (Oxford, second edition, 1994), Chapter IX, "Laws and Morals", pp. 185–6.

grounds, as a legal system: or at least, a legal order (the difference between a system and an order is probably a fruitful one, but I cannot go into it now).

In short, I think that much of the debate about positivism confuses (a) and (b) as I described them earlier: the factual question, what has been regarded as law, and the normative question, in what a society's laws should consist.

There are other issues connected with the positivist debates, which are really the province of moral philosophy, such as the old but interesting question, when is disobedience to the law justified. But that is beyond my present brief.[11]

THE NATURE OF PRINCIPLE

The distinction, which is a philosophical one, between factual and normative propositions can and should be harnessed to serve a better understanding of the development of legal principle. It serves us, for example, in the debate about ultra vires. What sort of statement is it to say that the ultra vires principle is, or is not, the foundation of judicial review? It is, surely, a normative statement; it expresses the author's view about how one aspect of the constitution ought to be arranged. But as the contentions and counter-contentions on this topic have shown, a number of different types of argument have been deployed on either side.

It is useful to identify these categories, since they may apply also to other questions about fundamental legal principles. And their identification and evaluation exemplifies philosophical method at work; it articulates, as Collingwood said, "what we are trying to do", in the formulation of the law's principles. I think the categories are as follows.

(1) There are arguments from logic

Thus it is said that ultra vires cannot account for review of the decisions of non-statutory bodies (which plainly it cannot), so that the ultra vires doctrine must be abandoned. The riposte is that a different theory of judicial review applies to non-statutory bodies; but this weakens the ultra vires doctrine, which must in light of this argument be seen as a partial account only of the judicial review jurisdiction.

The statement of a logical truth is neither factual nor normative. It is an *a priori* truth, of which mathematical propositions are a paradigm. $2 + 2 = 4$ does not depend on any experience of the world.[12] So also with any of Aristotle's syllogisms, of which the most tedious is: *All men are mortal; Socrates was a man;*

---

[11] On disobedience to bad laws, see for example Hart, op. cit., pp. 210–11; there are many discussions on the subject.

[12] Though since Godel's work in the 1930s, the idea that mathematical propositions may possess the quality of absolute truth has been called in question.

therefore Socrates was mortal. But it is interesting enough to contrast it with what would be a false syllogism: *Socrates was mortal; all men are mortal; therefore Socrates was a man*. It is, of course, a silly example. But what of this: *This applicant is a victim of discrimination; all successful applicants are victims of discrimination; therefore this applicant must succeed*. It is no less false. Elementary logic of this kind dispels loose thinking and unreflective prejudice.

(2) There are arguments from consequences

I have in mind Christopher Forsyth's reliance[13] on *Staatspresident v. United Democratic Front*,[14] in which the Supreme Court of South Africa upheld regulations restricting press freedom which were said to be so vague as to be null and void. But on the face of it they were protected by an ouster clause in the enabling Act; and the Supreme Court so held. Dicta from Rabie ACJ and Hefer JA cited by Forsyth show that this conclusion was arrived at by a rejection of the conventional ultra vires approach, so that *Anisminic* principles had no application. Thus in short Forsyth argues[15] that abandonment of ultra vires unwrites the *Anisminic* doctrine and deprives the courts of their best weapon to ensure that unfair or irrational decisions are not protected by ouster clauses. As I have said elsewhere[16], I think the argument is false, but I am not concerned to refute it here. I merely identify it as a category of argument which can be deployed to assault or support a normative proposition of principle.

The ascertainment of consequences is a factual inquiry, though it may well depend on probabilities.

(3) There are arguments from precedent

Forsyth makes much of Lord Browne-Wilkinson's speech in *R v. Hull University Visitor, ex parte Page*[17] (and would certainly draw support from the observation of Lord Steyn in the recent case of *Boddington*,[18] where he said "I see no reason to depart from the orthodox view that ultra vires is 'the central principle of administrative law' as *Wade and Forsyth, Administrative Law*, 7th ed., p. 41 described it").[19] But our rules of *stare decisis*, while of course they constrain courts bound by them, never close off the question whether the precedent is right. It is right (and I make no excuse for the Latin) *sub modo*; it may not be right *sub specie aeternitatis*. Where a question of principle is involved, academic

---

[13] In "Of Fig Leaves and Fairy Tales: The *Ultra Vires* Doctrine, the Sovereignty of Parliament and Judicial Review", [1996] 55 *CLJ* 122 and p. 29 above.

[14] 1988 (4) SA 830(A).

[15] Pages 131–2.

[16] Supperstone & Goudie, *Judicial Review* (2nd edition), ch. 4: *Illegality:The Problem of Jurisdiction* and pp. 73–81 above.

[17] [1993] AC 682.

[18] [1998] 2 AER 203.

[19] At 225f–g.

reliance on precedent again makes the mistake of confusing what is with what ought to be. If there were a precedent supporting the view that judicial review is an autonomous jurisdiction having nothing to do with the authority of Parliament, Forsyth would roundly criticise it, and would, very obviously, be quite entitled to do so. But there is a tension here. While scholars – or anyone, for that matter – are perfectly entitled to praise or criticise any particular precedent, the very notion of precedent has a self-standing value; it is an important guarantor of legal certainty, and is the medium by which the common law changes gradually, and not by coarse reversals.

The ascertainment of precedent is factual in the obvious sense that it is a matter of record what previous decisions have been made by the courts. But the precedent, once ascertained, is normative: it is one factor (short of the House of Lords, it may be compulsory and dispositive of the case) which drives the court's view of the result.

(4) There are, lastly, idealistic arguments

By this I mean arguments based on a perception of what kind of law, what kind of constitution, one wants to see in place. In the ultra vires issue, the difference is between those (like myself) who believe that the obviously autonomous standards which the courts have evolved for the proper legal control of public bodies should simply be recognised as such, and those who prefer the gross fiction that Parliament has willed the standards. The latter believe that the recognition of a judicial power to control the exercise of public power, if it is a power having nothing to do with the legislature's will, offends or even threatens the doctrine of parliamentary supremacy, and that this is a bad thing.

Ideals are, of course, purely normative. But they may be, and often will be, conditioned by the other three building blocks, as I will explain.

The building of principle is necessarily a normative exercise; and these four categories – logic, consequences, precedent, and idealism – which fly much further than ultra vires, are the foundations upon which, I think, all legal principle is constructed. Logic is a condition of any legal principle we would recognise as worth the name, since without reason, and thus without logic, any rule or proposition will be capricious, arbitrary, or even meaningless. But the requirement of logic is itself a function of what I have called idealism. It is no accident that the law avoids caprice. It is a reflection of man's inheritance as a rational being, which is one of his characteristics making morality both possible and necessary. An appreciation of the consequences of any putative principle in action is a self-evident requirement; but its relationship with the ideals we are to bring to bear – the fourth building-block – is not without subtlety. The mechanism of the construction of principle does not start with a sheet on which only ideals are written. The ideal to be achieved in any case may itself be qualified, changed, by reflection upon the consequences of this or that approach. The interplay of ideals and consequences is the *matrix* in which the three great conflicts to which I have referred are to be concretely resolved in any particular context. In all three, each arm of the dilemma itself represents an ideal, a value; otherwise, of course, the conflicts would not arise. Perceived consequences are likely to offer a route towards the decision, which ideal should prevail. And this exemplifies that hallmark of the common law to which I have referred, namely the achievement of a balance between competing values.

We apply, then, the discipline of logic to the interplay of consequences and ideals, and the process is modified by the use of precedent, which, in the legal context links, as Burke might have said, the dead, the living and the yet unborn in a common enterprise. The use of these four foundations is not optional. In large measure they define the common law. In the English tradition they are the necessary means by which the overall ideal of the rule of law is vindicated.

THE RULE OF LAW

These four foundations march with a theory of the rule of law which is substantive, not formal. There is now an extensive literature about what is meant by the rule of law, in which this antithesis between substance and form has been much debated. I will say only that, in my view, the formal theory – the notion that the rule of law may be satisfied by nothing more than the existence and fulfilment of requirements of manner and form as to the making and promulgation of law, and that this has no evaluative preconceptions as to what is good – is self-contradictory. In Supperstone and Goudie's book[20] I discussed a passage in Professor Paul Craig's *Administrative Law*[21] dealing with the rule of law. Perhaps I may repeat what I said:[22]

Craig says:[23]
"... if the rule of law is to be taken to demand certain substantive rights then it becomes tantamount to propounding a complete social and political philosophy and the concept would then no longer have a useful role independent of that political philosophy. Claims that a society did or did not adhere to the rule of law would simply become the mechanism for articulating these competing philosophies ... [Adherents of the substantive view] seek, therefore, to incorporate within the rule of law some substantive ideas, while at the same time trying to avoid tying these too closely to any specific substantive conception of justice ... The closer that one looks at certain formulations the more apparent does it become that the doctrines which are said to fall within the rule of law thus conceived are of two kinds. They are either in fact just recapitulations of the *formal* attributes of the rule of law, such as procedural due process, no retrospective punishment, and a formal conception of equality, all of which are accepted by those who espouse the first sense of the rule of law. Or they stray into the

[20] Op. cit.: see n. 13.
[21] Sweet and Maxwell, 3rd edition 1994.
[22] Pages 4.31–32.
[23] Op. cit. pp. 22–3.

adoption of a *particular substantive* view of a right, such as equality, which is reflective of one conception of justice."

. . . What I am concerned to do is to try and find the beginnings of an approach which will serve as a workable theory of the court's jurisdiction in place of ultra vires, and on which its development might be built. In this task the first imperative is to grasp Craig's nettle: the adoption of the rule of law as a substantive principle indeed involves a particular perception of social and political philosophy, or (as I would prefer to say) of moral philosophy. It cannot be otherwise: the very idea *means* an adherence to a set of ideals. But so does the formalistic approach. At the very least the latter implies . . . the existence of a rule of recognition as to what is to count as law. But the only point of such a rule's creation is a moral one. It is to distinguish the society where it is accepted from one which is purely anarchistic, or ruled by the whim of tyrants who get their place only by their guns and swords; and to prefer the former as a better place. And if the formalistic model includes such rules as due process and no retrospective punishment (which, logically, it need not) its moral content is all the plainer. In truth there is *no* conception of law which is, so to speak, value-free. This is not refuted by what one may call the minimal case, which might be a rule that whatever the sovereign for the time being dictates is law, unaccompanied by any other rules; for that cannot be distinguished from a situation where we would say there is no law at all – unless there are rules for the appointment of the sovereign and/or rules for the manner in which his will is expressed. But the need for or justification of such rules would be founded in morality; however modest, they would be there to diminish the arbitrary nature of the sovereign's power, because that is a good to be aimed for.

The very distinction between the formal and substantive approaches to the rule of law is therefore misleading. The more likely formal model includes as Craig says rules for the establishment of such goods as due process. In what sense is such a rule only *formal*? Only, I think, that it provides for procedures and not for results. But its rationale is an ideal of fairness. It claims moral ground as surely as "substantive" principles like *Wednesbury*, and of course the two are treated by Lord Diplock in *GCHQ* as having the same status. The real question is, what are the moral principles with which the common law of judicial review is necessarily concerned?

I recognise that some of this needs qualification. In particular I should revisit the statement that "there is *no* conception of law which is, so to speak, value-free". In looking at positivism I have said that the absence of any perceptible moral value in a legal system cannot debar the regime in question from qualifying, on linguistic or sociological grounds, as a legal system. The true position, I think, is that any regime purporting to constitute a legal order will necessarily reflect and exemplify the aspirations of its founders: as no doubt did the laws of Nazi Germany and Stalin's USSR. In this sense it is right that no legal order, or purported legal order, is value-free. It will reflect the values of its makers, which may be good or bad. They may be despicable. But where they are so, any legal order based on them will not reflect what I would see as the rule of law. Now this very proposition takes a normative stance. It attributes a worth to the concept of the rule of law, which I would not necessarily attribute to the mere idea of law itself.

It seems to me that any worthwhile notion of the rule of law's content must be closely associated with the process of building legal principle which I have described. I would, very roughly at least, unpack the substance of the rule of law as a constellation of freedom, justice and order,[24] a constellation respected by the State within which by force of law it has universal application. The constellation implies other requirements, such as an independent impartial judiciary. Any helpful discussion of the concept of the rule of law, of course, would have to take account of the very considerable literature on the subject,[25] and I cannot do that here. What I am concerned to say is that a substantive theory of the rule of law, vindicating core values such as the three I have mentioned, interlocks with the building blocks of common law principles. Each of the three values is, in truth, a function of the other two; hence the constellation. Their elaboration as a coherent whole requires the reflective process implied by the four foundations, which in turn conditions and refines what we *mean* by freedom, justice and order. It requires balances to be struck; and because it does so, it promotes a political or constitutional ethic which is moderate and pluralist. Thus the common law's method, and the substance of constitutional ideals, feed each other.

PARLIAMENT AND THE JUDGES

The common law's evolution of principle is a process which cannot be replicated in the processes of the sovereign Parliament in its legislative capacity, to which it is necessarily dissimilar. Parliament's dictates are inevitably *dirigiste*, precisely because it has the power to dictate anything. Thus any adherence to and respect for the concept of evolved principle on the part of Parliament is contingent, not necessary; and this constitutes a difference in nature, of great importance, between Parliament's law and the common law.

But our constitutional foundations are shifting; the relations between judiciary, executive and legislature are changing. The development of judicial review since the seminal cases in the 1960s – *Ridge* v. *Baldwin*,[26] *Padfield*,[27] *Anisminic*[28] – and the reforms to Order 53 of the Rules of the Supreme Court in 1977 have vouchsafed the submission of the executive to the rule of law. The tide of European law has been the genesis of profound change in the law of statutory interpretation, which has affected the relationship between legislature and judiciary. In particular, the doctrine of implied repeal – and therefore the rule that Parliament cannot bind its successors, which is an important dimension of traditional conceptions of parliamentary sovereignty – is now subject, at least, to heavy qualification.

[24] See *Supperstone and Goudie*, pp. 4.33–4.
[25] Certainly not omitting a piece by David Dyzenhaus, *The Politics of the Rule of Law*, first published in *Ratio Juris*, 3 (1990). It contains this majestic statement (which I am trying to take to heart): "On the whole, judges who become philosophically ambitious are bad judges".
[26] [1964] AC 40.
[27] [1968] AC 997.
[28] [1969] 2 AC 147.

The old rule was, of course, that where a later statute made provision inconsistent with what was laid down in an earlier Act, the earlier measure was *pro tanto* impliedly repealed. In the second *Factortame* case[29] the House of Lords granted an interlocutory injunction whose effect was to disapply for the time being certain provisions contained in the Merchant Shipping Act 1988, there being a question (which fell to be resolved upon a reference made by the House to the European Court of Justice under Article 177 (now 234) of the Treaty of Rome) whether they were repugnant to rights guaranteed by European Community law. The European Communities Act 1972 provided by section 2(4) that Community law was to prevail over Acts of Parliament "passed or to be passed". In the first *Factortame* case[30] Lord Bridge of Harwich said:[31]

> By virtue of section 2(4) of the Act of 1972 Part II of the Act of 1988 is to be construed and take effect subject to directly enforceable Community rights . . . This has precisely the same effect as if a section were incorporated in Part II of the Act of 1988 which in terms enacted that the provisions with respect to registration of British fishing vessels were to be without prejudice to the directly enforceable Community rights of nationals of any member state of the EEC.

This is, certainly, a plain departure from the old doctrine of implied repeal. Sir William Wade recognises it as such. He says in an important article:[32]

> When that Act [sc. the Act of 1972] was . . . held to prevail it seemed fair comment to characterise this, at least in a technical sense, as a constitutional revolution. The Parliament of 1972 had succeeded in binding the Parliament of 1988 and restricting its sovereignty, something that was supposed to be constitutionally impossible. It is obvious that sovereignty belongs to the Parliament of the day and that, if it could be fettered by earlier legislation, the Parliament of the day would cease to be sovereign.

After citing the passage from Lord Bridge's speech set out above, Sir William continues:[33]

> But this is much more than an exercise in construction. Lord Bridge's hypothetical section would take effect by authority of the Parliament of 1988, not the Parliament of 1972. To hold that its terms are putatively incorporated in the Act of 1988 is merely another way of saying that the Parliament of 1972 has imposed a restriction upon the Parliament of 1988. That is exactly what the classical doctrine of sovereignty does not permit.

Nothing in this passage or what follows in Sir William's article persuades me that in point of legal principle we are here dealing with anything other than the courts' approach to questions of statutory construction. In truth the doctrine of parliamentary sovereignty which Sir William is at pains to emphasise, namely that a later Act prevails over an earlier in the case of inconsistency, was never

---

[29]   [1991] 1 AC 603.
[30]   [1990] 2 AC 85.
[31]   At p. 140.
[32]   *Sovereignty – Revolution or Evolution?* (1996) 112 *LQR* 568 (at p. 568).
[33]   Pages 570–1.

more than a function of statutory interpretation. What else could it be? I think the true rule of sovereignty, as it were the bottom line, is and is only that Parliament may pass what law it chooses, and the courts are bound to apply any such law. How the courts apply Parliament's law depends, obviously, upon how they interpret it; and it is long established law that the interpretation of statutes is within the judges' province. The meaning of any statute at any time is ascertained and mediated to the people by the judges. In *X Ltd* v. *Morgan Grampian Ltd*[34] Lord Bridge of Harwich stated:

> In our society the rule of law rests upon twin foundations: the sovereignty of the Queen in Parliament and the sovereignty of the Queen's courts in interpreting and applying the law.

With respect this is precisely accurate. The rule of implied repeal belongs to the sovereignty of the Queen's courts.

There is thus a categorical difference between the rule of implied repeal and the principle that Parliament may enact what it chooses. Abolition of the former (as a universal rule) does not derogate from the latter. There is nothing "revolutionary" (to use Sir William's expression) about such a change. What it *does* mean is that in areas where implied repeal no longer has effect, Parliament, if it seeks to change the law, must enact in express terms. And the areas in question are, and will increasingly be identified as, those where constitutional fundamentals are involved.

By force, perhaps, of sheer political reality the law of Europe led the march towards this position. In *Factortame* a judicial decision which disapplied section 2(4) of the European Communities Act 1972 from the Merchant Shipping Act 1988, but, presumably, otherwise left the 1972 Act (and so our membership of the Community) intact, would plainly have been a legal and political – and logical – nightmare; the air round Luxembourg would have been thick with flying writs; and, as I recall, the government never argued for such a position.

But if the dam of implied repeal has been breached by Europe, it is not an isolated hole in the wall. As regards the common law, the decision in *Witham*[35] was concerned with the right of access to the Queen's courts: a statutory instrument required those without means or legal aid, along with everyone else, to pay substantial court fees to start or in some circumstances participate in litigation. The Divisional Court (Rose LJ and myself) held that, at least, "clear" legislation (per Rose LJ) would be required to produce such a result. Perhaps I may be forgiven for citing from my own judgment which was delivered first at Rose LJ's invitation:

> It seems to me . . . that the common law has clearly given special weight to the citizen's right of access to the courts. It has been described as a constitutional right . . . In this whole argument, nothing to my mind has been shown to displace the proposition that the executive cannot in law abrogate the right of access to justice, unless it is

[34] [1991] 1 AC 1, 48.
[35] [1998] 2 WLR 849.

specifically so permitted by Parliament; and this is the meaning of the constitutional right. But I must explain . . . what in my view the law requires by such a permission. A statute may give the permission expressly; in that case it would provide in terms that in defined circumstances the citizen may not enter the court door . . . I find great difficulty in conceiving a form of words capable of making it plain beyond doubt to the statute's reader that the provision in question prevents him from going to court (for that is what would be required), save in a case where that is expressly stated. The class of cases where it could be done by necessary implication is, I venture to think, a class with no members . . .

Access to the courts is a constitutional right; it can only be denied by the government if it persuades Parliament to pass legislation which specifically – in effect by express provision – permits the executive to turn people away from the court door.

Now, I accept entirely that there may be questions whether *express* provision is required to override a fundamental right.[36] But we are, at least, moving towards a common law recognition of the existence of such rights. In my view, to the extent that such rights are to be recognised, they can only be given effect in our uncodified constitution by a rule of statutory construction to the effect that express provision is required to override them. Such a rule preserves entirely the sovereignty of Parliament; it requires only that if Parliament is to override a fundamental right, it must say so unambiguously. No democrat, surely, would have difficulty with this.

But here there is a difficulty. Because we have no written constitution, no sovereign text, the identification of constitutional rights as opposed to much lesser rights (like walking your dog on the pavement) is on the face of it at large. The common law has gone some way here. *Witham* is an instance. This passage from Lord Bridge's speech in *Brind* is very important:[37]

But I do not accept that this conclusion [viz. that there is no presumption that a statutory discretionary power must be exercised within ECHR limits] means that the courts are powerless to prevent the exercise by the executive of administrative discretions, even when conferred, as in the instant case, in terms which are on their face unlimited, in a way which infringes fundamental human rights. Most of the rights spelled out in terms in the Convention, including the right to freedom of expression, are less than absolute and must in some cases yield to the claims of competing public interests. Thus, article 10(2) of the Convention spells out and categorises the competing public interests by reference to which the right to freedom of expression may have to be curtailed. In exercising the power of judicial review we have neither the advantages nor the disadvantages of any comparable code to which we may refer or by which we are bound. But again, this surely does not mean that in deciding whether the Secretary of State, in the exercise of his discretion, could reasonably impose the restriction he has

---

[36] In *Ex p. Pierson* [1998] AC 539 Lord Browne-Wilkinson said at 575C: "Although I must not be taken as agreeing with everything said in the judgment in that case [*Ex p Witham*] (in particular whether basic rights can be overridden by necessary implication as opposed to express provision), I have no doubt that the decision was correct for the principle reasons relied on by Laws J in his judgment. Such basic rights are not to be overridden by the general words of a statute since the presumption is against the impairment of such basic rights".

[37] [1991] 1 AC 696 at 748F–749B.

imposed on the broadcasting organisations, we are not perfectly entitled to start from the premise that any restriction of the right to freedom of expression requires to be justified and that nothing less than an important competing public interest will be sufficient to justify it. The primary judgment as to whether the particular competing public interest justifies the particular restriction imposed falls to be made by the Secretary of State to whom Parliament has entrusted the discretion. But we are entitled to exercise a secondary judgment by asking whether a reasonable Secretary of State, on the material before him, could reasonably make that primary judgment.

There is a big question how far it is for the judges to prescribe what are fundamental constitutional rights. They can go so far; access to justice, and the right to life and limb, are obvious enough. No one would suggest that a person might for instance be imprisoned save by express legal authority. But other cases, of actual or putative constitutional rights, are less clear. In relation to them the judges have to have well in mind that they are not elected. Hence the crucial importance, in what the judges do, of the requirement of public confidence which I have described. Without democratic validation, without a sovereign constitutional text, the development of a law of fundamental rights must remain a careful and conservative exercise. I think the common law can do it, without offence to other powers and interests in the State. But the deep constitutional importance of the Human Rights Act 1998 rests in the fact that it gives democratic validation to the concrete expression of constitutional rights.

Anxieties are expressed in some quarters that the balance of State power is, and more particularly will be by force of the Human Rights Act, tilted too far towards the unelected judges. They will have to make decisions on large questions involving value judgments upon issues about which there may be deep ethical and philosophical disagreement; and what is seen as rule by the subjective opinions of an unelected judiciary is regarded as objectionable. These concerns will be more readily allayed if the nature of judicial decision-making is better understood. The means by which principle is elaborated, the use of the four building blocks, is at the heart of it. While it would be simply idle to deny that judges, like anyone else, have their own opinions, often no doubt strongly held, the process I have described confines the judge's own views in a strict and objective context. It produces a high degree of continuity in the law, a union of past and future; and the conditions for the maintenance of public confidence in the common law will remain the same.

The application of the Human Rights Act in practice must come to be seen as the product of a partnership between legislature and judiciary. The demise of implied repeal, which I have discussed, will be carried further by the deployment of section 3 of the Act, subsection (1) of which provides:

> So far as it is possible to do so, primary legislation and subordinate legislation must be read and given effect in a way which is compatible with the Convention rights.

I will go so far as to say that I expect this provision will enable legislation to be read conformably with Convention Rights in all cases save where the right is expressly denied. Such an approach surely marches with the legislature's intention; and it should mean that declarations of incompatibility will be very rare. It sits with the emerging common law rule that constitutional rights may only be denied by express enactment. But now the rule will have the authority of Parliament.

Confucius was wrong to say that it is a curse to live in interesting times. We are witnessing the development of a constitutional philosophy which recognises fundamental values, and gives them effect in the mediation of law to the people. It is being done by the incremental process of the common law and the enactment of legislation which, as its makers must intend, invites an approach to its own interpretation and that of other statutes in which these values guide the judge's hand.

Written constitutions, I think, only work if they are made at the beginning of an era in the State's history. They must be the first page in the book. The book of England's law is far too many volumes long for such an enterprise. The great benefit of a written constitution is that it establishes fundamental norms whose authority is not in question, which are axioms upon which other law is based. The adventure on which we are presently engaged opens the door to like advantages in the setting of our uncodified constitution. The nature of common law principle, most active as it is in the developed law of judicial review, is a plinth well fitted to bear much of the weight.

Constitutional Reform and the Foundations of Judicial Review

9

The Foundations of Review, Devolved Power and Delegated Power

BRIGID HADFIELD

GENERAL INTRODUCTION

In accordance with what principles will a court[1] determine the validity of an Act of a devolved legislature? The potential answers to this question may, constitutionally, be "writ large" or "writ small", but, either way, the search for the answer involves seeking to identify the continuing adequacy of the "central organizational theme"[2] of the United Kingdom constitution. The classic view is (or has been) that the bedrock of both constitutional and administrative law is the doctrine of the sovereignty of the Westminster Parliament and, in administrative law, its corollary the doctrine of ultra vires. So, Lord Steyn in *Boddington* v. *British Transport Police*[3] said:

> Leaving to one side the separate topic of judicial review of non-legal powers exercised by non-statutory bodies, I see no reason to depart from the orthodox view that ultra vires is "the central principle of administrative law" . . .[4]

Quoting from Lord Browne-Wilkinson in *R* v. *Hull University Visitor, ex parte Page* ("The fundamental principle of judicial review is that the courts will intervene to ensure that the powers of public decision-making bodies are exercised

---

[1] The answers may, of course, vary according to within which legal jurisdiction the "devolution" case arises for decision. The Judicial Committee of the Privy Council, the ultimate court of appeal for United Kingdom devolution cases (subject to a residual discretion in the House of Lords) must, in this respect, be regarded as a "United Kingdom" court, although its location (and possibly also its composition) may be regarded as rendering it an "English" court. This may seem simplistic, but the idea that "geography" governs, if not judicial reasoning, then at least popular perceptions of the administration of justice lies at the heart of the decision to enable Welsh Devolution issues (Crown Office cases) to be heard in Cardiff: see Practice Direction: Welsh Devolution Issues, June 1999, paras. 14.2 and 14.3.

[2] Supreme Court of Canada, in *In re Secession of Quebec from Canada* [1998] 2 SCR 217, at para. 57.

[3] [1998] 2 All ER 203 (HL, E).

[4] *Ibid.*, at p. 225. The quotation is from H.W.R. Wade and C.F. Forsyth, *Administrative Law* (7th ed., 1994) at 41.

lawfully"),[5] Lord Steyn concluded: "This is the essential constitutional under-pinning of the statute-based part of our administrative law".[6]

One needs, therefore, to consider the constitutional nature of the ground occupied by devolved power. Is it the same as legislative power delegated to local authorities and other bodies having the power to make bye-laws; that is, is it simply one new aspect of the statute-based part of our administrative law – nothing other (legally) than a new (novel, even) manifestation of issues which the courts have long been used to resolving? If devolved power is but delegated power on a geographically larger scale, then the sole judicial caution in the review of devolved power like much delegated (but unlike much administrative)[7] power will lie in the recognition, in challenges on the ground of unreasonableness, to be accorded the body's electoral mandate. As Lord Russell CJ said in *Kruse* v. *Johnson*[8]:

> A by-law is not unreasonable merely because particular judges may think that it goes further than is prudent or necessary or convenient . . . Surely it is not too much to say that in matters which directly and mainly concern the people of the county, who have the right to choose those whom they think best fitted to represent them in their local government bodies, such representatives may be trusted to understand their own requirements better than the judges.[9]

Devolved power carries a greater electoral mandate, for it operates in the context not of a locality but, at its lowest, a "region" and at its highest "a nation". Furthermore, the popular or electoral mandate for the devolved legislatures is as it were a double one: the electorate of both Scotland and Wales were asked first to approve, in a referendum, the principle (and general outline) of devolution, in addition to the actual voting in the subsequent elections to the Scottish Parliament and Welsh Assembly. The question is, is this "national" electoral mandate of itself sufficient legally to distinguish in any material respect devolved power from delegated power?

It may be, by contrast, that devolved power approximates more closely to federalism. Devolution quite clearly is not the same as federalism, which requires the exclusive allocation of powers by a written constitution to federal and state/provincial legislatures of co-ordinate status with each other. The doctrine of parliamentary sovereignty cannot co-exist with federalism. Parliamentary sovereignty requires not co-ordinate legislatures, but a superordinate legislature

---

  [5] [1993] AC 682, at 701.

  [6] [1998] 2 All ER 203, at 225. See also *per* Lord Browne-Wilkinson, at 218: "I adhere to my view that the juristic basis of judicial review is the doctrine of ultra vires".

  [7] See *e.g.*, *Nottinghamshire County Council* v. *Secretary of State for the Environment* [1986] 1 All ER 199 (HL, E). This case actually involved guidance to be issued by the Secretary of State (and not delegated legislation *per se*), but the Local Government, Planning and Land Act 1980 required the guidance to be approved by resolution of the House of Commons. Payment of the rate support grant to local authorities could only be made in accordance with the resolution of the HC. Lord Scarman, at 202, said: ". . . these are matters of political judgment for him and for the House of Commons. They are not for the judges or your Lordships House in its judicial capacity".

  [8] [1898] 2 QB 91.

  [9] *Ibid.*, at 100.

(Westminster) and subordinate ones, that is, devolved legislatures with no exclusive powers and with what powers they do possess vulnerable to unilateral alteration by Westminster.

It is now, however, and with regard to Northern Ireland's previous experience of devolution,[10] has been for a time, fashionable to identify devolution, actually or potentially, as a form of quasi-federalism. The essence of this argument is that the strict legal form of devolution (which is *not* federalism) becomes softened into something closer to it, by the growth and operation of constitutional conventions.[11] The conventions which would be significant in this context would be a convention of Westminster non-intervention in devolved matters ("exclusive powers"?) and one of no fundamental amendment to the Scotland Act without the agreement of the Scottish Parliament (and people) ("the Scotland Act as a written constitution"?).

So the question becomes: is there in terms of strict law (there clearly is politically) any room between delegated power and federalism as may not only be *occupied* by devolution but also be *reflected* in the principles of interpretation, on *vires* questions, which are to be adopted by the courts? This question becomes more complex in many ways, given that the systems of devolution which have been introduced for Scotland, Wales and Northern Ireland are asymmetrical and will thus involve all the courts (especially the House of Lords and, to a much greater extent, the Judicial Committee of the Privy Council) in the resolution of different constitutional relationships between Westminster and the devolved legislatures.

While devolution may raise questions whether constitutional conventions (and the overall political context within which they will operate) can be sufficiently strong as to persuade the courts to regard devolved power as different from delegated power, it may also raise questions as the extent to which parliamentary sovereignty is (still) the constitutional bedrock. The "emergence" of parliamentary supremacy *post* 1688 and its entrenchment (through widespread acceptance by the key constitutional players) indicate a particular constitutional relationship between Parliament and the courts,[12] in which the essential

---

[10] See *e.g.*, H.Calvert, *Constitutional Law in Northern Ireland* (1968) (which bears the sub-title: "a study in regional government"), chap. 6 and *passim*, and B.Hadfield, *The Constitution of Northern Ireland* (1989), 80–8. Two analogies were actually used with regard to the relationship between the Westminster and Northern Ireland Parliaments and the bases for the analogies should be kept distinct. The first, as already mentioned, related to the quasi-federalism arguments; the second argued that the relationship was akin to that between Westminster and a Dominion Parliament.

[11] References to the case-law, for example, and especially *Gallagher* v. *Lynn* [1937] AC 863, is also made in this context. The point is not further pursued here (but see below) because in general terms, this point would beg rather than answer the questions concerning judicial response to devolved power.

[12] Geoffrey Wilson's summary of the doctrine in *Cases and Materials on Constitutional and Administrative Law* (1976, 2nd ed.) remains, it is submitted, a very percipient analysis of the doctrine. At 226, he writes:- ". . . useful as quotations from past cases are in illustrating the attitudes and rhetoric of particular judges and particular courts, they do not *establish* the present constitutional position or provide a conclusive answer as to how judges in the future in different and more important circumstances ought to behave. There can in a strict sense be no legal authority for the doctrine. *It is an*

principles are that judicial power is derived and subordinate and is not autonomous (and co-equal) with parliamentary power. With devolution, the courts in both Scotland and Northern Ireland (and ultimately too the House of Lords and especially the Judicial Committee of the Privy Council) will be engaging with what in some respects may accurately be termed *primary* legislation[13] in the context of a non-sovereign legislature and hence, at least indirectly, with Westminster's powers *vis-à-vis* the devolved legislature. Given that the democratic mandate (and democratic mandate plays a key part in the legal centrality of the Westminster Parliament) of the devolved legislature is *at the least* co-equal with that of Westminster in the devolved region or nation, one must ask in this regard (using Sir Anthony Mason's words in a different context) whether the doctrine of Westminster's legislative supremacy "cannot be taken so far as to support measures which would undermine the system of democratic government as we (now post-devolution) know it".[14]

There is also a point to be made here concerning the status of the Acts of Union as constituent Acts. It is perfectly possible – and legally compelling in many regards – to formulate an argument that Westminster is only a sovereign parliament when exercising its powers with regard to England. To assume that the doctrine applies equally to Scotland especially (and to Northern Ireland) is too simplistic. There are distinctively Scottish (and distinctively Northern Ireland) constitutional principles, not least regarding the Acts of Union as constituent Acts, and post-devolution these arguments will not be confined solely to their own courts.[15] These principles have been too often ignored in the debates on the centrality of parliamentary sovereignty. These principles facilitate an argument, that the basic constitutional *grundnorm* is not the sovereignty of

---

example of what is traditionally called a constitutional convention. That it is regarded as a basic convention by the present generation of judges does not make it any more immune to change than any other part of the unwritten constitution. It is a convention which is the product of historical development and of a view of the constitution which has for some time now been handed down without serious questioning from textbook to textbook, but *its real strength lies in the principles underlying it and the views and values which those principles express.* Should they change the doctrine may well turn out to be less sacrosanct than the authorities would have us believe". Author's own emphasis for the word "establish"; otherwise emphasis added.

[13] This is *not* the terminology which is employed under the Human Rights Act 1998 with regard to devolved legislation: see s. 21(1), and further below.

[14] Sir Anthony Mason, "One Vote, One Value v. The Parliamentary Tradition – the Federal Experience" in C.Forsyth and I.Hare (eds), *The Golden Metwand and the Crooked Cord* (1998), at 334. At 351, he writes: "The doctrine of parliamentary sovereignty is the servant not the master of the constitution in the United Kingdom".

[15] See *e.g.*, *MacCormick* v. *Lord Advocate* (1953) SC 396; *Gibson* v. *Lord Advocate* 1975 SLT 134; B.Hadfield, "Learning from the Indians: the Constitutional Guarantee re-visited" 1983 *PL* 351, and "The Belfast Agreement, Sovereignty and the State of the Union" [1998] *PL* 599; M.Upton, "Marriage Vows of the Elephant: The Constitution of 1707" (105) 1989 *LQR* 79. See also Lord King Murray: "Devolution in the U.K. – A Scottish Perspective" (96) 1980 *LQR* 35. (The article concerned the debates on and demise of the Scotland Act 1978). At 50 he writes: ". . . the orthodox doctrine of the sovereignty of Parliament may now be an obstacle to reasonable and progressive institutional reform in this country". See also N. MacCormick, *Questioning Sovereignty* (1999).

Parliament but that of the people,[16] or at the very least that the latter (at least as contained in the Acts of Union and the electorates' wishes concerning their evolution and modification) can serve to moderate the operation of the former. Section 2 of the Northern Ireland Act 1998 and section 37 of the Scotland Act, with all due respect, beg and do not answer these questions.[17] Devolution has given the courts throughout the United Kingdom the opportunity to consider what the key elements of the constitution are and it cannot be assumed that all courts throughout the United Kingdom will identify the elements identically. It is not being argued that the idea of the Acts of Union as constituent Acts is universally accepted. It is not.[18] As Martin Loughlin writes:

> Consider, for example, the argument touted by a number of Scottish lawyers in recent years, that the Articles of Union of 1707 are constitutive of the United Kingdom. Their argument undoubtedly has a certain logic to it. But . . . [the] fallacy of this Scottish position is to be located in the assumption that the constitutional significance of these Acts can be discerned by logical analysis. Because this Scottish argument fails to acknowledge that positive law is not foundational, its proponents fail to recognize that, in Pocock's words, the Union of 1707 was an "incorporating" rather than a "federating" union.[19]

The point which is being made here is the more prosaic one of indicating that there indubitably exist different approaches to the nature of the Acts of Union (whatever their respective merits) and that these arguments will undoubtedly be aired throughout the different legal jurisdictions of the United Kingdom. There are no obviously immediate *a priori* assumptions as to which argument will prevail where.

Certainly the language of the political and parliamentary debates for Scottish (but not Northern Irish) devolution – and during the Human Rights Act too – was redolent with the language of parliamentary sovereignty. Paradoxically, it may be that these Acts together sound the end of the doctrine – this, in spite of the fact, that the powers of the devolved legislatures are far more tightly drawn than is often the case with Acts of Parliament conferring powers on government ministers.

There is one last preliminary point to be made about the doctrine of parliamentary sovereignty and its influence upon the courts in their interpretation of legislation. The courts in discharging this responsibility frequently state that in so doing their prime task is to seek "the intention of Parliament". It is trite

[16] See, within the context of possible secession from a federation, *In re Secession of Quebec from Canada*, n. 2 supra at para. 85: "The Constitution is the expression of the sovereignty of the people of Canada. It lies within the power of the people of Canada, acting through their various governments duly elected and recognised under the Constitution, to effect whatever constitutional arrangements are desired within Canadian territory". See the debates which will (inevitably) take place as to the requisite procedures or "consents" for fundamental amendment of the Scotland Act itself. See *Issues around Scottish Independence* (The Constitution Unit, 1999).

[17] See also the Scotland Act, sched. 4, and sched. 5, Part 1, para. 1b.

[18] See *e.g.*, Colin Munro, *Studies in Constitutional Law*, (2nd edn., 1999) ch. 5.

[19] In "Rights Discourse and Public Law Thought in the United Kingdom" in G.Anderson (ed.), *Rights and Democracy: Essays in UK – Canadian Constitutionalism* (1999), at 202. Author's footnotes omitted.

constitutional law to state that, given the relationship between the government of the day and the Commons and the limited powers of the House of Lords, that what is *in fact* being sought is the intention of the government (as contained in the legislation enacted through a government-dominant process). Judges are as well aware of this as any one else. This is a point which has been further highlighted by the decision of the House of Lords in *Pepper* v. *Hart*[20] – and the subsequent practice of the sponsoring minister making "*Pepper* v. *Hart* statements" during the legislative process, which are often then resorted to later – whether or not the statutory provision is ambiguous and obscure. (The ruling in *Pepper* v. *Hart*, of course, also carries the "risk" that Bills may be drafted in an obscure way, leaving resort to ministerial statements inevitable).[21] Nonetheless, the fiction of the "intent of Parliament" – accepted by all as a fiction – continues to be resorted to. It may well be, however, that the courts and the government (particularly the government) should accept the reality of the situation and rearticulate the rule to accord with reality, namely that, statutory interpretation (particularly with regard to modern statutes) (often) involves the search for the *intent of the government through Parliament*. The dominance of the executive within the constitution should not continue to be masked by fictions, which all accept are fictions, and which, by implying the legal supremacy of the will of *Parliament* as of the representatives of the people, merely serve further to heighten the powers of the government *vis-à-vis* the courts. To what extent would a realistic reformulation of the parliamentary intent fiction lead to a reassessment of the constitutional acceptability of the centrality of parliamentary sovereignty?[22] The recitation of the doctrine of parliamentary sovereignty (especially by a government wishing to emphasise *its own* superordinate power as against the courts) has become something of a mantra, but in terms of its impact upon the development of constitutional principles, it is something of a praying mantis. The only effective counter to this point is for the Commons to put its own house in order and make the *parliamentary* aspects of executive control (more) real.

---

[20] [1993] AC 593 (HL, E).

[21] See, for example, the way in which explanations are provided of the meaning of section 6 of the Human Rights Act 1998.

[22] The force of this is often seen with regard to government response to adverse judicial rulings. See Andrew Le Sueur, "The Judicial Review Debate: from partnership to friction" (1996) 31 *Government and Opposition* 8; and M.Sunkin and Le Sueur, [1997] *PL* 470–4. See also Lord Woolf "Judicial Review – The Tensions between the Executive and the Judiciary" 1998 (114) *LQR* 579: "I have no doubt that there is and has been, particularly over the last five years, tension between the judiciary and the executive, and that the tension has from time to time increased as a result of the decisions of judges on applications for judicial review. I, however, do not regard this as a matter of concern. It is no more than an indication that judicial review has been working well during a period when the other restraints on the executive were not as great as ideally they should be".

Devolution is not coming to the courts "cold". The evolution of principles of constitutional adjudication in the context of European Community law, the European Convention on Human Rights, the Commonwealth jurisdiction of the Judicial Committee of the Privy Council and judicial review of delegated legislation is of considerable – albeit currently latent – significance. It may even be that *Dr Bonham's Case,*[23] the *fons et origo* of much debate, stemming from a pre-1688 constitutional era, may be ready for a revival, as the twenty-first century constitutional structures replace the (relative) stability of the preceding 300 years. All these points and the points made in the Introduction should be placed in the context of Lord Sankey's *dictum* – not perhaps quoted now as often as it was but of increasing significance –

> ... the Imperial Parliament could, as a matter of abstract law, repeal or disregard section 4 of the Statute of Westminster. *But this is theory and has no relation to realities.*[24]

The importance of this *dictum* may be illustrated by reference to the legislative supremacy of Westminster and its powers *vis-à-vis* European Community law. Those who argue that Westminster is still sovereign (post-*Simmenthal, Factortame et al*)[25] argue that the current limitations upon sovereignty are reversible; that the United Kingdom is free to legislate to withdraw from the Community. The Lord Chancellor (in his lecture to the Hong Kong Supreme Court, September 1998)[26] has argued that the doctrine of parliamentary sovereignty is not, in this regard, affected in terms of it still being the "fundamental and ultimate limit on the powers of British courts" because (1) the ultimate sovereignty of Parliament remains intact; (the Treaty of Rome may be repudiated); (2) "this reversible modification of the sovereignty principle operates only in the limited (*sic*) fields in which EU Law applies"; and (3) ". . . this alteration to the sovereignty doctrine is emphatically not the result of a unilateral initiative on the part of the courts".

It will remain a matter of debate, for some time at least, as to the extent to which this attitude reflects theory or reality, but reasoning or logic as such cannot dictate which is the "right" answer. In the interim, an increasing number of adjectives have been brought into play to indicate the current strains on the doctrine: limited sovereignty, pluralistic sovereignty, divided sovereignty, residual

---

[23] 1610 Co Rep at 118 a: "And it appears in our books, that in many cases, the common law will control Acts of Parliament, and sometimes adjudge them to be utterly void: for when an Act of Parliament is against common right and reason, or repugnant, or impossible to be performed, the common law will control it, and adjudge such an Act to be void". Cf J. Goldsworthy, *The Sovereignty of Parliament* (1999).

[24] *British Coal Corporation* v. *The King* [1935] AC 500, 520. For a postscript, see section 2 of the Canada Act 1982.

[25] [1978] ECR 629; and, *e.g.* [1989] 2 All ER 692 and [1991] 1 All ER 70.

[26] It is entitled "Principle and Pragmatism; The Development of English Public Law under the Separation of Powers". See www.open.gov.uk/lcd/speeches/1998.

sovereignty – to the point where it, at times, seems to have become "a freely adjustable commodity".[27]

DEVOLUTION: THE MECHANICS

This chapter now deals with the legal framework of devolution, for Scotland and for Northern Ireland (without equating all issues to which the two systems give rise).[28] Devolution, in many ways, occupies the complex constitutional terrain between the rock of parliamentary sovereignty and the hard place peopled by the spectres of judicial supremacists. This section deals not with all the details of the two schemes but with some particularly pertinent features in the context of this chapter. Most of the references deal with Northern Ireland, with comparative reference to Scotland, given the material available elsewhere on the Scotland Act.[29] The significance, however, lies not in the detail provided but in the issues to which they give rise.

Exclusive powers?

The Northern Ireland Act 1998 contains three categories of legislative power, as explained in section 4 and schedules 2 and 3. This is to be contrasted with the Scotland Act, which contains reserved and devolved or transferred matters only. In both Acts, the devolved matters are not enumerated; they constitute the residue once the enumerated (excepted and) reserved matters have been subtracted.

Excepted matters are enumerated in schedule 2 of the Northern Ireland Act. Lord Dubs in the House of Lords stated: "They are in substance not within the purview of the Assembly at all and cannot be transferred to it. They concern chiefly central government issues like international relations, defence and taxation".[30] Under the 1998 Act, excepted matters are outside the legislative competence of the Northern Ireland Assembly, unless the provision in the Assembly Act is "ancillary" to other provisions dealing with reserved or transferred matters. "Ancillary" is defined in section 6(3), and "deals with" is defined in section 98(2) (on these see further below).

---

[27] See H.W.R. Wade, "Sovereignty – Revolution or Evolution" (1996) 112 *LQR* 568, at 573.

[28] The system of devolution contained in the Government of Wales Act 1998 is not dealt with here, for the reason that that Act essentially introduces a system of devolution which is identified as delegated legislation. It is not, however, being suggested by this omission that Welsh Assembly devolved legislation equates in all regards to ministerial or local authority delegated legislation. Some of the points discussed below will, in more general terms, also have application to Wales.

[29] See *e.g.*, C.Himsworth and C.R.Munro, *The Scotland Act 1998* (1999), A.Page, C.Reid and A.Ross, *A Guide to the Scotland Act 1998* (1999) and J.McFadden and M.Lazarowicz, *The Scottish Parliament: An Introduction* (1999). For an outline of the Northern Ireland Act, see B.Hadfield, "The Nature of Devolution in Scotland and Northern Ireland: Key Issues of Responsibility and Control" 1999 (3) *Edinburgh Law Review* 3.

[30] 5 October 1998, vol. 593, col. 170.

Section 4(1) states that "excepted matters" means *any matter falling within a description* specified in schedule 2". An earlier draft of the Bill read: "means the *matters specified in* schedule 2". This change, which has greater relevance concerning the identical wording used for reserved matters (schedule 3),[31] was made in order to indicate that the "matters" specified in the schedule cover not only the "matters" expressly mentioned but also "matters" which fall within one of the descriptions there.

Reserved matters are enumerated in schedule 3. The Assembly may legislate on reserved matters only with the consent of the Secretary of State (section 8) and Westminster parliamentary control (section 15). Among the reserved matters are policing and criminal justice but the category is by no means confined to these matters. Lord Dubs pointed out that this category drew not only on the provisions of the Belfast Agreement but also on the pre-existing legal framework of, for example, the Government of Ireland Act 1920 and Northern Ireland Constitution Act 1973. Accordingly, said Lord Dubs:

> our starting point has to be the 1973 divisions. But some tidying up has been required . . . The reserved category includes a number of matters which the [Belfast] Agreement envisages as being suitable for transfer, in the fields of policing and justice. But not all reserved matters are, or were in 1973, envisaged as suitable for transfer . . .[32]

Under section 4 a reserved matter may become a transferred matter or *vice versa* under a cross-community supported Assembly resolution *and* a Westminster Order in Council. Hence, the reserved category (consisting of some forty-two matters) embodies the maximum amount of flexibility while adhering to the terms of the Belfast Agreement and the pre-existing legal framework. Matters in that category may be legislated on by Westminster (see here section 85) or by the Assembly, with Westminster/Secretary of State approval *or* may become a part of the transferred category. Schedules 2 and 3 specify the excepted and reserved matters. Under section 4(1) a "transferred matter" means any matter which is not an excepted or reserved matter. That is, transferred matters are *not* enumerated. The same is true of the Scotland Act, although it contains only two categories of legislation, those devolved and those reserved or not devolved. The Scottish "reserved" category should thus not be equated with the Northern Ireland Act's "reserved" category but with its "excepted" category. Also, the "broad brush" approach taken to the Northern Ireland Act's excepted and reserved matters, when contrasted with the highly specific and detailed style of the Scotland Act's schedule 5 reserved matters, is explained by Northern Ireland's statutory history of devolution and the constraints afforded by the 1920 and particularly the 1973 Acts. In Scotland, starting with a clean slate, the highly detailed approach was preferred. One issue to be considered concerning

[31] See *per* Lord Dubs, 19 October 1998, vol. 593, col. 1196: "We intend that any matter that falls within the reserved field, whether it is expressly mentioned in schedule 3 or merely falls within one of the descriptions there, should be capable of transfer . . ." (provided the requisite criteria in section 4 are satisfied).

[32] *Ibid.*, col. 1822.

Scotland's reserved category (which is relatively open-ended – see section 30(2))[33] and Northern Ireland's excepted category (amendable only by Westminster Act) is the extent to which they may be or may come to be regarded as Westminster's exclusive domain, *conjointly with* the matters devolved then lying within the *exclusive* domain of the devolved legislature. It is beyond argument that the legislation, by expressly preserving Westminster's power to legislate for Scotland and Northern Ireland,[34] creates no category of power which is withheld from *its* competence. This is, however, an area worth exploring with Lord Sankey's *dictum* in mind – especially concerning the conventions or procedures which will develop regarding Westminster's powers to debate or scrutinise devolved matters (and *vice versa* regarding Scotland and reserved matters). The legislative history of section 28(7) of the Scotland Act, preserving Westminster's supremacy, indicates the Government's (inevitably) ambivalent or vague approach to the constitutional ramifications of devolution. For the Government, this subsection ". . . capture[s] . . . the essence of devolution as opposed to some other model such as, perhaps, federalism". The counter-argument was to the effect that the subsection "is provocative and indeed positively offensive because it almost invites [Westminster] to meddle in the future in the law-making of Scotland on those matters which this [Act] devolves to Scotland". This was in turn countered by the promise that ". . . as happened in Northern Ireland earlier in the century, we would expect a convention to be established that Westminster would not normally legislate with regard to devolved matters in Scotland without the consent of the Scottish Parliament".[35]

The House of Commons' Select Committee on Procedure in its Fourth Report of May 1999 repeated the Government's juxtaposition of Parliament's power to legislate on any devolved matter, with the likelihood of the adoption of the convention of no legislation without consent. Indeed, the Government has also stated that it will, in general, oppose private member's legislation at Westminster in a devolved area, in the absence of consent from the devolved body. The Procedure Committee itself supported "the principles behind this statement and agree that the House should not legislate on devolved matters without the consent of the legislature concerned".[36]

The Government thus seeks to identify the essence of devolution as involving the sovereignty of parliament limited by a constitutional convention of non-exercise of its sovereign powers within the devolved areas. The question then of *Westminster's* legislative powers is *sought* to be removed from the courts. If the

[33] See Lord Dubs, *ibid*: "Under the Scotland Bill, there is a greater flexibility to change the constitutional categorisation of matters; under [the Northern Ireland] Bill, there is no mechanism for moving matters out of the excepted field".

[34] Scotland Act 1998, s. 28(7) and Northern Ireland Act 1998, s. 5(6).

[35] See Himsworth and Munro, *op.cit.*, n. 29, at p. 36, from where these quotations are taken.

[36] HC 185 (1998–9), 24 May 1999, para. 26. See also HC 814 (1998–9). The publication of the Memorandum of Understanding (Cm. 4444, October 1999, see especially paras 13–15, 26–7 and the Agreement on the Joint Ministerial Committee) post dates the writing of this chapter but the MoU and the Concordats confirm the writer's opinion that devolution should be regarded as *Sui generis* and not "quasi" anything else.

Westminster Government should seek to introduce legislation there dealing with a devolved matter, then that Bill when enacted would be covered by the statutory provisions in the devolution Act expressly preserving Westminster's supremacy (and the existence of the convention would be recognised but not enforced by the courts). These provisions are also reinforced by provisions locating the power to amend the devolution Acts in Westminster alone[37] and provisions ensuring that in the case of a "conflict of laws" in the devolved area, the Westminster Act will prevail.[38] The statutory provisions are also to be bolstered by political arrangements, for example, a Joint Ministerial Committee, as well as other more informal liaison, seeking to ensure that "demarcation disputes" would be resolved at an early stage. The role of the courts is, thus, to be confined to statutory interpretation concerning the express or implied reach of the Westminster Act on devolved matters. The issue of the "exclusivity" of devolved power, therefore, becomes one of (Westminster's) political choice not judicial resolution. By contrast, there would, on first appearance, appear to be a far greater role for the courts on questions concerning the *vires* of devolved legislation.

The devolved legislative competence

This is provided for – for the Northern Ireland Assembly – in section 6(1) to (3) of the Northern Ireland Act, which are as follows:-

> A provision of an Act is not law if it is outside the legislative competence of the Assembly.
> (This presumably will involve the courts in "severance"/"blue pencil" questions.)

> (2) A provision is outside that competence if any of the following paragraphs apply –
> (a) it would form part of the law of a country or territory other than Northern Ireland, or confer or remove functions exercisable otherwise than in or as regards Northern Ireland;
> (b) it deals with an excepted matter and is not ancillary to other provisions (whether in the Act or previously enacted) dealing with reserved or transferred matters;

[37] The Northern Ireland Act 1998, sched. 2, para. 22 and sched. 3, para. 42 and the Scotland Act 1998, sched. 4, para. 4, and s. 29(2)(c).

[38] The Scotland Act 1998, sched. 4, para. 2. The Northern Ireland Act 1998 s. 5(6) is rather different. Added at a late stage in the legislative procedure it provides (after declaring Westminster's sovereignty) ". . . but an Act of the Assembly may modify any provision made by or under an Act of Parliament in so far as it is part of the law of Northern Ireland". (See also the NI Constitution Act 1973, s. 4(4)). *Cf*, the Government of Ireland Act 1920, s. 6. Section 6(1) located the power to amend the 1920 Act (in most respects) in the Westminster Parliament. Section 6(2) provided that in a case of conflict of laws in the transferred area: ". . . The Act of . . . the Parliament of Northern Ireland shall be read subject to the Act of the Parliament of the United Kingdom [if passed after 1921], and so far as it is repugnant to that Act, but no further, shall be void". Section 6(2) was *in practice* avoided by the drafting device of inserting into a post 1921 Act of the Westminster Parliament a clause deeming that Act to have been passed *before* 1921. The Act of the NI Parliament, therefore, prevailed. Section 4(4) of the 1973 Act and s. 5(6) of the 1998 Act, thus, follow the NI *practice* since 1921. As far as s. 5(6) itself is concerned, (the) Westminster (government) could, if a legislative "ping-pong" match were envisaged, insert into one of its Acts in the devolved area a provision overriding the latter part of s. 5(6) for the specific purposes of that Act. The Westminster Act itself would then prevail.

(c) it is incompatible with any of the Convention rights;

(d) it is incompatible with Community law;

(e) it discriminates against any person or class of person on the ground of religious belief or political opinion;

(f) it modifies an enactment in breach of section 7. (These "entrenched" enactments include the Human Rights Act 1998 and the European Communities Act 1972).

(3) For the purposes of this Act, a provision is ancillary to other provisions if it is a provision –

(a) which provides for the enforcement of those other provisions or is otherwise necessary or expedient for making those other provisions effective; or

(b) which is otherwise incidental to, or consequential on, those provisions;

and references in this Act to provisions previously enacted are references to provisions contained in, or in any instrument made under, other Northern Ireland legislation or an Act of Parliament.

Section 29 of the Scotland Act makes equivalent provision, the major difference being the omission of an equivalent to section 6(2)(e) and the inclusion of special protection for the position of the Lord Advocate (and the provisions concerning schedule 4 of the Scotland Act).

Before considering the principles which the courts are likely to employ in determining devolved *vires* issues, consideration has to be given to the pre-enactment scrutiny required by the legislation.

There are various mechanisms providing for pre-enactment scrutiny regarding the *vires* of Parliament and Assembly Bills. They are:

—scrutiny by devolved *Ministers* – there is a *duty* incumbent upon them to make a statement, to the effect that in his or her view the Bill would be within the legislative competence of the Assembly.[39]

—scrutiny by *Presiding Officer* – Standing Orders in Northern Ireland must ensure that a Bill is *not introduced* if the Presiding Officer decides that any provision of it would not be within the Assembly's legislative competence. He is also under a duty (regarding a Bill both on its introduction and on its final stage) to refer any Bill to the Secretary of State which he considers to be outside the Assembly's competence. The Northern Ireland Presiding Officer's (i.e., the Speaker's) preventative powers are to be contrasted with those of the Scottish

---

[39] NI Act, s. 9, Scotland Act, s. 31(1). See also for Westminster, the Human Rights Act 1998, s. 19, which is already in force. If the devolved legislatures follow the Westminster practice of brevity, the importance will lie in the act of scrutiny rather than the provision of information to the legislature (and indirectly the courts) as to the substance of the scrutiny. Note also in this context, Lord Burlison (for the Government), HL 5 May 1999, WA 93: "If a section 19(1)(a) statement is to be made, a Minister must be clear that, at a minimum, the balance of arguments supports the view that the provisions are compatible. Lawyers will advise whether the provisions of the Bill are on balance compatible with the Convention rights. In so doing, they will consider whether it is *more likely than not* that the provisions of the Bill will stand up to challenge on Convention grounds before the domestic courts and the European Court of Human Rights in Strasbourg". Emphasis added.

[40] NI Act, s. 10, Scotland Act, s. 31(2). Given the NI Act's triple legislative categorisation, there are special provisions concerning NI's reserved category which are not considered here.

Presiding Officer, whose power is simply to inform the Scottish Parliament of his opinion on the *vires* of the Bill.[40]

—*the power of the Advocate General, the Lord Advocate or the Attorney General for Northern Ireland* (subject to certain time constraints) to refer the question of whether the provision of a Bill is *intra vires* to the Judicial Committee of the Privy Council (JCPC).[41]

The potential for conflicting legal advice here is clearly considerable – as is the potential for political conflict, because both the Scotland Act and the Northern Ireland Act contain provisions enabling the Secretary of State in certain circumstances to prevent a devolved Bill being submitted for the Royal Assent.[42] The first key to the resolution of much of this potential conflict would appear to be not so much the "longstop" provisions relating to references to the JCPC and their determinations, but rather to political "goodwill" (assumed rather than assured). Indeed Mr Henry McLeish, Minister of State in the Scottish Office in giving evidence to the Scottish Affairs Select Committee in its investigations into *The Operation of Multi-Layer Democracy* said:

> . . . I have no doubt that the [judicial representation on the JCPC] will be of a very high quality . . . [The] caveat is that it is about resolving *technical, legal issues* and not resolving politics or north/south (*sc* Scottish/English) differences between the two jurisdictions . . . If you have confidence in the judiciary, as I have and the Government have, then this is a process whereby we can resolve that very small band of *technical, legal issues*, which have not been resolved further down the line.[43]

One trusts that the Government's confidence in the ability of the judiciary to solve a very small band of technical legal questions will not be misplaced! Political goodwill, however, may not always be present and not all *vires* questions will be foreseen (or identified accurately)[44] and, therefore, *vires* questions will come before the courts, directly or collaterally, which will not necessarily be of a "technical, legal nature". The devolution legislation, therefore, provides for a procedure for the resolution of "devolution issues", which are essentially those relating to the competence of the devolved legislature (and executive).

The following summary of the procedure is drawn from the Northern Ireland legislation, but most of it, *mutatis mutandis*, applies in principle to Scotland

---

[41] NI Act, ss. 11 and 12; Scotland Act, ss. 33 and 34. Again, there are differences, not least because Scotland will have its own law officers. At least at the inception of devolution to Northern Ireland, the Attorney-General for Northern Ireland will continue to be the English Attorney-General. See the NI Constitution Act 1973, s. 10(2), not repealed by the NI Act 1998. Presumably, when s10(2) is repealed, the NI Act 1998, s. 11 which refers only to the AGNI will be amended to include also the AG to bring it into line with s.33 of the Scotland Act.

[42] NI Act s. 14, particularly s. 14(5), Scotland Act, s. 35(1). See also s. 35(2). The provisions are not identical in detail. There are also differences in wording in the grant of powers in the two Acts, which would make for interesting arguments on comparative grounds in any judicial review application.

[43] 1997–8 HC 460 – II 2 December 1998, Q.323 and Q.324. Emphasis added. See also MoU paras. 26–7, n. 36 above.

[44] Governments, at times, find it hard to accept that the *legal advice* they receive is not of equivalent status to a ruling of a court.

too. When a devolution issue arises before a tribunal from which there is no appeal, the issue must be referred to the Northern Ireland Court of Appeal. Any tribunal and any court from which there is an appeal *may* make such a reference. The Court of Appeal may refer any devolution issue arising in proceedings before it to the JCPC, but this does not apply to "devolution" references made to it by a lower court or tribunal. An appeal against this latter determination by the Court of Appeal lies (with leave) to the JCPC. Any devolution issue which arises in judicial proceedings in the House of Lords shall be referred to the JCPC unless the Lords consider it more appropriate, having regard to all the circumstances, that it should determine the issue. (This may be particularly pertinent where the devolution issue is a human rights issue). Part V of schedule 10 of the Northern Ireland Act also empowers the Attorney General, Attorney General of Northern Ireland, and First Minister and Deputy First Minister acting jointly to require any court or tribunal to refer to the JCPC any devolution issue which has arisen in proceedings before it to which he is or they are a party. The same parties also have the power to refer to the JCPC any devolution issue which is not the subject of proceedings, a power which may be particularly significant in Northern Ireland in a multi-party executive.

Under section 82(1) any decision of the JCPC in proceedings taken under the Northern Ireland Act is binding in all legal proceedings, other than proceedings before the Committee itself. One general query arises, but cannot be answered at this stage: on what criteria should a lower court or tribunal which has a discretion to refer the issue to the Court of Appeal exercise that discretion? Will Article 177 of the EC Treaty (now Article 234) provide any guidance here? (And will the same guidance apply when the Court of Appeal decides whether to refer a case to the JCPC?)

It is in accordance with the various procedures described here that devolution issues may arise before the courts. The devolution Acts lay down general principles to guide the courts in their resolution of these issues.

Section 83[45] of the Northern Ireland Act is, first, of relevance here, and the legislative "history" of section 83 is of interest. Clause 6(3) of the Bill (removed in the House of Lords and replaced by section 83) read:

> Any provision of an Act of the Assembly is to be read, so far as possible, so as to be within the legislative competence of the Assembly and is to have effect accordingly.

Notes on Clauses explained this issue:

> . . . so, in cases of doubt, where a court is faced with more than one plausible interpretation of an Act and one of these would render the Act ultra vires, it will endeavour to avoid the problems that might arise from the latter construction being arrived at and steer towards a construction that will keep the Act within the legislative competence of the Assembly.

---

[45] See also the Scotland Act, s. 101, and Himsworth and Munro, *op. cit.*, pp. 125–7. The wording of the two provisions is not identical, but is intended to have identical effect.

Clause 6(3) was deleted from the Bill at the Lords' Committee stage for reasons of "technical deficiency".[46] What is now section 83 was added at Report stage and, through use of different wording, seeks to achieve the same result: namely the legislative provision is to read in such a way as to render it *intra* not *ultra vires*.[47] The new clause was explained, for the Government, by Lord Williams thus:

> this is a technical clause about the way in which the court should interpret Acts of the Assembly, subordinate legislation and indeed measures of a wide range of public authorities, including Ministers of the Crown. The point of the amendment is quite simple. If there are alternative readings of the provisions of the legislation concerned, the reading which would lead to a conclusion of validity is to be preferred. It is as simple as that.[48]

This requirement upon the courts has also to be read in conjunction with the more specific provisions of sections 6 and 98(2) of the Northern Ireland Act and section 29(3) of the Scotland Act.

Under section 6(2)(b) a provision is outside the legislative competence of the Northern Ireland Assembly, if it *deals with* an excepted matter and is not ancillary (see section 6(3) above) to other provisions (whether in the Act or previously enacted) dealing with reserved or transferred matters. Section 98(2) defines "deals with" for the purposes of the Act as meaning "*affects* otherwise than incidentally" (and see the recurrence of this phrase in Lord Sewel's statement below).

By contrast, section 29(3) of the Scotland Act invokes a purposive approach for the courts. The Scottish Parliament is precluded from legislating *in relation to* a "reserved" matter (the broad equivalent of a Northern Ireland excepted matter). Subsection (3) states that whether a provision of an Act of the Scottish Parliament "relates to" a reserved matter is to be determined by reference to "the purpose of the provision having regard (among other things) to its effect in all the circumstances". Lord Sewel explained this provision as follows:

> The White Paper indicated that it was proposed to define the legislative competence of the Scottish Parliament by listing the matters which were reserved. Everything not specifically reserved would be devolved. This approach is given effect to in the Bill by providing (in section 29) that the Scottish Parliament can make laws except where the provision "relates to" the reserved matters listed in Schedule 5. In interpreting what is meant by "relates", it is intended that the courts should rely upon the respection doctrine which they developed in dealing with cases arising from the Commonwealth constitutions and the Government of Ireland Act 1920. The classic statement is found in the words of Lord Atkin in *Gallagher* v. *Lynn* in 1937 (decided under the 1920 Act) where he stated:

---

[46] Lord Williams of Mostyn vol. 593, col. 1216.

[47] See HL, 10 Nov. 1998, vol. 594, col. 721; see also Third Reading, 17 Nov. 1998, vol. 594, col. 1219.

[48] 10 Nov. 1998, vol. 594, col. 721.

"It is well established that you ought to look at the true nature and character . . . the pith and substance of the legislation. If, on the view of the statute as a whole, you find that the substance of the legislation is within the express powers, then it is not invalidated if incidentally it affects matters which are outside the authorised field".

In other words, it is intended that any question as to whether a provision in an Act of the Scottish parliament "relates to" a reserved matter should be determined by reference to its "pith and substance" or its purpose and if its purpose is a devolved one then it is not outside legislative competence merely because "incidentally it affects" a reserved matter. A degree of trespass into reserved areas is inevitable because reserved and other areas are not divided into neat watertight compartments.[49]

As far as Scotland at least is concerned, therefore, the 1998 Act indicates a test (drawn from a federal, that is Canadian, system) which relates to the devolved parliament's intent, not that of the parent Act. It is a test which will, as against Westminster and when read with the interpretative presumption, tend to enhance the powers of the Scottish Parliament, but must be placed in the overall political "liaison" commitment mentioned above.

One other aspect of the restriction on the devolved legislatures' powers may be mentioned. It is outside their legislative competence if a provision of an Act is incompatible with any of the rights contained in the European Convention on Human Rights. The issues relating to devolution and the protection of human rights are of considerable importance, but the matter is being referred to here solely to reinforce the point that, while normally devolved Acts will be regarded as "primary" legislation, for the purposes of the Human Rights Act they are *subordinate legislation* and will be treated as such under the Human Rights Act and by the courts. While this division between Westminster Acts and other legislation is inevitable, given the dominant consideration to preserve Westminster's sovereign powers, it is a further illustration of the difficulties involved in identifying the constitutional nature of devolution.

This is further compounded by the provisions in the devolution Acts dealing with non-judicial aspects of post-enactment *vires* questions. Section 80 of the Northern Ireland Act gives the Secretary of State *legislative* power to remedy devolved ultra vires acts, including "any provision of an Act of the Assembly which is not, *or may not be*, within the legislative competence of the Assembly or any purported exercise by a (Northern Ireland) Minister or Department of his or her functions which is not, or *may not be*, a valid exercise of those functions". This *delegated* legislative power (which includes the power to make provision having retrospective effect) is to be done by statutory instrument, laid subject to

---

[49] HL, 21 July 1998, vol. 592, col. 818 et seq. There are undoubted difficulties with this test, as a fuller consideration of Lord Atkin's dictum (at [1937] AC 863, at 870) indicates. See on this H.Calvert, *Constitutional Law in Northern Ireland* (1968), chap. 11, *passim* and see also *R(Hume)* v. *Londonderry Justices* [1972] NI 91. See also H.Calvert, "Gallagher v Lynn Re-examined – a Legislative Fraud" [1972] *PL* 11. The resort to parliamentary debates will remove at least some of the likelihood of "legislative fraud". Professor Calvert's conclusion is well worth quoting: "I am very dubious about entrusting to our supreme fora the tasks of ensuring smooth constitutional development within a regionally-structured United Kingdom. Do you blame me?".

Westminster's affirmative resolution procedures. The Scotland Act 1998 section 107, section 113, section 114 contain effectively similar provision in principle.

This provision went into the Northern Ireland Bill at the Lords' Report stage, and the italicised phrase "may not be" is a clearly substantial power to vest in a non-judicial person. The "reassurances" given by Lord Williams for the Government on the exercise of this power include:

- the Secretary of State would be open to judicial review proceedings;
- under section 96(2) the Secretary of State's Order (a Statutory Instrument) would be made subject to the prior affirmative resolution procedure at Westminster;
- where there has been no court decision, it is the Government's intention to use these powers only with the consent of the devolved Ministers.[50]

Later, Lord Dubs (for the Government) was asked: "Can he assure the House that there will be no circumstances in which legislation will be issued to affect judicial proceedings before they are terminated". Lord Dubs replied . . . "I believe the answer to that is yes. I am reluctant to be 100 per cent categoric, but I understand that the answer is yes".[51]

The role of the courts[52] is thus to some extent modified, just as the position of the devolved legislature is expressly rendered subordinate to the Secretary of State and delegated legislation. It is, in many ways, a constitutional enormity to confer a judicial power ("may be" ultra vires) on a Secretary of State. It becomes even more problematic when the "purely" legislative power, to remedy an Act declared by the courts as ultra vires, is conferred upon a Westminster minister through Westminster's *delegated legislative procedures, to remedy the Acts of a devolved legislature.*

CONCLUSIONS

This chapter has concentrated only on certain aspects of devolved *legislative* power. (Although the nexus of relationships concerning executive power is politically as significant, those issues legally fit into a more traditional pattern). Is devolution nothing other than delegated legislative power, to be accommodated within the doctrine of parliamentary sovereignty and the statute-based part of our administrative law? The answer is, on one level quite clearly, yes. Parliament, retaining its sovereign powers, confers certain powers on a devolved legislature; there is no exclusive allocation of powers; Westminster (in the main) retains the sole power to amend the "parent" Act and retains, and intends to exercise, considerable scrutiny over the exercise of those powers. Indeed the amount of potential *governmental* (*cf* parliamentary, *cf* judicial) power *vis-à-vis* the devolved legislature is extensive – there are many situations which can be foreseen when political "goodwill", "co-operation", "negotiation" and "liaison" will become

---

[50] HL Debs, 10 Nov. 1998, vol. 594, col. 718–9.

[51] HL Debs, 17 Nov. 1998, vol. 594, col. 1218.

[52] For their powers on a devolution issue, see NI Act, s. 81 and Scotland Act, s. 102. More generally, see also s. 23 of the Judicature (NI) Act 1978.

euphemisms for a Westminster diktat. At the pre-enactment stage, Westminster has a (consultative, liaison, scrutiny?) role to play; the same is true of the post-enactment stage and the courts are to be left with a few "technical legal issues". The prorogation (and later abolition) of the Northern Ireland Parliament by Westminster Act in 1972 is often said (rightly) to have occurred in extreme or highly unusual circumstances. That point, however, relates to the conditions under which the power was exercised, not (of course) to the validity of the exercise of the power. Furthermore, the Northern Ireland Parliament had by then existed for fifty years. It is hard, if not impossible, to predict with any certainty what the position will be with regard to Westminster and Scotland and Wales fifty years hence (*a fortiori* Northern Ireland).

These last remarks, however, bring the topic closer to political considerations (and indeed the constitutional conventions which may emerge to reflect them) and further away from strictly legal ones. It is, however, surely wrong to assume that the dynamo of devolution will be driven solely by the Westminster government of the day. There are many variables, both legal and political, which should not be ignored or brushed aside, but which will (eventually) have a considerable impact upon the evolution of devolution. These factors include most crucially the fact that there will be courts in the four territorial jurisdictions of the United Kingdom considering devolution issues and consequently different lines of judicial reasoning, different constitutional principles and outlook will inform the jurisprudence of the Judicial Committee of the Privy Council. Furthermore, as the chapter has indicated above, there are various central "reserve" powers in the legislation; for example, the power of the Secretary of State in effect to bar a Bill from receiving the Royal Assent and the Secretary of State's powers to remedy ultra vires Acts. These, along with the pre-enactment scrutiny responsibility of Ministers and of the Presiding Officer, are all (arguably) subject to judicial review. Certainly both the Northern Ireland Act (section 5(5)) and the Scotland Act (section 28(5)) contain a (differently worded) provision to the effect that the validity of a Parliament/ Assembly Act is not affected by any invalidity in the Parliamentary/ Assembly proceedings leading to its enactment. This provision (which *is* of a different nature from the lesser procedural protection, if any, usually afforded delegated legislation) is designed to extend to devolved legislation, once enacted, some of the aspects of Westminster parliamentary privilege and thus (probably) at most protects *procedural* deficiencies from founding a challenge to a devolved Act *once enacted*. It does not arguably serve to protect from judicial review the Secretary of State, devolved Ministers or the Presiding Officer in the exercise of the powers just mentioned. While the courts may hesitate over intervening in the "political processes" involved or from doing so at too premature a stage, the possibility of judicial review cannot be precluded. This means, that especially here, the "reserve" powers of the Secretary of State (which may be viewed as going against the political *raison d'etre* of devolution) may be subject to judicial scrutiny, leaving the courts in this regard as key determinants of the "nature" of devolution – and this chapter has only dealt with a selection of such potential issues.

Other matters which may come to influence the evolution of devolution include: devolution and the "English question"; the impact of the Human Rights Act on all the legislatures, including (albeit more indirectly) Westminster; the variable/varying political relationships which will emerge from coalition or multi-party executives and Westminster; the recommendations of the Royal Commission on the House of Lords concerning the separation of powers and the debate about the desirability of creating a Supreme or Constitutional Court.

It is less than thirty years since the United Kingdom became a member of the Common Market or European Economic Community. Is it still accurate today to describe the position of the United Kingdom within the European Union in the same (legal) terms as were employed in 1972? At what point, does legal theory yield to reality – or look ill-informed and archaic if it does not. Devolution is not a static event, but a process which will be influenced by "independent constitutional organs" other than the Westminster government.

When the seeds are first sown, it is not immediately clear exactly what the harvest will be. It is, at least, arguable that the devolution Acts and the Human Rights Act have sown the seeds of a new constitutional order in which the bedrock of the constitution is not the sovereignty of parliament and the justification for the courts' review powers is not the ultra vires doctrine. The European dimensions, human rights and fundamental constitutional principles, indeed devolution itself, combine to create a new constitutional order, an embryonic written constitution, under which the judges will interpret *all* manifestations of legislative and executive power in accordance with new constitutional doctrines, subject only perhaps to a political questions doctrine. The requirements of constitutional interpretation should not be solely or purely those of statutory interpretation.

Schedule 5, Part 1 of the Scotland Act in its reference to "the following aspects of the constitution" has paved the way for a long overdue recognition and then formulation in United Kingdom constitutional law of a coherent and rational constitutional order.

The time is now ripe for the courts to reach an accommodation between the principles stemming from the fiction of the sovereignty of parliament (and the fictions flowing from it) and those stemming from the reality of the sovereignty of the Westminster government *vis-à-vis* the United Kingdom Parliament and of the dispersal of political power.

Lord Irvine, the Lord Chancellor, in his Paul Sieghart Memorial Lecture on 20 April 1999 quoted (in the context of human rights instruments) from Benjamin Cardozo:

Statutes are designed to meet the fugitive exigencies of the hour . . . A Constitution states or ought to state not rules for the passing hour, but principles for an expanding future.[53]

---

[53] www.open.gov.uk/lcd/speeches/1999. See also 1999 *EHRLR* pp. 350–72. The quotation from Cardozo is from *The Nature of the Judicial Process* (1921), p. 83.

The courts are now boundary riders in which the power of all legislatures within the United Kingdom is contained within a triangle. (Time will tell whether the triangle is equilateral or isosceles). The three sides are the European Union, the European Convention on Human Rights (or human rights more generally)[54] and the United Kingdom as a Union and not a unitary State.[55] Devolution at the least politically and maybe judicially too makes that distinction crucial, for it cannot be assumed that devolution is purely a one-way relationship *from* Westminster. There are too many key constitutional players involved in the resolution of devolution issues for it (ultimately) to be equated with delegated power.

[54] See e.g., Lord Hoffmann in *R* v. *Secretary of State for the Home Department, ex parte Simms* [1999] 3 All ER 400 at 412 on the principle of legality: "in the absence of express language or necessary implication to the contrary, the courts therefore presume that even the most general words were intended to be subject to the basic rights of the individual. In this way the courts of the United Kingdom, though acknowledging the sovereignty of Parliament, apply principles of constitutionality little different from those which exist in countries where the power of the legislature is expressly limited by a constitutional document". The UK-wide ramifications of human rights issues also being devolution issues may be seen, e.g., in *Starr and Chalmers* v. *Procurator Fiscal, Linlithgow*, High Court of Justiciary, 11 November 1999 and in the powers of the NI Human Rights Commission under sections 69 and 70 of the Northern Ireland Act 1998.

[55] "The unitary state [is] built up around one unambiguous political centre which enjoys economic dominance and pursues a more or less undeviating policy of administrative standardisation ... [In the] union state ... [i]ntegration is less than perfect." This quotation from Stein Rokkan and Derek Unwin is in V.Bogdanor, *Power and the People* (1997), 30 and see generally his chapter 2. See also N. MacCormack, n. 15 *supra*.

10

The Courts, Devolution and Judicial Review

PAUL CRAIG and MARK WALTERS

Legislation enacted by the Labour government has had a fundamental impact on the structure of political and legal authority in the United Kingdom. The devolution of power to Wales and Scotland[1] is one significant element in the government's overall strategy for constitutional reform. It poses challenging problems for public lawyers who will have to come to grips with complex legislation. This article seeks to explore one aspect of devolution in detail, judicial review. It will be readily apparent from the discussion which follows that judicial review is of central importance to the legislation. The way in which the courts interpret this power may well have a profound impact on the whole enterprise of devolution.

The article will begin by considering the legislation concerning Wales and will make clear the nature of the power which has been devolved. This will be followed by an analysis of the ways in which challenges to the validity of Assembly action can arise. The same exercise will then be done in relation to Scotland. This is essential if the provisions which are concerned with judicial review are to be understood. The discussion will then turn to the key issues which will affect the way in which the courts will exercise the powers accorded to them. We will draw on experience from other Commonwealth jurisdictions in order to inform this aspect of the discussion.

WALES, EXECUTIVE DEVOLUTION AND THE ASSIGNMENT OF LIMITED
COMPETENCE

The analysis of the political structure in Wales post-devolution is necessarily limited. The object is to give the reader the background which is necessary in order to make sense of the provisions on judicial review. It is important to recognise at the outset two central features of the Welsh scheme which shape the functions of the Assembly, both of which stand in contrast to the position in relation to Scotland. The first is that the strategy in the Government of Wales Act 1998

---

[1] Considerations of space preclude treatment of Northern Ireland.

(GWA) is to assign the Assembly competence field by field. The Scottish Parliament, by way of contrast, has a general legislative competence, albeit subject to a wide range of limitations. The second feature of the GWA is that the competence afforded to the Assembly is in relation to the passage of secondary legislation. It is this which serves to explain the title "executive devolution". With these features in mind we can now look briefly at some of the key features of the legislation.

Section 1(1) of the GWA establishes the National Assembly for Wales. Ordinary elections for the return of the entire Assembly will normally take place every four weeks.[2] The Assembly is to consist of one member for each Assembly constituency, and members for each Assembly electoral region,[3] with the consequence that voters have two votes. The result is an Assembly of 60 members, 40 of whom will be elected from Assembly constituencies, the other 20 from regions. The procedure of the Assembly is to be regulated by standing orders which it makes.[4]

The GWA mandates a number of important procedural and substantive principles as to the operation of the Assembly. The English and Welsh languages are to be treated equally,[5] and the Assembly is instructed to have due regard to the principle that there should be equality of opportunity for all people.[6] Proceedings of the Assembly are to be held in public.[7] There is a Welsh Administration Ombudsman to investigate complaints.[8]

The Assembly elects from among its members a presiding officer and a deputy presiding officer, who cannot be from the same party.[9] The Assembly also elects one of its members to be Assembly First Secretary, who then appoints Assistant Secretaries.[10] The GWA makes provision for the establishment of committees. Some of these are stipulated by the Act, others can be set up at the discretion of the Assembly.[11]

The most important of the statutorily mandated committees is the Executive committee which operates rather like a cabinet. The Executive committee consists of the Assembly First Secretary, who occupies the chair, and the Assembly Assistant Secretaries.[12] The GWA also mandates the establishment of subject committees.[13] These are to mirror the subject-matter division of function of

---

[2] GWA, s. 3(2).
[3] *Ibid.* s. 2(2).
[4] *Ibid.* ss. 46(1)–(2).
[5] *Ibid.* s. 47.
[6] *Ibid.* s. 48.
[7] *Ibid.* s. 70.
[8] *Ibid.* s. 70(5).
[9] *Ibid.* s. 52.
[10] *Ibid.* s. 53.
[11] *Ibid.* s. 54.
[12] *Ibid.* s. 56.
[13] *Ibid.* s. 57.

those who sit on the Executive committee. The subordinate legislation scrutiny committee is also mandated by the Act.[14]

The way in which the Assembly operates in practice, and the practical locus of power, will depend in part on how the broad powers to delegate given by the GWA are exercised. It is the Assembly which is accorded powers by the GWA. It is empowered to delegate its functions to any of its committees, or to the First Secretary.[15] There are broad powers for committees to delegate to sub-committees.[16] The Executive committee itself can delegate its functions to the First Secretary or to an Assistant Secretary.[17]

The functions of the Assembly are set out principally in sections 21 and 22. Section 21 stipulates that the Assembly shall have the functions which are transferred to, or made exercisable by, the Assembly, by virtue of the GWA, or conferred or imposed on the Assembly by or under the GWA or any other Act. It is, however, section 22(1) which gives the clearest guidance on the functions which will be performed by the Assembly. This section provides that Her Majesty may, by Order in Council:

(a) provide for the transfer to the Assembly of any function so far as exercisable by a Minister of the Crown in relation to Wales,

(b) direct that any function so far as exercisable shall be exercisable by the Assembly concurrently with the Minister of the Crown, or

(c) direct that any function so far as exercisable by a Minister of the Crown in relation to Wales shall be exercisable by the Minister only with the agreement of, or after consultation with, the Assembly.

Section 22(2) directs the Secretary of State for Wales, before the first election to the Assembly, to lay before each House of Parliament the draft of such an Order in Council for the transfer of such functions in each of the fields specified in Schedule 2 as he considers appropriate. The fields listed in Schedule 2 are: agriculture, forestry, fisheries and food; ancient monuments and historic buildings; culture; economic development; education and training; the environment; health and health services; highways; housing; industry; local government; social services; sport and recreation; tourism; town and country planning; transport; water and flood defence; and the Welsh language.

The main task of the Assembly will therefore be to take over the functions previously exercised by the Secretary of State for Wales, who in an average year made approximately 150 instruments on his own, and 400 with other ministers.[18] The Act makes it clear that the normal Westminster procedures for the making of subordinate legislation do not, with some limited exceptions, apply in relation to matters which have been transferred to the Assembly.[19] Standing

---

[14] *Ibid.* s. 58.
[15] *Ibid.* s. 62(1).
[16] *Ibid.* s. 62(2).
[17] *Ibid.* s. 62(3)(a).
[18] R. Rawlings, "The New Model Wales" (1998) 25 *Jnl. Law and Society* 461 at p. 488.
[19] GWA, ss. 44–45.

orders must provide for the procedures which are to apply to the making of sub-ordinate legislation.[20] The Act itself does however specify some novel substantive and procedural features for the making of such legislation as compared with the traditional Westminster machinery.

In substantive terms, the GWA provides for what is termed "regulatory appraisal". This requires there to be a cost-benefit analysis of compliance with the proposed subordinate legislation before a draft of the statutory instrument containing the legislation is laid before the Assembly.[21] Such an appraisal need not be carried out however where it is "inappropriate or not reasonably practicable".[22] In procedural terms, the "default position" is that general subordinate legislation may not be made unless the draft statutory instrument has been laid before, and approved by, a resolution of the Assembly itself.[23] Moreover, the draft instrument must not be approved by the Assembly until it has considered the report of the subordinate legislation scrutiny committee, and the regulatory appraisal published in relation to it where there is one.[24] These requirements can be dispensed with if the Executive committee determines that it is not reasonably practicable to comply with them.[25]

The other main type of power accorded to the Assembly enables it to take over, or transfer to another body, the functions presently exercised by certain bodies listed in the Act. It should be noted that while the Assembly does not possess primary legislative power, sections 27 and 28 contain "Henry VIII" clauses. These sections enable the Assembly to amend primary legislation by means of an order.

It is clear that the Assembly has certain duties as well as powers. Section 106(7) states that the Assembly has no power to act in a way which is incompatible with Community law. Section 107 makes provision for the application of the Human Rights Act 1998 to the Assembly. The application of international obligations to the Assembly is governed by section 108.

JUDICIAL CHALLENGE TO THE COMPETENCE OF THE ASSEMBLY

There are complex provisions for legal challenge lest the Assembly strays beyond its limited powers. The rules are contained in Schedule 8. The key phrase throughout this part of the legislation is "devolution issue". A court or tribunal can disregard a devolution issue if the claim is frivolous or vexatious.[26] Devolution issue is defined in Schedule 8, paragraph 1(1) to mean:

---

[20] GWA, s. 64.
[21] *Ibid.* s. 65.
[22] *Ibid.* s. 65(2).
[23] *Ibid.* s. 66(2).
[24] *Ibid.* s. 66(5).
[25] *Ibid.* s. 67(1).
[26] *Ibid.* Sched. 8, para. 2.

(a) a question whether a function is exercisable by the Assembly.

(b) a question whether a purported exercise of power or proposed exercise of a function by the Assembly is, or would be, within the powers of the Assembly (including a question whether a purported or proposed exercise of a function by the Assembly is, or would be, outside its powers by virtue of section 106(7) or 107(1)),

(c) a question whether the Assembly has failed to comply with a duty imposed on it (including a question whether the Assembly has failed to comply with any obligation which is an obligation of the Assembly by virtue of section 106(1) or (6)), or

(d) a question whether a failure to act by the Assembly is incompatible with any of the Convention rights.

A devolution issue may well arise in proceedings which are begun in England and Wales, Scotland, or Northern Ireland. The GWA therefore makes provision for all these jurisdictional possibilities, but the rules do not differ in principle. The discussion which follows will concentrate on the rules which apply where a devolution issue arises in England and Wales. There are four principal ways in which devolution issues can come before the courts.

(a) Direct reference to the Privy Council

A devolution issue an be resolved by direct reference to the Judicial Committee of the Privy Council. This can occur in three types of case.

First, there is the possibility of *pre-enactment challenge and scrutiny*. Schedule 8, paragraph 31(1) states that the Attorney-General or the Assembly may refer to the Judicial Committee of the Privy Council any devolution issue which is not the subject of civil or criminal proceedings. Paragraph 31(2) then states that where the reference is made by the Attorney-General and relates to the proposed exercise of a function by the Assembly, the Attorney-General is to notify the Assembly of that fact, and the Assembly must not exercise the function in the manner proposed from the date of receiving the notification until the reference has been decided or disposed of.

Secondly, it is clear that there can be *post-enactment challenge even where the devolution issue has not arisen in independent proceedings*. This follows from the wording of paragraph 31(1). Thus the Attorney-General or the Assembly may have passed certain subordinate legislation which is later felt to have exceeded the bounds of the powers accorded to it under the Transfer of Functions Order. The matter can be referred to the Privy Council even though the subordinate legislation has not been contested in any other proceedings.

Thirdly, it is open to the *Attorney-General to require a court or tribunal to transfer a case to the Privy Council*. Paragraph 30(1) of Schedule 8 authorises the Attorney-General to require any court or tribunal to refer to the Privy Council any devolution issue which has arisen in any proceedings before it to which he is a party. Courts and tribunals are under an obligation to give notice of devolution issues which arise in any proceedings to the Attorney-General and the Assembly.[27] The person or body to which notice is given is entitled to take part in the proceedings so far as they relate to the devolution issue.[28]

(b) Institution of proceedings by a Law Officer

The GWA allows the relevant law officer to institute proceedings for the determination of a devolution issue.[29] The law officers have the power to require the devolution issue to be referred to the Privy Council, as described above, but may choose not to exercise this power.

(c) Reference through other Courts

A devolution issue can also arise before a court which is empowered by the GWA to refer the matter on to another court. It is the devolution issue which is referred to the higher court. Once this matter has been decided the case will then return to the lower court for final resolution of the case. The relevant rules distinguish between civil and criminal proceedings.

The rules on civil proceedings are that a magistrate's court may refer a devolution issue which arises in such proceedings before it to the High Court.[30] A court may refer a devolution issue which arises in civil proceedings before it to the Court of Appeal,[31] but this does not apply to a magistrates' court, the Court of Appeal or the House of Lords, nor to the High Court taking a reference from a magistrates' court pursuant to paragraph 6. Civil proceedings are defined by the Act to mean any proceedings other than criminal proceedings.[32] It would therefore include proceedings for judicial review.

If the devolution issue arises in criminal proceedings then a court, other than the Court of Appeal or the House of Lords, may refer the issue to the High Court in the case of summary proceedings, or to the Court of Appeal if the proceedings are on indictment.[33]

It is open to the Court of Appeal to refer a devolution issue which has come before it other than by way of reference from a lower court on to the Privy Council. This option will be open to it where the devolution issue emerges in proceedings before the Court of Appeal itself.

The discussion thus far has concentrated on courts themselves which are given a power to refer as described above. Tribunals are treated somewhat dif-

---

[27] GWA, Sched. 8, para. 5(1).
[28] *Ibid.* Sched. 8, para. 5(2).
[29] *Ibid.* Sched. 8, paras. 4, 13, 23.
[30] *Ibid.* Sched. 8, para. 6.
[31] *Ibid.* Sched. 8, para. 7(1).
[32] *Ibid.* Sched. 8, para. 1(2)(b).
[33] *Ibid.* Sched. 8, para. 9.

ferently. A tribunal from which there is no appeal must refer the devolution issue to the Court of Appeal. Where there is an appeal from the tribunal's findings it has a discretion to refer, but does not have a duty to do so.[34]

Provision is made for an appeal against a determination of a devolution issue by the High Court or the Court of Appeal when a reference has been made to those courts in the manner described above. The appeal lies to the Privy Council, but only with the leave of the court concerned, or failing such leave, with special leave from the Judicial Committee.[35]

If a devolution issue arises in judicial proceedings before the House of Lords it is to be referred to the Privy Council unless the Lords consider it more appropriate to determine the issue.[36]

(d) Decisions made by the Court immediately seized of the matter

It is important to realise that the provisions described above give courts a discretion whether to refer devolution issues. They do not have the duty to do so. The court before which the issue is raised is therefore entitled, subject to the discussion in the section which follows, to decide the case for itself. It might be thought that this point is merely academic since courts would normally wish to avail themselves of the referral power. Many courts will undoubtedly wish to do so. It should however be recognised that, for example, the High Court exercising its judicial review jurisdiction may well feel able to resolve devolution issues itself, and be wary, moreover, of overburdening the Court of Appeal through too ready an exercise of the referral power.

There is, however, an indirect qualification to the courts' discretion to retain cases. We have seen that a court or tribunal before which a devolution issue arises must give notice to the Attorney-General who can then take part in the proceedings. Once the Attorney-General is part of the proceedings he can then use the power given to him by paragraph 30 of Schedule 8 to require the court to refer the matter to the Privy Council.

(e) Devolution issues which "arise": the relevance of the general law on collateral challenge

Schedule 8 of the GWA is framed in terms of devolution issues "arising" before a particular court. It is clear that such issues will often arise directly, as in the context of a judicial review action. There will, subject to the normal rules on such actions, be no difficulty about raising the vires of Assembly subordinate legislation in this manner.

[34] *Ibid.* Sched. 8, para. 8.
[35] *Ibid.* Sched. 8, para. 11.
[36] *Ibid.* Sched. 8, para. 29.

Devolution issues will also arise collaterally where, for example, Assembly subordinate legislation is being enforced and the applicant claims that it is ultra vires. Recent decisions of the courts have been more liberal in allowing collateral challenge, although there are still some uncertainties.[37] This raises the interesting question as to how far these general rules concerning collateral challenge and vires issues will apply in this context.

It could be argued that the GWA itself resolves the matter by giving a right to challenge devolution issues collaterally as well as directly. The strongest argument in favour of this conclusion is that the court's power of referral implies, as argued above, a power not to refer and to decide the matter for itself. This presumes that it has the authority to decide the matter for itself. This is not self-evidently correct. It could equally be argued that any constraints imposed by the general law on collateral attack will structure the circumstances in which a court does have authority to decide this type of matter for itself. The courts' more liberal attitude to collateral challenge should, however, mean that, even if the general legal rules on collateral challenge are applied, applicants will normally be able to raise vires issues collaterally as well as directly.

(f) The result of a finding that the Assembly exceeded its power

The consequences of finding that the Assembly exceeded its power when making subordinate legislation might be far reaching. Section 110 therefore empowers a court or tribunal to make an order removing or limiting any retrospective effect of its decision, or suspending the effect of the decision for any period and on any conditions to allow the defect to be corrected. When deciding whether to make such an order the court or tribunal must have regard to the interests of persons who are not parties to the proceedings. It must also give notice of its intention to make such an order to the relevant law officer and the Assembly.

SCOTLAND, LEGISLATIVE DEVOLUTION AND THE DEMARCATION OF LEGISLATIVE
COMPETENCE

Section 1 of the Scotland Act 1998 (SA) establishes the Scottish Parliament. Ordinary general elections for the Scottish Parliament are to be held every four years.[38] The voting system is very similar to that which applies in the case of Wales. A member is returned for each constituency under the simple majority system,[39] and members are also elected from regions under the additional member system of proportional representation.[40] A Presiding Officer of the Scottish

---

[37] *Boddington v. British Transport Police* [1998] 2 WLR 639.
[38] SA, s. 2(2).
[39] *Ibid.* s. 1(2).
[40] *Ibid.* s. 1(3).

Parliament, plus two deputies, are appointed from the elected members.[41] The proceedings of the Parliament are to be regulated by standing orders which may or must make provision for a range of matters.[42] The Scottish Executive is composed of the First Minister, such ministers as he or she appoints, and the Lord Advocate and Solicitor General for Scotland.[43] They are known collectively as the Scottish ministers.[44]

The *legislative powers* of the Scottish Parliament stand in marked contrast to those of the Welsh Assembly. The Scottish Parliament is given the power by section 28 of the SA to make primary laws which are to be known as Acts of the Scottish Parliament. The Parliament's prima facie general legislative capacity is, however, then qualified by other provisions of the Act. The power of the Westminster Parliament to make laws for Scotland is not affected by Scotland's power to make laws.[45] More important in practical terms is the fact that the legislative competence of the Scottish Parliament is bounded, and section 29(1) provides that an Act will not be law so far as any provision exceeds these limits.[46] The member of the Scottish Executive who is in charge of a Bill must, on or before the introduction of the Bill in the Parliament, state that in his or her view the provisions of the Bill would be within the legislative competence of the Parliament.[47] The Presiding Officer must also do so.[48] Section 29(2) defines the bounds of the Scottish Parliament's competence. It states that a provision is outside the Parliament's competence if:[49]

(a) it would form part of the law of a country or territory other than Scotland, or confer or remove functions exercisable otherwise than in or as regards Scotland,
(b) it relates to reserved matters,
(c) it is in breach of the restrictions in Schedule 4,
(d) it is incompatible with any Convention rights or with Community law,
(e) it would remove the Lord Advocate from his position as head of the systems of criminal prosecution and investigation of deaths in Scotland.

Section 29(2)(b) requires further explanation. The list of reserved matters is set out in Schedule 5. Whether a provision of an Act of the Scottish Parliament relates to a reserved matter is to be determined by reference to the purpose of the provision having regard, *inter alia*, to its effects in all the circumstances.[50] Schedule 5 is very lengthy and therefore it can only be described in outline here. It is divided into three parts.

---

[41] *Ibid.* s. 19.
[42] *Ibid.* s. 22(1).
[43] *Ibid.* s. 44(1).
[44] *Ibid.* s. 44(2).
[45] *Ibid.* s. 28(7).
[46] *Ibid.* s. 29(1).
[47] *Ibid.* s. 31(1).
[48] *Ibid.* s. 31(2).
[49] *Ibid.* s. 29(2).
[50] *Ibid.* s. 29(3). See also, s. 29(4) which touches on this same issue.

Part I deals with General Reservations and lists a number of matters which are outside the competence of the Scottish Parliament. Important aspects of the *Constitution* are one such category.[51] A second general reservation relates to the *registration and funding of political parties.*[52] The *conduct of foreign affairs*, including relations with the E.C., other international organisations, and the regulation of international trade, is not surprisingly another reserved matter.[53] The other general reservations relate to *the public service, defence and treason.*[54]

Part II of Schedule 5 deals with Specific Reservations.[55] A glance at this part of the Act makes one realise that it will be difficult for the Scottish Parliament to determine with certainty whether it has legislative competence or not. Part II contains a large number of reserved heads which are listed as "Head A-Financial and Economic Matters", "Head B-Home Affairs", "Head C-Trade and Industry" and so on, there being 11 such heads in total.[56] Each of these Heads is then sub-divided into a number of sections labelled in the case of, for example Head C, which is Trade and Industry, from C1–C15. The list of the sections which apply for Trade and Industry are: business associations; insolvency; competition; intellectual property; import and export control; sea fishing; consumer protection; product standards, safety and liability; weights and measures; telecommunications and wireless telegraphy; Post Office, posts and postal services; Research Councils; designation of assisted areas; Industrial Development Advisory Board; and the protection of trading and economic interests.

The legal advisor's task is made even more difficult by the style of drafting which is used in Part II. On some occasions the reserved heads are set out at a high level of generality, without mentioning any particular existing statute. On other occasions the reserved heads will specify a particular section of a particular statute which is off-limits for the Scottish Parliament. On yet other occasions, it will stipulate that the subject matter dealt with by an entire statute is outside its legislative competence. The format of Part II is further complicated by the fact that any of the styles mentioned thus far will often be accompanied by exceptions, which allow the Parliament to legislate within the area thus stipulated, by interpretative statements designed to clarify the reach of the reserved head, and by illustrations aimed at clarifying the meaning of generally worded statements. It is, moreover, the case that these differing techniques will not infrequently be used within the same section,[57] and any one section may have six or more different references.

---

[51] SA, Sched. 5, Pt. I, para. 1.

[52] *Ibid.* Sched. 5, Pt. I, para. 6.

[53] *Ibid.* Sched. 5, Pt. I, para. 7(1).

[54] *Ibid.* Sched. 5, Pt. I, paras. 8–10.

[55] It is also the case that Sched. 4, para. 1, prevents the Scottish Parliament from modifying certain legislative provisions including, *inter alia*, the Human Rights Act 1998.

[56] The other Heads are: Energy, Transport, Society Security, Regulation of the Professions, Employment, Health and Medicines, Media and Culture and Miscellaneous.

[57] See, *e.g.* Sched. 5, Pt. II, sections D1, E1, E3 and F1.

Part III of Schedule 5 has a more institutional focus. The gist of this Part of the Schedule is to reserve certain bodies, or to clarify which bodies are not reserved. Thus, for example, a body mentioned by name in Part II of Schedule 5 is a reserved body, as is the Commission for Racial Equality, the Equal Opportunities Commission and the National Disability Council.[58] The effect of being denoted as such a body is to reserve its constitution, and its functions.

The force of section 29(2)(b) and Schedule 5 is reinforced by section 29(2)(c). This latter section brings Schedule 4 into play. Paragraph 2(1) of Schedule 4 states that an Act of the Scottish Parliament cannot modify, or confer power by subordinate legislation to modify, the law on reserved matters. It is clear that the "law on reserved matters" covers any enactment the subject matter of which is a reserved matter which is comprised in an Act of Parliament or subordinate legislation made thereunder. It also covers any rule of law which is not contained in an enactment where the subject matter is a reserved matter.[59] There is an exception where the modification is incidental to provision made which does not relate to the reserved matter, provided that the modification does not have a greater effect on reserved matters than is necessary to give effect to the purpose of the provision.[60] It is however open to the Scottish Parliament to restate the law.[61]

It is also important to have some understanding of the *powers of the executive*. Specific statutory functions can be conferred on the Scottish Ministers by name through any enactment.[62] The SA also makes a general transfer to the Scottish Ministers of functions which were hitherto exercised by a Minister of the Crown.[63] The Scottish Ministers are therefore prima facie given the powers exercised by Ministers of the Crown in relation to Scotland.[64] These functions are however only transferred in so far as they are exercisable within "devolved competence".[65] The exercise of a function will be outside a devolved competence if it would be outside the legislative competence of the Scottish Parliament itself.[66] The executive cannot therefore act so as to circumvent the limits placed on the legislative competence of the Parliament. It inexorably follows that all the difficulties of interpreting the boundaries of legislative competence charted above will apply whenever the executive itself seeks to act, irrespective of the form which the act takes.

The Scotland Act also makes provision for the passage of *subordinate legislation*, which involves the exercise of power by both the legislature and the

[58] *Ibid.* Sched. 5, Pt. III, para. 3.
[59] *Ibid.* Sched. 4, para. 2(2).
[60] *Ibid.* Sched. 4, para. 3(1).
[61] *Ibid.* Sched. 4, para. 7(1).
[62] *Ibid.* ss. 52(1), 52(7).
[63] *Ibid.* s. 53(1).
[64] Notwithstanding the generality of the transfer of functions described in the preceding paragraph, the Act stipulates that the functions under certain statutes are to be exercisable by a Minister of the Crown as well as the Scottish Ministers, ss. 56–57.
[65] *Ibid.* s. 53(1).
[66] *Ibid.* ss. 54(2)–(3).

executive. The Act gives extensive powers in this respect.[67] This includes "Henry VIII" clauses. Thus, subordinate legislation can be used to cure defects in an Act of the Scottish Parliament which has been found to be ultra vires.[68] The procedures which have to be followed when passing subordinate legislation vary. Suffice it to say for the present that Schedule 7 sets out 11 different procedures which can apply to the making of subordinate legislation under the Act. It is clear that on some occasions approval must be gained from the Westminster Parliament as well as from the Scottish Parliament.[69]

POLITICAL CHALLENGE TO THE COMPETENCE OF THE SCOTTISH PARLIAMENT

The Scotland Act contains provisions enabling the Secretary of State to intervene in certain cases. Two sections of the Act are of particular importance in this respect.

Section 35 allows the Secretary of State to make an order prohibiting the Presiding Officer from submitting a Bill for Royal Assent if it contains provisions which he or she has reasonable grounds to believe would be incompatible with any international obligations, or the interests of defence or national security. The Secretary of State can also make such an order where the Bill has provisions which modify the law as it applies to reserved matters, and which he or she has reasonable grounds to believe would have an adverse effect on the operation of the law as it applies to reserved matters. Reasons must be given for making such an order. It appears, moreover, that this power can be exercised even where a reference has been made to the Privy Council which has disposed of the matter.[70]

Section 58 contains a parallel power for the Secretary of State to intervene on the same grounds in relation to subordinate legislation made by the Scottish Executive.[71] In such instances the Secretary of State may by order actually revoke the legislation.

JUDICIAL CHALLENGE TO THE COMPETENCE OF THE SCOTTISH PARLIAMENT

The Scotland Act places, as we have seen, significant limitations on the legal competence of the Scottish Parliament. Schedule 6, which is made operative by section 98, is central in this respect. It defines "devolution issue" to mean:[72]

---

[67] *Ibid.* s. 104(1).
[68] *Ibid.* s. 107.
[69] *Ibid.* Sched. 7, paras 1(2), (2).
[70] *Ibid.* s. 35(3)(c).
[71] *Ibid.* s. 58(4).
[72] *Ibid.* Sched. 6, para. 1.

(a) a question whether an Act of the Scottish Parliament or any provision of an Act of the Scottish Parliament is within the legislative competence of the Parliament,

(b) a question whether any function (being a function which any person has purported, or is proposing, to exercise) is a function of the Scottish Ministers, the First Minister or the Lord Advocate,

(c) a question whether the purported or proposed exercise of a function by a member of the Scottish Executive is, or would be, within devolved competence,

(d) a question whether a purported or proposed exercise of a function by a member of the Scottish Executive is, or would be, incompatible with any of the Convention rights or with Community law,

(e) a question whether a failure to act by a member of the Scottish Executive is incompatible with any of the Convention rights or with Community law,

(f) any other question about whether a function is exercisable within devolved competence or in or as regards Scotland and any other question arising by virtue of this Act about reserved matters.

Section 101 imposes an interpretative obligation on courts to try and read Acts and Bills of the Scottish Parliament, and subordinate legislation, as being intra vires rather than ultra vires. Where any provision could be read so as to be ultra vires, section 101(2) states that it is to be read as narrowly as is required for it to be within competence,[73] if such a reading is possible.

The Scotland Act, like the Government of Wales Act, contains detailed rules as to the different types of legal challenge.

(a) The resolution of devolution issues: direct reference to the Privy Council

A devolution issue may be resolved through direct reference to the Privy Council. There are three types of case where this can occur.

First, there can be *pre-enactment scrutiny*. The Advocate General, the Lord Advocate or the Attorney-General may refer the question of whether a Bill or any provision of a Bill would be within the legislative competence of the Parliament to the Judicial Committee of the Privy Council for a decision.[74] The Presiding Officer must not submit a Bill for Royal Assent at any time when such a law officer is entitled to make a reference, or where the reference has been made but the Privy Council has not yet disposed of the matter.[75] Decisions made by the Privy Council are binding in all legal proceedings, other than proceedings before the Privy Council itself.[76] If the Privy Council decides that the Bill is ultra vires then the Presiding Officer cannot submit it for Royal Assent in its

---

[73] "Competence" is defined in relation to an Act of the Scottish Parliament, or a Bill, to mean the legislative competence of the Parliament; in relation to subordinate legislation it is defined to mean the powers conferred by the SA, s. 101(3).

[74] *Ibid.* s. 33(1). Such a reference can be made within four weeks beginning with the passing of the Bill, and any period of four weeks beginning with the subsequent approval of the Bill in accordance with standing orders which are made, s. 33(2).

[75] *Ibid.* s. 32(2).

[76] *Ibid.* s. 103(1).

unamended form.[77] Special provision is made for cases which might be referred by the Privy Council to the European Court of Justice.[78]

Secondly, there is the possibility of a direct reference to the Privy Council *from existing proceedings.* Law officers must be notified of a devolution issue which arises in particular proceedings, and they are then entitled to take part in the proceedings so far as they relate to the devolution issue.[79] The Lord Advocate, the Advocate General, the Attorney-General and the Attorney-General for Northern Ireland may then require the court or tribunal to refer the devolution issue to the Privy Council.[80]

Thirdly, there can be a direct reference of a devolution issue *which is not the subject of existing proceedings.* The same law officers can exercise this power.[81]

(b) Institution of proceedings by a Law Officer

The Scotland Act allows the relevant law officer to institute proceedings for the determination of a devolution issue. The Lord Advocate will normally be the defendant in such actions.[82] The law officers have the power to require the devolution issue to be referred to the Privy Council, as described above, but may choose not to exercise this power.

(c) Reference to other Courts

The discussion thus far has focused on the role of the law officers in enforcing the limits to the Scottish Parliament's power. It is, however, readily apparent that devolution issues will often arise in the course of proceedings involving individuals, or between an individual and a public body. The Act clearly contemplates such actions.[83] It makes provision in such instances for the referral of devolution issues from one court to another. The rules in this respect are very similar to those which apply in the Government of Wales Act. Proceedings which raise devolution issues may occur in Scotland itself, in England and Wales or in Northern Ireland. The Scotland Act establishes a reference system for all three jurisdictions. The description which follows applies in relation to England and Wales.

In non-criminal proceedings, magistrates' courts can refer devolution issues to the High Court.[84] Other courts may refer such issues to the Court of

---

[77] *Ibid.* s. 32(3).
[78] *Ibid.* s. 34.
[79] *Ibid.* Sched. 6, paras. 5–6, 16–17, 26–27. Which Law officers must be notified depends on where the proceedings initially arise, Scotland, England and Wales or Northern Ireland.
[80] *Ibid.* Sched. 6, para. 33.
[81] *Ibid.* Sched. 6, paras. 34–35.
[82] *Ibid.* sched. 6, paras. 4, 15, 25.
[83] *Ibid.* Sched. 6, paras. 4(3), 15(3), 25(3).
[84] *Ibid.* Sched. 6, para. 18.

Appeal.[85] In criminal cases, a court, other than the Court of Appeal or the House of Lords, can refer a devolution issue to the High Court, in the case of summary proceedings, or the Court of Appeal in the case of proceedings on indictment.[86] Tribunals from which there is no appeal must refer to the Court of Appeal, and may make a reference in other instances.[87]

The Court of Appeal can refer any devolution issue which comes before it, other than on a reference as described above, to the Privy Council.[88] Where a devolution issue arises in judicial proceedings in the House of Lords it must be referred to the Privy Council unless the House decides that it would be more appropriate in all the circumstances for it to hear the issue.[89]

Appeals from the High Court or the Court of Appeal on devolution issues lie to the Privy Council. Leave is required for such an appeal from the High Court or Court of Appeal, or from the Privy Council.[90]

(d) Decision made by the Court immediately seized of the matter

The situation here is the same as that in Wales. The court immediately seized of the matter has the power to refer the matter in the manner described above. It does not have the duty to do so, subject to being compelled to make a reference by the intervention of a law officer requiring the case to be referred to the Privy Council. The comments made on the way in which this power might be exercised are equally applicable here.[91]

(e) Devolution issues which "arise": the relevance of the general law on collateral challenge

This issue was discussed in relation to the Government of Wales Act. The language used in the Scotland Act is the same, and reference should therefore be made to the previous discussion.[92]

---

[85] *Ibid*. Sched. 6, para. 19, with the exception of magistrates' courts, the Court of Appeal or the House of Lords, or the High Court where acting under para. 18.

[86] *Ibid*. Sched. 6, para. 21.

[87] *Ibid*. Sched. 6, para. 20.

[88] *Ibid*. Sched. 6, para. 22.

[89] *Ibid*. Sched. 6, para. 32.

[90] *Ibid*. Sched. 6, para. 23.

[91] See above, p. 219.

[92] See above, pp. 219–20.

(f) The result of finding that the Scottish Parliament acted outside its competence

The Scotland Act makes provision as to what should occur if an Act of the Scottish Parliament, or subordinate legislation, is found to be *ultra vires*.

In political terms, the Act does, as we have seen, contain a broad "Henry VIII" clause allowing the passage of subordinate legislation to amend an Act of the Scottish Parliament, or other subordinate legislation, which has been found to be ultra vires.[93] The subordinate legislation which performs this corrective function will, however, be subject to scrutiny by the Westminster Parliament.[94]

In legal terms, the SA empowers a court or tribunal which has decided that an Act of the Scottish Parliament, or subordinate legislation, is ultra vires, to make an order removing or limiting any retrospective effect of that decision, or suspending the effect of that decision for any period and on any conditions to allow the defect to be corrected.[95] The court, in deciding whether to make such an order, must take into account, *inter alia*, the extent to which persons who are not party to the proceedings would otherwise be adversely affected.[96] The appropriate law officer must be given an intimation that such an order might be made, and can then join the proceedings for this issue.[97]

JUDICIAL DETERMINATION OF LEGISLATIVE COMPETENCE:
THREE CENTRAL ISSUES

With this overview of the GWA and SA in mind, it is now possible to consider how judges might deal with disputes about the competence of either the Assembly or the Scottish Parliament. In so far as courts are required to rule upon the validity of subordinate legislation enacted by the Assembly, they will be on relatively familiar ground, since they are accustomed to reviewing secondary legislation. The GWA no doubt complicates this task, but it does not alter the fundamental nature of judicial review. In contrast, under the SA courts will have a power to review the *primary* legislation of a Parliament.

In adapting to their new role, however, judges need not operate in a vacuum. Consideration of previous British experience with devolution may prove helpful, and the analysis may be expanded to include consideration of judicial review under federal constitutions. Federalism and devolution represent different methods of ordering regional or national components within a single constitutional system, but the judicial task of determining legislative competence is, in conceptual terms, essentially the same in both. Judges must identify the

---

[93] SA, s. 107.
[94] *Ibid*. Sched. 7, para. 1(2).
[95] *Ibid*. s. 102(3).
[97] *Ibid*. s. 102(4).

subject matter of the impugned statute, and then determine whether it falls within or outside the subject matters over which the legislature has authority.

There are, of course, limits to the value of comparative analysis. Legal, constitutional, political and historical factors will differ as between different systems, and will render some comparisons less appropriate than others. The following analysis is therefore restricted to a consideration of historical and modern examples from the United Kingdom and the Commonwealth in which judges sharing a common juridical tradition have interpreted statutes of the United Kingdom Parliament establishing either devolved or federal constitutional orders. Particular attention is given to the South Africa Act 1909 and Government of Ireland Act 1920 (GIA), which created systems of devolution as between the South African colonies and as between the United Kingdom and Northern Ireland respectively,[98] and the British North America Act 1867 (BNA Act), now called the Constitution Act 1867, and the Commonwealth of Australia Constitution Act 1900, enacting the Australian Constitution, which create federal systems for Canada and Australia respectively.

We are not suggesting that the case law from other jurisdictions can be applied directly to problems arising under the GWA or SA. It will, however, be argued that an appreciation of the judicial experiences in other systems is critical to the development of an appropriate normative framework for the interpretation of the concept of "legislative competence" under the GWA and SA.

It should, moreover, be recognised that *any* division of legislative power will raise certain fundamental issues which must be resolved by the courts and which will shape the entire nature of that division of authority. Three issues are particularly seminal in this respect: the choice of interpretative perspective; the manner in which, and the degree to which, legislative power is divided; and the task of classifying impugned legislation according to subject matter. These issues will be considered in turn.

THE INTERPRETATIVE PERSPECTIVE: STATUTORY OR CONSTITUTIONAL INTERPRETATION?

The GWA and SA are statutes of the United Kingdom Parliament, but they are statutes with obvious constitutional significance. Should they be interpreted, according to the normal canons of statutory construction, in a conservative, literal manner which emphasises text above other factors? Or should they be read, as constitutions tend to be read, in a liberal, progressive manner which emphasises not only text but also shifting social and political context? Experience

[98] The Government of India Act 1919 also established devolution as between central and provincial legislatures, but judicial review of legislative competence was prohibited: Sir I. Jennings and C.M. Young, *Constitutional Laws of the Commonwealth* (Oxford: Clarendon Press, 1952), pp. 357–359. The Northern Ireland (Constitution) Act 1973 established a devolved legislature for Northern Ireland, but it functioned only briefly.

under similar statutes suggests that courts seek to combine rules of statutory and constitutional construction, and that parliamentary intent gradually loses its significance as an interpretative factor the longer the Act survives.[99]

For example, the Privy Council initially insisted that Canada's BNA Act 1867 be subjected to the "same methods of construction and exposition" as other statutes, and that the legislative powers of the federal and provincial legislatures created by that Act were simply those powers that "the Imperial Parliament intended to give".[100] By 1930, however, judicial attitudes had clearly shifted. Lord Sankey L.C. concluded that the BNA Act was to be read as a "Constitution" and not like an Act passed to "regulate the affairs of an English parish", for it had "planted in Canada a living tree capable of growth and expansion within its natural limits".[101] Thus, the Act was to be given "a large and liberal interpretation" so that the provincial and federal legislatures might (within their respective spheres of competence) exercise full authority over their own affairs.[102] As Sir Ivor Jennings observed, in this "remarkable" decision Lord Sankey "wiped out the rule that the Canadian Constitution is a statute, to be interpreted like other statutes".[103] For Canadian courts parliamentary intent is, at best, only the starting point in the analysis.[104] They now view the jurisprudential root of the Constitution Act 1867 as being the popular sovereignty of the Canadian people rather than the United Kingdom Parliament.[105]

The significance of a *constitutional* interpretative perspective is that the text's meaning may become detached from its author's intent. As a *statute* the 1867 Act created a centralised federation in which broad powers were given to the federal Parliament and government; as a *constitution*, however, it has been judicially interpreted to secure a decentralised federal order in which extensive legislative autonomy is secured for provincial legislatures.[106] In contrast, the text of Australia's Constitution suggests a decentralised federation with strong state legislatures, but judicial interpretation has secured a predominant role for the federal, or Commonwealth, Parliament.[107] This change in the Constitution's meaning was influenced by, as Windeyer J. acknowledged, an emerging sense of nationhood that necessitated a reworking of Australia's normative constitutional foundation.[108] Evolving judicial interpretation of the Constitution's text was the medium through which this legal change was achieved. The

---

[99] G.P. Browne, *The Judicial Committee and the British North America Act* (Toronto: University of Toronto Press, 1967), p. 14.

[100] *Bank of Toronto v. Lambe* (1887) 12 App.Cas. 575 at 579, 586.

[101] *Edwards v. Attorney General for Canada* [1930] AC 124 at 136–137.

[102] *Ibid.* see also, *British Coal Co. v. The King* [1935] AC 500 at 517–518.

[103] Sir I. Jennings, "The Statute of Westminster and Appeals to the Privy Council" (1936) 52 LQR 173 at p. 181.

[104] *Martin Service Station Ltd v. Minister of National Revenue* [1977] 2 SCR 966 at 1006.

[105] *Reference re Secession of Quebec* [1998] 2 SCR 217 at para. 85.

[106] P. Hogg, *Constitutional Law of Canada* (Toronto: Carswell, 3rd ed., 1992), pp. 108–111.

[107] See, in general, C.D. Gilbert, *Australian and Canadian Federalism, 1867–1984: A Study of Judicial Techniques* (Melbourne, Melbourne University Press, 1986).

[108] *Victoria v. Commonwealth (Payroll Tax case)* (1971) 122 CLR 353 at 395–396.

Constitution was regarded as a fundamental law and judicial interpretation thereof could "vary and develop in response to changing circumstances".[109]

The label "fundamental law" is not unknown to judicial and academic discourse surrounding the Scottish-English union, but courts have been reluctant to infuse even the Acts of Union 1706–7 with a degree of justiciable force different from regular statutes.[110] However, it may be argued that the GWA and SA should be interpreted as constitutional instruments, and that this could be done (as it was, initially at least, in relation to the BNA Act and the Australian Constitution) without compromising United Kingdom parliamentary sovereignty. Viewing the GWA and SA as constitutions subject to constitutional interpretative principles may, however, be problematic. There are a number of distinguishing features between these two sets of statutes.

First, the BNA Act 1867 and Commonwealth of Australia Act 1900 created what were at the time *colonial* constitutions for distant settlements with a view toward gradually loosening imperial control. The political context of the GWA and SA is rather different: these statutes re-order legislative power within the United Kingdom in such a manner as to ensure (supposedly) the on-going legal, constitutional, political and economic integration of Wales and Scotland within the United Kingdom.[111]

Secondly, there are critical differences between the GWA and SA, and the 1867 and 1900 Acts for Canada and Australia. The lists of federal and provincial legislative powers in sections 91 and 92 of the BNA Act and the list of Commonwealth parliamentary powers in section 51 of the Australian Constitution are vague and, one could say, constitution-like. The list of reserved matters in Schedule 5 of the SA is, as we have seen, textually dense and much more statute-like. When legislative competence is defined by reference to particular statutory provisions it becomes much more difficult to justify departure from normal rules of statutory construction when defining the scope of that competence. Thus, it is unlikely that a particular section of a reserved United Kingdom statute could, at some future date, be construed so as to enhance Scottish legislative competence in order to reflect whatever new political and social reality may have emerged to inform judicial conceptions of the Scottish-English union. This applies *a fortiori* in relation to Wales where the Assembly only has competence in the fields specifically assigned to it.

Thirdly, the degree to which judges read the SA as a constitution may depend in part upon the ease with which it can be legislatively amended. Section 30 allows modifications to be made to Schedules 4 and 5 by Order in Council. If, however, a constitutional convention develops preventing the United Kingdom

---

[109] *Ibid.* see also, *Attorney-General for New South Wales* v. *Brewery Employees Union of NSW* (1908) 6 CLR 469 at 611–612 and *Jumbunna Coal Mine NL* v. *Victorian Coal Miners' Association* (1908) 6 CLR 309 at 367–368.

[110] *e.g. MacCormick* v. *Lord Advocate* 1953 SC 396; *Gibson* v. *Lord Advocate* 1975 SLT 134; C. Munro, *Studies in Constitutional Law* (London: Butterworths, 1987), pp. 66–78.

[111] *Scotland's Parliament*, Cm. 3658 (1997); *A Voice for Wales*, Cm. 3718 (1997).

Parliament from amending the SA unilaterally,[112] then perhaps a more flexible judicial interpretation, like that used in relation to the 1867 and 1900 Acts, may be appropriate. In relation to the Government of Ireland Act 1920 it was argued that the dynamic interpretative approach adopted in relation to the BNA Act and the Australian Constitution was inappropriate, in part because "from time to time" United Kingdom statutes were made to remove "difficulties" caused by the restrictions placed on the devolved Northern Ireland Parliament.[113] The difference, then, was that no convention limited the United Kingdom Parliament's ability to alter the GIA unilaterally,[114] whereas such conventions did develop (and were confirmed by the Statute of Westminster 1931) in relation to the BNA Act and the Australian Constitution.[115]

While it may therefore be difficult for the courts to adopt a constitutional perspective of the kind taken in relation to Canada and Australia it should also be recognised that there is considerable scope for an interpretative approach that is sensitive to the fact that the courts will be reviewing the actions of democratically elected bodies. It is very likely that this will have an impact on challenges to validity. The courts will require clear evidence of, for example, trespass on a reserved matter before rendering the relevant provisions ineffective, all the more so given the interpretative obligation contained in the SA. The courts will also be reluctant to intervene on procedural grounds, for example that the Assembly failed to consult as required by the GWA, unless the error can be clearly proven.

Review for irrationality will be possible in theory for Assembly subordinate legislation, as it is in the case of statutory instruments approved by the House of Commons.[116] Applicants will, however, have to show something extreme before the courts are willing to strike down action on this ground. Whether irrationality would be a round for challenge even in theory in relation to primary legislation passed by the Scottish Parliament is more debatable. If the SA is regarded as a constitutional instrument establishing a Parliament with primary legislative power, then the Scottish Parliament should be regarded, within its sphere of legislative competence, as occupying the same status as the United Kingdom Parliament, which is not susceptible to judicial review on grounds of irrationality when acting "legislatively". When the United Kingdom Parliament established legislatures in the past, legislative power was typically granted to make laws for the "peace, order and good government" of a certain territory. According to the courts, such legislatures were not "agents" or "delegates" of the United Kingdom Parliament; rather, they had, within their prescribed

---

[112] The possibility was acknowledged in the *Report of the Royal Commission on the Constitution, 1969–1973*, Cmnd. 5460 (1973), para. 768.

[113] *Regina (Hume)* v. *Londonderry Justices* [1972] NI 91 at 114–115.

[114] H. Calvert, *Constitutional Law in Northern Ireland* (London and Belfast: Stevens & Sons, Ltd, 1968), pp. 88–92.

[115] Sir K.C. Wheare, *The Statute of Westminster and Dominion Status* (Oxford: Oxford University Press, 5th ed., 1953).

[116] *Nottinghamshire County Council* v. *Secretary of State for the Environment* [1986] AC 240 at 250.

spheres of legislative competence, "plenary powers of legislation as large, and of the same nature, as those of Parliament itself".[117] Thus, the Acts of these legislatures could not be reviewed on grounds of unreasonableness.[118] Although the "peace, order and good government" formula was used in the Government of Ireland Act 1920, it is not used in the SA. One could therefore argue that it must have been the intention of Parliament to deny to the Scottish Parliament the same "plenary" legislative powers as these other legislatures, and that judicial review on *Wednesbury* grounds is warranted just as it is in relation to local authorities. This would, however, be a startling assertion for any court to make. Indeed, there is nothing magic about the "peace, order and good government" formula. Under the system of devolution established by the South Africa Act 1909, the "peace, order and good government" formula was not used in granting legislative authority to provincial councils, yet it was held that the ordinances of such "legislative" councils were not to be treated as "byelaws" subject to review as "unreasonable".[119] The provincial councils had the "same power" as the central Parliament to make even retrospective laws, and if these laws were unjust or "inexpedient" it was for Parliament to repeal them.[120] In short, there is authority for the proposition that legislatures in a similar position to the Scottish Parliament are not amenable to judicial review for irrationality.

THE DIVISION OF POWER: MANNER AND DEGREE

There are two factors which are crucial in any division of power: the manner in which the power is divided and the degree of power accorded to the different legislative authorities. These factors are related but distinct. They will be examined in turn.

(a) The manner in which power is divided

Legislative competence may be divided between two or more legislatures in a number of different ways. One method is to attempt to identify the subject matters over which each legislature has competence. Thus if there are two levels of legislature, there will be two lists that enumerate legislative powers. This method may be labelled the double enumeration model. Another method is to list the subject matter over which one legislature is competent, and simply

---

[117] *Regina* v. *Burah* (1878) 3 App.Cas. 889 (re India); *Riel* v. *Queen* (1885) 10 App.Cas. 675 at 678 (re Canada); *Powell* v. *Apollo Candle Co. Ltd* (1885) 10 App.Cas. 282 (re New South Wales).

[118] *Bank of Toronto* v. *Lambe* (1887) 12 App.Cas. 575.

[119] *Middelburg Municipality* v. *Gertzen* [1914] AD 544. See also, *Hodge* v. *The Queen* (1883) 9 App. Cas. 117 (re Ontario); *Thakur Jagannath Baksh Sing* v. *The United Provinces* [1946] AC 327 at 335 (re India).

[120] *Marshall's Township Syndicate Ltd* v. *Johannesburg Consolidated Investment Co. Ltd* [1920] AC 420 at 425–426.

allocate the unenumerated residue to the other. Finally, a legislature may be granted competence over an unenumerated area, but be restricted from legislating in relation to a list of reserved matters. These last two methods are variations of what may be called the single enumeration model. In each, there is only one subject matter list. In Canada, the Constitution Act 1867 follows the double enumeration model: sections 91 and 92 list exclusive federal and provincial legislative powers respectively, with the residual power vested in the federal Parliament. Under the Australian Constitution the single enumeration model is followed: state legislative powers are unlisted (section 107 preserves their pre-federation powers, except where limited by the Constitution), whereas the Commonwealth Parliament has only those powers that are expressly listed. Commonwealth legislative powers are found mainly in section 51 and are not exclusive, though by section 109 Commonwealth legislation prevails over conflicting state legislation. Finally, the Government of Ireland Act 1920 adopted a different variation of the single enumeration model. The matters over which the devolved Northern Ireland Parliament was competent were unlisted. It was simply granted general authority subject to a list of matters over which it could not legislate. The structure of the SA is similar to that of the GIA.

In assessing the relevance of cases from other jurisdictions to the interpretation of the SA, it is important to consider the implications of the structure of the division of legislative competence. Does the adoption of a double enumeration model affect judicial interpretation of legislative competence, thereby rendering cases under that model unhelpful when interpreting legislative competence under a single enumeration model? Will judicial approaches to legislative competence vary depending upon which sort of single enumeration model is used? Answers to these questions are necessary before the substantive principles of interpretation from one model can be applied to another model.

Some judges and commentators have argued that Canadian cases on legislative competence under the Constitution Act 1867 are inapplicable to questions of legislative competence under either the Australian Constitution or the GIA, because the former uses a double enumeration model and the latter use single enumeration models. It has been argued, for example, that the Canadian practice of examining the underlying purposes and actual effects of an impugned statute to determine whether it falls within an area over which the legislature is competent is necessitated by the double enumeration model, and that a more narrow, textually-based interpretation of contested statutes is appropriate under a single enumeration mode.[121] The strength of this argument is, however, questionable. While there are, as will be seen, competing approaches to the interpretation of contested legislation, there is no reason to conclude that the

---

[121] For arguments distinguishing the BNA Act from the Australian Constitution on this basis, see *South Australia* v. *Commonwealth (First Uniform Tax case)* (1942) 65 CLR 373 at 425–426. For arguments distinguishing the BNA Act from the GIA on this basis, see *Regina (Hume)* v. *Londonderry Justices* [1972] NI 91 at 110–111 and Calvert, *op. cit.* pp. 187–196.

choice of approach is determined by whether a single or double enumeration model is used.

A more plausible reason why the double enumeration in the Canadian federal model may reduce the value of the Canadian judicial approach as guidance for judges in devolved or federal systems using a single enumeration model was articulated by Evatt J. in *Huddart Parker* v. *Commonwealth*,[122] an Australian case in which the federal "trade and commerce" power was at issue. It was argued that the restrictive interpretation of the equivalent federal "trade and commerce" power in Canada should be adopted in Australia. Under the Constitution Act 1867, the Canadian Federal Parliament was given legislative authority over "The Regulation of Trade and Commerce". Although this phrase is not explicitly qualified, it has been limited by courts to foreign and inter-provincial trade and commerce to account for the fact that provinces are granted exclusive legislative authority over "Property and Civil Rights in the Province", which the courts have said must include *intra*-provincial trade and commerce.[123] This led Evatt J. to say that the "double enumeration" of exclusive federal and provincial powers in Canada requires judges "to visualize and recognize both powers at the same moment".[124] In his view, however, the judicial task in Australia is "essentially different": only the Commonwealth Parliament is granted "express powers", and therefore the existence of unenumerated, residual state powers "does not control or predetermine those duly granted to the Commonwealth".[125] Commonwealth powers are ascertained first, independently of state powers, and "[w]hatever self-governing powers remain belong exclusively to the States".[126] The consequences of adopting this approach are striking: Australian courts are more willing to permit federal regulation of intra-state trade than Canadian courts are to permit federal regulation of intra-provincial trade, even though in Australia the federal power *is* expressly limited to foreign and inter-state trade whereas in Canada the equivalent limitation arises through mere judicial construction.[127] In more general terms, it is fair to say that the interpretative approaches have contributed significantly to the decentralisation of federalism in Canada and the centralisation of federalism in Australia: without the boundary line provided by a second enumeration of subject matters, the powers defined by a single enumeration may be allowed to expand to the limits that language will allow.

The Australian Constitution adopts a single enumeration model in which the *powers* of the Parliament are expressly listed, whereas the SA adopts a single enumeration model in which the *restrictions* on the powers of the Scottish Parliament are expressly listed. Despite this difference, it could be argued that,

---

[122] (1931) 44 CLR 492.
[123] *Citizens' Insurance Co. of Canada* v. *Parsons* (1881) 7 App.Cas. 96.
[124] *Huddart Parker* v. *Commonwealth* (1931) 44 CLR 492 at 526–527.
[125] *Ibid.*
[126] *Ibid.*
[127] Gilbert, *op. cit.* pp. 39–68.

because there is only one list in the SA, the Australian and not the Canadian interpretative perspective is appropriate. Thus, the reserved matters listed in Schedule 5 of the SA should be given their natural, literal meaning, and whatever powers happen to be left over fall within the devolved competence of the Scottish Parliament. If accepted, this approach would probably lead to a narrowing of the Scottish Parliament's powers just as it led to the narrowing of Australian state powers.

The single enumeration model under both the GIA and the SA is, however, different from that under the Australian Constitution. In abstract terms, the formulae for the grant of legislative authority under the Australian Constitution and the SA respectively may be represented as follows:

(1) Legislature A may make laws on a, b, c . . . n; the remainder of the legislative power is vested in Legislature B.

(2) Legislature B may make any law, except laws that relate to a, b, c . . . n, which are matters reserved for Legislature A.

If the content of a, b, c . . . n was capable of definition with mathematical precision, then, in terms of strict logic, Legislature B should have the same legislative competence in both formula (1) and formula (2). However, the content of subject matters a, b, c . . . n cannot be known with such precision: they are open to broad and narrow interpretations, and the choice between a broad or narrow interpretation may be influenced by the formula in which they are found. Since formula (1) seems to focus attention on Legislature A's powers, and formula (2) focuses attention on Legislature B's powers, it may be appropriate to give a, b, c, . . . n a relatively broad reading in (1) and a relatively narrow reading in (2).

This argument is strengthened when the formulae are put into their broader constitutional contexts. The Australian Constitution follows formula (1), but because state legislatures have *concurrent* authority over subjects a, b, c . . . n, and state power is only ousted by conflicting federal laws, the state/federal power imbalance is not as great as formula (1), interpreted without a notional sphere of state power, might suggest. Similarly, the SA follows formula (2), but the United Kingdom Parliament has *concurrent* and *supreme* legislative authority over devolved matters, and so a narrow interpretation of reserved subjects a, b, c . . . n that accounts for a notional sphere of devolved legislative authority would not severely imbalance the legal relationship between Scotland and the United Kingdom.

(b) The degree of power accorded to the different legislative authorities

The preceding discussion of the manner in which legislative authority is divided must be viewed in conjunction with the equally important issue regarding the degree of power accorded to the different legislative authorities. There may be two systems both of which use a single enumeration model, and both of which express this in terms of general legislative power accorded to the devolved body, with a list of matters which are then reserved to the central legislature. The GIA and the SA both follow this format. The crucial difference between them resides in the degree of power accorded to the two legislatures. The list of reserved powers contained in the former is relatively short, and relatively general. The list contained in the SA is very long, contains general reservations and a plethora of much more detailed specific reservations. This serves not only to limit more markedly the powers of the Scottish Parliament; it can also have a significant impact on the way in which courts will construe the reservations when challenges to competence arise.

The breadth of the list of reserved matters in the SA is mitigated to some extent by section 101, which directs judges to avoid finding Scottish Acts ultra vires where possible. This presumption of legality could be achieved by (a) reading the list of reserved matters narrowly, (b) reading the impugned Act narrowly to exclude reserved matters, or (c) by combining elements of both approaches. In fact, section 101 of the SA provides that an impugned Scottish Act must be read "as narrowly as is required for it to be within competence". The inclusion of section 101 in the SA could be said to preclude the adoption of approach (a) above. However, it is perhaps better to assume that section 101 creates a rule of construction for impugned Acts which applies only after the issue of "competence" has been determined, and "competence" may be established through whatever reading of the SA judges conclude is appropriate, including (perhaps) one that reads the reserved list conservatively to account for a notional sphere of devolved power.

THE UNAVOIDABLE TASK: THE CLASSIFICATION OF IMPUGNED LEGISLATION BY SUBJECT MATTER

Whenever a legislature's authority is limited or restricted, the legality of its legislation can only be determined by a process of reasoning that involves *classifying* the impugned legislation according to subject matter, and then seeing whether or not that subject matter falls within the area over which the legislature has authority.[128] The contested Act will be valid if it is made "in relation to"[129] or "with respect to"[130] a subject matter over which the legislature is competent. Conversely, the Act will be invalid if it is made "in respect of"[131] or if it "relates to"[132] a subject matter over which the legislature has no competence.

---

[128] See W.R. Lederman, "Classification of Laws and the British North America Act", in *Continuing Canadian Constitutional Dilemmas: Essays on the Constitutional History, Public Law and Federal System of Canada* (Toronto: Butterworths, 1981).

[129] Constitution Act 1867, ss. 91 and 92; South Africa Act 1909, s. 85.

[130] Australian Constitution, s. 51.

[131] Government of Ireland Act 1920, s. 4(1).

[132] Scotland Act 1998, s. 29(2)(b).

It is important to emphasise that, unless some form of concurrent legislative authority arises, a law is invalid because it encroaches upon a *subject matter* over which the legislature has no authority, not because it conflicts with a *law* made by another legislature that does have authority over that subject matter. The wording of section 29 is framed so as to preclude Scottish legislation which *relates* to the list of reserved matters. Thus, even if the impugned measure improperly touches upon a prohibited subject matter in a way which is consistent with existing laws on that subject matter, it is invalid.

The difficulty is, of course, that statutes rarely touch upon only one subject matter. Human activity cannot be neatly pigeon-holed in this way, and nor can laws that regulate human activity. Statutes may therefore touch upon several issues, some of which are within the competence of the legislature, others not. The struggle to develop methods of identifying the *constitutionally-relevant* subject matter of an impugned statute has pre-occupied courts from each of the jurisdictions we have considered. There has, moreover, been disagreement as to the criteria which should be used as the discussion below will reveal.

(a) The colourability doctrine

A contested Act may appear on its face to relate to a subject matter over which the legislature has authority, but it may have a purpose or effect that relates to a subject matter over which the legislature does not have authority. The Canadian cases describe such Acts as "colourable", and declare them ultra vires. Thus, in the *Alberta Bank Taxation* case, a provincial statute imposing high rates of tax on banks was held invalid because although the tax was, in *form*, within provincial competence it was, in *effect*, a tax that would have discouraged the establishment of banks in the province, and the regulation of banking is within the federal Parliament's authority.[133] In determining the effect of a statute a court may take "judicial notice" of "any public general knowledge" and "may in a proper case require to be informed by evidence as to what the effect of the legislation will be".[134]

The idea that a law might be valid in form but invalid because of underlying purpose or actual effect has been rejected by the Australian High Court. In Australia, courts look only to the "duties, rights or powers" that the law "creates, abolishes or regulates" when classifying the law's subject matter.[135] Thus, if a Commonwealth statute imposes a tax it is valid pursuant to the federal taxation power no matter how great the effect (intended or not) on matters within exclusive state jurisdiction.[136]

---

[133] *Attorney-General for Alberta* v. *Attorney-General for Canada (Alberta Bank Taxation case)* [1939] AC 117.

[134] *Ibid.* pp. 130–131.

[135] *South Australia* v. *Commonwealth (First Uniform Tax case)* (1942) 65 CLR 373 at 424–426.

[136] *e.g. Department of Taxation* v. *WR Moran Pty Ltd* [1940] AC 838; *Fairfax* v. *Commissioner of Taxation* (1965) 114 CLR 1; *Commonwealth* v. *Tasmania* (1983) 46 ALR 625; Gilbert, *op. cit.* pp. 8–26.

Gallagher v. *Lynn*[137] applied the Canadian approach to Northern Ireland. There was at that time, a steady stream of Privy Council cases from Canada, yet comparatively few from Australia,[138] and it is therefore understandable that Lord Atkin drew upon the Canadian jurisprudence. However, the linkage was criticised. It has been argued that juridical inquiry into the underlying purpose and actual effect of impugned legislation was required in Canada because of the double enumeration of federal and provincial powers there, and in systems adopting a single enumeration of powers or restrictions, like the Australian Constitution and the GIA, resort to extrinsic evidence in construing legislation was unnecessary, unwarranted and overly subjective.[139]

The "purpose and effect" approach to construing contested legislation under a double enumeration model does ensure that one list of powers is not destroyed by "colourable" legislation made under the other list. However, there is no reason why it could not also be employed under a single enumeration model to ensure that a legislature with listed powers does not improperly intrude upon a sphere of power notionally reserved to the other level of legislature (as in Australia), or to ensure that a legislature whose unlisted powers are subject to a list of reservations does not improperly circumvent those reservations (as under GIA or SA). The real reason why judges in Australia refused to adopt a colourability rule was probably its incompatibility, when applied in the Australian context, with the prevailing judicial conception of Australian federalism.[140]

The choice between the Canadian and Australian approaches is therefore dependent upon a political choice about the right balance to strike between legislatures, and perhaps it was to relieve the United Kingdom courts from having to make this political choice that the SA expressly adopts a "purpose and effect" approach. Section 29(3) of the SA states that the question whether a Scottish Act relates to a reserved matter is to be determined by reference "to the purpose of the provision, having regard (among other things) to its effect in all the circumstances". Thus, section 29(3) removes from the judicial armoury an important tool for enhancing the Scottish Parliament's powers: adoption of the Australian approach would have shielded Scottish Acts from at least certain forms of challenge. In light of section 29(3) it must be concluded that the Australian cases on the classification of impugned legislation offer little or no assistance to the classification of Scottish Acts. However, some value might be derived from the Canadian cases. It might be useful, for example, to consider what sorts of effects

---

[137] [1937] AC 863. The Canadian approach was also adopted in the South African context, *Middelburg Municipality* v. *Gertzen* [1914] AD 544; *Marshall's Township Syndicate Ltd* v. *Johannesburg Consolidated Investment Co. Ltd* [1920] AC 420 at 421 (*per* counsel).

[138] V.C. MacDonald, "The Privy Council and the Canadian Constitution" (1951) 29 Can. Bar Rev. 1021; B. Galligan, *Politics of the High Court: A Study of the Judicial Branch of the Government of Australia* (St Lucia: University of Queensland Press, 1987), p. 177.

[139] Calvert, *op. cit.*, pp. 187–196, cited with approval in *Regina (Hume)* v. *Londonderry Justices* [1972] NI 91 at 312. Latham C.J. makes a similar argument in relation to Australia: *South Australia* v. *Commonwealth (first Uniform Tax case)* (1942) 65 CLR 373 at 424–426.

[140] Gilbert, *op. cit.* pp. 25.

Canadian courts have considered, and what sorts of extrinsic evidence they have examined, when determining the constitutionally relevant subject matter of contested statutes.[141] It may also be useful in relation to the pre-assent review jurisdiction to be exercised by the Privy Council under the SA to consider how the Supreme Court of Canada determines the "effect" of legislation in the absence of a factual dispute when exercising its advisory jurisdiction.[142]

(b) The pith and substance doctrine

Whenever a legislature's authority is limited some rule must be adopted to address the possibility that a law may touch upon subject matter within and outside legislative competence. For a court to strike down all legislation affecting matters outside the legislature's competence, however remote the effect, would leave the legislature with little scope for action. The Constitution Act 1867 contains no express rule on this issue, but the courts use the so-called "pith and substance" doctrine to address the problem: as long as the predominant aspect (or "pith and substance", or "true nature and character") of the contested measure is within legislative competence then the measure is valid even though it affects incidentally subject matter over which the legislature has no authority.[143] Such a law is valid in all respects, and therefore the pith and substance rule implies *concurrent* legislative authority in such incidental areas. However, for the law's incidental encroachment on a prohibited subject matter to be valid, it must have a "rational, functional connection" to the main part of the legislation.[144] Indeed, recent cases have gone further, suggesting that if the incidental effect is a major encroachment on a subject matter it can only be justified if it is "truly necessary" or "essential" to the legislative scheme.[145] This proportionality-type rule has, however, been criticised.[146] Finally, the pith and substance rule, because it contemplates concurrent legislative competence, must operate in conjunction with some rule of paramountcy dealing with conflicting legislation. In Canada, the rule is, again, one of judicial construction: when a provincial and a federal statute come into *operational* conflict (in the sense of requiring, on the facts of the case, inconsistent conduct or results) then the federal statute prevails and the provincial statute is, to the extent of the inconsistency, inoperative (as opposed to invalid).[147]

---

[141]   *e.g.* courts may have regard to economic effects of a contested law *Central Canada Potash Co.* v. *Government of Saskatchewan* [1979] 1 SCR 42, or the manner in which it is actually enforced by police *Saumur* v. *Quebec* [1953] 2 SCR 299.

[142]   *e.g. Reference re Anti-Inflation Act* [1976] 2 SCR 373.

[143]   The phrase was first used by Lord Watson in *Union Colliery Co.* v. *Bryden* [1899] AC 580. For a recent application, see *Ontario Home Builders' Association* v. *York Region Board of Education* [1996] 2 SCR 929. See, in general, Hogg, *op. cit.* pp. 377–388.

[144]   *Multiple Access* v. *McCutcheon* [1982] 2 SCR 161.

[145]   *General Motors* v. *City National Leasing* [1989] 1 SCR 641.

[146]   Hogg, *op. cit.* pp. 407.

[147]   *Ibid.* Chap. 16.

In Australia, the Constitution itself expressly provides for similar rules. The Commonwealth Parliament may legislate on "[m]atters incidental" to matters over which it is granted power (section 51(xxxix)); there is concurrent state and federal authority over most matters (section 107), and in the event of "inconsistency" state laws are "invalid" (although operational conflict is not required; rather it is sufficient if the Commonwealth statute "covers the field" for state authority to be ousted[148]).

The Canadian pith and substance rule can be, and has been, applied in the context of devolution. The South Africa Act 1909 and the GIA did not contain express provisions dealing with incidental effect, but the courts applied the pith and substance doctrine as a matter of judicial construction.[149] The relevance of the doctrine to the SA, however, is complicated by provisions that seem to address the question of incidental effect, but do so in a novel way. Aside from the special provisions concerning Scots criminal and private law, the main provision is found in Schedule 4, Part I, paragraph 3. This provision contains what may be called an *incidental modification* rule. Paragraph 3 states that paragraph 2, which provides that the Scottish Parliament cannot modify rules of law (enacted or otherwise) on reserved matters, does not apply to "modifications" which are (a) "incidental to, or consequential on" a provision which does not relate to a reserved matter, and (b) "do not have a greater effect on reserved matters than is necessary to give effect to the purpose of the provisions". Thus, the Schedule 4 rule purports to address not incidental *effect* on *subject matters* but incidental *modification* of *rules of law*, subject to a rather strict form of proportionality requirement. It could be interpreted in two different ways.

First, it could be seen simply as a combined "pith and substance" and "Scottish paramountcy" rule: Scottish Acts predominantly concerned with non-reserved matters may incidentally affect reserved subject matter, and when these incidental provisions conflict with rules of law in the reserved sphere they prevail and serve to modify those rules of law so far as they would otherwise apply for Scotland. If this interpretation is accepted then Schedule 4's incidental modification rule, together with section 29(3)'s purpose and effect principle, may be said to render the classification analysis under the SA very similar to the classification analysis under the Constitution Act 1867. Thus, Canadian cases on pith and substance may be helpful in so far as they illustrate, in general terms, the sorts of factors courts consider when distinguishing between the primary and incidental aspects of a statute. It must be acknowledged, however, that no value-neutral criteria exist to govern this distinction, and judicial classification of legislation is ultimately informed by some normative conception of the constitution as a whole.[150] Obviously, the Canadian cases will not provide answers as

---

[148] *e.g. Ex parte McLean*(1930) 43 CLR 472 at 483.

[149] *Middelburg Municipality v. Gertzen* [1914] AD 544; *Marshall's Township Syndicate Ltd* v. *Johannesburg Consolidated Investment Co. Ltd* [1920] AC 420 at 421 (*per* counsel); *Gallagher v. Lynn* [1937] AC 863.

[150] Lederman, *op. cit.*

to which normative conception of the United Kingdom constitution judges should adopt.

There is, however, another possible reading of Schedule 4's incidental modification rule. Because it addresses the modification of *rules of law*, it may be interpreted as inapplicable to incidental effects that do not modify rules of law. In Canada, provincial legislatures may incidentally affect federal subject matter but, due to me federal paramountcy rule, they may not thereby modify federal legislation on federal subject matter. Thus, it seems to be acknowledged that laws may incidentally affect a subject matter without modifying rules of law (or at least rules of statute law) on that subject matter. Could it be argued that, in certain circumstances, a Scottish Act on a non-reserved matter may touch upon, in an incidental manner, a reserved subject matter even though it does not expressly purport to modify the law on that reserved matter and even though it is not inconsistent with any identifiable rule of law (enacted or otherwise) on that reserved matter? It might be said that such an Act is jurisprudentially impossible: an Act could not affect a subject matter without modifying *some* rule of law (enacted or otherwise) on that subject matter, (thus, in the Canadian example above the provincial law could be seen as altering the state of the common law on the federal subject matter). However, if "rule of law" in Schedule 4 means some existing, identifiable rule of law as opposed to an implicit, as yet unarticulated, common law rule, then a Scottish Act could exist that affects a reserved subject matter without modifying a rule of law on that subject matter, and it would not be saved by the Schedule 4 incidental modification rule since it does not modify any rule of law. It might then be said that such a Scottish Act would be invalid because it "relates to" a reserved matter. This would, of course, be an anomalous conclusion: it would mean that the Scottish Parliament has a power to modify rules of law on reserved matters incidentally, but has no power to enact laws that simply touch on reserved matters incidentally without actually modifying an identifiable rule of law on the reserved matter.

There are two solutions to this anomaly. One would be simply to accept that there is no jurisprudential distinction between a law incidentally affecting a subject matter and a law incidentally modifying a rule of law on a subject matter: any and all incidental effects of a Scottish Act on reserved matters fall within the scope of, and are only valid if they meet the requirements of, Schedule 4's incidental modification rule. The second solution is to accept that the distinction between affecting incidentally reserved matters and modifying incidentally rules of law on reserved matters is possible, but to conclude that Scottish Acts that do the former are not invalid, even though outside the scope of the incidental modification rule, for the following reason. Although such Acts would not be saved by the incidental modification rule, they would still have to "relate to" a reserved matter in order to be found ultra vires. Judges have, in the past, consistently held that phrases like "relate to" catch only those Acts that relate *in pith and substance* to prohibited subject matters.

It is important to distinguish between these two different solutions because they may lead to very different results. If the second approach is taken, then Scottish Acts that incidentally affect a reserved matter without seeking to modify rules of law on that matter can only take effect subject to the law on that reserved matter. Such Acts would be in a position not unlike provincial statutes in Canada that incidentally affect federal matters, and, as in Canada, the courts would have to develop a rule about paramountcy. For example, they could take the Canadian approach and enforce the Scottish Act unless there was *operational* conflict with an existing rule of law; or they could adopt the Australian approach and enforce the Scottish Act only where there is no set of laws *covering the field*. The second major difference between the two solutions relates to the proportionality requirement. If the second solution is adopted, then, because Schedule 4's incidental modification rule does not apply, the strict proportionality requirement of that rule does not apply either. It may however be that some form of proportionality test is implicit in the pith and substance rule itself.

CONCLUSION

Devolution is intended to provide some measure of policy choice for Scotland and Wales. This freedom of action will, so it is hoped, help cement the Union, and assuage separatist demands, thereby giving the lie to Tam Dalyell's sentiment that devolution is a motorway to independence with no exit.[151] Whether this proves to be so, only time will tell. Certain matters are however clear and they do not portend well.

In economic terms neither the Assembly, nor the Scottish Parliament, have any significant financial autonomy. This is to notwithstanding the considerable attention devoted to Scotland's power to raise income tax by up to three pence from the base rate. Even if this power is exercised to the full, which is unlikely in political terms, it will still only bring in around £500 million, which is pretty small compared to the £14 billion from central government. The room for independent policy choice is further circumscribed when it is realised that changes in the level of central grant are tied to the Barnett formula which renders any such alteration difficult.

In legal terms, the GWA only assigns limited powers to Wales, and the SA, while giving Scotland general legislative power, then limits this through a broad list of reservations. At the minimum, this means that the Scottish Parliament will have to become accustomed to living with the "judge over its shoulder". Proposed legislation will have to be scrutinised assiduously lest it fall foul of one

---

[151] It is clear from experience elsewhere that devolution does not necessarily lead to independence for the regions or countries to which power has been devolved: R. Hazell and B. O'Leary, "A Rolling Programme of Devolution: Slippery Slope or Safeguard of the Union?", *Constitutional Futures, A History of the Next Ten Years* (R. Hazell ed., Oxford University Press, 1999), Chap. 3.

of the many heads of reserved subject matter. Neil MacCormick[152] opined of the Scotland Act 1978 that its drafting meant that it would be all but impossible for anyone other than a lawyer to give any meaningful guidance on the complex list of powers and reservations, and argued that this offended the principle of intelligibility which is so important in constitutional documents. The same might well be said of the Scotland Act passed twenty years later. The need for constant recourse to lawyers who will, in many instances, indicate that proposed action cannot be taken, is bound to generate frustration and anger in Scotland. These sentiments are likely to be reinforced if the courts take a very strict view of the words "relate to", and even more so if they interpret the list of reserved matters expansively. Many of the questions surrounding the role of the judiciary in determining difficult issues of legislative competence have been addressed before, in slightly different contexts. While it would be a mistake to seek authoritative answers from these other systems on specific points of interpretation under the GWA and SA, consideration of judicial experience elsewhere is useful in understanding the endemic problems which a system of divided legislative competence poses for the courts. The courts are inevitably faced with a grave responsibility: the way in which they interpret the SA may be a significant factor in deciding whether devolution proves to be the reform which cements the union, or whether it is the first step towards its dissolution.

---

[152] "Constitutional Points" in D. Mackay (ed.), *Scotland: The Framework for Change* (1979), pp. 53–54.

11

Convention Rights and Substantive Ultra Vires

DAVID FELDMAN

I. THE MEANINGS OF "ULTRA VIRES" AND THE PURPOSE OF THIS ESSAY

The foundations of judicial review (and I use the plural with care) are contentious. Among those foundations, the theory of ultra vires, and especially the field of substantive ultra vires with which this essay is concerned, tends to attract arcane metaphysical arguments using elaborate and esoteric metaphors. Lawyers talk of being within the "four corners" of a power,[1] of "crossing the threshold" of a power,[2] or of reliance on the will of the legislature to bolster the doctrine of ultra vires as a "fig-leaf".[3] Indeed, it is widely accepted that the doctrine of ultra vires often relies on a fiction, and (as other contributions to this volume demonstrate) the dispute between the protagonists of different positions often turns on questions about the value of maintaining the fiction, whether for day-to-day use or aesthetic effect. If it is correct to say that the difference between neurotics and psychotics is that the former see castles in the air while the latter live in them,[4] one can see much of the debate as a contest between the "neurotic" faction which sees and sometimes admires the elegance of the doctrine of ultra vires but doubts its utility, and the "psychotic" faction which is happy to inhabit it and make daily use of it. This curious disagreement can induce confusion among spectators (and occasionally, one suspects, participants).

This essay deals mainly with substantive ultra vires in the context of Convention rights under the Human Rights Act 1998. The way in which the Act will be implemented is currently, at best, a matter for informed speculation. In combining this uncertainty with the curious nature of the ultra vires debate as a

---

[1] It has never been properly established whether the figure which is envisaged is two- or three-dimensional, and it probably does not matter.

[2] This phrase clearly implies a three-dimensional image, although the significance of this is obscure.

[3] Sir John Laws, "Law and democracy" [1995] *PL* 72–93 at 79. The fig-leaf was presumably plucked by, rather than from, the "least dangerous branch": see Alexander Bickel, *The Least Dangerous Branch* (New York, Bobbs-Merrill, 1962), and *cp.* Lord Steyn, "The least dangerous department of government" [1997] *PL* 84–95.

[4] I am grateful to Jill Feldman for this succinct explanation.

whole, one risks either losing or alienating readers when one has barely begun. The foundations of judicial review and the nature of and justifications for the theory of substantive ultra vires have been analysed and debated by other contributors to this volume so extensively and learnedly that nothing I could say would add usefully to their work.[5] It is, however, important to know what any author means when he or she uses the terms "ultra vires" and "substantive ultra vires". I hope, therefore, to be forgiven for starting with a bald statement of my position, for which I will offer little argument (not wishing to retrace paths already mapped admirably by others). This may help to clarify the assumptions which lie behind my paper, although I recognise that none of them is uncontroversial, and that the likelihood of upsetting readers will probably increase in direct proportion to any clarification which may be achieved. Readers who prefer to skip this preliminary matter can proceed directly to Section II, probably without missing anything of much value.

The term "ultra vires" is commonly used in at least three different senses which are liable to be confused with each other unless care is taken. First, it can be used as a single, self-sufficient meta-normative principle which provides legitimacy for judicial review of administrative, executive and sometimes legislative action. Secondly, ultra vires can be seen as one facet of one part of the rule of law, namely the principle of legality, providing only one aspect of a complex web of justifications for judicial review which operate complementarily but independently at a meta-normative level. Thirdly, it can be used as an umbrella term to describe the principles which courts apply at a normative level when conducting judicial review, or (more narrowly) to refer only to that group of normative principles which Lord Diplock, in *Council of Civil Service Unions* v. *Minister for the Civil Service*,[6] named "illegality", as distinct from other grounds which he grouped under the titles of "procedural impropriety" and "irrationality".

In its first sense, meta-normative principle legitimating judicial review is thought by ultra vires theorists to be needed because, unlike Parliament, the judiciary has no source of legitimacy in an expression of popular will through the ballot box, unless it can be said that it is directly or indirectly upholding the will of the democratically accountable Parliament (or, more accurately, House of Commons). In this manifestation, the doctrine of ultra vires is usually taken to rest on a claim that the courts enforce the express or implied will of Parliament in respect of powers granted to subordinate decision-makers.[7] Judicial

---

[5] As well as the papers written for this volume, see particularly Dawn Oliver, "Is the ultra vires rule the basis of judicial review?" [1987] *PL* 543–569 pp. 3–27 above; Sir John Laws, "Law and democracy", above n. 3, and "Illegality: the problem of jurisdiction", in Michael Supperstone and James Goudie, *Judicial Review* (London: Butterworths, 2nd edn. 1997), ch. 4 pp. 73–81 above; Christopher Forsyth, "Of Fig Leaves and Fairy Tales: The Ultra Vires Doctrine, the Sovereignty of Parliament and Judicial Review" [1996] *CLJ* 122–140 pp. 29–46 above; Paul Craig, "Ultra Vires and the Foundations of Judicial Review" [1998] *CLJ* 63–90 pp. 47–71 above; Lord Woolf, "Droit Public – English Style" [1995] *PL* 57–71 at 66.

[6] [1985] AC 374, HL, at 410–11.

[7] See the articles by Christopher Forsyth and Paul Craig cited in n. 5, above.

intervention in the activities of a public body are held to be justified or legitimated by the need to ensure that the ultimate legislative supremacy of Parliament is respected. While it does not follow logically that any particular example of judicial review is justified on that ground, advocates of meta-normative ultra vires doctrine argue that the basis for the legitimacy of the institution of judicial review would be weakened, perhaps fatally, unless it is assumed that Parliament approves what the courts are doing, and that this approval can be presumed from the failure of Parliament to stop courts doing it.

In the simple case of powers conferred or limitations imposed on a body established by statute to perform specified public functions, one can see why this approach might be taken. Where delegated legislation is made in circumstances which fall outside the power delegated by Parliament, it is clearly ultra vires in this simple sense. Parliament has not authorised the exercise of legislative power in that way. In a trivial sense, the judiciary shares the role of setting the limits of legality, as the language of Parliament takes effect through the medium of interpretation by judges, but at least the judges' claim to be giving effect to the will of Parliament is not wholly fictitious.

In more complex cases, however, the link between the sovereignty of Parliament and ultra vires as a justification for or ground of judicial review with it is more tenuous. Where a statute grants special powers or imposes duties on a body which already exists for other purposes, both the powers of and the limitations on the body may be derived from a variety of juridical sources, some of which can be portrayed as an expression of the will of the legislature more convincingly than others. For example, where it is alleged that a public official is acting ultra vires because he or she is giving advice which conflicts with the general law (perhaps by encouraging people to commit a crime), the will of Parliament may have been expressed in circumstances which took no account of the position of the official or the nature of the advice in question.[8] In such a case, the notion that the limits of legality have been set by Parliament is only a partial truth, as the will of Parliament in the circumstances of the case is entirely a judicial construct.

Sometimes the limits of legality are overtly shaped by the common law rather than Parliament. The principles of natural justice were judicial creations. Review of administrative action for unreasonableness is based on a judicial assessment of the proper purposes or scope of a statutory power or duty in respect of considerations not usually expressed in the statute. Both of these grounds of review go to the *vires* of a decision-maker, and make the decision "void" or "unlawful" or "a nullity" (for at least some purposes), as Lord Reid and others recognised in the great trio of cases[9] which began the re-conceptualisation of administrative law in the 1960s. *A fortiori* any set of fundamental common-law rights, operating as a

---

[8] See e.g. *Gillick* v. *West Norfolk and Wisbech Area Health Authority* [1986] AC 112, HL.

[9] *Ridge* v. *Baldwin* [1964] AC 40, HL, at 80 *per* Lord Reid; *Padfield* v. *Minister for Agriculture, Fisheries and Food* [1968] AC 997, HL, at 1058 *per* Lord Upjohn; *Anisminic Ltd.* v. *Foreign Compensation Commission* [1969] 2 AC 147, HL, at 171 *per* Lord Reid.

constraint on the executive or even Parliament, and generating presumptions for use in statutory interpretation, would be virtually impossible to justify by reference to a meta-normative theory founded on the intention of Parliament.[10] The attempt by Lord Diplock in *Council of Civil Service Unions* v. *Minister for the Civil Service*[11] to limit the intrusiveness of judicial review into the work of the executive and administration by dividing the grounds of review into three (illegality, procedural impropriety and irrationality), concealing the fact that all these heads relate to forms of illegality, ultimately failed to undermine the essentially inclusive and multi-faceted nature of the doctrine of ultra vires.

The use of ultra vires as a meta-normative principle uniquely capable of legitimating judicial review, and the theoretical assumptions which accompany it, seem to me to be flawed. They are based on an unsound presupposition, namely that the exercise of public power must always be justified by reference to a democratic mandate or democratic accountability. If that were so, a very large part, if not most, of the exercise of public power in the United Kingdom would be illegitimate. Perhaps it is, but I prefer to think that there are other factors which, under appropriate conditions, may justify the use of public power without direct or indirect electoral approval. The factors which suffice will depend on the functions of the person or body exercising the power, the purpose for which it is being exercised, and (where the power is one of judicial review) the nature of the activity being reviewed.

Let us turn to the second sense in which the term "ultra vires" may be used: to describe a strand in the principle of legality, one of the elements of the rule of law. The principle of legality requires that public power should be exercised in ways which are demonstrably compatible with positive law and fundamental, constitutional principles. It is the least common of the three usages of the term "ultra vires", but it is highly significant. Under a constitution which controls public power by reference to democratic law-making procedures, this sense of ultra vires provides an important link between judicial review and democratic legitimacy. A similar task is performed by ultra vires in the first sense, as a meta-normative principle based on parliamentary supremacy. But it is not necessary to be a democrat to believe in the principle of legality, and it is not necessary to be a parliamentary supremacist to believe that it is justifiable for anyone, and particularly for judges, to uphold the principle of legality. Nor is the principle of legality the whole of the rule of law. There are other justifications for upholding the principle of legality, some of which can be found within the rule of law itself, which are at least as compelling and convincing as democracy as justifications for judicial review.[12] A claim

---

[10] For accounts which recognise that such principles must be based on rule-of-law or fundamental-rights principles rather than the will of Parliament, see T. R. S. Allan, *Law, Liberty, and Justice: The Legal Foundations of British Constitutionalism* (Oxford, Clarendon Press, 1993), and Sir John Laws, *op. cit.*, n. 3 above.

[11] [1985] AC 374, HL, at 410.

[12] Although this is not an original insight, I have pursued it and some of its implications at tedious length several times. See e.g. David Feldman, "Democracy, the Rule of Law and Judicial Review" (1990) 19 *Federal Law Review* 1–30.

that an action or decision is ultra vires may be based on rules derived from any number of sources of law, of which Parliament is only one. The sovereignty of Parliament is a very significant source of limitations on powers, not least because of the democratic legitimacy which it confers on judicial review where it can be invoked. However, judicial review on ultra vires principles can be justified on grounds other than democracy, of which the rule of law is one of the most powerful. Others include the manifold values which support or are derived from a wide variety of fundamental rights and freedoms.

We can now turn to the third sense of ultra vires, encompassing the various principles controlling the grounds on which judicial review is exercised. Within the realms of ultra vires in this sense, substantive ultra vires gives rise to particular uncertainty of meaning. This is in practice often linked to the meta-normative use of the term. When Lord Reid attempted to use the meta-normative conception of ultra vires to justify an extended use of judicial review, he did it partly by treating a violation of any principle of administrative law as making decisions presumptively ultra vires and hence invalid.[13] The move depended for its success on unsupported assertions about the principles which Parliament must have assumed decision-makers would respect. The assertions owed more to meta-normative principles about what Parliament should have intended than to empirical evidence about what it actually contemplated.

Despite being linked in practice, the second sense of ultra vires as a collective term for several principles of judicial review is conceptually distinct from the first sense of ultra vires as a meta-normative principle. A couple of examples make clear both the distinction and the link between them. Lord Diplock's classification of grounds of review into the categories of illegality, procedural impropriety and irrationality[14] operates at the normative level but may give rise to a need for judicial review on different grounds to be justified in different ways. The same is true of Sir Stephen Sedley's development of the idea of the "bi-polar sovereignty of the Crown in Parliament and the Crown in its courts, to each of which the Crown's ministers are answerable – politically to Parliament, legally to the courts".[15] The way the term "ultra vires" is used in its second, normative sense will therefore often depend on the user's view of the proper scope of a particular kind of meta-normative justification. Sometimes the adjective "substantive" is used to distinguish between "procedural" and other grounds of review.[16] At other times "substantive" refers to the type of review which is being conducted, or the type of standard being applied in the review, or as a synonym for review of the merits of a decision as opposed to the forms of, and reasoning processes supporting, the decision. When used in this way, it is

---

[13] See the cases cited in n. 9, above.

[14] *Council for Civil Service Unions* v. *Minister for the Civil Service* [1985] AC 374, HL, at 410.

[15] Sir Stephen Sedley, "Human Rights: a Twenty-First Century Agenda" [1995] *PL* 386–400 at 389. See also *X Ltd.* v. *Morgan-Grampian (Publishers) Ltd.* [1991] 1 AC 1, HL, at 48 *per* Lord Bridge of Harwich.

[16] See e.g., *Director of Public Prosecutions* v. *Bugg* [1993] QB 473, DC, at 494–500 *per* Woolf LJ, overruled on this point in *Boddington* v. *British Transport Police* [1998] 2 WLR 639, HL.

usually as part of a warning against judges being too ready to make a finding of irrationality, because of the difficulty in justifying judges making such judgments when they have been remitted by Parliament to another type of decision-maker.[17]

Review of the merits is a type of review on non-procedural grounds, but there may be non-procedural grounds of review (such as those relating to the reasoning or purposes supporting a decision) which do not necessarily require a reviewing court to evaluate the decision itself. Nevertheless, this type of review may be conducted by reference to standards which are substantive in the sense that they are concerned with the *value* of the decision, action or rule itself, albeit not with its *correctness*. The same may be true of some reviews conducted on procedural grounds.[18]

There is a thread in the literature which treats non-procedural, and particularly merits-based, judicial review as particularly hard to justify because it is assumed to allow judges to impose on decision-makers standards for which there is no democratic authority. This is simplistic. The minimum standards of procedural fairness which courts apply when reviewing decision-making procedures are judge-made, and are amply justified on non-democratic grounds (notably by reference to the value of equality before the law which is part of the doctrine of the rule of law). The criteria which judges use to evaluate processes of reasoning or justifications for decisions, or the legal merits of the decision itself, are sometimes provided in legislation and only interpreted by the judges. Different types of review and grounds for review are appropriate in different settings, and have to be justified in varied ways in diverse circumstances. We should beware of arguments which mask the complexity of the issues. Law seeks to impose system on some of the normative implications of the infinite variety of human interactions. Its success depends on classification of actions and effects in a manner which avoids either pressing life into the strait-jacket of too limited a range of categories or, on the other hand, creating such a chaotic mass of legal categories that they fail to offer a helpful structure for planning action or resolving disputes.

Ultra vires theories face this challenge. It will already have become clear that I consider that those who use ultra vires in its first sense seek to over simplify, which is why their approach would require judges to live in a fictional universe divorced from much important reality. I prefer to use it in its second, meta-normative, sense, and in the narrower of the third, normative, pair of senses. Having explained my starting point, I can now explore both the ways in which the notion of ultra vires (particularly substantive ultra vires in its various senses) as a foundation of review may affect the protection of Convention rights in judi-

---

[17] See e.g., *In re Lonrho Plc* [1990] 2 AC 154, HL; *R. v. Secretary of State for the Home Department, ex parte Hargreaves* [1997] 1 WLR 906, CA.

[18] For discussion, see Denis Galligan, *Due Process and Fair Procedures: A Study of Administrative Procedures* (Oxford, Clarendon Press, 1996).

cial review proceedings (Section II), and the effect which the Convention rights may themselves have on the principles of ultra vires (Section III).

II. THE EFFECT OF ULTRA VIRES THEORIES ON THE PROTECTION OF CONVENTION RIGHTS

This section considers the way in which the theory of ultra vires may influence the way in which the courts are able to protect Convention rights. In this respect, it will be argued, the fundamental change which the Human Rights Act 1998 effects is to turn contravention of a Convention right into a ground of ultra vires in the limited sense of illegality. While such review will inevitably require the courts to base their decisions on substantive values, this is justifiable by reference to the broad, meta-normative principle of ultra vires, because it accords with the express intention of Parliament.

In the past, judicial review has been of limited effect in protecting the human rights and fundamental freedoms guaranteed under international human-rights instruments such as the European Convention for the Protection of Human Rights and Fundamental Freedoms ("the ECHR").[19] There are various reasons for this. Several of them apply equally to all forms of legal procedure. Our common-law tradition has been to approach most issues by fashioning remedies for wrongs. Rights have tended to emerge as correlatives to or logical inferences from duties which have been defined at least as much by reference to what amounts to wrongful conduct in a defendant as by reference to what a plaintiff's rights were. Various interests have always been treated as worthy of special concern, but the rules which have resulted have tended to overlap, rather than coincide with, the categories of rights and freedoms which have been developed so fast in international law in the second half of this century. Statute is a more promising source of declarations of rights than the common law, but in practice statutes rarely grant rights, at least of the fundamental variety. Although there are exceptions (such as the rights of suspects under the Police and Criminal Evidence Act 1984), generally statutes impose duties or confer powers (often interfering with liberty) rather than grant rights. Even the ground-breaking anti-discrimination legislation, arguably the most significant human-rights legislation this century in the United Kingdom until the Human Rights Act 1998, and going in many respects further than the 1998 Act in protecting the right to be free from arbitrary discrimination, used the drafting technique of defining wrongs rather than conferring rights.

Another major obstacle to the effective protection of fundamental rights as such has been the dualist nature of the United Kingdom's constitution, which (at

---

[19] Murray Hunt, *Using Human Rights Law in English Courts* (Oxford, Hart Publishing, 1997) and Rabinder Singh, *The Future of Human Rights in the United Kingdom* (Oxford, Hart Publishing, 1997), chs. 1, 3 and 5, provide good analyses and critiques of the traditional approach of English judges.

any rate according to orthodox theory) has made it impossible to create free-standing causes of action out of rights contained in international treaties.

This brings us to a third obstacle, which relates particularly to judicial review. Because human rights have not generally been part of English law (unlike humanitarian law, parts of which, dealing with genocide, torture and the treatment of refugees, have been incorporated), violating a right under the European Convention on Human Rights or the International Covenant on Civil and Political Rights has not been a jurisdictional error, either of law or of fact. Instead, compliance with human rights has been seen as one of a number of considerations which may be relevant to a decision-maker's consideration of a case but which is not decisive. In a number of cases, parties have argued that failure to take proper account of human rights had made a decision irrational. However, courts have generally been unwilling to hold that failing to consider the relevant international law of human rights makes a decision so unreasonable that no reasonable decision-maker could have made it. Their reluctance is especially marked where the decision-maker is accountable to Parliament, or some other democratic forum, for the reasonableness of the decision. There is a category of cases affecting life and liberty in which judges have said that they will subject the reasoning of decision-makers to particularly anxious scrutiny, and in other cases human rights have been said to form part of the background against which the rationality of decision-making will be assessed. It may be that the commitment to a new standard of "anxious scrutiny" where it is alleged that human rights have been violated has produced a new "super-*Wednesbury*" test for unreasonableness in human-rights cases.[20] However, if such a test exists in practice there are few signs that it has ever caused a court to reach a decision different from that which it would have reached otherwise. When arguments are couched in terms of failure to give due weight to relevant considerations, the response tends to be that there are sufficient countervailing considerations to justify the decision. This has all made it difficult, if not impossible, to treat a decision-maker's failure to consider (*a fortiori* comply with) the State's international human-rights obligations as a reviewable error in judicial review proceedings.[21]

How will the effect of ultra vires doctrine, and particularly substantive ultra vires, change when applied to the Convention rights which become part of English law under the Human Rights Act 1998? The first point to note is that judicial and collateral review of administrative acts and decisions and of subordinate legislation for incompatibility with Convention rights is no longer to be dependent on the grounds of review which relate to irrationality or failure to take account of a relevant consideration. Once it is shown that an act, omission,

---

[20] See e.g., *Bugdaycay* v. *Secretary of State for the Home Department* [1987] AC 514, HL; *R.* v. *Secretary of State for Defence, ex parte Smith* [1996] QB 517, CA.

[21] The *locus classicus* is *R.* v. *Secretary of State for the Home Department, ex parte Brind* [1991] 1 AC 696, HL, although the speeches were actually more liberal than some commentators have allowed.

decision or piece of subordinate legislation done or made by a public authority is incompatible with a Convention right, section 6(1) of the Act provides that it is automatically to be treated as unlawful. This has the effect of turning incompatibility with Convention rights from being a possible ground for holding it to be irrational into a jurisdictional error of law, unless (under section 6(2)) the incompatibility is unavoidable in the light of the demands of primary legislation which cannot itself be interpreted (in accordance with the interpretative obligation imposed on courts and tribunals by section 3) so as to be compatible with the right in question. There might seem superficially to be room for argument about whether incompatibility with a Convention right automatically goes to jurisdiction or falls into that shadowy area in which the unlawfulness of a decision or order may not fatally flaw it. However, section 6(1) is in absolute terms, and is directed to public authorities including courts, making it tolerably clear that it should be interpreted as constituting a limitation on the legal powers of all public authorities (subject to the other provisions of section 6). When one considers also the special status (both politically and, as I have argued elsewhere,[22] legally) of the Human Rights Act 1998, it would be perverse to treat incompatibility with a Convention right as anything other than an automatic ground for holding the decision to be ultra vires.

The fundamental role of the Convention rights in helping to set the boundaries of public authorities' powers is emphasised by Parliament's use of them in circumscribing the legislative powers of the Scottish Parliament and the Welsh and Northern Ireland Assemblies. In the case of the Scottish Parliament and the Welsh Assembly, the constitutive legislation provides that neither body's legislative competence extends to making legislation which is incompatible with a Convention right.[23] In the case of the Northern Ireland Assembly, the Human Rights Act 1998 itself provides that the Assembly's legislation is to be treated as subordinate legislation,[24] so that it will be invalid to the extent of any incompatibility with a Convention right unless the incompatibility is compelled by primary legislation. If the United Kingdom Parliament considered that it was appropriate to limit the powers of those subordinate legislatures (although not its own powers as section 6, subsections (2), (3), and (6) make clear) by requiring compliance with Convention rights, there can be little room for doubting that the correct interpretation of section 6(1) of the Human Rights Act 1998 in relation to other, lesser, public authorities is that their powers are absolutely limited to acting in accordance with Convention rights unless section 6(2) applies.

Saying that the powers of public authorities are absolutely limited by the scope of Convention rights naturally leaves open the possibility that a court, having held that an act or decision of a public authority is incompatible with a

---

[22] David Feldman, "The Human Rights Act 1998 and Constitutional Principles" (1999) 19 *Legal Studies* 165–206 at 178ff.

[23] Scotland Act 1998, s. 29(2); Government of Wales Act 1998, s. 107.

[24] Human Rights Act 1998, s. 21(1), definition of "subordinate legislation".

Convention right, might in its discretion refuse a remedy, or at any rate refuse to quash or declare the absolute invalidity of the act or decision. We are familiar with the spectre of the decision which, although invalid, has some legal effect in the sense that people may be allowed to rely on it until such time as it is quashed or authoritatively declared to be ultra vires. Some judicial voices, strongly committed to coherency and principle in public law, have been raised against this possibility,[25] but at present it cannot be safely said that an ultra vires decision or rule has no legal effect for any purpose.[26] However, in view of the fundamental quality of the rights and freedoms protected by the Convention rights, it would be a brave judge who would hold that someone's Convention right had been violated but then refuse to grant an effective remedy, particularly as the Lord Chancellor said in the course of debate on the Human Rights Bill in the House of Lords that it was unnecessary to include Article 13 among the Convention rights because the remedial scheme within the Bill was adequate to provide an effective remedy for any violation.

It should nevertheless be noted that there is an exception to this, because of the strange way in which "primary legislation" is defined to include certain legislation made by a body other than Parliament. Because (for instance) an Order in Council made under the Royal Prerogative is primary legislation under the terms of the Human Rights Act 1998, it may be ultra vires by reason of an incompatibility with a Convention right, but cannot be quashed or declared to be invalid, or subjected to collateral review, on that ground. It can only be subjected to a declaration of incompatibility under section 4. The makers of such legislation are under a duty to comply with Convention rights, but that rule is one of incomplete obligation. Of course, the Order in Council may be quashed or declared to be invalid in the usual way on other grounds for judicial review, but not for incompatibility with a Convention right. This is an anomalous result, but it seems to follow unavoidably from the way in which the Act has been drafted.

If all this is correct, the effect of applying orthodox notions of ultra vires to most acts, rules and decisions which violate Convention rights is to produce two new ways in which any public authority may be held to have acted unlawfully and (at least presumptively) to have made a decision or rule which is of no legal

---

[25] See e.g. *Boddington* v. *British Transport Police* [1998] 2 WLR 639, HL, at 646–7 *per* Lord Irvine of Lairg LC. On the effect on the availability of damages for false imprisonment, see *R.* v. *Governor of Brockhill Prison, ex parte Evans (No. 2)* [1999] 2 WLR 103, CA (a governor's decision about a prisoner's release date which was technically ultra vires and led to the applicant's detention for a longer period than was proper), and *Roberts* v. *Chief Constable of the Cheshire Constabulary* [1999] 1 WLR 662, CA (a review officer's failure to conduct a review of detention at the appropriate time under the Police and Criminal Evidence Act 1984).

[26] See e.g., *Olotu* v. *Home Office* [1997] 1 WLR 328, CA; *Percy* v. *Hall* [1997] 3 WLR 924, CA; *Boddington* v. *British Transport Police* [1998] 2 WLR 639, HL, at 655 *per* Lord Browne-Wilkinson, 656 *per* Lord Slynn of Hadley, and 662 *per* Lord Steyn; and Christopher Forsyth, " 'The Metaphysics of Nullity' – Invalidity, Conceptual Reasoning and the Rule of Law", in Christopher Forsyth and Ivan Hare (eds), *The Golden Metwand and the Crooked Cord: Essays on Public Law in Honour of Sir William Wade Q.C.* (Oxford, Clarendon Press, 1998), 141–60.

effect. *First*, rules or decisions may on their face be incapable of being interpreted in a way which does not purport to authorise a violation of a Convention right. Such rules and decisions are ultra vires. There is, however, an interpretative obligation under section 3 of the 1998 Act which will limit the impact of this. Where a rule takes the form of subordinate legislation within the meaning of the Act, a court or tribunal will be required by section 3 to interpret it so far as possible to make it compatible with Convention rights. If this obligation stimulates judges to interpret the legislation as they do when required to avoid an incompatibility with EC law, apparent incompatibilities should rarely survive interpretation, and subordinate legislation will therefore rarely be invalid for incompatibility with Convention rights. For example, a rule might impose a duty or confers a power on a public authority which is generally compatible with a Convention right but, in particular circumstances, could violate one. Such a rule would fairly easily be read down so that the duty or power was construed as not authorising or requiring acts or decisions which, on the facts of a particular case, would violate a Convention right. On the other hand, where one is dealing with a decision of generalised effect, or a rule which is contained in quasi-legislation issued by a public authority, the interpretative obligation under section 3 of the Act does not apply, and the decision or rule will more often have to be quashed for incompatibility with a Convention right. Of course, the courts might choose to treat other types of rules and decisions by analogy as if section 3 applied to them. Applying statutory rules by analogy to circumstances not covered by the legislation is an unusual and generally unsafe way of proceeding, because it often has the effect of extending the impact of legislation which interferes with people's rights to situations in which there is no legislative authority for interfering with them. But in relation to the obligation on courts and tribunals under section 3 of the Human Rights Act 1998 to interpret legislation so far as possible to be compatible with Convention rights, the effect would *prima facie* be to extend protection for, rather than interference with, rights (although there might be circumstances in which extending the protection of Convention rights would interfere with someone else's previously vested legal right by way of an indirect horizontal effect). This might make the extended use of a power of robust interpretation less objectionable than usual.

Secondly, a general rule which is not facially incompatible with a Convention right, or which is facially incompatible but is contained in primary legislation which cannot be quashed or read down to secure compatibility, might confer discretion on a public authority or official which can be exercised in ways which, under certain conditions, would violate such a right. Such an exercise of discretion or power would be ultra vires by virtue of section 6(1) of the Act. Even primary legislation cannot authorise the use of discretion (as opposed to the performance of a duty) in ways which violate Convention rights, unless the discretion is so drawn that any conceivable exercise of it would necessarily violate a Convention right. If a way of exercising discretion compatibly with Convention rights can be found, any other exercise of it will be unlawful by reason of section 6(1). Were this not so, section 3(2)(c) and section 6(2) of the Act, saving incompatible subordinate legislation and actions of public authorities where the incompatibility is required by the terms of primary legislation, would be otiose. Subordinate legislation conferring powers is *a fortiori* incapable of authorising the use of those powers in a manner incompatible with a Convention right.

To what extent does all this give rise to a new form of substantive, as opposed to procedural or formal, ultra vires? This depends on the sense in which "substantive" is being used. Review for incompatibility with a Convention right is usually concerned with either the substantive *values* affected by a rule, act or decision, or the *normative quality* of the decision itself by reference to the right, rather than the *procedure* by which it was reached. But this will not always be the case. Some Convention rights relate to values which are procedural, such as those which are explicitly protected by Article 6 (fair trial) and to some extent Articles 5 (process rights for those suspected of crimes) and 7 (non-retroactiveness of criminal legislation). A judicial decision that a rule or act interferes with the right to a fair trial (for example) involves assessing the lawfulness of the trial (and sometimes the pre-trial) process by reference to criteria of quality which encapsulate process values rather than values which are concerned with the quality of the outcome.

Even where a Convention right appears to protect substantive values, such as respect for private life, process values may have a place. For example, the right to respect for private and family life under Article 8 does not preclude State interference in the family, but constrains the manner in which the interference may be conducted and justified. There are decisions of the European Court of Human Rights under Article 8 of the ECHR which hold that the right to respect for private life imposes obligations in relation to the procedures to be followed if an interference with private life is to be justifiable as being in accordance with the law and necessary in a democratic society (importing a requirement of proportionality) for one of the purposes particularised in Article 8(2).[27] Similar procedural or organisational requirements have been imposed in relation to justifications for killing by security forces under Article 2.[28] The same approach is likely to be taken in respect of some other articles. If the English courts follow the Strasbourg line, review for compatibility of decisions, actions or rules with at least some Convention rights may thus involve assessing not only the substantive quality of the impugned decision, act or rule, but also the quality of the

---

[27] See e.g. *O, H, W, B and R* v. *United Kingdom*, Eur Ct HR, Series A, Nos. 120 and 121, Judgments of 8 July 1987, holding that it violated Article 8 to make child-care decisions without hearing the parents and taking their rights and interests into account.

[28] See *McCann* v. *United Kingdom*, Series A, No. 324, Judgment of 27 September 1995: where death is caused by State forces preventing crime, relevant organisational and institutional matters for the Court when assessing whether the force was absolutely necessary for the purposes of Article 2 include the way in which officers have been trained and how evidence of necessity for lethal force is assessed in the chain of command before a decision to use force is taken. The same principles apply where the victim was an innocent hostage: *Andronicou and Constantinou* v. *Cyprus* (1997) 26 EHRR 491.

procedure adopted when deciding to act or to make the rule or decision. The quality of procedures may be relevant either when deciding whether a procedural right (for example, under Article 6) is implicated at all, or when deciding whether a public authority can justify an infringement of a right under any of the articles (for instance, when considering whether the infringement was in accordance with the law and necessary in a democratic society for one of the permitted purposes). Substantive and procedural evaluation are thus intimately connected, to the point where it will often be difficult to separate them for practical purposes.

Review for substantive ultra vires in this sense is not novel, although the immediate source of the unlawfulness, violation of a Convention right, is new. It has always been the case that holding an act, rule or decision to be outside the four corners of the legal powers of a public authority has necessitated reference to standards which enable the legal quality of the authority's behaviour to be substantively rather than procedurally evaluated, unless the impugned action has breached a mandatory procedural precondition to the exercise of a power or performance of a duty. For present purposes, I take the legitimacy of such review on the ground of substantive ultra vires (in the sense of a non-procedural reason for holding an authority to have exceeded its power or acted without power) to be relatively uncontroversial. If that is correct, conducting such review on the ground of incompatibility with a Convention right will be no more difficult to justify (to put it at the lowest) than review for non-compliance with other statutory requirements.

Another sense of "substantive" refers to review of the merits of a decision rather than review of more formal features, such as the methods of reasoning leading to it, the terms in which it is justified, and the procedures leading up to it. There will certainly be circumstances in which acts, rules or decisions will be challenged on the ground that they produce an outcome which is said to be substantively wrong, in that it fails adequately to respect a party's Convention right. In the past, where a statute (as interpreted by the courts) has required public authorities to seek to achieve some defined objective, planning for some incompatible objective instead has been ultra vires, either as a plan pursuing an improper purpose or as action exceeding the four corners of the authority's powers.[29] These purposive limits on powers have been specific to a particular public authority or field of activity.[30] Review on deontological grounds has previously been confined to forming aspects of review for *Wednesbury* unreasonableness. When courts have asked about the intrinsic goodness or badness of a decision, act or rule only when asking whether the decision, etc., was so unreasonable that no reasonable body could have made it, deontological considerations were among a number of factors relevant to the overall reasonableness or

---

[29] See e.g. *R*. v. *Greater London Council, ex parte Bromley London Borough Council* [1983] 1 AC 768, HL.

[30] Even delimitations of powers by reference to generally expressed purposes, such as those in Local Government Act 1972, s. 111, have been restricted to particular types of public authority.

unreasonableness of the decision. Now, for the first time, the 1998 Act has introduced generalised rather than specific limitations on the powers of all public authorities, and the limitations are defined principally deontologically (by reference to the values enshrined in Convention rights) rather than teleologically or purposively.[31] This is one of the distinctive features of the Act, and it will have a significant impact on judicial review: the vires of all public authorities will now be systematically structured for most purposes by reference to criteria which will require courts and tribunals to make sensitive moral, social and political judgments about the substantive goodness of the outcome of official decisions, actions and rules. Deontological standards, while still relevant to questions of unreasonableness, have also been imported into the area of strict ultra vires in the sense in which Lord Diplock, in *Council for Civil Service Unions* v. *Minister for the Civil Service*,[32] used the word "illegality".

Using human-rights standards in this way has been resisted by the common law for many years on the ground that it would amount to unconstitutionally incorporating international human-rights instruments by the back door, a task which can properly be achieved only on the authority of an Act of Parliament. Nothing in the Human Rights Act 1998 undermines that constitutional orthodoxy. Parliament has spoken. Novel as it is for Parliament to require judges to use deontological standards to set limits to the powers of public authorities, there can be no constitutional objection to judges doing so when both the requirement and the standards are contained in an Act of Parliament.

Some people might dispute the claim that there is nothing illegitimate in using substantive human-rights standards to review the powers of public authorities, including makers of subordinate legislation. Normally, they might argue, the limits on the substantive powers of a public authority are contained (expressly or by implication) in the legislation which confers the power. In interpreting statutes, we are used to reading the statute as a whole, but we are not usually required to look outside it in order to interpret the scope of the powers conferred by it. Yet using Convention rights under the Human Rights Act 1998 to limit specific statutory powers contained in another Act involves interpreting the will of Parliament in passing the latter Act as if it were of a piece with the will of Parliament in enacting the 1998 Act. This, it might be said, is illegitimate, particularly where the other Act was passed before the 1998 Act.

That would be a persuasive argument, were it not for countervailing considerations which seem conclusively to outweigh it. In relation to Bills introduced to Parliament by a minister since section 19 of the 1998 Act came into force, the responsible minister is required to make a statement as to his or her view of the compatibility of the provisions of the Bill with Convention rights. This gives both the minister and Parliament the opportunity to consider whether in effect to exclude reference to Convention rights in English courts by stating that the

---

[31] By contrast, most of the permitted justifications for interfering with rights are teleological. See e.g., Articles 8(2), 9(2), 10(2) and 11(2).

[32] [1985] AC 374, HL, at 410.

Bill is not compatible with the Convention rights, and to draft the Bill in such a way that it cannot conceivably be read down so as to comply with the rights in the course of interpretation. For example, a combination of clear and unambiguous language coupled with the phrase, "Notwithstanding any requirements of Convention rights under Schedule 1 to the Human Rights Act 1998 to the contrary", or, in the interpretation section, "Section 3 of the Human Rights Act 1998 shall not apply to this Act". Where this course is not taken, it will be reasonable for the courts to assume that it was the will of Parliament both to comply with the Convention rights and to have the rule of interpretation in section 3 of the 1998 Act applied to the later legislation.

Even in relation to Acts passed before the Human Rights Act 1998, it is no more exceptional to look to the 1998 Act to help to interpret the scope of the earlier Act than it would be to apply the presumptions contained in the Interpretation Act 1978 to an Act passed before 1978. It is worth remembering in this context that the courts have long assumed, as a matter of interpretation, that Parliament does not intend to legislate in a manner inconsistent with the United Kingdom's international obligations, particularly human-rights obligations (an assumption which continues to operate in respect of human-rights instruments other than the provisions incorporated in the Human Rights Act 1998). Indeed, there is more reason to apply the 1998 Act to earlier legislation than to apply the Interpretation Act 1978 retrospectively. First, the interpretative obligation imposed by the 1998 Act expressly applies to prior as well as subsequent legislation, as section 3(2)(a) makes clear. Secondly, the 1998 Act goes beyond providing an interpretative obligation. It also provides, by the clearest possible implication from section 3(2)(a) and (c) and section 6(1) read together, that subordinate legislation whenever made is invalid to the extent of any incompatibility with a Convention right.

In the light of this, it is clear that the 1998 Act is intended to be read as imposing a general limitation on the powers of all public authorities under all previous legislation, except for primary legislation which cannot be interpreted in a manner compatible with the Convention rights. Orthodox notions of parliamentary sovereignty make such a move entirely unexceptionable. One Parliament is normally free to revisit the enactments of its predecessors, imposing additional limits on powers, amending legislation in other ways, or repealing it. Paradoxically, this could mean that there is a stronger, or at least less contentious, constitutional justification for using the doctrine of ultra vires to enforce Convention rights against authorities exercising powers under earlier legislation than under subsequent legislation. However, for the reasons given in the paragraph before last, the justification for applying it to powers under subsequent legislation which purports to be compatible with the Convention is coherent and outweighs countervailing arguments.

One standard which, it has been suggested in the past, is becoming or could become a new substantive ground for judicial review is proportionality. It may be that proportionality (or lack of it) is becoming a ground for reviewing decisions in English administrative law independently of the Human Rights Act 1998. However, the status of proportionality as a ground of judicial review seems unlikely to be directly affected by the Human Rights Act 1998. Professor Jeffrey Jowell and Lord Lester of Herne Hill QC have argued persuasively[33] for the use of proportionality as a substantive ground of ultra vires, although this gives rise to disagreement as to the nature of proportionality and its relationship with strong *Wednesbury* unreasonableness. However, in connection with review for violation of Convention rights, proportionality will probably not function as a ground of review at all. Instead, it will have a subordinate role, and will have even that role only if the case-law of the Strasbourg organs on the subject is followed. In that case-law, proportionality comes into play only after an applicant has established an infringement of a right, and the State seeks to justify the infringement. In relation to most rights infringement of which can be justified, the State must show that the infringement was in accordance with or prescribed by law (terms which import broad rule-of-law values going beyond merely finding a legal authority for the infringement in positive national law), and that it was necessary (incorporating the idea of a pressing social need for State action) in a democratic society for one of a number of specified purposes. Only if the State shows that the infringement was in accordance with the law and was directed to a legitimate purpose does the reviewing body have to consider whether the infringement in its nature and extent was proportionate to the pressing social need. If it was disproportionate, it will not be regarded as having been necessary in a democratic society, so the infringement will be unjustified and a violation will be found.

In other words, proportionality under the case-law of the Strasbourg organs, so far from being a substantive ground for review of State action, is a criterion for assessing the acceptability of a justification advanced by the State for an established infringement of a right. The applicant challenging a decision or act of a public authority will not have to establish that it was disproportionate. Instead, the public authority will carry the burden of proving proportionality with appropriate evidence.[34] Furthermore, the margin of appreciation which is allowed by the Strasbourg organs to States when assessing the acceptability of justifications for infringements in international law is entirely inappropriate for use in the setting of a national court reviewing the legality of action by one of the public authorities of the same State (although this is not to say that other acceptable doctrinal grounds for limiting judicial review of the proportionality of otherwise legitimate interferences with rights may not be found in national

[33] Jeffrey Jowell and Anthony Lester QC, "After *Wednesbury*: Substantive Principles of Judicial Review" [1987] *PL* 368–82; Jeffrey Jowell and Anthony Lester QC, "Proportionality: neither Novel nor Dangerous", in Jeffrey Jowell and Dawn Oliver (eds), *New Directions in Judicial Review* (London, Stevens & Sons, 1988), 51–73. However, the position is not uncontroversial. See the essays in Evelyn Ellis (ed.), *The Principle of Proportionality in the Laws of Europe* (Oxford, Hart Publishing, 1999), particularly those by Professor Craig at 85–106 and Lord Hoffmann at 107–15.

[34] See David Feldman, "Proportionality and the Human Rights Act 1998", in Ellis (ed.), *op. cit.*, n. 33 above at 117–44.

law, as David Pannick QC has argued).[35] Because the function of proportionality in arguments based on Convention rights is entirely different from its potential function as a ground of substantive ultra vires, it is not relevant to the subject of this paper (although it is perfectly possible that growing familiarity with the concept of proportionality in the context of Convention rights will encourage the judges to experiment with the concept in the very different context of an independent head of review).

In the light of the discussion in this section, it is both inevitable and justifiable under orthodox constitutional principles that the 1998 Act will lead to review for substantive ultra vires through non-compliance with a Convention right. The Act extends the scope of review for substantive ultra vires, but that is compatible with and follows directly from even the most traditional form of ultra vires theory justifying review by reference to Parliament's intention.

III. THE EFFECT OF CONVENTION RIGHTS ON THE THEORY OF ULTRA VIRES

The previous section examined the effects of applying ultra vires theory in two of its forms to the review of public authorities for violation of Convention rights under the 1998 Act. In this section, we turn to the way in which that process may affect our understanding of ultra vires principles. Professor Paul Craig has drawn attention to the importance of the link between theories of judicial review and underlying constitutional theories.[36] The link is as significant in the context of judicial review under the Human Rights Act 1998 as it is elsewhere. What is more, the 1998 Act is part of an ambitious attempt at a major constitutional resettlement, particularly as it sits alongside the devolution legislation for Scotland, Wales and Northern Ireland. This can be seen as re-juridifying the constitution. The years of Conservative government between 1979 and 1997 witnessed a process of de-juridification and de-politicisation, as both legal and political theory were subordinated to economic theory in constitutional matters. The famously flexible nature of the national constitution before that period[37] made it possible to bend it to the ends of policies driven by economics. Monetarism, a modified public choice theory and a rhetorical commitment to the free market, led to a process in which democratic accountability and responsible government were progressively replaced by privatisation, internal

---

[35] David Pannick, "Principles of Interpretation of Convention Rights under the Human Rights Act 1998 and the Discretionary Area of Judgment" [1998] *PL* 545–551. See also Feldman, *op. cit.*, n. 34 above, at 124–7.

[36] P. P. Craig, *Democracy and Public Law in the United Kingdom and the United States of America* (Oxford, Clarendon Press, 1991), especially ch. 1.

[37] It is because of this flexibility that Professor Martin Loughlin suggested during discussion at the conference on which this volume is based that the raft of 1998 legislation should be regarded as having juridified, rather than re-juridified, the constitution. For present purposes, the divergence of expression is not significant, although it reflects radically different attitudes to twentieth-century politico-constitutional history.

markets and agencies whose standards of performance were set by codes of practice, regulators or charters rather than by democratically accountable officers. Alongside this weakening of the democratic infrastructure went a decline of concern in government for the traditional constraints of the rule of law. Whatever the other effects of the tranche of constitutional legislation passed in 1998 may have, it undoubtedly embodies and requires us to take seriously an attempt to inject major elements of democracy (at least at regional level) and legality into the constitution. Judicial review under the Human Rights Act 1998 will make an important contribution to realising this programme. In doing so the foundations of ultra vires may well develop in interesting ways, because the theory of judicial review should be affected by the changing weights of different principles (particularly democracy, liberty and economic freedom) in the constitution which underpins it. This section draws attention to six such possible effects, in a spirit of tentative prediction on the basis of informed speculation (although some of these are less speculative than others). Time may show that the real impact is entirely different and would have been completely unpredictable (or simply that I have got it wrong).

First, it follows from the argument in the previous section that the substantive right-based values[38] which are protected by the Convention rights contained in Schedule 1 to the 1998 Act will become part of the grounds of jurisdictional error of law. It is likely that these values will be held to include dignity, autonomy, pluralist democracy, tolerance, open-mindedness, equality, and respect for the rule of law, which have variously been regarded by the European Court and Commission of Human Rights as underpinning all or some of the Convention rights. I say that it is likely, rather than being categorical about it, because section 2 of the Act requires courts and tribunals to "take into account" the case-law of the Strasbourg organs, and not necessarily to follow it, when interpreting Convention rights. It is possible that courts and tribunals in the UK might develop a jurisprudence of human rights on the basis of different values, or (more likely) give different relative weights to the various values, from those which the Strasbourg organs have articulated. There could be a number of good reasons for such a development, which I have discussed elsewhere.

It is also entirely possible that different values, and hence different weighting of rights, will come to dominate the separate jurisdictions in England and Wales, Scotland and Northern Ireland. As interpretation of rights within a constitution is affected by the structural and institutional arrangements in the State (such as whether the State is unitary or federal, and, if federal, what type of federalism is in place), there could even be an argument for applying the values

---

[38] The word "values" is capable of having a variety of meanings, including goods to be pursued, considerations which are relevant to the choice of and relative weight to be attached to different goods, and considerations which should be taken into account when deciding how, and how far, to pursue goods. For present purposes, I will generally use the word in its second sense; the goods to be pursued and the factors relevant to deciding how and how far to pursue them are specified in the text of the various articles read together with the Strasbourg case-law. Other values mainly affect the relative weighting of the rights where they conflict.

of Convention rights differently when judicially reviewing legislation of the Welsh Assembly from the way they apply to subordinate forms of legislation in England.

For present purposes, the important point to note is that, whatever values end up being dominant in the English case-law, the injection of generalised substantive values into the legal rules which delimit the four corners of public authorities' powers has occurred with parliamentary sanction. Not only has Parliament, in the Human Rights Act 1998, approved the text of the rights which are to be applied in this way, and expressly or by necessary implication authorised this use of them, but it has done so in the knowledge that the full meaning of the rights would become clear only from judicial decisions after the main provisions of the Act come into force. We can thus look forward to review for substantive ultra vires *stricto sensu* in which both the nature of the review and the judges' interpretative role in it will be justifiable, in line with classical ultra vires doctrine, by reference to the will of Parliament. In this context, there will be no need to trouble ourselves about whether or not the doctrine of ultra vires is a fiction or a fig-leaf.

Secondly, the substantive values of the Convention will affect procedural ultra vires as well as substantive ultra vires. The procedural rights of litigants and those suspected of crimes under Articles 5 and 6 of the Convention, and the implications which some of the substantive Convention rights have for administrative procedure (for example, Article 8 in relation to child-care decisions),[39] may well interact in interesting ways with the rules of natural justice and fairness as understood both in administrative law and in criminal and civil procedure. As this happens, it is likely to reduce the significance of the distinction between substantive and other grounds of review, both in practice and as a matter of theory. Although one must not lose sight of the need to justify review and keep it within the bounds of the available justifications, it is unlikely to be easy to keep separate, in everyday practice, the foundations of those aspects of the duty of fairness which are derived from the common law and those which are based on the Human Rights Act 1998. Justifying review on the basis of parliamentary supremacy is so easy in relation to Convention rights under the Act that it would not be surprising if the right-based approach appropriate to the Convention rights were to spill over to the common-law principles, ultimately producing a single body of law theorised on the foundation of the central role of rights. That in turn will further reduce the significance of the distinction between substantive and procedural ultra vires at the normative level (that of principles of review), and make it harder to maintain that ultra vires at the meta-normative level provides the only or specially privileged source of legitimacy for judicial review.

Thirdly, although substantive review for compatibility with Convention rights under the Human Rights Act 1998 will move from the irrationality ground for review (often characterised as a form of substantive ultra vires which

---

[39] See text at n. 27, above.

presents special problems of justification on the basis of the intention of Parliament) to the error-of-law ground which is far easier to justify by reference to statutory authority, other rights under international human-rights instruments will still be available to be taken into consideration as part of the backdrop against which (as at present) the reasonableness of official action will be assessed. Using unincorporated rights for this purpose might seem to be difficult to support, once Parliament has provided for a specific range of rights to be part of English law. However, there are good arguments in favour of the continued use of a wider range of rights for the purposes of assessing rationality. Whatever the merits or deficiencies of justifications of review of rationality based on the implied intention of Parliament, reference to the United Kingdom's international treaty obligations has both an interpretative justification and an institutional one. The presumption, in interpreting legislation, that Parliament does not intend to legislate in a manner incompatible with the United Kingdom's obligations in international law is bolstered by the institutional consideration, which applies to executive and administrative action as well as legislation, that courts and tribunals are emanations of the State. As the State is responsible in international law for ensuring that its international obligations are met, the courts are institutionally proper bodies for treating decisions, actions or rules which appear to breach those obligations as presumptively unreasonable and so unlawful. The finding of unlawfulness can be avoided by reference to clear words in statutes or, to a lesser extent, countervailing considerations of policy or principle. However, the onus should lie on a public authority to justify it, rather than on the individual who is adversely affected to show that a public authority which breaches international law has acted wholly unreasonably in doing so. Making reference to instruments not included among the Convention rights can be seen as gaining additional legitimacy from the terms of section 2 of the 1998 Act. When interpreting Convention rights, section 2 enjoins courts and tribunals to take into account the Strasbourg case-law, and the Strasbourg organs make reference to a range of international instruments outside the ECHR when it is useful to explicate the meaning of Convention rights. If this justifies our courts in making use of unincorporated human-rights texts as an aid to interpreting Convention rights for the purpose of error-of-law ultra vires review, there would seem to be no reason to exclude those unincorporated texts from consideration in relation to questions of substantive rationality.

Fourthly, quite apart from use of Convention rights as a substantive basis for ultra vires review, it would seem sensible to regard them as relevant considerations to be taken into account by a public authority which makes a decision or takes action which potentially might affect a right. Indeed, a wider range of material than the incorporated rights may be treated as relevant for judicial review purposes. As noted in the previous paragraph, where rights incorporated in the 1998 Act are invoked section 2 requires courts and tribunals to take account of decisions of the Strasbourg organs, which in turn have regard to unincorporated instruments including Article 13 of the ECHR, the provisions of the International Covenant on Civil and Political Rights, and the UN Convention on the Rights of the Child. It would not seem absurd to regard such texts as giving rise to relevant considerations for the purpose of reviewing decisions of public authorities. This is not entirely straightforward, because under section 2 only courts and tribunals are under an obligation to take account of Strasbourg case-law. Other public authorities are not compelled to do so. Therefore there might not always be an obligation to consider the wider range of material as a relevant consideration. However, it would be strange if a court reviewing a decision of another public authority for compliance with Convention rights was under an obligation to have regard to Strasbourg case-law, but the primary decision-maker were to be regarded as free to ignore it. Any sensible public authority, knowing that its decisions might be reviewed by reference to the Strasbourg interpretation of Convention, will do its best to take account of that case-law in its decisions. The principles of review should take account of that practical relevance.

Fifthly, we may need to reconsider the generality of the rule that the High Court does not act beyond its jurisdiction when it gets the law wrong.[40] It has been held in the past that an order of the High Court, even if wrongly made as a matter of law, is valid unless and until quashed on appeal, and must be obeyed (even by a minister of the Crown).[41] This was a valuable assertion of the need for certainty and, in context, of the rule-of-law principle subjecting the executive to the authority of the courts. However, the decision presupposed that a decision of the High Court vitiated by an error of law was not invalid on that account. That presupposition can no longer apply where the error of law consists of an incompatibility with a Convention right, because the presumption is at least arguably overridden by the terms of the Human Rights Act 1998. All courts and tribunals are subject both to section 6(1) and to section 2 of the Act. One can therefore argue that if the High Court makes a decision which is incompatible with a Convention right it will be acting ultra vires, since Parliament has expressly limited the vires of all public authorities by reference to the standards embodied in Convention rights.

Although section 9(1) and (2) of the Act provides in effect that the only proceedings which a person who is the victim of such an ultra vires decision can initiate to seek a remedy will be by way of appeal, section 9(1) leaves the victim the option of ignoring the decision and relying on the incompatibility by way of defence in subsequent proceedings (for example, for contempt of court). Allowing scope for this sort of collateral review of a High Court decision creates the possibility of uncertainty, but should not undermine the subjection of the executive to law, because (by virtue of the nature of Convention rights) the executive will never be a victim of a decision of a court which violates a

---

[40] *In re Racal Communications* [1981] AC 385, HL, reversing *In Re A Company* [1980] Ch 138, (CA); *M v. Home Office* [1994] 1 AC 377, HL.
[41] *M v. Home Office* [1994] 1 AC 377, HL.

Convention right.

Sixthly, there is one new type of judicial review which will require the application of substantive standards but which, unlike other kinds of review under the Act, will not be capable of being theorised by reference to the meta-normative doctrine of ultra vires. This type of review will arise where a superior court decides that a piece of primary legislation as defined by the 1998 Act is incapable of being interpreted under section 3 so as to be compatible with a Convention right, or that primary legislation prevents a piece of secondary legislation from being so interpreted. If a litigant then seeks a declaration of incompatibility under section 4 of the 1998 Act in respect of the incompatible legislation, and the declaration would relate directly or indirectly to an Act of Parliament, the court will have to embark on a new kind of inquiry. The review of the primary legislation, stopping short of invalidating it but leading to a declaration that it is in some sense contrary to law, will have been authorised by Parliament in section 4 of the Act. However, it will not strictly involve an application of ultra vires doctrine, because under the 1998 Act Parliament does not act beyond its powers in legislating in a manner incompatible with Convention rights. The role of the courts in granting declarations of incompatibility will be more advisory than an exercise in the implementation of the rule of law, although the substantive standards applied in the process of conducting the review will be legal standards (the Convention rights).[42]

IV. CONCLUSION

I have tried to show that, whatever the weaknesses or limitations of ultra vires theory may be in general as the main or only meta-normative foundation for the legitimacy of judicial review, the Human Rights Act 1998 will generate new developments in substantive review which all have either express or clearly implied authority from Parliament within the terms of the Act itself, unlike several of the existing grounds for judicial review and such conceptual tools as common-law fundamental rights. So far as the Convention rights open a new direction for judicial review, the path-finding judges will be able to legitimate their creativeness by reference to a sound foundation in the classical doctrine of ultra vires. This will apply whether the ground of review is substantive or procedural, and whether it goes to the merits of an action, decision or rule or to the process of reasoning by which it was reached or justified. Judges will not be subject to the strictures which have been aimed at those who in the past have sought to develop substantive grounds of review through the medium of the principle of unreasonableness or that of fundamental common-law rights. Parliament's words, in the form of generalised right-based criteria, applicable to all public authorities, for assessing the limitations of their powers, will provide all the

---

[42] For further discussion, see Feldman, *op. cit.*, n. 22 above, at 186–7.

legitimacy which is needed.

This is not to say that further justification could not be provided. The rule of law, the duty of States in international law to comply with their obligations under treaties, and the values which underpin the Convention rights, all provide powerful arguments for taking Convention rights seriously as aspects of normative, rather than meta-normative, ultra vires. Such arguments would justify judicial review in a range of cases where it would not be convincing to rely on the will of Parliament to legitimate the review. However, I have presented no such argument here. Instead, I have argued only that, in the context of review for incompatibility with Convention rights, it is unnecessary (although it may be useful) to look beyond the traditional boundaries of ultra vires doctrine, either at the normative or at the meta-normative level, to justify a significantly increased level of review for substantive ultra vires (in all the senses of that term).

The Convention rights will set minimum standards below which it will be unlawful for public authorities, including courts, to fall. These standards will be pervasive and multi-faceted. Some will overlap with existing procedural principles, while others will go further, necessitating substantive review. The separation between procedural and substantive grounds of judicial review, and the common-law and Convention-based principles, will probably be progressively broken down over time. This should not, however, be allowed to obscure the need to be sensitive to the range of different implications of Convention rights. Courts will have to grapple with these in many kinds of proceedings. Where there is a matter of general application, it should be approached as far as possible in similar ways under similar circumstances, regardless of the nature of the proceedings. For example, the interim effect of rules or decisions which are later held to be invalid by reason of incompatibility with a Convention right will have to be worked out in the law of tort as well as in judicial review. The answer will affect the availability of legal remedies and the nature of those remedies which are available in a variety of types of litigation. It is important that there should be a principled and consistent approach to such problems. The same can be said of the exercise of judicial discretion in respect of remedies other than damages: it is hard to imagine that theoretically discretionary remedies will really be regarded as discretionary when a public authority has been shown to have violated a Convention right, save to the extent that there is a choice between possible remedies and it is necessary to decide which of them (alone or in combination) will provide an adequate remedy for the victim.

When approaching these issues, courts and tribunals will need to set the Human Rights Act 1998 in its constitutional context. Where a public authority has interfered with a right, and tries to justify the interference, the weight to be attached to proposed justifications will depend on the type of instrument, act or decision which is impugned and the type of body which is challenged. Developments in the constitution, particularly in respect of devolution, mean that the justifications for infringements which are permitted under the various articles in Schedule 1 to the Act may be interpreted in different ways, or given different weights, in the several constituent parts of the United Kingdom, because of the constitutional natures of their various legislative and executive organs. Courts must be sensitive to the constitutional framework when making decisions under the Act, or there will be a danger that applying the doctrine of ultra vires without regard to constitutional context will produce results which derail good, as well as bad, government. If operated with proper sensitivity, ultra vires will be one of the bases for judicial review of violations of Convention rights at the meta-normative level, and will bolster the protection for such rights at the normative and remedial levels.

12

Fundamental Rights as Interpretative Constructs: The Constitutional Logic of the Human Rights Act 1998*

MARK ELLIOTT

I. INTRODUCTION

The incorporation of the European Convention on Human Rights (ECHR) into English law is one of the longest-awaited and potentially most far-reaching changes to affect the British constitution in its recent history.[1] One of the central issues which arose when incorporation[2] was contemplated concerned the extent to which the Convention rights should be entrenched: whether, in other words, fundamental rights ought to have been placed beyond legislative interference by conferring on the judiciary the power to strike down primary legislation which abrogated them.

It was long held that, irrespective of the merits or demerits of an entrenched bill of rights, the English doctrine of parliamentary sovereignty meant that

---

* I am grateful to Dr Christopher Forsyth and Sir William Wade QC for reading and commenting upon earlier drafts of this paper.

[1] There exists a huge literature on the subject of the incorporation of the ECHR. Lord Lester, "Democracy and Individual Rights" (Fabian Tract No. 390, 1968) and Lord Scarman, *English Law – The New Dimension* (London, 1974) are generally credited with sparking the incorporation debate. For discussion of the advantages and disadvantages of incorporation, see M. Zander, *A Bill of Rights?* (London, 1997, 4th ed.) For reaction to the method of incorporation adopted, see H.W.R. Wade, "Human Rights and the Judiciary" [1998] *EHRLR* 520; J. Beatson, C.F. Forsyth and I.C. Hare (eds), *Constitutional Reform in the United Kingdom: Practice and Principles* (Oxford, 1998); Lord Bingham, "The Way We Live Now: Human Rights in the New Millennium" [1998] 1 *Web Journal of Current Legal Issues*; G. Marshall, "Interpreting Interpretation in the Human Rights Bill" [1998] *PL* 5; D. Pannick, "Principles of Interpretation of Convention Rights under the Human Rights Act and the Discretionary Area of Judgment" [1998] *PL* 545; N. Bamforth, "Parliamentary Sovereignty and the Human Rights Act 1998" [1998] *PL* 572.

[2] The language of incorporation in relation to the Human Rights Act 1998 (hereinafter "HRA 1998") is used in this paper and elsewhere as convenient shorthand for the Act's giving of greater effect to the ECHR in English law. However, strictly speaking, the Convention rights will not be incorporated in the sense that they will "not . . . become part of our domestic law" (583 HL Deb., col. 522 (Lord Irvine); see also Marshall in Beatson, Forsyth and Hare (eds), op. cit., n. 1, at p. 75). The significance of this point will become apparent below.

entrenchment was simply not a constitutional possibility.[3] However, subsequent experience in the field of European Community law has proved that this view was not wholly accurate.[4] Consequently a broad spectrum of methods of incorporation was open to the United Kingdom, ranging from the relatively weak – albeit largely successful[5] – interpretative approach preferred in New Zealand,[6] through the Canadian methodology which permits judicial invalidation of statutes that infringe rights subject to limited and express legislative derogation,[7] to a fully entrenched catalogue of fundamental rights such as that which obtains in the United States.[8]

It is, by now, well known that the model which has been adopted in the United Kingdom will function largely by recourse to interpretative techniques,[9] subject to the possibility of a judicial declaration that legislation is irreconcilable with one or more of the rights enshrined in the European Convention;[10] this, in turn, will trigger an administrative competence to amend the offending legislation.[11] In this manner the theory of parliamentary sovereignty is preserved by withholding from judges the competence to invalidate primary legislation, while ensuring that – through interpretative methodology and, where this fails, the political pressure to change English law which will result from a declaration of incompatibility – a considerable degree of protection is conferred on human rights norms. Lord Lester acknowledges that this is "an ingenious and successful reconciliation of the principles of parliamentary sovereignty and the need for effective domestic remedies".[12] Judges, too, have welcomed this careful balancing of rights protection and parliamentary supremacy: Lord Bingham CJ, for instance, believes it to be "vastly preferable" that judges should

---

[3] See, e.g., the evidence of the Special Advisor to the House of Lords Select Committee on a Bill of Rights: D. Rippengal, "Minutes of Evidence Taken Before the Select Committee on a Bill of Rights" (House of Lords, 1977). For the Committee's report, see *Report of the Select Committee on a Bill of Rights* (House of Lords, 1978).

[4] As is well known, it has been held that section 2 of the European Communities Act 1972 requires that directly effective EC law takes priority over incompatible domestic primary legislation, thereby abrogating – or at least suspending – the traditional orthodoxy of legislative supremacy. See *R. v. Secretary of State for Transport, ex parte Factortame Ltd.* [1991] 1 AC 603; *R. v. Secretary of State for Employment, ex parte Equal Opportunities Commission* [1995] 1 AC 1.

[5] See P.T. Rishworth, "Affecting the Fundamental Values of the Nation: How the Bill of Rights and the Human Rights Act affect New Zealand Law" in P.T. Rishworth (ed.), *Rights and Freedoms* (Wellington, 1995).

[6] See New Zealand Bill of Rights Act 1990.

[7] See Canadian Charter of Rights and Freedoms and, for comment, R. Penner, "The Canadian Experience with the Charter of Rights: Are there Lessons for the United Kingdom?" [1996] *PL* 104.

[8] Although the US Constitution does not explicitly vouchsafe the entrenchment of the rights which it enumerates against legislative interference, it was held in *Marbury v. Madison* (1803) 1 Cranch 137 that it follows implicitly from the Constitution that adjudication on the constitutionality of legislation is an inherent part of the judicial function.

[9] See HRA 1998, section 3(1).

[10] See ibid., section 4.

[11] See ibid., section 10.

[12] HL Deb., 18 November 1997, col. 521.

not be involved in the disapplication of statutes which affront fundamental rights, because this is "not part of our constitutional tradition".[13]

Against this background, it is the purpose of the present paper to demonstrate that care must be taken when conceptualising the manner in which the Human Rights Act will operate in the field of administrative law. The most attractive and straightforward rationalisation of the Act's impact on judicial review (which is described below) is, upon careful analysis, incompatible with the legislation's stated objective of reconciling rights with sovereignty. It will be argued that only by drawing upon notions of statutory interpretation and the methodology of ultra vires, which has long been accepted[14] as the constitutional foundation of the existing, procedure-oriented law of judicial review, is it possible to explain the functioning of the Human Rights Act in a manner which is consistent with its non-entrenched status and with continuing respect for parliamentary supremacy.

II. HUMAN RIGHTS AS SUBSTANTIVE RULES OF GOOD ADMINISTRATION

A. A rule-based approach to human rights review

According to the ultra vires doctrine, all of the existing principles of judicial review take effect as interpretative constructs. However, as I explained above,[15] this conceptualisation of administrative law has been challenged by a number of leading writers who maintain that it is unconvincing and artificial.[16] It will be recalled that such commentators advocate the reconceptualisation of the heads of review: they are not, it is said, interpretative constructs but take effect, instead, as free-standing common law rules of good administration which have nothing to do with the intention of the legislature.[17] Notwithstanding that this approach possesses certain superficial attractions, Christopher Forsyth and myself have argued at length – in papers which can be found above – that abandoning the essence of the ultra vires rule as the basis of judicial review is neither necessary (because it is possible, by recognising the sophistication of the doctrine and the constitutional setting within which it operates, to explain review convincingly by reference to it) nor constitutionally possible (since such a course

---

[13] "Bingham Rejects New Privacy Law", *The Daily Telegraph*, 9 October 1997.

[14] Although ultra vires has been subjected to a good deal of academic and extra-curial criticism, on which see the papers cited in n. 16, the courts continue to accept it as the juridical basis of judicial review. For recent and authoritative confirmation, see *Boddington* v. *British Transport Police* [1998] 2 WLR 639, 639, *per* Lord Steyn, 650, *per* Lord Irvine L.C., 655, *per* Lord Browne-Wilkinson.

[15] See above, "The Ultra Vires Doctrine in a Constitutional Setting: Still the Central Principle of Administrative Law", at pp. 83–109.

[16] See, *inter alios*, D. Oliver, "Is the Ultra Vires Rule the Basis of Judicial Review?", above pp. 3–27; Sir John Laws, "Illegality: The Problem of Jurisdiction", above pp. 73–81; Lord Woolf, "*Droit Public* – English Style" [1995] *PL* 57; P.P. Craig, "Ultra Vires and the Foundations of Judicial Review", above pp. 47–71, and "Competing Models of Judicial Review", below pp. 373–92.

[17] See n. 16.

would preclude the reconciliation of the supervisory jurisdiction with the principle of legislative sovereignty).[18]

This is not the place to revisit the detail of those arguments, although their central thrust will be referred to where this is necessary. The important point for present purposes is that the Human Rights Act appears to facilitate an approach to rights-based judicial review which obviates the need to make recourse to the ultra vires doctrine's construction-based methodology which has been so strongly criticised. This putative foundation of a simple rule- rather than interpretation-based approach to review finds expression in section 6(1) of the Act, which provides that: "It is unlawful for a public authority to act in a way which is incompatible with a Convention right." By setting out such a clear duty to respect human rights, this provision ostensibly places rights-based review on an altogether different and more straightforward footing than the traditional grounds of review. It seems that the courts will not be required to cast their judgments under the Human Rights Act in the language of statutory interpretation; instead, they will simply be enforcing a set of rules based on respect for human rights. Any administrator found breaking the rules will find his action tainted with the stigma of illegality.[19] Thus it appears that the legislation ensures that review on rights-based grounds is not open to the same criticisms as the traditional law of judicial review, by making the new substantive rights capable of vindication otherwise than via the circuitous methodology of statutory construction which – according to traditional theory – explains the existing law of review.

This simple,[20] rule-based conception of human rights review carries with it a further advantage. I noted above that the ultra vires doctrine's reliance on statutory implication means that it is incapable of explaining why the existing grounds of judicial review can apply in areas – such as the exercise of prerogative and de facto governmental powers – where they cannot, in logic, be conceptualised as implied statutory terms.[21] The same problem would not beset human rights review if it was rationalised – as section 6(1) appears to suggest it should

---

[18] See above, C.F. Forsyth, "Of Fig Leaves and Fairy Tales: The Ultra Vires Doctrine, the Sovereignty of Parliament and Judicial Review" above, p. 29; Elliott, op. cit., n. 15. See also M.C. Elliott, "The Demise of Parliamentary Sovereignty? The Implications for Justifying Judicial Review" (1999) 115 *LQR* 119.

[19] Unless the enabling provision necessarily requires the infringement of human rights: see section 6(2).

[20] It is the structural methodology by which rights adjudication is facilitated that is, on this view, simple; it is not submitted that the substantive issues raised by judicial enforcement of human rights can be anything other than complex and challenging, irrespective of the methodology by which they are given effect.

[21] See above, pp. 105–7. It is now well-established that review lies in these non-statutory fields (although the courts have not explained how this is to be constitutionally justified given the inapplicability of the ultra vires doctrine). See, *inter alia, R.* v. *Criminal Injuries Compensation Board, ex parte Lain* [1967] 2 QB 864; *Council of Civil Service Unions* v. *Minister for the Civil Service* [1985] AC 374; *R.* v. *Panel on Take-overs and Mergers, ex parte Datafin plc* [1987] QB 815. For an explanation of how the ultra vires doctrine, properly understood, fits into a regime of judicial review which extends beyond statutory power, see above, pp. 105–7.

be – as a straightforward duty to respect fundamental rights which is incumbent upon all public authorities, irrespective of whether their power derives from statute. Since the section 6(1) approach does not characterise human rights as implied statutory requirements, it provides an all-encompassing juridical foundation which secures rights protection for individuals as they interact with all manners of public decision-makers.

It will be argued below that, superficially attractive though this approach may be, it cannot be adopted unless the Human Rights Act is conceptualised as an entrenched guarantee of fundamental rights.[22] First, however, it is necessary to emphasise the nature of the distinction between *rule-based* and *vires-based* models of judicial review.

B. The distinction between rule-based and vires-based review

Christopher Forsyth maintains that the temptation to replace ultra vires with a set of common law rules of good administration must be resisted, in relation to the existing, uncodified law of judicial review. Forsyth's argument is set out, in his own words, elsewhere in this volume; it is, therefore, necessary at this juncture only to summarise its main points.[23]

When Parliament grants a discretionary power to an administrator, it must follow in logic that, as a matter of empirical fact, such power either is or is not subject to limitations requiring adherence to such precepts as the *Wednesbury* principles and the rules of natural justice.[24]

If the power to act unfairly or *Wednesbury* unreasonably is withheld from the decision-maker then judicial review, consistently with ultra vires theory, involves the courts' ensuring that the limits which Parliament is taken to have applied to the administrative power are not transgressed. It follows that, within this framework, common law rules of good administration would be otiose since they would simply replicate the duty to act fairly and rationally which, by virtue of his implicitly limited powers, would already be incumbent upon the administrator.

[22] See below, section C.
[23] See Forsyth, op. cit., n. 18, and "Heat and Light: A Plea for Reconciliation", below pp. 393–409. It should be emphasised at this point that Forsyth's argument relates to the imperative of reconciling judicial review with the framework of the constitution. It is no part of his thesis that the ultra vires doctrine, properly understood, should not form the basis of a dynamic and progressive corpus of administrative law. The same is true of the argument advanced in the present paper, according to which the ultra vires doctrine facilitates the development of public law by providing the constitutional mechanism by which human rights are given legal force in the field of executive decision-making.
[24] Forsyth, op. cit., n. 18, at pp. 39–40. Although Forsyth's analysis has been questioned by Laws, op. cit., n. 16, pp. 73–81, and Craig, "Ultra Vires and the Foundations of Judicial Review", op. cit., n. 16, pp. 47–71, I argued above, at pp. 88–100, that these criticisms do not withstand analysis. I have also sought to demonstrate that Forsyth's analysis holds good, so that ultra vires remains constitutionally necessary, even if it is thought that the traditional doctrine of parliamentary sovereignty has been eclipsed by a more limited conception of legislative competence: see "The Demise of Parliamentary Sovereignty? The Implications for Justifying Judicial Review", op. cit., n. 18.

Conversely, it may be that when the administrative power is granted, it is taken to be free from any tacit conditions requiring it to be used only in a fair and rational manner. The absence of any implied limitations thus precludes the operation of the ultra vires doctrine, given that it can only function when there exist such limits for the courts to police. However, this absence of implied limits logically also precludes the application of a set of common law rules of judicial review. If it is assumed that Parliament has desisted from attaching implied constraints to the relevant discretionary power – and this assumption *must* be made if the common law rules of good administration are not, as they were in the first model, to be otiose – then judicial application of common law limits to the exercise of that power would reduce the scope of the power which Parliament must be taken to have created. Conceptualised thus, judicial review, rather than fulfilling legislative intention, cuts across the will of Parliament, thereby assaulting the doctrine of parliamentary sovereignty.

Hence the distinction between *vires-based* and *rule-based* review is that the former entails judicial enforcement of the internal limits of discretionary powers, while the latter involves the courts' removing from administrators certain competencies – such as the ability to act unfairly or unreasonably – which, in the absence of an interpretative approach and for the reasons given above, it must be assumed that Parliament originally granted to them. The implications of this analysis for the existing law of judicial review are explored in detail elsewhere in the volume, in papers by Christopher Forsyth and myself.[25] The remainder of this paper is concerned with the relevance of this analysis to the juridical foundations of the new, rights-based regime of judicial review which is about to be ushered in by the Human Rights Act.

C. Rule-based review, entrenchment and sovereignty

The constitutional impropriety which is entailed in any attempt to explain the present regime of judicial review in terms of common law rules rather than interpretative constructs can be explained in simple terms: it involves, as the previous section explained, setting up the common law against the will of Parliament which, according to classic theory, is constitutionally anathema.

The rule-based approach to human rights review described above does not, however, suffer from the same shortcoming. The "rules" which exist within that model are statutory, having their basis in legislation – *viz.* section 6(1) of the Human Rights Act – rather than the common law. There is, therefore, no question that rule-based review on substantive rights grounds involves the setting up of the common law against the sovereign will of Parliament. Nevertheless, a rule-based approach founded on section 6(1) still raises considerable constitutional problems. It is necessary to substantiate this proposition in two stages by

---

[25] See Forsyth, op. cit, nn. 18 and 23; Elliott, op. cit., nn. 15 and 18, and "Legislative Intention versus Judicial Creativity? Administrative Law as a Co-operative Endeavour", below.

considering the *analytical* and then the *constitutional* implications of adopting section 6(1) as a rule-based foundation for human rights review.

The *analytical* implications of a rule-based approach to review under the 1998 Act are identical to the analytical consequences of conceptualising the existing grounds of judicial review as common law rules. If human rights find expression in the administrative law sphere as straightforward rules which decision-makers must obey, rather than as interpretative principles which shape the internal contours of discretionary powers, then, just as with common law rules of good administration, they must be viewed as cutting down the scope of decision-making powers and, therefore, as removing from administrators powers which Parliament initially granted to them.

Once this proposition is accepted, it becomes necessary to analyse its *constitutional* implications. In order to do so, a distinction must be made between judicial review of the exercise of statutory discretionary power created *before* and *after* the enactment of the human rights legislation.

First, consider a piece of legislation enacted in, say, 1990, which creates a particular ministerial decision-making power. The rule-based approach to judicial review tells us that, properly interpreted, the minister's power is not subject to any implied conditions requiring it to be exercised compatibly with the Convention rights: as discussed above, acceptance of the contrary proposition renders the rule-based model otiose. However, section 6(1) requires respect for human rights and, subject to section 6(2), renders "unlawful" any use of the discretionary power which is "incompatible with a Convention right". There therefore arises a discrepancy between the Acts of 1990 and 1998. The former vests a broad competence in the minister to exercise his discretion in a manner which need not be compatible with Convention rights,[26] while the latter directs that it is unlawful to use the discretionary power in such a way. In this situation, orthodox theory provides that the later legislation should prevail, so that, according to a rule-based analysis, the Human Rights Act operates so as to remove from decision-makers powers which, properly construed, earlier enabling legislation conferred upon them.

This raises two points. First, the rule-based analysis does not, in relation to judicial review on rights grounds of discretions created before the enactment of the Human Rights Act, raise any constitutional problem, since it is perfectly clear that later legislation can prevail over earlier legislation. Secondly, however, it is apparent that this is not the approach which the promoters of the 1998 Act had in mind. The White Paper which accompanied the draft human rights legislation stated that:

> It has been suggested that the courts should be able to uphold the [Convention] rights in preference to any provisions of earlier legislation which are incompatible with those

---

[26] Subject to the overarching requirement that his disregard of Convention rights may not be so flagrant as to be irrational. However, as the judgment of Simon Brown LJ in *R.* v. *Ministry of Defence, ex parte Smith* [1996] QB 517 demonstrates with striking clarity, the rationality doctrine is no substitute for a direct obligation to respect human rights.

rights. This is on the basis that a later Act of Parliament takes precedence over an earlier Act if there is a conflict. But the Human Rights Bill is intended to provide a new basis for judicial interpretation of all legislation, not a basis for striking down any part of it.[27]

Consequently the Act provides that the courts' duty to attempt to interpret enactments consistently with human rights and their power to issue declarations of incompatibility when this proves impossible shall have no impact upon the "validity, continuing operation or enforcement" of primary legislation.[28] Although these provisions of the Act and of the White Paper are primarily intended to demonstrate that judges should not, under the new law, possess the power to strike down legislation, it nevertheless follows that the implications of the rule-based analysis identified above – according to which the Human Rights Act would remove from administrators powers which earlier statutes had conferred upon them – are inconsistent with this ethos. Hence, in the context of rights review of pre-HRA discretions, it can be said that the rule-based model, while constitutionally workable, is certainly incompatible with the principle on which the rights legislation is supposed to be founded.

Adherence to the rule-based model raises more profound constitutional difficulties in respect of judicial review, on rights grounds, of discretionary powers created *after* the enactment of the Human Rights Act. Consider an enactment of, say, 2003 which creates, in broad terms which make no reference to respect for human rights, a certain ministerial discretion. According to the rule-based analysis, the scope of that discretion, properly interpreted, would not be subject to any implied obligation to observe human rights standards:[29] as discussed above, if the position were otherwise, no "rules" would be needed. Consequently it would be necessary to argue that the earlier Human Rights Act rendered unlawful (by operation of section 6(1)) something which, according to the later enabling legislation, would not be unlawful. The Act of 1998 would therefore purport to take away from the minister a power which, properly interpreted, the Act of 2003 conferred upon him. For this to be possible, the Human Rights Act 1998 would have to be an entrenched enactment, capable of prevailing over later legislation which – positively or by omission, expressly or implicitly – was inconsistent with the 1998 Act's policy of securing respect for human rights. Although the European Communities Act 1972 has apparently been entrenched in this manner, it is very clear that the same is not true of the Human

---

[27] Cm 3782, *Rights Brought Home: The Human Rights Bill* (London, 1997), p. 10.

[28] HRA 1998, sections 3(2)(b) and 4(6)(a).

[29] It would, of course, be difficult to justify reading the legislation thus if a ministerial statement had been made under HRA, section 19, to the effect that the legislation was thought to be compatible with respect for ECHR rights. In light of section 19, it would be much more natural to hold that provisions creating discretionary powers were intended to be implicitly limited by reference to Convention standards. This is one reason why the vires-based model, set out below, is to be preferred over the rule-based model presently under discussion.

Rights Act: the White Paper confirms this conclusion in terms,[30] and there exists no provision in the Act which suggests otherwise.[31]

This analysis discloses a striking symmetry between the constitutional consequences of embracing a rule-based approach to the existing grounds of judicial review and the new rights-oriented heads of challenge. Just as it is impossible to set up the common law against legislation, so it is not possible for earlier non-entrenched legislation (such as the Human Rights Act) to cut down or take away powers granted by later legislation (in the form of enabling provisions giving rise to discretionary power which, unless an interpretative approach is adopted, will not be subject to any internal rights-based limits). In each instance the same reasoning explains the result: within the British hierarchy of legal norms, the common law is inferior to legislation, just as earlier legislation cannot be set up against later legislation. Both of these propositions are logical functions of the doctrine of parliamentary sovereignty, according to which the contemporary will of Parliament is the ultimate source of law in the constitution, prevailing over the common law and earlier legislation alike.

It may be thought that the direction in section 6(1), that it shall be unlawful for public decision-makers to infringe Convention rights, creates an interpretative background against which future grants of discretionary power should be viewed as being subject to internal limits on human rights grounds. Perhaps this is so; however, far from rescuing the rule-based model from constitutional unworkability, such an approach necessarily entails the rejection of that model. If section 6(1) is viewed as giving rise to such an interpretative backdrop, thereby leading to the implied limitation of future grants of discretionary power on rights-based grounds, this reflects an altogether different approach, based on interpretation. Indeed, it takes us back to the familiar implication-based methodology of the ultra vires principle, to which we must now turn.

III. HUMAN RIGHTS AS INTERPRETATIVE CONSTRUCTS

A. A vires-based, not a rule-based, model of judicial review

Having rejected a rule-based conceptualisation of judicial review under the Human Rights Act in light of the constitutional difficulties which it raises, it is necessary to articulate a theory which gives effect to fundamental rights in the administrative law sphere in a manner which is consistent with the non-entrenched status of the Act.

The solution to this conundrum is clear. The Convention rights, as they apply to the administrative decision-making process, must be rationalised as interpretative constructs which shape the internal contours of enabling provisions,

---

[30] Op. cit., n. 27, pp. 9–11.
[31] Compare the European Communities Act 1972, section 2, which does provide a peg on which to hang the argument that it was intended to constitute an entrenched measure.

thereby ensuring that the courts, in effecting judicial review on rights-based grounds, enforce the limits of discretionary powers which enabling legislation – properly interpreted – sets, rather than cutting down the scope of such powers and thereby giving rise to the problems, identified above, which inhere in the rule-based approach. The Human Rights Act provides, in section 3(1), the foundations for precisely this methodology: "So far as it is possible to do so, primary and subordinate legislation must be read and given effect in a way which is compatible with the Convention rights." The Act provides no indication of how sections 3(1) and 6(1) relate to one another. At first glance, the most likely answer is that section 6(1) deals specifically with administrative law, placing public decision-makers under a simple, direct obligation to respect human rights: in other words, a rule-based approach to judicial review on Convention grounds. Within this framework, section 3(1) would relate to areas other than administrative law, imposing upon the courts a broad obligation to adopt, where possible, a rights-oriented construction of legislation generally, such as that relating to criminal procedure and evidence: many such statutes, although likely to be significantly affected by incorporation, have nothing to do with the exercise of discretionary power and are therefore outwith the reach of section 6(1). This approach is attractive, at least superficially: not only does it place judicial review on a straightforward footing; it also allots clear, distinct roles to sections 3(1) and 6(1), thereby helping to make sense of the structure of the Act.

However, it has already been established that this model cannot be adopted. For this reason the focus, in the administrative law field, must be on section 3(1) rather than section 6(1). Since it is not constitutionally possible to conceptualise human rights as rules-based limits, rights-oriented review must instead be facilitated by reliance on the familiar methodology of ultra vires. In this manner fundamental rights must be internalised: they must be given effect interpretatively rather than directly. Section 3(1) must therefore be relied on as an interpretative tool so that all discretionary power – whether created before or after the entry into force of the human rights legislation – is read as being inherently limited by reference to human rights norms.

There therefore exists an important distinction between the rule- and vires-based models. Whereas the rule-based approach involves the taking away (by the Human Rights Act) of power which is conferred by enabling legislation, the vires-based model holds that grants of discretionary power never, in the first place, confer upon decision-makers any vires to breach the Convention rights. It follows from this that – unlike the rule-based method – the vires-based model is able to reconcile judicial review on human rights grounds with the non-entrenched status of the Human Rights Act since, within that model, there is no attempt to use the Act in order to remove power which was conferred by enabling legislation.

The interpretative model thus raises no constitutional difficulties. It is well-established that earlier legislation can contribute to the interpretative framework within which later legislation is construed. The Interpretation Act 1978 is a good example of this. Provided that earlier legislation does not seek to over-ride later legislation, no problems arise: subsequent legislation must therefore prevail if it is not possible to give effect to it in a manner which is consistent with the interpretative direction contained in the earlier measure. Hence, in the present context, later legislation must be given effect when it clearly confers on decision-makers the power to act in a manner which involves a breach of human rights. Precisely this approach is embodied in the Human Rights Act through its qualification of the interpretative obligation in section 3(1) by the caveat "so far as it is possible to do so".

B. The vires-based model and the relationship between sections 3(1) and 6(1)

It is clear from the foregoing that within the vires-based model – which must, for reasons already stated, be preferred – section 6(1) of the Human Rights Act is not directly in play when the courts are involved in reviewing, on substantive rights grounds, the exercise of statutory discretions. In spite of this, section 6(1) still serves two important functions.

First, it elucidates the meaning of section 3(1). In the *Brind* case,[32] Lord Lester, as counsel for the applicant, argued that, even in the absence of any statutory incorporation of the ECHR, discretionary powers should (subject, of course, to specific contrary provision) be interpreted as containing implied limits requiring adherence not only to the established principles of good administration but also to the substantive guarantees contained in the Convention. It is well-known that this argument failed before the House of Lords, on the basis that it would have entailed judicial – or "back door"[33] – incorporation of the European Convention. Indeed it is noteworthy that, although English courts have been willing to take the unincorporated ECHR into account in a number of contexts,[34] its relevance has been particularly limited in the administrative law field; in particular, the judges have refused to countenance it as a direct fetter on discretionary power.[35] It appears that this position obtains in light of the courts' reluctance to usurp both legislative functions (by transgressing the dualism principle) and executive functions (since the institution of human rights review would significantly reduce the administration's area of decision-making autonomy).[36]

Reading sections 3(1) and 6(1) together, it becomes clear beyond any doubt that, once the Act enters into force, the interpretation of statutory provisions

---

[32] R. v. *Secretary of State for the Home Department, ex parte Brind* [1991] 1 AC 696.

[33] Ibid., at p. 762, *per* Lord Ackner.

[34] For a useful summary of the (pre-HRA 1998) relevance of the Convention in English law, see Lord Bingham, HL Deb., 3 July 1996, cols. 1465–7.

[35] For discussion, see M. Hunt, *Using Human Rights Law in English Courts* (Oxford, 1997), especially ch. 4; F. Klug and K. Starmer, "Incorporation through the Back Door?" [1997] *PL* 223.

[36] See further on this point Lord Irvine, "Constitutional Change in the United Kingdom: British Solutions to Universal Problems" (an as yet unpublished lecture delivered in Washington DC, May 1998).

giving rise to discretionary powers will henceforth reveal the existence of implied limits relating to both the traditional grounds of judicial review *and* the substantive rights which are enshrined in the ECHR. Section 6(1) therefore confirms that the interpretative duty contained in section 3(1) extends to the discovery of implied rights-based limits in legislative provisions which create discretionary powers, thereby effectively reversing the House of Lords' decision in *Brind*.

Section 6(1) serves a second, equally important purpose. It has, thus far, been argued that considerations of constitutional propriety require the adoption of a vires-based model of human rights review which is founded on the interpretative machinery contained in section 3(1). It is immediately apparent, however, that common sense dictates that this approach is wholly inapplicable to public decision-making powers which do not derive from legislation. Two obvious examples are the Crown's prerogative powers and the de facto powers of bodies such as the City Panel on Take-overs and Mergers. Section 6(1) clearly envisages that all public power must, in the future, be exercised in a manner which respects fundamental rights. Judicial enforcement of this policy in relation to non-statutory powers will therefore be founded on the obligation to act compatibly with Convention rights which is contained in section 6(1).

It is submitted that this difference in approach between human rights review of statutory and non-statutory powers is a strength, not a weakness, of the present analysis. The objective of securing compliance with human rights standards by public decision-makers remains constant, while the juridical basis of enforcement differs in order to accommodate the constitutional distinctions between the two forms of power. In this manner, the policy of the Human Rights Act is effectuated in a way which reconciles principle and pragmatism: human rights are embraced as interpretative constructs in relation to statutory powers in order to avoid the constitutional difficulties concerning entrenchment which would otherwise arise, while they are characterised as free-standing rules or obligations in other contexts so as to render them effective in relation to public authorities which wield non-statutory powers.

C. Broader Perspectives: Preclusive Provisions and Collateral Challenge

It has been observed that the adoption of an interpretation- rather than a rule-based approach to review of statutory power on human rights grounds is necessary in order to ensure that, as a matter of constitutional logic, the Human Rights Act is able to function satisfactorily as a non-entrenched measure. In addition to this theoretical advantage of the vires-based model, it is desirable to point to two further benefits which it entails and which are of a rather more practical nature.

1. Preclusive provisions

It is a well-known fact that English courts jealously guard their public law juris-diction, resisting, wherever possible, legislative attempts to oust judicial review. Thus it is now said that access to justice is a "constitutional right" of the citi-zen.[37] This principle was classically established in the case of *Anisminic Ltd.* v. *Foreign Compensation Commission*.[38] It will be recalled that in this decision the House of Lords held that a strongly worded preclusive provision, properly con-strued, was incompetent to protect errors of the tribunal which went to its juris-diction. Subsequent cases have held that all reviewable errors committed by administrators cause them to act ultra vires;[39] hence, Lord Irvine LC recently remarked that, viewed thus, "The *Anisminic* decision established . . . that there was a single category of errors of law, all of which rendered a decision ultra vires".[40] It follows that since all reviewable errors are species of ultra vires, *Anisminic* reasoning operates to prevent standard ouster provisions from pre-cluding review in the face of any violation of the principles of modern adminis-trative law.[41]

The connection between the ultra vires doctrine and the courts' capacity to resist ouster provisions was illuminated by the South African Appellate Division's decision in the *UDF* case in the late 1980s.[42] The Public Safety Act 1953 granted the State President extensive powers to make regulations. The validity of certain regulations, which, it was said, had been made under section 3 of the Act, was challenged on the ground that they were vague. However, sec-tion 5B provided that "no court shall be competent to enquire into or give judg-ment on the validity of any proclamation [made] under section 3 [of the Act]". The question therefore arose whether the court had jurisdiction to review the

---

[37] See e.g., *R.* v. *Lord Chancellor, ex parte Witham* [1998] QB 575, 580, *per* Laws J.

[38] [1969] 2 AC 147. For further examples, see *Raymond* v. *Honey* [1982] 1 All ER 756; *R.* v. *Secretary of State for the Home Department, ex parte Anderson* [1984] QB 778; *R.* v. *Secretary of State for the Home Department, ex parte Leech* [1994] QB 198; *Witham*, op. cit., n. 37.

[39] See especially *R.* v. *Lord President of the Privy Council, ex parte Page* [1993] AC 682.

[40] *Boddington* v. *British Transport Police* [1998] 2 WLR 639, 650.

[41] This does not, however, mean that it lies beyond Parliament's competence to preclude judicial review in particular contexts. The question is always whether Parliament has used language which is so clear that it rebuts the very strong presumption that citizens should enjoy access to the ordinary courts. Some legislation embodies ouster provisions which are stronger than that which was at stake in *Anisminic*. For example, the Interception of Communications Act 1985, section 7(8), and the Security Service Act 1989, section 5(4), prevent review, *inter alia*, of decisions "as to jurisdiction". It may well be that this formula is strong enough to rebut the presumption in favour of access to justice.

[42] *United Democratic Front* v. *Staatspreident* 1988 (4) SA 830. The judgments are in Afrikaans; for comment in English, see N. Haysom and C. Plasket, "The War Against Law: Judicial Activism and the Appellate Division" (1988) 4 *South African Journal on Human Rights*; E. Mureinik, "Administrative Law" [1998] *Annual Survey of South African Law* 34; J. Grogan, "The Appellate Division and the Emergency: Another Step Backward" (1989) 106 *SALJ* 14; M.L. Matthews, "Vandalizing the Ultra Vires Doctrine" (1989) 5 *South African Journal on Human Rights* 481; A. Breitenbach, "The Justifications for Judicial Review" (1992) 8 *South African Journal on Human Rights* 513; Forsyth, op. cit., n. 18.

regulations for vagueness in spite of section 5B. The majority held, contrary to the weight of previous South African authority, that a number of the grounds of judicial review – including the prohibition on vague regulations – existed as common law *rules* rather than as *interpretative* constructs. It followed from this that, properly interpreted, section 3 of the 1953 Act *did* confer upon the State President a competence to make regulations which extended to the making of vague regulations: it was a separate *common law* rule which prohibited this latter activity. Consequently the vague regulations in question were "made under section 3" and were therefore protected, by section 5B, from judicial review.

The position would have been very different had the court not abandoned the logic of ultra vires. If the prohibition on vague regulations had been conceptualised as an interpretative construct, the State President's power would, *ab initio*, have been limited accordingly, with the result that the Act, properly construed, would never have conferred upon him any power to make such regulations. His action would therefore not have been committed "under section 3" of the Act, with the result that judicial review would have been available.

The implications of this South African case are highly significant to the present discussion concerning the juridical foundations of review under the British Human Rights Act. The rule-based approach to human rights adjudication, discussed above, conceptualises fundamental rights, in the administrative law sphere, as obligations incumbent upon decision-makers which are unrelated to the scope of the discretion granted to them by Parliament in enabling legislation. In this manner, they do not constitute limits on the jurisdiction or the vires of administrators. It follows that *Anisminic* logic would not vouchsafe judicial review on human rights grounds in the face of an ouster provision. An administrative decision which breached fundamental rights *would* constitute a decision "made under" the relevant empowering legislation, because the obligation to respect human rights would derive not from the limited scope of Parliament's delegation of power but, rather, from a separate rule unrelated to the ambit of the discretion conferred by the enabling statute.[43]

This would lead to the strange position that ouster provisions would bite on human rights review, but not on judicial review on traditional, procedure-oriented grounds (which would continue to be rationalised through the ultra vires doctrine and, therefore, to which *Anisminic* reasoning would be applicable). The framers of the Human Rights Act surely cannot have intended this result. It is therefore appropriate that they placed the implication- based methodology of ultra vires at its heart. Embracing human rights as interpretative constructs ensures that the logic of the *Anisminic* case can be deployed in order to minimise the impact of preclusive provisions on the operation of the courts' new rights-based review jurisdiction.

[43] It should be noted that the conceptualisation of human rights as rules, rather than as interpretative constructs, in relation to non-statutory power is of no relevance in the present context, because statutory ouster provisions are only ever an issue in relation to judicial review of statutory power.

2. Collateral challenge

The vires-based model is to be preferred over its rule-based counterpart for a second, connected reason. It is a logical function of the doctrine of ultra vires that administrative action which is committed beyond the powers of the decision-maker is void as a matter of law. Once this important point is appreciated, it becomes apparent that ultra vires decisions should be capable of being questioned not only directly in judicial review proceedings, but also collaterally in any other relevant proceedings.

These conclusions follow from first principles. In order for a public administrator to make a decision or commit an act which impacts upon the legal rights or obligations of others, the rule of law – or, more specifically, the principle of legality – requires the existence of positive legal justification.[44] This proposition was classically established in *Entick* v. *Carrington*.[45] The ultra vires doctrine is concerned with the scope of the executive's power and, more particularly, with the question whether, in a particular case, an administrator has remained within or trespassed beyond the limits of his power. Hence to determine that a decision was reached ultra vires is to hold that it lacks the requisite legal authorisation and must, therefore, be void.[46] As I remark elsewhere in this volume,[47] it follows that, provided ultra vires is recognised as the basis of administrative law, the issue whether an executive decision has been reached in contravention of the principles of good administration should be capable of being raised not only directly in judicial review proceedings, but also collaterally in other proceedings. It would affront the rule of law if, for instance, a defendant in a criminal trial could not raise in his defence the argument that the regulations under which he was charged did not, in truth, rest on any satisfactory legal basis.

However, this analysis would not necessarily hold if ultra vires were abandoned as the foundation of judicial review. Under such an approach, the obligation to abide by the principles of good administration and human rights norms would be supplied respectively by the common law and section 6(1) of the Human Rights Act 1998. Crucially, enabling legislation which conferred decision-making authority upon administrators would not be inherently limited by reference to any obligation to adhere to the principles of good administration or to human rights standards. Consequently any analysis of administrators' power

---

[44] Indeed in *R.* v. *Somerset County Council, ex parte Fewings*, Laws J in the Divisional Court ([1995] 1 All ER 513, 524) and Sir Thomas Bingham MR in the Court of Appeal ([1995] 3 All ER 20, 25) went further by suggesting that there must exist positive legal justification for *anything* which a public authority does because, unlike individuals, such authorities possess no residual liberties (although *cf. Malone* v. *Metropolitan Police Commissioner* [1979] Ch. 344 and the views of T.C. Dainith, "The Techniques of Government" in J. Jowell and D. Oliver, *The Changing Constitution* (Oxford, 1994, 3rd ed.), p. 211).

[45] (1765) 19 St. Tr. 1030; 95 ER 807.

[46] See e.g., *F. Hoffman-La Roche and Co. AG* v. *Secretary of State for Trade and Industry* [1975] AC 295, 365, *per* Lord Diplock.

[47] See below, "Legislative Intention versus Judicial Creativity? Administrative Law as a Co-operative Endeavour" below pp. 364–8.

in terms of the jurisdiction conferred by enabling legislation would reveal legal authority for the commission of acts which abrogated procedural and substantive public law norms. It would not, therefore, necessarily follow that decisions reached in breach of those norms would be void and susceptible to collateral challenge. On the contrary, it would be possible to conclude that such decisions ought to stand until and unless they were set aside in judicial review proceedings.

I point out elsewhere in this volume that the Divisional Court's decision in *Bugg v. Director of Public Prosecutions*[48] points towards the correctness of this argument. Woolf LJ delineated two categories of defect in the administrative decision-making process.[49] Decisions which were "substantively invalid" – because, for example, their subject-matter fell outwith the competence conferred by statute – were to be treated as void and therefore susceptible to collateral challenge.[50] It was implicit that Woolf LJ accepted this was a vires or jurisdictional issue; indeed, his Lordship has acknowledged, extra-curially, that the ultra vires doctrine forms an adequate foundation for this aspect of administrative law.[51] Different reasoning, however, applied to decisions which had been adopted pursuant to a faulty decision-making process: such "procedurally invalid" action could not be challenged collaterally (in which case it would have to be characterised as voidable, not void).[52] Given that voidness and amenability to collateral challenge are ineluctable consequences of ultra vires executive action, it must follow that, according to Woolf LJ's analysis, procedural defectiveness was not to be treated as a jurisdictional issue, so that judicial review on grounds such as natural justice would have to be rationalised by reference to a rule-based, not a vires-based, model. Indeed Woolf LJ acknowledged in relatively clear terms that his conclusions regarding voidness and collateral challenge were based on the view that certain principles of good administration, such as those which relate to procedural fairness, rest on foundations other than the ultra vires principle;[53] thus he said that he would "not categorise procedural invalidity as being properly a question of *excess* or abuse of power".[54]

---

[48] [1993] QB 473.

[49] *Bugg* was concerned with byelaws; however, since the principles enunciated were of general application, references will be made to administrative decisions, which term shall be used to include the making of byelaws.

[50] [1993] QB 473, 494.

[51] "*Droit Public* – English Style" [1995] *PL* 57, 65.

[52] [1993] QB 473, 494.

[53] This approach, which envisages two categories of grounds of review, one founded on ultra vires and the other on the common law, echoes the approach of the South African Appellate Division in the *UDF* case, op. cit., n. 42.

[54] [1993] QB 473, 500 (emphasis added). However, in *R. v. Secretary of State for the Home Department, ex parte Fayed* [1997] 1 All ER 228, 231, Lord Woolf MR resiled from this position: implicitly acknowledging that procedural fairness is a facet of ultra vires, he stated that when the courts insist that administrators adopt a fair decision-making procedure, they are simply "ensuring that decisions of the executive are taken in the manner required by Parliament".

Orthodoxy has now been restored by the decision of the House of Lords in *Boddington* v. *British Transport Police*.[55] The applicant had been prosecuted for the breach of a byelaw which he claimed had been unlawfully activated. Their Lordships held that individuals who find themselves in this position must be able to raise *any* relevant defects in the regulations under which they are charged, including what Woolf LJ would have characterised as procedural defects.[56] This conclusion followed from the fact that ultra vires was the organising principle of administrative law: any legally recognised shortcoming in the decision-making process is therefore to be characterised as a species of ultra vires, with the result that defectiveness necessarily entails voidness and amenability to collateral challenge.

Thus it becomes apparent that the manner in which the juridical basis of judicial review under the Human Rights Act is characterised may have important practical consequences. If the rule-based model, described above, was adopted as the rationalisation of rights-oriented review, fundamental rights would not constitute jurisdictional limits on the powers of public decision-makers with the consequence that abrogation of rights standards would not necessarily render administrative action void and vulnerable to collateral challenge. This is significant since, as Lord Steyn observed in *Boddington*, "The possibility of judicial review will . . . in no way compensate [a defendant] for the loss of *the right* to defend himself by a defensive challenge to the byelaw".[57]

Now that *Boddington* has reaffirmed the logical consequences of the fact that all of the existing grounds of review are species of ultra vires, it would be lamentable and anomalous if the new rights-oriented grounds of review were characterised in rule- rather than vires-based terms, with the result that breach of fundamental rights would not necessarily render an administrative act collaterally impeachable. Such an approach, said Lord Steyn, would be "unacceptable . . . in a democracy based on the rule of law" since the consequences – particularly for defendants in criminal proceedings – "are too austere and indeed too authoritarian to be compatible with the traditions of the common law".[58] Although these remarks concerned the existing principles of administrative law, they apply with equal force to the new grounds of challenge which the Human Rights Act will introduce.

It should be noted, at this point, that there exists a fairly obvious retort to the contention, advanced above, that the related concepts of vires and voidness are necessary in order to vouchsafe the collateral impeachability of executive action which affronts human rights. Section 7(1)(b) of the Human Rights Act provides that an individual may "rely" on a breach of Convention rights "in any legal proceedings". At first glance, it may seem that this statutorily guarantees the availability of collateral challenge in cases where Convention rights have been

---

[55] [1998] 2 WLR 639.
[56] Unless, of course, Parliament has made clear contrary provision: see *R.* v. *Wicks* [1998] AC 92.
[57] *Boddington*, op. cit., n. 55, pp. 663–4.
[58] Ibid.

infringed, meaning that such challenge would be possible irrespective of whether a vires-based or rule-based model was used to explain human rights review. However, such reasoning is faulty. Notwithstanding section 7(1)(b), it is necessary to retain the ideas of vires and voidness if collateral attack is to be possible on human rights grounds. This proposition is best substantiated by example.

Assume that an individual is prosecuted, in a magistrates' court, for breaching a certain byelaw. The defendant wishes to argue, in his defence, that the relevant byelaw was made in breach of one or more of the Convention rights. He will, therefore, bring this matter to the attention of the magistrates, as he is entitled to do under section 7(1)(b). If the magistrates are satisfied that there has been a breach of the Convention, it becomes necessary to determine what they can do about it. It is at this point that the distinction between the vires-based and rule-based models becomes crucial.

If it is acknowledged that human rights take effect as interpretative constructs, so that they represent inherent limits on statutory powers, no problem arises. The byelaw is ultra vires and hence void. The defendant can therefore successfully raise the breach of Convention rights, and can escape conviction on the ground that the byelaw under which he was charged is without legal effect.

However, if human rights are free-standing rules which have nothing to do with the internal contours of statutory powers, the position is very different. Notwithstanding that section 7(1)(b) allows the defendant to rely on his Convention rights, there is nothing which the magistrates' court can do in response to such reliance. The reasoning is as follows. Within the rule-based model, the byelaw is not ultra vires and therefore need not be conceptualised as void; instead, it may be voidable, as the reasoning in *Bugg* illustrates.[59] Voidable administrative action is valid and legally effective unless and until it is quashed by a court of competent jurisdiction. However, a magistrates' court does not have the power to quash unlawful administrative action. Moreover, section 8(1) of the Human Rights Act is of no avail here, since it merely allows a court to "grant such relief or remedy" as is "within its powers": *certiorari* is quite clearly outwith the powers of a magistrates' court. In result the byelaw, which has been made in breach of the Convention, remains valid unless it is quashed on judicial review.

It may be argued that it is implicit in section 7(1)(b) that there exists a power, in cases of collateral challenge, to quash executive action which is in breach of Convention rights. However, this would represent a very strained construction of the Act. The most natural interpretation is to accept that the reliance which section 7(1)(b) allows litigants to place on Convention infringements presupposes – in line with orthodox administrative law reasoning – that executive action which is unlawful for breach of the Convention is ultra vires and therefore void. Adopting this approach carries the dual benefits that section 7(1)(b)

---

[59] *Bugg v. Director of Public Prosecutions* [1993] QB 473.

can be accorded a natural construction, while litigants are truly able to rely on their Convention rights collaterally as well as directly. Once again, it becomes apparent that the theory of ultra vires is central to the effective functioning of the Human Rights Act.

Forsyth comments that the *Boddington* decision shows with great clarity that "the rule of law, the ultra vires doctrine and the voidness [and amenability to collateral challenge] of unlawful administrative acts are linked together", thereby forming the foundations of administrative law.[60] It is these same foundations upon which judicial review under the Human Rights Act must rest, and conceptualising fundamental rights, in the administrative law sphere, as interpretative constructs vouchsafes this position. Not only is this conclusion dictated by the principle of parliamentary sovereignty; it follows equally from a consideration of more tangible matters such as the impact of preclusive clauses and the amenability to collateral challenge of administrative action which fails to respect human rights. The vires-based model is therefore to be preferred both for reasons of constitutional theory and in the light of its consequences for individuals and the rule of law.

IV. CONCLUSION

One of the defining features of the Human Rights Act 1998 is its apparent capacity to reconcile the promotion of fundamental rights with the hallowed principle of parliamentary sovereignty. The constitutional controversy and difficulty which would have arisen had any attempt been made at entrenchment has been obviated by the provision of a strong interpretative obligation together with the novel[61] declaration of incompatibility. The purpose of this paper has been to demonstrate that the reconciliation between rights and constitutional theory which the framers of the Human Rights Act have sought to effect raises particular issues in the administrative law field. Special care must be exercised so as to rationalise the theoretical underpinnings of judicial review on human rights grounds in a way that is consistent with the Act's desire to conform to the dictates of parliamentary sovereignty.

The shortcomings of the ultra vires doctrine as it is traditionally understood have long militated in favour of its abandonment as the foundation of the existing law of judicial review, in favour of a set of common law rules of good administration. Although it has been argued elsewhere that such an approach is neither necessary nor constitutionally appropriate,[62] the temptation

---

[60] C.F. Forsyth, "Collateral Challenge and the Foundations of Judicial Review: Orthodoxy Vindicated and Procedural Exclusivity Rejected" [1998] *PL* 364. See also M.C. Elliott, "*Boddington*: Rediscovering the Constitutional Logic of Administrative Law" [1998] *Judicial Review* 144.

[61] Although this idea is not altogether new: H. Lauterpacht, *An International Bill of the Rights of Man* (New York, 1945), p. 193, suggested that such an approach would effect a useful compromise between the sovereignty principle and the need for effective protection of human rights.

[62] See Forsyth, op. cit., nn. 18 and 23; Elliott, op. cit., nn. 15 and 18.

to conceptualise the new, rights-oriented heads of review as straightforward rules rather than as interpretative constructs is greater still, given that section 6(1) of the Human Rights Act appears to offer an explicit basis for such an approach.

Nevertheless, it has been argued in this paper that to characterise the new grounds of review in rule-based terms is to render the non-entrenched Human Rights Act constitutionally unworkable. It is the familiar, implication-based ultra vires doctrine which must be drawn upon in order to facilitate, in terms of constitutional logic, the operation of the human rights legislation in the field of judicial review. Only by recourse to such interpretative methodology is it possible to fashion a juridical basis for the new rights-based public law jurisdiction which is compatible with the orthodoxy of legislative supremacy, a principle which is itself embraced by the Human Rights Act.

It may be thought surprising that the ultra vires doctrine is of such continued importance as English public law begins to reinvent itself by embracing a new, rights-based legal culture. Such a perception, however, overlooks the realities of the constitutional order. Just as the implication-oriented ultra vires principle has effected the reconciliation of the dramatic expansion of judicial review in recent decades with the theory of parliamentary sovereignty, so it will also play a fundamental role in the juridical underpinning of the further development of judicial review as human rights eventually become part of English law. It is the deep foundations of constitutional logic on which the ultra vires principle rests – and, in particular, its recognition of the need to reconcile respect for individuals' rights, whether procedural or substantive, with the constitutional framework – which explains its ubiquitous relevance to both the long history of English administrative law and the new dawn of constitutionalism which is now breaking.

Judicial Review of Statutory and Non-Statutory Discretion

13

Public Power and Private Power

SIR STEPHEN SEDLEY

English Law is entering what is certainly a new phase, possibly a new era. By passing the Human Rights Act 1998 Parliament has not simply added another statute to an already crammed statute book. Rather it has called on the executive and judicial arms of the state, and has in effect pledged itself, to respect the norms set out in a treaty, the European Convention on Human Rights, to which the United Kingdom has been a party since its inception in 1950. Despite, however, being one of the prime movers in the drafting of the Convention, it was not until 1966 that the United Kingdom gave its citizens the right of individual petition to the European Court of Human Rights, and it is only now that the United Kingdom Parliament has made the Convention rights a part of its domestic law.

Lord Denning, in one of the first judgments on the effect of the European Communities Act 1972, likened the Treaty of Rome in a striking simile to an incoming tide flowing into the estuaries and up the rivers of our geographical and political island.[1] The Human Rights Act deserves a different metaphor – perhaps that of a dye which will colour the fabric of our law except in those places where the fabric is impervious to it. This is because the Act, at least on the face of it, follows the New Zealand model of infiltrating rights to the extent that the statute book will tolerate them. We already have some experience under the European Communities Act 1972 of reshaping the language of domestic legislation – even mildly torturing it – to make it speak the words of European directives;[2] and we may well find that the exercise of doing the same with Convention rights is not unduly casuistic or offensive to our linguistic sensibility in the great majority of cases.[3] For the common law, for delegated legislation, and for administrative

---

[1] *Bulmer Ltd* v. *Bollinger SA* [1974] Ch. 401 at 418.

[2] See *Pickstone* v. *Freemans* [1989] AC 66, *per* Lord Oliver at 125–128.

[3] In a paper delivered in 1998 to the Franco-British Lawyers' Association in London, Roger Errera, Conseiller d'Etat, said that he had traced only two cases in which the French courts had been unable to make domestic legislation conform with the Convention. This may have in part to do with the laconic and open-textured mode of French legislative drafting. In Canada provincial and federal legislation has repeatedly been found incompatible with the Charter: see the comprehensive schedule in Peter Hogg and Alison Bushell, "The Charter Dialogue between Courts and Legislatures" (1997) 35 Osgoode Hall L.J. 75. This is, at least in part, because the Canadian courts, armed with the power to strike down, have declined to adopt more catholic canons of construction in order to avoid conflict: see Andrew Butler, "A presumption of statutory conformity with the Charter" (1993) 19 Queens L.J. 209. Somewhere in between stands New Zealand's experience with section 6 of the Bill of Rights Act 1990: see Michael Taggart, "Tugging on Superman's Cape" [1998] PL 266 at section 280–286; *cf* Paul Rishworth's early exhortation "The potential of a Bill of Rights" [1990] NZLJ

policies and practices, there is no such problem: they must all yield to the Convention rights.

Where, however, the Human Rights Act encounters primary legislation which simply will not accommodate it, the courts have been given a new tool – the declaration of incompatibility. Furnished with such a declaration, ministers will have the power to amend the offending statute by the use of "remedial orders". They will also, in a relevant sense, have a duty to do so because – and it is this which distinguishes the United Kingdom's situation sharply not only from that of New Zealand but from that of every other common law country with a Bill of Rights – the entire state, Parliament included, is under a treaty obligation to conform to the Convention. What remains to be seen is how government will respond to a judicial declaration of incompatibility with which it disagrees. Governments appear now to have no right of appeal to the Court of Human Rights in Strasbourg: it is only the aggrieved individual who may petition the Court.[4] Will government therefore respect the court's ruling whatever its reservations, or will it have to adopt the inelegant expedient of refusing to change the law and compelling the individual to take the state before the Strasbourg court for non-compliance, so that Her Majesty's Government can argue that Her Majesty's courts have got it wrong?

It would be pleasant if the unpredictabilities ended here, but they don't. One major imponderable is the measure of the courts' receptivity to human rights issues. There is no doubt that across the common law world the atmosphere has changed in the last two decades. We have seen the Supreme Court of India beginning to draw out of the once dormant constitution a striking series of social, economic and environmental rights.[5] In Canada, where the now forgotten Bill of Rights 1960 had sunk like a lead balloon, the 1982 Charter of Rights and Freedoms in the hands of a creative Supreme Court has transformed the country's legal and political culture. The High Court of Australia has discovered an unexpected batch of civil rights in a constitution which for almost a century had been thought to contain none.[6] New Zealand has established that the omission from its 1990 Bill of Rights of any provision for special remedies will not prevent the courts giving damages for violations.[7] There is no reason to think that the courts of the United Kingdom will be insensitive to this wind of

68 at 69–70. But Lord Cooke of Thorndon has said that he "may be wrong" in his dictum in *Ministry of Transport* v. *Noort* [1992] 3 NZLR 260 at 272 that section 6 "does not authorise a strained interpretation": see "The British embracement of human rights", [1999] 3 EHRLR 243. (The error, if error there is, may lie in no more than the choice of epithet.)

⁴ ECHR (as amended by Protocol 11), Art. 34. The former Art. 48, giving wider recourse, has gone.

⁵ See, for a seminal instance, *People's Union for Democratic Rights* v. *Union of India*, Bhagwati and Islam JJ., May 11, 1982; published as *Observe Labour Laws* by the Baliga Foundation. *Cf* the 1996 Constitution of South Africa, Arts 22–29, which spells out a series of such rights.

⁶ See *Australian Capital TV Pty Ltd* v. *Commonwealth* (1992) 177 CLR 106; *Nationwide News Pty Ltd* v. *Wills* (1992) 177 CLR 1. I have commented on these remarkable decisions in "The Sound of Silence: constitutional law without a constitution" (1994) 110 LQR 270 at 276.

⁷ *Simpson* v. *A-G (Baigent's Case)* [1994] 3 NZLR 667.

change. But it may be a mistake to suppose that the success or failure of a rights instrument is no more than a matter of judicial inclination. It is going to be fully as much a consequence of how lawyers shape up to the task. If Convention rights are used simply as fallbacks where other arguments have failed, the Human Rights Act may well become devalued. Convention rights will acquire the throwaway status of *Wednesbury* unreasonableness – a contention so regularly used as a makeweight that in the handful of cases where it really might be relevant it provokes unwarranted scepticism. If on the other hand lawyers (especially those now coming through the law schools) learn to discern the viable human rights issues in fact situations and to argue these with discrimination and skill as organic elements of their case, the courts themselves will be helped to understand the relevance and purpose of the Human Rights Act and a human rights culture may begin to take root.

Let me assume the best – that the legal system will adapt to the new approach, and that judges, academics and practitioners will learn steadily from each other as time goes by. I assume it readily because I think it is the likeliest scenario. If so, I believe that there are two major tranches of jurisprudence which are going to demand continuing attention. The first is the question of substantive as opposed to formal equality before the law. The second, which I want to focus on in this lecture, is what is commonly but misleadingly called the horizontal effect of human rights. What it signifies is the proposition that it is not only the state but individuals and, importantly, corporations who are required to respect the human rights of others: in other words, that in the field of human rights the substantive division of the public from the private sphere is or ought to be immaterial.

This is certainly not the pure paradigm of rights from which instruments such as the European Convention derive. Historically such rights belong with the nineteenth-century liberal view that the state, at best a necessary evil, is the natural enemy of the individual. In my first lecture I looked at some of the implications for the common law of this too-ready conflation of liberty with individualism. The function of a rights instrument, taken on this premise, is to show the state a red light in its dealings with its citizens.[8] Insofar as the state is credited with a potentially benign role – a green light role – it is to be found in the exceptions which follow all but the absolute rights in the Convention: for example where the individual right of peaceful association with others is qualified by a limited power of restriction in the interests of public safety, public order and so forth.[9] But there is nowhere in the European Convention an articulated concept of the state as a repository of obligations which citizens have the right to expect it to discharge: obligations, for example, to assure so far as

---

[8] As this paper, I hope, indicates, I do not accept that the sole role of public law is to show the state a red light. Like amber-light theorists I would regard public power as a necessity, not simply as a necessary evil. See M. Partington, "The reform of public law in Britain" in McAuslan and McEldowney, ed., *Law, Legitimacy and the Constitution* (1985).

[9] Article 11.

possible a life free from fear or a safe environment. These are not economic rights, which of course throw up questions of affordability; they are, no doubt social rights in the sense that they are enjoyed either collectively or not at all; but that they would feature in any human rights instrument being written today is, I would suggest, beyond doubt.

Yet even accepting, as one must, that history (and a measure of politics) has given us in the course of the twentieth century a series of rights instruments with more to connect them with the nineteenth century than with the twenty-first, the question of the public and the private keeps presenting itself. Horizontality is a convenient portmanteau term, but the image it calls up is not really apposite.[10] It is predicated on a model of human rights as essentially a bottom-upward process, travelling in the vertical plane from individual to state. By way of contrast it posits a horizontal cross-flow from individual to individual. Described in this way, the two axes correspond precisely with the assumed dichotomy of law's public and private spheres, and the metaphor reinforces the sense that these are as different as any two dimensions are. But the reasoning which questions the division of the public from the private has nothing to do with turning Convention rights through 90 degrees. It has to do with the much more direct issue of how the state is to fulfil the obligations which individual human rights thrust upon it, and this in turn has to do with the nature and meaning of the state in the context of the Convention and the new Human Rights Act.

The Act is unequivocal in imposing its obligations on the judicial and executive arms of the state. "It is unlawful", it says, "for a public authority to act in a way which is incompatible with one or more of the Convention rights"; and a public authority is explicitly defined so as to include the courts but to exclude Parliament. It will mean that both the substantive doctrines of the common law and equity and the orders made by the courts must meet the Convention's standards. Now the common law at present possesses no tort of invasion of privacy. Article 8 of the Convention, however, says "Everyone has the right to respect for his private and family life, his home and his correspondence." This is straightforward enough when the threat to a person's privacy comes from the state: the court can intervene to ensure that any interference lies within the permitted exceptions. Equally, if one simply regards the activities of non-state entities as lying along a different axis, the court will be powerless whether the threat to privacy comes from the next-door neighbour or a transnational news corporation. But what then becomes of the court's own obligation to act compatibly with the Convention? Does it extend to developing a body of law which will protect individuals from all violations of their Convention rights from whatever source? Because the metaphor has become part of the argument, and because – for reasons I have given – horizontality

---

[10] Its immediate lineage is in the jurisprudence of the European Union, where a geometric image of the possible reach of directives is more apposite.

seems to me to assume the very thing that needs to be debated, I propose to call this not horizontal but cascade effect.[11]

A great deal may turn, under the new United Kingdom Human Rights Act, on the deliberate inclusion of the courts – the judicial arm of the state – in the general obligation to give effect to the Convention rights. This may seem an obvious requirements of a rights instrument, but the Canadian Charter does not have this effect: early in its life the Supreme Court held that its structure and wording were such that the courts were free to make orders which themselves violated the Charter.[12] Other jurisdictions, by contrast, including the European Court of Human Rights have validated at least the availability of a cascade effect by holding that the courts themselves, being part of the state which is required to assure the delivery of rights, may be under an obligation to take legal steps to prevent interference by non-state actors with a Convention right.[13]

[11] Any metaphor risks misleading, but Lord Cooke's image of "interweaving" the scheduled rights into the common law (*op. cit.*) is a valuable one. Geometric vocabulary might drive one to say that Ireland is the only common law country to have achieved complete horizontality: see *Meskell v. Coras Iompair Eireann* [1973] IR 121 at 132–133, *per* Walsh J. I hope to be forgiven for not using the German coinage *Drittwirkung der Grundrechte* (third-party effect of basic rights), which again suggests an artificial extension of the natural ambit of rights – in the language of the common law, a *jus quaesitum tertio*. Murray Hunt in his incisive article "The 'horizontal effect' of the Human Rights Act" [1998] PL 423 postulates a spectrum in order to escape from the polarities of the geometric metaphor. An elegant exposition of the universality of rights can be found in the dissenting judgment of Kriegler J. in *Du Plessis* v. *de Klerk* 1996 (3) S.A. 850 at 914–915.

[12] *Dolphin Delivery* 33 DLR (4th) 174 (1985); [1986] SCR 573. But see *R.* v. *Lerke* 25 DLR (4th) 403 (1986) (Alberta CA), holding that a citizen's arrest was subject to the same Charter restrictions as a police arrest. This has recently been followed in New Zealand: *NZ Police* v. *Song Van Nguyen* (Wellington DC) July 21, 1998. See also *Slaight Communications* v. *Davidson* 59 DLR (4th) 416 at 442–444 (1989).

[13] *X and Y* v. *The Netherlands* (1986) 8 EHRR 235 at 239–240 (no. 29); *Plattform "Aertzte für das Leben"* v. *Austria* (1988) 13 EHRR 204 at 210 (#32); *Gustavfsson* v. *Sweden* (1996) 22 EHRR 409 at 435–436 (45); *Young et al* v. *U.K.* (1982) 4 EHRR 38; *A* v. *U.K.* (Commission, September 18, 1997). Similar conclusions have been reached by the Inter-American Court of Human Rights (*Velasquez Rodriguez* v. *Honduras* 9 HRLJ 212–249 (1988)). The UN Human Rights Committee, in comments issued under Article 40(4) of the International Covenant on Civil and Political Rights (the basis of New Zealand's Bill of Rights Act 1990) has expressed the clear view that the rights of privacy and of freedom from inhuman treatment are entitled to state protection whether the threat to them comes from public or private sources (44th session, 1992; 32nd session, 1988). The New Zealand Court of Appeal has recognised the force of the argument, without so far explicitly adopting it: see *R.* v. *H.* [1994] 2 NZLR 143 at 147; *Lange* v. *Atkinson* [1997] 2 NZLR 22 at 32 (Elias J. affirmed on appeal), following *Duff* v. *Communicado Ltd* [1996] 2 NZLR 89 (Blanchard J.). Valuable academic comment on the possibility of a cascade effect of the Human Rights Act includes Sir William Wade Q.C., "Human rights and the judiciary" (Judicial Studies Board Lecture, 1998); Murray Hunt, *op. cit.* [1998] PL 423; Andrew Butler, "The NZ Bill of Rights and private common law litigation, [1991] NZLJ 261] and, from a more sceptical standpoint, Ian, Leigh, "Horizontal rights . . . lessons from the Commonwealth" (1999) 48 Int. and Comp. L.Q. 57. For illuminating comparative studies see Andrew Butler, "Private litigation and constitutional rights under the 1996 [S.A.] Constitution – assistance from Ireland" (1999) 116 SALJ 77, and B.S. Markesinis, "Privacy, freedom of expression and the horizontal effect of the Human Rights Bill: lessons from Germany" (the 1998 Wilberforce Lecture), (1999) LQR 47. It is noteworthy that the cascade effect, doubted by Sydney Kentridge Q.C. among others under the 1993 Interim Constitution of South Africa, is now spelt out in the final version by section 8 of the definitive Constitution. The effect seems in any event to flow inexorably from conflicts between two guaranteed rights: see *Re J* [1996] 2 NZLR 134, concerning a clash between a parent's freedom of religion and a child's right to life; and see ECHR, Art. 17.

There are convincing reasons why the courts might well consider giving a cascade effect to the Article 8 guarantee of privacy. The case for privacy legislation has been cogently made in a paper given by the present Lord Chief Justice, Lord Bingham.[14] He argues that the need is apparent and that none of the objections – interference with freedom of expression, difficulty of definition, the preferability of self-regulation and the alternative possibility of a common law solution – is convincing. Lord Hoffmann has advanced a separate and equally powerful case for a non-Convention-based common law right of privacy.[15] The *Guardian*'s editor Alan Rusbridger has also cautiously added his voice:

> Is it conceivable that . . . there is a case for a privacy law, if drafted carefully and interpreted sensibly by a discerning judiciary? That self-regulation has frequently been a fig-leaf behind which we have disguised our unease?[16]

The correspondingly strong case for a cascade application of Convention rights under Article 8 meets, however, what is both a jurisprudential and a psychological block in the mindset which allocates rights and remedies to a domain which has to be either public or private. It is this that I want to examine and, as will become apparent, contest.

Twelve years ago the present Master of the Rolls, Lord Woolf, delivered a seminal paper called "Public and private: why the divide?" He answered his own question with a convincing analysis of the need for separate sets of rules to govern challenges to public bodies and contests between natural or legal persons. In short, as pointed out, there are requirements of speed and certainty which make it necessary for the rules governing public law claims to differ significantly from those governing civil litigation. Analogous arguments hold good for many other branches of legal practice. But to accept this is not necessarily to accept that there is, or ought to be, a comparable jurisprudential divide between the private and the public.

Let me start with what is perhaps the most fundamental of all public law concepts, the notion of ultra vires. The process of doggerelisation which has turned this adverbial or adjectival phrase into a noun can stand as a symbol of its metamorphosis from a doctrine of company law into one of public law. The early attitude of the law to limited companies was that, once brought into being, typically by the exercise of the Royal Prerogative, they could operate as freely, and if they wished as capriciously, as natural persons. In tandem with this, the courts from an early date[17] developed a hands-off policy towards the internal affairs of limited companies, culminating in 1843 in the decision in *Foss* v. *Harbottle*,[18]

---

[14] "Should there be a law to protect rights to personal privacy?" (1996) 5 EHRLR 450. See also Rabinder Singh, "Privacy and the media after the Human Rights Act" [1998] EHRR 712.

[15] "Mind your own business", the 1996 Goodman Lecture.

[16] Alan Rusbridger, *The Freedom of the Press and other Platitudes* (James Cameron Memorial Lecture, 1997).

[17] See *Carlen* v. *Drury* (1812) 1 Ves. & Bea. 154, *per* Lord Eldon L.C.

[18] (1843) 2 Hare 461. The doctrine has had to be diluted to deal with the worst abuses, including ultra vires acts: see *Edwards* v. *Halliwell* [1950] 2 All ER 1064 at 1066–1067.

forbidding the use of legal process by a minority of shareholders to challenge the propriety of what the majority is up to. There is sense in this, not only on Lord Eldon's original ground of caseload control but because the policy of the Companies Act 1844 and its successors was to permit incorporation at will, so long as it was on standardised terms with obligatory registration and disclosure, and thereafter to let the company manage its own affairs. Even so, the hands-off policy of the courts towards limited liability companies contrasts uncomfortably with their interventionism towards (if not all, then some) municipal corporations, culminating in the surcharging of the Poplar councillors in 1925[19] for attempting, ultra vires as it was finally held to be, to pay fair and equal wages to men and women on their staff.

Seward Brice, the earliest scholarly commentator on the ultra vires principle,[20] argued convincingly that it was the abuse of the colossal powers conferred by private Acts of Parliament on the early joint stock railway companies which prompted the courts to set enforceable limits to their powers. The birth of the doctrine in 1846, fully grown like Pantagruel, is to be found in the Master of the Rolls' judgment in *Colman* v. *Eastern Counties Railway Co. Ltd*,[21] holding that things done beyond the ambit of the powers expressly conferred on the company were to be treated by the law as not done at all: were, in other words, null and void (one of the tautologies in which the vocabulary of the law is so rich). With the growth in the powers of municipal corporations and regulatory bodies the doctrine, intelligibly enough, became transferred to them. But the limited liability company, though every bit as much a creature of statute as the municipal corporation, was by the development of the rule in *Foss* v. *Harbottle* progressively cut free of judicial control, turning the doctrine of ultra vires into a rogue's charter by which a company could avoid liability by pleading its own want of power,[22] and returning much of company law to the arena of self-

---

[19] *Roberts* v. *Hopwood* [1925] AC 578, upholding the surcharge and creating the fiduciary obligation which remains central to local government law. The decision does not sit comfortably with the Court of Appeal's earlier decision overturning a surcharge on Westminster City Council for buying horsefeed from the highest bidder (*R.* v. *Roberts* [1908] 1 KB 407).

[20] Brice, *Treatise on the Doctrine of Ultra Vires*, preface to 1st ed., 1874.

[21] (1846) 16 LJ Ch. 73; 10 Beav. 1, blocking the operation of the rule in *Foss* v. *Harbottle* in cases in which a majority could be shown to be taking the company outside its lawful powers.

[22] *Riche* v. *Ashbury Railway Carriage Co. Ltd* (1874) LR 7 HL 653. Brice's comment in 1874 (*loc. cit.*) was: ". . . the Doctrine of Ultra Vires is constantly cropping up in unexpected quarters, and manifesting its effects in an unforeseen and unwelcome manner. One of its first onslaughts was upon the time-honoured maxim of the Common Law that a man cannot stultify himself [n. *Beverley's Case* 4 Rep. 123b.] – that the lunatic, the fool, the drunkard, and the knave, who have made a contract, shall not subsequently repudiate the same by alleging that neither they nor their agents had at the time sufficient brains or authorisation to make it. This maxim the Doctrine of Ultra Vires soon demolished, and corporations may set up their incapacity whenever it is inconvenient for them to carry out their engagements. It next ran full tilt against the less rigid but more equitable principles laid down by the Courts of Lincoln's Inn. 'Who seeks equity must do equity' and 'Who comes for aid to Chancery must come with clean hands' are two of the most elementary principles of the Chancellor's jurisdiction. But the new doctrine refused to allow them to be applied to corporations, and after much wrangling it came off victorious, and corporations can now be relieved from Ultra Vires contracts, and yet keep the benefits thereof [n. with the exceptions and qualifications set forth *post*]."

regulation. The process of "humanisation" of private corporations perhaps reached its zenith with the recommendation of the Cohen Committee in 1945[23] that the anomaly should be resolved by enacting that "every company . . . should, notwithstanding anything omitted from its memorandum of association, have as regards third parties the same powers as an individual" – a well-meant endeavour to stop companies repudiating their own contracts, but adopting a means which revealed just how far limited companies had been allowed to travel away from being statutory corporations and towards a quasi-human status.[24]

Yet it remains the historical and jurisprudential fact that limited liability and the entities which enjoy it are entirely creatures of statute. They are not conceived of as public bodies because what they do is regarded as by definition their own affair, and courts of judicial review correspondingly take no interest in their activities. But this approach overlooks two major realities, one physical, one legal.

The physical reality is that there are corporations which now carry out functions that until recently *were* the state's, and others which deploy more power in their field of activity than the state does. For the former, it is difficult to see how a function ceases to be a public function simply because of a change in who carries it out. After all, private functions are not regarded as becoming public functions simply because it is the state which conducts them.[25] The rights and obligations of a plumber who is called in to fix the toilets in an office building will not differ depending on whether the building is a government office or a corporate HQ; whichever it is, she will be able to sue for her charges if she is not paid, and no member of the public, however directly affected, is going to have standing to question the necessity for her visit. Why then is the same not true, *mutatis mutandis*, of functions which have an incontestably *public* character? Modern public law has come to recognise that it is the nature and purpose of a power, not necessarily its source or its repository, which determines whether or not its exercise is a public function.[26]

---

[23]   Cmd. 6659.

[24]   The Jenkins Committee in 1962 (Cmnd. 1749) advised the more modest course of giving third parties statutory protection against rogue repudiations. The whole concept of legal personality recalls the episode in Anatole France's satire on the Dreyfus case, *L'Ile des Pingouins*, in which a short-sighted early missionary baptises the population of an island inhabited entirely by penguins in the belief that they are human beings, creating an acrimonious debate among the saints in heaven as to whether the act of baptism has invested the penguins with immortal souls or is, as lawyers would say, ultra vires, null and void. Janet McLean has drawn my attention to the contrast between early north American jurisprudence, treating each company as a "little commonwealth" with corresponding public obligations, and the abrupt holding of the U.S. Supreme Court in *Santa Clara* v. *S. Pacific Railroad* 118 U.S. 394 (1886) that corporations were persons for all Fourteenth Amendment purposes.

[25]   Cf. The Human Rights Act 1998 section 6(5) for an argument that this need not exclude employment rights, see G. Morris, "The Human Rights Act and the public/private divide in employment law" (1998) 27 ILJ 293.

[26]   See Lord Woolf, "Droit public – English style" [1995] PL 57 at 63–64: ". . . it should be the nature of the activity and not the nature of the body which should be decisive . . ."; Krishna Iyer J. in *Som Prakash* v. *Union of India AIR* (1981) SC 212 at 219: "The true test is functional. Not how

The legal reality is something which runs counter to the entire mindset that modern lawyers have absorbed through their professional education and internalised in practice. It is that, in spite of a massive body of doctrinal fiction, legal personality and human personality are two different things. The fiction that the law can invest an abstraction with the qualities of a person of course serves a purpose: to invest with legal rights and liabilities an entity to which the law has given an existence independent of the individuals behind it. But to call such an entity a person, albeit a legal as opposed to a natural person, is mere witch-doctoring to the extent that it pretends to invest the corporation with attributes beyond those which are necessary for its existence. This is of course why the illusion breaks down at those relatively few points where the ultra vires doctrine or some other branch of the law prevents a limited company from doing something that an individual could not be stopped from doing. But such points are not located consistently so as to assimilate private to public corporations; rather the reverse. True, a company is not entitled to spend its money without regard to its shareholders' interests;[27] but the generous leeway permitted by law in terms of directors' perks and corporate hospitality compares unhappily with the decision of Sir Peter O'Brien C.J. in the Irish High Court in 1894 that the cost of a picnic for the Dublin councillors on the occasion of their annual inspection of the Vartry waterworks in the Wicklow Hills should be disallowed and surcharged on the members.

> I now come to deal with the expenditure in respect of the lunch. . . . I think it is relevant to refer to the character of this luncheon. I have before me the items in the bill. Amongst the list of wines are two dozen champagne – Ayala 1885 – a very good branch – at 84s. a dozen; one dozen Marcobrunn hock – a very nice hock; one dozen Chateau Margaux – an excellent claret; one dozen fine old Dublin whiskey – the best whiskey that can be got; one case of Ayala; six bottles of Amontillado sherry – a stimulating sherry; and the ninth item is some more fine Dublin whiskey. . . . There is an allowance for brakes; one box of cigars, 100; coachmen's dinner; beer, stout, minerals in syphons, and ice for wine. There is dessert and there are sandwiches, and an allowance for four glasses broken – a very small number broken under the circumstances. . . .

> The Solicitor-General in his most able argument – I have always to guard myself against his plausibility – appealed pathetically to common sense. He asked, really with tears in his voice, whether the members of the Corporation should starve; he drew a most gruesome picture; he represented that the members of the Corporation would really traverse the Wicklow Hills in a spectral condition unless they were sustained by lunch. I do not know whether he went so far as Ayala, Marcobrunn, Chateau Margaux, old Dublin whiskey and cigars. In answer to the Solicitor-General we do not

---

the legal person is born but why it is created." For a New Zealand perspective, see Janet McLean, "Contracting in the corporatised and privatised environment"; (1996) 7 PLR 223; Michael Taggart, "Public utilities and public law" in Joseph, ed., *Essays on the Constitution* (1995). New Zealand has arguably led the way both politically (in corporatising and privatising public enterprises) and jurisprudentially (in developing an analysis of the consequences).

[27] See Bowen's L.J.'s celebrated "cakes and ale" judgment in *Hutton* v. *West Cork Railway Co.* (1883) 23 Ch. 654.

say that the members of the Corporation are not to lunch. But we do say that they are not to do so at the expenses of the citizens of Dublin.[28]

To take a very different and grimmer example, large numbers of people are the tenants, or the dependants of tenants, of small or medium-sized property companies. Most of them lack security of tenure and an increasing proportion are on short-term lets. If someone in lower or middle management decides for reasons of caprice or spite to refuse to renew the tenancy of a particular family, neither public nor private law offers any redress. Yet if the same were to happen at the hands of a local authority, judicial review would almost certainly be available. In other words, the assimilation of legal to natural persons has travelled well over the boundary between fiction and fact. Among its consequences is the ability of bodies – limited liability companies – which owe their existence entirely to statute to behave as capriciously as an individual is on principle free to do[29] with, at present, uncontrollable consequences for some of people's most basic needs.

This is an issue which is going to become more acute with the introduction of a human rights regime into English law. Are corporations going to rank as persons for the enjoyment of human rights? In Canada, partly because of the phraseology of the Charter, the answer has been a qualified "Yes".[30] The European Court of Human Rights, to whose decisions we are enjoined by the new Act to have regard but not necessarily to adhere, has held that corporations rank as persons under the Convention. In New Zealand, section 29 of the Bill of Rights Act says expressly that they do. I no longer regard this issue, as I once did, as an acid test of the desirability of enacting a domestic Bill of Rights. The fact that corporations are not human, whatever the law tries to say, does not necessarily preclude their arguing for the rights of individuals in their own corporate interests. And in any case no amount of formal exclusion will stop them funding individuals to carry their Convention baggage. My point is the distinct one that unless they are brought within a cascade effect of the Human Rights Act, corporations will be getting both the penny and the bun: a multi-national news corporation will rank as a potential victim of human rights abuse at the hands of the state, able to complain loudly of official violations of its right of free expression – yet people whose privacy it invades in the name of free expression will be said have no constitutional redress against it. They will be left to scrab-

---

[28] *R (Bridgeman)* v. *Drury* [1894] 1 IR 489 at 495–497. The case is conclusive authority for the proposition that there is no such thing as a free lunch.

[29] Antony Shaw has drawn to my attention G.B. Shaw, *Everybody's Political What's What* (1944), p. 44: 2: 4 "Mr British Everyman thinks that he is governed by two authorities only: the House of Commons, elected by his vote, and the House of Lords, which he hopes will soon be abolished, although it is far more representative of him, coming into the world as it does, like himself, by the accident of birth. Really he is governed by as many authorities as the Russians: by his trade union or professional association, by his cooperative society, by his employers federation, by his church, by his bankers, by his employers and by his landlords. Most of these have practically irresponsible powers over him to which no responsible state department dare pretend."

[30] See *R.* v. *Big M Drug Mart Ltd* 18 DLR (4th) 321 (1985).

ble uncertainly in the present patchy law of breach of confidence. I know of no principle of law or justice which can validate such a paradigm of rights. A cascade model, by contrast, will carry a flow of rights and remedies from the Convention through the Act and into the courts, and from the courts into enforceable forms of recourse to the Convention right of privacy, whoever is responsible for the breach.

So far so good. But Article 8(1), which confers the primary right, is followed by Article 8(2) which sets out a series of grounds upon which the state can justify an invasion of it. It starts: "There shall be no interference by a public authority with the exercise of this right except . . .". A corporation, however large, is not a public authority. What are the courts then to do about the plain need for a free press to be able to investigate and expose serious wrongdoing, as at least one element of the British broadsheet press has done with conspicuous success in recent years? The answer lies in the cascade itself: although a corporation is not, a court *is* a public authority. To the same extent as it is empowered to give effect to the primary right of privacy it will be empowered to permit such interference "as is in accordance with the law and is necessary in a democratic society in the interests of national security, public safety or the economic wellbeing of the country, for the prevention of disorder or crime, for the protection of health or morals, or for the protection of the rights and freedoms of others". The elegance of this solution lies in the fact that it does not put the news corporation on a par with the state: the licence accorded to each is limited by what is necessary in a democratic society – a test which is likely to produce different answers for a police investigation and a tabloid stakeout.[31]

I do not want to suggest that this is at present more than a fruitful line of inquiry. The courts will have in due course to consider not only the questions I have been exploring but the significance of the omission from the Act of Article 13 of the Convention, which guarantees a remedy for every violation "notwithstanding that the violation has been committed by persons acting in an official capacity".[32] We shall also need to give careful attention to the composition of

---

[31] I am happier with this solution, in any event, than with the Privacy and Defamation Bill proposed by the Guardian's editor Alan Rusbridger. This offers a trade-off: a right of privacy, couched in the language of Article 8, in return for a *Sullivan* defence of reasonable belief to libel actions. It exempts corporations (and, more dubiously, partnerships) from the protective ambit of the right of privacy. But the right is also made subject to a public interest defence which includes "preventing the public from being misled by some statement or action of a public figure". This seems to take us back to where we started.

[32] Whether this is a restrictive provision which confines justiciable violations to those committed by officials, or an expansive one which underlines that act of state is by itself no answer to a breach, it seems likely that the omission has been made by Parliament to achieve (among other things) consistency with the prohibition on disapplying incompatible primary legislation. Instead the Act itself, by section 8, gives the courts power to grant any appropriate remedy within their jurisdiction. This overlooks, however, the fact that there are many persons other than MPs and judges who, acting in an official capacity, can and arguably should give an effective remedy for violations of people's Convention rights. Francis Jacobs (Advocate General at the European Court of Justice) and Robin White in *The European Convention on Human Rights* (2nd ed.), pp. 18–19, reach the unequivocal conclusion that "Article 13, by providing in effect that it should not be a defence that the violation

section 6 of the Act: does the inclusion of public bodies imply the exclusion of private ones? Alongside these high-profile questions we shall have to learn to handle Article 17 which, echoing the classic statement of Article 4 of the 1789 *Déclaration des Droits de l'Homme* that freedom is the right to do anything that does not harm others, forbids the use of Convention rights to undermine the Convention rights of others. If this is not a horizontal or cascade effect, albeit negatively couched, I do not know what is.

I need to return from here to the issue I touched on earlier – the learned response of our generation of public lawyers that the ultra vires principle is the basis of all public law.[33] Historically there is an apparent symmetry in the transfer from private to public corporations of doctrines of limited power during the years of the nineteenth century in which the corporate state began to take shape. Some of the leading decisions of the Victorian judiciary make it pretty plain that they were consciously setting about controlling the power of a state which was interfering on a growing scale with an entrepreneurial society of such vigour that it was jeopardising the conditions of its own existence. But the truth is that judicial supervision of public authorities antedated by centuries this conflict-ridden growth in the machinery of state.[34] Equally, it is surviving, with if anything greater vigour, the disestablishment of much of the corporate state in almost all the world's developed societies. The reason is that at one level or another and by one means or another, by direct intervention or by devolution or by licence, states have to make a certain measure of provision for the orderly meeting of social needs. Whatever its current governing ideology, the state has no other *raison d'etre*. And whatever rhetoric of liberty is used, all but the smallest and simplest forms of human society need an ordered distribution of power if they are to function at all. While this is not a sufficient condition of the rule of law (it would, for example, include a dictatorship) it is a necessary one. The role of public law in this elementary scheme is not well or adequately described as keeping the state within the limits of its lawful powers: the metaphor of the state as a limited company breaks down when its powers and their limits have sometimes to be invented in order to be defined. What public law is about, at heart, is the restraint of abuses of power. It has been so since the earliest recorded cases, and it continues to be so.[35] There is in my view no other theory

was committed by a person acting in an official capacity, presupposes that it cannot be a defence that it was committed by a private individual".

[33] Among the growing literature on this topic, see D. Oliver "Is ultra vires the basis of judicial review?" [1987] PL 543 and at Chapter One pp. 3–27 above; P. Craig, "Ultra vires and judicial review" [1988] CLJ 63 and at Chapter Three pp. 47–71 above; Sir J. Laws, "Illegality: the problem of jurisdiction" in Supperstone and Goudie ed., *Judicial Review* (1992) and at Chapter Four pp. 73–81 (extract) above; C. Forsyth, "Of fig-leaves and fairy tales" [1996] CLJ 122 and at Chapter Two pp. 29–46 above, 122; D. Dyzenhaus, "Reuniting the brain: the democratic basis of judicial review" [1998] PLR 98. Reference might also be made to the officious backbencher as a parodic explanation of the doctrine of presumed parliamentary intent: see M. Nolan and S. Sedley, *The Making and Remarking of the British Constitution* (1997), p. 16.

[34] The Commissioners of Sewers, instituted in the early 15th century, had by the end of the 16th century faced judicial review for acting ultra vires: *Rooke's Case* (1598) Co. Rep. 99b.

[35] *Nottinghamshire County Council* [1986] AC 240, *per* Lord Scarman at 249.

capable of explaining how, for example, the courts today have a supervisory juris-diction over the exercise both of the Royal Prerogative[36] and of powers exercised by bodies with no legal underpinning at all.[37]

If this is right, one can come back to non-state repositories of power with a different perspective. Some may be exercising public functions – typically the allocation of resources of basic importance to the whole population. Control of these can, of course, be expected to be governed by procedural rules which recognise the special public need for speed and certainty of decision-making, and even by rules of standing designed to exclude mere busybodies; but it can also be powerfully argued that the substantive law applied to such bodies ought not to differ significantly from that which is applicable to the state itself. Other bodies – the press and broadcast media are a prime example – will be exercising functions not of a traditionally state character but still of radical importance to large numbers of people. Where such bodies invade what are now to be the con-stitutional rights of individuals, I have suggested that the means may exist in the Human Rights Act to ensure that such invasions are either justified or stopped. But is this an unacceptably novel configuration of rights and remedies? Is it one which impermissibly conflates the private and the public?[38]

I ask the first question because the common law, like the god Janus, is for ever facing both the future and the past. As the great Scottish jurist Stair pointed out in the seventeenth century, statute law possesses the great virtue of certainty but the unavoidable drawback of rigidity.[39] The common law's great advantage is its ability to respond to change or to adapt to the unexpected; but if it does so in a baldly reactive fashion it risks destroying the stability which a society is enti-tled to look for in its legal system. So the common law likes to travel back to the future, looking constantly for precedents that will blunt the edge of the anxiety that it is sacrificing stability on the altar of innovation. Sometimes we get awk-wardly close to Professor Cornford's principle of unripe time, with its axiom that nothing should ever be done for the first time;[40] but the search for precedent is never entirely cosmetic. It reflects the equal and opposite pulls of adaptability and certainty.

Is there then anything in the common law's past which pre-figures this sym-biosis of the public with the private? The answer is an emphatic "Yes". Two

[36] *R. v. Criminal Injuries Compensation Board, ex p. Lain* [1967] 2 QB 864.

[37] *R. v. Panel on Takeovers and Mergers, ex p. Datafin* [1987] QB 815. In New Zealand see *Electoral Commission v. Cameron* [1997] 2 NZLR 421 concerning a voluntary body with powers of censorship.

[38] Novel it is not: see G. Borrie, "The regulation of public and private power" [1989] PL 552; D. Oliver, "Common values in public and private law and the public/private divide" [1997] PL 630, and "The underlying values of public and private law" in M. Taggart ed., *The Province of Administrative Law* (1997) p. 217; P.P. Craig, "Public law and control over private power", *ibid.*, p. 196.

[39] Stair, *Inst.* I.1.15: "But in statutes the lawgiver must at once balance the conveniences and the inconveniences; wherein he may and often doth fall short . . ." (quoted by F.A. Bennion, *Statutory Interpretation*, (3rd ed.), p. 783).

[40] F.M. Cornford, *Microcosmographia Academia* (1908), Chap. VII.

examples must do service here, drawn from the law of trade and employment. Lawyers still tend to believe that, in spite of modern statutory controls, trade and employment are areas where freedom of action is the common law's universal groundrule. At common law you can sell goods and services to and buy them from whom you please. At common law you can hire and fire, take or leave a job, without anybody being entitled to question the fairness or rationality of what you are doing. Or can you?

Since the eighteenth century, perhaps earlier, the common law has set its face against unreasonable restraints on the free movement of labour and on the availability of necessary public services. Covenants, albeit voluntarily entered into, which restrict an employee's freedom to move on and take his skills and knowledge with him have for the better part of three centuries been subjected by the courts to a stringent test of what is reasonable – reasonable, moreover, not in the deferential *Wednesbury* sense that a rational person could decide to do it, but in the direct sense that it is in the court's own judgment tolerable on public policy grounds.[41] Similarly, a person who was granted a legal monopoly or who held a virtual monopoly of a service on which a section of the public depended was for centuries forbidden by the English courts to levy more than what the court regarded as a reasonable charge.[42] The doctrines of restraint of the abuse of private monopoly power, although for the present they have drifted out of sight in England, have remained alive and well in the United States.[43] They formed part of a complex legal regime for the governance of markets in a period (from the sixteenth to the end of the eighteenth century) which we tend mistakenly to regard as one of laissez-faire practices. During this period, first by statute but then at common law, the cornering and distortion of markets was caught by the now forgotten crimes of forestalling, regrating and engrossing: profiteering by buying up goods before they reached the market; by buying them up in order to resell them in the same market; and by buying them in bulk in order to create scarcity. An overt part of the rationale of these crimes was the preservation of public order, and the eclipse of them coincided with two things: the raising and garrisoning of armed troops all over Britain for war with France, but capable equally of putting down bread riots; and the acquisition of almost scriptural status among judges as well as politians of Adam Smith's *Wealth of Nations*[44] (an early analogue of the modern law and economics movement). But there was plainly, too, a strong moral component in the creation and prosecution of these

---

[41] *Mitchel* v. *Reynolds* (1711) 1 P. Wms. 181 at 195. See Halsbury's *Laws of England* (4th ed.), Vol. 42, paras. 21, 24.

[42] P.P. Craig, "Constitutions, property and Regulation" [1991] PL 538; M. Taggart, "Public Utilities and the Law", in Joseph ed., *Essays on the Constitution* (1995). The doctrine reappears in the 20th century in the Privy Council's decision in *Minister of Justice for Canada* v. *City of Levis* [1919] AC 505.

[43] See *Munn* v. *Illinois* 94 U.S. 77 (1877) and the articles by Craig and Taggart (previous note) *passim*.

[44] See Douglas Hay, "The State and the Market in 1800", *Past and Present*, Vol. 162 (February, 1999), pp. 101–162. The last major proponent of market crimes was Lord Kenyon C.J.; his main opponent was Lord Ellenborough C.J. who not only survived him but sat in Cabinet. See generally

offences, and none the less so for its eclipse by a different morality still familiar to us.

Perhaps the most striking modern concatenation of the public and the private has been in the law of what used to be called master and servant – employment law. In England much of its development during the twentieth century was bound up with the law of trade unions, because it was often members and officials, contending that they had been unjustly expelled from or dismissed by what were in law mere voluntary associations, who resorted to the courts for redress. In a series of cases running into the 1980s the courts, continuously reverting to earlier authority, developed and applied a coherent body of principles of natural justice which members and, importantly, office-holders could rely on to protect them from arbitrary action.[45] By 1970 the need for uniform legal protection of employees against arbitrary dismissal had become so apparent that the House of Lords[46] went as close as it could to introducing a right to natural justice into every contract of employment. Within a year Parliament had introduced such a right by statute.[47] But for the legislative intervention it is highly likely that the common law would have completed the task itself. One of the most interesting aspects of the common law development was that it did not operate by implying terms into the contract: in the famous phrase of Byles J.[48] the justice of the common law was supplying the omission of the legislature. And it did so not by according a right to damages but by declaring unfair dismissals from office void – a remedy we have come to think of as distinctively one of public law.

It seems to me, therefore, that the moment of introduction of a human rights regime into the law of the United Kingdom, though millennial, is not arbitrary. It comes, of course, at the end of a long trek by a handful – of whom I was not one – of far-sighted campaigners led by Lord Scarman.[49] But it comes also at a

---

P.S. Atiyah, *The Rise and Fall of Freedom of Contract*, pp. 363–366; E.P. Thompson, "The Moral Economy reviewed" in *Customs in Common* (1991). Hay (n. 17) cites evidence of laws against engrossing and profiteering in ancient Athens.

[45] See S. Sedley, "Public law and contractual employment" (1994) 23 ILJ 201; J. Laws, "Public law and employment law: abuse of power" [1997] PL 455; P. Davies and M. Freedland, "The impact of public law on labour law 1972–1997" (1997) 26 ILJ 311.

[46] In *Malloch* v. *Aberdeen Corporation* [1971] 1 WLR 1578, decided in 1970, Lord Wilberforce said: "One may accept that if there are relationships in which all the requirements of the observance of natural justice are excluded (and I do not wish to assume that this is inevitably so), these cases must be confined to what have been called 'pure master and servant cases', which I take to mean cases in which there is no element of public employment or service, no support by statute, nothing in the nature of an office or a status which is capable of protection. If any of these elements exist then, in my opinion, whatever the terminology used, and even though in some inter partes aspects the relationship may be called that of master and servant, there may be essential procedural requirements to be observed, and failure to observe them may result in a dismissal being declared to be void."

[47] Industrial Relations Act 1971, s. 22(1): "In every employment to which this section applies every employee shall have the right not to be unfairly dismissed by his employer . . ."

[48] In *Cooper* v. *Wandsworth Board of Works* (1863) 14 CB, NS 180 at 194.

[49] Lord Scarman's 1974 Hamlyn Lectures, *English Law, the New Dimension*, make prescient reading. He called among other things for a new constitutional settlement with entrenched rights and restraints on the exercise of state power, and for a supreme court to handle constitutional and devolution issues.

stage of development of our constitutional common law when it is more possible than ever before to see how artificial the segregation of the public from the private has become in all but procedural terms. The old presumption that the Crown was not bound by statutes unless they expressly said so has become all but redundant: legislation today routinely binds the Crown – as employer, as occupier, as contractor, as landlord – to observe the same legal standards as everybody else. The historic decision of the House of Lords in *M* v. *Home Office*[50] that ministers of the Crown are answerable to the courts for breach of their orders has restored constitutional law to a principled course from which it had been deviating for over a century: though we still have a certain distance to go in recognising the state itself as a legal entity.[51] By a fine irony of history, Dicey's well-known view that we had no need of a system of administrative law because everyone from the postman to the prime minister was governed by the ordinary law, is more nearly true now than it was when he wrote it – for our public law *is* our ordinary law, the common law.

In the historic decision of the New Zealand Court of Appeal in *Baigent's Case*,[52] Hardie Boys J. quoted some words of Anand J. of the Supreme Court of India:[53]

> The purpose of public law is not only to civilise public power but also to assure the citizen that they live under a legal system which aims to protect their interests and preserve their rights.

My argument is not that the state is just another corporation, nor that (as was held in the great mid-eighteenth century cases arising out of the raid on the North Briton) ministers should still be liable as private individuals for torts committed in office. It is that the rule of law, if it is to mean anything, has to embrace state, corporation and individual alike; that the law's chief concern about the use of power is not who is exercising it but what the power is and whom it affects; and that the control of abuses of power, whether in private or in public hands, is probably the most important of all the tasks which will be facing the courts in a twenty-first century democracy. The sea in which, as citizens, we all have to swim in inhabited not only by Leviathan – an alarmingly big but often benign creature – but by Jaws; and the law needs to be on the watch for both.

---

[50] [1994] 1 AC 377.
[51] See S. Sedley, "The Crown in its own Courts" in C. Forsyth and I. Hare ed., *The Golden Metwand and the Crooked Cord* (1998), pp. 253–266.
[52] [1994] 3 NZLR 667.
[53] *Nilabati* v. *State of Orissa* (1993) Crim. L.J. 2899.

14

Review of (Non-Statutory) Discretions

DAWN OLIVER

In this paper I consider the operation of supervisory jurisdictions in relation to the exercise of non-statutory discretions.[1] By supervisory jurisdiction I mean jurisdictions in which the courts prescribe decision-making processes and procedures. Not all supervisory jurisdictions involve the idea, familiar to public lawyers, that the court may not itself exercise a discretion or dictate how it should be exercised. I focus initially on private law. I shall suggest that the principles of judicial review – broadly duties of legality, rationality and procedural propriety, to adopt Lord Diplock's shorthand in the *CCSU* case[2] – are not essentially public law principles. These duties of what I prefer to call "considerate decision-making" have been developed by the common law (and by the courts of equity) to apply in situations which are purely "private", as well as to "public" decision-making. They are not, or not only, principles of statutory interpretation. Their application in judicial review is not explicable by the doctrine of legislative intent. They are general principles, which govern exercises of discretionary decision-making power when certain conditions are satisfied, and certain countervailing considerations do not apply. The conditions include situations where a decision will adversely affect an individual's vital interests, such as his or her security, status, or autonomy; or where other reasons of public policy (as in restraint of trade cases or where decisions are being made in the exercise of public or governmental functions) lead the courts to impose such duties. Often the situations in which these duties of considerate decision-making arise involve relationships where there is an imbalance of power.

The limits of my argument need to be made clear at the outset. I am not suggesting that whenever a private or public body exercises a discretion that will adversely affect an individual, the common law or equity impose duties of considerate decision-making. There are countervailing considerations which may lead the courts to exclude these duties. For instance, the decision-maker's own vital interests may be at stake: this will often be the case in purely personal private relationships. Or the needs of the market or of management or other prerogatives, or considerations of justiciability may militate against imposing such duties. But similar countervailing considerations operate to preclude duties of

---

[1] This argument is expanded in my book *Common Values and the Public–Private Divide*, 1999, Butterworths.

[2] *Council for Civil Service Unions* v. *Minister for the Civil Service* [1985] AC 374.

considerate decision-making in both public and private law. This argument clearly has profound implications for the public law private law divide and the exclusivity rule in *O'Reilly* v. *Mackman*[3] and for the ultra vires rule. These will be briefly considered at the end of the paper.

FIDUCIARY RELATIONSHIPS

In the space available it is only possible to illustrate my hypothesis by a few examples. Let us start with a look at the principles governing the exercise of discretion in fiduciary relationships, notably those of trustees-beneficiaries, and company directors-companies. These are of particular interest because their existence undermines any assumption that principles of considerate decision-making are essentially the creatures of the common law (rather than equity) and within the common law, of public law.

I propose to adopt Paul Finn's interpretation of fiduciary law, he suggests that:

> First, but by no means uniquely, fiduciary law's concern is to impose standards of acceptable conduct on one party to a relationship for the benefit of the other where the one has responsibility for the preservation of the other's interests. Secondly, again in common with other bodies of law, it does this by proscribing one party's possible use of the power and of the opportunities his position gives, or has given, him to act inconsistently with that responsibility.[4] . . . The fiduciary duty originates in public policy, a view of desired social behaviour.[5] . . . A fiduciary relationship, ultimately, is an imposed not an accepted one. If one needs an analogy here, one is closer to tort law than to contract; one is concerned with an imposed standard of behaviour.[6]

The relationships which give rise to fiduciary duties are very diverse. In some cases, as in local government, public decision-makers may be regarded as being in a fiduciary relationship with their public, the council tax payers.[7] In private law, fiduciary relationships include the relationship of trustee and beneficiary, some contractual relationships, and other relationships not necessarily based in contract, as where information is received in confidence. So the trust, to which we now turn, is just one example of a range of fiduciary relationships.

Trusts

The trust is particularly interesting because it involves principles of decision-making as well as standards of considerate behaviour.

---

[3] [1983] 2 AC 237.

[4] P.D. Finn, "The fiduciary principle" in T.G. Youdan, (ed.), *Equity, Fiduciaries and Trusts*, 1989, p. 2.

[5] Ibid., p. 27. See also P.D. Finn, "Fiduciary law and the modern commercial world", in E. McKendrick, (ed.), *Commercial Aspects of Trusts and Fiduciary Obligations*, 1992.

[6] Ibid., at p. 54.

[7] See for instance *Bromley LBC* v. *GLC* [1983] 1 AC 768. See De Smith, Woolf and Jowell, *Judicial Review of Administrative Action*, 5th edn., 1995, para. 6–096.

The principles for the exercise of duties and discretions by trustees are well settled, but they will be summarised here to bring out the similarities and contrasts with principles of decision-making in other supervisory jurisdictions, particularly judicial review.[8] Generally trustees must be disinterested – they must not profit from the trust; they must distribute to beneficiaries in accordance with the terms of the trust, exercising any discretion for the benefit of the beneficiaries (which generally means the financial benefits of the beneficiaries)[9] and not in accordance with a whim. Trustees are under a duty not to delegate powers unless they have authority to do so.[10]

In exercising discretions, trustees as fiduciaries must not act capriciously or outside the field permitted by the trust, they must act fairly as between the beneficiaries and they must take all relevant considerations into account.[11] Trustees' powers must be used to effectuate the purpose for which they were conferred and not to secure indirectly some other purpose (the doctrine of "fraud on the power".) Sir Richard Scott summed up the supervisory jurisdiction over trustees in *Edge and Others* v. *Pensions Ombudsman and another*[12] as follows: a judge may only interfere if the trustees had "taken into account irrelevant, improper or irrational factors, or their decision was one that no reasonable body of trustees properly directing themselves could have reached".

As far as duties of procedural fairness in trusts are concerned, in principle there is no duty to consult on the part of trustees before exercising a discretion that may adversely affect, for instance, a beneficiary.[13] However, Robert Walker J in *Scott and another* v. *National Trust*[14] indicated that, although trustees are not under any general duty to give a hearing before making decisions, a beneficiary may have a legitimate expectation that a discretionary benefit will continue to be paid, and if the trustees are considering terminating the payments the beneficiary might be entitled in equity to a warning and an opportunity to try to persuade the trustees to continue the payment, at least temporarily. Interestingly, from the viewpoint of public lawyers, Robert Walker J. indicated that failure to do this might amount to "capricious" behaviour on the part of the trustees which would enable the court to intervene.

Beneficiaries are entitled to be provided with information which will enable them to determine whether the trust is being administered correctly; they have a right to see the trust accounts, to know how trust money is invested, to inspect documents and so on (though documents about discussions between trustees about the exercise of discretion are privileged). The court may order that a

---

[8] For summaries of the duties of trustees see Robert Walker J in *Scott and another* v. *National Trust* [1998] 2 All ER 705.

[9] *Cowan* v. *Scargill* [1984] 3 WLR 501, Sir Robert Megarry V-C.

[10] *Re Hay's Settlement Trusts* [1981] 3 All ER 786.

[11] *Re Baden's Deed Trusts (McPhail* v. *Doulton)* [1971] AC 424, per Lord Wilberforce.

[12] [1998] 2 All ER 547, Sir Richard Scott V-C.

[13] A rare example of a duty to consult before a decision is made that may adversely affect others in trust law is provided by section 11 of the Trusts of Land Act 1996, under which there is a limited duty to consult beneficiaries with an interest in possession under a trust of land.

[14] [1998] 2 All ER 705, p. 718.

beneficiary be informed of the identity of trustees to enable them to exercise these rights.[15] But beneficiaries are not entitled to be given reasons or explanations for trustees' decisions, although, as Robert Walker J noted in the *Scott* case, if a decision of trustees is challenged in legal proceedings they may well have to disclose the substance of their reasons.[16]

Comparisons with judicial review

There are significant differences between trusts and judicial review. For instance, the court may itself execute a trust, thus substituting its own view of what should be done for that of the trustees. Thus if, for instance, the trustees fail in their duty to consider whether and if so how to exercise their discretions, the beneficiaries may seek the aid of the court, and the court will take whatever course seems appropriate: it may appoint fresh trustees; or apply the maxim equality is equity and order that the property should be divided equally (though this will often not be appropriate or in line with the settlor's intentions); or itself direct how a trust power is to be exercised or how property is to be distributed.[17] No such usurpation of a decision-making function is permitted in judicial review.

A second example of a striking difference between trusts and judicial review appears to be the absence of rights on the part of beneficiaries to be consulted. But often beneficiaries will be in the equivalent position of "applicants" in judicial review cases, especially in the case of discretionary trusts. In other words, frequently beneficiaries will not have a sufficient vested interest to give rise to a duty of consultation. As the comments by Robert Walker J in *Scott* show, there may be duties of natural justice in some trust situations. And the rule that a trustee must not benefit from the trust provides a parallel with the rule against bias in judicial review.[18] Entitlements to see documents and know the identity of trustees may be viewed as, in practice, requirements of procedural propriety or natural justice, though far less developed than duties in judicial review.

The similarities between the equitable jurisdiction in trusts and the common law jurisdiction in judicial review are strong and highly significant. The origin of the trust is the need to prevent trustees from abusing their powers as legal owners of trust property by applying it for their own benefit. This is similar to the idea in constitutional theory and public law that ministers and other public officials should not abuse their powers by acting in their own interests, but must be altruistic. In both trusts and judicial review, decision-makers are under duties of selflessness and altruism.[19] Looked at from the point of view of a modern

---

[15]   *Murphy* v. *Murphy* [1999] 1 WLR 282.

[16]   See per Robert Walker J in *Scott* v. *National Trust*, supra. at p. 718–9, referring to *Dundee Hospitals* case [1952] 1 All ER 896, p. 900, per Lord Normand.

[17]   *Re Baden's Deed Trusts (McPhail* v. *Doulton)* [1971] AC 424.

[18]   See De Smith, Woolf and Jowell, chapter 12.

[19]   See for instance *Padfield* v. *Minister of Agriculture* [1968] AC 997 on selflessness by public decision-makers, and the parallel equitable principle that trustees must not benefit from the trust.

public lawyer the other rationale that would spring to mind, at least in relation to a trust from which a person had already benefited, would be that the beneficiary might have a legitimate expectation that the benefit would continue to be received. This view is reflected in the comments of Robert Walker J in *Scott and others* v. *National Trust*:

> The beneficiary has no legal or equitable right to continued payment, but she or he has an expectation. So I am inclined to think that legitimate expectation may have some part to play in trust law as well as in judicial review cases . . .[20]

The requirements in relation to discretionary decisions by trustees are, it is obvious, very close to the duties of legality and *Wednesbury* reasonableness which were imposed by Lord Greene MR in that case in public law.[21] The comments by Sir Richard Scott in *Edge,* noted above, must represent a deliberate borrowing from judicial review. These similarities are not surprising. Lord Greene was a distinguished trust and equity lawyer, and he may well have been drawing deliberately on equitable principles in formulating the grounds for review in the *Wednesbury* case.[22] Sir Richard Scott, in turn (another Chancery lawyer) must have been borrowing back from judicial review in the *Edge* case.

Public decision-makers and trustees must act in accordance with the intention of the body from whom their power derives – respectively Parliament (normally) or the settlor. Neither public decision-makers nor trustees must act capriciously or "*Wednesbury* unreasonably", nor must they act for ulterior or improper purposes.[23] Both must take account of relevant considerations, and not be influenced by irrelevant considerations. They may take into account ethical considerations, as long as they do not allow these to run counter to the overall purpose of their functions.[24] They must exercise discretions with an open mind.[25] They may not delegate their discretions to others,[26] or fetter their discretion.[27]

The particular significance of the parallels between rules for the exercise of discretion in trusts and in judicial review is fivefold. First, they indicate that the rules governing decision-making in judicial review are not uniquely "public", so that these rights are not accurately described as "public law rights" as Lord Diplock described them in *O'Reilly* v. *Mackman.* Secondly, they show that

---

[20] [1998] 2 All ER 705.

[21] *Associated Provincial Picture Houses* v. *Wednesbury Corporation* [1948] 1 KB 223, (CA).

[22] Ibid.

[23] See De Smith, Woolf and Jowell, chapter 6, esp. paras. 6–059 – 6–083. On ulterior purposes in trusts see *Re Baden's Deed Trusts (McPhail* v. *Doulton)* [1971] AC 424, per Lord Wilberforce.

[24] *R.* v. *Somerset County Council, ex parte Fewings* [1995] 3 All ER 20, at pp. 28, 31, 34 (CA); cf *Roberts* v. *Hopwood* [1925] AC 578. On ethical considerations in trusts see *Cowan* v. *Scargill* [1984] 3 WLR 501; *Harries* v. *Church Commissioners for England* (1991) *The Times,* 30 October 1999.

[25] *British Oxygen Co.* v. *Ministry of Technology* [1971] AC 610. Cf *Turner* v. *Turner* [1984] Ch. 100.

[26] *Lavender (H) and Son Ltd.* v. *Ministry of Housing and Local Government* [1970] 1 WLR 1231. On the exercises of discretion in judicial review see generally De Smith, Woolf and Jowell *Judicial Review of Administrative Action*, 5th edn., 1995, chapter 6.

[27] See De Smith, Woolf and Jowell, *Judicial Review of Administrative Action*, 1995, chapter 11.

duties of rational and considerate decision-making (except the *audi alteram partem* rule) have roots both in equity and in the common law. These duties form part of a legal framework for the control of power which is not by any means confined to public law. Thirdly, the duties in decision-making in trusts are *imposed* by equity, and are not – or not solely – derived from the intentions of the settlor, the terms of the trust or the agreement of the parties: in other words, equity, via fiduciary duties, provides examples of duties arising in decision-making which cannot be rationalised in terms of the equivalent of legislative intent, the consent of the parties, or a policy that those performing public or governmental functions are (uniquely) under duties of considerate decision-making imposed by law. These duties are imposed as a matter of justice and public policy, and thus provide support for the position that it is not contrary to principle or tradition for the courts to impose obligations of considerate decision-making on those in positions of power. Fourthly, these duties in decision-making are suitable for the protection of individuals whose security or other interests are threatened by decision-making, as well as for the general purpose of controlling the exercise of power on public policy grounds, including the need to prevent abuse of power and frustration of the wishes of the settlor or donor of a power. And fifthly, in private law as well as in public law, there are duties of altruism: public bodies are not alone in being under duties of disinterestedness and consideration.

Company law

Duties analogous to those imposed in judicial review also arise in relation to company directors. There is not the space here to explore the duties of directors in detail.[28] It will suffice for present purposes to focus on the most obvious parallels with judicial review and other supervisory jurisdictions.

The sources of the duties of directors are varied – equity, statute and the common law. In equity, directors are not strictly trustees of the company property,[29] but they resemble trustees in that they owe fiduciary duties towards the company (but not towards its individual members).[30] This entails that they must each and all act bona fide in the interests of the company and, subject to their interests as shareholders and the articles of the company, not in their own interests (the self-dealing rule)[31] or those of third parties.

If a question arises as to whether directors have breached their duty to the company, the court exercises a supervisory jurisdiction. Directors must direct

---

[28] For a full account see P. Davies *Gower's Principles of Modern Company Law*, 6th edn., 1997, (henceforth Gower) chapter 22. See also Mrs Justice Arden "Codifying directors' duties" in R. Rawlings (ed.), *Law, Society and Economy*, 1997, pp. 91–108.

[29] Gower p. 598.

[30] Gower, pp. 599–623. *Percival* v. *Wright* [1902] 2 Ch. 421.

[31] See *Movitex Ltd.* v. *Bulfield and Ors.* (1986) 2 BCC 99, 403, Vinelott J.

their minds to the question whether a transaction was in fact in the interests of the company. (A transaction may be held not to be binding on a company if a director fails in this respect.)[32] Certain matters are prescribed as relevant in decision-making: directors must take into account the interests of shareholders, and this entails that they may have some regard to their own interests if they happen to be shareholders. Thus they are:

> not required by the law to live in an unreal region of detached altruism and to act in a vague mood of ideal abstraction from the obvious fact which must be present to the mind of any honest and intelligent man when he exercises his powers as a director.[33]

But the court holds that it is for the directors and not the court to consider what is in the interests of the company.

Directors must exercise their powers for the purpose for which they were conferred, and not for improper purposes. An improper purpose would include the advancement of the directors' own interests if this is contrary to the interests of the company as a whole.[34] The criteria for determining a proper purpose are objective, drawn from the articles of association (and in this respect are comparable to the "legality" ground in judicial review).

Directors must not in general fetter their future discretion, and they must exercise their own independent judgment.[35] However, this does not prevent them from entering into a contract under which they agree to take further action in future in order to carry out the contract. Outside the realm of contract, the rule against fettering of discretion still applies; for instance directors may not fetter their discretion as to the advice they will give shareholders on a matter on which the shareholders have the right to decide in the future.[36]

Lastly, as far as duties in equity are concerned, in principle and unless the articles of association provide otherwise (which they usually do) directors must not place themselves in a position where their personal interests or duties to others are liable to conflict with their duties to the company, unless the company gives its informed consent.[37]

The formal position of directors then has considerable similarities with those of decision-makers in public law. However, the reality of the matter is to some degree different, since the majority of shareholders determine whether the company should pursue complaints against directors and frequently the majority will not wish to do so.[38] (It is impossible to resist drawing an analogy here with

---

[32] Gower, pp. 601–5; *Re W. & M. Roith Ltd* [1967] 1 WLR 432.

[33] *Mills* v. *Mills* (1938) 60 CLR 150, Australian HC, quoted by Gower p. 602.

[34] Gower, pp.605–8.

[35] Gower, pp. 608–10.

[36] *John Crowther Group plc.* v. *Carpets International* [1990] BCLC 460; Gower p. 609.

[37] Gower, pp. 610–23.

[38] See *Foss* v. *Harbottle* (1843) 2 Hare 461, 67 ER 189; *Smith* v. *Croft (No. 2)* [1987] 3 All ER 909, Knox J.

the ability of a majority party in Parliament to protect a government from accountability for its mishandling of its responsibilities.)[39]

Comparisons with judicial review

Each of these points has interesting parallels, at least formally, in judicial review, which will be briefly pointed up here. The parallel between articles of association and enabling statutes has already been noted. The parallel in company law with the public law requirement that decision-makers are to be impartial and must act in the public interest and within the purpose of the enabling statute[40] is the requirement that directors must act in the interests of the company and according to its articles of association. Both directors and public decision-makers must act in good faith in the area with which their powers are concerned, and for a proper purpose. In judicial review the duty of altruism is strict, and may involve the rule against bias. It also entails that a minister should not be influenced by the political flak that an unpopular decision may attract.[41] This is not the case with directors. However, just as there are exceptions to a director's duty of impartiality (i.e. where he is a shareholder) so in public law a minister may decide in favour of a policy to which he is committed[42] (i.e. about which he or she is not impartial) and may even take the view that it is in the public interest for his or her own party to remain in power.[43]

In public law statutory provisions may make clear that particular sectional interests are relevant in certain decisions (for instance the interests of property owners in compulsory purchase, and of neighbours in planning cases) just as the Companies Act provides for employees' interests to be taken into account in directors' decisions. Statute will also be a guide to what is a proper purpose in public law.[44]

As in company law, discretion must not be fettered in public decision-making,[45] though the position in public law in relation to contracts which may reduce the area of free decision-making in the future is complex.[46]

As far as remedies are concerned, at least formally there are clear parallels with remedies for breach of directors' duties, in the availability of injunctions

---

[39] Under section 459 of the Companies Act a petition may be brought alleging that the company has been conducted in a manner which is "unfairly prejudicial" to the petitioner, usually a minority shareholder.

[40] See De Smith, Woolf and Jowell, paras. 6–059–6–084.

[41] *Padfield* v. *Minister of Agriculture* [1968] AC 997, (HL).

[42] *Franklin* v. *Minister of Town and Country Planning* [1948] AC 87, (HL).

[43] *R.* v. *Waltham Forest LBC, ex parte Baxter* [1988] QB 419.

[44] *Padfield* v. *Minister of Agriculture*, and De Smith, Woolf and Jowell, supra.

[45] See De Smith, Woolf and Jowell, chapter 11.

[46] Contracts entered into by the Crown are not to be construed as being subject to implied terms that would exclude the exercise of general discretionary power for the public good, and are to be construed as incorporating an implied term that such power remain exercisable: De Smith, Woolf and Jowell, p. 518. But "How and where the line is to be drawn is not clear." De Smith, Woolf and Jowell, para. 11–014; *Ayr Harbour Trustees* v. *Oswald*(1883) 8 App. Cas. 623; *Rederaktiebolaget Amphitrite* v. *R.* [1921] 3 KB 500.

and declarations in judicial review. In practice orders of *certiorari*, prohibition and *mandamus* in judicial review fulfil many of the same functions as declarations and injunctions in company law. In reality, however, a majority of shareholders is in a position to block actions against directors.

The significance of the parallels between the law relating to directors' duties and judicial review is similar to the significance of the parallels in trusts. They show that duties in decision-making may be *imposed* – by equity; principles of legality, rationality and procedural propriety are not only common law principles; such duties need not rest on an ultra vires doctrine or legislative intent; duties such as those laid down in the *Wednesbury* case are not uniquely public law in nature but have some of their roots in equity and thus in private law; and they are apt for the protection, *inter alia*, of the interests of individuals such as shareholders and employees. The rules also indicate, however, how important rules of standing can be for the protection of interests, in the facts that employees cannot enforce the duties of consideration owed to them by directors, and in practice only companies, controlled by the majority of the shareholders (who may not wish to sue the directors) can enforce directors' duties.

THE COMMON LAW

Let us now turn from the ways in which equity has developed duties of legality, rationality and even procedural propriety on the part of some decision-makers, to the common law, which has developed principles of legality, rationality and procedural propriety in both what we would now call private law and public law. In private law examples can be found in contract and in public policy – though in the latter it is hard to distinguish between common law and equity, and indeed between public and private law.

Contract

A problem that Beatson identifies, which separates contract law from judicial review (and from trusts and company law) is that "contract law has difficulty in dealing with discretion . . ."[47] The starting point, historically at least, has been until recently that a discretion granted by contract is unfettered. This point is well illustrated by the case of *Weinberger* v. *Inglis*[48] in which the House of Lords refused to interfere with a refusal by the Committee of the London Stock Exchange to re-elect the plaintiff to the Exchange, because he was of German birth. The rules of the exchange empowered the Committee to admit such persons as it "shall think proper". However, this case may be characteristic of a

---

[47] J. Beatson "Judicial review in contract" in J. Beatson and D. Friedmann, (eds.), *Good Faith and Fault in Contract Law*, 1995, p. 263.
[48] [1919] AC 606.

period where the justice of exchange dominated contract law. Other cases demonstrate a preference for what Collins has called "justice ideals of the social market", namely fairness of exchange, individual autonomy and co-operation in the treatment of discretionary power enjoyed under contracts. For instance, in the shipping case of *Tillmanns and Co* v. *SS Knutsford Ltd* the master of a ship had a contractual power to land a cargo at a port other than the port of discharge, where that port was unsafe or inaccessible. It was held that he must "exercise that discretion fairly as between both parties, and not merely to do his best for the shipowners, his masters, disregarding the interests of the charterers".[49] Beatson gives further examples of how tests similar to those which are currently applied in applications for judicial review have been employed in contract cases to control the possible abuse of discretion or power for many years. The themes that emerge from these cases include the lack of the right to act partially, or entirely selfishly.[50] Beatson's conclusion is that contract law *generally* has not been influenced either by public law principles or by the rules of statutory regulatory regimes, and that it is only in a number of particular situations that a limited concept of "abuse of rights" has been recognised in a contractual context.

In his consideration of the ways in which the exercise of contracting power by government is controlled, Daintith seeks comparisons in the way in which the courts have treated disputes about the exercise of discretionary powers in private contracts. In a constitutive contract where the contract is a way of regulating the continuing relationship of a group with a common purpose such as a club, a trade union or a company, he argues, if the common purpose is clear then the courts will use it as a criterion against which to measure the exercise of discretion;[51] in the absence of such guidance, the courts have relied on the fiduciary position of the controlling group, and have founded on this a general obligation to act in good faith, not corruptly, or arbitrarily or capriciously.[52] In commercial contracts too, Daintith shows, power – for instance power to approve of goods or of improvements by a lessee – must be exercised in good faith, not capriciously, in accordance with the presumed intentions of the parties.[53] Daintith observes that, as far as substantive requirements of, broadly, reasonableness, are concerned, leaving special cases aside, ". . . one is struck by the

---

[49] [1908] 2 KB 385, at 406.

[50] See J. Beatson and D. Friedmann, (eds), *Good Faith and Fault in Contract Law*, 1995, pp. 268–9.

[51] T.C. Daintith, "Regulation by contract" [1979] *CLP* 41, p. 55–6. Cases on this include *Punt* v. *Symons and Co Ltd.* [1903] 2 Ch. 506; *Hogg* v. *Cramphorn Ltd.* [1967] Ch 254. See also *Stevenson* v. *United Road Transport Union* [1977] ICR 893. However, in the case of trade unions the courts have not shown sympathy with the collective objectives of the organisation: see S. Deakin and G. Morris, *Labour Law*, 1998, chapter 10.

[52] See Daintith, op. cit., p. 56. On trade unions see *Maclean* v. *Workers Union* [1929] 1 Ch 602; on clubs see *Dawkins* v. *Antrobus* (1861) 17 ChD 615.

[53] Daintith, ibid p. 57. Cases on this point include *Dallman* v. *King* (1837) 4 Bing, (NC) 105; *Braunstein* v. *Accidental Death Insurance Co.* (1861) 1 B and S 782; *Andrews* v. *Belfield* (1857) 2 CB (NS) 779.

similarity of the results obtained by applying, on the one hand, administrative law tests to the exercise of discretionary statutory power, and on the other, common law tests to discretionary contractual power".

The well known lines of cases on duties of procedural propriety in decisions by membership associations in respect of their members illustrate this approach. For instance, trade unions must act in accordance with principles of natural justice in dealing with their officers,[54] sporting associations in relations with their members including those disciplined by them,[55] and universities in relations with their students.[56]

The parallels between aspects of contract law and judicial review were made explicit in *Shearson Lehman Hutton Inc* v. *Maclaine Watson and Co Ltd.* in which Webster J questioned the assumption that public law rules cannot be applied in private law.[57] His view was that the differences between private and public law rights were to do with the procedures by which they might be protected rather than their substance.

There are, then, obvious and strong parallels between aspects of contract law and judicial review. Considering what is happening in contract in Australia, Judge Paul Finn argues that there is a strong trend in modern contract law to develop duties of fairness – "decency in human dealings" – which is evidenced in the implied duty to act reasonably, to use best endeavours,[58] to give reasonable notice,[59] opportunity,[60] etc.[61] Finn relates this to a policy adopted by the Australian courts to control exercises of power, to uphold standards of conduct, notably fairness, fidelity and moral responsibility, and to uphold basic human values including dignity, integrity, security of one's property, and reputation, and the rights of parents in relation to their children.

It is clear that duties of, broadly, legality, rationality and procedural propriety do not arise in all contractual situations. The duties seem to arise where a decision is likely to affect an individual's vital interests, for instance in their security or status or autonomy. Many contractual relationships are purely commercial, the parties are not individuals, and these particular individual-oriented considerations in favour of duties of considerate decision-making are not present. On the other hand there may be other public policy reasons to impose or imply into the contract such duties.

---

[54] *Breen* v. *AEU* [1971] 2 QB 175, *Stevenson* v. *United Road Transport Union* [1977] ICR 893;

[55] *Law* v. *National Greyhound Racing Club* [1983] 1 WLR 1302.

[56] *Herring* v. *Templeman* [1973] 3 All ER 569.

[57] [1989] 2 Lloyd's Rep 570 at 625.

[58] His example is *Perri* v. *Coolangatte Investments Pty Ltd* (1982) 166 CLR 623 at 654.

[59] His example is *Laurinda Pty Ltd* v. *Capalabe Park Shopping Centre Pty Ltd* (1989) 166 CLR 623 at 654.

[60] His example is *Presmist Pty Ltd* v. *Turner Corporation Pty Ltd* (1992) 30 NSWLR 478.

[61] See *Renard Constructions (ME) Pty Ltd* v. *Minister for Public Works* (1992) 26 NSWLR 234.

Public policy

Let us now shift our focus from contractual to other relationships where a supervisory jurisdiction is exercised at common law. The position of bodies exercising monopoly power or providing services of importance to members of the public (often the case in judicial review) illustrates the point that duties of legality, rationality and procedural propriety in decision-making may be imposed on both public and private bodies.

Despite the fact that the courts nowadays do not consider regulatory bodies in sport and many other "private" bodies exercising regulatory or legislative power as being subject to judicial review,[62] duties of legality, rationality and procedural propriety which closely resemble the duties imposed in public law are imposed by the common law on private bodies in a range of non-contractual situations. The point is illustrated by *Law* v. *National Greyhound Racing Club*,[63] in which the plaintiff member of the NGRC had issued an originating summons to challenge the decision of the club in relation to him in the Chancery Division. The respondents were arguing that proceedings should have been commenced in the Queens Bench Division under Order 53 of the Rules of the Supreme Court (RSC). The Court of Appeal held that he was entitled to start proceedings in the Chancery Division, and that a remedy by way of declaration would be available.[64] The pegs on which this jurisdiction hung were, first, contract, in that a court could imply a duty of fairness or rationality in the membership contract of the club, and secondly, public policy, including policy against restraint of trade.

Nagle v. *Feilden*[65] provides an interesting example of the operation of restraint of trade doctrine, and of possible other public policy bases for the award of remedies for breach of duties of fairness and rationality, notably discrimination, in the common law Although *Nagle* was pleaded in both restraint of trade and on public policy grounds, Lord Denning did not base his judgment on restraint of trade. On the strength of *Nagle*, if a person was refused a trainer's licence for discriminatory reasons not covered by European law or British legislation, such as their religion, sexual orientation, the colour of their hair, their political affiliations or personal animosity on the part of a member of the licensing body, the court could find that this was unlawful, expressing it either as an unlawful restraint of trade or as contrary to a wider public policy: in effect the court could impose duties of reasonableness (as in the common callings cases) or of rational decision-making on the regulatory body.

---

[62] *Law* v. *National Greyhound Racing Club* [1983] 1 WLR 1302.

[63] Ibid.

[64] The declaration sought was that the decision was void and ultra vires, in that (i) it was a breach of an implied term of the agreement between the parties that all actions taken by the stewards which could deprive the plaintiff of his licence would be reasonable and fair and made on reasonable grounds, and (ii) it was in restraint of trade and contrary to public policy. It is not known what the outcome of the case was.

[65] [1966] 2 QB 633.

The case of *McInnes* v. *Onslow Fane*[66] provides an interesting contrast with *Nagle* v. *Feilden* as it was not based in restraint of trade at all, but on other public policy considerations. The plaintiff's application for a boxing manager's licence was refused and he was complaining of the lack of a hearing. There was no contractual relationship in which to base duties towards the plaintiff. The plaintiff failed because this was an application case, not a case of forfeiture or legitimate expectation, and there had been no breach of the relevant duties in dealing with the application. But Megarry VC laid down requirements of decision-making procedures in application, forfeiture or legitimate expectation cases affecting a "liberty to work" which, developed by subsequent case law, now also form part of the requirements in judicial review. In effect these principles require the interests of the plaintiff to be considered fairly and rationally when decisions affecting him are made. They include a duty, in application cases, "to reach an honest conclusion without bias and not in pursuance of any capricious policy"" – a formulation, like that in *Nagle*, that is reminiscent of *Wednesbury* reasonableness. In renewal and forfeiture cases additional duties are imposed, because these affect the existing interests of licensees in ways in which applications do not.

In *McInnes* Megarry VC was drawing analogies with a wide range of cases on immigration, reputations, privacy and status as well as livelihood. The foundation of the jurisdiction to control the decision-making processes of private regulators with various degrees of intensity, and outside contract, appears to have been public policy, in this case policy in favour of enabling people to earn their living in their own way – in favour of their autonomy. But, given Megarry VC's reference to other areas of the law in which rationality is imposed, public policy may also require degrees of rationality where other subject matter than livelihoods and other interests than autonomy are at stake – dignity, status and security in particular.

A question that arises is whether the jurisdiction in private law with which these cases have been concerned survives more recent judicial comments about the public/private divide and the exclusivity rule. In *RAM Racecourses* Simon Brown J commented that cases such as *Nagle*, if they had arisen then, "would have found a natural home in judicial review proceedings". But this approach cannot stand with the decisions in *Law, Aga Khan*[67] and other cases to the effect that such decisions by such bodies are not subject to judicial review. It is in my view quite consistent with general legal policy and developments in other areas of law for duties of considerate decision-making to be imposed in private law, so that the availability of judicial review is not essential to the remedy in such cases.

Doubts have been expressed about the wisdom of the courts interfering with the decisions of self-regulatory bodies through a supervisory jurisdiction, whether in judicial review or in private law. This is indeed an issue. It has been

[66] [1978] 1 WLR 1520
[67] R. v. *Disciplinary Committee of the Jockey Club, ex parte Aga Khan* [1993] 1 WLR 909, (CA).

argued that such bodies are well qualified to make these decisions themselves and they provide a workable "alternative dispute resolution" system.[68] This is certainly a legitimate consideration to take into account when the courts are considering the granting of remedies; but it should not of itself be taken to justify findings that the bodies are public or private, or their functions are public, governmental or private, or that they are not subject to duties of fairness and rationality in their actions.

There are a number of other fields in which duties of non-discrimination, fairness and rationality are imposed on decision-making by private bodies exercising power that adversely affects individuals in significant ways outside doctrines of contract or restraint of trade – and even outside monopoly situations. In *Wood* v. *Woad*,[69] a case on expulsion of the plaintiff from a mutual insurance society, Kelly CB founded his decision in favour of the plaintiff not on implied contractual terms, but on the basis that the *audi alteram partem* rule "is applicable to every tribunal or body of persons invested with authority to adjudicate upon matters involving civil consequences to individuals". This proposition was approved by Lord Macnaghten in *Lapointe* v. *L'Association de Bienfaisance et de Retraite de la Police de Montreal*[70] (a Privy Council case). That case concerned the decision of the board of a pension fund trust to deprive the plaintiff of his pension. Lord Macnaghten based his decision that the rules of natural justice applied on both "the rules of the society" and, significantly for our purposes, "the elementary principles of justice". It is worth observing at this point that insurance companies, banks, building societies, pension schemes and personal investment organisations often have in their hands the security of individuals – in fact arrangements with these bodies are often far more likely to provide individuals with security than, for example, employment or traditional property rights, or even the welfare state. These financial institutions are in positions of power in relation to their clients or members in the sense that their negligence or arbitrary action or wrongdoing can cause serious damage to the security of those dependent upon them. It is suggested that it is this factor that has led the courts, through the development of the common law and equity, and Parliament, to impose duties of natural justice upon them.

Another field in which duties of legality, fairness and rationality are imposed on decision-makers is employment: under the Employment Rights Act's provisions on unfair dismissal the courts, drawing on the ACAS Codes, have developed a supervisory jurisdiction over employers' decisions that requires them to act "within a band of reasonableness" (within four corners, perhaps?) and to follow a procedurally fair procedure.[71]

[68] See James A.R. Nafziger, "International sports law as a process for resolving disputes" (1994) 45 *ICLQ* 130. See also Julia Black, "Constitutionalising self-regulation" (1996) 59 *MLR* 24 for a discussion of the subjection of self-regulating bodies to judicial review.

[69] (1874) LR 9 Ex. 190

[70] [1906] AC 535, at 538–40, PC.

[71] Per Browne-Wilkinson J in *Iceland Frozen Foods Ltd.* v. *Jones* [1983] ICR 17, pp.24–5; *West Midland Co-operative Society Ltd.* v. *Tipton* [1986] AC 536.

TOWARDS GENERAL PRINCIPLES OF DECISION-MAKING

We have only been able , in the time and space available, to identify a limited number of examples of the imposition or implication of duties of considerate decision-making in private law situations. These, it is suggested, undermine the common assumption that these are essentially public law principles. This is far too narrow a view. There is scope for the common law and equity to continue to develop the law relating to decision-making so as to protect individuals from decisions that may adversely affect them and to promote public policies against abuse of power. In my view the decision in *O'Reilly* v. *Mackman* ran quite counter to the ways in which the common law and equity had been developing in purely private law areas, and the sooner we recognise that there are general principles of considerate decision-making in the course of development, which would apply both to the exercise of non statutory powers by public bodies and to private bodies, the better.

The point that duties, for instance, of natural justice, are not essentially based in the ultra vires rule or in public law, and that they are of longstanding pedigree in private law, has been illustrated by some of the examples given above. In 1911 Lord Loreburn – in a public law case – asserted that the duty of natural justice rests upon "anyone who decides anything".[72] These sentiments were echoed by Lord Denning in *Breen* v. *Amalgamated Engineering Union*:[73] "Call it prejudice, bias, or what you will. It is enough to vitiate the discretion [of] any body, statutory, domestic or other".[74] Lord Reid in *Ridge* v. *Baldwin*[75] also endorsed the proposition of Kelly CB in *Wood* v. *Woad*. There is also the line of cases on the duties of universities in private law to comply with rules of fairness and natural justice in their dealings with their students;[76] in other cases the duty is imposed in public law[77] because the university was a "public institution discharging public functions" (per Sedley J); and in others where there is a visitatorial jurisdiction the visitor has exclusive jurisdiction, but the visitor is subject to judicial review.[78] In these cases students, who are generally in vulnerable positions with no established status in society and no qualifications, receive some protection against the university authorities' exercise of their power, in that they can control student access to university property, and punish students by withdrawing co-operation.

These relationships, in which it is established that duties of fairness or rationality in decision-making are imposed, have a number of features in common. In many of them the vital interests of individuals are at stake, notably their

---

[72] *Board of Education* v. *Rice* [1911] AC 179.
[73] [1971] 2 QB 175; [1971] 1 All ER 1146.
[74] [1971] 1 All ER 1148, p. 1155.
[75] [1964] AC 40, 70.
[76] For example, *Herring* v. *Templeman* [1973] 3 All ER 569.
[77] For example, *R.* v. *Manchester Metropolitan University, ex parte Nolan* (1993) CLY 1646, DC.
[78] *R.* v. *Hull University Visitor, ex parte Page* [1993] AC 682.

interests in their autonomy, dignity, respect, status or security. They are also relationships in which a private decision-maker is in a position of power over other parties

It is suggested that, in the light of these developments, the courts can be seen to be developing general principles of considerate decision-making which span the public private divide. This jurisdiction to control exercises of power by imposing requirements on decision-making is an aspect of the jurisdiction to right wrongs and injustices[79] that was asserted in the early cases of *Bagg's case*[80] and *R. v. Barker*,[81] and of "the justice of the common law" referred to by Byles J in *Cooper v. Wandsworth Board of Works*.[82] The jurisdiction is not confined to public law. In effect the common law, equity – and statutes – in imposing duties on private bodies, are requiring what might be termed "civil citizenship" which resembles in many ways the civic duties imposed on public bodies in public law. These developments have in common that they democratise, rationalise and equalise public and private relationships.

THE LIMITS OF DUTIES OF CONSIDERATE DECISION-MAKING IN PUBLIC AND PRIVATE LAW

In both public and private supervisory jurisdictions there are countervailing considerations which may militate against judicial intervention, though there is not the space to go into them here more than in passing. There are clear parallels between the refusal of equitable remedies on grounds of delay or prejudice to third parties in private actions, and restrictions on the award of remedies in judicial review. The needs of the market, or managerial prerogatives (as in judicial review – the interests of good administration – and in employment)[83] may explain the non-application of duties of considerate decision-making in contract and precontractual situations. Where individual, as opposed to corporate, interests are not at stake there may be no reason to impose such duties, unless for instance a public policy such as that against restraint of trade or abuse of private monopoly power is engaged.

---

[79] See P Craig, "Ultra Vires and the foundations of judicial review" 57 *CLJ* (1998), 63, at pp. 77–8; M. Beloff, "Pitch, Pool, Rink – Judicial review in the sporting world" [1989] *PL* 95; and M. Beloff in M. Supperstone and J. Goudie, (eds.), *Judicial Review*, op. cit., pp. 8.21–8.22.

[80] (1615) Co Rep 93b; 77 ER 1273.

[81] (1763) 3 Burr 1265.

[82] (1863) 14 CB NS 180.

[83] See for instance, *Hollister v. National Farmers Union* [1979] ICR 542, at 541; and see H. Collins, "Market power, bureaucratic power, and the contract of employment" (1986) 15 *Industrial Law Journal* 1.

IMPLICATIONS FOR THE PUBLIC PRIVATE DIVIDE

The implications of this thesis are many. First, there is no substantive public law private law divide: the question whether prima facie duties of considerate decision-making arise does not depend upon whether the function under challenge is public or governmental in nature, or on the source of the power, or upon the nature of the decision-maker. It depends upon the effect of the proposed decision on an individual, or on other public policy considerations. Even where a decision will have an adverse effect on important interests of an individual, there may be countervailing considerations against imposing duties of considerate decision-making, or against granting discretionary remedies. Here the identity of the respondent as a public body or a body exercising public or governmental functions may be relevant, since such a body does not have its own interests to place in the balance against being under duties of considerate decision-making, or there may be considerations of natural security or non-justiciability to weigh against these prima facie duties.

There are also important implications for remedies. In trusts and company law, declarations and injunctions and other equitable remedies are available. So, under Lord Cairns' Act are damages. At common law there may be awards of damages for breach of contractual duties of natural justice or rational decision-making, or injunctions or declarations. Damages – or equitable remedies – may also be awardable in restraint of trade and other public policy situations in which duties of fairness and rationality are imposed, as in the torts connected with abuse of monopolies and breaches of the duties of those in common calling, which there has not been the space to discuss here. Duties of considerate decision-making shade into duties of considerate action in those areas. If I am right that the existence of duties of considerate decision-making does not depend upon whether the function in issue is public or governmental, but upon general legal principles to do with the control of power, protection of individuals and general public policy, it would seem to follow logically that damages might also be available where public or governmental functions are under challenge. The "wrong" of inconsiderate decision-making may be an equitable or a common law wrong, or both, it may be virtually tortious, and it is not intrinsically "public" in nature.

In the light of this set of considerations, the procedural and remedial divides (for that is all they are) introduced by the House of Lords in *O'Reilly* v. *Mackman* seem particularly inappropriate. *O'Reilly* boils down to nothing more than a rule that in some cases in which public or governmental functions are at issue, permission must be obtained for proceedings and a tight time limit is imposed. This looks very like a quasi-immunity. It is difficult to find a rational justification for a situation in which duties of legality and fairness and rationality are imposed broadly across the spectrum of public and private law, and yet procedural and remedial protections apply in certain types of case because public or governmental functions are being exercised and certain remedies are being claimed. This is particularly odd since the protections apply regardless of whether in fact in a particular case it would be against the interests of good administration to exercise the jurisdiction, and they apply regardless of whether the decision-maker is a private or public body (see *Datafin*). Short (six month) limitation periods in civil actions against public bodies were abolished by the Law Reform (Limitation of Actions) Act 1954, and it seems quite anomalous that the judicial review limit should remain when the substantive law in a case is not peculiarly "public". A short time limit in a case that is public ought surely not to be applied without any consideration to whether interests of good administration or other considerations weigh against the imposition of prima facie duties of legal, rational and fair decision-making.

My thesis also has implications for the theory that the ultra vires rule and the doctrine of legislative intent form the basis of judicial review. There are some rather unconvincing parallels between the doctrine of legislative intent in judicial review and duties in trusts and contract which might be loosely linked to the intentions of the parties to a contract or the settlor of a trust. But in practice it is quite clear that equity *imposes* duties in fiduciary relationships and the trust instrument simply enables the duties to be given some of their content; similarly the duties of directors are largely imposed, though the articles and resolutions of the company and its shareholders are relevant considerations. In this respect legislation, contracts, articles of association and trust instruments have much in common. Those of us who deny that the doctrine of legislative intent is the rationale for judicial review of statutory powers do not deny the relevance and often (European law and the Human Rights Act 1998, section 3 provide major exceptions) the overriding importance of the express terms of the statute, just as parties to a contract or a trust would not deny the relevance of those documents. But in situations where the interests of individuals or other public policy interests are at stake and either there are imbalances of power in relationships or power may be abused to the detriment of the public interest, the courts have for long *imposed* duties of legality, rationality and procedural propriety on decision-makers. We ought to admit that such duties may legitimately be imposed by the common law and equity in such situations, and that the justification for imposing such prima facie duties has nothing to do with legislative intent or its private law equivalents, or with questions about public or governmental functions.

Such an approach would release the energies and creativity of equity and the common law and avoid the illogicality of assuming that bodies wielding private power, such as the regulatory bodies in sport, cannot be placed under duties of legality rationality and fairness unless their activity is of a public or governmental character – in which case, quite illogically, they will be entitled to the protections of section 31 of the Supreme Court Act 1981 and Order 53 RSC. An open approach would remove the temptations on the courts to squeeze essentially private bodies into a public pigeon hole in order to impose such duties upon them when, given the chance to do so, equity and the common law could develop such duties without jumping through that uncomfortable hoop and being met with the procedural and remedial obstacles presented by the rules for applications for judicial review.

15

Of Vires and Vacuums: The Constitutional Context of Judicial Review*

JEFFREY JOWELL

What justifies the power of judges to strike down decisions of public officials? It seems odd that so many years after judicial review began to develop so rapidly we are still arguing about this fundamental question, but there are two opposing views on the matter, each of which receives significant support.

The first view contends that judicial review of official action is justified by the doctrine of ultra vires;[1] the second that it is justified by the inherent power of the courts to develop the common law.[2] Under the first justification (ultra vires) it is said that the courts through judicial review are implementing the will of Parliament – express or implied. Under the second (common law), judicial review is a "judicial creation",[3] applying standards of a higher-order law that is "logically prior"[4] to the command of the legislature.

These two alternative justifications rest upon different constitutional foundations. Ultra vires rests securely and wholly upon the supremacy of Parliament

* The author would like to thank Stephen Guest and Martin Loughlin for their helpful comments on an earlier draft of this article.

[1] e.g. H.W.R. Wade and C.F. Forsyth, *Administrative Law* (7th ed., 1994), p. 342; C. Forsyth, "Of Fig Leaves and Fairy Tales: The *Ultra Vires* Doctrine, The Sovereignty of Parliament and Judicial Review" (1996) 55 CLJ 122 and Chapter Two pp. 29–4 above; M Elliott, "The Demise of Parliamentary Sovereignty? The Implications for Justifying Judicial Review" (1999) 115 LQR 119, and "The *Ultra Vires* Doctrine in a Constitutional Setting: Still the Central Principle of Administrative Law" [1999] CLJ 129 and Chapter Five 83–109 above.

[2] e.g. Dawn Oliver, "Is the *Ultra Vires* Rule the Basis of Judicial Review?" [1987] PL 543 and Chapter One pp. 3–27 above; Sir John Laws, "Illegality: The Problem of Jurisdiction" in M. Supperstone and J. Goudie, *Judicial Review* (1998) and Chapter Four pp. 73–81 (extract) above, Ch. 4; Sir John Laws, "Law and Democracy" [1995] PL 72; Lord Woolf M.R., "Droit Public – English Style" [1995] PL 57; D. Dyzenhaus, "Reuniting the Brain: The Democratic Basis of Judicial Review" (1998) 9 Pub. L. Rev. 98; P. Craig, "*Ultra Vires* and the foundations of Judicial Review" [1998] CLJ 63 and Chapter Three pp. 47–71 above. See also P. Craig below at p. 373.

[3] The words of Sir John Laws, "Law and Democracy", above at p. 79.

[4] Sir John Laws, above p. 86, quoting R. Latham, *The Law and the Commonwealth* (1949) p. 523. This phrase was employed by Laws J. in *R. v. Lord Chancellor, ex p. Witham*, [1997] 2 All ER 799, when he held that the introduction of new court fees deprived the citizen of his constitutional right of access to the courts. Such rights were not "the consequence of the democratic political process but would be logically prior to it."

and leaves no doubt that the courts in our system are subordinate to the legislature. All power is derived power – derived from the legislature, which is the supreme law-making authority. The courts are Parliament's bureaucrats, implementing the legislature's designs as agents rather than principals.

Under the second justification, the courts possess a source of authority which is independent from the legislature. Although bound to follow and enforce the will of Parliament where that is expressed clearly, situations of ambiguity release judges to establish their own regime as principals rather than agents. That regime is governed by the common law, rather than Parliament's law.

Both justifications employ the rule of law as a guiding precept under which official action may be constrained – but place different emphasis upon different aspects of the rule of law. The ultra vires justification views the rule of law largely as a principle of legality in its broadest sense. Courts thus implement the rule of law by requiring officials to execute their power in accordance with the scope under which it was conferred. The courts thus ensure that officials obey the rule of law by not straying outside their given powers. The common law justification views the rule of law largely as a disabling principle – one that limits the scope of officials (in the absence of parliamentary purpose to the contrary) to breach a catalogue of independent tenets incorporated within the rule of law – such as legal certainty, consistency, rationality and access to justice.

Both these justifications bristle with problems. Ultra vires is artificial because it supplies an intention to the legislature which is wholly fictional; the legislature is unlikely ever to have considered the matter, and, if it had, might well have formed a different conclusion from the one implied by the courts. Ultra vires is also incomplete, in that it fails to explain judicial review's dominion over prerogative power or the power of non-statutory bodies exercising public functions.

The common law doctrine has the attraction of frankness; it does not hide behind fiction and artificiality. It candidly admits the independent role of the judiciary. In doing so, however, it presents a provocative challenge to traditional British constitutional doctrine by seemingly conferring an open-ended law-making power on unelected judges, leading perhaps to the review even of primary legislation.

If standards of judicial review are being developed apace, as they are, and if these standards are generally accepted as right and just, does it matter whether they are modestly attributed by the courts to the implied intent of the legislature, or brashly asserted as independent creations of their own? Since, after all, implied intent is a judicial construction, the judges can be as bold in their manipulation of that construct as they can under the model of the common law. So why the fuss?

The proper justification for judicial review does matter, not only because it provides a reason for intervention, but also because it indicates the limits of judicial power and its legitimate scope. It is thus crucial to the future relationship between the judiciary and the legislature and to the development of standards that delineate the appropriate balance between official power and individual rights in a constitutional democracy.

To test which of the justifications is to be preferred, or to decide how the two may be reconciled or modified, we should begin by examining the accepted grounds or principles which the courts have applied through judicial review of discretionary powers, seeing how they fit with either justification.

It is often said that judicial review should not concern itself at all with the substance of an official decision, but only with the way decisions are reached.[5] This invokes the image of a path leading up to an official decision and requiring the judge, when reviewing that decision, not to look forward from the decision to assess its impact after it was made. Unlike Lot's wife, the judge is confined only to looking back from the decision along the path, ensuring that the decision-maker did not irrelevantly stray from the path en route to the decision, and that no unfair obstacles were placed in the way of affected parties.

This image directs our attention to both the scope and limits of judicial review. It comfortably allows courts to assess the "legality" of official action – ensuring that the decision-makers interpreted their powers correctly and kept within their assigned pathway. It also allows the courts to ensure that the affected parties were not unfairly denied an adequate opportunity to present their case (review for lack of procedural fairness). But it suggests that the courts are not able to evaluate the substantive consequences of a decision (at least outside of the situation of manifest absurdity).

Let us then examine the two extremes of the spectrum of judicial review – instances where it is generally agreed that the courts do, and do not, respectively, have the power to strike down official action. First, review for procedural fairness (where the courts clearly do have power to intervene) and secondly, review for substance (where it is said that the courts do not have the power to substitute their judgment for the primary decision-maker on the so-called merits of a decision).

Procedural review

At the first end of the spectrum, it is beyond contention that the courts may always intervene to strike down a decision which is flawed for want of a fair hearing or natural justice. How then do we justify the power of the courts, in the face of a statute that is silent on the matter, to require, for example, the Home

---

[5] *e.g.* Lord Brightman in R. v. *Chief Commissioner of North Wales Police, ex p. Evans* [1982] 1 WLR 1155 at 1173F: "Judicial Review is concerned not with the decision but with the decision-making process".

Secretary to receive representations from an applicant for British citizenship before refusing his application?[6] After all, it is the Home Secretary, and not the court who is the donee of the statutory power. So what is it that invites the necessary implication that Parliament did not intend the Home Secretary to be the master of his own procedures (as the ultra vires justification would contend)? Or that the courts are entitled to supply the omission of the legislature by their own justice (as the common law justification would contend)?

Competence

In seeking to justify judicial review on any ground, we must surely begin with a notion of competence. In order to second-guess the primary decision-maker the courts must first establish that the decision is within their appropriate realm of decision. There are two senses of competence, *constitutional competence* and *institutional competence*, both of which are necessary to ground the court's jurisdiction. The question of constitutional competence involves a normative assessment of the proper role of institutions in a democracy. It starts with the assertion that it is not the province of courts, when judging the administration, to make their own evaluation of the public good, or to substitute their personal assessment of the social and economic advantage of a decision. We should not expect judges therefore to decide whether the country should join a common currency, or to set the level of taxation. These are matters of policy and the preserve of other branches of government and courts are not constitutionally competent to engage in them.[7]

The question of institutional competence involves a practical evaluation of the capacity of decision making bodies to make certain decisions. It starts with the recognition that some matters are not ideally justiciable. It thus focuses not upon the appropriate role of the judge, but upon the inherent limitations of the process of adjudication. This is because courts are limited in their capacity to decide matters which admit of no generalised or objective determination. Such matters (such as whether a local authority's expenditure was "excessive",[8] or the question of a university department's rating for research[9]), are not amenable to decision by a non-specialist. In addition, the adjudicative process is not ideally suited to deciding polycentric questions – those which cannot be settled in isolation from others which are not before the court – such as whether scarce resources should be allocated to one project or proposal in preference to others whose claims are not in issue.[10]

---

[6] As in R. v. *Secretary of State for the Home Department, ex p. Fayed* [1997] 1 WLR 228 (CA).

[7] See R. Dworkin, *Taking Rights Seriously* (1977), pp. 82–87.

[8] R. v. *Secretary in State for the Environment, ex p. Hammersmith and Fulham L.B.C.* [1991] AC 521, *per* Lord Bridge at 596–597.

[9] R. v. *Higher Education Funding Council, ex p. Institute of Dental Surgery* [1994] 1 WLR 242.

[10] For a fuller account of justiciability and polycentricity, see L. Fuller, "The Forms and Limits of Adjudication" (1978–9) 92 Harv. L. Rev. 395; J.W.F. Allison, *A Continental Distinction in the*

Returning now to the ground of procedural fairness, the reason we accept it as an appropriate basis for judicial review is that the decision whether a public body failed to afford an individual a fair hearing is a matter clearly within both the institutional and constitutional competence of the courts. In respect of constitutional competence, the tenets of procedural fairness do not require an utilitarian evaluation of preferred outcomes. They are not based upon policy evaluations best suited to elected officials or their agents in a democracy. Procedural fairness is based on principle, which is the proper role of judicial decision. This does not mean that decisions about procedure are immune from political controversy or do not require searching evaluation of their proper limits. For example the judicial introduction of a right to reasons for decisions may arouse much contention on the part of administrators who will count their cost carefully. Nevertheless, it is not seriously contended that the imposition of procedural norms is beyond the constitutional capacity of judges, who aim thereby not to achieve any particular social or economic objective but to ensure only that the decision was fairly arrived at.

Courts are also clearly institutionally competent to decide matters of procedure. Judges are seeped in matters procedural and their own decision-making is hedged with safeguards assuring participation by affected parties who thus have a fair opportunity to influence the result. Being experts in one area of decision-making, it is an easy step to apply those principles and techniques, appropriately modified to another. Procedure is a quintessentially justiciable issue, summoning arguments of principle addressed to discernible criteria and imposing no undue strain upon the adjudicative process.

Qualifying on the ground of constitutional and institutional competence is only the first step to judicial review. Once it is established that the courts have the capacity to decide a matter involving procedure, a further exercise is then required, that of justification on grounds of principle. Reasons must be found to legitimate the constraints imposed by the courts upon the powers of bodies on whom broad discretionary power has been conferred by Parliament. The deeper, principled justification for procedural fairness is not hard to find. One such justification is the concern and respect for human dignity: individuals should not have decisions made about their vital interests without having an opportunity to influence the outcomes of those decisions. Another justification is based on the aim of rationality and the avoidance of the arbitrary decision. Participation of affected parties in the decision, proper opportunity to present evidence, the requirement of reasons, all promote a more informed and therefore accurate decision and one for which the decision-maker is more easily able to be held accountable for error. Participation in decision-making also assists access to justice, by permitting a person to protect the substantive interest to which he has a legitimate claim of entitlement. Finally, procedural fairness may

Common Law: A Historical and Comparative Perspective on English Public Law (1996). Note that lack of constitutional and institutional competence may coincide in respect, *e.g.* of a decision whether to site an airport on site A, B or C.

be required in order to protect a legitimate expectation which is under threat of being disappointed.[11]

These reasons for procedural fairness do not constitute isolated claims of institutional morality. They are simply too rich to be attributed to the intention of a legislature when passing a statute on a possibly mundane matter. They address fundamental questions of the respective roles of state and individual in a democratic society. These justifications all invoke fundamental constitutional principle – such as the concern for human dignity, for official rationality, and the rule of law.

Substantive review

At the other end of the spectrum from procedural judicial review is review on the ground of the substantive content of the decision. It is generally accepted that, when a power is conferred by Parliament upon a public body, a court reviewing a decision of that body should not substitute its substantive decision for that of the reviewed body. Thus, where power is given to the Home Secretary to decide whether the character of an applicant justifies his grant of citizenship, the court should not substitute its view of the applicant's character for the view of the Home Secretary as if the court were entitled to make that primary decision.

What are the limits to substantive judicial review and what justifies those limits? We must begin here by noting the obvious distinction between judicial review and judicial appeal. Courts on appeal may be permitted to reassess *ab initio* both the lawfulness of a decision and its substantive content. Judicial review deals with lawfulness alone. But what is substantive review, and what justifies its exclusion from judicial review's grasp (if excluded it is)?

Sir John Laws rests this prohibition on the courts' power on the rule of law which, he contends, requires the courts to recognise that they themselves are not the donee of the relevant statutory power. The courts have a duty, he says, to ensure "that the statute is not usurped by anyone – including the courts themselves".[12] Insofar as Laws is sating that the courts are not Parliament's chosen instruments to achieve the substantive purpose of their statute, then his argument is surely correct. Indeed our procedures of judicial review do not permit the courts to substitute their decision for that of the primary decision-maker, but only to quash, enjoin or prohibit its implementation or to remit it for reconsideration.[13] However, short of wresting power in such an obvious way, courts do in practice interfere with official decisions on substantive grounds in two sit-

---

[11] For a full account of these various justifications see D.J. Galligan, *Due Process and Fair Procedures* (1996).

[12] In "Law and Democracy", above, n. 2, at p. 78.

[13] See CPR, Ord. 53.

uations (which mostly are, but sometimes are not, labelled under the general ground of review known as unreasonableness or irrationality).

First courts review on the ground of a defect in the *process* by which the decision was reached. Process must be distinguished from procedure. Procedure deals with the mechanisms of participation in the decision-making process itself. Process deals with the way decisions are justified or reasoned, or the factors taken into account *en route* to the decision. Courts do comfortably strike down decisions infected by defective process. Examples include decisions that are strictly irrational and apparently arbitrary; where improper motives were taken into account; where there was no evidence to justify the decision, or where the reasoning was incoherent. But even beyond process, the courts also feel themselves able to hold unlawful decisions on the ground of their *impact* on affected persons and to strike them down because they are unduly oppressive because they interfere with a person's rights (such as a prisoner's right of access to justice,[14] or to a person's right not to be treated unequally[15]) or with their legitimate expectations (such as a decision to implement a retrospective penalty[16]) or because they cause unnecessary hardship to their interests.[17] Where broad discretionary power is conferred upon the primary decision-maker, how do courts justify their intercession on the ground of failure to observe the proper process of decision-making or the unduly oppressive impact of the decision?

Again there, we must look first to the notion of competence. The courts in this area of substantive review are more limited in their institutional competence than they were in procedural review. A number of questions are not justiciable because courts are not able objectively to evaluate their respective merits, or because the decisions are polycentric, such as those which require the allocation of scarce resources (for example, whether to order a hospital to provide a child with an expensive urgent operation with very little hope of success; the provision of the operation would have the effect of reducing the resources available to the hospital for other needed activities[18]). Institutional competence also requires expertise, which is why the courts will be hesitant to overturn a decision which required the weighing of respective relevant considerations by holding that excessive weight was placed by the decision-maker on one or other of those considerations. Courts would be reluctant, therefore, themselves to weigh the relevant merits of granting a planning permission for a new building against the desirability of preserving an existing building.[19] Judges may have views on these matters, but they do not possess the expertise required to decide them on our behalf.

[14] R. v. *Secretary of State for the Home Department, ex p. Leech (No. 2)* [1994] QB 198.

[15] See, *e.g.* R. v. *Immigration Appeal Tribunal, ex p. Manshoora Begum* [1986] Imm.A.R. 385.

[16] *Pierson* v. *Secretary of State for the Home Department* [1998] AC 539.

[17] For further examples of review for process or impact see de Smith, Woolf and Jowell, *Judicial Review of Administrative Action* (1995) Chapter 13.

[18] R. v. *Cambridge District Health Authority, ex p. B* [1995] 2 All ER 129, CA.

[19] See, *e.g.* *London Residuary Body* v. *Lambeth L.B.C.* [1990] 1 WLR 744.

Courts may also be disabled from substantive review on the ground of their lack of constitutional competence. Decisions of social and economic policy are constitutionally allocated to our elected officials and it is not for the courts to engage in matters involving a utilitarian calculus of social good.

What is then the justification for intervention on substantive grounds of review within this relatively narrow range of competence? Here we are often confused by the fact that the courts, sensing that they are on thinner constitutional ground in substantive review than on procedural review, do all they can to cover their tracks by laying false clues and donning elaborate camouflage. When judges deny that they ever engage in substantive review the denial is invariably disingenuously qualified by the phrase "outside of *Wednesbury* unreasonableness".[20] But on most of the occasions when the courts have intervened on the ground that the decision is unreasonable, the official body being reviewed has behaved in a manner that was coolly rational and far from the *Wednesbury* formulation, and the ultimate reason for intervention could as easily have been cast in principle as in pragmatism – and increasingly is.[21]

As with procedural review, it is fundamental constitutional principle that supplies the justification for substantive review – whether specifically acknowledged or not. The rule of law provides much of the justification, requiring legal certainty,[22] access to justice not to be unfairly impeded,[23] consistent application of laws and legitimate expectations to be fulfilled.[24] But outside of the rule of law other principles are also found, such as equality[25] and freedom of expression.[26]

The above excursus leads us to a position where we find that, to be seized of judicial review of a particular matter, the courts must be both constitutionally competent (in the sense that the task they seek to perform is not more appropriately conferred on another instrument of governance) and institutionally competent (in the sense of deciding on matters that are capable of resolution by means of adjudication and not requiring expertise which the courts lack). Once qualified in these ways, the courts decide matters both about procedure (which

[20] See, *e.g.* Lord Brightman's qualification to his statement in *ex p. Evans*, cited in n. 4, above, at p. 1175B–C.

[21] See Lord Cooke's subtle attack on *Wednesbury* in R. v. *Chief Constable of Sussex, ex p. International Traders' Ferry Ltd* [1998] 3 WLR 1260 at 1288G–1289B.

[22] *e.g. Wheeler* v. *Leicester City Council* [1985] 1 AC 1054; R. v. *Secretary of State for the Home Department, ex p. Pierson* [1998] AC 539.

[23] R. v. *Secretary of State for the Home Department, ex p. Leech (No. 2)* [1994] QB 198. And see R. v. *Secretary of State for, the Home Department, ex p. Simms* [1999] 2 All ER 400, HL.

[24] For examples see de Smith, Woolf and Jowell, above, paras. 13–026–025. See P.P. Craig, "Substantive Legitimate Expectations in Domestic and Community Law" [1996] CLJ 289.

[25] See de Smith, Woolf and Jowell, paras. 13–036–045. See also *Matadeen* v. *Pointu and the Minister of Education and Science* [1999] AC 98 (PC) where is was said that equality "in one of the building blocks of democracy and necessarily permeates any democratic constitution" and was a "general axiom of rational behaviour" *per* Lord Hoffmann at 109.

[26] *Derbyshire County Council* v. *Times Newspapers Ltd* [1993] AC 534 (HL) – not a judicial review but see, *e.g.* R. v. *Ealing L.B.C., ex p. Times Newspapers* [1987] 85 LGR 316. See also the powerful statement by Lord Steyn in *ex p. Simms*, above, note 22, at 407F–408J.

is generally accepted as being within their scope) or about the substance of a decision (where their power to review is more contested). Under either of those heads, the justification for review is ultimately based not on mere notions of fairness applied pragmatically to the instant case, but rooted in deeper constitutional principle.

Three further points should now be made. The first is the obvious one that constitutional principles are not rules.[27] They lack that element of specificity. They are prescriptive in character but indeterminate in content. Their content crystallises over time when concrete problems throw up the need to settle competing claims of power and authority and rights. Judging these claims requires a strong empirical sense that allows an evaluation, within the bounds of democracy's inherent requirements, of changes in practice and expectations. New principles emerge by a process of accretion reflecting a constitution's changing imperatives and shifting settlements. These are based upon altering notions of the proper scope of governmental power[28] as well as upon other fundamental social values which become endorsed over time.[29] Secondly, we should note that, unlike rules, evidence of principle is not found solely in the authoritative command of officials (whether courts or other enforcement officers of one kind or another, or the command of a statute). The moral force of a constitutional principle can be discerned in cases of inaction as well as action, for example, the fact that a governmental proposal seeking to breach a constitutional principle was defeated in Parliament. This happened with the Police Bill 1997, which threatened the principle of the sanctity of a person's home and privacy, but failed to receive parliamentary approval. The failure to enact the legislation in such a case may indicate not that Parliament was unable in law to breach the principle, but that Parliament was persuaded, against the initial judgement of the majority of its members, not to withstand the rule of law's moral strictures.

Finally, we should observe that constitutional standards are not confined to Dicey's duo of the supremacy of Parliament tempered by the rule of law. The rule of law is a key principle of institutional morality, but it is not the sole such principle. The rule of law does have a broad scope and seeks to achieve aims that are both procedural and substantive. It requires access for the individual to the courts and an independent judiciary; it requires congruence between legislative purpose and official action; it forbids arbitrary or irrational decisions and, perhaps above all, it requires what we now call legal certainty – the absence of retrospective laws and the fulfilment of legitimate expectations. It is through that

[27] For a useful analysis of the difference between rules, which are relatively specific in their direction, and other standards, see J.M. Black, " 'Which Arrow?' Rule Type and Regulatory Policy" [1995] PL 94.

[28] *e.g.* proportionality may be taking root as a general principle of democratic governance. See *International Traders' Ferry*, above, note 20 and Lord Hobhouse in *ex p. Simms*, above, note 22, at 422G.

[29] *e.g.* the values common to public and private law suggested by Dawn Oliver, namely, autonomy, dignity, status, respect and security. D. Oliver, "The Underlying Values of Public and Private Law" in Michael Taggart (ed.), *The Province of Administrative Law* (1997), p. 217.

route of legal certainty that the rule of law embraces a notion of formal equality – requiring law to be enforced equally between rich and poor; official and citizen. But it surely stretches the rule of law to breaking point to ask it to
encompass notions of substantive equality, to require equal laws; or to embrace
other principles such as proportionality.[30]

For our purposes the rule of law does not need to be spread beyond its capacity[31] for there are other constitutional principles, such as equality in its own
right, or freedom of expression, of movement, of association, and so on, which
can stand these days, unaided by any support from the rule of law, as fundamental principles in any democracy properly so-called – and irrespective of
whether they are endorsed in statutory form.[32]

VIRES IN CONSTITUTIONAL CONTEXT

We are now ready to return to our question about the proper justification of
judicial review. At first sight it seems as if the ultra vires justification is less convincing than that of the common law. In our scheme the courts, once qualified
by means of competence to enter review, have played their search-lights upon a
order higher than any statute in order to identify their ultimate reason for intervention. If a governing constitutional principle is found, then it prevails, at least
in the absence of a statutory command to the contrary. The theory of implied
intent cannot accommodate this approach, which reaches beyond the realm of
the statute whose intent is in issue. Yet we are uncomfortable with the notion of
courts free to impose their judicial creations without identifiable constraints – a
freedom that could logically lead to a damaging turf war between our institutions of governance. And the common law justification also has to contend with
powerful judicial dicta stating clearly that ultra vires is indeed the foundational
principle of judicial review.[33]

---

[30] Trevor Allan invests the rule of law with such a broad scope. See T.R.S. Allan, "The Rule of
Law as the Rule of Reason: Consent and Constitutionalism" (1999) 115 LQR 221. See J. Jowell, "Is
Equality a Constitutional Principle?" [1994] CLP 1; J. Jowell, "The Rule of Law Today", in J. Jowell
and D. Oliver (eds.), *The Changing Constitution*, (3rd ed., 1994), p. 57.

[31] Despite its elasticity. See the example its extension to the prohibition of the Home Secretary's
taking into account "public clamour" as a consideration in deciding to extend a prisoner's sentence
in *R. v. Secretary of State for the Home Department, ex p. Venables* [1998] AC 407 (HL).

[32] The Human Rights Act 1998 will of course put into statutory form those rights contained in
the European Convention on Human Rights. Strictly speaking, breach of those rights will, once the
Act is in force, offend the ground of judicial review of legality rather than irrationality or indeed procedural propriety. However, the Act is likely to attain a broader constitutional significance. See
A. Barak, "The Constitutionalisation of the Israeli Legal System as a Result of the Basic Laws and
its Effect on Procedural and Substantive Criminal Law" (1997) 31, Israeli L. Rev. 3. Lord Lester,
"The Art of the Possible. Interpreting Statutes Under the Human Rights At" [1998] EHRLR 665.

[33] See in particular Lord Brown-Wilkinson in *R. v. Lord President of the Privy Council, ex p. Page*
[1993] AC 682 at 701–702, and Lord Steyn in *Boddington* v. *British Transport Police* [1998] 2 WLR
639 at 662, HL.

These dicta may well, however, have been guided by shrewd judicial politics based upon a desire in the courts not to provoke the other arms of government at a sensitive moment. We should also note that the very general statement that ultra vires is the foundation of judicial review massively begs the question of what we mean by *vires*. In its strict sense, *vires* refers to the powers conferred by statute. The accepted ground of review of legality then permits the courts quite properly to ensure that discretionary powers have been exercised within the circumference of those powers. But there is a broader sense of *vires*, which it is open to the courts to recognise. This sense was recently expressed by Lord Steyn (one of the authors of the dicta referred to above) in the *Pierson* case. He said this:

> Parliament does not legislate in a vacuum. It legislates for a European liberal democracy founded on the principles and traditions of the common law. And courts may approach legislation on this initial assumption. But this assumption only has prima facie force. It can of course be displaced by a clear and specific provision to the contrary.[34]

And in the same case, Lord Browne-Wilkinson (the author of the other dictum) said:

> A power conferred by Parliament in general terms is not to be taken to authorise the doing of acts by the donee of the power which adversely affects the legal rights of the citizen or the basic principles on which the law of the United Kingdom is based unless the statute conferring the power makes it clear that such was the intention of Parliament.[35]

Under this approach the judicial delineation of *vires* need not involve the court in interpreting a conferred power by reference to the legislature's implied intent (as the "modified version") of the ultra vires justification contends[36]). The courts are able to engage directly with constitutional principle and need not summon the medium in the statute to thump out a message on the table on behalf of that principle. *Vires* becomes power in context; it respects identifiable legislative intent, but draws the very practical inference that our legislature is legislating in and for a society governed by a framework of democracy, of which the legislature is a vital but not the only part, and in which the supremacy of Parliament and the rule of law are crucial but not the only guiding tenets.

Does this approach amount to the same as the common law justification of judicial review? Not quite. The courts are neither the agents of the legislature nor the unconstrained masters of the common law. The judicial task is relatively circumscribed; it is not to impose its "creations" upon officials, but to articulate the foundations of a system in which both courts and the legislature are

---

[34] R. v. *Secretary of State for the Home Department, ex p. Pierson* [1998] AC 539 at 575. See also, The Rt. Hon. Lord Steyn, *The Constitutionalisation of Public Law* (Constitution Unit, May 1999).

[35] *Ibid.* at 575.

[36] This is the view put forward by Elliott in the articles referred to in n. 1 above, and so ably criticised by Paul Craig at p. 373 below.

essential features with their own distinct institutional limits. Whether judges "make" or "find" the law, they do so within a relatively confined space in which a focused search for the concrete application of constitutional and institutional principle takes place. Another feature of this approach is its acceptance of Parliament's supremacy; if Parliament goes so far as to exclude a constitutional principle (and we have seen that it has the power to do so, although the moral strictures of constitutional principle will weigh in the opposite direction) the courts (at least under the present constitutional dispensation) will have to accept that. But, in order to command that acceptance, Parliament will have to make itself clear. Even ambiguity may not be enough to coax the courts into agreeing to displace democracy's foundational features.[37]

THE SEPARATION OF POWERS AND JUDICIAL INDEPENDENCE

We have now reached a position where constitutional principle governs all governmental action, subject to the important qualification that Parliament, being the supreme law-making institution in Britain's democracy, can, if it wishes, override constitutional principle. Democracy may be dented as a result, but, until we move to a new constitutional settlement, it is the prerogative of Parliament so to dent it. We have not been able quite to adapt the ultra vires justification of judicial review to this position, but there is a final problem with the common law justification. To what extent can it coexist with a concession which disables its effect in respect of primary legislation? If it is agreed that (a) the courts cannot strike down primary legislation, and (b) Parliament can reverse a decision by the courts on the lawfulness of a public power, is there any room left for an independent role for the courts upon which the common law justification depends?

The answer is surely yes. Courts are not bureaucracies. Whether courts are themselves creations of statutes or possess inherent powers, the essence of their function is to adjudicate on the lawfulness of official action (at least outside of legislation). That function involves the courts forming their own view of the matter in this area of their competence. For the courts to decide these questions on the basis of an assessment of how the legislature would have decided the matter had it been a judge in its own cause amounts to an exercise in divination[38] and is ultimately an abdication of judicial responsibility.

---

[37] The legislative provision in *Pierson*, n. 33 above, was held not to be ambiguous but nevertheless permitted the constitutional principle of the rule of law to prevail. This contradicts the approach in *Brind* [1991] 2 AC 696 (HL), where it was held that the conferment of a broad discretionary power effectively rebutted any presumption that a treaty obligation could apply in domestic law. In the recent case of *ex p. Simms*, note 22 above, the majority of the House of Lords endorsed the approach of Lords Steyn and Browne-Wilkinson in *Pierson*. See Lord Hoffmann at 412G–J; Lord Steyn at 411G–J. And see Sir Rupert Cross, *Statutory Interpretation* (3rd ed., 1995), pp. 165–166.

[38] Interpretation was distinguished from divination by Kentridge A.J. in giving the judgment of the South African Constitutional Court in *State* v. *Zuma* [1995] (4) BCLR 401 at 412.

Once we accept, as we surely must, that the judiciary in the United Kingdom, despite its present limitations in respect of primary legislation,[39] are and must be independent, the common law justification of judicial review must therefore be preferred – but subject to a final modification, which has already been explored: that although judges are not bureaucrats, neither are they policy-makers. Judicial review is by no means an unbounded exercise allowing the judiciary freedom to impose unconstrained standards. And it requires a sensitive appreciation of the institutional and constitutional limitations of all decision-making bodies, including those of the courts themselves, as well as those of Parliament, the executive and other bodies exercising public functions.

REVIEW OF NON-STATUTORY BODIES

A final reason for preferring the common law justification of judicial review is that it avoids the black hole of the ultra vires justification, namely, its failure to accommodate judicial review of non-statutory power. To say, as Forsyth does,[40] that such review is justified on the basis of the power of the courts to control monopoly power, begs a myriad of questions about the competence of the courts to pursue a policy about the appropriate role of competition in the economy. To justify such review on the ground that the legislature would have regulated the body's power had it had the opportunity to do so (which is sometimes suggested by the courts)[41] again amounts to a fanciful guess at legislative intent. Non-statutory bodies with regulatory powers – over the activities of individuals or classes of individuals or professions that they control – should be called to legal account on the basis of standards similar to those imposed upon statutorily-created regulatory bodies. It would be wrong to impose different standards of behaviour upon bodies on the basis of the happenstance of the source of their power. Both statutory and non-statutory bodies should be governed by those principles that govern the exercise of power in a democracy, if the functions they perform are equivalent.

CONCLUSION

It is an inescapable feature of an unwritten constitution that its dimensions emerge in the course of concrete decisions raising questions about the appropriate balance of power between different instruments of government and about the proper lim-

---

[39] When the Human Rights Act 1998 takes effect on October 5, 2000, courts will be able to review primary legislation which may not conform with the provisions of the European Convention. However, under section 4 of the Act, the courts will not be able to strike down such legislation but only issue a declaration of incompatibility.

[40] "Of Fig Leaves and Fairy Tales", cited fully at n. 1 above, pp. 124–126, and pp. 31–3 above

[41] Sometimes known as the "but for" test, and applied in *e.g. R. v. Disciplinary Committee of the Jockey Club, ex p. Aga Khan* [1993] 1 WLR 909 (CA) by Bingham M.R. (at 923). See also de Smith Woolf and Jowell, above, paras. 3–023–034.

its of the state. That process requires due regard to be had to a mix of principle and empiricism – an appreciation of the moral rights of individuals and the appropriate reach of state power in the light of shifting institutional arrangements between different sources of authoritative decision.

Legitimate judicial review must always begin with an assessment of vires – of the powers intended by a legislative scheme. But it needs to proceed further; first to examine the competence of both the reviewed body and the court to decide the matter, and then to identify the underlying principles which should govern the decision. These principles do not exist in a vacuum. For judges to seek them in the general notions of fairness that may reside in the common law may prove helpful, but it is more helpful still for them to engage openly with the necessary qualities of a modern constitutional democracy.

16

Legislative Intention Versus Judicial Creativity? Administrative Law as a Co-operative Endeavour*

MARK ELLIOTT

I. INTRODUCTION

The debate concerning the juridical basis of judicial review has, on occasion, tended to be a divisive one. Writers are separated into opposing camps, and the different theories are often presented – or at least perceived – as competing rivals. Discussion centres upon the contemporary relevance of the ultra vires doctrine, which holds that judicial review entails nothing more than the enforcement of implied statutory limits on discretionary powers.[1] The two principal schools of thought in this area are distinguished by their approach to the question whether legislative intention is relevant to the justification of judicial review in a modern democracy based on the rule of law. Ultra vires theorists maintain that it is, while proponents of an autonomous approach to review argue that the common law alone is able to supply adequate justification for curial supervision of executive action.[2]

The common law theorists make a very powerful case.[3] They point out that, to the extent that it presents review as the product of judicial divination and implementation of legislative intention, ultra vires is entirely unconvincing.[4] It is perfectly clear to all concerned that, in the words of Sir John Laws, the

* I am grateful to Dr. Christopher Forsyth for his valuable comments on an earlier draft of this paper.

[1] For detailed accounts of the ultra vires principle, see H.W.R. Wade and C.F. Forsyth, *Administrative Law* (Oxford, 1994, 7th ed.), pp. 41–9; P.P. Craig, *Administrative Law* (London, 1994, 4th ed.), pp. 4–17.

[2] On the distinction between the ultra vires and common law schools, see further M.C. Elliott, "The Ultra Vires Doctrine in a Constitutional Setting: Still the Central Principle of Administrative Law" [1999] CLJ 129, 129–31 and pp. 83, 83–6 above.

[3] The criticisms of ultra vires are helpfully stated by P.P. Craig, "Ultra Vires and the Foundations of Judicial Review" [1998] CLJ 63 and pp. 47–71 above.

[4] The inability of ultra vires to explain review of prerogative and other non-statutory power, which is a further drawback of the orthodox theory, is beyond the scope of the present paper. For an explanation of how a modified version of ultra vires theory can co-exist in a constitutionally coherent manner with judicial review of non-statutory powers, see Elliott, op. cit., n. 2, pp. 154–6.

principles of judicial review "are, categorically, judicial creations".[5] Thus arises the temptation to abandon the ultra vires doctrine in its entirety, replacing it with a wholly new justification for judicial review based on the normative resonance of the values which the common law has historically embodied. Such an approach holds that the grounds of review "have nothing to do with the intention of Parliament, save as a fig leaf to cover their true origins".[6] We do not, say the common law theorists, need that fig leaf any longer.

It is this type of reasoning – according to which the important part played by judicial creativity precludes *any* role for legislative intention in the constitutional explanation of judicial review – that leads to the perception that the common law and ultra vires schools are rivals which must be chosen between. It is high time that closer attention was paid to the common values and ideas that underpin these two approaches, and which indicate that the dispute which has dominated this subject in recent years is, at least to some extent, more apparent than real. It is submitted that, far from being divided by a gulf of disagreement, the parties to the present debate occupy a good deal of common ground.

Few people, if any, doubt the need to replace the conventional ultra vires principle with a more convincing explanation for judicial review. In particular, it is necessary to articulate a theory which acknowledges the creativity of the judges and the normative foundations upon which they have built modern administrative law. The purpose of this paper is to demonstrate that, in spite of the imperative of moving beyond conventional ultra vires theory, there are still good reasons for retaining legislative intention as *part* of the constitutional explanation for judicial review.

Christopher Forsyth and myself have already argued that such an approach is necessary in order to reconcile the supervisory jurisdiction with the principle of parliamentary sovereignty (irrespective of whether Parliament remains fully sovereign in the orthodox sense).[7] In this paper I shall argue that there exists a series of further, more pragmatic, reasons for preferring a theoretical model of judicial review which connects it with, rather than divorces it from, the related ideas of vires, jurisdiction and intention. In doing so, my aim is not to obscure the arguments concerning sovereignty which have already been made elsewhere; rather, my purpose is to show that preserving a link between judicial review and parliamentary intention carries with it a set of additional, perhaps more tangible, benefits. In this manner, the conceptualisation of judicial review as a co-operative endeavour, encompassing both judicial creativity and legislative will, makes good sense in not only constitutional but also practical terms.

---

[5] "Law and Democracy" [1995] *PL* 72, 79.

[6] Ibid.

[7] C.F. Forsyth, "Of Fig Leaves and Fairy Tales: The Ultra Vires Doctrine, the Sovereignty of Parliament and Judicial Review" [1996] *CLJ* 122 and p. 29 above; M.C. Elliott, "The Demise of Parliamentary Sovereignty? The Implications for Justifying Judicial Review" (1999) 115 *LQR* 119; M.C. Elliott, "The Ultra Vires Doctrine in a Constitutional Setting: Still the Central Principle of Administrative Law" [1999] *CLJ* 129 and p. 83 above.

Before turning to these matters, it is necessary briefly to set out what is meant by the modified ultra vires theory.[8]

II. THE MODIFIED ULTRA VIRES PRINCIPLE

A. The nature of the modified ultra vires principle

It is clearly unconvincing to suggest that the courts, as they apply the principles of review to discretionary powers, are doing nothing more than ascertaining and implementing Parliament's will. The problem with this orthodox conception of the ultra vires doctrine lies in its assertion that there exists a straightforward, direct relationship between intention and review, such that review is no more than the effectuation of a specific, albeit unwritten, legislative intention.[9] As Forsyth observes, "[n]o-one is so innocent as to suppose that judicial creativity" has not contributed to the development of administrative law.[10]

However, as I have argued at length elsewhere,[11] the conclusion that a direct relationship between intention and review is fundamentally implausible need not ineluctably lead to the rejection of the possibility of some other form of connection. It is quite feasible to postulate an indirect relationship between legislative intention and the principles which the courts apply upon judicial review.

As Lord Steyn has explained, it is a fundamental principle of both constitutionalism and interpretation that:

> Parliament does not legislate in a vacuum. Parliament legislates for a European liberal democracy founded on the principles and traditions of the common law. And the courts may approach legislation on this initial presumption.[12]

This is the premise on which courts approach all legislation, including that which confers decision – and rule-making powers on executive agents. It follows that, when a court seeks to ascribe meaning to such legislation and to determine the extent and scope of such powers, it will assume – in the absence of very clear contrary provision – that Parliament intended to confer a power the nature and contours of which are consistent with the values embodied in the contemporary rule of law doctrine as it is understood within the British constitutional framework. Consequently, when the court articulates and enforces limits on the exercise of discretionary powers by reference to the established principles of fairness, reasonableness and so on, it fulfils the general intention underlying the

---

[8] See further the articles cited at n. 7.

[9] As has already been indicated, a number of further problems have been identified in relation to the ultra vires doctrine. However, I have argued (see op. cit., n. 2, pp. 148–57 and pp. 100–7 above) that, once the ultra vires principle is understood within its proper constitutional setting, these difficulties are avoided. It is not the purpose of the present paper to repeat those arguments.

[10] Forsyth, op. cit., n. 7, p. 136 and p. 42 above.

[11] Op. cit., n. 2.

[12] R. v. *Secretary of State for the Home Department, ex parte Pierson* [1998] AC 539, 587.

legislative scheme. On this approach, there is no attempt to impute to Parliament specific intention concerning the precise content of the principles of judicial review. Rather, the wholly plausible step is taken of ascribing to Parliament a general intention that the rule of law should be upheld and, therefore, that the discretionary powers to which legislation gives rise should be subjected to legal limits based on the rule of law doctrine. Judicial review thus becomes a co-operative endeavour in which the courts give concrete legal effect to Parliament's presumed general intention that executive power should be limited by reference to constitutional principle.

Thus arises a modified conception of the ultra vires doctrine which locates the orthodox principle within its proper constitutional setting, thereby allowing it to function as a relatively straightforward presumption concerning Parliament's intention. By envisaging an indirect connection between parliamentary intention and the grounds of review, the traditional ultra vires doctrine's implausible assertion that there exists a direct relationship is avoided, and the creativity of the judges in developing modern administrative law can be openly acknowledged because, within the modified model, Parliament is taken to have left it to the good sense of the courts to determine the precise content of the grounds of review through the incremental method of the common law tradition.

B. The utility of the modified ultra vires principle

Not only does the modified ultra vires principle constitute a substantial advance on the traditional doctrine; it is also to be preferred to the common law model, which denies the existence of any connection between intention and review. Specifically, the modified doctrine's principal advantage over the common law theory is that it facilitates the reconciliation of review with the theory of legislative supremacy. The reasons underlying the necessity of retaining a relationship between intention and review in order to avoid challenging parliamentary sovereignty are complex, and it is not the purpose of this paper to repeat arguments which have been set out in detail elsewhere.[13]

Instead, the remainder of this paper is devoted to an exploration of a set of additional advantages which flow from the postulation of a relationship between curial supervision and legislative frameworks. It is submitted that consideration of these matters demonstrates that both the pure ultra vires doctrine and the alternative common law model are inadequate on their own and that, in order to articulate a justification for judicial review which is both constitutionally satisfying and pragmatically workable, it is necessary to combine the points made by the theorists on both sides of the present debate.

However, before developing these ideas further, it is appropriate to examine the criticisms which some writers have levelled at the modified theory of ultra vires.

---

[13] See the literature cited at n. 7.

C. Criticism of the modified ultra vires principle

Due to considerations of space, discussion of the criticisms which have been made of the modified ultra vires doctrine will be kept brief and will be confined to four specific points.[14]

1. The purpose of the modified ultra vires principle

The first matter which requires consideration is the purpose of the modified ultra vires principle, in light of the argument recently advanced by Nicholas Bamforth that it fails to secure its objective.[15] He remarks that the aim of ultra vires theory is the protection of parliamentary sovereignty, and goes on to suggest that it "fails to achieve this goal" which, in turn, "must force us to conclude that there is an inconsistency between the theory's aims and its outcome". Bamforth reaches this conclusion by reasoning as follows. According to Sir William Wade's classic exposition of sovereignty theory,[16] the constitutional status of legislation ultimately turns on the courts' willingness to recognise parliamentary enactments as valid law. Given this, says Bamforth, the ultra vires doctrine can only be judged to be a success if, in potentially revolutionary situations (that is, where the courts' adherence to legislative expression is placed under particular strain), its effect is to vouchsafe judicial obedience to parliamentary intention. Bamforth concludes that the ultra vires doctrine has no such effect and therefore fails to fulfil the purpose which its proponents are said to claim for it. This argument prompts two responses.

First, it may be something of a simplification to suggest that ultra vires is of no relevance in potentially revolutionary situations. It is clear that the *legal* doctrine of ultra vires cannot absolutely guarantee the sovereignty of Parliament given that – as Wade explains – the latter exists as an ultimately *political* phenomenon within the British constitutional framework. However, it is certainly possible to argue that one of the virtues of ultra vires is that it reflects and reinforces the correct mode of institutional interrelation which obtains under the United Kingdom's constitutional settlement. As Forsyth notes:

> [Ultra vires theory maintains that] judicial review does not challenge but fulfils the intention of parliament. By their ready acceptance of ultra vires the judges show that they are the guardians, not the subverters, of . . . [the] existing constitutional order. This fact is not a "fig-leaf" nor is it a "fairy tale"; it marks the maintenance of the

---

[14] The criticisms of the modified ultra vires doctrine which are discussed in the following paragraphs can be found in the papers, published in this volume, by Nicholas Bamforth and Professor Paul Craig, respectively entitled "Politics, Ultra Vires and Institutional Interdependence" pp. 113–39 and "Competing Models of Judicial Review" pp. 373–92. Of necessity, the passages from those papers which are cited and discussed below are taken from the draft papers which were circulated at the conference on the foundations of judicial review at the Cambridge Centre for Public Law in May 1999.

[15] "Politics, Ultra Vires and Institutional Interdependence" (see elsewhere in this volume).

[16] See "The Basis of Legal Sovereignty" [1955] *CLJ* 172.

proper balance of powers between the elected and non-elected parts of the constitution. Adherence to ultra vires is a gentle but necessary discipline.[17]

On this view, ultra vires exerts a symbolic influence which locates public law principles within a constitutional framework that requires judicial deference to parliamentary enactment. In this way it is possible to argue that adherence to ultra vires embodies a form of constitutional practice which reinforces the idea of sovereignty, thereby militating – albeit indirectly – in favour of respect for Parliament's supremacy in potentially revolutionary situations.

There is, however, a second, and perhaps more obvious, response to Nicholas Bamforth. His central criticism of ultra vires is that it fails to protect parliamentary sovereignty, which, he says, is the doctrine's *raison d'être*. This begs the question what precisely is meant by "protecting parliamentary sovereignty". There are, in fact, two prinicpal competing meanings which this expression may bear.

One possibility is that it may refer to the protection of parliamentary supremacy against a constitutional revolution; as already discussed, it is this goal which Bamforth ascribes to ultra vires. However, saying that ultra vires "protects parliamentary sovereignty" may mean something quite different. When a commentator who supports ultra vires refers to its capacity to uphold parliamentary sovereignty, it is most likely that he is alluding to the doctrine's ability to effect a constitutional reconciliation which permits the co-existence of judicial review of executive action and the principle of legislative supremacy. In this sense, the purpose of ultra vires theory is not to guarantee the existence of parliamentary sovereignty in the event of constitutional change. Rather, its function is to vouchsafe the legitimacy of judicial review – by furnishing the theoretical means by which to explain its existence in a manner which is compatible with the principle of parliamentary sovereignty – so long as the present constitutional order, and the supremacy doctrine which it embodies, continues to subsist. It follows that the true purpose of ultra vires is to vouchsafe the legitimacy of judicial review, not to protect the existence of the doctrine of parliamentary sovereignty.[18] Whether ultra vires – in its traditional or modified form – actually succeeds in that endeavour is a keenly debated point; nevertheless, it is crucial that any evaluation of ultra vires should be founded on an accurate understanding of the goal which it claims to secure. It is submitted, with respect, that Nicholas Bamforth's assessment of ultra vires does not rest on such a foundation.

2. Statutory agencies and private law

Professor Paul Craig makes some more specific criticisms of the modified ultra vires theory.[19] As explained above, the theory holds that statutory agencies are required to respect public law principles because, when Parliament legislatively

---

[17] Op. cit., n. 7, pp. 136–7 and 42–3.

[18] This is apparent from the accounts of ultra vires offered by Wade and Forsyth, loc. cit., n. 1 and Forsyth, op. cit., n. 7. The same is true of my own work on ultra vires (op. cit., n. 7).

[19] See "Competing Models of Judicial Review" p. 378 below.

confers authority upon them, the grant is inherently limited by a general intention that public bodies should act in accordance with those principles; meanwhile, it is left to the courts to determine precisely how the broad principles of good administration should be translated into specific legal requirements. Craig remarks that, if this is so, the application to public bodies of private law principles must be explained symmetrically, by reasoning that:

> Parliament in a constitutional democracy intends a just system of civil liability, and that it then delegates the detailed implementation of this task to the courts to be decided in accordance with the normative principles which should govern such a system.

Such reasoning, says Craig, fails to reflect accepted thinking about the relationship between private law and public agencies.

There are, in fact, two aspects to that relationship. On the one hand, it would be both unorthodox and counterintuitive to assert that private law doctrine has been developed at the tacit behest of Parliament. It is perfectly clear that it is the courts which have developed the regime of civil liability which obtains in English law. The corpus of private law – like public law – therefore owes its *existence* to the creativity of the judiciary and the incremental method of the common law. It is therefore important to emphasise that modified ultra vires theory does not require the denial of this. Rather, it merely requires acknowledgment of the fact that, when Parliament creates a statutory power, it cannot sensibly be taken to intend anything other than that it should be exercised according to law. It therefore follows that, within the modified ultra vires framework, intention does not explain the *existence* or development of the legal rules – public or private – which apply to statutory agencies; rather, intention is relevant only to the *application* of public and private law principles to such agencies, in the sense that Parliament is plausibly taken to intend that the bodies which it creates should be subject to law.

Within this model, legislative intention and judicial creativity are of a piece with one another, serving complementary functions at different levels of specificity. The courts, acting within their proper constitutional sphere, develop principles of private (and, for that matter, public) law liability, while Parliament, acting within its legislative province, ordains that the agencies which it creates should be subject to the values which underpin public and private law[20] and to the specific legal rules which the courts have developed in order to give practical effect to those values. The fact that statutory agencies are regulated by private law therefore presents no obstacle to the modified ultra vires theory. That theory does not necessitate recourse to the fiction that private law has been developed pursuant to parliamentary will, and nor does it require the normative values which underpin private law to be denied or disguised. In truth, modified ultra vires theory merely requires recognition of the fact that Parliament legislates in a legal

---

[20] Indeed, Professor Dawn Oliver identifies a high degree of symmetry between the values which are upheld by public and private law. See, for example, her contribution to this volume pp. 307–25.

environment which embodies private (and, of course, public) law principles and must surely be taken to intend that the bodies which it creates should be subject to, rather than above, the law. As with public law, so with private law: the imputation to Parliament of this modest intention ensures that the application of legal rules to statutory bodies fulfils rather than cuts across legislative schemes and, in this manner, judicial regulation of public agencies is rendered consistent with, rather than a challenge to, the legislative supremacy of Parliament.[21]

3. Legislation which regulates matters in the private sphere

Professor Craig makes a related, but distinct point, concerning legislation which regulates matters in the private sphere. He suggests that whenever such regulation exists – for example, in the area of employment protection – it logically follows from the modified ultra vires principle that the entire body of law in the relevant area must be related to legislative intention. Common law doctrine relating to the employment relationship would, on this view, have to be legitimated by reference to an assumption that Parliament is taken to intend a just relationship between employers and employees. In truth, the modified ultra vires doctrine produces no such consequences.

It is important, in the present context, to distinguish between the legal regulation of *statutory power* on the one hand and *residual liberty* on the other. Whenever an agency exercises statutory power, it logically follows that it must either act within or beyond the scope of its derived competence. That is why it has been argued at length that judicial regulation of the exercise of statutory power must be rationalised in terms of the delineation and enforcement of the scope of the conferred power; any other approach would involve conflict with the legislative scheme and would therefore be an affront to sovereignty theory.

However, the same position does not obtain in relation to the regulation of private matters. Take, for example, the employer-employee relationship. When someone decides to employ a worker, he does not act pursuant to any power which has been conferred by Parliament; rather, he exercises the freedom – which every British citizen possesses – to do as he pleases (save to the extent that the law confines such freedom). Since no exercise of statutory power is at stake in this context, it is unnecessary to relate curial regulation to legislative intention. The motivation for articulating such a connection in the context of statutory agencies is to ensure that the control of statutory power traces, rather than

---

[21] It has been explained elsewhere, in considerable detail, why it is constitutionally necessary to embrace a connection between, on the one hand, the legislative scheme which gives rise to a particular agency and, on the other hand, the legal regulation of such an agency by the courts: see above, n. 7. It will be argued below (see sections III and IV of this paper) that there exists a set of complementary, pragmatic considerations which also militate in favour of such an approach. However, for present purposes, the important point is that acceptance of the modified ultra vires theory as the constitutional justification for the application to statutory agencies of public law principles on judicial review does not require the adoption of an unrealistic or unorthodox conception of the relationship between statutory agencies and private law.

cuts across, the contours of the grant of power, thus avoiding conflict with legislative intention. However, no such imperative exists in private contexts, given that no statutory power is in play. Thus it must be concluded that Craig is incorrect to assert that modified ultra vires theory renders legislative intention the "central principle" in every area of law which is touched by legislation. That theory is directed towards the specific question of how judicial regulation of statutory power may be justified in constitutional terms. It does not impact upon private matters in which statutory power is not, in the first place, in issue, and – contrary to Professor Craig's assertion – the modified ultra vires doctrine certainly does not require "writers in areas as diverse as labour law, company law, commercial law and tax" to "re-write" their subjects.

4. Judicial review and legislative intention

It is appropriate, at the present juncture, to refer to one further criticism which Craig makes of the modified ultra vires theory. As is well known, the central issue in the ultra vires debate concerns the question whether judicial review should be related to legislative intention. There are, in fact, two senses in which intention may be relevant to review.

Most commentators agree that, in this context, intention certainly possesses what may be termed *negative relevance*. This means that if Parliament makes sufficiently clear provision – by means, for example, of an adequate preclusive clause – the operation of the principles of good administration can be excluded. In his most recent paper, published in this volume, Professor Craig readily accepts that intention is relevant in this residual sense.

Ultra vires theorists, however, go further: they ascribe a second, *positive relevance* to legislative intention. For reasons which have been advanced elsewhere, they maintain that it is constitutionally necessary to hold that judicial review entails the identification and enforcement of the limits of discretionary power which inhere in the legislative scheme. In this manner, intention does not merely operate residually to exclude review; it is also responsible, in the first place, for the application of public law limits to statutory powers.

It is this positive relevance which the modified ultra vires doctrine ascribes to legislative intention that Professor Craig questions in his most recent paper, in which he insists that intention is relevant only in the negative sense. However, this must be contrasted with a paper which Craig published in 1998. He wrote that, in order to render judicial review constitutionally legitimate, and to meet the concerns of the ultra vires school:

> there would be a common law presumption that the common law proscription against the making of vague regulations [or any other conduct in breach of the principles of good administration] would be prohibited, unless there was some very clear indication from Parliament to the contrary.[22]

[22] Op. cit., n. 3, p. 74 and p. 57.

In this passage, it is relatively clear that Craig attaches both positive and negative relevance to parliamentary intention: the courts are justified in enforcing limits on statutory power because Parliament is presumed to permit the enforcement of such limits (positive relevance), unless this presumption is displaced by sufficiently clear contrary provision (negative relevance). In this manner, Professor Craig appeared to accept that there must exist some form of connection between legislative intention and the law of judicial review, according to which intention would serve an active, legitimating function, not merely a residual, prohibitive function.

It is important to draw attention to this matter, since the question of the precise nature of the relationship between legislative schemes and judicial review remains the principal source of disagreement between the commentators. The analytical debate on this point is exhaustive, and it would not be profitable to repeat it here. Instead, it is necessary to return to the main theme of this paper which seeks to highlight a set of more pragmatic, tangible benefits which flow from recognising that judicial review is a co-operative endeavour which embraces both legislative intention and judicial creativity.

III. AN UNWELCOME DISTINCTION IN ADMINISTRATIVE LAW

A. Introduction

Critics of ultra vires tend to distinguish between two applications of the doctrine. On *narrow review* the courts are concerned to ensure the presence of those "things which are conditions precedent to the tribunal having any jurisdiction to embark on an enquiry".[23] This ensures that "the relevant agency [has] . . . the legal capacity to act in relation to the topic in question: an institution given power by Parliament to adjudicate on employment matters should not take jurisdiction over non-employment matters".[24] The basis of this form of review is therefore straightforward, since the limits which the courts impose on narrow review are "to be found from a consideration of the legislation" which marks out the scope of the delegate's competence.[25] For this reason even critics of ultra vires, like Lord Woolf, accept that it "can readily be applied" to explain narrow review.[26]

---

[23] *Anisminic Ltd.* v. *Foreign Compensation Commission* [1969] 2 AC 147, 195, *per* Lord Pearce.

[24] Craig, op. cit., n. 3, p. 65. See e.g., *White and Collins* v. *Minister of Health* [1939] 2 KB 838.

[25] *Anisminic Ltd.* v. *Foreign Compensation Commission* [1969] 2 AC 147, 207, *per* Lord Wilberforce.

[26] Lord Woolf, "*Droit Public* – English Style" [1995] *PL* 57, 65. It is, perhaps, no longer wholly accurate to call Lord Woolf a critic of ultra vires given that, in *R.* v. *Secretary of State for the Home Department, ex parte Fayed* [1998] 1 WLR 763, 766–7, he opined – in strikingly orthodox terms – that, on judicial review, "the court is ensuring that decisions of the executive are taken in the manner required by Parliament".

It is the courts' *broad review* jurisdiction that critics of the orthodox ultra vires principle concentrate upon, pointing out the substantial implausibility which is involved in the assertion that the complex principles of good administration simply spring from Parliament's legislative silence.

The situation thus arises that narrow review is undeniably based on vires and intention (given that the limits which are judicially enforced in such cases are apparent from the relevant legislative framework), while many commentators assert that the broad principles of good administration rest on distinct, common law foundations. Once it is recognised that this is the true position of the common law theorists, it becomes apparent that the drawing of a dividing line between ultra vires and common law grounds of review is unavoidable. This raises some significant problems.

Two particular points need to be addressed. First, it will be noted that it is very difficult, in practical terms, to force the grounds of review into two such watertight compartments. Secondly, the reasons which underpin this difficulty will be examined, and it will be argued that they ultimately point towards the futility and illogicality which inheres in any attempt to establish a category of common law grounds of review that are unrelated to the enabling statutory scheme.

B. The practical difficulty illustrated

In its decision in *Bugg* v. *Director of Public Prosecutions*,[27] the Divisional Court set out a distinction between substantively and procedurally defective executive action, holding that the former, but not the latter, could be challenged collaterally by defendants in criminal proceedings. It was the difficulty of satisfactorily demarcating the boundary between these two quite separate classes of defect which substantially contributed to the doubts which the House of Lords expressed about the *Bugg* decision in *R.* v. *Wicks*[28] and, ultimately, to its decision in *Boddington* v. *British Transport Police*[29] that *Bugg* had been wrongly decided. As the Lord Chancellor said in *Boddington*:

> . . . the distinction between orders which are "substantively" invalid and orders which are "procedurally" invalid is not a practical distinction which is capable of being maintained in a principled way across the broad range of administrative action . . . Many different types of challenge, which shade into each other, may be made to the legality of byelaws or administrative acts. The decision in *Anisminic* freed the law from a dependency on technical distinctions between different types of illegality. The law should not now be developed to create a new, and unstable, technical distinction between "substantive" and "procedural" invalidity.[30]

---

[27] [1993] QB 473. *Bugg* was concerned with byelaws; however, the making of delegated legislation is merely a facet of administrative action. The implications of that decision, had it been allowed to stand, would have affected the exercise of all forms of discretionary power.

[28] [1998] AC 92.

[29] [1998] 2 WLR 639.

[30] Ibid., 650–1.

Lord Steyn took this point, too:

> There is . . . a formidable difficulty of categorisation created by *Bugg*'s case . . . A distinction between substantive and procedural invalidity will often be impossible or difficult to draw. Woolf LJ recognised [in Bugg] that there may be cases in a grey area, e.g. cases of bad faith . . . I fear that in reality the grey area covers a far greater terrain.[31]

Thus the House of Lords recognised that it is extremely difficult to establish a clear division between two different classes of defect for the purposes of determining whether collateral challenge can lie because, as Lord Greene MR remarked in *Wednesbury*, the different grounds of review tend to "run into one another".[32] Hence, in *Boddington*, their Lordships concluded that it was necessary to abandon any attempt to demarcate a class of defects which rendered administrative action merely voidable and, therefore, collaterally unimpeachable.

C. Distinguishing ultra vires and common law grounds of review

Just as Woolf LJ's attempt to divide the grounds of review into procedural and substantive classes was beset with practical problems, so any attempt to establish a boundary between those grounds of review which are attributable to legislative intention and those which rest on common law foundations would also, to adopt Lord Steyn's expression, raise "formidable difficulties of categorisation". It is instructive, in this context, to look at the experience of those jurisdictions – notably South Africa and Australia – which have embraced the idea of common law grounds of review.

It is now received wisdom in Australia that the rules of natural justice are creations of the common law, having nothing to do with deemed intention. This new orthodoxy, which followed from the decision of the High Court in *Kioa v. Minister for Immigration and Ethnic Affairs*,[33] has been explained in the following terms by the Chief Justice of New South Wales:

> [In traditional theory, the] role of the Courts is the limited role of ensuring that administrative decisions are kept within the bounds which Parliament has itself laid down. Administrative law has now gone beyond these limits by the recognition that common law principles apply of their own force and not on the basis of the intention of Parliament. It now appears that many of the grounds for judicial review are not merely propositions of statutory construction. Rather they are imposed on the exercise of public power by the common law . . . The best established case concerns the principles

---

[31] [1998] 2 WLR 661.
[32] *Associated Provincial Picture Houses Ltd.* v. *Wednesbury Corporation* [1948] 1 KB 223, 228. See further M. Fordham, *Judicial Review Handbook* (Chichester: John Wiley, 1997, 2nd edn.), pp. 514–21.
[33] (1985) 159 CLR 550.

of natural justice and, particularly, the requirement to give persons a fair hearing. This is a requirement which the common law attaches to the exercise of public power.[34]

Once the rules of natural justice are categorised as autonomous common law grounds of challenge, it becomes necessary to determine whether other heads of review – rationality, relevancy, legitimate expectation, and so on – should be similarly conceptualised. The difficulty lies in deciding where to draw the line. As an Australian commentator remarked, "The distinction may seem so problematic that it should be avoided".[35]

The South African courts faced similar problems in the aftermath of the very widely criticised decision in *Staatspresident* v. *United Democratic Front*, in which the Appellate Division held – contrary to previous authority and established principle – that vagueness was a common law ground of review rather than a species of ultra vires.[36] Once this conclusion had been reached, Friedman J felt obliged, in a later case, to hold that the doctrine of unreasonableness also fell outside the ambit of ultra vires.[37] Similarly the requirements of fairness were held to constitute a common law ground of challenge, unrelated to the scope of the power which the legislature initially granted.[38]

However, a large grey area must remain. Particular problems arise in relation to such principles of review as the obligation to take all relevant, but no irrelevant, factors into account, and to use statutory power only to further, never to frustrate, the purpose for which it was created. Grounds of challenge such as these are particularly difficult to categorise, given that they can possess concrete meaning and content only when they are located within the context of a specific statutory scheme. In this manner, the determination of purpose and relevancy is possible only by reference to, *inter alia*. ideas of intention.[39]

These practical difficulties arise in part because the grounds of review do tend to run into one another. However, it is also possible to identify more

---

[34] J.J. Spigelman, "The Foundations of Administrative Law" (the 1998 Spann Oration, Sydney, Australia, 7 September 1998).

[35] P. Bayne, "The Common Law Basis of Judicial Review" (1993) 67 *ALJ* 781, 782.

[36] 1988 (4) SA 830. The decision was widely criticised not only because of the doctrinal confusion which it introduced into South African administrative law, but also due to the fact that it substantially removed the courts' ability to read ouster clauses narrowly by applying the reasoning in *Anisminic Ltd.* v. *Foreign Compensation Commission* [1969] 2 AC 147. This was of particular importance bearing in mind the political regime which prevailed in South Africa at the relevant time. For discussion, see E. Mureinik, "Administrative Law" [1988] *Annual Survey of South African Law* 34; J. Grogan, "The Appellate Division and the Emergency: Another Step Backward" (1989) 106 *SALJ* 14; M.L. Matthews, "Vandalizing the Ultra Vires Doctrine" (1989) 5 *South African Journal on Human Rights* 481; Forsyth, op. cit., n. 7.

[37] *Natal Indian Congress* v. *State President* 1989 (3) SA 588.

[38] *Administrator, Transvaal* v. *Traub* 1989 (4) SA 731.

[39] F. Wheeler, "Judicial Review of Prerogative Power in Australia: Issues and Prospects" (1992) 14 *Sydney Law Review* 432, 468–71, argues that grounds of challenge such as relevancy of considerations and propriety of purpose may be applicable to prerogative powers notwithstanding the absence of a statutory framework; nevertheless, she concedes that this framework is highly relevant when statutory powers are reviewed on these grounds, and that the scope for deploying these heads of review when no such framework exists is severely limited. This follows because it is the statutory scheme which pre-eminently confers content upon such heads of review.

fundamental reasons which explain why it is ultimately meaningless to seek to establish a bright line distinction between grounds of review which are and are not related to legislative intention. It is to these matters which we must now turn.

D. Distinguishing ultra vires and common law grounds of review: explaining the difficulty

Three particular factors can be identified which help to illuminate the underlying difficulties which would attend any attempt to articulate two distinct categories of review based respectively on ultra vires and the common law.

1. *Legislative intention and the grounds of review: a spectrum of relevance*

It is clear that there are some grounds of review which are more transparently and closely related to the will of Parliament than others. For instance, the connection between review for narrow jurisdictional error and legislative intention is particularly clear, while the complex rules of natural justice are less obviously a straightforward product of legislative intention. However, to deduce from this that there exist two quite separate classes of review, one of which is a simple function of legislative intention, the other having absolutely nothing to do with it, is unduly simplistic.

All of the principles of good administration are, in some manner, context-sensitive in their application. As noted above, this is particularly apparent in relation to such matters as propriety of purposes and relevancy of considerations. The determination of purpose and relevancy can only be undertaken by reference to, *inter alia*, the framework established by and the intention underlying the enabling legislation. However, this is true of other grounds of review which are perhaps less overtly related to the will of Parliament. For instance, Friedman J noted, in a South African case, that:

> where one is dealing with questions of unreasonableness, any argument based on unreasonableness must of necessity be directed towards the empowering provision.[40]

In the High Court of Australia, Mason J made the same point with regard to fairness:

> Where the decision in question is one for which provision is made by statute, the application and content of the rules of natural justice or the duty to act fairly depends to a large extent on the construction of the statute.[41]

---

[40] *Natal Indian Congress* v. *State President* 1989 (3) SA 588, 594. Friedman J's conclusion that unreasonableness was nevertheless a common law ground of challenge was reached reluctantly, on the basis that the Appellate Division's *UDF* decision dictated this outcome.

[41] *Kioa* v. *Minister for Immigration and Ethnic Affairs* (1985) 159 CLR 550, 584.

Lord Parker CJ also emphasised the importance of referring to the relevant legislation in order to evaluate what fairness requires in any particular case:

> Good administration and an honest or bona fide decision must, as it seems to me, require not merely impartiality, nor merely bringing one's mind to bear on the problem, but acting fairly; and to the limited extent that the circumstances of any particular case allow, and *within the legislative framework under which the administrator is working*, only to that limited extent do the so-called rules of natural justice apply.[42]

The principles of good administration are therefore flexible requirements, the precise content of which cannot be determined without reference to the legislative intention manifested in enabling legislation.

It follows from this that it makes no sense to argue in favour of a category of grounds of review to which legislative intention is wholly irrelevant. To posit a watertight division between heads of challenge to which intention is respectively relevant and irrelevant is thus untenable. It is more realistic to acknowledge – as does the modified ultra vires doctrine – that there exists, in relation to the principles of good administration, a spectrum of relevance of legislative intention. At one end of this continuum, where grounds of review such as narrow jurisdictional error are found, the relevance of intention is highly conspicuous. At the other end of the continuum, legislative intention is still relevant, but less obviously and less directly: such principles as natural justice and reasonableness fall into this category. This approach recognises that the precise content and impact of the principles of good administration must always ultimately be determined by reference to, *inter alia*, the legislative framework giving rise to the administrative discretion in question. In this manner it is possible to avoid the simplistic and artificial attempt of the common law theory to establish a set of grounds of review which are wholly unrelated to legislative intention.

2. The absurdity of propounding the absolute irrelevance of legislative intention

The assertion of common law theorists that the broad grounds of review are judge-made constructs which have nothing to do with the intention of Parliament appears, at least at first glance, appealingly simple. In truth, however, to argue in favour of a category of grounds of review to which legislative intention is entirely irrelevant is to embrace the manifestly absurd.

Take the South African Appellate Division's *UDF* decision that to make vague regulations is not to exceed the powers which legislation confers.[43] This entails that Parliament is taken to confer rule-making powers which are not limited by any requirement to avoid making vague regulations. Now, a regulation which is so vague as to be vulnerable to judicial review is one which is so unclear and imprecise as to be incapable of being reasonably complied with and which

---

[42] *Re H.K. (An Infant)* [1967] 2 QB 617, 630 (emphasis added).
[43] 1988 (4) SA 830.

therefore serves no useful purpose. It must follow that a vague regulation is made outwith the purposes for which Parliament, in the first place, created the rule-making power: "Delegated legislation which [is so vague that it] serves no purpose, or purposes which cannot be ascertained, falls as far short of the purposes stipulated in an enabling provision as that which serves some ulterior or improper purpose".[44]

The upshot of this is that it is illogical to argue that legislative intention has nothing whatsoever to do with striking down regulations which are unacceptably vague. Unless an absurd intention is attributed to the legislature, it *must* be presumed that it did not intend the rule-making power which it conferred to be used to create regulations which are purposeless, impossible to comply with or which run counter to the purpose for which the power was in the first place created. To suggest – as common law theorists certainly do – that parliamentary intention is irrelevant to the prohibition on vague regulations is to impute absurdity to the legislature; as Haysom and Plasket observe, it means that "the legislature in conferring power on an official to make regulations allows him, in the absence of an express prohibition, to make meaningless regulations".[45]

The same point can be made in relation to the other grounds of review. It is implicit in any suggestion that the rationality doctrine is not part of the ultra vires rule that Parliament grants discretionary power without attaching any condition which prevents the making of a decision that is "outrageous in its defiance of logic or of accepted moral standards".[46] Similarly, if the principle of fairness is no part of the ultra vires doctrine, it must follow that Parliament grants discretionary powers which are not limited by any requirement to act fairly: on this view, Parliament's will would not be frustrated or contradicted by the official who sits as judge in his own cause or by the Home Secretary who decides how long a life sentence a prisoner should serve without regard to even the most basic precepts of natural justice; yet the attribution of such absurd intentions to the legislature is an unavoidable function of the common law theory of judicial review.

It is certainly true that the traditional ultra vires doctrine, which proposes a direct relationship between intention and the grounds of review, is highly artificial. However, to suggest that legislative intention is of absolutely no relevance to the principles of review is equally artificial and, it is submitted, wholly implausible. The common law theory, by holding that intention is irrelevant to judicial review, represents an overreaction to the traditional model's overreliance on intention. In contrast, the modified ultra vires principle steers a

---

[44] J. Grogan, "The Appellate Division and the Emergency: Another Step Backward" (1989) 106 *SALJ* 14, 22–3.

[45] N. Haysom and C. Plasket, "The War and Against Law: Judicial Activism and the Appellate Division" (1988) 4 *South African Journal on Human Rights* 303, 329. Such absurdity can, of course, be avoided by embracing the ultra vires theorists' argument that legislative intention is relevant in both negative and positive senses (as discussed above).

[46] *Council of Civil Service Unions* v. *Minister for the Civil Service* [1985] AC 374, 410, *per* Lord Diplock.

middle course which accepts that both intention and judicial creativity have a role to play in this area.

3. The basis of judicial review and the canons of statutory construction

It is necessary to point out one further difficulty which would underlie any attempt to distinguish between grounds of review based respectively on ultra vires and the common law. It is a cardinal principle of statutory construction in English law that the courts approach legislation on the initial presumption that Parliament intends that the rule of law should be upheld.[47] This principle is of broad application, and extends far beyond the administrative law sphere. Take, for instance, the strong presumption that Parliament does not intend to create criminal offences which have retroactive effect: as Lord Reid explained in *Waddington* v. *Miah*, the courts approach penal statutes on the basis that "it is hardly credible that any government department would promote or that Parliament would pass retrospective criminal legislation".[48]

The breadth of the presumption regarding Parliament's intention to legislate consistently with the rule of law was made clear by Lord Steyn in *Pierson*, in a dictum cited above.[49] It is precisely this presumption which forms the basis of the modified ultra vires doctrine. However, it is the obverse assumption which necessarily inheres in the common law theory of review: it holds that legislative intention has nothing at all to do with the principles of good administration (which, in turn, are founded in the contemporary rule of law doctrine). In this manner, the common law approach is fundamentally inconsistent with the English courts' long-established approach to statutory construction. While the courts generally presume that Parliament intends to uphold the rule of law, common law theorists direct that the judges must, when approaching legislation which creates discretionary power, suspend that presumption. Instead, the courts must hold that, at worst, Parliament grants powers which are so ample that they encompass the competence to disregard the rule of law or, at best, Parliament is agnostic as to whether decision-makers possess the competence to abrogate the principles of fairness and reasonableness which the rule of law doctrine embodies. Indeed, Sir John Laws has acknowledged that it is central to the constitutional workability of the common law model of review that Parliament must be assumed to be entirely neutral about the limits which apply to and condition the exercise of statutory powers.[50] Consideration of the principle of access to justice reveals, in particularly stark terms, this flaw in the common law model of review.

---

[47] See generally T.R.S. Allan, "Legislative Supremacy and the Rule of Law: Democracy and Constitutionalism" [1985] CLJ 111.

[48] [1974] 1 WLR 683, 694.

[49] See text to n. 12.

[50] See below, n. 60.

The constitutional right of recourse to the courts finds practical expression in two particular circumstances. First, the judges vindicate it by approaching preclusive provisions in primary legislation on the initial presumption that Parliament does not intend to abrogate the rule of law by interfering with citizens' access to the courts.[51] It will be argued below that only by adopting an *interpretative* approach to ouster clauses, based on this *presumption*, is it possible to justify departure from their prima facie meaning; an approach not based on interpretation and presumption would necessarily involve judicial disobedience to Parliament. For present purposes, it is sufficient to note that an interpretative attempt to attribute to preclusive provisions a meaning which is compatible with the rule of law is of a piece with the courts' long-standing approach to the construction of legislation within a framework based on that constitutional principle.

Secondly, access to justice finds expression as a ground of judicial review. The courts regularly hold that the executive should not use its decision- and rule-making powers to impede access to court.[52] However, the common law theory of review maintains that the limits which the courts apply to the administration's discretionary powers are, "categorically, judicial creations . . . They have nothing to do with the intention of Parliament".[53] On this approach, Parliament must be taken either to grant to officials the power to impede access to justice or, at best, to be agnostic about the matter.

A contradiction thus arises. The courts generally approach primary legislation on the presumption that Parliament does not intend to inhibit access to justice (which is one facet of the broader presumption that Parliament legislates consistently with the rule of law); in this manner, the judges limit the impact of provisions in primary legislation which, at least on their face, appear to curtail the jurisdiction of the courts. However, the common law theory of review maintains that the principles of good administration – one of which is that officials should not make decisions or regulations which impede access to justice – rest on common law foundations and have nothing to do with the intention of Parliament. This necessarily implies that Parliament does not entertain any bias in favour of access to justice, and is therefore wholly incompatible with the well-established presumption that Parliament does not intend to fetter citizens' access to the courts. Once again, it becomes apparent that the common law model of review entails a high degree of artificiality, according with neither the reality of judicial practice nor the logic of constitutional theory.

The true position is that the constitutional principle which favours access to the courts rests on the same foundations whether it is applied to primary legis-

---

[51] See, e.g., *Pyx Granite* [1960] AC 260, 286, *per* Viscount Simonds: "It is a principle not by any means to be whittled down that the subject's recourse to Her Majesty's courts for the determination of his rights is not to be excluded except by clear words".

[52] See, *inter alia*, *Raymond v. Honey* [1983] 1 AC 1; *R. v. Secretary of State for the Home Department, ex parte Leech* [1994] QB 198; *R. v. Lord Chancellor, ex parte Witham* [1998] QB 575.

[53] Laws, op. cit., n. 5, p. 79.

lation or to administrative action. It is, categorically, an interpretative rule based on the presumption that Parliament does not intend to abrogate access to justice. The courts approach *all* legislation on this basis. Just as it is presumed that Parliament itself does not intend to inhibit recourse to the courts (via ouster clauses, for example), so it is also presumed that Parliament does not intend to confer on officials the competence to attenuate access to justice. Thus, whenever the courts uphold the citizen's right of access to the courts, they do so on the basis that, once the relevant legislation is properly construed, it becomes apparent that it was never meant to sanction interference with access to justice. This is of a piece with the modified ultra vires doctrine, which is based on the proposition that the courts approach all legislation, including provisions which create discretionary powers, on the presumption that Parliament intends to legislate consistently with the norms which lie at the centre of our constitutional system.

4. Conclusion

Embracing a common law theory of review introduces a distinction into administrative law between those grounds which are vires-based and those which constitute autonomous common law constructs. The practical difficulty which would be involved in maintaining such a distinction is unsurprising, given that any attempt to do so would be fundamentally inconsistent with the basis on which the courts have long approached statutory construction. Such problems are avoided if it is accepted that, as the modified ultra vires doctrine suggests, administrative law constitutes a co-operative enterprise which embraces both Parliament and the courts. It is now necessary to explain why the distinction between vires-based and common law principles of review would not only be difficult to sustain in practice, but would also damage the coherence of administrative law and its capacity to protect individual citizens against maladministration.

IV. THE UNDESIRABLE CONSEQUENCES OF THE UNWELCOME DISTINCTION

A. The Courts' Treatment of Preclusive Provisions

One of the traditional flash-points in the debate between ultra vires and common law theorists has been the courts' approach to legislative provisions which appear to exclude the possibility of judicial review. It will be argued in the following paragraphs that the ultra vires principle – in its modified form – may actually provide a *more* convincing justification than the common law model for a robust attitude to ouster clauses. After all, the perceived contradiction between ultra vires theory and the judiciary's treatment of ouster clauses is that the courts appear simultaneously to *invoke* legislative intention as the justificatory foundation of administrative law while choosing to *disregard* it in contexts where adherence to parliamentary will would be inconvenient. It is worth pointing out that, once it is accepted that the ultra vires doctrine is ultimately about giving practical effect to Parliament's intention that the rule of law should be upheld, this apparent contradiction can more easily be resolved, and the judiciary's treatment of ouster clauses explained more convincingly. It is also important to note that the common law theory's approach to ouster clauses is not without problems.

The courts' treatment of ouster provisions may be characterised in three principal ways. It will be suggested that only one of these methods is both convincing and constitutionally legitimate, but that those who propound the common law theory of review are logically precluded from adopting that approach.

1. Straightforward implementation of legislative will

First, it may be said that the judges' treatment of ouster provisions constitutes nothing more than the implementation of the plain and natural meaning of the words which Parliament uses. This explanation is consistent with the traditional ultra vires doctrine, which posits that judicial review itself is about nothing more than the straightforward and direct vindication of legislative intention. However, this explanation is untenable: the courts' approach to ouster clauses quite clearly goes much further.

2. Non-interpretative approaches to ouster provisions

Alternatively, it might be that, as Sir William Wade argues, preclusive clauses really do mean that review should not occur, but that the courts effect review in spite of this.[54] Now, whether parliamentary sovereignty is perceived as a positive or negative feature of the British constitution, two points cannot easily be disputed: first, at their present stage of evolution, the United Kingdom's constitutional arrangements still embody a principle of legislative supremacy; secondly, an explanation of judicial treatment of ouster provisions which relies on the courts' disregarding them is necessarily inconsistent with that principle. Thus, although Wade's reasoning is attractively straightforward, it does not fit easily into the broader framework of the constitution.

Sir John Laws has set out a further approach to ouster clauses. Like Wade, he seeks to avoid the difficulties which inhere in the interpretative model. However, unlike Wade, he claims that his approach is consistent with the sovereignty principle.

Laws suggests that the courts' response to ouster provisions rests on the axiom that "Parliament can only abrogate the rule of law by an express measure to that effect".[55] Judicial treatment of ouster clauses is therefore referable to

---

[54] See H.W.R. Wade, "Constitutional and Administrative Aspects of the *Anisminic* Case" (1969) 85 *LQR* 198; Wade and Forsyth, op. cit., n. 1, pp. 734–9.

[55] "Illegality: The Problem of Jurisdiction" in M. Supperstone and J. Goudie (eds.), *Judicial Review* (London, Butterworths, 1997, 2nd edn.), p. 4.26.

"constitutional principle" and has little to do with interpretation.[56] In this manner Laws seeks to avoid the complexities of construction by invoking a simple constitutional rule to the effect that review obtains unless Parliament expressly excludes it. This raises two points.

First, there arises the difficult practical problem of ascertaining what constitutes an "express" ouster clause. This, in itself, must necessarily raise questions of construction. It must therefore be concluded that presenting the courts' approach to ouster clauses as the application of a straightforward constitutional principle, which permits the exclusion of review only by the use of express language, does not circumvent the difficulties of statutory interpretation which have long beset this area of public law.

Secondly, if Laws's approach is to be legitimate, it must be based upon the *presumption* that Parliament intends the rule of law to be upheld, so that only very clear – indeed, on Laws's view, express – language is capable of rebutting that presumption. It is necessary to emphasise this point. If a presumptive model is embraced in the present context, it is possible to reconcile Laws's approach to ouster provisions with the theory of parliamentary sovereignty: it is assumed that any such provision which does not expressly exclude review was not, in truth, intended to have that effect. This permits theoretical reconciliation of a robust approach to ouster provisions with the doctrine of legislative sovereignty: the courts do not *refuse* to apply non-express preclusive clauses; rather, they *interpret* them such that they do not, properly understood, preclude review. Disobedience to Parliament is thus avoided, at least at a formal level.

However, if the idea of presumption is jettisoned, the situation must arise in which the courts simply refuse to apply non-express ouster provisions *without* justifying such action by reference to the assumption that Parliament could not have intended to abrogate review other than via express language. Unless the effect of the non-express ouster clause is neutralised by such a presumption, the courts' failure to give effect to it amounts to outright disobedience to Parliament.

Thus the position is reached that, so long as Parliament remains competent to suspend and modify the application of the principles of good administration, the courts' approach to ouster clauses can be founded on nothing other than statutory construction. A "rule" to the effect that Parliament must use express language to preclude review is quite beside the point. The real – and only – question is whether, properly interpreted, Parliament legislated to preclude review. As a matter of pragmatics, it is certainly true that Parliament must use very clear language in order to displace the principles of judicial review. This, however, does not follow from any constitutional rule which allows the courts to *disregard* purported ouster provisions which are not "express". Rather, it follows from the application of a rule of *construction* which is based on the presumption that Parliament would not wish to abrogate citizens' basic rights. There

---

[56] Ibid., pp. 4.20–4.26.

can, therefore, be no question of the courts' *ignoring* Parliament's intention: they may only *interpret* legislative provisions from a particular starting-point, *viz.* a presumption that the rule of law should be upheld.

This approach finds support in the House of Lords. In *Witham*,[57] Laws J sought to establish a straightforward rule to the effect that citizens' access to the courts may be abrogated only by express provision in primary legislation.[58] However, in *Pierson*, Lord Browne-Wilkinson questioned the correctness of this proposition. While he agreed that the courts should certainly seek to uphold the rule of law by attempting to preserve access to justice, he made it very clear that this task can only be undertaken interpretatively. Thus very clear legislative language is required in order to abrogate access to justice not because the courts are entitled to *ignore* purported ouster provisions which are not "express" but, rather, because the courts *presume* that Parliament does not intend to abrogate fundamental rights:

> Such basic rights [as access to justice] are not to be overridden by the general words of a statute since the *presumption* is against the impairment of such basic rights.[59]

Clearly this is the correct approach; the crucial point for present purposes is that while it is eminently consistent with the modified ultra vires doctrine, it logically cannot be adopted by those who propound a common law basis of review, as the following paragraphs explain.

3. *Statutory interpretation within a framework based on the rule of law*

According to the modified theory of ultra vires, the law of judicial review is based on the simple proposition that Parliament intends that the discretionary power which it creates should be limited by reference to the constitutional principle of the rule of law. This justifies both the application of limits to statutory agencies' powers and the courts' endeavours to interpret ouster provisions in a manner which preserves the operation of those limits. The basic premise of the modified ultra vires principle thus accommodates an interpretative, and therefore legitimate, explanation of the courts' approach to ouster clauses.

The same is not true, however, of the common law model of review. Indeed, a contradiction exists at the heart of that theory. Sir John Laws, a leading common law theorist, acknowledges that in order for the common law model to be constitutionally legitimate, it must be presumed that Parliament is neutral about the application of limits to discretionary power.[60] However, as the previous

---

[57] R. v. *Lord Chancellor, ex parte Witham* [1998] QB 575.

[58] Or by secondary legislation made pursuant to primary legislation which expressly confers the power to abrogate the right.

[59] R. v. *Secretary of State for the Home Department, ex parte Pierson* [1998] AC 539, 575 (emphasis added).

[60] See Laws, op. cit., n. 55, pp. 4.17–4.18. Space does not permit analysis of the reasons for and the implications of this aspect of Laws's argument: for discussion of this point, see Elliott, op. cit., n. 2, pp. 134–48 and 87–100 above.

section sought to demonstrate, the courts' treatment of ouster clauses can only be rendered constitutionally proper if a presumption is applied to the effect that Parliament, in the absence of clear contrary provision, is taken to intend that the principles of good administration should be operative and enforceable, in order that individuals may have recourse to courts of public law jurisdiction. Only by making a presumption about what Parliament meant is it possible to justify substantial departure from the plain and natural meaning of the ouster provision without recourse to notions of illegitimate judicial disobedience. By presuming that Parliament is neutral about the application and operation of the principles of good administration, common law theorists thus preclude the adoption of a legitimate approach to ouster clauses, based on interpretation and presumption.

In the context of ouster clauses, therefore, the common law and modified ultra vires theories differ markedly. The latter embraces the idea that the entire administrative law enterprise constitutes an endeavour shared by courts and Parliament to secure government under the rule of law. The same idea – of judicial interpretation of legislation against the background presumption that Parliament intends to uphold the rule of law – explains both the application of the principles of review and the courts' enthusiasm to apply those principles to all discretionary powers unless there is very clear contrary provision.

The common law model falters because it seeks to make judicial review an exclusively judicial endeavour. The artificial neutrality which is thus ascribed to Parliament vis-à-vis the limitation of discretionary power (which, as Laws acknowledges, is necessary to legitimate a common law system of review) deprives the courts of any adequate interpretative machinery which can be employed in relation to ouster provisions.

4. Conclusion

The foregoing analysis demonstrates that there exists a clear relationship between, on the one hand, the courts' ability to limit the impact of preclusive provisions and, on the other hand, the manner in which the theoretical basis of judicial review is constructed.

Provided that ultra vires theory is adhered to, it is possible to adopt a legitimate, interpretative approach to ouster clauses which permits their impact to be attenuated by judicial interpretation. However, as discussed above, adherence to the common law model demands recognition of two sets of grounds of review: narrow limits remain vires issues, while the broad principles of good administration are conceptualised as common law matters in relation to which Parliament possesses no intention. The foregoing analysis demonstrates that, while it is possible to justify judicial review on vires-based grounds in the face of an ouster clause, the same is not true of review on common law grounds. It is therefore likely that, if a common law theory of review were adopted, ouster provisions would immunise executive action which breached common law principles of good administration, while they would remain ineffective in the face of official action which was categorised as ultra vires in the narrow sense. Such a situation would present two particular problems.

First, assume that two individuals have both suffered an abuse of power by a particular administrative agency the decisions of which are protected by an ouster clause. Assume further that the illegality in the first case consists of the breach of a narrow, vires-based limit on the agency's competence, while the second applicant's complaint relates to the transgression of a broader common law rule of good administration. It is likely that the ouster provision would operate to defeat the second, but not the first, applicant. Two victims of unlawful administrative action would therefore have their cases treated in very different ways because of a technical distinction between the juridical bases of different forms of administrative defect. Perhaps even more perversely, a single victim of a variety of abuses of power would be precluded from making some complaints, but not others.

Secondly, the distinction between those administrative defects which are protected by ousters and those which are not would be extremely difficult to draw in practice. It has already been observed that any attempt to distinguish between ultra vires and common law grounds of review would be plagued by practical difficulties. Therefore, not only would victims of unlawful executive action have their cases treated differently; it would also be extremely difficult, in light of the nebulous nature of the distinction between ultra vires and common law grounds, to predict which unlawful acts would be protected by an ouster.

This differential treatment and unpredictability is fundamentally inconsistent with the existence of a developed and coherent system of administrative law which aims to provide citizens with effective protection against executive abuse.

B.   The theoretical basis of review, voidness and collateral challenge

1.   The logical connection between ultra vires and voidness

It is a logical consequence of the ultra vires doctrine that administrative action which is committed in excess of jurisdiction is void, as Lord Diplock explained:

> It would . . . be inconsistent with the doctrine of ultra vires as it has been developed in English law . . . if the judgment of a court . . . that a statutory instrument was ultra vires were to have any lesser consequence in law than to render the instrument incapable of ever having had any legal effect upon the rights and duties of the parties to the proceedings.[61]

This conclusion follows from the simple fact that executive action which is ultra vires lacks any basis in law. Although there remains a certain amount of confu-

---

[61]   F. Hoffman-La Roche and Co. AG v. *Secretary of State for Trade and Industry* [1975] AC 295, 365.

sion regarding the practical effects of action which is ultra vires and void,[62] the important point for present purposes is that such action can be challenged not only directly in judicial review proceedings, but also collaterally in any other proceedings in which it is relevant.[63] Forsyth captures the logical connection between ultra vires, voidness and collateral challenge when he writes that:

> Where a matter is properly raised by collateral challenge, then, once the unlawfulness of the act has been established, the court has no discretion, and rightly so, but to uphold the law. Indeed, this underlies the necessity that the unlawful act should be void. When the matter is raised collaterally, the unlawful act is denied effect without its having been quashed by the court; how can this be unless the unlawful act is void? Collateral challenge and the voidness of unlawful acts stand or fall together.[64]

While there is an inevitable connection between ultra vires action, voidness and collateral challenge, the same position does not obtain within a common law model of review. Ultra vires action is necessarily void and collaterally impeachable because it constitutes action committed without any legal justification: the condemnation of ultra vires entails that the administrator has acted outwith the scope of his legal powers, so that his action is void as a matter of law. The common law model, in contrast, maintains that the principles of good administration are autonomous rules which are unrelated to the perimeter of the power conferred by enabling legislation. The analysis is not, according to this approach, directed towards the question whether the action was within or outwith the conferred authority; in result, holding that executive action is in breach of a common law rule of good administration does not necessarily mean that it is outside the scope of the conferred power and hence devoid of legal authority. There is, therefore, no ineluctable connection between administrative action which is unlawful at common law and the ideas of voidness and collateral impeachability.

This argument is illuminated by the Divisional Court's decision in *Bugg* v. *Director of Public Prosecutions*.[65] It was explained above that, in this case, Woolf LJ distinguished between procedurally and substantively defective administrative action: the former was voidable, meaning that it had to be

---

[62] The better view, it is submitted, is that which is advanced by C.F. Forsyth, "'The Metaphysic of Nullity': Invalidity, Conceptual Reasoning and the Rule of Law" in C.F. Forsyth and I.C. Hare (eds), *The Golden Metwand and the Crooked Cord* (Oxford, Clarendon Press, 1998). Ultra vires action is thus void as a matter of law, but may nevertheless exist as a matter of fact (see *Percy* v. *Hall* [1997] QB 924, 951, *per* Schiemann LJ: "Manifestly in daily life the [ultra vires and void] enactment will have an effect in the sense that people have regulated their conduct in the light of it"). As Forsyth, op. cit., p. 159, explains, if further legal decisions are taken in reliance on an earlier ultra vires act, the legality of those decisions depends on whether the "second actor has legal power to act validly notwithstanding the invalidity of the first act". In *Boddington* v. *British Transport Police* [1998] 2 WLR 639, 662, Lord Steyn adopted this analysis and accepted that, although ultra vires action may thus produce practical consequences, this does not detract from its voidness as a matter of law.

[63] Provided that Parliament does not provide otherwise: *R.* v. *Wicks* [1998] AC 92.

[64] Forsyth, op. cit., n. 62, p. 157.

[65] [1993] QB 473.

treated as valid until and unless a court of public law jurisdiction quashed it, whereas the latter was void, and therefore amenable to collateral challenge.

It is important to note that Woolf LJ's attack on the traditional view – that defective administrative action is void and hence collaterally impeachable – was intimately connected with a departure from ultra vires theory. His Lordship tacitly signalled his desire to discard ultra vires as the foundation of some parts of the law of judicial review when he stated that he would "not categorise procedural invalidity as being properly a question of excess . . . of power".[66] The *Bugg* decision thus clearly demonstrates the connection between ultra vires and the voidness of unlawful administrative action, and indicates that abandonment of the ultra vires doctrine would be likely to herald a departure from the voidness – and amenability to collateral challenge – of such action.[67]

The lapse represented by *Bugg* was corrected by the decision of the House of Lords in *Boddington*. Lord Irvine LC explained that:

> The *Anisminic* decision established . . . that there was a single category of errors of law, all of which rendered a decision ultra vires. No distinction is to be drawn between a patent (or substantive) error of law or a latent (or procedural) error of law. An ultra vires act or subordinate legislation is unlawful simpliciter and, if the presumption in favour of its legality is overcome by a litigant before a court of competent jurisdiction [which includes a criminal court], is of no legal effect whatsoever.[68]

This clearly illustrates the logical connection between the ultra vires doctrine and the voidness of unlawful execution action, and the *Boddington* decision is to be welcomed as a significant reassertion of the constitutional logic which lies at the heart of English administrative law.[69]

2. Abandoning ultra vires: the consequences for voidness and collateral challenge

It is apparent from the foregoing that, if the views of the critics of ultra vires were adopted, such that some grounds of review rested on common law foundations, important implications would arise vis-à-vis voidness and collateral challenge. This conclusion follows from the fact that, while voidness is an inevitable consequence of ultra vires administrative action, it is not – as *Bugg* so

---

[66] Ibid., p. 500. However, it was observed above, n. 26, that Lord Woolf MR has now resiled from this position and appears, at least in his judicial capacity, to subscribe to the orthodoxy of ultra vires.

[67] This conclusion is confirmed by the courts' jurisprudence on error on the face of the record. At one time, that was considered to be an exceptional, non-jurisdictional ground of review. Being unconnected to the ultra vires doctrine, such errors rendered executive action merely voidable, with the consequence that no collateral challenge was possible. Of course, such errors are now to be regarded as species of ultra vires (see *R. v. Lord President of the Privy Council, ex parte Page* [1993] AC 682), so voidness and collateral impeachability must logically follow. See further Wade and Forsyth, op. cit., n. 1, pp. 324 and 340.

[68] [1998] 2 WLR 639, 650, *per* Lord Irvine LC.

[69] For further discussion, see M.C. Elliott, "*Boddington*: Rediscovering the Constitutional Logic of Administrative Law" [1998] *Judicial Review* 144.

vividly illustrates – a necessary concomitant of executive action which merely breaches common law principles of good administration. Two particular points arise.

First, it would be thoroughly objectionable were a category of administrative action to exist which was unlawful (by virtue of contravening a common law rule of good administration) but collaterally unimpeachable. As Lord Steyn observed in his speech in *Boddington*, such a situation would be "unacceptable . . . in a democracy based on the rule of law" since the consequences – particularly for defendants in criminal proceedings – "are too austere and indeed too authoritarian to be compatible with the traditions of the common law".[70] Moreover, "[t]he possibility of judicial review will . . . in no way compensate [a defendant] for the loss of *the right* to defend himself by a defensive challenge to the byelaw".[71] His Lordship noted that a number of factors – including the inconvenience and cost of launching judicial review proceedings while also mounting a defence in criminal proceedings; the problems associated with obtaining legal aid for judicial review; the need to apply for leave, and the discretionary nature of remedies following judicial review – make it less than ideal for defendants to have to institute separate proceedings in order to challenge the legality of the secondary legislation under which they are charged. Thus the rule of law requires unlawful administrative action to be susceptible to collateral challenge, and the ultra vires doctrine – together with voidness, which is its logical product – vouchsafes this position.

Secondly, for the reasons advanced above, the dividing line between those defects which would and would not be able to be questioned collaterally would be lamentably unclear. Defendants in criminal proceedings – and others – would be faced with very considerable uncertainty as to the possibility of raising faults in the decision-making process which foreshadowed the relevant subordinate legislation or administrative decision. This point demonstrates, perhaps more powerfully than most, that the way in which the theoretical foundation of administrative law is constructed can produce practical – and potentially very serious – implications for individuals. This did not escape Lord Nicholls in *R. v. Wicks*:

> There is . . . an imperative need for the boundary line [between defects which can and cannot be challenged collaterally] to be fixed and crystal clear. There can be no room for an ambiguous grey area . . . [T]he boundary is not merely concerned with identifying the proceedings in which, as a matter of procedure, the unlawfulness issue can be raised. Rather, the boundary can represent the difference between committing a criminal offence and not committing a criminal offence.[72]

Although his Lordship was speaking in the context of the putative distinction between substantively and procedurally defective executive action, his remarks

---

[70] [1998] 2 WLR 639, 663–4.
[71] Ibid. (original emphasis).
[72] [1998] AC 92, 108.

apply with precisely the same force to the suggested distinction between ultra vires and common law species of unlawful administrative action.

The Lord Chancellor has noted that:

> The decision in *Anisminic* freed the law from a dependency on technical distinctions between different types of illegality. The law should not now be developed to create a new, and unstable, technical distinction between "substantive" and "procedural" invalidity.[73]

Any attempted distinction between administrative action which is unlawful at common law on the one hand, and under the ultra vires doctrine on the other, would be equally unstable. It would undermine the theoretical foundation on which English administrative law rests and would produce practical consequences for individuals that would be inimical to the rule of law.

V. CONCLUSION

The on-going discussion between ultra vires and common law theorists, concerning the underlying constitutional justification for judicial review, is a stimulating one. Although there remain significant points of disagreement, there is also a good deal of common ground. All modern writers recognise the necessity of moving beyond the unconvincing dogma of the orthodox ultra vires principle. All concerned are equally keen to allow open acknowledgment and discussion of the normative values which are vindicated by means of the supervisory jurisdiction. And there is surely broad agreement, too, that it is necessary to articulate a juridical foundation for administrative law which vouchsafes both its constitutional legitimacy and its practical ability to protect citizens against the misuse of public power.

One of the principal points which common law theorists consistently raise is the inappropriateness, within a modern democracy based on the rule of law, of arguing that the legitimacy of judicial review depends on nothing other than its conceptualisation as the product of legislative intention. It would indeed be surprising – and lamentable – if constitutional theory could furnish a rationalisation of review no richer than that. At the same time, however, a desire to acknowledge the normative foundations of the values which are protected by way of judicial review need not inexorably lead to the wholesale divorce of administrative law from legislative intention.

Consideration of the values upon which judicial supervision of the executive is based reveals that they are norms which have a deep constitutional resonance. Indeed, they are pervasive constitutional norms which have long subsisted within the environment in which Parliament legislates, the courts interpret and the executive operates. In order to acknowledge that the credit lies with the courts for the translation of these norms into enforceable legal principles, it is not necessary to

---

[73] *Boddington v. British Transport Police* [1998] 2 WLR 639, 651.

deny that Parliament has long been taken to respect those values. There is no shame in admitting that judicial development of administrative law is consistent with the legislative intention of Parliament. This is not the hallmark of a blinkered polity which can see no further than the legislative command of the sovereign; it is, rather, the characteristic of a mature democracy in which respect for the most fundamental values permeates each branch of the constitution.

The modified ultra vires doctrine, which was defined above, postulates an indirect connection between legislative intention and the law of judicial review. I have suggested elsewhere that such an approach to the juridical foundation of review can overcome the shortcomings of the orthodox ultra vires principle which common law theorists have identified.[74] It is able to account for the evolutive nature of administrative law and is capable of accommodation within a broader regime of review which encompasses judicial supervision of non-statutory powers. Perhaps most importantly, however, it discards the implausibility of the orthodox principle's direct relationship between intention and review, thereby permitting open acknowledgment of the contribution of the courts and allowing judicial review to be conceptualised as much more than curial enforcement of the sovereign's will.

Recognising that there is a connection between legislative intention and judicial review also carries with it a set of pragmatic advantages. A defining feature of the growth of modern administrative law in England has been the judiciary's willingness to free it from the archaic shackles which so inhibited the development of public law in the past. In particular, a series of technical distinctions has been abandoned in an attempt to make judicial review an accessible and useful mechanism for the protection of individuals. Thus the distinctions between administrative and judicial functions, statutory and non-statutory powers, public and private bodies and, most recently, substantive and procedural defects have been abandoned or at least marginalised. It would be a great pity if, at the dawn of a new era of rights-oriented English public law, a novel and potentially destructive distinction – between grounds of review based respectively on the ultra vires doctrine and the common law – were introduced into this area. The distinction is formidably difficult to draw, and threatens the theoretical coherence and practical utility of administrative law.

It is submitted that there is, in truth, no need to embrace such a distinction. By acknowledging a modest and realistic conception of the relationship between parliamentary intention and judicial review, it is possible to articulate a foundation for administrative law which combines the best features of the two models which have, hitherto, been perceived as competitors. In this manner, judicial review can properly be presented as a co-operative endeavour which engages both Parliament and the courts, and the justification of review emerges as a joint enterprise which draws upon the work of both the common law and the ultra vires theorists.

[74] Op. cit., n. 2, pp. 148–56.

Conclusion

17

*Competing Models of Judicial Review**

PAUL CRAIG

The debate concerning the foundations of judicial review has, as will be seen, taken a new turn. Supporters of the ultra vires doctrine have responded to critics by deploying a modified version of that doctrine which they claim can and must be the foundation of judicial review, for so long as we retain the conception of parliamentary sovereignty. This article challenges that claim. It will be argued that the common law model of judicial review entails no conflict with the sovereignty of Parliament, expresses the proper relationship between the rule of law and sovereignty and best captures the practice of the courts. It may be helpful at the outset to describe the contending models around which the debate has focused.

THE STORY THUS FAR: THE CONTENDING MODELS

Before outlining the relevant models it is important to be clear about a point which is obvious once stated, but all too often lost sight of. The magic phrase "ultra vires" is indicative of action being beyond power. It does not, in and of itself, tell us whether an act is beyond power because the legislature has intended to place certain limits on an agency, or whether these limits are more properly regarded as a common law creation of the courts. It is this issue which divides the two camps in the debate about the foundations of judicial review.

The *traditional ultra vires model*, or *specific legislative intent model*, was based on the assumption that judicial review was legitimated on the ground that the courts were applying the intent of the legislature. The courts' function was to police the boundaries stipulated by Parliament. The ultra vires principle was regarded as both a necessary and sufficient basis for judicial intervention. It was necessary in the sense that any ground of judicial review had to be fitted into the ultra vires doctrine in order for it to be acceptable. It was sufficient in the sense that if such a ground of review could be fitted into the ultra vires principle it obviated the need for further independent inquiry. On this view, the very doctrines which make up administrative law derived their legitimacy and content

* I am grateful for the comments received at the Conference and for more particular comments from Trevor Allan, Nicholas Bamforth, Mark Freedland and Dawn Oliver.

from the fact that the legislature intended them to apply in a particular way in a particular statutory context.

Advocates of the *common law model of illegality* challenged these assumptions. They argued that the ultra vires principle as articulated above was indeterminate, unrealistic, beset by internal tensions, and unable to explain the application of public law principles to those bodies which did not derive their power from statute.[1] Critics of the ultra vires principle are of course concerned to keep bodies within their assigned spheres. It is moreover self-evident that the enabling legislation must be considered when determining the ambit of a body's powers. This is not, however, the same thing as saying that the heads of review, their meaning or the intensity with which they are applied can be justified by legislative intent. The central issue is therefore how far these relevant legal rules and their application can be satisfactorily explained by reference to legislative intent. Proponents of the common law model argue that the principles of judicial review are in reality developed by the courts. They are the creation of the common law. The legislature will rarely provide any indications as to the content and limits of what constitutes judicial review. When legislation is passed the courts will impose the controls which constitute judicial review which they believe are normatively justified on the grounds of justice, the rule of law, etc. They will therefore decide on the appropriate procedural and substantive principles of judicial review which should apply to statutory and non-statutory bodies alike. Agency action which infringes these principles will be unlawful. If the omnipotent Parliament does not like these controls then it is open to it to make this unequivocally clear. If it does so the courts will then adhere to such dictates. If Parliament does manifest a specific intent as to the grounds of review the courts will also obey this, in just the same way as they will obey such intent in other areas where the primary obligations themselves are the creation of the common law. There is, in this sense, nothing odd or strange about a set of principles derived from the common law, which are then supplemented or complemented by specific legislative intent if and when this is to be found. This is indeed the paradigm in areas such as contract, tort, restitution, and trusts. It has indeed been forcefully argued by Dawn Oliver[2] that the very principles of legality, rationality and procedural propriety are but part of a broader set of duties founded on "considerate decision making" which have been developed by the courts and apply to private as well as public decision making.

[1] D. Oliver, "Is the Ultra Vires Rule the Basis of Judicial Review?" [1987] PL 543 and Chapter One pp. 3–27 above; S. de Smith, Lord Woolf and J. Jowell, *Judicial Review of Administrative Action* (5th ed., 1995); Sir John Laws, "Illegality: The Problem of Jurisdiction", *Judicial Review* (M. Supperstone and J. Goudie eds., 2nd ed., 1997). Chapter Four pp. 73–81 above; P. Craig, "*Ultra Vires* and the Foundations of Judicial Review" [1998] CLJ 64 and Chapter Three pp. 47–71 above; D. Dyzenhaus, "Reuniting the Brain: The Democratic Basis of Judicial Review" (1998) 9 Pub. Law. Rev. 98; N. Bamforth, "Politics, *Ultra Vires* and Institutional Interdependence", Chapter Six pp. 113–39 above. J. Jowell, "Of Vires and Vacuums: The Constitutional Context of Judicial Review" [1999] PL 448.

[2] "Review of (Non-Statutory) Discretions", Chapter Fourteen pp. 307–25 above. See also, D. Oliver, *Common Values and the Public–Private Divide* (1999).

There is now a *modified ultra vires model*, or *general legislative intent model*. Supporters of the ultra vires doctrine, notably Christopher Forsyth and Mark Elliott[3] have accepted many of the criticisms voiced by proponents of the common law model. They have in particular conceded that the legislature will rarely have any specific intent as to the content of the rules which make up judicial review. They have accepted also that it is legitimate for the courts to impose the controls which constitute judicial review directly on bodies which do not derive their power from statute. They acknowledge that the very normative force of these principles justifies this. They maintain, however, that ultra vires must still be the central principle of judicial review. It is argued that legislative intent *must* be found in order to vindicate judicial review, since to discard the ultra vires principle would entail a strong challenge to parliamentary sovereignty, and would also involve the exercise of untrammelled power by the courts. They further maintain that legislative intent *can* be found to legitimate the exercise of judicial power. They acknowledge that it is unrealistic to imagine that Parliament has any specific intent as to how the grounds of review should apply in any particular instance. The argument is now put in terms of general legislative intent. Parliament is taken to intend that its legislation conforms to the basic principles of fairness and justice which operate in a constitutional democracy. However, because Parliament itself cannot realistically work out the precise ramifications of this general idea it delegates power to the courts which then fashion the more particular application of this idea in accordance with the rule of law.

We are now in a position to assess the claim that legislative intent, as conceived by proponents of the modified ultra vires doctrine, is the central principle of administrative law. This claim will be examined in relation to the substance of judicial review, the substance of other areas of the law and in relation to the formal basis for judicial review.

LEGISLATIVE INTENT AS THE CENTRAL PRINCIPLE OF ADMINISTRATIVE LAW?
THE SUBSTANCE OF JUDICIAL REVIEW

(a) The different roles played by legislative intent in the two versions of the ultra vires doctrine

It is important at the outset to understand the very real difference between the traditional ultra vires model and the modified version of that doctrine. The traditional ultra vires doctrine saw particular legislative intent operating as the tool

---

[3] C. Forsyth, "Of Fig Leaves and Fairy Tales: The *Ultra Vires* Doctrine, the Sovereignty of Parliament and Judicial Review" [1996] CLJ 122 and Chapter Two pp. 29–46 above; M. Elliott, "The Demise of Parliamentary Sovereignty? The Implications for Justifying Judicial Review" (1999) 115 LQR 119, and "The *Ultra Vires* Doctrine in a Constitutional Setting: Still the Central Principle of Administrative Law" [1999] CLJ 129 and Chapter Five pp. 83–109 above.

through which Parliament's specific will would delineate the ambit of judicial review in the instant case. It was meaningful to call it an ultra vires doctrine precisely because it was meant to provide not only the *legitimation* for intervention, but also the *content* of judicial review in the particular case. The fact that it so patently failed to do the latter is of course one of the grounds for the critique of the doctrine. The modified ultra vires doctrine, is in reality, a very different idea, and the fact that the words "legislative intent" appear in both should not be allowed to conceal this. The modified ultra vires doctrine sees general legislative intent merely as a key to unlocking the door to allow the courts to decide on the ambit of judicial review in accord with the rule of law. On this version of the doctrine legislative intent is said to provide the formal legitimation for review, but it tells us nothing as to the specific content thereof. This will be determined by the courts in accord with whatsoever they choose to include within it pursuant to the rule of law ideal.

This shift of position in itself concedes a very large part of the argument advanced by supporters of the common law model. It is accepted that specific legislative intent will rarely tell us anything about the scope of review, its intensity, or how the heads of review change across time. The real substance of judicial review, its content, will be decided by the courts in a manner which is just the same as, or very similar to, that being argued for by proponents of the common law model. Supporters of the common law model have made it clear that they believe that the content of judicial review should be decided in accordance with the rule of law, or normative considerations of justice, which warrant the imposition of constraints on the exercise of discretion.[4] The choice of the precise label need not concern us here. My own preference has been to use the latter formulation, in part because of the different meanings attached to the concept of the rule of law. I am however perfectly happy to employ the terminology of the rule of law, provided that it is understood that the substantive concept of the rule of law necessarily entails some vision of justice and rights.

It is then not surprising that the modified ultra vires doctrine can cope with many of the problems associated with the traditional ultra vires doctrine. This is, of course, because the reasoning underlying the former is, once you get beyond the formal bow to general legislative intent, very similar to that propounded by the common law model. The difficulties of understanding how legislative intent can make sense of the detailed application of the principles of judicial review in a particular instance, or how it can explain how these rules develop across time, are clearly obviated if one moves to the general conception of legislative intent. This is because the idea of general legislative intent, coupled with delegation to the courts to work out the detailed meaning of ideas such as rationality, fairness, etc., operates to unlock the door for the courts to develop the rules of review as they see fit, both in the present and across time.

---

[4] Above, n. 1.

It is, moreover, not clear what function would be served by judicial invocation of the language of ultra vires in terms of general legislative intent. The use of such phraseology would necessarily have a "self-referential" quality: it would simply direct the parties to the case to the very reasoning used by the court to justify the conclusion which it had reached in its capacity as delegate of the legislature in applying the rule of law.

(b) The different normative force of specific and general legislative intent

There is a less obvious objection to the argument that general legislative intent should be conceived as the central principle of administrative law, so far as concerns the substance of judicial review. It seems clear that Elliott regards specific and general legislative intent as being of the same nature, the only difference residing in their relative generality. The more one thinks about this, the less obvious does it become.

The reason why we attach importance to specific legislative intent is that "in a democracy people have at least a strong prima facie moral right that courts enforce the rights that a representative legislature has enacted".[5] In this sense it follows that "if it is clear what the legislature has granted them, then it is also clear what they have a moral right to receive in court".[6] It follows that insofar as we might be able to find specific legislative intent which relates to the grounds of review it is then meaningful to talk in terms of that intent as being determinative of the content of review. If such indications of specific intent were generally available in the context of different statutes it would also be possible to sustain the thesis that legislative intent was the "central principle"of administrative law. This was the force and attraction of the traditional ultra vires doctrine. The fact that such indications of specific legislative intent were normally not to be found was, as we have seen, one of the principal reasons for the critique of that model.

This reasoning cannot readily be transferred to the idea of an implied, general legislative intent. This is in part because of the very fact that legislative intent set at such a general level will not in any sense be determinative of what rights an individual should receive in court. The legislature will, by definition, not have any clear idea of what particular meaning it wishes to accord to rationality or fairness. It will, therefore, be for the courts to fill out the detailed meanings of such general intent in the cases which come before them. It is in part because an implied, general legislative intent, to the effect that Parliament should be taken to intend fairness and rationality when it enacts legislation, does not mean that legislative intent conceived in such terms is creative or constitutive of these basic precepts. The normative force of, for example, formal equality is not created

---

[5] R. Dworkin, *A Matter of Principle* (1985), p. 16.
[6] *Ibid.* p. 16.

because we can construct some general legislative intent of the kind suggested by Elliott.

It is important to pause and take stock at this point. It has been shown that general legislative intent as manifested in the modified ultra vires doctrine will tell us nothing in and of itself about the detailed content of review. Proponents of that doctrine argue that the ultra vires principle, thus conceived, must nonetheless be seen as the central principle of administrative law. The fact that Parliament in a constitutional democracy is to be assumed to wish to act fairly and rationally, coupled with delegation to the courts to work out the details, is regarded as the foundation for this assertion. This proposition is put forward forcefully. There is an implicit challenge to opponents to deny the proposition that Parliament intends to act fairly and rationally. The very generality of this argument, to the effect that Parliament intends to be just, and therefore that legislative intent thus conceived can be seen as the "central principle" underlying an area of the law, has far-reaching implications for all areas of the law.

The thesis was developed so as to justify the existence of judicial review, but the underlying argument, if true, must be equally applicable in other contexts. It should be remembered that the central kernel of the argument is that where Parliament has passed a statute it is not open to the courts to impose controls unless they can be legitimated by reference to legislative intent: what the all powerful Parliament does not prohibit it must be taken to authorise expressly or impliedly. It is for this reason that legislative intent must be found in order to legitimate the imposition of any constraints on the way in which power is exercised. This legislative intent can be either specific, or general, but some species thereof must be found to authorise the imposition of any control. In the absence of such a finding the existence and application of the controls which the courts might otherwise be minded to impose cannot be justified. Because this is so it is said to be valid to regard legislative intent as the "central principle" underlying the relevant area of the law. It is interesting to test this assumption to see whether it makes sense of the way in which we conceive of the relationship between statute and controls developed by the courts.

We can do so by looking at the way in which we justify the imposition of the principles of contract, tort, restitution and the like to public bodies which derive their power from statute. If we subscribe to the modified ultra vires doctrine we would have to argue as follows. Parliament has passed a statute which has given power to a particular public body. We are not entitled to impose any limits on the way in which that power is exercised unless we can find justification in terms of legislative intent. If therefore we wish to argue that the public body should be subject to rules of contractual, tortious or restitutionary liability then the requisite legislative intent must be found. There may be some specific legislative intent that we can point to, but this will often be absent, since Parliament will not have the necessary expertise, time, etc., to manifest a specific intent on the matter. So we have to fall back on some general legislative intent. This could, doubtless, be constructed. It could be argued that Parliament in a constitutional democracy intends a just system of civil liability, and that it then delegates the detailed implementation of this task to the courts to be decided in accordance with the normative principles which would govern such a system. If no such intent can be found then the existence and application of such principles cannot be justified. If we are satisfied that the requisite intent can be found then we can and must say that the "cental principle" of this area of the law is legislative intent. We must, moreover, say this notwithstanding the fact that the principles of civil liability which are thus applied to public bodies have a normative force of their own which warrants their application to public bodies and to private parties where there is no relevant background statute.

It is clear that this reasoning does not accord with how we think of the application of the rules of civil liability to public bodies, nor does it capture the way in which the courts approach the matter. It is of course the case that legislative intent is of relevance in this area, but the role played by such intent is very different from that described above. This is no place to engage in a detailed exegesis about the rules of civil liability and public bodies, but the essence of the judicial approach is surely as follows. The courts develop the principles of civil liability which they believe best capture the underlying aims of contract, tort and restitution. These common law principles are formally valid because pronounced by courts which are competent over the subject matter. They have substantive force because of the normative principles which comprise their content. The courts will decide whether such principles should be applied to bodies which derive their power from statute. They will limit the application of these principles where Parliament unequivocally states that liability should, for example, be contingent on proof of bad faith. The courts may also do so where they decide that there is something in the nature of the statutory scheme which makes it necessary to exclude or modify these principles. It is also open to the courts to develop and modify these principles over time, and to do so in accord with changing normative conceptions which affect the subject as a whole, or part thereof, as exemplified by the extension of restitutionary liability in the case of ultra vires payments. The process described in this paragraph captures the approach of the courts and provides an example of the common law model in operation.

The modified ultra vires doctrine can also be tested in the context of statutes which deal with matters in the private sphere. Much legislation is enacted on topics relating to commercial law, banking, trusts, employment law, land law and the like. It is not uncommon for such legislation to afford some measure of discretion to a private party, or to contain terms which require interpretation by the courts. If we adhere to the strictures of Forsyth and Elliott then we must say that legislative intent is the "central principle" of the relevant area of the law. Specific legislative intent will often not be present. We must therefore construct some species of general legislative intent. It might be argued that Parliament in a constitutional democracy intends there to be a just relationship between, for example, banks and their customers, and that Parliament intends to delegate the working out of this relationship to the courts. When the courts fashion the relevant rules they will doubtless draw on pre-existing concepts from the law of contract, trusts, restitution, etc., which have a normative force of their own, and are often applied in circumstances where there is no statutory background. Notwithstanding this, supporters of the modified ultra vires doctrine would insist that if no such intent can be found then no limits are warranted, and that if such general intent can be found then this justifies the conclusion that legislative intent is the "central principle" in the relevant area. If this is true then writers in areas as diverse as labour law, company law, commercial law, and tax will have a good deal of re-writing to do in their subjects.

LEGISLATIVE INTENT AS THE CENTRAL PRINCIPLE OF ADMINISTRATIVE LAW?
THE FORMAL BASIS FOR JUDICIAL INTERVENTION

The discussion thus far has shown the real difference between the traditional ultra vires doctrine and the modified version sketched by Forsyth and developed in greater detail by Elliott. It has been argued that the modified form of the doctrine concedes almost all of the substance argued for by those in the other camp. Forsyth and Elliott continue to insist however that constitutional orthodoxy demands that we accept their view that judicial review is still based on legislative intent, albeit in the modified form explained above. They argue that to do otherwise entails a strong challenge to sovereignty.

It might be felt at this juncture that little harm would be done if we accepted this compromise. The common law school of thought wins on substance, in the sense that it is accepted by all sides that the detailed doctrines of judicial review are developed by and through the common law courts. The ultra vires school wins on form, in the sense that constitutional orthodoxy is preserved by legitimating the exercise of judicial power through the idea of legislative delegation in the manner described above. Some might be content with such a compromise, or feel that it is in any event demanded if judicial review is to be squared with constitutional orthodoxy.

I do not believe that this is correct. It will be argued that constitutional orthodoxy is not offended in any way by the picture of judicial review articulated by, inter alia, Laws, Craig and Oliver. It will moreover be argued that the modified ultra vires doctrine articulated by Elliott entails a novel view of the relationship between courts and the legislature in our country which is not warranted in terms of orthodox constitutional principle or constitutional history.

(a) The argument from analytical logic

The principal foundation for the claim that constitutional orthodoxy requires adherence to the ultra vires doctrine, albeit in its modified form, is to be found in what I have termed in an earlier article the analytical impasse.[7] The essence of this claim, to be examined in detail below, is that abandonment of the ultra vires doctrine as the foundation for judicial review in reality amounts to a strong challenge to sovereignty. It is therefore contended that while the traditional notion of sovereignty continues to hold sway, judicial review must be premised on the ultra vires doctrine in some form. This first appeared as but one part of the argument advanced by Forsyth as to the dangers of abandoning the ultra vires doctrine as the foundation of judicial review.[8] It has since been promoted to centre stage. Elliott has written an article expressly premised on the soundness of this argument.[9] He argues that the traditional conception of sovereignty remains intact, and that, even if it were modified so that the courts did not always accept the unequivocal will of Parliament, such limits on Parliament would not touch the great generality of administrative law cases. His conclusion is unequivocal. If judicial review is premised on any thing other than the ultra vires doctrine, then this will entail a strong challenge to sovereignty. While the traditional vision of sovereignty remains as the cornerstone of the constitution ultra vires must therefore continue to be the foundation for judicial review. While this argument is cast in analytical terms it also carries, and is intended to carry, a "political" punch. It is clearly intended to convince judges that they must adhere to the ultra vires doctrine or be guilty of the gravest constitutional heterodoxy.

I do not believe that adherence to the common law model of illegality entails this consequence. There is, as will be shown, nothing in the views of those who are opposed to legislative intent as being the foundation of judicial review which in any way leads to a strong challenge to sovereignty. To understand why this is so, and to lay this argument to rest, it is necessary to be clear about the analytical claim.

Forsyth's version of the analytical impasse is presented in the following quotation. It formed but one part of his general thesis as to why it was necessary to retain the ultra vires doctrine as the foundation of judicial review.[10]

Suppose that a Minister in the apparent exercise of a statutory power to make regulations, makes certain regulations which are clearly so vague that their meaning cannot be determined with sufficient certainty. Classic theory tells us that Parliament never intends to grant the power to make vague regulations – this seems an entirely

---

[7] Craig, "*Ultra Vires* and the Foundations of Judicial Review" [1998] CLJ 63 at pp. 73–74 and pp. 55–7 above.

[8] Forsyth, "Of Fig Leave and Fairy Tales", p. 133 and p. 39 above.

[9] M. Elliott, "The Demise of Parliamentary Sovereignty? The Implications for Justifying Judicial Review" (1999) 115 LQR 119.

[10] Forsyth, "Of Fig Leaves and Fairy Tales", p. 133, p. 39–48 above.

reasonable and realistic intention to impute to Parliament – and thus the vague regulations are ultra vires and void: there would be no difficulty in the court striking down the regulations. But classic theory has been abandoned: the grounds of review derive, not from the implied intent of the legislature, but from the common law. It follows that although the regulations are intra vires the minister's powers, they are none the less invalid because they are vague.

The analytical difficulty is this: what an all powerful Parliament does not prohibit, it must authorise either expressly or impliedly . . . Thus, if the making of the vague regulations is within the powers granted by a sovereign Parliament, on what basis may the courts challenge Parliament's will and hold that the regulations are invalid?

Elliott deploys the same argument in more detail in his work. He argues that when Parliament confers ostensibly unfettered discretionary power there are two ways in which to justify the imposition of unwritten limits on the exercise of such discretion. The traditional methodology of the ultra vires doctrine is to say that the imposition of, for example, procedural fairness, is subject to "an implied statutory provision to that effect".[11] No transgression of sovereignty has occurred since the "courts simply articulate and enforce those limits on power which Parliament is taken to have demarcated implicitly as part of its original grant of power".[12] The alternative approach is based on the premise hat Parliament really does not intend there to be any limits on the exercise of the discretion. If this is indeed so then it means that, for example, the exercise of discretion without a hearing is intra vires, in the sense that it is within the ambit of power which Parliament has chosen to grant. If therefore the courts intervene and impose limits on such power, they are transgressing the will of Parliament. Elliott's conclusion is captured in the following quotation.[13]

Therefore, so long as the sovereignty principle survives, judicial review can be reconciled with constitutional orthodoxy only by holding that it involves the enforcement of those limits on power which Parliament is taken to have intended. The alternative explanation – based on judicial imposition of autonomous common law requirements of legality – necessarily entails constitutional impropriety because it involves the courts holding unlawful administrative action which must logically be lawful according to Parliament (given that rejection of the ultra vires doctrine must involve acceptance of the proposition that Parliament makes ample grants of discretionary power unfettered by an implied statutory restrictions based on the requirements of fairness and rationality).

There is in reality nothing in the view presented by opponents of the legislative intent model which entails a strong challenge to sovereignty. The common law model holds that the principles of judicial review are developed by the courts. They are the creation of the common law. The legislature will rarely provide any indications as to the content and limits of what constitutes judicial review,

---

[11] Elliott, "The Demise of Parliamentary Sovereignty?", p. 121.
[12] *Ibid.* p. 121.
[13] *Ibid.* p. 123.

as is conceded by advocates of the ultra vires doctrine.[14] When legislation is passed the courts will impose the controls which constitute judicial review which they believe are normatively justified on the grounds of justice, the rule of law, etc. They will therefore decide on the appropriate procedural and substantive principles of judicial review. Agency action which infringes these principles will be unlawful. It will not, in any sense, by intra vires. If the omnipotent Parliament does not like these controls then it is open to it to make this explicitly clear. If, for example, the courts decide that proportionality should be a head of judicial review, but the legislature disagrees, either generally or in some specific context, then it is open to the legislature to make this clear. If it does so then the courts will accept this. This is how the courts conceived of judicial review in historical terms,[15] and it is what underlies Stephen Sedley's[16] dual constitutionalism and much of John Laws'[17] work, as well as my own. There is therefore nothing in the common law model which involves a strong challenge to sovereignty.[18] It is based on the assumption that it will be for Parliament expressly, or in some other unequivocal manner, to demonstrate that it does not wish the normally applicable judicially developed controls to apply in a particular instance. This is however quite different from acceptance of a strong challenge to sovereignty. The latter entails the proposition that the courts will continue to apply their judicially developed tools even where there is an express or unequivocal Parliamentary intention to the contrary.

It is of course the case that in this sense legislative intent is of relevance for those who adopt the common law model. This is, however, true of *any* body of jurisprudence developed by the courts on *any* subject. It is always open to Parliament to decide that the legal rules which govern an area should be different from those developed at common law by the courts. There is however the world of difference between saying that legislative intent is of relevance in this residual sense, and the claim that the entire fabric of judicial review is founded on legislative intent.[19] No one would seriously contend that because an all powerful Parliament can choose to limit the application of the common law principles of contract or tort to public bodies (or indeed anyone else), therefore the very existence of that entire body of principle should or could be rationalised in terms of legislative intent.[20]

We are now in a position to understand why the common law model does not involve any strong challenge to sovereignty of the kind postulated by Forsyth and Elliott. Their claims is based on two assumptions.

---

[14] Elliott, "The *Ultra Vires* Doctrine in a Constitutional Setting", p. 141, p. 94 above.

[15] Craig, "*Ultra Vires* and the Foundations of Judicial Review", pp. 79–86, pp. 61–9 above.

[16] Sir Stephen Sedley, "Human Rights: A Twenty-First Century Agenda" [1995] PL 386.

[17] Sir John Laws, "Illegality: The Problem of Jurisdiction", *Judicial Review* (M. Supperstone and J. Goudie eds., 2nd ed., 1997), Chapter 4 and Chapter Four pp. 73–81 above.

[18] Although it is of course the case that proponents of this view might also believe in a strong challenge to sovereignty on one of a variety of other grounds.

[19] The failure to distinguish between these two propositions can be seen in Elliott's observations in, "The *Ultra Vires* Doctrine in a Constitutional Setting", p. 136 and p. 89 above, n. 28.

[20] See above, pp. 375–78 for further discussion.

First, there is the *substantive assumption* that unless we preserve the ultra vires doctrine then the limits on agency power will somehow disappear. This will not withstand examination. The fact that some might choose to reject the ultra vires doctrine based on legislative intent as the justification for judicial review does not mean that the limits to an agency's powers thereby alter. The argument as put thus elides the existence of limits to an agency's power with the conceptual basis for those limits. The live issue is whether one believes that such limits are really to be derived from legislative intent or more honestly from judicial creation through the process of the common law. Under the latter approach one would simply say that there is a common law principle that regulations cannot be too vague, that statutes which empower the making of regulations will be read subject to this principle and therefore that the minister did *not* have power to make such vague regulations.

Secondly, there is the *constitutional assumption* expressed by Forsyth that "what an all powerful Parliament does not prohibit, it must authorise expressly or impliedly".[21] This is the premise for the argument that the controls which constitute judicial review are only justified if we can find some *positive, albeit implied, legislative intent* to the effect that such controls should exist. We must, on this view, find that the all powerful Parliament intends to prohibit the making of vague regulations, etc., in order for such judicial controls to be constitutionally acceptable. If we cannot do so then it is argued that the legislature must be taken to have authorised the making of, for example, vague regulations. It is this which is said to compel continued adherence to the ultra vires doctrine as the foundation of judicial review. This causality is denied by those in the common law school. We maintain that *unless the all powerful Parliament has clearly authorised action which is inconsistent with the judicially created controls* then such controls should be operative and the relevant action should be prohibited. There is no need to find any positive legislative intent to justify the imposition of the controls which constitute judicial review. There is no necessity to manufacture legislative intent to fill the gap between legislative silence and the imposition of judicial controls. The courts develop and impose the controls which they believe are normatively justified. Agency action which infringes these controls is therefore illegal, unless Parliament clearly stipulates to the contrary. There is, on this view, no difference in this respect between contract and tort, and judicial review. The core principles which constitute all these subjects are the creation of the common law. They will apply unless Parliament has indicated otherwise.

(b) The argument concerning judicial supremacism

Elliott deploys a second argument, based on a critique of the work of Sir John Laws, as to why judicial review *must* be founded on legislative intent. Elliott

[21] Forsyth, "Of Fig Leaves and Fairy Tales", p. 133, p. 39 above.

contends that to forsake the ultra vires principle and legislative intent involves an unwarranted manifestation of judicial supremacism. This is said to be inconsistent with any legal duty of judicial fidelity to the will of Parliament, with the consequence that it thereby "sweeps away the constitutional theory of sovereignty on which the ultra vires doctrine is based".[22] Indeed, he goes further and contends that Sir John Laws' argument renders otiose any attempt to justify judicial review. Elliott's point would be very important if it were correct. It is, however, clear this is not what Sir John Laws was saying. Elliott relies on two passages to sustain his conclusion.

In the first Sir John Laws states that the legal power of the courts is not dependent upon an imprimatur from an external source, and there is in that sense no higher order law for them. From this it "follows that any analysis of their jurisdiction, if it is not to be confined to the simplest statement that the court reviews what it chooses to review, must consist in a description of the nature and extent of judicial review in practice".[23] The courts possessed ultimate freedom of movement, with the consequence that if they chose to push out the boundaries of judicial review in a particular case, they could, said Sir John, not be accused of any constitutional solecism. The second passage on which Elliott relies is one in which Laws is talking about the meaning of the term jurisdiction. Sir John Laws states that jurisdiction is a protean word, the most common application of which is where a body acts outside the limited powers conferred on it by another body. He then states that the superior courts are not constituted on any such basis, and they "have, in the last analysis, the power they say they have".[24]

There is nothing in either passage to warrant the conclusion that *sovereignty and fidelity to Parliament have been swept away*. The first quote taken from Sir John Laws occurs in the middle of a discussion about sovereignty and the role of the courts. The nub of his point is simply that sovereignty, in the sense of Parliamentary omnipotence free from constitutional review, exists in part because the courts have chosen to recognise this state of affairs. This is entirely in accord with standard thinking on this matter, which goes back to Sir William Wade's seminal article.[25] Sir John Laws correctly emphasises that whether the courts could do otherwise is not "in the end a proposition about the theoretical limits of the court's jurisdiction, but about the historical and political dictates on which the relationship between judiciary and legislature is factually based".[26] He then, once again correctly, points out that subordinate authorities are manifestly subject to the courts' control. The passage from which Elliott quotes occurs immediately after this. It is, however, clear that all that Sir John

---

[22] "The *Ultra Vires* Doctrine in a Constitutional Setting", p. 132, p. 86 above.

[23] Sir John Laws, "Illegality: The Problem of Jurisdiction", *Judicial Review* (M. Supperstone and J. Goudie, 1st ed., 1992), pp. 69–70.

[24] Sir John Laws, "Illegality: The Problem of Jurisdiction", *Judicial Review* (M. Supperstone and J. Goudie, 2nd ed., 1997), Chapter 4, p. 1.

[25] "The Basis of Legal Sovereignty" [1955] CLJ 172.

[26] Sir John Laws, "Illegality: The Problem of Jurisdiction", *Judicial Review* (M. Supperstone and J. Goudie, 1st ed., 1992), p. 69.

Laws is saying is that the very existence of the courts' *general power* of judicial review is not dependent on the existence of any external source, and therefore that if the courts choose to extend the ambit of review they are free to do so. He is clearly not saying that if Parliament expressly and unequivocally curtailed this power in some manner, by for example limiting the availability of a ground of review, the courts would ignore this expression of sovereign will. This is equally apparent from the second quotation on which Elliott relies. Sir John Laws is discussing the general foundation for the courts' power of review. The essence of his argument is simply that while Parliament might well have confirmed the existence of the courts' power of review, and regulated its exercise, "the ancient jurisdiction of Queens Bench to call up the decisions of inferior bodies was never conferred by Parliament".[27] There is nothing which indicates in any way that the courts should ignore the express will of Parliament where it relates to the ambit of judicial review. The argument is simply that the doctrine of judicial review in general was not based on a conferral of power by Parliament to courts. This is clearly correct in historical terms. It is of course the case that, as is well known, Sir John Laws has argued that there should be some limits placed on parliamentary sovereignty.[28] The circumstances in which this should occur are carefully delineated by him. There is however nothing in the common law model of review generally, or in the version developed by Sir John Laws, which entails a strong challenge to sovereignty.

There is also nothing in these passages to warrant the other conclusion which Elliott draws, to the effect that Laws' thesis *renders otiose any attempt to justify judicial review*. There is no inconsistency between saying that the existence and ambit of judicial review are dependent on the view of the courts, subject to any unequivocal statement from Parliament on the matter, and that in making that determination the courts should use justice, the rule of law, etc., as guiding criteria. Sir John Laws has indeed written at length concerning the substantive conception of the rule of law which he believes does and should underpin judicial review.[29]

(c) Constitutional principle: the relationship between sovereignty and the rule of law

The discussion thus far has concentrated on the analytical argument presented by supporters of the ultra vires doctrine. It is, however, still open to supporters of the modified ultra vires doctrine to claim that their view best conforms to constitutional principle quite independently of the analytical argument. They

[27] Sir John Laws, "Illegality: The Problem of Jurisdiction", *Judicial Review* (M. Supperstone and J. Goudie, 2nd ed., 1997), Chapter 4, p. 1.

[28] Sir John Laws, "Law and Democracy" [1995] PL 72, and "The Constitution, Morals and Rights" [1996] PL 622.

[29] See, *e.g.* Sir John Laws, "Illegality: The Problem of Jurisdiction", *Judicial Review* (M. Supperstone and J. Goudie eds., 2nd ed., 1997), Chapter 4 and Chapter Four pp.73–81 (extract) above.

would doubtless contend that the idea of legislative delegation to the courts of the power to develop the rules of judicial review in accordance with the rule of law is empirically plausible and achieves the best accommodation between sovereignty and judicial power. This may be felt to be an attractive way in which to legitimate judicial review.

It will be argued that we should think long and hard before accepting this rationalisation, since it has far reaching implications for the relationship between sovereignty and the rule of law. It will be shown that it is in fact that common law model which best captures the relationship between sovereignty and the rule of law, the twin principles which underpin our constitutional order.

The meaning of the rule of law has been much debated, as has the concept of sovereignty. The nature of the relationship between the two has received rather less attention, and it is this with which we are concerned here. Elliott's thesis provides a stark answer on this point. To understand why this is so we need to pay close attention to his argument. There are two strands to his thesis: legislative intent *can* provide the foundation for judicial review, and legislative intent *must* do so if judicial review is to be legitimate. These will be examined in turn.

The argument that legislative intent *can* provide the foundation for judicial review takes the following form. Elliott argues that the disagreement between proponents of the intention-based and common law models stems from the question of what role, if any, should be ascribed to parliamentary intention *vis-à-vis* the grounds of review.[30] He argues that the entire range of possible views can be expressed in terms of five competing propositions, and that all but one of these must be rejected. The first is that Parliament might intend there to be no implied limits on the exercise of discretionary power. This is rejected as being absurd.[31] The second possibility, that Parliament intends to specify every detail and nuance of the principles of good administration which the courts can apply is likewise rejected as being equally absurd, it being unrealistic to suppose that Parliament has any specific intent as to the detailed requirements of good administration.[32] The third possibility is that Parliament when it grants discretionary power must do so in accord with the principles of good administration. This too is dismissed since it entails a strong challenge to sovereignty for which there is said to be no warrant.[33] It is the fourth model which Elliott favours. On this view it is assumed that Parliament intends to legislate in accordance with the rule of law. The fleshing out of the detailed norms which comprise the rule of law is delegated to the courts.[34] The relationship between legislative intent and judicial review is perceived as being indirect, but real nonetheless: the details of judicial review are not attributed to legislative intent, but the "judicially-created rules of good administration should nevertheless be viewed as

---

[30] "The *Ultra Vires* Doctrine in a Constitutional Setting", p. 140, p. 93 above.
[31] *Ibid*. pp. 140–141, pp. 93–4 above.
[32] *Ibid*. p. 141, pp. 94–5 above.
[33] *Ibid*. pp. 141–142, pp. 94–6 above.
[34] *Ibid*. p. 143, p. 96 above.

having been made pursuant to a constitutional warrant granted by Parliament".[35] The final conceptualisation of the relation between legislative intent and review, which is attributed to Sir John Laws and myself, is that there is no relationship. Elliott takes Laws to task for suggesting such a thing, and argues that it is implicit on this model that Parliament is wholly neutral about the extent of the administrative power which it grants, and the manner in which it is exercised. This is said to be both absurd and implausible.[36] This is to misunderstand the nature of the argument advanced by Sir John Laws.[37]

Let us now turn to the other strand of Elliott's thesis, which is that legislative intent *must* be found in some form if judicial review is to be legitimate. It is clear that this is required if his overall thesis is to be sustained: the mere fact that legislative intent can be constructed does not in and of itself tell us that it must be present. Elliott does not shy away from this aspect of his claim. It is the explicit foundation for the analytical argument discussed in the earlier section. It surfaces once again in his later work. This can be seen in the way in which he addressed the objection made against the traditional ultra vires doctrine, that it could not be readily applied to cases where public law principles were being applied to bodies which did not derive their power from statute. He argues that these difficulties are circumvented if one accepts the modified version of the ultra vires doctrine.[38] He acknowledges that there are good normative considerations based on the rule of law to justify the direct imposition of public-law type controls on such bodies. It is accepted therefore that the application of these principles to such bodies is clearly warranted in and of itself by reason of their normative force. The application of such constraints to bodies which derive their power from statute must, by way of contrast, be based on legislative intent, since this is said to be required in order to reconcile the rule of law with sovereignty.

We are now in a position to appreciate the implications which this analysis has for the relationship between sovereignty and the rule of law. It is accepted that the principles which make up the rule of law have a normative force of their own which warrants their direct application to non-statutory bodies. Sovereignty is said nonetheless to require that legislative intent can and must be found before the application of the principles which comprise the rule of law is to be regarded as legitimate in relation to those bodies which derive their power from statute. This legislative intent can be specific, but it is accepted by Elliott that this will not normally be present. It is for this reason that he falls back on the general formulation as to legislative intent set out above. On this view the

---

[35] "The *Ultra Vires* Doctrine in a Constitutional Setting", p. 143, p. 96 above.

[36] *Ibid.* p. 146, pp. 98–9 above.

[37] The argument advanced by Sir John Laws was based on the traditional ultra vires doctrine, since the modified version thereof had not been developed at that time. It is perfectly plausible to suggest, both empirically and conceptually, that the legislature might have no specific intent one way or the other as to the incidence or intensity of review in a particular context.

[38] "The *Ultra Vires* Doctrine in a Constitutional Setting", p. 155, pp. 106–7 above.

principles which constitute the rule of law have no application or existence in relation to bodies which derive their power from statute unless we can find the requisite legislative intent. Delegation by Parliament, based on general legislative intent, is the *sine qua non* for the development and application of the rule of law by the courts.

This argument is presented as constitutional orthodoxy. If this is right then courts and commentators have been guilty of a constitutional heresy for three hundred and fifty years. This view is not supported by the case law which laid the foundations for judicial review, nor by academic opinion. These will be examined in turn.

Let us begin with the *case law* itself. In an earlier article I examined the foundations for judicial review and the way in which the courts conceived of the relationship between the norms which constitute judicial review and the will of Parliament.[39] It is clear from that case law that the courts did not conceive of the principles which constitute judicial review as being dependent on the finding of legislative intent in the manner argued for by Elliott. For Coke, Holt and Mansfield the central idea was the capacity of the common law to control governmental and non-governmental power. If Parliament desired to limit such controls, so be it. The courts would then pay heed to such dictates, provided that they were sufficiently clear and unequivocal. They did not, however, act on the assumption that the existence and application of the norms which constitute the rule of law were dependent on a finding of legislative intent. This jurisprudence is an expression of the common law model set out above.

It is surprising that those who argue for constitutional orthodoxy pay no attention to the constitutional jurisprudence which created and developed judicial review. The response can only be conjectured at, but I imagine that it would take the following form. It would be argued that this case law is of no relevance since it pre-dated the emergence of the modern sovereign Parliament. Constitutional propriety would now be said to demand a relationship between sovereignty and the rule of law of the kind articulated by Elliott.

This line of argument is dependent on an empirical assumption as to when the "modern Parliament" might be said to have emerged. Some might think that this was post-1689, others might put the date in the mid-eighteenth century, yet others might choose the late nineteenth century or early twentieth century. It is however clear that references to legislative intent as a way of legitimating the existence of particular grounds for review only really begin to appear in the late nineteenth and early twentieth century. It is therefore only if one believes that the "modern Parliament" emerged after this date that one can dismiss the relevance of the earlier case law.

This view is also dependent on the further empirical assumption that the more modern case law reflects the assumptions of the modified ultra vires doctrine. This is questionable to say the very least. While some cases sought to legitimate

---

[39] Craig, *"Ultra Vires"*, pp. 79–85, pp. 62–7 above.

the existence of particular grounds of review on legislative intent, it should also be recognised that there were far more instances where the courts created and developed the grounds of review without any conscious need to find positive support in terms of legislative intent. The general approach was, as it always had been, for the courts to develop the grounds as they saw fit. If Parliament did not like the result it could make this unequivocally clear, and the courts would then abide by the result.

There is, moreover, a less obvious flaw in the argument that the historical case law is irrelevant. It is based on the premise that while it might well have been legitimate for the courts to act as they did before the emergence of the modern Parliament, it ceased to be so once that body did assume its modern form. This premise cannot be sustained. The body politic as conceived in, for example, the eighteenth century was one in which power was divided between the King, Commons and Lords. This division of authority *was* regarded as legitimate at that time, and the Parliament thus composed *was* sovereign. This was the very way in which Blackstone saw the sovereign Parliament. It was the Parliament "thus conceived" which was regarded as omnipotent in the famous quotation from Blackstone.[40] Notwithstanding this, the courts continued during this period to develop judicial review in the manner captured by the common law model. The courts did not feel any necessity to ground the existence of particular heads of review in a finding of legislative intent.

Let us now turn to *academic opinion* on the relationship between sovereignty and the rule of law. Space precludes any exhaustive survey as to how academics have conceived of the relationship between sovereignty and the rule of law. This would require an article or a book in its own right. We can however gain some impression by considering the work of particular writers. The Diceyan account is of particular interest, given the prominence which he accords to both sovereignty and the rule of law in his work. Dicey devotes a specific chapter directly to this issue.[41] His object is to show that parliamentary sovereignty favours the rule of law, and that the rule of law favours parliamentary sovereignty. There is much which makes good sense within this account, and also much which oversimplifies the relationship between the two concepts in his desire to show their compatibility. At no stage does Dicey suggest that the norms which comprise the rule of law are dependent upon a showing of legislative intent and delegation in the manner argued for by Forsyth and Elliott. The closest that he comes to addressing the issue is in his discussion of the way in which the rule of law favours parliamentary sovereignty. His reasoning is as follows.[42] If the executive requires discretionary authority it must obtain this from Parliament in the form of a statute. Recourse to such discretionary power may well be necessary, particularly in times of disorder

---

[40] Sir W. Blackstone, *Commentaries on the Law of England* (16th ed., 1825), Vol. I, Book 2, pp. 146–161.

[41] A.V. Dicey, *An Introduction to the Study of the Law of the Constitution* (10th ed., 1967), Chapter XIII.

[42] *Ibid.* pp. 411–414.

or war. The fact that the "most arbitrary powers of the English executive must always be exercised under Act of Parliament places the government, even when armed with the widest authority, under the supervision"[43] of the courts. Such powers are not unlimited, but are confined by the words of the enabling legislation and "what is more, by the interpretation put upon the statute by the judges".[44] He continues in the following vein.[45] This is not the language of someone who conceives of the relationship between the rule of law and supremacy in the manner being argued for by supporters of the modified ultra vires doctrine.

> Parliament is supreme legislator, but from the moment Parliament has uttered its will as lawgiver, that will becomes subject to the interpretation put upon it by the judges of the land, and the judges, who are influenced by the feelings of magistrates no less than by the general spirit of the common law, are disposed to construe statutory exceptions to common law principles in a mode which would not commend itself either to a body of officials, or to the House of Parliament, if the Houses were called upon to interpret their own enactments.

Jeffrey Jowell's work can be taken as representative of modern mainstream thinking about the rule of law.[46] We are not concerned with the details of the thesis, but with the relationship between the principles which constitute the rule of law, and sovereignty. For Jowell, sovereignty enables powers to be exercised by government, whereas the rule of law disables the government from abusing its power.[47] In countries which have written constitutions the text will normally provide the enabling features of the constitution, as well as its disabling features. In Britain with its unwritten constitution it is the rule of law which performs a similar disabling function.[48] It is in this sense conceived of as a principle of institutional morality, which is only to be excluded where Parliament makes this expressly clear.[49] It is regarded as proper and legitimate for the courts to supply the omission of the legislature, and it is accepted that Parliament will often be unclear as to what the aims or purposes of legislation actually are.[50] There is no warrant on this account for the proposition that the norms which comprise the rule of law can only be taken to exist if one can point to some specific or general legislative intent by way of justification.

CONCLUSION

The common law model of illegality best captures what the courts have done for the last three hundred and fifty years, and it continues to do so. This is so even

[43] *Ibid.* p. 413.
[44] *Ibid.* p. 413.
[45] *Ibid.* pp. 413–414.
[46] "The Rule of Law Today", *The Changing Constitution* (J. Jowell and D. Oliver eds., 3rd ed., 1994), Chapter 3.
[47] *Ibid.* p. 72.
[48] *Ibid.* pp. 72–73.
[49] *Ibid.* p. 73.
[50] *Ibid.* pp. 73–74.

when courts or judges proclaim adherence to the ultra vires model. This can be exemplified by the recent case law on collateral challenge. It is well known that in *Boddington*[51] Lord Steyn explicitly stated that ultra vires should still be regarded as the foundation for review. It is not clear from his Lordship's judgment which version of that doctrine he had in mind. The traditional ultra vires model, based on specific legislative intent, could not, with respect, provide the rationalisation for the judgment, since the plethora of legislation which raises the possibility of collateral attack will rarely contain any indication as to the relationship between direct and collateral challenge. Nor does Lord Steyn base his judgment on any such reasoning. The actual reasoning used fits perfectly with the common law model. Lord Steyn provides an excellent set of normative and pragmatic reasons why collateral attack should, prima facie, be generally available in criminal cases. It is a classic example of a judgment developing review, in this instance the ambit of collateral challenge, on grounds of principle which are normatively warranted in terms of justice, the rule of law, etc. Legislative intent features in the judgment in just the manner claimed by proponents of the common law model. It performs a residual function. The general presumption that collateral challenge should, on grounds of principle, be available, may be rebutted where there is some clear indication from Parliament that it should be more limited, as in *Wicks*.[52]

Elliott concludes his article by wondering why critics such as myself are against the idea of legislative intent. I hope that the preceding discussion has made it clear that those who support the common law model have nothing, in and of itself, against the idea of legislative intent. The essential dividing line between supporters and opponents of the ultra vires model is as to how far legislative intent can provide a satisfactory explanation for the norms which constitute judicial review. The previous exchanges on this subject focused on the traditional ultra vires model, since that was the only version of the legislative intent model on offer. The weaknesses of that model now seem to be accepted by all. It is those who support the ultra vires doctrine who have shifted ground by proposing a modified version of that doctrine. This article has sought to challenge this latest version. It has been argued that there is no warrant for the claim that general legislative intent can be regarded as the foundation for judicial review, in terms of the substance of review itself. It has moreover been argued that there is no basis for the claim that the ultra vires model must be adhered to as the formal basis for review. The argument that this must be so, since to do otherwise would entail a strong challenge to sovereignty, or unchecked judicial supremacism, is unfounded.

The foundations of judicial review laid by the courts over three hundred years ago were based on the common law model. They continue to provide a fitting picture of the relationship between courts and Parliament. It is time we acknowledged our past, and recognised its continuing relevance for our future.

---

[51] *Boddington* v. *British Transport Police* [1998] 2 WLR 639.
[52] *R.* v. *Wicks* [1998] AC 92.

18

Heat and Light: A Plea for Reconciliation

CHRISTOPHER FORSYTH

The time has come for what I hope will be my final contribution to the debate over the foundations of judicial review. I believe in the value of academic debate as an anvil upon which the truth may be beaten out. But there is a danger when forceful counter-riposte follows riposte in short order that that the debate will descend into trivial or arcane points of detail that are not of general interest and, in the end, of little value. That heat rather than light will be generated. But I have been silent since my article "Of Fig Leaves and Fairytales",[1] defending the ultra vires doctrine as the foundation of the judicial review of statutory discretions, was published in early 1996. I have lost track of the number of people who have felt it necessary to explain (sometimes several times) in print how mistaken I was. There are so many of them that it is undeniable that I have a right of reply. But the views put forward in "Fig Leaves" have found a staunch and effective defender in Dr Mark Elliott to whom I am much indebted. Apart from anything else his detailed work allows me to respond to the critics in broader and in briefer terms than would otherwise be the case. I will try to bring light – and, perhaps, in some cases reconciliation.[2]

THE VANISHING OF THE "STRONG" CRITICS

I would like to start by noting the changes that there have been in the terms of the debate since I wrote "Of Fig Leaves and Fairytales". At that time several leading English judges had expressed themselves in public speeches and in print – although never on the bench – as opposed to the ultra vires doctrine; and had used its deficiencies as a step towards the proposition that the judges could strike down Acts of Parliament if the judges considered them too outrageous. One

---

[1] Above p. 29. The concerns expressed in the article clearly touched a nerve and I received, from all over the common law world, many appreciative letters from persons, some very eminent, who shared my concerns. I was touched by all these letters and grateful for them – especially as the number of critics mounted.

[2] It would be quite impossible for me to deal with every criticism of every aspect of "Fig Leaves". It should not be assumed that because I do not deal with a criticism that I accept it. In particular I will try to avoid criticisms that are simply assertion, sometimes robust, of a different position.

does not need to a defender at all costs of parliamentary sovereignty, to find such statements disconcerting.[3] Parliament speaks, and one trusts, always will speak, with a democratic legitimacy the judges, however independent and no matter how respected, will always lack. Thus the idea that a small group of unelected (and unrepresentative) officials – however eminent – could decide, without reference to anyone else, to shift the ultimate constitutional power from the hands of the elected representatives into their own hands has to be offensive to the democratic heart. And this is so even if those judges acted for the best of reasons. Indeed it would be worse if they acted for the best of reasons, for the unconstitutional seizure of power would be masked by their noble purpose and thus more difficult to resist and rectify.

But these judicial statements challenging parliamentary supremacy have ceased. There are doubtless many reasons for this.[4] There have been signs of recantation from those who originally made the statements. Perhaps there was never really a threat of judicial supremacism. Perhaps it was nothing more, in the Lord Chancellor's words, than "extra-judicial romanticism".[5]

The last word on parliamentary sovereignty has not been spoken;[6] and who knows what developments we may see in the future.[7] For the present it seems to me that we are in a curious position. The factual limits on the power of Parliament have grown greatly. As a matter of practical politics, for instance, it is difficult to envisage Parliament legislating expressly contrary to the European Convention on Human Rights and Fundamental Freedoms or to disapply European legislation, in general or in particular, or to abolish the Scottish

---

[3] And for the record I wish to remark that I, being far too well acquainted with the horrors that can result when a sovereign parliament is captured by anti-democratic forces (as was the case in South Africa), will not be found in the last ditch defending parliamentary sovereignty. In the UK the ingrained democratic nature of constitutional practice, in general, and of the House of Commons in particular ameliorates this danger considerably. But differing views of the merits of parliamentary sovereignty are irrelevant. The United Kingdom has, at present, a sovereign parliament and that is the context in which a justification for judicial review must be found.

[4] The enactment of the Human Rights Act 1998 must have been an important factor in that it eased judges's frustration in being unable to protect human rights directly and this lay, in large measure, behind the desire to clip Parliament's wings. But the 1998 Act, and in particular the device of a "declaration of incompatibility", is carefully crafted to ensure that it does not challenge Parliament's supremacy. Lord Irvine's robust assertion of orthodoxy shortly before he ascended the Woolsack must also have played a role ([1996] PL 59) as did the debate he initiated in the House of Lords on the relationship between the branches of government in which several of the critics of sovereignty were present, but remained silent notwithstanding strong assertions of orthodoxy (HL Debs. Vol. 572, 5 June 1996, cols. 1254–1313). A senior judge has written to me that "Fig Leaves" played a part in his change of mind.

[5] [1996] PL 59 at 77. Not all academic critics are persuaded though.

[6] For a recent valuable contribution see Goldsworthy, *The Sovereignty of Parliament* (OUP, 1999).

[7] The people of the United Kingdom, speaking through their representative institutions or by plebiscite, may choose to adopt a written constitution that limited the power of the legislature. Though there seems to me to be little public support for such a step. (I am not unaware of the technical difficulties with the abandonment of sovereignty but these could be readily overcome if the will to abandon sovereignty were present in Parliament.)

Parliament and the Welsh Assembly. Yet as a matter of pure constitutional law Parliament now seems as secure in its position of supremacy as it ever was.[8]

Anyway the significance of this for the debate over the foundations of judicial review is that one whole class of critics that I identified in "Fig Leaves" – the "strong critics", those who challenged the sovereignty of Parliament – has vanished. And all that is left are the "weak critics" who forswear any challenge to Parliament but rest their case on the artificial nature of the doctrine – or other deficiencies.

THE EMERGENCE OF CONSENSUS ON JUDICIAL REVIEW OF NON-STATUTORY DISCRETION

One further change since "Fig Leaves" has been the emergence of some consensus over the basis of the judicial review of non-statutory bodies.[9] Self-evidently it is not meaningful when a body lacks legal power to talk about it acting in excess of its legal powers. Yet the developed law of judicial review extends to non-statutory bodies that do not exercise legal powers. Ultra vires cannot be the juristic basis of judicial review in such circumstances.

In "Fig Leaves" I proposed, in reliance upon earlier work of Professor Craig, that there was a common law root for such judicial review.[10] The common law imposed a duty to act reasonably upon those who exercised monopoly power even when that power simply existed *de facto*. This, it seemed me, required little extension to provide the juristic basis for the judicial review of non-statutory bodies – such as the Panel on Take-overs and Mergers which wielded great *de facto* power. This is a view that others seem to share and I hope that it is not too contentious to say that, although there is much that remains to be worked out in this area, there is little dispute over this.[11]

These two developments – the disappearance of the "strong critics" and agreement on the common law's capacity to support the judicial review of non-statutory bodies – are to be welcomed; and amount to implicit acceptance of important parts of the argument of "Fig Leaves". But there remained the "weak critics".

---

[8] See *R v. D.P.P. ex p. Kebiline* [1999] 3 WLR 972 (HL), 980–82 for a recent decision taking the continuing sovereignty of parliament for granted.

[9] Judicial review of the prerogative was not discussed in "Fig Leaves" and is not much discussed elsewhere. I recommend Mark Elliott, *The Constitutional Legitimacy of Judicial Review in English Law* (unpublished PhD thesis, Cambridge, 1999), chapter 5.3.

[10] Above, pp. 31–3.

[11] See Laws, "Public Law and Employment Law: Abuse of Power" [1997] PL 455, 460–4. Above, pp. 59–60 (Craig). cf. Jowell, above, p. 339 who elsewhere recognises the importance of the common law powers to control monopolies in this area (de Smith, Woolf and Jowell, *Judicial Review of Administrative Action* (5th ed., 1995), para 3–027 (3), 3–051, 3–053).

BIG-ENDIANS AND LITTLE-ENDIANS

As I argued in "Fig Leaves" "weak critics" are easily reconciled with the modified or developed doctrine of ultra vires that I (and more recently Mark Elliott)
have advanced.[12] But it takes two to tango. And some "weak critics" refuse to
be reconciled. Many at the conference, perceiving how close that reconciliation
is, expressed themselves as unable to see what the fuss was about. Once it is
clear that there is no challenge to Parliament's supremacy does it make much
difference whether one formulates the basis for judicial review in accordance
with the first or the second statement that now follows?

> 1. *Unless Parliament clearly intends otherwise, the common law will require decision-*
> *makers to apply the principles of good administration as developed by the judges in*
> *making their decisions.*
> (This is a statement of the position of the "weak critics".)

> 2. *Unless Parliament clearly indicates otherwise, it is presumed to intend that*
> *decision-makers must apply the principles of good administration drawn from the*
> *common law as developed by the judges in making their decisions.*
> (This is a statement of the position of those who support the modified ultra vires doc-
> trine.)

These statements both recognise the creativity of the judiciary in developing
judicial review. They also both recognise the supremacy of Parliament. The difference between them is simply over the articulation of what is plainly an artificial construct: the intention of Parliament. Should Parliament be presumed to
have authorised the application by the judges of the principles of good administration or should that authorisation come from the common law? I have a great
deal of sympathy with those who do not understand the passion that seems to
be generated in support of the one formulation or the other. I am surprised that
in the welter of metaphors no one has yet invoked the clash between the Big-
endians and the Little-endians.[13]

So I am a little amused by all the fuss generated by the "weak critics" but also
disappointed. There is so much common ground between the two positions reconciliation should not be so far off. It is also disappointing to discover the frailty
of language: that an argument – or even just a statement of a position- advanced
with the greatest clarity that I can muster is so readily misunderstood. But even
if I can understand and share the views of those that are mystified by the passion
that erupts – particularly on one side of the debate – I have to say that there
remain important differences between the two opposing positions (although the

[12] Professor Craig in his latest writing (above, p. 375) on the subject seems to suggest that Mark
Elliott and myself have "shifted" our position and have "conceded a very large part of the argument
advanced by supporters of the common law model" . But in fact we have always been in favour of
the modified or developed ultra vires doctrine although the way in which we have expressed it has
varied between us. But see below, p. 409.

[13] These were two parties in the empire of Lilliput in bitter dispute over the proper end at which
to break a boiled egg. The little-endians were the orthodox party.

disappearance of the "strong critics" renders the dispute less urgent). For reasons of principle and pragmatism, in my opinion, the modified ultra vires remains distinctly preferable to the common law model. And so, lest that point of view be smothered, or assumed to be smothered, by the clamour of the critics, I think I should take up my pen and explain the reasons why I remain a, somewhat bemused, Little-endian.

Before doing so I want in the interests of clarity to make clear what the modified ultra vires doctrine is and what it is not. It does not assert that every nuance of every ground of judicial review is to be found in the implied intent of the legislature. There is no summoning of "the medium in the statute to thump out a message on the table".[14] It simply asserts that when the courts do turn to common law principle to guide their development of judicial review they are doing what Parliament intended them to do. Parliament thus authorises the courts to develop the law in the way that they do. Parliament seldom spells out this authorisation expressly but it is in accord with precedent and principle to presume that it does, save where its intent is clearly different. The creativity of the common law and the supremacy of statute are thus reconciled; and the constitutional foundations of the judicial review jurisdiction are rendered secure.

THE LEGAL STATUS OF THE ULTRA VIRES DOCTRINE

The first point, and it is an important point to make, is that the modified ultra vires doctrine is the law. There are four recent decisions of the House of Lords[15] in which the leading speeches clearly favour the modified ultra vires doctrine (or something very similar).[16] Lord Steyn said in *R. v. Home Secretary, ex p. Pierson*:[17]

---

[14] See Jowell, above, p. 337.

[15] *R. v. Lord President of the Privy Council ex parte Page* [1993] AC 682 (not mentioned in the text) is the third such decision. Lord Browne-Wilkinson, citing Sir William Wade's views with approval, said: "intervention [by judicial review] . . . is based upon the proposition that such powers have been conferred on the decision-maker on the underlying assumption that the powers are to be exercised only within the jurisdiction conferred, in accordance with fair procedures and, in a *Wednesbury* sense reasonably". Cf. Professor Craig, above, p. 62 seeking some comfort from the fact that elsewhere in his speech Lord Browne-Wilkinson refers to a body acting ultra vires "if it reaches it conclusions on a basis erroneous under the general law " (at 702F). But no comfort is to be had for, it seems, the judge has in mind a co-operative endeavour between legislature and common law of exactly the type envisaged by the modified ultra vires doctrine. See further, "Fig leaves", above pp. 30 n. 5 and pp. 80–1 (Laws). The fourth such decision is *R v. Home Secretary ex p. Abdi* [1996] 1 WLR 298 (HL) "Parliament assumes that procedural fairness will be observed, and legislates on that basis. In an appropriate case the courts have power to supplement the procedure laid down by Parliament" (Lord Lloyd at 313. There are many other decisions that recognise implied restrictions on discretions and favour ultra vires. See, for instance, *R. v. Boundary Commissioner for England and Wales, ex parte Foot* [1983] QB 600 (CA) (Sir John Donaldson, MR) *Daymond v. South West Water Authority* [1976] AC 609 (HL) *Spackman v. Plumstead DBW* (1885) 10 App. cas. 229, 240 and *A. G. v. Ryan* [1980] AC 718.

[16] I think I should mention, in passing, Professor Jowell's essay (above, p. 327) "Of Vires and Vacuum: the Constitutional Context of Judicial Review" where he refers to the dicta that follow and in reliance upon them advances a theory of "*Vires* in context" which does "not involve the court in

Parliament does not legislate in a vacuum. It legislates for a European liberal democracy founded on the principles and traditions of the common law and the courts may approach legislation on this initial assumption. But this assumption only has prima facie force. It can of course be displaced by a clear and specific provision to the contrary.

Lord Browne-Wilkinson spoke to like effect in the same case when he said:[18]

A power conferred by Parliament in general terms is not to be taken to authorise the doing of acts by the donee of the power which adversely affects the legal rights of the citizen or the basic principles on which the law of the United Kingdom is based unless the statute makes it clear that such was the intention of the Parliament.

And in a leading speech in *Boddington v. British Transport Police*[19] Lord Steyn expressly approved Sir William Wade's classic words that the ultra vires doctrine – and it is clear that Sir William had something akin to the modified ultra vires doctrine in mind – remains "the central principle of administrative law".[20] This was not a chance or throwaway remark and *all* the other speeches in that case recognised the necessity for ultra vires as the basis of the review of statutory discretions. "[T]he juristic basis of judicial review is ultra vires" said Lord Browne-Wilkinson.[21] "[A]ny misdirection in law would render the relevant decision ultra vires and a nullity", said the Lord Chancellor.[22] An act "undertaken pursuant to [an invalid byelaw] is ultra vires and unlawful" said Lord Slynn.[23] And one might also mention the complete absence of any case, concerning a statutory discretion, in which the ultra vires doctrine is rejected. Now, of course, the House of Lords may change its mind. But until that happens the normative force of these dicta cannot be ignored. As Sir John Laws rightly says in his essay in this volume:

interpreting a conferred power by reference to the legislature's implied intent . . . *Vires* becomes power in context . . ."(at p. 337). Although Professor Jowell plainly considers he is advancing something different from the modified ultra vires doctrine I do not think that he is.

[17] [1998] AC 539 at 518.

[18] At 575.

[19] [1998]2 WLR 639. For comment see [1998] PL 364, [1999] JR 165 (Forsyth), [1998] JR 144 (Elliott) and (1998)114 LQR 534 (Craig). Professor Craig's note is a curiosity of the debate in that it barely mentions the question of vires (although the phrase *intra vires* is used once)!

[20] Wade and Forsyth, *Administrative Law* (7th ed., 1994), p. 41 approved by Lord Steyn in *Boddington v. British Transport Police* [1998]2 WLR 639 (HL) at 662D. Professor Craig p. 392 above, however, states that it is "not clear" which version of the doctrine Lord Steyn had in mind. But Sir William's words must be seen in their context which Lord Steyn could hardly have overlooked. In explaining these words Sir William says: "It is presumed that Parliament did not intend to authorise abuses, and that certain safeguards against abuse must be implied in the Act. These are matters of general principle, embodied in the rules of law which govern the interpretation of statutes. Parliament is not expected to incorporate them expressly into every Act that is passed. They may be taken for granted as part of the implied conditions to which every Act is subject and which the courts extract by reading between the lines, or (it may be truer to say) insert by writing between the lines" (at p. 42). That is what Lord Steyn was approving.

[21] At 655D.

[22] At 646B.

[23] At 655G.

While scholars – or anyone for that matter – are perfectly entitled to praise or criticise any particular precedent, the very notion of precedent has a self-standing value; it is an important guarantor of legal certainty, and it is the medium by which the common law changes gradually, and not by coarse reversals.[24]

So "coarse reversals" are not to be expected. The primary reason for this judicial support for the ultra vires doctrine is not judicial blindness to reality but judicial wisdom. The judges know they need a constitutional justification for judicial review and that the ultra vires doctrine is the best one available. To the detail of this proposition we now turn.

THE CONSTITUTIONAL JUSTIFICATION FOR JUDICIAL REVIEW

The most fundamental reason why the judiciary should cleave to the doctrine of ultra vires is that otherwise the judges have no good answer to the officious but pertinent question: who are you to interfere in the exercise of a discretion, clearly within the requirements of the statute, and entrusted to a democratically accountable decision-maker by a democratically elected parliament? In the absence of a written constitution, limiting the powers of the legislature and granting a warrant, express or implied, to the judges to police those limits, this is a real question that needs an answer. Windy rhetoric about the age old wisdom of the common law locked in the bosom of the judges will not do.

There is, of course, much learning about the weakening of accountability to the legislature requiring greater accountability to the law, about the protection of fundamental rights being an important facet of democracy, and about the rule of law. But all of this addresses the desirability of judicial review, something which is not in dispute. None of it addresses the legal basis of judicial review in terms of hard legal rule and principle. It seems to me too that it is no reply to this question to point, as Professor Craig does, to ancient cases which, he claims, did not have regard to the intent of the legislature in imposing standards upon decision-making bodies.[25] These decisions antedate the development of our sovereign Parliament in its modern form and the current question simply did not arise in this way in those days.[26]

But the ultra vires doctrine provides, it seems to me, the most satisfactory answer available to that question. In Lawrence Baxter's words the "application [of the ultra vires doctrine] consists of nothing other than the an application of the law itself, and the law of Parliament to boot".[27] Judicial review thus implies no challenge to the democratic legislature – it is the legislature's will that is being

---

[24] Above, p. 182.

[25] Above, pp. 62–7

[26] And it seems to me to be irrelevant whether the "modern parliament" developed three hundred and fifty years ago or only one hundred and fifty ago. It did develop, and it is now democratic, so the question arises and demands an answer. Cf. Craig, above, p. 389. see Goldsworthy, op. cit. for a thorough discussion of sovereignty in earlier centuries.

[27] *Administrative Law* (Juta & Co., 1984), at 303.

upheld. Political wisdom underlies the judicial acceptance of ultra vires. Especially when a decision is bold or controversial the wise judge will almost invariably spell out expressly the relationship of his conclusions to the relevant statute. Thus we find Simon Brown LJ declaring regulations that denied asylum seekers all social security benefits (unless they had applied for asylum on entry) void in these words: [28]

> [these regulations are] so uncompromisingly draconian in effect that they must indeed be held ultra vires . . . Parliament cannot have intended a significant number of genuine asylum seekers to be placed on the horns of so intolerable a dilemma . . .[29]

Similarly in R. v. *Lord Chancellor ex parte Witham*[30] Lord Justice Laws found that the Lord Chancellor's general powers to "prescribe the fees to be taken in the Supreme Court" in section 130 of the Supreme Court Act 1981 were subject to certain *implied* limitations in favour of a constitutional right of access to the courts.

As I said in "Fig Leaves"

> By their ready acceptance of ultra vires the judges show that they are the guardians, not the subverters, of this existing constitutional order. This fact . . . marks the maintenance of the proper balance of powers between the elected and non-elected parts of the constitution. Adherence to ultra vires is a gentle but necessary discipline . . .[31]

IS ABANDONING ULTRA VIRES A CHALLENGE TO PARLIAMENTARY SOVEREIGNTY?

A fundamental part of the argument in "Fig Leaves", was that those who would abandon ultra vires are necessarily driven to challenge the supremacy of Parliament. If this argument is right, "weak" critics, whether they intend it or not, are transmuted into "strong" critics. "weak critics" thus have, if they are to challenge "Fig Leaves", to counter this argument or recognise themselves as "strong critics".

Of all those whose responded critically to "Fig Leaves" Sir John Laws was the one who most clearly accepted this point and came up with the most telling challenge to it. It will be recalled that I argued that:[32]

---

[28] R. v. *Secretary of State for Social Security ex parte Joint Council for the Welfare of Immigrants* [1997] 1 WLR 275. It may be noted that Simon Brown LJ buttressed his conclusion by quoting from Lord Ellenborough CJ in R. v. *Inhabitants of Eastbourne* (1803) 4 East 103 at 107: "the law of humanity, which is anterior to all positive laws, obliged us to afford them ['poor foreigners'] relief, to save them from starving". And to like effect R. v. *Home Secretary ex parte Jammeh* [1997] *The Times*, 11 September and several other cases.

[29] But Parliament reinstated the regulations by primary legislation shortly thereafter. See [1997] PL 394 (Harvey). There is unlikely ever to be a better opportunity to challenge the validity of part of an Act of Parliament on the grounds of its infringement of fundamental rights. After all it had just been condemned by a leading judge as "uncompromisingly draconian". It was a pity that no challenge was launched on the back of the views of the "strong critics" but the applicants were doubtless, quite correctly, advised that such a challenge was bound to fail.

[30] [1998] 2 WLR 849.

[31] Above, pp. 42–3.

[32] See above, pp. 39–40.

... what an all powerful Parliament does not prohibit, it must authorise expressly or impliedly. Likewise if Parliament grants a powers to a minister, that minister either acts within those powers or outside those powers. There is no grey area between authorisation and prohibition or between empowerment and the denial of power.

Consequently, I argue, if the relevant statute did not intend that a particular decision should be exercised in accordance with the principles of procedural justice, but the common law were so to specify, the common law would be challenging the will of Parliament. But if, as the modified ultra vires doctrine contends, Parliament is presumed to intend that those common law principles should be applied by the judges, there is no challenge: judicial review becomes a co-operative endeavour between statute and common law.

Sir John contends that in so arguing I neglect:[33]

> "the undistributed middle" – an obscure, but useful, academic expression, meaning that although X and Y may be opposites, like praise and blame, they do not cover the whole field; there might be Z, which involves neither. Thus Forsyth mistakes the nature of legislative sovereignty, which is trumps, not all four suits, specific not wall to wall.

Thus although Parliament might not intend the application of the procedural justice this does not mean that Parliament has prohibited it; the common law – the undistributed middle – might still require its observance.

Mark Elliott has shown this approach leads to the imputation of unrealistic intentions to Parliament.[34] Instead of imputing to Parliament the plausible intention that when it grants power to a decision-maker it intends that that power should be exercised in accordance with the principles of good administration (as determined by the judges), Sir John's approach requires that Parliament should be agnostic, or indifferent, to the fairness of the exercise of the power. Parliament does not enjoin procedural justice but neither does it prohibit it, it is undecided. This is self-evidently unrealistic – even the most dim-witted legislator, or officious backbencher, will, if asked, say that in legislating they intend that the powers granted should be fairly exercised! [35]

But there is a deeper difficulty with Sir John's reasoning. He neglects the relatively well known and useful academic concept of "mutual exclusivity". While it is possible, but implausible, that Parliament is agnostic about procedural fairness there is no such uncomfortable middle ground with the concept of ultra

---

[33] See above, p. 78.

[34] Above, pp. 93–9.

[35] And if Sir John were to say that in truth Parliament leaves it, or may be presumed to leave it, to the judges to decide the measure of procedural justice appropriate in the particular circumstances, he is reconciled to the modified ultra vires doctrine. This, it seems to me, is exactly what he recognises when he argues (above, p. 189) that section 3(1) of the Human Rights Act 1998 enables legislation to be read conformably with the Convention "save where the right is expressly denied. Such an approach surely marches with the legislator's intention". Later he says that the recognition of fundamental values "is being done by the incremental process of the common law and the enactment of legislation which, as its makers must intend, invites an approach to its own interpretation and that of other statutes in which these values guide the judge's hand". But this is the logic of the modified ultra vires doctrine, which, try as he might, Sir John cannot escape.

vires. The concepts of ultra vires and intra vires are mutually exclusive: a decision-maker either acts within or outside his or her powers, there is no middle ground. It is like pregnancy, you are either pregnant or you are not, or like a light switch which is either on or off. If, say, a decision-maker, in denying a hearing in certain circumstances, acts within the powers granted by Parliament the common law cannot impose a duty of fairness upon that decision-maker without challenging parliament's power to allow him or her to make valid decisions without a hearing. Otherwise you have the position where every requirement for validity laid down expressly or impliedly by Parliament is satisfied yet the common law is imposing an additional requirement for validity. That is a challenge to parliamentary supremacy. And "weak critics" become "strong critics".

In this first response to "Fig Leaves" Professor Craig seems to consider that it is enough to meet this point to deny that he is a "strong critic". But in his latest work[36] he seeks to meet it by generalising the argument and showing that, in his view, absurd consequences follow. Thus he argues that a public body, established by statute, would not be bound by the rules of contractual or tortious liability unless there could be shown to be, at least presumed, legislative intent that they should be so bound. This he says is not the way in which we think about the contractual and tortious liability of public bodies; and we would not take seriously the proposition that statutory intention was "the central principle" of this area of law. Similarly in regard to statutes in the sphere of private law that accord a measure of discretion to a private party, it would not be considered that legislative intent was the "central principle" of this area of the law.

Let me deal with the second of these examples first. Where a statute grants a discretionary power to a private party it is obviously true that the reach of that power and its mode of exercise is a matter of statutory interpretation. But when statute does enter the field of private law it is intruding into a complex web of pre-existing relationships between pre-existing persons founded on the common law. The central principles of that area of law are to be found in the rules governing those relationships, not in the statute that intrudes upon one aspect.[37] On the other hand with public law – in the statutory field at any rate – one is dealing with bodies that would not exist but for the statute, exercising powers that would not exist but for the statute. The statute will have created the entire relevant relationship between public bodies and the citizens concerned. The two situations are completely different.

There may, of course, be circumstances where an analysis similar to the modified ultra vires doctrine is relevant in determining the limits of the statutory power granted to a private person. But these circumstances will be very rare because there is a world of difference between a discretion exercised by a private

---

[36] Above, pp. 378–80.

[37] Of course, when statute does become so obtrusive that it dominates an area of law, e.g., the Bills of Exchange Act 1882, it may be that that statute contains the central principles of the law in that area.

party – which may generally be exercised as the individual wishes without regard to fairness or the public good – and a discretion granted to a public party – where fairness and the public interest are paramount. But this is saying nothing more than that what is to be implied from the statute depends upon the context.

I turn now to Professor Craig's first example, the imposition of civil liability upon public bodies. Part of the thrust of his argument I accept. A public body cannot enter into a contract unless it is given power to do so, expressly or impliedly, in the statute setting it up. But this is surely uncontroversial: administrative law is littered with the consequences of public bodies which entered into contracts when they lacked the power to do so. Similarly, if there is no statutory duty there can be no breach of statutory duty. But Professor Craig does not have these issues in mind. He has, I think, in mind the rules of, for instance, the law of contract that apply once the question of vires has been determined. These rules are the same rules that would apply when a private party entered into a similar contract. Is the *existence* of these rules the result of legislative intention? The answer to this question is surely no. Those rules are preexisting and would exist whatever the statute said. The statute is relevant to the application of those ordinary rules of civil liability, i.e., if a statute sets up a body with contractual capacity but says nothing about the law of contract that is to apply, then it is reasonable to impute to Parliament the intention that the normal rules should apply. Indeed, the very purpose of granting (by statute) legal personality to a public body is so that it may be the bearer of rights and duties under the ordinary law! Thus the *application* of the law of contract to the contracts of a statutory body may be implied from a statute, but the *existence* of the law of contract is, contrary to Professor Craig's argument,[38] not governed by statute.

The way Professor Craig puts this latest argument is curious. Craig's argument is phrased in terms of whether *legislative intent* is the central principle of a particular area of law. But it is no part of the modified ultra vires doctrine that *legislative intent* is the central principle of administrative law. The argument rages over whether the ultra vires *doctrine* is the central principle of administrative law. This is significant, first, because it shows that the logic of modified doctrine only applies where there is some question of the limits of power. But, secondly, because the modified ultra vires doctrine recognises common law principles relevant to administrative law that are not derived from legislative intent. The implied legislative intent upon which we rely does not specify those principles, or give life to those principles, or bring them into existence, it simply *authorises* their application in the circumstances. This misunderstanding seems to be at the heart of this particular strand of criticism.

Notwithstanding the criticism of Lord Justice Laws and Professor Craig, the reasoning of "Fig Leaves" still seems, as a matter of pure logic, compelling: if a

---

[38] He clearly argues that the modified ultra vires doctrine holds that both "the existence and the application of [contractual] principles" must be justified by legislative intent (above, p. 379).

decision-maker complies with all the requirements of the statute for validity, the common law surely cannot impose an additional requirement without challenging the will of Parliament. It is a solecism to challenge the will of Parliament, so this must be wrong; yet those common law principles, as developed by the judges, are a vital part of modern administrative law. How is a reconciliation to be achieved? Through the assumption, backed both by judicial precedent and common sense, that when Parliament grants power to a decision-maker it intends that those common law principles should be applied. This is the modified ultra vires doctrine in a nutshell.

THE THEORETICAL CRITICISM

This is the point at which it is appropriate to deal with some of the theoretical critics, primarily Professor Dyzenhaus.[39] I am sorry to say that I have not been much helped by their writings. It seems to me that they develop their theories of judicial review on the assumption that they have a clean sheet on which to write. But the courts, and those of us who support the modified ultra vires doctrine, are grappling with a real problem in a particular constitutional context. However interesting the theorists' thoughts might be and however valuable their theories might be in other contexts, we are down in the mud trying to find a workable constitutional warrant for a sophisticated law of judicial review in a constitution with a sovereign parliament.

Elementarily, our constitution is not about tearing up everything that has gone before. This is not the land of the *tabula rasa* or of revolution. The materials of the past are fashioned into the solutions for today. Thus the construction of a constitutional justification for judicial review does not begin with a search for a fresh blueprint. We do not begin again. So if we are to consider the foundations of judicial review we must start not by wondering what these foundations might be in an ideal world, but what they *are* in our existing constitutional order or if they are unclear, how might clarity be built from the materials at hand.

It may be that some of this theoretical work could be brought to bear in a meaningful way on the concrete task we face. For the present I take comfort from the fact that when Dyzenhaus ceases to be relentlessly abstract and considers judicial review in a concrete context, he recognises that there may be legal orders where:

---

[39] Above, p. 141 and in several other places. I will add a word here about Nick Bamforth's paper, "Ultra Vires and Institutional Interdependence" (above, p. 113). The argument of this interesting paper is built upon what seems to me to be – for this author – an uncharacteristic error, viz., that part of the function of the ultra vires doctrine is to "provide a reliable defence for Parliamentary Sovereignty" (above, p. 114). But the ultra vires doctrine is the *consequence* of parliamentary sovereignty; it is not a defence of it. It is thus no criticism of the doctrine of ultra vires to point (as Bamforth does) to its alleged deficiencies in the event of a transformation of the relationship between the courts and the legislature that leads to the demise of sovereignty. The modified ultra vires doctrine simply does not address that issue.

the sovereign's commands will be recognised as law as long as he complies with certain minimal criteria pertaining to the steps that have to be followed in the law-making process. In such a legal order, it would follow that the only legitimate basis for judicial review of administrative action is something like the ultra vires doctrine, which says that the judges must enforce only those legal limits on administrative action which the legislature intended them to enforce . . . For judges to conclude otherwise, for example, by finding limits in common law principles would amount to an illegitimate arrogation of authority.[40]

We, of course, operate, for good or ill, in just such a legal order. And these words grasp the difficulty that we face, even if the abstract theorising seems to have little useful to say in resolving that difficulty.

THE CONSEQUENCES OF ABANDONMENT FOR ADMINISTRATIVE LAW

Thus far the modified ultra vires principle has been considered from the point of view of principle and precedent. But it is at least as important to consider the consequences for the law of judicial review that would or would be likely to flow from the abandonment of the doctrine. These are very considerable although largely overlooked by the critics.

The effectiveness of ouster clauses

"Fig Leaves" drew attention to the fact that the ultra vires doctrine had in fact – just as the critics urged – been abandoned as the central principle of administrative law in another jurisdiction with a sovereign parliament, apartheid South Africa. This abandonment had an immediate consequence quite unforeseen by the critics: straightforward ouster clauses were thereby rendered effective to preclude judicial review. The leading case of *Staatspresident en andere* v. *United Democratic Front*[41] concerned the making of vague regulations by a minister. Since the requirement of clarity now came from the common law and was not implied from the statute, the allegedly vague regulations were now within his powers under the relevant Act; and an ouster clause precluding judicial challenge to regulations made "in terms of the Act" was effective to preclude judicial review. The classic reasoning that administrative lawyers learn at their mother's knee, viz., that Parliament did not intend that the minister should have power to make vague regulations, thus the vague regulations were ultra vires, thus they were not made "in terms of the Act" and thus the ouster clause did not

---

[40] Above, pp. 153–4. Interestingly both Sir John Laws, n. 35 above, and Professor Craig, n. 28 above, express themselves in similar terms, i.e., they recognise and accept the logic of the modified ultra vires doctrine. Given how reluctant they are to find any merit in this doctrine, this recognition is a tribute to its logical power and vigour.

[41] 1988(4) SA 830(A). Discussed above, pp. 35–9.

apply to them,[42] was no longer available. The arguments that prevailed in the *UDF* were ones which followed perfectly logically from the abandonment of ultra vires. They could be pressed upon a UK court. They might be accepted. But then they lead to the evisceration of judicial review wherever there is a straightforward ouster clause.

Now, of course, this is a result that few would welcome. But how is it to be resisted? I am not impressed by the critics' response. This is to stress the importance of access to the court and thus a "clause which purported to do this would therefore be restrictively construed so as to apply only to decisions which were not vitiated by errors of the kind which could be changeable under the standard heads of review".[43] But this is a mixture of hope and assertion which lacks the hard legal argument apt to win round a court minded to accept *UDF* style reasoning. Restrictive interpretation is one thing and ignoring the words used by Parliament is another. I can see innumerable reasons of policy and pragmatism why *UDF* style interpretations should be resisted; I have yet to hear a cogent legal argument showing where the logic of the *UDF* reasoning is flawed. Hence I consider, all other considerations aside, rather than render ouster clauses effective the doctrine of ultra vires should be retained.

The evisceration of planning law

The critics have not dealt with or answered in any detail a matter which I raised in "Fig Leaves": the evisceration of planning law if ultra vires were abandoned. Section 288(1) of the Town and Country Planning Act 1990 provides that a "person aggrieved" by an order made under the 1990 Act may apply within six weeks of its confirmation to the High Court to test its validity. As several well known decisions have made clear this is the *only* way in which such challenges may be mounted; the application for judicial review is not available.

The only grounds on which such challenges may be mounted are "that the order is not within the powers of this Act or that any of the relevant requirements have not been complied with." The "relevant requirements" are defined elsewhere as "any requirements of this Act or of the Tribunals and Enquiries Act 1971 or of any order, regulations or rules made under this Act or under that Act . . .". Although the classic grounds of judicial review are not expressly mentioned as requirements in the Act, it is well established that they are impliedly included. As Lord Denning said in hallowed words in *Ashbridge Investments* v. *Minister of Housing and Local Government*:[44]

> Under this section [the precursor of s 288] it seems to me that the court can interfere with the Minister's decision if he has acted on no evidence; or if he has come to a conclusion to which on the evidence he could not reasonably come; or if he has given a

---

[42] Professor Craig calls this "the strained idea that Parliament did not intend such clauses to protect nullities" (above, p. 55).

[43] Above, *ibid.* (Craig).

[44] [1965] 1 WLR 1320.

wrong interpretation to the words of the statute; or if he has taken into consideration matters which he ought not to have taken into account . . . It is identical with the position when the court has power to interfere with the decision of a lower tribunal which has erred in point of law . . .

But if the modified ultra vires doctrine has been abandoned and the classic grounds of challenge come directly from the common law, this reasoning is not available: a section 288 challenge must restrict itself to the requirements of the Act – and these no longer include the classic grounds. Thus the Secretary of State can act perversely in planning matters, need not restrict himself to relevant considerations, and may depart from the principles of natural justice (save to the extent that they are laid down expressly in the "relevant requirements") for none of these matters are expressly "within the powers of this Act". Now, of course, this is once more a consequence that no one desires. But it follows perfectly logically from the abandonment of ultra vires. How is it to be resisted? Other than by cleaving to ultra vires, I do not know. When this point was put at the conference there was a fair bit of assertion along the lines of "The judges would never let it happen, etc. . . ." But I heard nothing that revealed the legal or logical error of this argument.

But whether cogent legal arguments showing that ouster clauses would not be rendered effective and the planning law would not be eviscerated exist or not, it seems to me that the uncertainty and confusion that would result from raising these issues by the abandonment of ultra vires is in itself enough to suggest that the prudent course is to stick with the devil we know.

Undermining the conceptual foundations of judicial review

Boddington v. *British Transport Police*,[45] barely touched upon by the critics, is a most important case in the debate over the foundations of judicial review. Its importance lies not only in the House of Lords' formal and unequivocal approval of the ultra vires doctrine as the juristic basis of judicial review, but in the fact that it shows how all the fundamental concepts of judicial review are linked together and interrelated. The case establishes that a person charged with a breach of a byelaw, may raise the invalidity of that byelaw as a defence to the charge and was not restricted to challenging it, other than when it was "bad on its face", by way of an application for judicial review. Any other conclusion would mean that an individual unable (through lack of means, delay, denial of leave or otherwise) to apply for judicial review might be coerced by a prosecution founded upon an illegality. A person could be sent to gaol for doing a lawful act. This was a conclusion "too austere and . . . too authoritarian to be compatible with the traditions of the common law" and "an unacceptable consequence in a democracy based upon the rule of law".[46]

---

[45] [1998] 2 WLR 639.
[46] Per Lord Steyn at 664B, 663G. And see above pp. 366–8 (Elliott).

Now the magistrates' court before which the invalidity of a byelaw might be raised as a defence has no power to issue *certiorari* and quash an invalid byelaw. Thus the success of such a collateral (or defensive) challenge depends upon the invalid byelaw being void, not voidable (for otherwise the byelaw would still exist in law and have to be applied by the court). And an act done beyond the legal power of the actor (i.e. an ultra vires act) is non-existent in law or void. Thus the rule of law requires that collateral challenge should be generally available, which requires that unlawful acts should be void not voidable which requires that they should be ultra vires.

Now there are, of course, some who would abandon voidness as readily as they would abandon ultra vires; and whose support for the rule of law is sufficiently malleable to allow them to tolerate the consequent widespread denial of collateral challenge. But the message of *Boddington* is that the conceptual foundations of judicial review are not be attacked in this way. Apart from anything else think of the confusion that would be caused if all the conceptual foundations of judicial review were cast aside in this way.

CONCLUSION

It should not be supposed that the supporters of the ultra vires doctrine are unaware of its defects. There is a measure of artificiality about the modified doctrine;[47] it is true that there is some awkwardness over explaining how the grounds of judicial review may change over time although the relevant statute remains the same;[48] there is some truth in the charge that the modified doctrine is without content in that it provides little guidance to the actual reach or intensity of judicial review in a particular area.[49] But these defects should not be exaggerated and allowed to obscure the doctrine's strengths.

The first of those strengths is, of course, that it provides a firm constitutional foundation for judicial review – and enough has been said about that above.

[47] The intention of Parliament is inevitably an artificial construct. But it is not unreasonable or implausible to impute to Parliament the intention that decision-makers should comply with the principles of good administration.

[48] But see Lord Mustill in R. v. *The Home Secretary ex parte Doody* [1994]1 AC 531: "where an Act of Parliament confers an administrative power there is a presumption that it will be exercised in a manner which is fair in all the circumstances . . . The standards of fairness are not immutable" (at 540).

[49] But there remains a tangible link between implication from the statute and the intensity of judicial review. Consider procedural justice. In well known words Lord Bridge said in *Lloyd* v. *McMahon* [1987] AC 625 that "what the requirements of fairness demand . . . depends on the character of the decision-making body [which depends upon the statute setting it up], the kind of decision it makes [which will depend upon the powers which the statute gives it] and the statutory framework . . . in which it operates . . ." Thus what fairness requires in any particular case (beyond what is expressly specified in the statute) depends upon other factors which are largely derived from the statute. Where the statute seems silent the common law does not spring forward to prescribe in detail what is required. On the contrary, inferences based upon the relevant statutory provisions and statutory background are crucial. The interplay between the common law and implication from the statute is subtle and the relationship intimate. The modified ultra vires doctrine indeed grasps this truth rather better than those who would base judicial review upon the common law.

For a full discussion see Elliott, above pp. 363–4. He points out that the common law theorists

But there is a second and deeper strength that is nearly as important. The modified doctrine incorporates judicial creativity into the orthodox constitutional structure of judicial subservience to statute. This permits the judiciary to continue to develop and extend the principles of judicial review as they have done so successfully over the past forty years.

The analogy with other institutions is appropriate. Beneath the form of a powerful monarchy a democracy flourishes. Behind the facade of a legally weak prime minister is an all powerful figure at the heart of government. This is a characteristic of our constitution. Statute apart, reform takes place incrementally: the solutions for the problems of today are made by small but subtle changes to the materials at hand. Thus over time things come to appear different from what they are; and so the modified ultra vires doctrine, while speaking the language of judicial subservience, in fact makes the judges and the legislature partners in the vital task of ensuring that the executive remains answerable to the law. This reconciliation between the creativity of the judiciary and the supremacy of parliament is a distinct and valuable constitutional achievement. It is embedded in our ancient constitutionalism yet it serves a modern and important purpose. It should be cherished as an expression of the pragmatic genius of our constitutional arrangements, not idly discarded on what are in the end unpersuasive grounds.

As the judiciary turns to the great task of putting flesh on the bones of the Human Rights Act 1998, there is no longer any sign that the judges are considering discarding the modified doctrine. And this is as it should be: there will be difficulty and confusion enough without attempting to transform the relationship between the judiciary and parliament in a way that is bound to be controversial. After all, what would be gained? The modified doctrine allows judges to be just as creative – provided they are true to their relationship with parliament – but it does not threaten the conceptual foundations of administrative law and promise widespread confusion. All that the Big-Endians can say is that their approach is franker and avoids the "artificiality" of the modified doctrine. But who is misled by the modified doctrine? No one that I know of.

The work of the Big-Endians, though, should not be dismissed. Their contribution to the development of the modified doctrine has been profound and should be gratefully acknowledged. The process has been dialectical. The Big-Endians have put forward the anti-thesis to the thesis of the classical and undeveloped ultra vires doctrine. The modified doctrine is the resulting synthesis that incorporates the best of both. But now the time has come to go forward. The energies and abilities of both Big-Endians and Little-Endians should be bent to the tasks that lie ahead as our constitutional order changes. But to devote further energy to debate over the ultra vires doctrine is unnecessary and a distraction.

---

must accept that, if they are right, there are two classes of grounds of review: those implied from the statute and those based in the common law. But it is difficult to distinguish between them although it will frequently be necessary to do so.

Comments from some Participants

The Rule of Law as the Foundation of Judicial Review

T.R.S. ALLAN*

The most remarkable feature of the present English debate about the basis of judicial review is that almost all participants appear to agree about almost every significant issue of substance. Adherents to the conception of ultra vires based on legislative intent readily accept that the relevant legal principles are judge-made, finding the relevant connection with Parliament in the grant of the necessary "imprimatur" to the judges; and those who insist on the common law basis of judicial review, rejecting reliance on fictions or fig-leaves, agree that parliamentary sovereignty remains inviolate – at least for the purposes of the debate. The truth of the complaint that any relevant legislative intent is only tacit and general is frankly acknowledged; but tacit approval of judicial creativity could, it is fairly pointed out, always be withdrawn if legislative sovereignty truly remains unqualified.[1] In these circumstances, it is often hard to understand, or share, the passion and excitement which the debate seems to generate.

We should be grateful, however, to Mark Elliott for a careful and considered analysis which has the particular merit of revealing how little truly divides the opposing camps. In his account, the courts' jurisdiction and jurisprudence are rightly grounded in the rule of law; and the integrity of the constitutional order is preserved by the reasonable presumption that Parliament intends the rule of law to be upheld. While the rule of law provides the basis of review directly in the case of non-statutory sources of power, review of the exercise of statutory power obtains its legitimacy from the necessary presumption of parliamentary intent. It is unreasonable to suppose that Parliament intended to confer unlimited discretionary power on an executive agency, and unrealistic to argue that the statute fully prescribes the relevant limits. The conclusion is drawn that Parliament has delegated to the courts the task of defining the boundaries of the agency's jurisdiction, pursuant to the rule of law.

* The helpful comments of David Dyzenhaus and Nils Jansen are gratefully acknowledged.

[1] See esp. Christopher Forsyth, "Of Fig Leaves and Fairy Tales: The Ultra Vires Doctrine, the Sovereignty of Parliament and Judicial Review" [1996] *CLJ* 122; Paul Craig, "Ultra Vires and the Foundations of Judicial Review" [1998] *CLJ* 63; Sir John Laws, "Illegality: The Problem of Jurisdiction", in Supperstone and Goudie (eds), *Judicial Review* (London, 1997). Note, however, Sir John Laws's defence of "the imperative of higher-order law" in "Law and Democracy" [1995] *PL* 72.

Elliott's work also clarifies what, if anything, is truly at stake in the debate over ultra vires. He insists that any *irreconcilable* conflict between parliamentary intention and the rule of law must be resolved in favour of the former.[2] Even if one accepts an "attenuated sovereignty principle", rejecting unqualified legislative supremacy, Parliament remains "competent to grant or withhold the power to contravene the principles of good administration".[3] Elliott observes that critics of absolute parliamentary sovereignty envisage only a modest attenuation of legislative competence; and the well-established tradition of offering extreme and unlikely examples to test the limits of the legislative capacity for evil might seem to support his conclusion that such attenuation is actually "minimal". He therefore seeks to distinguish between Parliament's (arguable) inability to "abrogate the most basic tenets of the British democratic tradition", on one hand, and its liberty to alter the complex rules governing administrative decision-making, on the other. As he fairly points out: "Completely abolishing all review in every context is an entirely different enterprise from statutory modification of the intensity, nature or availability of review in a particular instance."[4]

It does not follow, however, that an intervention of the latter kind is necessarily legitimate; for the essentially procedural rules enforced by judicial review lie at the very core of the rule of law, and hence at the heart of our constitutional foundations. There would be no point in denying Parliament legislative capacity to interfere with the "most fundamental rights and interests", as the present argument assumes is possible, if it were free to authorise the executive to override them – in the exercise of its discretion – by the arbitrary treatment of individuals. The scope for legislative modification of the "principles of good administration", while extensive, is not therefore unlimited. The denial of natural justice in the case of a deprivation of personal liberty – except on special grounds, such as a credible threat to national security – would for example constitute the most serious violation of the rule of law. While we may well agree that legislative supremacy is a valuable and accepted feature of our democracy, for the purposes of collective decision-making about many matters of political substance, we cannot concede even to an elected majority absolute power to determine every question of procedure. For it is only our constitutional commitment to principles of fair procedure in the treatment of individuals which makes majority will a tolerable, let alone attractive, basis of governance.

The fundamental status of procedure is the principle theme of David Dyzenhaus's valuable and wide-ranging discussion of conflicting theoretical bases for judicial review.[5] Dyzenhaus commends a culture of justification, in

---

[2] Mark Elliott, "The Ultra Vires Doctrine in a Constitutional Setting: Still the Central Principle of Administrative Law" [1999] *CLJ* 129, p. 153.

[3] Elliott, "The Demise of Parliamentary Sovereignty? The Implications for Justifying Judicial Review" (1999) 115 *LQR* 119, p. 133.

[4] *Ibid.*, p. 135.

[5] David Dyzenhaus, "Form and Substance in the Rule of Law: A Democratic Justification for Judicial Review?", in this volume.

which the ideals of participation and accountability take centre stage, rejecting a "substantivist" theory of adjudication which (in Ronald Dworkin's version) makes democracy subservient to liberalism. Although there is much in common between his approach and mine, as Dyzenhaus observes, he points to a difference of emphasis in our accounts of the ideal of equal citizenship.[6] While my version of that ideal focuses on the substance of the law before which the citizen is equal, his version celebrates the citizen as active participant in the legal order. However, these are ultimately two ideals, which in any decent society – of the kind in which most of us want to live – are closely related and exist in tandem: together they constitute the core of liberal democracy. We need both the rule of law and democracy, and it would be a grave mistake to settle for one without the other. Moreover, the principles of procedure (such as those of natural justice) which Dyzenhaus rightly makes central to the rule of law cannot be wholly divorced from questions of substance, for their main point is to facilitate the fair treatment of individuals – according to whatever principles those in authority purport to recognise. Procedure, in other words, is ultimately the handmaid of equality, in the sense of reasoned consistency, excluding arbitrary discrimination.

Dyzenhaus objects that my analysis of the rule of law, which rejects Joseph Raz's largely formal account in favour of a broader principle of equality, may not be "incompatible with contemporary positivist understandings of the rule of law, especially in their inclusive versions". I gladly accept this charge since I consider the defeat of legal positivism, whether inclusive or otherwise, to be irrelevant to my task. I offer my account of the rule of law as an attractive ideal, already embedded in our institutions and fundamental political commitments, and in no way dependent on the truth or falsity of positivism. It is precisely because positivism has lost its moorings in political theory since Austin's (and Kelsen's) insistence on its purely conceptual character, as Dyzenhaus observes, that in its modern form it is largely irrelevant to practical questions of governance and legitimacy. Legal positivism, understood simply as the claim that there is no necessary connection between law and morality, is, as Dyzenhaus himself points out, "consistent with any role for judges you like". It is better, then, left on one side in the debate about the foundations of judicial review. Admittedly, I recognise the similarities between my account and Ronald Dworkin's work and invoke his idea of "integrity" in support.[7] However, it is doubtful whether Dworkin's project required his sustained assault on legal positivism of the purely descriptive or conceptual kind: H.L.A. Hart's view was that Dworkin's brand of interpretative jurisprudence was simply a different enterprise from his own largely descriptive endeavour.[8]

---

[6] See Allan, "The Rule of Law as the Rule of Reason: Consent and Constitutionalism" (1999) 115 *LQR* 221.

[7] Ronald Dworkin, *Law's Empire* (London, 1986).

[8] H.L.A. Hart, *The Concept of Law*, (2nd ed., Oxford, 1994), *Postscript*.

I also agree with Dyzenhaus's view that Dworkin fails to establish a necessary connection between law and morality; but it does not follow, as Dyzenhaus assets, that the rule of law – interpreted as a liberal ideal – collapses into a substantive account of justice. The rule of law consists in application of the principle of equality, as I have elaborated it. It requires faithful adherence to a coherent conception of the common good and allegiance to the principles of justice that that conception supports. It is certainly true that if the society or polity is infected by "a pernicious moral ideology", that ideology will inform the relevant conception of the common good. That is exactly why the ideal of the rule of law does not collapse into a specific, and inevitably contentious, theory of justice: although an attractive ideal, which has intrinsic moral value, the rule of law is compatible with a variety of different theories of justice, some of which we may well find abhorrent. It remains the professional and moral responsibility of lawyers to fight against arbitrariness and inconsistency, insisting on fair treatment according to clearly established standards of justice, even when, as private citizens, they entertain conflicting – sometimes sharply conflicting – political commitments and ideals. If the rule of law were not an independent ideal, which could claim the allegiance of citizens of different political persuasions, the distinction between law and politics would disappear, along with individual freedom – freedom from the exercise of arbitrary power (using "arbitrary" in the sense of lacking justification according to a determinate conception of the common good, rather than contrary to any particular theory of justice).[9]

In addition to respect for fair procedures, the rule of law entails a limited, largely uncontroversial substance, compatible with a wide variety of otherwise conflicting theories of justice. Democracy and the rule of law alike require the preservation of those civil and political liberties which ensure that debate about the requirements of justice can flourish – especially freedoms of speech, association and assembly. There is, admittedly, wide scope for judgment about the scope of these rights in different contexts, and equivalent room therefore for judicial deference to legislative decision; but unlimited deference would amount to betrayal of the culture of justification. Divorced from every constraint of substance, and without judicial intervention to ensure respect for procedural fairness in particular cases, majoritarian democracy would be quite as unattractive as Dworkin's vision of a state in which every question of political principle is ultimately for judges to determine, in their role as guardians of a highly specific, and contentious, version of liberalism. Unqualified legislative sovereignty, giving the majority unlimited power over every question of both procedure and substance, is as objectionable as a power of judicial review which makes the validity of legislation wholly dependent on compliance with common law principles.

Moreover, the persecution of minorities – the imposition of constraints on their freedom which find no plausible justification in values to which a majority

---

[9] This ambiguity in the notion of arbitrariness has been responsible for much confusion over the meaning of the rule of law, as Dyzenhaus observes.

of citizens are genuinely committed – must be resisted by judges committed to equal citizenship. That a majority of the legislature has, after due deliberation, adopted a measure can provide a legitimate *part* of the justification for judicial obedience; but it cannot provide the whole. The rule of law requires the majority to govern the minority according to the principles of justice it applies to itself: the justification of coercive acts must consist in appeal to reasons which are truly consistent with a conception of the common good – one to which it is reasonable to think that all could and should acknowledge as a fair basis for governance. Reasons which appeal only to the will of the majority to promote its own advantage, at the minority's expense, clearly should not count. The judge cannot, in the last resort, escape the responsibility to determine whether the commitment to justification, of the appropriate kind, has been understood and honoured by those in power.

Certain forms of liberalism are hostile to the welfare-regulatory state and therefore find no place for administrative law. Hayek's conception of the rule of law excludes the exercise of coercive discretionary powers by public officials on the ground that it is intrinsically arbitrary, making the citizen or his property an instrument of the state.[10] It may also be the case, as Dyzenhaus argues, that Dworkin's theory of law makes insufficient allowance for the place of administrative agencies and is generally ill-adapted to the requirements of official discretion. There is clearly a problem with the current approach of English courts towards so-called errors of law by agencies and tribunals; and Dworkin's theory might appear to support the notion that every question of law has, in principle, a single correct answer which it is ultimately the preserve of the court to supply.[11] The view that in general any decision of an administrative tribunal may be quashed for error of law takes no account of the expertise of a specialist body, whose decisions about the best interpretation of its governing statute are normally entitled to respect.[12] Moreover, the lapse of the distinction between jurisdictional and non-jurisdictional errors makes statutory ouster clauses entirely futile: the strongest indications of a legislative intention to restrict judicial intervention are simply disregarded. It is also true that Dworkin has sometimes neglected the independent value of procedural rights, treating them as wholly subservient to substantive rights; and in the context of administrative discretion, where entitlements depend on considerations of policy, as determined by the relevant agency, such an approach would deny procedural rights altogether.[13]

Dworkin's account of adjudication could no doubt be modified to meet these objections, even if Hayek's theory of law could not. The ideal of the rule of law

---

[10] See generally F.A. Hayek, *Law, Legislation and Liberty* (London, 1982).

[11] See esp. Ronald Dworkin, *A Matter of Principle* (Oxford, 1986), ch. 5.

[12] The leading case is now R. v. *Lord President of the Privy Council, ex p. Page* [1993] AC 682.

[13] See Dworkin, *A Matter of Principle*, pp. 98–100; D.J. Galligan, *Due Process and Fair Procedures* (Oxford, 1996); Genevra Richardson, "The Legal Regulation of Process" in Richardson and Genn (eds), *Administrative Law and Government Action* (London, 1994), pp. 112–13.

is, in any case, independent of Dworkin's idiosyncratic presentation of it; and since, indeed, it remains distinct from any particular liberal theory of justice, even though constituting an integral part of every kind of liberalism, it is perfectly compatible with the administrative state. There is nothing in the ideal of equality, properly understood, that either prohibits recourse to official discretion, on one hand, or excludes judicial oversight of the adoption and implementation of policy, on the other. Just as the courts may properly defer to legislative judgment about the needs of the common good, so they may equally defer to an administrative determination when the agency's powers are duly authorised by the legislature. The same logic, moreover, justifies a qualified judicial deference to an agency's view about the limits of its statutory jurisdiction: the rule of law merely insists that the scope of such deference should be settled by reason – the reasons for giving weight, in the circumstances, to the agency's expertise, set against those for overriding its judgment. That is exactly what is apparently envisaged by Dyzenhaus's model of "deference as respect": elsewhere, he has argued that recourse to the courts from the decisions of administrative bodies must always be available, but only "on the basis of the question whether the tribunal's decision was supportable by the reasons it in fact and could in principle have offered".[14]

It is clearly implicit in any recognition of the legitimacy of official discretion that the courts must accept the validity of many decisions whose correctness they doubt or deny: hence the basic distinction between appeal and review. The principle of equality none the less excludes arbitrary decision-making: distinctions between persons must be rationally made for defensible public purposes, reasonably regarded as falling within the agency's sphere of authority. It is true that judicial review of administrative action may be understood as chiefly concerned with the enforcement of procedural, rather than substantive, rights – the right of each citizen to have his case fairly considered in the light of the policies adopted by public authorities for specific purposes, and against the background of those basic constitutional principles which are more enduring components of the common good. Such procedural rights, however, are themselves only the necessary consequence of the overriding principle of equality: their enforcement by the courts ensures that the interests of all citizens are fairly taken into account and that unjustified discrimination is excluded.

It does not follow that all kinds of interests have the same weight, or even the weight ascribed by any particular theory of justice which commands a specific judge's allegiance. There must, however, be similar treatment for everyone, according to consistent principles, openly avowed by the various arms of government and subject to public criticism; and the central core of the basic political liberties must be preserved for all in recognition of each person's equal political status. The common law approach, which presumes a legislative intention to safeguard fundamental rights and requires explicit enactment in order to

---

[14] David Dyzenhaus, "The Politics of Deference: Judicial Review and Democracy" in Michael Taggart (ed), *The Province of Administrative Law* (Oxford, 1997), p. 305.

effect their abridgement, is perfectly capable of achieving an acceptable balance between private and public interests. The more serious the apparent abridgement, and the more fundamental the right concerned, the more readily the statutory language will resist a literal construction, in breach of deeply rooted constitutional assumptions. There is no need for declarations of invalidity in the case of primary legislation – a prospect from which all apparently recoil in horror. It is sufficient to determine its meaning and effect in the particular case.[15] In the same way, while policy choices are rightly left to the agency charged with the relevant public function, at least within reasonable limits, the courts can preserve equality by ensuring that policies are fairly applied to particular cases, and that legitimate expectations are upheld whenever possible without serious damage to the public interest.[16] Understood as a constitutional ideal, in the way I have defended it, the rule of law provides the true foundation of judicial review, just as majoritarian democracy is the basis for a carefully qualified, though broad and generous, principle of parliamentary sovereignty.

[15] *Anisminic Ltd.* v. *Foreign Compensation Commission* [1969] 2 AC 147 is a familiar example of the mode of judicial interpretation consistent with the requirements of the rule of law; *R.* v. *Secretary of State for the Home Dept., ex p. Fayed* [1997] 1 All ER 228 provides a more recent illustration.

[16] See further Allan, "Fairness, Equality, Rationality: Constitutional Theory and Judicial Review" in Forsyth and Hare (eds.), *The Golden Metwand and the Crooked Cord* (Oxford, 1998).

Judicial Review in a Modern Context

STEPHEN BAILEY

The vigorous debate on the foundations of judicial review is both necessary and timely. It is necessary because the relationship between the judiciary and those who are subject to their decisions (which may lead to orders enforceable through proceedings for contempt of court) is peculiarly sensitive where the respondents are, or are exercising powers conferred by, a democratically elected body. It is timely given that the implementation in the near future of the Human Rights Act 1998 will bring about a significant shift in that relationship.

In this debate, any appeal to history for assistance in identifying and articulating an underlying theory of judicial review is likely to be unconvincing. It must be remembered that the existence of "judicial review of administrative action" as a principled area of judicial activity is very much a product of the middle to late twentieth century, owing an enormous amount to the academic work of de Smith and Wade, to the judicial lawmaking of, among others, Lords Reid, Denning and Diplock, and to the procedural reform founded on the work of the Law Commission.

For some centuries, much of what we now think of as judicial review as of course found in two separate bodies of law administered by different courts with different kinds of respondent, and developed over different timescales in history. The strand that began life first, the law governing the prerogative writs, can be understood in terms of the royal courts in the name of the Crown either controlling bodies such as justices that exercised *judicial* power over others (*certiorari*, probation), or compelling performance of a legal duty (*mandamus*). In a number of instances in the nineteenth century the court's power to control particular bodies through *certiorari* was itself by statute. As late as 1882, it could be argued by the Solicitor General, albeit unsuccessfully, that prohibition did not lie against a department of central government as that department did not act judicially (R. v. *Local Government Board* (1882) 10 QBD 309). Only in the 1960s and 1970s did it become accepted that *certiorari* and prohibition were not confined to control of judicial functions. The other strand, the use of declarations and injunctions by the Court of Chancery to keep statutory companies to their powers as authorised expressly or impliedly by Act of Parliament, was of course in terms based on the ultra vires doctrine. Reference to these two strands does not provide a complete picture. Contributions to the development of the law (benign or otherwise) could also come, for example, from actions in tort (*e.g.*

Cooper v. *Wandsworth Board of Works* (1863) 14 CB (NS) 180) and statutory review (*e.g. Roberts* v. *Hopwood* [1925] AC 678). These strands, whether taken separately or together, do not, it is submitted provide fertile ground for discovering a theory for the modern doctrine of judicial review. Indeed, if anything, they sit more comfortably with the possibility that different theories may be needed in different contexts.

In any event, it might well be better to accept that judicial review is a modern construct and can only sensibly be analysed in its modern context. Here, it is clear that by far the greater proportion of the voluminous modern case law has arisen out of a statutory background. Judicial decisions based on an interpretation of the express words used by Parliament are firmly based on the ultra vires doctrine. Decisions based on implied limits as to considerations and purposes also flow directly from the statutory and administrative context. Decisions based on a discrete finding of irrationality are very rare, and not uncontroversial. Legal requirements of fairness of process can also be seen as matching and reinforcing values generally recognised and accepted in modern public administration, and therefore part of the background assumed by Parliament in legislating. Accordingly, there is little difficulty in accepting the view that judicial review in a statutory context is based on express or implied Parliamentary intent. This position is not undermined by the fact that a different theory (or different theories) may be necessary in non-statutory contexts. Indeed, the search for one over-arching theory may have the disadvantage of inhibiting progress in establishing an appropriate judicial role in reviewing the activities of those who exercise monopoly power (just power) over others without the authority of an Act of possibly Parliament. (As regards control of prerogative powers it is of course difficult to agree on a theory that justifies review when we cannot agree on a definition of prerogative power itself. Furthermore, it does not follow from the fact that the *content* of the limits applied by courts in a non-statutory context may well be similar to that found in statutory contexts (*e.g.* basic rationality and fairness of process) that the underlying theories justifying imposition must be identical. Fairness and rationality can, after all, be regarded as desirable and, indeed, expected in all sorts of contexts; my children, for example, expect me to be fair and rational in my dealings with them (allegations of "unfairness" covering in practice both elements).

Overall, any attempt to identify a unifying theory incorporating the rag-bag that is the non-statute-based case law of judicial review to date, requires a considerable leap of imagination and faith. It is certainly fun, but it is submitted that the development of a series of context-specific theories is more likely to be helpful for the foreseeable future.

No Need for a Single Foundation

SIR ROBERT CARNWATH

"This was a highly successful and stimulating conference. To me, however, it demonstrated that there neither is nor needs to be a single set of 'foundations' for judicial review The ultra vires principle is a valid and useful tool, in those parts of the law which depend on a statutory or other constitutional foundation. (For example, I discussed the role of ultra vires in relation to local government in 'The reasonable limits of local authority power' (1996 PL 244).) Since the decision of the House of Lords in *Page* v. *Hull University Visitor* [1993] AC 682, it no longer has to be assumed that principles applying in one area of public law are automatically transferable to another. Judicial review has reverted to its proper place as a form of procedure, not a system of substantive law.

What the conference also demonstrated is that in areas of law to which the ultra vires principle cannot be readily applied, there are other important principles derived from the common law, such as abuse of monopoly power and fundamental rights, which can contribute to a principled approach. Dawn Oliver's paper also demonstrated that these principles are not peculiar to public law, but have a much deeper foundation in the law generally".

Whither the Constitution?

MARTIN LOUGHLIN

Although the main theme of the seminar concerns the foundations of judicial review, it seems obvious that once that issue is raised, a multitude of more basic questions lurk in its shadow. If we are motivated to ask "what is it that justifies the power of judges to quash decisions of the Executive?" it seems evident that neither "the ultra vires principle" nor "the common law" is likely to provide a satisfactory answer. The question forces us to engage with some rather unsettling issues concerning the authority structure of the British State. It is difficult to say anything sensible on such a large issue within the constraints of a short comment on the seminar papers. Nevertheless, the title of Lord Steyn's paper, "The Constitutionalisation of Pubic Law" (The Constitution Unit, 1999), is helpful: it identifies a middle ground between positive law and political theory and thus provides the peg on which a few remarks might be hung.

The most important point I wish to make is that while all participants might agree that the theme of "constitutionalisation" is important, not many appear to recognise that it is also controversial. The British constitution is, or at least traditionally has been acknowledged to be, the epitome of a political constitution. Consider, for example, the classic work of the nineteenth century, Bagehot's *The English Constitution*. This is a text which, though unrivalled in its insights into the workings of the constitution, manages scarcely to mention law and the judiciary; indeed it would hardly be an exaggeration to suggest that Bagehot attributes greater weight to the Corporation of the City of London than to the judiciary in providing a bulwark for English liberties.

When we turn to the contemporary debate, however, it is evident that Bagehot's perspective is one that has been almost totally eclipsed. For the fact of the matter is that the judiciary, in recent years, have to all intents and purposes appropriated the constitution. The constitution, Sir Stephen Sedley comments, "remains a common law ocean dotted with islands of statutory provision" and is therefore a subject on which the judiciary speak with authority. And they have. According to Lord Steyn, "the House of Lords *held* that the British constitution is firmly based on the separation of powers" (emphasis supplied). But the most explicit admission of judicial appropriation of the constitution comes from Sir John Laws. Writing extra-curially he asks the basic question and answers it without ambiguity: "What *is* a constitution? It is that set of *legal* rules which governs the relationships in a state between the ruler and the ruled" (former emphasis in original, latter supplied).

I have said enough, I hope, at least to intimate why the issue of the constitutionalisation of public law might be a particularly important question for lawyers to address. We appear to be evolving from a political constitution towards a constitution based on the foundation of legal principle. This presents a major challenge for the English legal tradition. Since judges traditionally have viewed their role (in Lord Wright's words) as one of proceeding "from case to case, like the ancient Mediterranean mariners, hugging the coast from point to point and avoiding the dangers of the open sea of system and science", nothing less than a sea-change in the philosophy of the common law seems to be required. If, as Sir John Laws now suggests, lawyers – presumably as an essential part of their craft – now "need to think about moral and political philosophy" the challenge becomes obvious. What, for example, are these foundational constitutional principles? Whence are they derived? What is it within the background, education, training and experience of the judiciary which enables them not only to identify the principles (the relatively easy bit) but also to unpack them and set them to work to resolve particular social disputes concerning the appropriate exercise of public power?

Many amongst the judiciary now recognise the importance of these questions (how else can we explain the recent outpouring of learned articles by senior judges on various aspects of the relationships between law, morality, democracy, justice, freedom and rights?). But, important though it is, "grasp[ing] the theory of the thing" (as Sir John Laws urges) is only the starting point for the engagement. As the most distinguished of our constitutional historians recognised, "the more we study our constitution whether in the present or the past, the less do we find it conform[s] to any such plan as a philosopher might invent in his study." To subject it to rational analysis for the purpose of moving towards "a principled constitutional order" is almost inevitably to change it. Further, there is a danger in asserting, as Sir John Laws does, that the notion of morality lies at the foundation of the constitution. The constitution is the product of a quintessentially political relationship and to assume that the claims of morality must succeed whenever there is a clash between politics and morality rests (as Hegel recognised) "on superficial ideas about morality, the nature of the state, and the state's relation to the moral point of view". The judiciary once acknowledged this, though mainly through accommodation of governmental power and the acceptance of limitations on their jurisdiction. If these jurisdictional limits are now to be removed and law is to provide the foundation for our system of government, then in grasping at the nature of the thing we must take Hegel's warning seriously.

Ultra Vires as Distraction

MICHAEL TAGGART*

Whether one came to Cambridge to praise the ultra vires doctrine or to bury it, there is no doubting the doctrine's enduring fascination for British public lawyers. It remains the cuttlebone upon which the beaks of established and soon-to-be-established scholars are honed.[1] Seemingly the prize for the most incisive analysis is a large one: no less than establishing the legitimacy of the enterprise of judicial review of action emanating directly or indirectly from statute. But most of the protagonists in this debate have so much in common that the debate is a little unreal, and it seems to me to distract attention from more important developments.

The rule of law envelopes and subsumes the ultra vires doctrine. Grounding the ultimate justification for judicial invalidation of administrative action under statute in the intent of Parliament maintains a democratic pedigree and supposedly insulates the judges from the criticism of over-reaching. This is the "rule of law, not men" strand of the rule of law.[2] But the rule of law is a coat of many colours, and it contains many principles, ideas, values and conventions,[3] most of which predate modern democratic government in Great Britain.[4] This is "lore" as well as "law", and in accordance with the "folk ways" of common lawyers statutes are read in accordance with these values, and the judges have fashioned the grounds of administrative law so as to give expression to them. Lawyers on both sides of the ultra vires debate acknowledge these "folk ways", and most approve of this form of judicial behaviour. It is the rule of law in this sense, as Dicey recognised long ago, that balances the British constitution,

* Faculty of Law, The University of Auckland. My attendance at the Cambridge conference on "The Foundations of Judicial Review" was made possible by grants from The University of Auckland Research Committee and the Faculty of Law contestable conference funds. I am grateful for that support and thank Christopher Forsyth for the invitation.

[1] I recall a French scholar using this metaphor in relation to Dicey's work, but cannot locate the source.

[2] I have retained the sexism of the formulation because of its historical accuracy. Cf. Radin, "Reconsidering the Rule of Law" (1989) 69 *BULR* 781, n. 1.

[3] The literature is large, but the following recent articles give a fair sampling of the literature and opinions: Craig, "Formal and Substantive Conceptions of the Rule of Law: An Analytical Framework" [1997] *PL* 467 and Fallon, " 'The Rule of Law' as a Concept in Constitutional Discourse" (1997) 97 *Col LR* 1.

[4] See generally Kiser and Barzel, "The Origins of Democracy in England" (1991) 3 *Rationality and Society* 396.

providing the counterweight (in addition to pubic opinion) to the theoretically omnipotent legislature. That is why ultra vires is a fig leaf.

The issue is how can the rule of law be squared with democracy? Does one leave the fig leaf in place or discard it? Must the rule of law be reduced to a formal or process-based concept to avoid clashing with legislative policies? Should the rule of law be given liberal substance *à la* Hayek or some other "academic scribbler"?[5] Or is there some middle road, whereby the rule of law may have some substantive content but falling short of a highly contestable, full-blown substantive theory? Whatever the answer, the courts retain (at a minimum) the awesomely powerful job of interpreting texts. The common law/private right interpretative backdrop is now being overlapped by human rights instruments.[6] Today this process of imbrication of old and new "rights" is ubiquitous.

The new rights-based approach, which draws on international, regional and national human rights instruments, is transforming the old remedies-based common law system. This accentuates the challenge to sovereignty; simultaneously coming from within the domestic system and from without. Some of these rights are of a piece with those protected by the rule of law, but many more are new or at least were insufficiently developed at common law. The patchy common law record of preventing racial and other types of discrimination is but one illustration. This has spawned statutory solutions, which in turn often appear partial and create pressures for judicial supplementation.[7] The line between public and private spheres of activity (and law) is indistinct, and ultimately may be seen to have been drawn with disappearing ink.

Moreover, the "contracting State" is raising new challenges, and leaving the ultra vires debate somewhat high and dry. Much less is done by statute than used to be. Interestingly, the historical justification given for the *Datafin*-style extension of judicial review to non-statutory bodies by both supporters and detractors of the ultra vires doctrine is rather ancient case law controlling abuse of de facto monopolistic power by individuals and entities. Rather than signalling a separate justification for review of non-statutory bodies, distinct from control of statutory decision-makers by means of the ultra vires doctrine (as supporters of the doctrine assert),[8] this case law and the history of judicial

---

[5] "Madmen in authority, who hear voices in the air, are distilling their frenzy from some academic scribbler of a few years back": J.M. Keynes, *The General Theory of Employment, Interest and Money* (Harcourt, Brace and Company, New York, 1936) 383.

[6] For insightful discussion of these and other interpretative backgrounds in administrative law cases, see J. Evans, H.N. Janisch and D.J. Mullan, *Administrative Law: Cases, Text, and Materials* (Emond Montgomery, Toronto, 4th ed., 1995) chs 1 and 9.

[7] See Taggart, "The Province of Administrative Law Determined?" in M. Taggart (ed.), *The Province of Administrative Law* (Hart Publishing, Oxford, 1997) 1, 6–17; Witelson, "Retort: Revisiting *Bhadouria* and the Supreme Court's Rejection of a Tort of Discrimination" (1999) 10 *National Journal of Constitutional Law* 149.

[8] See Forsyth, "Of Fig Leaves and Fairy Tales: The Ultra Vires Doctrine, the Sovereignty of Parliament and Judicial Review" [1996] *CLJ* 122, 124–7.

review more generally may sustain a generic principle about controlling abuse of power.[9]

A weakness in some of the supporters' defence of ultra vires is their approval of the courts' circumvention of privative clauses in cases like *Anisminic*, where seemingly one of the rule of law values (namely, access to court) trumps legislative intent. Whereas the advancing adminsitrative State used "privative" clauses, the retreating State "privatises"; both are designed to keep the courts out. In the former, the intent is to keep the courts out of "public" business, and in the later it is to stop judges wielding public law yardsticks by which "private" action might be measured. It is uncertain that this line will hold. "Social forces like armies can sweep around a fixed position and make it untenable", as Justice William Douglas once remarked.[10]

As public lawyers plumb the sociologists' observation of "compenetration" of State and civil society and the economists' enthrallment with efficient markets, the ultra vires doctrine appears increasingly beside the point.

---

[9] See *Vector Ltd* v. *Transpower New Zealand Ltd*, as yet unreported decision of the New Zealand Court of Appeal, CA 32/99, 31 August 1999; particularly the concurring judgment of Thomas J.

[10] Douglas, "Stare Decisis" (1949) 49 *Col LR* 735.

Constitutional Realities and Judicial Prudence

SIR WILLIAM WADE

We all understood the realities and knew perfectly well that the judges created their own powers as they went along. Furthermore, their claims to independence were already recognised in the law to some extent. Lord Woolf's suggestion that the courts might refuse to enforce an Act abolishing judicial review was only saying what the House of Lords had said, though in a much more involved way, in *Anisminic* and what Lord Woolf himself had held in the *Al Fayed* case when disregarding the ouster clause. The Lord Chancellor had fastened on the wider ideas put forward by Lord Woolf, Lord Cooke, Lord Justice Laws and Lord Justice Sedley and had called them claims to judicial supremacism prompted by judicial romanticism. Nevertheless the judges, having now taken the bit firmly between their teeth, will certainly not be deterred by these accusations.

They might, however, be ill-advised to advertise their creative powers. The public can see that they are getting a great accretion of power under the Human Rights Act, on top of their greatly extended powers of judicial review. If in addition they are seen to be building a yet greater empire and claiming to be independent of Parliament, they will only encourage the familiar charge of being unelected and unaccountable and undemocratic. It behoves them, surely, to be circumspect in their claims. There is wisdom, therefore, in the House of Lords' firm support of the traditional ultra vires doctrine which is founded, however unrealistically, on the presumed intentions of Parliament, and has eloquent support in the writings of Christopher Forsyth and Mark Elliott.

Index